Studies of Chinese Religion:
A Comprehensive and Classified
Bibliography of Publications
in
English, French, and German through 1970

Compiled by

LAURENCE G. THOMPSON

University of Southern California

With the Research and Editorial Assistance of

JUSTINE PINTO

Dickenson Publishing Company, Inc.
Encino, California & Belmont, California

ISBN-0-8221-0187-4
Library of Congress Catalog Card Number: 76-1313

Printed in the United States of America
Printing (last digit): 9 8 7 6 5 4 3 2 1

Cover Design/Mark Kochan

152935

To My Friend

Fred Streng

With Respect and Appreciation

Contents

Preface   v

Acknowledgements   vi

Abbreviations

    A. General   vii

    B. Publications   viii

Details Concerning Serial Sources   xiii

PART ONE
BIBLIOGRAPHY AND GENERAL STUDIES

1. Bibliography   2   2. General Studies   3

PART TWO
CHINESE RELIGION EXCLUSIVE OF BUDDHISM

1. Terminology	12	22. Meditation - General	65
2. Antiquity	12	23. Folk Religion - General	65
3. Mythology	15	24. Local Studies - Mainland	67
4. Art and Symbolism	17	25. Deities and Images - General	70
5. Religion and History	23	26. Specific Deities and Cults	71
6. Religious Thought	26	27. Festivals - Customs - Religious Calendar	74
7. Confucius and Confucianism	29	28. Temples and Mountains	78
8. Ethics and Morals	36	29. Rites and Ceremonies	81
9. Filial Piety	38	30. Divination	82
10. Ancestral Cult	38	31. Shamanism and Mediums	83
11. Feng-shui	41	32. Magic and Sorcery	84
12. State Religion	42	33. Medicine and Religion	86
13. Taoism - General	46	34. Religion in Folklore, Tract, Literature and Drama	88
14. Lao Tzu and Tao Te Ching	49	35. Sects and Secret Societies	91
15. Other Taoist Texts - The Canon	53	36. Modern (pre-1949) Religion	94
16. Taoist Theory	55	37. Religion under Communism	96
17. Taoism - History	57	38. Taiwan	98
18. Taoist Immortals	59	39. Overseas (including Hong Kong)	99
19. Taoist Pantheon and Cults	60	40. Comparative Studies	101
20. Taoist Monachism	60	41. Miscellaneous	105
21. Taoist Yoga and Alchemy	61		

PART THREE
CHINESE BUDDHISM

1. Reference Works   108
2. General Studies   109
3. Texts in Translation   113
4. Studies of Texts and Terms   117
5. Theory and Doctrine   123
6. History   125
7. Schools (except Ch'an)   133
8. Individuals (except Ch'an)   133
9. Ch'an   135
10. Saṅgha - Monachism -
    Monasteries   139
11. Pilgrims   140
12. Rites - Practices - Cults - Instruments 144
13. Arts and Iconography   145
    A. General   145
    B. Iconography - Motifs   146
    C. Specific Temples   147
    D. Architecture (except pagodas)   148
    E. Pagodas   149
    F. Sculpture   150
    G. Stelae   153

    H. Painting (including woodcuts
       and frescoes)   154
    I. Historical Emphasis   155
    J. Miscellaneous   156
14. Caves and Mountains   156
    A. General   156
    B. Yün-kang   156
    C. Lung-men   157
    D. T'ien-lung Shan   157
    E. O-mei Shan   158
    F. Wu-t'ai Shan   158
    G. P'u-t'o Shan   158
    H. Tun-huang   159
    I. Miscellaneous   160
15. Specific Deities   161
16. Popular Buddhism - Buddhist Stories   162
17. Buddhism and Chinese Culture   163
18. Modern (pre-1949) Buddhism   164
19. Buddhism under Communism   166
20. Taiwan and Overseas (including Hong Kong) 167
21. Comparative Studies Related to Buddhism 168
22. Miscellaneous   169

Index of Authors, Editors, Compilers, Translators, Photographers and Illustrators   172

Preface

The present volume had its origin in no more exalted an ambition than the compiler's intention to build a modest card file that would enable him to gain control of the literature in the field. As the accumulation of cards progressed over several years it became apparent that this literature was far more extensive than had been imagined. Frustration with the various inadequacies of existing bibliographies eventually led to recognition that halfway measures were futile, and to the determination to make a comprehensive catalog. After these unanticipated labors had reached a certain stage it was inevitable that the idea should occur of formalizing this catalog and publishing it.

The obvious need for a comprehensive bibliography was not the only reason for taking this final step. The compiler had also become sensible of the fuzzy definition of the field of Chinese religion evident, for example, in a general tendency to confuse the subject matter of the Confucian Canon, the writings of the philosophers, and religious data properly speaking. The compiler himself shared in this sort of confusion at the outset of his work, and one of the benefits of the labor that has gone into the present bibliography is clarification of this matter in his own mind. It is our view that it is as possible and necessary to distinguish religion from philosophy in the case of China as in the case of the West. The present bibliography therefore deals solely with Chinese **religion**, and includes items pertaining to the so-called Classics and philosophy only when these address themselves to religious matters. It goes without saying, on the other hand, that the Confucian Classics and certain of the philosophers themselves have much religious material in them; however, to have included all the translations and studies of such works would have enormously expanded our list and would at the same time have duplicated other bibliographical compendia.*

Restricting the definition of the field will, it is believed, be helpful, but we are equally convinced of the need for expanding it. As our numerous headings indicate, we have cast a wide net so as to include all topics relevant to the understanding of Chinese religion. This has on the one hand brought within the field some sorts of studies that have seldom been incorporated into bibliographical lists on Chinese religion, and on the other has suggested categories that we trust will sharpen perceptions of the subject's many facets. We wish to emphasize that these categories have been arrived at after the facts, and were not established because of any preconceived notions as to how the subject-matter should be arranged.

For the convenience of the user we have taken pains to cross-reference generously under appropriate headings. In those cases where to follow this procedure fully would have resulted in undue duplication we have advised the user of various categories to be consulted for additional materials.

As in several earlier works in the field we have here taken Chinese religion to be essentially a manifestation of the Chinese culture. We have considered only Buddhism, of all the foreign religions historically known in China, to have permeated this culture to such an extent that it became an integral part of Chinese religion. The other foreign religions have not, therefore, been included. Furthermore, we have limited our collection to the Han Chinese religion, and have excluded materials pertaining to ethnic minorities and peripheral cultures. Several other subjects are also excluded from the scope of this volume:

1. The so-called"term-question." For references on this subject one may consult Cordier's **Bibliotheca sinica** 3, col 1279-1294.

2. In the section on Sects and Secret Societies, the voluminous literature on the T'ai-p'ing rebellion.

3. The Confucian Canon and studies primarily concerned with textual, literary, or philosophical aspects of its components.

4. The question of Fu-sang. For references consult Cordier's **Bibliotheca sinica** 4, col 2653-2658.

---

*The standard bibliography of Chinese philosophy in Western languages is Chan Wing-tsit, **An outline and an annotated bibliography of chinese philosophy.** Yale university (1961) with several later supplements.

5. A number of studies deriving from the writings of Chinese Buddhist pilgrims, that concern non-religious topics.

6. Writings on medicine whose contents do not include the religious aspects of traditional theory.

7. The huge general travel and descriptive literature in which religion is often mentioned more or less incidentally.

8. General and historical treatments of art, and album-volumes, which include Buddhist art as part of their broad coverage; to have listed all these works would have expanded our listings unnecessarily. It should be noted, however, that the present volume provides an extensive bibliography of the field of Chinese Buddhist art that will in itself, we hope, be a useful new tool.

It would no doubt have been desirable to include items in Western languages other than the three here represented, but in fact the great bulk of the material is in English, French, and German. We should also mention that there are many as yet unpublished* studies such as theses and dissertations. The more valuable of these will eventually become available in published form, and we anticipate the opportunity to include them in a later supplement or revision of this bibliography. Needless to say, we shall also welcome all corrections, additions, and comments that would improve such a future edition.

The word 'comprehensive' in our title must thus be taken as somewhat less than literally true. Comprehensiveness is in any case a chimerical goal. Our hopes will be abundantly satisfied if the material here brought together proves useful in providing an overview of what had been accomplished to the terminal date by scholarship in the field, in furnishing leads for new researches, and in defining the field in its whole extent and in its parts.

Laurence G. Thompson

University of Southern California

ACKNOWLEDGEMENTS

Financial support for this work was provided from the Faculty Research Fund of the College of Letters, Arts, and Sciences of the University of Southern California in the form of two small, but crucially important grants. Publication was made possible by an additional grant from The Institute for Advanced Studies of World Religions in New York. To these two sources of assistance we express our gratitude.

Special appreciation is due to the compiler's dear friend Mark Kochan, whose help was invaluable in the publication of the book.

---

*"Publication," in the present work, refers to the book, pamphlet, and magazine or journal, as these are commonly understood.

Abbreviations

A. GENERAL

abbrev/abbreviated
abrmt/abridgement
add/additional, additions
ann/année(s)
annot/annotated, annotations
app/appendix(es)
arch/architecture, architectural
art/article(s)

bd/band
betw/between
bibliog/bibliography
bk/book
bl-&-wh/black and white

chap/chapter(s)
chin/china, chinese, chinois
chron/chronology
col/column(s), color
collab/collaboration, collaborator
comm/commentary
comp/compiled, compiler(s)
corr/corrected, corrigenda

d/date(d)
dept/department
diagr/diagram(s)

ed/edited, edition, editor(s)
engl/English, England
enl/enlarged
esp/especially

fasc/fascicule(s)
fig/figure(s)
fr/from

gloss/glossary

illus/illustration(s), illustrated
incl/includes, including, included
intro/introduction

jap/Japan(ese)

lith/lithographs

mél/mélanges
M.I.T./Massachusetts institute of technology

no/number(s)
n.d./no date
n.p./no place
n.s./new series
N.Y./New york

offpr/offprint
orig/original(ly)

p/page(s)
pl/plate(s)
pref/preface
Proc/Proceedings
pseud/pseudonym
pt/part(s)
publ/publication, published, publisher

ref/references
reimp/reimpression
repr/reprint(ed)
republ/republished
rev/review(ed), revised

s/seite
sec/section(s)
sep/separate(ly)
ser/series
sér/série
summ/summary
suppl/supplement

t/tome
trad/traduit
Trans/Transactions
tsl/translated, translation, translator

übers/übersetzt
univ/university
unk/unknown

vol/volume(s)

B. PUBLICATIONS*

AA	Artibus asiae	AUFS	American universities field staff
AAA	Archives of asian art	AV	Archiv für völkerkunde
AArch	Art and archaeology	A&T	Art & thought, issued in honour
AB	Art bulletin		of dr. ananda k. coomaraswamy
AC	Aspects de la chine. Paris, musée guimet (1959)		on the occasion of his 70th birthday. London (1947)
ACASA	Archives of the chinese art society of america	BAAFC	Bulletin de l'association amicale franco-chinoise
ACF	Annuaire du collège de france	BAF	Bulletin asie-française
ACP	Annales de chimie et de physique	BAIC	Bulletin of the art institute of chicago
ACSS	Annual of the china society, singapore	BAV	Boas anniversary volume; anthropological papers written in honor
ActaA	Acta asiatica		of franz boas . . . N.Y. (1906)
AdSin	Adversaria sinica	BCL	D.R. Bhandarker et al (ed) B.c.
AEO	Annales de l'extrême-orient		law volume. Calcutta, pt 1 (1945)
AIPHO	Annuaire de l'institut de philologie et d'histoire orientale		pt 2 (1946)
AL	Annali lateranensi	BCMA	Bulletin of the cleveland museum of art
AM	Asia major		
AMG	Annales du musée guimet	BCUP	Bulletin of the catholic university of peking
AMH	Annals of medical history		
AMHAV	Asia major: hirth anniversary volume (introductory vol of this journal, pref by editor Bruno Schindler d Oct 1922)	BDIA	Bulletin of the denver institute of arts
		BDetIA	Bulletin of the detroit institute of arts
AMZ	Allgemeine missions-zeitschrift	BEA	Bulletin of eastern art
ANA	Art news annual	BEFEO	Bulletin de l'école française
AO	Acta orientalia (Copenhagen)		d'extrême-orient
AP	Aryan path	BFoggMA	Bulletin of the fogg museum of
APC	Annales de philosophie chrétienne		art
AQ	Art quarterly	BHM	Bulletin of the history of medicine
AQR	Asiatic quarterly review	BIHM	Bulletin of the institute of the
AR	Asiatic review		history of medicine
ARW	Archiv für religionswissenschaft	BlM	Blackwood's magazine
ArchOr	Archiv orientální	BM	Burlington magazine
ArtsAs	Arts asiatiques	BMFA	Bulletin of the museum of fine
AS	Asiatische studien		arts (Boston)
ASAB	Annales de la société royale d'archaeologie, bruxelles	BMFEA	Bulletin of the museum of far eastern antiquities (Stockholm)
ASBIE	Academia sinica, bulletin of the institute of ethnology (Taipei)	BMFJ	Bulletin de la maison franco-japonaise
ASBIHP	Academia sinica, bulletin of the institute of history and philology (Taipei)	BMMA	Bulletin of the metropolitan museum of art (N.Y.)
		BMQ	British museum quarterly
Asiatica	Asiatica; festschrift friedrich weller zum 80. geburstag überreicht. Leipzig (1954)	BMSAP	Bulletin et mémoires de la société d'anthropologie de paris
		BOR	Babylonian and oriental record
ASONT	Marjorie Topley (ed) Aspects of social organization in the new territories, hong kong. Hong kong (1965)	BROMA	Bulletin of the royal ontario museum of archaeology
		BSAB	Bulletin de la société royale belge d'anthropologie, bruxelles
AsSur	Asian survey	BSEIS	Bulletin de la société d'études indochinoises de saigon

*Book or journal titles consisting of more than one word have been abbreviated if they occur more than twice in this bibliography.

BSOAS	Bulletin of the school of oriental and african studies (Univ london)
BTLVK	Bijdragen tot de taal-, land- en volkskunde
BUA	Bulletin de l'université l'aurore (Shanghai)
BVAMG	Bibliothèque de vulgarisation des annales du musée guimet
CalR	Calcutta review
CB	Current background (U.S. consulate general, hong kong)
CBWK	Chinesische blätter für wissenschaft und kunst
CC	Chinese culture (Taipei)
CCJ	Chung chi journal
CCS	Collectanea commissionis synodalis. Peking (1935)
CCY	China christian yearbook
CD	B.C. Henry, The cross and the dragon. N.Y. (1885)
CDA	Chinesisch-deutsch almanach
CF	Ching feng
CHM	Cahiers d'histoire mondiale
ChRec	Chinese recorder
ChRep	Chinese repository
ChRev	China review
CIHR	Congrès internationale d'histoire des religions
CISE	Congrès internationale des sciences ethnographiques, session de 1878
CJ	China journal
CL	Chinese literature
CM	Charles A. Moore (ed) The chinese mind. Univ hawaii (1967)
CMBA	China missionary; later China missionary bulletin; later Mission bulletin; later Asia
CMG	Conférences faites au musée guimet
CMH	China mission hand-book
CMI	Church missionary intelligencer
CMJ	Chinese medical journal
CNA	China news analysis
CP	Arthur F. Wright and Denis Twitchett (ed) Confucian personalities . Stanford univ (1962)
CPOL	Congrès provinciale des orientalistes, lyon, 1878
CQ	China quarterly
CR	Contemporary review
CRAIBL	Comptes rendus de l'académie des inscriptions et belles-lettres
CRJ	Contemporary religions in japan
CRecon	China reconstructs
CSM	Chinese students' monthly
CSPSR	Chinese social and political science review
CSSH	Comparative studies in society and history
CTI	John K. Fairbank (ed) Chinese thought and institutions. Univ chicago (1957)

CW	Catholic world
CWayRel	Laurence G. Thompson (ed) The chinese way in religion. Encino and belmont, calif.(1973)
CWR	China weekly review
CYT	E.T. Williams, China yesterday and today. N.Y. (1923 et seq; 4th ed 1928)
DR	J.M. Reid (ed) Doomed religions: a series of essays on great religions of the world. N.Y. and cincinnati (1884)
DV	Justus Doolittle (ed) Vocabulary and handbook of the chinese language. Foochow (1872)2 vol.
EA	East of asia
EArt	Eastern art
EB	Eastern buddhist
EH	Eastern horizon
EJ	Eranos jahrbuch
EM	Encyclopédie moderne
EMM	Evangelisches missions-magazin
EncyB	Encyclopaedia britannica
EORL	Études d'orientalisme, publiées par le musée guimet à la mémoire de raymond linossier. Paris (1932)
EP	Essays in philosophy by 17 doctors of philosophy of the university of chicago. Univ chicago (1929)
ER	Études religieuses
Études	Études des pères de la compagnie de jésus
EW	Eastern world
EWCR	East-west center review
EZT	Essays on the history of buddhism presented to professor zenryū tsukamoto. Kyoto university (1961)
E&W	East and west
FA	France-asie
FA:BPB	René de Berval (ed) Présence du bouddhisme (FA 16, 1959)
FCR	Free china review
FE	Far east
FEER	Far eastern economic review
FEQ	Far eastern quarterly
FF	Fortschungen und fortschritte
FKCS	Maurice Freedman (ed) Family and kinship in chinese society. Stanford univ (1970)
FLJ	Folk-lore journal
FO	Ferne osten
FRWVSP	Folk religion and the worldview in the southwestern pacific. Tokyo (1968)
FS	Folklore studies
GBA	Gazette des beaux-arts
GE	La grande encyclopédie
GM	Geographical magazine

HERE	James Hastings (ed) Encyclopaedia of religion and ethics. 13 vol (1908-26)	JHI	Journal of the history of ideas
HJ	Hibbert journal	JHKBRAS	Journal of the hong kong branch, royal asiatic society
HJAS	Harvard journal of asiatic studies	JHMAS	Journal of the history of medicine and allied sciences
HKS	Symposium on historical, archaeological and linguistic studies on southern china, south east asia and the hong kong region. Hong kong (1967)	JIA	Journal of the indian archipelago
		JIBS	Journal of indian and buddhist studies: Indogaku bukkyōgaku kenkyū
		JISOA	Journal of the indian society of oriental art
HM	Histoire de la médecine	JMBRAS	Journal of the malayan branch, royal asiatic society
HMRC	Henri Maspero. Les religions chinoises. Mélanges posthumes sur les religions et l'histoire de la chine, t 1. Paris (1950)	JMGS	Journal of the manchester geographical society
		JNCBRAS	Journal of the north china branch, royal asiatic society
HPEW	S. Radhakrishnan (ed) History of philosophy, eastern and western. London (1952)	JOR	Journal of oriental research (Madras)
HR	History of religions	JOS	Journal of oriental studies (Univ hong kong)
HRAF	Human relations area files	JOSA	Journal of the oriental society of australia
HTR	Harvard theological review		
HZ	Hansei zasshi	JPOS	Journal of the peking oriental society
IA	Indian antiquary		
IAC	Indo-asian culture	JPTS	Journal of the pali text society
IAE	Internationales archiv für ethnographie	JR	Journal of religion
		JRAS	Journal of the royal asiatic society
IAQR	Imperial and asiatic quarterly review	JRASB	Journal of the royal asiatic society of bengal
ICG	Indo-chinese gleaner	JRH	Journal of religious history
ICO	International congress of orientalists	JSBRAS	Journal of the straits branch, royal asiatic society
ICHR	International congress for the history of religions	JSMVL	Jahrbuch der stadtliches museums für völkerkunde zu leipzig
ICR	International congress of religions	JSR:HS	Japan science review: humanistic studies
IHQ	Indian historical quarterly	JSR:LPH	Japan science review: literature, philosophy and history
India antiqua	India antiqua. A volume of oriental studies presented to jean philippe vogel. Leiden (1947)	JSS	Journal of social science, national taiwan university college of law
		JWCBorderResS	Journal of the west china border research society
IPQ	IPQ: International philosophical quarterly		
IQB	Iqbal, later Iqbal review	KGUAS	Kwansei gakuin university annual studies
IRM	International review of missions		
JA	Journal asiatique	LD	Light of dharma
JAAS	Journal of asian and african studies	LO	M. Kern (ed) Das licht des ostens. Stuttgart (1922)
JAFL	Journal of american folk-lore		
JAK	Jahrbuch der asiatischen kunst	MAI	Mémoires de littérature tirés des registres de l'académie des inscriptions
JAOS	Journal of the american oriental society	MAIBL	Mémoires de l'académie des inscriptions et belles-lettres
JAS	Journal of asian studies	MB	Maha bodhi
JBBRAS	Journal of the bombay branch, royal asiatic society	MC	Missions catholiques
JCE	Journal of chemical engineering	MCAM	Mémoires couronnés et autre mémoires, académie royal de belgique
JCS	Journal of the china society, taipei		
JEAC	Journal of esthetics and art criticism	MCB	Mélanges chinois et bouddhiques

MCLC	Mémoires concernant l'histoire, les sciences, les arts, les moeurs, les usages etc des chinois, par les missionaires de pékin	OA	Oriental art
		OC	Open court
		OE	Oriens extremus
		OL	Orientalische literaturzeitung
MCSJ	Mémoires du comité sinico-japonais	OR	Ostasiatische rundschau
		OSCEP	Val Dastur Cursetji Pavri (ed) Oriental studies in honor of cursetji evachji pavri. London (1933)
MDGNVO	Mitteilungen der deutschen gesellschaft für natur- und völkerkunde ostasiens, tokyo		
MIHEC	Mélanges, paris universitaire institut des hautes études chinoises	OstL	Ostasiatische lloyd (Shanghai)
		OZ	Ostasiatische zeitschrift
		PA	Pacific affairs
MIOF	Mitteilungen, deutsche (preussische) akademie der wissenschaften zu berlin (institut für orientforschung)	PAAAS	Proceedings of the american academy of arts and sciences
		PC	People's china
MJ	Museum journal	PCEW	Charles A. Moore (ed) Philosophy and culture east and west. Univ hawaii (1962)
MLA	Magazin für die literatur des auslandes		
MMDFL	Hugo Kuhn and Kurt Schier (ed) Märchen, mythos, dichtung: festschrift zum 90. geburtstag friedrich von der leyens. . . München (1963)	PCIEEO	Première congrès internationale des études d'extrême-orient, hanoi (1902)
		PEW	Philosophy east and west
MN	Monumenta nipponica	PFV	Paranavitana felicitation volume on art and architecture presented to senarat paranavitana. Colombo (1966)
MRW	Missionary review of the world		
MS	Monumenta serica		
MSGFOK	Mitteilungen der schweitzerischen gesellschaft der freunde ostasiatische kultur	PIAHA	Proceedings of the 2nd bienniel conference, international associa-tion of historians of asia. Taipei (1963)
MSL	Mémorial sylvain lévi. Paris (1937)		
MSOS	Mitteilungen des seminars für orientalische sprachen	PIAJ	Proceedings of the imperial academy of japan
MSPD	Mélanges de sinologie offerts à paul demiéville. Paris (1966)	PJGG	Philosophisches jahrbuch der görres-gesellschaft
MSVC	Wolfram Eberhard. Moral and social values of the chinese: collected essays. Taipei (1971)	PS	Popular science monthly
		PT	People's tribune
		PTP	Phi theta papers
MW	Middle way	PW	Pacific world
Nachr-DGNVO	Nachrichten der deutschen gesellschaft für natur- und völkerkunde ostasiens, hamburg	QJCA	Quarterly journal of current acqui-sitions, u.s. library of congress
		QNCRR	Quarterly notes on christianity and chinese religion (Hong kong)
NC	Nineteenth century	RA	Revue archéologique
NCELYY	Frederic Wakeman, jr (ed) 'Nothing concealed': essays in honor of liu yü-yün. Taipei (1970)	RAA	Revue des arts asiatiques
		RC	Relations de chine (Kiangnan)
		RCCS	Albert R. O'Hara. Research on changes of chinese society. Taipei (1971)
NCH	North china herald		
NCR	New china review		
NGM	National geographic magazine		
NLIP	Natural law institute proceedings (Univ notre dame)	RDM	Revue de deux mondes
		RE	Revue d'ethnologie
NO	New orient	REO	Revue de l'extrême-orient
NPMB	National palace museum bulletin (Taipei)	RGI	Revue géographique internationale
		RHR	Revue de l'histoire des religions
NQ	Notes and queries on china and japan	RIC	Revue indochinoise
		RMM	Revue de métaphysique et de morale
NR	Nouvelle revue		
NRJ	National reconstruction journal	ROA	Revue de l'orient et de l'algérie
NZM	Neue zeitschrift für missionswissen-schaft	RofR	Review of religion
		RR	Revue des religions

RS	Religious studies	TICHK	Marjorie Topley (ed) Some
RSJ	Religious studies in japan. Tokyo		traditional chinese ideas and
	(1959)		conceptions in hong kong social
RSO	Revista degli studia orientali		life today. Hong kong (1967)
RSW	Religious systems of the world.	TJ	Tsinghua journal of chinese
	London and n.y. (1889 et seq)		studies
SA	Robert K. Sakai (ed) Studies on	TJR	Tenri journal of religion
	asia 1963. Univ nebraska (1963)	TM	À travers le monde
SAWW	Sitzungsberichte der . . . akademie	TOCS	Transactions of the oriental
	der wissenschaften in wien (phil.		ceramic society
	-hist. klasse)	TP	T'oung pao
SCFRE	Wolfram Eberhard. Studies in	TPJS	Transactions and proceedings
	chinese folklore and related		of the japan society
	essays. Indiana univ (1970)	UPUMB	University of pennsylvania mu-
SCMM	Survey of china mainland magazines		seum bulletin
	(U.S. consulate general, hong kong)	USJPRS	U.S. joint publications service
SCT	Arthur F. Wright (ed) Studies in	VBA	Visva-bharati annals
	chinese thought. Univ chicago	VBQ	Visva-bharati quarterly
	(1953)	Waifs	Frederic H. Balfour. Waifs and
SEAJT	South east asia journal of theology	and	strays from the far east, being a
SG	S. G. Brandon (ed) The saviour	Strays	series of disconnected essays on
	god: comparative studies in the		matters relating to china.
	concept of salvation. Manchester		Shanghai (1877)
	univ (1963)	WBKKGA	Wiener beiträge zur kunst- und
SIEW	Charles A. Moore (ed) with assis-		kulturgeschichte asiens
	tance of Aldyth V. Morris. The	Wen-lin	Tse-tsung Chow (ed) Wen-lin;
	status of the individual in east		studies in the chinese humanities.
	and west. Univ hawaii (1968)		Univ wisconsin (1968)
SIJ	Sino-indian journal	WMM	Wesleyan methodist magazine
SIS	Sino-indian studies	WPDMD	Ram Jee Singh (ed) World per-
SJFAW	Sino-japonica; festschrift andré		spectives in philosophy, religion
	wedemeyer zum 80. geburstag.		and culture: essays presented to
	Leipzig (1956)		professor dhirenda mohan datta.
SJV	Silver jubilee volume, kyoto uni-		Patna (1968)
	versity jimbun kagaku kenkyū-sho	WPR	John Henry Barrows (ed) The
	(1954)		world's parliament of religions.
SM	Studia missionalia		Chicago (1893) 2 vol.
SOERF	Maurice Freedman (ed) Social	YE	Young east
	organization. Essays presented	ZBK	Zeitschrift bildende kunst
	to raymond firth. London (1967)	ZCE	R. C. Zaehner (ed) Concise en-
SS	Studia serica		cyclopaedia of living faiths.
SSBKD	Søren, Egerod (ed) Studia serica		London (1959)
	bernhard karlgren dedicata.	ZDMG	Zeitschrift der deutschen
	Copenhagen (1959)		morgenländischen gesellschaft
SSMT	William Theodore DeBary (ed)	ZE	Zeitschrift für ethnologie
	Self and society in ming thought.	ZMK	Zeitschrift für missionskunde
	Columbia univ (1970)	ZMR	Zeitschrift für missionswissenschaft
SW	W. S. McCullough (ed) The seed		und religionswissenschaft
	of wisdom: essays in honor of		
	t. j. meek. Univ toronto (1964)		
SWJA	Southwestern journal of		
	anthropology		
TASJ	Transactions of the asiatic society		
	of japan		
TBMRD	Tōyō bunko, memoirs of the re-		
	search department		
TC	James T. C. Liu and Wei-ming Tu		
	(ed) Traditional china. Englewood		
	cliffs, n.j. (1970)		
THM	T'ien hsia monthly		

Details Concerning Serial Sources
Justine Pinto

The following list assembles publication data for most of the serials named in the bibliography. Reference is made to our abbreviations in the left-hand column. Because it was not possible in many cases to determine date of termination, the absence of such an indication should not be taken as implying that the serial continued publication through 1970. Where we have been unable to find sufficient information to be useful, the serial has been omitted from this list.

ASBIE   Academia sinica. The institute of ethnology. Taipei. **Bulletin**, 1, march 1956- .

ASBIHP   Academia sinica. The institute of history and philology. Peking and taipei. **Bulletin** 1, october 1928-.

           Académie des inscriptions et belles-lettres. Paris- . Publ the following five ser:

CRAIBL   **Comptes-rendus des séances.** 1, 1857- .

           Histoire et mémoires. 1-51, 1666/1710-1784/93. Publ 1736-1843. Individual numbers with **Mémoires de littérature tirés des registres.** See below.

MAIBL   **Mémoires.** 1, 1803-. Publ 1815-. May be listed as new ser.

           Mémoires concernant l'asie orientale, inde, asie centrale, extrême-orient. 1-3, 1913-1919.

MAI   **Mémoires de littérature tirés des registres.** 1-81, 1666/1710-1773/1776. Repr from vol 1-41 of the **Histoire.**

           Académie des sciences. Paris. **Comptes-rendus hebdomadaires des séances,** 1, 1835- .

           Académie imperiale des sciences. St Petersburg. **Bulletin.** See Akademiia nauk. SSSR, Leningrad.

           Académie royale de belgique. Classe des lettres et des sciences morales et politiques. **Bulletin.** See Academie royale des sciences. . . brussels.

           Académie royale des sciences, des lettres et beaux-arts de belgique, brussels. **Bulletin,** 1, 1832-98. Classe des lettres et des sciences morales et politiques, **Bulletin,** 1899- . Also publ:

MCAM   **Mémoires couronnés et autre mémoires,** 1840-1904. Title varies as **Mémoires couronnés et mémoires des savants étrangers.**

Academy   **Academy and literature.** London. 1, 1869- . Title varies.

ActaA   **Acta asiatica.** Tokyo. 1, 1960- .

           Acta orientalia academiae scientiarum hungaricae. See Magyar tudomanyos. Akademia.

AO   **Acta orientalia.** Copenhagen. 1, 1922- .

           Acts of various congresses, institutions, etc. are listed by name or title of congress or institution.

           Adyar library bulletin. Madras. 1, february 1937- .

           Akademie der wissenschaften (Royal Prussian Academy of Science) Berlin. See also under Institut für orientforschung. **Abhandlungen.** 1804-1907 in one volume a year including publications of various klasses. 1908- as **Abhandlungen** under Philosophisch-historische and physikalisch-mathematische klasse.

Akademie der wissenschaften. Leipzig. The name of the institute varies as Königlich sächsische gesellschaft der wissenschaften; Sächsische akademie der wissenschaften. **Berichte über die verhandlungen,** 1846-48. Philologisch-historische klasse, **Berichte.** 1, 1849- .

SAWW   Akademie der wissenschaften. Vienna. Philosophisch-historische klasse, **Sitzungsberichte.** 1, 1848-.

Akademiia nauk. SSSR, Leningrad. **Bulletin.** Ser 3, 1, 1860- . Previously divided by class. **Izvestiia.** Ser 7, 1928-. Earlier titled **Bulletin.**

All the year round. London. April 30, 1859-95.

AMZ   **Allgemeine missions-zeitschrift.** Berlin. 1-50, 1874-1923. Superseded by **Neue allgemeine missions-zeitschrift.**

Ambix. Society for the study of alchemy and early chemistry. London. 1, May 1937- .

PAAAS   American academy of arts and sciences. **Proceedings.** See **Daedalus.**

American anthropologist. Washington, n.y., pa. 1, 1888-.

American antiquarian and oriental journal. n.p. 1, 1878- .

American journal of economics and sociology. Lancaster, pa. 1, 1941-.

JR   **American journal of theology.** Baltimore. 1-15, 1880-95. Chicago. 1-24, 1897-1920, united with **Biblical world** to form **Journal of religion.**

American magazine of art. See **Magazine of art.**

JAOS   American oriental society. New haven, conn. **Journal.** 1, 1843-.

AUFS   American university field staff. Reports service: **East Asia series.** N.Y. August, 1952- .

Anatomical record. Wistar institute of anatomy and biology. Baltimore; philadelphia. Nov 1906- .

Ankara, Turkey. Université. Dil ve tarih-cografya fakultesi. **Dergisi.** 1, 1942- . Title page in french, Université d'ankara, **Revue de la faculté de langues, d'histoire et de géographie.**

Annales, annuals, annuairie, etc. of institutions, societes, etc, see under the name or location of the organization.

ACP   **Annales de chimie et de physique.** Paris. 1, 1789- .

Annales d'hygiène et de médecine coloniales. See **Annales de médecine et de pharmacie coloniales.**

AEO   **Annales de l'extrême-orient et de l'afrique.** Paris. 1, 1878-91. 1-3 as **Annales de l'extrême-orient; bulletin de la société académique indochinoise.**

Annales de médecine et de pharmacie coloniales. Paris. 1, 1898- . 1-17 titled **Annales d' hygiène et de médecine coloniales.**

APC   **Annales de philosophie chrétienne.** Paris. 1-166, 1830-1913.

Annales des voyages de la géographie, de l'histoire et de l'archéologie. Paris. 1-188, 1819-70. 1819-65 as **Nouvelles annales des voyages.**

AL   **Annali lateranensi.** (Rome lateran. Museo lateranense. Pontificio museo missionario ethnologico) 1, 1937- .

AMH   **Annals of medical history.** N.Y. 1, 1917- .

Année sociologique. Paris. Ann 1-12, 1896/97-1909/12; n.s. 1-2 1923-25; 3e sér 1940/48- . 1934-42 superseded by **Annales sociologique.**

Antaios. Athens. 1, 1945- .

Anthropological institute. Journal. See Royal anthropological institute of great britain and ireland and/or the ethnological society of london.

Anthropological quarterly. Washington, d.c. 1, 1928- .

Anthropologie. Paris. 1, 1890- . Suspended 1941-46.

Anthropos; ephemeris internationales ethnologica et linguistic. Salzburg, vienna, fribourg. 1, 1906- .

Antiquity; a quarterly review of archaeology. Gloucester. 1, 1927- .

Apollo; journal of the arts. London. 1, 1925- .

Archaeologia, or miscellaneous tracts relating to antiquity. London. 1, 1770- .

Archaeology. Cambridge, mass. 1, 1948- .

Archiv für geschichte der philosophie. Berlin. 1, 1888- . Vol 37-39 (1925-30) as **Archiv für geschichte der philosophie und soziologie;** vol 8-39 (1895-1930) as n.s. vol 1-32.

ARW   **Archiv für religionswissenschaft.** Heidelberger akademie der wissenschaften. Leipzig, etc. 1-37, 1898-1941.

AV   **Archiv für völkerkunde.** Museum für völkerkunde. Vienna. 1, 1946- .

ArchOr   **Archiv orientálňi.** Prague. 1, 1929- .

Archives d'anthropologie criminelle, de médecine légale et de psychologie normale et pathologique. Paris. 1-29, 1886-1914. 1886-92 as **Archives de l'anthropologie criminelle et des sciences pénales.**

Archives de sociologie des religions. Paris. 1, 1956- .

Archives suisses d'anthropologie générale. Genève. 1, 1914- .

AAA   **Archives of asian art.** See Chinese art society of america.

ACASA   **Archives** of the Chinese art society of america. See Chinese art society of america.

Aristotelian society for the systematic study of philosophy. Proceedings. London. 1, 1887- ; n.s. 1, 1900- .

Ars islamica. Michigan university research seminar in islamic art; Detroit institute of arts. Ann arbor. 1-15/16, 1934-51. Superseded by **Ars orientalis.**

AArch   **Art and archaeology.** Archaeological institute of america. Baltimore/washington d.c. 1-35, 1914-34.

Art and letters; india and pakistan. London, 1, 1925-26; n.s. 1, 1927+ 1925-47 as **Indian art and letters.**

AB   **Art bulletin.** College art association of america. N.Y. 1913- .

Art in america. N.Y. 1, 1913- .

ANA   **Art news (annual)** N.Y. 1, 1902- .

AQ   **Art quarterly.** See Detroit institute of arts of the city of detroit.

             Art studies; medieval, renaissance and modern. Ed members of the departments of fine arts
             at harvard and princeton universities. 1-8, 1923-31. Note also that these were issued as
             extra numbers of the **American journal of archaeology** in 1923, 1925-28.

             Artes; monuments et mémoires. Copenhagen. 1-8, 1932-40.

AA   **Artibus asiae; quarterly of asian art and archaeology for scholars and connoisseurs.** Ascona,
             switzerland. 1925- . There is also a ser of **Supplementa** issued from 1937.

ArtsAs   **Arts asiatiques.** Annales du musée guimet et du musée cernuschi. Paris. 1, 1954- .

AP   **Aryan path.** Bombay. 1, 1930- .

             Asia. N.Y. See **Asia and the americas.** From march 1917 to october 1942 title was simply
             Asia.

             Asia. Asia society, N.Y. 1, spring 1964- .

CMBA   **Asia.** Shanghai and hong kong. 1, 1948- . Title varies as follows: jan 1948-june 1949,
             China missionary; sep 1949-july 1953, **China missionary bulletin;** sep 1953-dec 1959,
             Mission bulletin.

             Asia; asian quarterly of culture and synthesis. Saigon. 1-4, 1951-55.

Asia   **Asia and the americas.** N.Y. 1-46, 1898-1946. Title varies as follows: 1898-jan 1917,
             Journal of the american asiatic association; mar 1917-oct 1942, **Asia.**

AM   **Asia major** London, leipzig. 1-10, 1924-34/35; 1944; London 1, 1949- .

AMHAV   **Asia major; Hirth anniversary volume.** Oct 1922. The introductory issue, not included in
             vol numbering.

AH   **Asian horizon.** London. 1-3, spring 1948-winter 1950/51.

             Asian review. London etc. 1, 1886- . Title varies as follows: 1886-90, 1913, **Asiatic quarterly**
AQR   **review;** 1891-1912, **Imperial and asiatic quarterly review;** or **Oriental and colonial record;**
AR   1914-52. **Asiatic review.**

AsSur   **Asian survey.** Berkeley. 1, 1961- . Supersedes **Far eastern survey.**

             Asiatic journal. See Asiatic journal and monthly review.

             Asiatic journal and monthly register. See **Asiatic journal and monthly review.**

             Asiatic journal and monthly review. London. 1816-45. Title varies as follows: ser 1-2,
             Asiatic journal and monthly register; ser 3, **Asiatic journal and monthly miscellany.**
             United with **Colonial magazine** and **East india review** to form **Colonial and asiatic review.**

AQR   **Asiatic quarterly review.** See **Asian review.** London.

AR   **Asiatic review.** See **Asian review.** London.

             Asiatic society of bengal, calcutta. 1936- as Royal asiatic society of bengal. **Asiatic**
             researches; or **Transactions** of the society. Calcutta. 1-20, 1788-1839. Superseded by
             Journal. Title varies. **Journal.** 1-33, 1832-64. Continued in the following: **Journal and**
JRASB   **proceedings,** n.s. 1-30, 1905-34; ser 3, 1, 1935- . **Proceedings.** 1865-1904. Continued
             in preceding title.

JBBRAS   Asiatic society of bombay. 1804-27, Literary society of bombay; 1827-1955, Royal
          asiatic society of great britain and ireland, bombay branch. **Journal.** 1841-1922/23;
          n.s. 1925- . Proc incl. **Transactions.** 1-3, 1804/5-1819-21.

          Asiatic society of great britain and ireland. See Royal asiatic society of great britain and
          ireland.

TASJ   Asiatic society of japan. **Transactions.** 1, 1872/73- . Various series.

AS   **Asiatische studien.** Bern. 1, 1947- . French title, **Études asiatiques.**

          Asiatisches magazin. Weimar. 1-2, 1802.

BAF   **Asie française; bulletin mensuel.** Paris, Comité de l'asie française. 1, 1901- . 1901-10 as
          Bulletin de la comité.

          Asien. Berlin. 1-16, 1901-19. Superseded by **Ostasiatische rundschau.**

BAAFC   Association amicale franco-chinoise. **Bulletin.** See **Revue franco-chinoise.**

          Association françoise des amis de l'orient. **Bulletin.** Paris. No 1-6, 1921-23; n.s. no 1-11,
          mar 1925-déc 1927; no 77, oct 1929. N.S. in **Revue des arts asiatiques** q.v. Nothing publ
          in 1924, 1928.

          Association of american geographers. n.p. **Annals.** 1, 1911- .

          Athenaeum; journal of literature, science, the fine arts, music and the drama. London.
          1828-1921.

          Atlantic monthly. Boston. 1, nov 1857- .

          Ausland. Stuttgart. 1-66, 1828-93. Merged into **Globus.**

          Aussenpolitik. Stuttgart. 1, 1950- .

BOR   **Babylonian and oriental record.** London. 1-9, 1886-1901.

          Baessler-archiv; beiträge zur völkerkunde. Leipzig, berlin. 1-25, 1910-43; n.s. 1, 1952- .

          Basavangudi, bangalore. Indian institute of culture. **Transactions.** See Indian institute of
          world culture.

          Belgrade. Institut imeni N. P. Kondakova. **Annaly.** 1-11, 1927-40. 1927-36 as **Sbornik
          statei po arkheologii i vizantinoiedieniiu seminarium kondakovianum.**

          Berichte der K. - Sach. ges. d. wiss. phil-hist.cl. see Akademie der wissenschaften. Leipzig.
          Berichte.

          Berichte des rheinischen missionsgesellschaft. See Rheinische missionsgesellschaft.

          Berlin. Staatliche museen. Ethnologische abtheilung. **Mitteilungen.** 1, 1885-86.

          Berlin. Staatliche museen. Museum für völkerkunde. **Veröffentlichungen.** 1-12, 1889-
          1919. Vol 11 not publ. 12 publ in 1907.

MSOS   Berlin. Universität. Ausland-hochschule. Through 1935, this organization was the
          university's seminar für orientalische sprachen. **Mitteilungen.** 1, 1898- .

          Berliner gesellschaft für anthropologie, ethnologie und urgeschichte. **Verhandlungen.**
          1869-1902. May be bound with **Zeitschrift für ethnologie.**

Berliner museum (museen). Amtliche berichte aus den preussischen kunstsammlungen. Berlin. 1-64, 1880-1943.

Biblical world. Chicago. 1, 1882-1920. United with the **American journal of theology** to form the **Journal of religion.**

Bibliotheca sacra; a theological quarterly. Oberlin. 1, 1844- .

Bibliothèque d'école hautes. See Paris. École pratique des hautes études.

BVAMG   **Bibliothèque de vulgarisation des annales du musée guimet.** See Paris. Musée guimet.

BTLVK   **Bijdragen tot de taal-, land- en volkskunde von nederlandsche-indie.** The hague. 1, 1853- .

Biologie médicale. Paris. 1, 1903- .

BlM   **Blackwood's magazine.** Edinburgh, london. 1, 1817- . 1817-1905 as **Blackwood's edinburgh magazine.**

Bombay. University. **Journal.** 1, july 1932-. Also numbered in various sub-ser.

BMFA   **Boston.** Museum of fine arts. **Bulletin.** 1, 1903- .

British academy for the promotion of historical, philosophical and philological studies. London. **Proceedings.** 1, 1903- .

British journal of sociology. London. 1, 1950- .

BMQ   **British museum quarterly.** London. 1, 1926- .

AIPHO   **Brussels.** Université libre. Institut de philologie et d'histoire orientales et slaves. **Annuaire.** 1, 1932/33- .

Buddhism in england. See **Middle way.**

The buddhist annual. Colombo. 1, 1964- .

Buddhist text society. Calcutta. **Journal.** 1-7, 1893-1906. The name of the organization varies and is superseded by the Indian research society.

Buecherei (bûcherei) der kultur und geschichte. Bonn, leipzig. 1-30, 1919-23?

BAF   **Bulletin asie-française.** See **Asie française.**

Bulletin de géographie historique et descriptive. See under France. Comité des travaux historiques et scientifiques.

Bulletin de l'académie impériale des sciences de st. petersburg. See Akademiia nauk, SSSR; Leningrad.

BAAFC   **Bulletin** de l'association amicale franco-chinoise. See **Revue franco-chinoise.**

BMFJ   **Bulletin** de la maison franco-japonaise. See under Tokyo. Maison franco-japonaise.

Bulletin de la société saint-jean-baptiste. See **Information nationale.**

Bulletin des missions. Bruges. 1, 1899- . Title varies.

BAAFC   **Bulletin franco-chinoise.** See **Revue franco-chinoise.**

Bulletin médical franco-chinois. Peking. 1, 1920- .

BEA **Bulletin of eastern art.** Tokyo. No 1-19/20, 1940-41.

BHM **Bulletin of the history of medicine.** Johns hopkins university. Institute of the history of
BIHM medicine. 1, 1933-. From 1933-38 as **Bulletin of the institute of the history of medicine.**

    Bulletin of the john herron institute. See under indianapolis. Art association of indianapolis.
    John herron art institute.

    Bulletins of other societies, libraries, museums, etc. are listed by name or place of the
    institution.

BM   **Burlington magazine.** London. 1, 1903- .

CHM **Cahiers d'histoire mondiale.** Paris. 1, 1953- .

CalR **Calcutta review.** Calcutta. 1, 1844- .

    Canadian magazine of politics, science, art and literature. Toronto. 1-91, 1893-1939.
    1925-37 titled **Canadian.**

    Canadian review of sociology and anthropology. 1, 1964- .

BCUP Catholic university of peking. See under Peking.

CW   **Catholic world; monthly magazine of general literature and science.** N.Y. 1, apr 1865- .

    Central asiatic journal. The hague. 1, 1955- .

    Century, a popular quarterly. N.Y. 1-120, 1870-1930. Title varies as follows: 1870-81 as
    Scribner's monthly; 1881-1925 as **Century illustrated magazine;** 1925-29 as **Century
    monthly magazine.** United with **Forum** to form **Forum and century.**

    Century illustrated magazine. See **Century, a popular quarterly.**

    Century magazine. See **Century, a popular quarterly.**

BAIC Chicago. Art institute. **Bulletin.** 1, 1907- 1-45 as **Bulletin** and now **Quarterly.**

    China-analysen. Frankfurt-am-main. 1, 1962- .

CCY **China Christian yearbook.** Shanghai. 1910-35. 1910-25 as **China mission yearbook.**

    China informatie. Delft. 1, 1967- .

    China institute bulletin. China institute in america. N.Y. 1936-47, 1949- .

CJ   **China journal.** Shanghai. 1-35, 1923-41. 1-5 as **China journal of science and arts.**

    China magazine. Hankow, chungking, n.y. 1-19, 1938-49. 1-15 as **China at war.**

    China magazine. N.Y. 1, 1924- . 1-10 as **China.**

    China mail. Hong kong.

CMH **China mission hand-book.** Shanghai. 1, 1896. Only one published.

China mission yearbook. See China christian yearbook.

CMBA   China missionary or China missionary bulletin. See Asia. Shanghai; hongkong.

China monthly; the truth about china. N.Y. 1-11, 1931-50.

CWR   China monthly review. Shanghai. 1-124, 1917-53. Title varies as follows: 1917-21, Millard's review; 1921-23, Weekly review of the far east; 1923-50, China weekly review.

CNA   China news analysis. Hongkong. 1, 1953- .

China notes. China committee. Far eastern office division of foreign missions. N.Y. 1, 1962- . Supersedes China bulletin.

China pictorial. Peking. 1951- .

CQ   China quarterly. Paris. 1, 1960- .

China quarterly. Shanghai. 1-6, 1935-41.

CRecon China reconstructs. Peking. 1, 1952- .

ChRev   China review. Hongkong. 1-25, 1872-1901.

China review. London. 1-5, 1931-38.

ACSS   China society. Singapore. Annual. 1948- (Chung-kuo hsüeh-hui)

JCS   China society. Taipei. Journal. 1, 1961- . Alternate listing under Chung-kuo hsüeh-hui, taipei.

China society occasional papers. London. N.s. 1, 1942- .

China today. N.Y. 1937-42.

China today. Taipei. 1958- .

CWR   China weekly review. See China monthly review.

La chine; revue bi-mensuelle illustrée. Peking. 1-73, 1921-25.

Chine et sibérie. Brussels. 1-2 (no 1-40), 1900-01.

Chinese and japanese repository of facts and events in science, history, and art, relating to eastern asia. London. 1-2 (no 1-29) 1863-65.

ACASA   Chinese art society of america. N.Y. Archives. 1, 1945/46- . With vol 20, 1966/67,
AAA   changed to Archives of asian art.

Chinese buddhist. Pure karma buddhist association. Shanghai. 1-2, 1930-31(?)

CC   Chinese culture. Taipei. 1, 1957- .

CL   Chinese literature. Peking. Autumn, 1951– (Wen-hsüeh nien-pao)

CMJ   Chinese medical journal. Shanghai. 1, 1887- .

ChRec   Chinese recorder. Shanghai. 1, 1868- . Supersedes Missionary recorder.

ChRep   Chinese repository. Canton. 1-20, 1832-51.

Chinese review. London. 1-4, 1914.

CSPSR	**Chinese social and political science review.** Peking. 1-24, 1916-41.
CSM	**Chinese students' monthly.** Baltimore. 1-26, 1905-30.
	Chinese year book. Shanghai. 1-7, 1935/36-1944/45.
CDA	**Chinesische-deutscher almanach.** Frankfurt-am-main. China-institut. 19–; probably 1926.
	Chinesische blätter für wissenschaft und kunst. 1, 1925/27. See also: **Sinica.**
CF QNCCR	**Ching feng.** Hong kong. 1957-. 1-7 has title **Quarterly notes on christianity and chinese religion and culture.**
	Ch'ing hua hsüeh-pao. See **Tsinghua journal of chinese studies.**
	Ch'ing-shih wen-t'i. New haven. 1, 1965-.
	Christian century. Chicago. 1, 1884-.
	Christliche welt. Marburg. 1, 1886-.
CCJ	**Chung chi journal.** Hongkong. July, 1961-.
	Chung-kuo hsüeh-hui. See China society, taipei, or China society, singapore.
	Chung mei yüeh-k'an. Taipei. 1, 1956-. **West and east** is the engl title of this journal.
CMI	**Church missionary intelligencer.** See **Church missionary review.**
	Church missionary review. London. 1-78, 1849-1927. From 1849-1906 as **Church missionary intelligencer.**
	Church missionary society. London. **Annual report of the committee of the church missionary society for africa and the east.** 1, 1801-. Title varies as **Proceedings** of the society for missions to africa and the east, or **Proceedings** of the church missionary society.
	Ciba symposia. New jersey. 1-11, 1939-51. Engl companion vol to **Ciba zeitschrift.**
	Ciba zeitschrift. Basel. 1-11, 1933-52. See also **Ciba symposia.**
	Cina. Rome. Istituto italiano per il medio estremo oriente. 1-8, 1956-64.
	Claremont quarterly. Claremont, california. 1-11, 1956/57-64.
BCMA	Cleveland. Museum of art. **Bulletin.** 1, 1914-.
	Club alpin français. Paris. **Annuaire.** 1-30, 1874-1903.
	Colonial and asiatic review. See **Asiatic journal and monthly review.**
	Comité japonais des sciences historiques. A section of the XIe Congrès international des sciences historiques. Stockholm, 1960.
	Comité sinico-japonais. See Société sinico-japonaise. Paris.
	Common cause. Chicago. 1-4, 1947-51.
	Common cause. London, n.y. 1, 1944-.
CSSH	**Comparative studies in society and history, an international quarterly.** The hague. 1, 1958-.
	Comptes rendus. See under name of institution or organization.

Concilium; internationale zeitschrift für theologie. Zürich, mainz. 1, 1965- .

CAM **Conférences faites au musée guimet.** See under Paris. Musée guimet.

Conferenze tenute all' istituto italiano per il medio ed estremo oriente. See under Istituto italiano per il medio ed estremo oriente.

CIHR Congrès international d'histoire des religions. (Société ernest renan) Paris, 1923. **Actes,** Paris, 1925, 2 vol. See also International congress for the history of religions.

Congrès international des sciences anthropologiques et ethnologiques. See International congress of anthropological and ethnological sciences.

ICO Congrès international d'orientalistes. See International congress of orientalists.

CPOL Congrès provincial des orientalistes français. Lyon, paris. **Compte rendu.** 1-3, 1875-78.

Congrès scientifique international des catholiques. 1888- . 4e congrès. Fribourg, 1897. **Compte rendu.** Fribourg, 1898, 11 vol in 3 vol.

CRJ **Contemporary religions in japan.** Tokyo. 1, 1960- .

CR **Contemporary review.** London. 1, 1866- .

La controverse et la contemporain. Paris. 1, 1845-89.

Cornhill magazine. London. 1, 1860- .

CB **Current background.** Hong kong. American consulate general. No 1, 1950- .

Current science; science in the making. Bangalore, india. 1, july 1932- .

The cycle; a political and literary review. Shanghai. 1st ser may 1870-june 1871. All publ in 1871.

Daedalus. American academy of arts and sciences. Cambridge, mass. 1, no 1, may 1846- . The Academy's **Proceedings.**

Dan viet nam. École française d'extrême-orient. Hanoi. No 1-3, 1948-49.

BDetIA Detroit institute of arts of the city of detroit. **Art quarterly.** 1, winter 1938- . **Bulletin.**
AQ 1, 1904- ; n.s. 1919- .

DGNVO Deutsche gesellschaft für natur- und völkerkunde ostasiens. See under Gesellschaft für natur- und völkerkunde ostasiens.

ZDMG Deutsche morgenländische gesellschaft. Leipzig. **Zeitschrift.** 1, 1847- .

Deutsche rundschau für geographie. Vienna, leipzig. 1-37, 1878-1915. 1-32 titled **Deutsche rundschau für geographie und statistik.**

Diogène. Paris. No 1, 1952- . French edition of **Diogenes.**

Diogenes: an international review of philosophy and humanistic studies. N.Y. No 1, 1952- .

Discovery; a popular journal of knowledge. London, cambridge. 1, 1920- .

Les documents du progrès. Paris. 1, 1909- . See following item. **Dokumente des fortschritte; internationale revue.** Berlin. 1-11, 1907-18. Affiliated with **Documents du progrès.** Paris. Occasionally art are duplicated. **Records of progress** is the american ed.

Dublin review. London. 1, 1836- .

E&W   **East and west.** Rome. 1, 1950- .

EA   **East of asia; an illustrated quarterly.** Shanghai. 1-5, 1902-06. This is engl ed of **Ferne osten,**
           q.v.

EWCR   **East-west center review.** Honolulu. 1-4, 1964-68.

EArt   **Eastern art.** College art association of america. Philadelphia. 1-3, 1928-31.

EB   **Eastern buddhist.** Kyoto. 1, 1921-1937; n.s. 1, 1965- .

EH   **Eastern horizon.** Hongkong. 1, 1960- .

EW   **Eastern world.** London. 1, 1947- .

           Eclectic magazine of foreign literature. N.Y., boston. 1-148, 1844-1907.

           École des hautes études. See Paris. École pratique des hautes études.

BEFEO   École française d'extrême-orient. Hanoi. **Bulletin.** 1, 1901- .

           École pratique des hautes études. See under Paris.

           Education. France. Haut- commissariat de france pour l'indochine. Saigon. 1, 1948.

           Eine heilige kirche. Munich. 1-22 no 2, 1919-41. Vol 1-15 as **Hochkirche.** Superseded by
           Ökumenische einheit.

           Encounter. London. 1, 1953- .

           Endeavour; revue trimestrielle, publiée en cinq langues et destinée à tenir registre du progrès
           des sciences au service du genre humain. Imperial chemical industries. London. vol 1,
           1942- .

EJ   **Eranos-jahrbuch.** Zürich. 1933- .

           Etc.; a review of general semantics. Chicago. 1, 1943- .

           Ethics. Chicago. 1, 1890- . Vol 1-48, 1890-1938 titled **International journal of ethics.**

           Ethnographie. Paris. 1-22, 1860-1903. N.s no 1, oct 1913- . Vol 1-2 as **Comptes rendus**
           of Société d'ethnographie; vol 3-8 as **Actes** of the society. Vol 1-22 also numbered in ser.

           Ethnological society of london. Journal. 1848-71. 1861-69 as **Transactions.** This society
           united with the anthropological society of london to form the Royal anthropological
           institute of great britain and ireland.

           Ethnologisches notizblatt. Königliche museum für völkerkunde. Königliche museum,
           berlin. 1-3, 1894-1904.

           Ethnos. Staten etnogtafiska museum. Stockholm. 1, 1936- .

AS   **Études asiatiques.** See **Asiatische studien.**

           Études sociales. Paris, 1, 1881- . 1881-1930 as **La reforme sociale.**

Études   **Études des pères de la compagnie de jésus.** Paris. 1, 1856- . Title varies as follows: 1856-61
ER   as **Études de théologie, de philosophie et d'histoire;** 1862-94 as **Études religieuses,**
           philosophique et historiques.

ER   **Études religieuses.** See **Études des pères.** . . .

Evangelischen missionen, illustriertes familienblatt. Güterslah. 1, 1895- .

EMM   Evangelisches missions -magazin. Basel. 1816-1939. In 1940 merged with NAM, ZMR, and Orient (Potsdam?) to form Evangelische missionszeitschrift. Stuttgart. 1, 1940- .

Évidences. Paris. No 1, 1949- . Preceded in mar 1949 by one unnumbered issue.

l'Explorateur: Journal géographique et commercial. Paris. 1-4, 1875-76.

FE   The far east. Shanghai? 1, no 1-12, 1905-06.

FEER   Far eastern economic review. Hongkong. 1, 1946- .

FEQ   Far eastern quarterly. See Journal of asian studies.

Far eastern review. Shanghai. 1-38, 1904-41.

FO   Ferne osten. Shanghai. 1-3, 1902-05. See also East of asia.

Fogg museum of art. See Harvard University. William H. Fogg art museum.

Folk-lore; quarterly review of myth, tradition, institution and custom. London. 1, 1890- .

FLJ   Folklore journal. London. 1-7, 1883-89.

FS   Folklore studies. Catholic university. Museum of oriental ethnology. Peking, nagoya. 1, 1942- . In 1963, title changed to Asian folklore studies.

FF   Forschungen und fortschritte; korrespondenzblatt der deutschen wissenschaft und technik. Berlin. 1-41?, 1925-67(?)

Fortnightly. London. 1-182, 1865-1954. From 1865-1934 titled Fortnightly review.

France. Comité des travaux historiques et scientifiques. Section de géographie. Bulletin. 1, 1886- . From 1886-1912 titled Bulletin de géographie historique et descriptive.

FA   France-asie; revue de culture et de synthèse franco-asiatique. Saigon. 1, 1946- .

Frankfurter hefte. Stadtisches völkermuseum. Frankfurter universität. 1-39, 1915-31. N.s. 1946- . 1, 1946- .

Fraser's magazine. London. 1, 1869-82.

FCR   Free China review. Taipei. 1, 1951- .

Freer galley of art. Washington, d.c. Occasional papers. 1, 1947- .

GBA   Gazette des beaux-arts. Paris. 1, 1859-1939. American ed n.y. Ser 6, vol 22, 1942- .

Geist des ostens. Munich. 1-2, 1913-15.

Geisteswissenschaften. Leipzig. No 1-39, 1913-14.

Geisteswissenschaftliche forschungen. Stuttgart. 1, 1936- .

Gentleman's magazine. London. 1-303, 1731-1907.

Geographical journal. Royal geographical society of london. London. 1, 1893- . Supersedes the society's Proceedings.

GM   Geographical magazine. London. 1-5, 1874-78. Superseded by the Royal geographical society of london, Proceedings.

Geographical magazine. London. 1, 1935- .

Géographie. Paris. 1-72,no 3, 1900-39. Supersedes **Bulletin** of the Société de géographie (Paris) See also listing under the Société.

MDGNVO
Nachr
DGNVO
Gesellschaft für natur- und völkerkunde ostasiens. Tokyo to 1945. Deutsche gesellschaft für natur- . . . is an earlier name of the institution. **Mitteilungen.** 1-32E, 1873/76-1943. **Nachrichten.** Tokyo, wiesbaden. No 1, 1926- . No 1-70, 1926-45 as **Nachrichten aus der gesellschaft.**

Globus. Hildburghausen, brunswick 1-98, 1861-1910. Merged into **Petermanns geographische mitteilungen.**

Goldthwaite's geographical magazine. N.Y. 1-7, 1891-95.

Gregorianum Rome. 1, 1920- .

Gutenberg jahrbuch. Mainz. 1, 1926- .

Han-hiue. Paris. Université. Centre d'études sinologiques de Pékin. 1-3.4, 1944-49. Vol 1 titled **Bulletin** de la centre.

HZ
Hansei Zasshi. See **Orient.** Tokyo.

Harper's magazine. N.Y. 1, 1850- . 1-101 as **Harper's new monthly magazine;** 102-28 as **Harper's monthly magazine.**

Harper's weekly. N.Y, 1-62, 1857- .

Harvard divinity bulletin. Harvard university. Divinity school. Cambridge, mass. 1, 1935/36- . Title varies as follows: **Harvard divinity school annual; Harvard divinity school bulletin; Harvard divinity school.**

HJAS
Harvard journal of asiatic studies. Cambridge, mass. 1, 1936- .

HTR
Harvard theological review. Harvard University. Theological school. 1, 1908- .

Harvard university. Center for east-asian studies. **Papers on China.** 1, 1947- .

BFoggMA
Harvard university. William H. Fogg art museum. **Bulletin.** 1, 1931- .

Hermes; recherches sur l'expérience spirituelle. Paris. 1, 1963- .

HJ
Hibbert journal; quarterly review of religion, theology and philosophy. London, boston. 1, 1902- .

HM
Histoire de la médecine. Paris. 1, 1951- .

HR
History of religions. Chicago. 1, 1961- .

History today. London. 1, 1951- .

Hitotsubashi academy annals. Tokyo. Annals. 1-10, 1950-59. In 1960, vol one of the **Hitotsubashi journal of arts and sciences** partially superseded the Annals. May also be listed under Tokyo. Hitotsubashi Daigaku.

Hobbies; the magazine for collectors. N.p. Begins with vol 36, 1931- .

Hochland; monatschrift für alle gebiete des wissens, der literatur und kunst. Munich; kempton. 1, 1903- .

Honolulu academy of arts. **Special Studies.** 1, 1947- . Supersedes its **Annual bulletin.** 1-3, 1939-41(?)

HRAF Human relations area files, inc. Country survey series. New haven. 1, 1956- .

Illustrated london news. London. 1, 1842- .

Illustration. Paris. 1-102, 1843-1944.

PIAJ Imperial academy of japan. **Proceedings.** See Japan academy. Tokyo. **Proceedings.**

IAQR **Imperial and asiatic quarterly review.** See Asian review. London.

IA Indian antiquary. Bombay. 1-62, 1872-1933. Superseded by **New indian antiquary.**

Indian art and letters. See **Art and letters: India and pakistan.**

Indian culture. Calcutta. 1, 1934- .

IHQ **Indian Historical quarterly.** Calcutta. 1, 1925- .

Indian institute of culture. See Indian institute of world culture.

Indian institute of world culture. Basavangudi, bangalore. **Transactions.** No 1, 1948- .

Indian journal of social research. Baraut, india. 1960- .

Indian journal of (the) history of medicine. Madras. 1, 1956- .

JISOA Indian society of oriental art. Calcutta. **Journal.** 1-19, 1933-52/53. Superseded by **Rupam.**

Indianapolis. Art association of indianapolis. John herron art institute. **Bulletin.** 1, 1911- .

IAC **Indo-asian culture,** New delhi. 1, 1952- .

ICG **Indo-chinese gleaner.** Malacca. 1-3 (no 1-20) 1817-22.

Information nationale. Montreal. 1953- . Vol 1-10 as **Bulletin** de la société saint-jean-baptiste de montreal.

AIPHO Institut de philologie et d'histoire orientales. See under Brussels. Université.

MIOF Institut für orientforschung. Deutsche akademie der wissenschaften. Berlin. **Mitteilungen.** 1953- .

Institute of pacific research. China academy. Taipei. **Journal** or **Bulletin.** 1, 1967- .

IAE **International archives of ethnography.** Leiden. 1, 1888- . Title varies as **Internationales archiv für ethnographie; Archives internationales d'ethnographie,** etc.

PIAHA International association of historians of asia. **Conference proceedings.** 1st biennial conference. Manila. 1960. 2nd biennial conference. Taipei. 1962.

ICfO International conference of orientalists in Japan. **Transactions.** 1, 1956- .

ICHR International congress for the history of religions. Proceedings title varies with host country. 1900- . 2nd congress Basel (1904) **Verhandlungen.** Basel (1905) 382p. 3rd congress. Oxford (1908) **Transactions.** Oxford (1908) 2 vol. 7th congress. Amsterdam (1950) **Proceedings.** Amsterdam (1951) 196p. 11th congress. Claremont, calif (1965) **Proceedings.** Leiden (1968?) 3 vol. See also under Congrès international d'histoire des religions, paris, 1923, for data on a congress which is not one of this ser.

International congress of anthropological and ethnological sciences. 1st congress. London. 1934. **Proceedings.** 2nd congress. Copenhagen. 1938. **Proceedings.** 6th congress. Paris. 1960. 3 vol **Proceedings.**

ICO International congress of orientalists. Transactions. Title varies with host country. 2nd congress. London. (1874) **Transactions.** 1876. 4th congress. Florence (1878) **Atti.** 2 vol 1880-81. 6th congress. Leiden (1883) **Actes.** 4 vol 1884-85. 9th congress. London (1892) **Transactions.** 2 vol 1893. 10th congress. Genève (1894) **Actes.** 3 vol (Leide) 1895-97. 11th congress. Paris (1897) **Actes.** 5 vol 1898-99. 13th congress. Hamburg (1902) **Verhandlungen** (Leiden) 1904. 14th congress. Algiers (1905) **Actes.** 3 vol in 4 (Paris) 1906-8. 18th congress. Leiden (1931) **Actes.** 1932. 21st congress. Paris (1948) **Actes.** 1949. 26th congress. New delhi (1964) **Daily bulletins.**

International journal of ethics. See **Ethics**

IPQ **IPQ: International philosophical quarterly.** N.Y. 1, 1961- .

IRM **International review of missions.** Edinburgh. 1, 1912- .

Ipek; jahrbuch für prähistorische ethnographische kunst. Leipzig. 1-22, 1925-69.

IQB **Iqbal review.** Karachi, pakistan. 1960- . Alternately in engl and urdu.

Isis, international review devoted to the history of science and civilization. Brussels, bern. 1, 1913- .

Is.MEO Istituto italiano per il medio e l'estremo oriente. Conferenze tenute all'is (tituto italiano per il) M(edio e l') e(stremo) o(riente) 1952- .

Izvestiya (izvestiia) akademiya nauk. See under Akademiia nauk, SSSR Leningrad. **Izvestia.**

JAK **Jahrbuch der asiatischen kunst.** Leipzig. 1-2. 1924-25.

JSMVL **Jahrbuch der städtliches museum für völkerkunde.** See under Leipzig.

Jahrbuch für psychologie, psychotherapie und medizinische anthropologie. Munich, etc. 1, 1952/53- . Title varies. Vol 1-6 (1952-59) as **Jahrbuch für psychologie und psychotherapie.**

Jahresberichte der geschichtswissenschaft. Berlin. 1-36, 1878-1913.

Jahrbuch für prähistorische ethnographische kunst. See **Ipek.**

Janus; revue internationale de l'histoire des sciences, de la médecine, de la pharmacie et de la technique. Leiden. 1, 1896- .

PIAJ Japan academy. Tokyo. **Proceedings.** 1, 1912- . From 1912-47 listed as published by the imperial academy of japan.

Japan quarterly. Tokyo. 1, 1954- .

JSR:HS **Japan science review: humanistic studies.** Tokyo. 1, 1950- . Vol 1-9, 1950-58 as **Japan**
JSR:LPH **science review: literature, philosophy and history**

JSR:LPH **Japan science review: literature, philosophy and history.** See **Japan science review: humanistic studies.**

TPJS Japan society, London. **Transactions and Proceedings.** 1, 1892- .

Japanese studies in the history of science. (Nippon kagakusi gakkai) Tokyo. 1, 1962- .

John herron institute. See under Indianapolis. Art association.

John rylands library. Manchester, england. **Bulletin.** 1, 1903- .

JP
NouvJA
Journal asiatique. Paris. 1, 1822- . 1828-35 as **Nouveau journal asiatique.**

Journal des savans. Paris. 1665-1792. Superseded by **Journal des savants.**

Journal des savants. Académie des inscriptions et belles - lettres. Paris. No 1-12, 1797; sér 2, 1, 1816- .

Journal d'hygiène. Paris. 1-40, 1875-1914.

JAFL   **Journal of american folklore.** Boston, lancaster. 1, 1888- .

JEAC   **Journal of aesthetics and art criticism.** N.Y. 1, 1941- .

JAAS   **Journal of asian and african studies.** Leiden. 1, 1966- .

JAS   **Journal of asian studies.** Ann arbor. 1, 1941- . Years 1941-56 titled **Far eastern quarterly.**

JCE   **Journal of chemical engineering, China.** Chinese institute of chemical engineers. Tientsin. 1, 1934- .

JIBS   **Journal of indian and buddhist studies (Indogaku bukkyŏgaku kenkyū)** Tokyo. 1, 1952- .

Journal of indian art and industries. London. 1-17, 1884-1916.

JOR   **Journal of oriental research.** See under University of madras. **Annals of oriental research.**

Journal of oriental research. Kuppuswami sastri research institute. Madras. 1, 1927- .

JOS   **Journal of oriental studies.** Hongkong. 1, 1954- .

JR   **Journal of religion.** Chicago. 1, 1921- .

JRH   **Journal of religious history.** University of Australia. Sydney. 1, 1960- .

Journal of religious psychology including its anthropological and sociological aspects. Worcester, mass. 1-7, 1904-15.

JSS   **Journal of social science.** National taiwan university. College of law. 1, 1956- . May be catalogued by chin title: **She-hui k'o-hsüeh lun-ts'ung.**

Journal of unified science. Leipzig, the hague. 1, 1930- . Supersedes **Annalen der philos-ophie und philosophischen kritik** (1-8 no 9/10, 1919- apr 1930). Vol 1-7 no 5/6, 1930- april 1939, as **Erkenntniss.**

Journal société finno-ougrienne. See under Suomalais-ugrilainen seura. Helsingfors.

JHI   **Journal of the history of ideas.** N.Y., lancaster. 1, 1940- .

JHMAS   **Journal of the history of medicine and allied sciences.** N.Y. 1, 1946- .

JIA   **Journal of the indian archipelago and eastern asia.** Singapore. 1, 1847- . Superseded by **Journal of eastern asia.** Singapore. 1, 1875- .

Journals of societies and institutions are listed under the name or locations of their respective organizations.

Kairos; religionswissenschaftliche studien. Salzburg. 1,1964-.

Kairos; zeitschrift für religionswissenschaft und theologie. Salzburg. 1, 1959-.

Die katholischen missionen. Freiberg i.b; st. louis, mo.; aachen, etc. 1, July 1873- . Numbering irregular.

Königlichen museum für völkerkunde. See under Berlin. Staatliche museem.

Kokka, an illustrated monthly journal of the fine and applied arts of Japan and other eastern countries. No 1, 1889-. Subtitle varies.

Koloniale rundschau. Berlin, leipzig. 1-34, 1909-43. May have the title **Kolonial-deutsche, wissenschaftliche beihefte.**

KGUAS   Kwansei gakuin university. Nishinomiya, japan. **Annual studies.** 1, 1953-.

Lancet. London, 1823-.

Laval théologique et philosophique. Quebec. 1, 1945-.

JSMVL   Leipzig. Städtisches museum für völkerkunde. **Jahrbuch.** 1-9, 1906-22/25; 10,1926/51-. **Mitteilungen.** No 1-17, 1960-64; 1965-.

Leipzig. Univerität. **Wissenschaftliche zeitschrift. Gesellschafts und sprach-wissenschaftliche reihe.** 1951/52-.

Life. N.Y. 1936-72.

LD   **Light of dharma.** San francisco. 1-6, 1901-07.

Littell's living age. Boston. 1844-1941.

Litterae orientales. Leipzig, wiesbaden. 1-84, ?-1939; n.s. no 1-44, 1953-1958.

BSOAS   London. University. School of oriental and african studies. **Bulletin.** 1, 1917-.

London. University. Warburg Institute. **Journal of the warburg and courtauld institutes.** 1, 1937-.

London and china express. London. 1-73, 1858-1931. Title varies.

Lotus. See under Société sinico-japonais. Paris.

Lyons. Université. **Annales.** 1-9, 1891-98; n.s. 1, **Sciences, médecine,** no 1-50, 1899-1934; n.s. 2, **Droit, lettres,** no 1-48, 1899-1934; Both superseded by n.s.3, **Science,** 1936-.

MacMillan's magazine. London, etc. 1, 1859-1907.

Magasin littéraire. Paris. 1-15, 1884-98. 1884-93 as **Magasin littéraire et scientifique.**

MLA   **Magazin; monatschrift für literatur, kunst und kultur.** Berlin. 1832-1915. Title varies as follows: 1832-80, **Magazin für die literatur des auslandes,** 1881-90, **Magazin für die literatur des in- und auslandes;** 1890-1904, **Magazin für litteratur;** 1904-05, **Neue magazin;** 1906-07, **Magazin für literatur des in- und auslandes.**

Magazine of art. Washington, n.y. 1-46 no 5, nov 1909- may 1953. 1909-15 as **Art and progress;** 1916-36 as **American magazine of art.**

Magyar tudomanyos akademia. Budapest. **Acta orientalia.** 1, 1950-.

Maharaja sayajirao university of baroda. **Journal.** 1, 1952-.

MB   **Maha Bodhi; a monthly journal of international buddhist brotherhood.** Calcutta. 1, 1892-. Title varies as follows: 1892-1901, **Journal of the Maha Bodhi society**; 1901-23, **Maha-bodhi and the united buddhist world.**

Main currents in modern thought. N.Y. 1, 1940-.

BMFJ   Maison franco-japonaise. See under Tokyo.

Man. Royal anthropological institute of great britain and ireland. London. 1,1901-.

JMGS   Manchester geographical society. Manchester, england. **Journal.** 1, 1885-.

Marco polo. Shanghai. 1, 1939-.

Mariner's mirror. London. 1, 1911-.

MCB   **Mélanges chinois et bouddhiques.** Louvain. 1, 1932-.

MIHEC   **Mélanges,** Paris universitaire, institut des hautes études chinoise. See under Paris. Université.

Mélanges sinologiques. Centre d'études sinologiques. Peking. 1951-.

Mémoires concernant l'asie orientale, inde, asie-centrale, extrême-orient. See Académie des inscriptions et belles-lettres.

MCLC   **Mémoires concernant l'histoire, les sciences, les arts, les moeurs, les usages etc. des chinois; par les missionnaires de pékin.** Ed C. Batteux, L.G. Oudert, Feudrix de Brequigny, J de Guignes, and A. J. Silvestresle Sacy. Paris. 1-16, 1776-1804.

MCAM   **Mémoires couronnés et autre mémoires.** See under Académie royale des sciences, des lettres et beaux-arts de belgique.

MAIBL   **Mémoires de l'academie des inscriptions et belles-lettres.** See under Académie des inscriptions. . .

MAI   **Mémoires de littérature tirés des registres de l'académie des inscriptions.** See under Académie des inscriptions et belles-lettres.

Mémoires de la société d'émulation de roubaix. See under société d'émulation. . . .

Merkur; deutsche zeitung für europäisches denken. Stuttgart, baden-baden. 1, 1947-.

WMM   **Methodist magazine.** London. 1, 1778-. Title varies as follows: 1778-97, **Arminian magazine**; 1798-1821, **Methodist magazine**;1822-1912, **Wesleyan methodist magazine**; 1914-26, **Magazine of the wesleyan methodist church.**

Methodist review. N.Y. 1-114, 1818- 1931. Title varies as follows: 1818-28, **Methodist magazine**; 1830-40, **Methodist magazine and quarterly review**; 1841-84, **Methodist quarterly review.**

BMMA   Metropolitan museum of art. See under New York.

MW   **Middle way.** London. 1, 1926-. Vol 1-17 as **Buddhism in england**.

Ministry; a quarterly theological review for east and south africa. Moriji, basutoland. 1, 1960-.

Minneapolis institute of art. Minneapolis. Bulletin. 1, 1905.

Mission bulletin. Shanghai, hongkong. See **Asia**.

Missionary recorder. Foochow 1, no 1-2, 1867. Superseded by **Chinese recorder.**

Missionary research library. New York. **Bulletin.** 1, 1928-. This publication coincides with dating of **Occasional bulletin.**

MRW   **Missionary review of the world.** London, etc. 1-62, 1878-1939. 1878-87 as **Missionary review.**

MC   **Missions catholiques.** Paris. 1, 1868-.

Mitteilungen aus der ethnologischen abteilung der königl- museen zu berlin. See Berlin. Staatliche museen. Ethnologische abtheilung.

MSGFOK   **Mitteilungen** der schweitzerischen gesellschaft der freunde ostasiatische kultur. See schweitzerische gesellschaft für asien-kunde.

MSOS   **Mitteilungen** des seminars für orientalische sprachen. See under Berlin. Universität. Ausland-hochschule.

MIOF   **Mitteilungen** deutsche preussiche akademie der wissenschaften zu berlin. See Institut für orientforschung.

MDGNVO   Mitteilungen der deutsche gesellschaft für natur- und völkerkunde ostasiens, tokyo. See Gesellschaft für natur- und völkerkunde.

Moderne welt. Cologne. 1, 1959-.

Monde moderne et la femme d'aujourdhui. Paris. 1-28, 1895-1908. 1895-1905 as **Monde moderne.** Merged into **Revue hebdomadaire.**

Monist, a quarterly magazine devoted to the philosophy of science. Chicago. 1-46, 1890-1936.

Moniteur universel: Journal officiel. Paris. 1789-1868.

MN   **Monumenta nipponica.** Tokyo. 1, 1938-.

MS   **Monumenta serica.** Peking, nagoya, los angeles, st. augustin (germany) 1, 1935/36-.

Muséon. Société des lettres et des sciences. Paris, louvain. 1, 1882-.

Museum; tijdschrift voor filologie geschiedenis. Groningen, leyden. 1-64, 1893-1959?

Museum journal. See under Pennsylvania. University. University museum.

BMFEA   Museum of far eastern antiquities. See under Stockholm.

BMFA   Museum of fine arts (Boston) See under Boston.

Nachr   **Nachrichten** der deutsche gesellschaft für natur- und völkerkunde ostasiens. See
DGNVO   Gesellschaft für natur- und volkerkunde ostasiens.

NGM   **National geographic magazine.** Washington, d.c. 1, 1888-.

National medical journal. London. 1, 1914-.

National medical journal of china. Shanghai. 1915-.

NPMB   **National palace museum bulletin.** Taipei. 1, 1966-. May be catalogued under **Kuo-li ku-kung po-wu-yüan.**

NRJ   **National reconstruction journal.** N.Y. 1-8, 1942-47.

National review. Shanghai. 1-20, ?-1916.

NLIP **Natural law institute proceedings.** Notre dame university. Law school (college of law) 1-15, 1947-51. Superseded by **Natural law forum.**

Nature. London. 1, 1869-.

Nature. Paris. 1, 1873-.

Neue orient. Berlin. 1-17, 1917-43.

Neue orient; abhandlungen zur geographie, kultur und wirtschaft der länden des ostens. Halle-a-saale. 1-13, 1905-18.

Neue schweizer rundschau. Zürich. 1-41, 1907-33; n.s. 1-22, 1933-55. 1907 as **Wissen und leben.**

NZM **Neue zeitschrift für missionwissenschaft.** Beckenreid, switz. 1, 1945-.

New age. Communist party of india. New delhi. 1, sep 1952-? n.s. 1, apr 1964-.

New asia; an organ of oriental culture and thought. Calcutta. 1-2, 1939-40?

New century review. London. 1-8, 1897-1900.

NCR **New china review.** Shanghai. 1-4, 1919-22.

NewIA **New indian antiquary; a monthly journal of oriental research in archaeology, art, epigraphy.** Bombay. 1, 1938-. Supersedes **Indian antiquary.** See also **New Indian antiquary. Extra series.**

NewIA **New indian antiquary. Extra series.** Bombay 1, 1939-.

New orient. N.Y. 1-3, 1923-27. Vol 1 as **Orient; an international magazine of art and culture.** Superseded by **Oriental magazine.**

NO **New Orient.** Prague. 1, 1960-.

New world; a quarterly review of religion, ethics and theology. Boston. 1-9, 1892-1900.

BMMA New York. Metropolitan museum of art. **Bulletin.** 1, 1905-.

New zealand institute. See Royal society of new zealand.

NC **Nineteenth century.** See **Twentieth century.** London.

Nineteenth century and after. See **Twentieth century.** London.

North american review. N.Y., boston. 1, 1815-.

NCH **North China herald.** Shanghai. 1850-?

NQ **Notes and queries on china and japan.** Hongkong. 1-4, 1867-70.

NouvJA **Nouveau journal asiatique.** See **Journal asiatique.**

NouvClio **Nouvelle clio.** Brussels. 1, 1949-.

NR **Nouvelle revue.** Paris. 1, 1879-.

Nouvelle revue française. Paris. 1-31, 1909-43. N.s. 1, 1953- . Title varies as
La nouvelle nouvelle revue.

Nouvelles annales des voyages. See Annales des voyages, de la géographie, de l'histoire et
de l'archéologie.

Nucleus. American chemical society. Boston. 1, 1924-.

Numen; international review for the history of religions. Leyden, 1, 1954-.

Numismatic and antiquarian society of philadelphia. Proceedings. Philadelphia
1, 1865/66-.

Occult review. See Rider's review. London.

Occult review. Boston. 1888-97.

Österreichische monatschrift für den orient. Vienna. 1-44, 1875-1918.

Okurayama oriental research institute. Proceedings. 1, 1954-. Engl title of Okurayama
gakuin. Yokohama. Okurayama Gakuin Kiyo.

OC   Open court, a quarterly magazine. Chicago. 1-50, 1887-1936.

Oriens. Leiden. 1, 1948-.

OE   Oriens extremus. Wiesbaden. 1, 1954-.

Orient. Hongkong. 1-6, 1950-56.

HZ   Orient. Tokyo, 1-16, ? - 1901. Vol 1-13 titled Hanzei zasshi.

Orient et occident. Geneva. 1-2, 1934-36.

OA   Oriental art. London. 1-3, 1948-51; n.s. 1- 1955-.

TOCS   Oriental ceramic society. London. Transactions. 1, 1921-.

JOSA   Oriental society of australia. Sydney. Journal. 1, 1960-.

Orientalia suecana. Uppsala. 1, 1952-.

Orientalische archiv. Leipzig. 1-3, 1910-13.

OL   Orientalistische literaturzeitung. Berlin, leipzig. 1, 1898-.

Oriente poliana. Istituto italiano per il medio e l'estremo oriente. Rome.

OstL   Ostasiatische lloyd. Shanghai. 1-31, 1866-1917.

Ostasiatische rundschau. Berlin. 1-25, 1920-44.

OZ   Ostasiatische zeitschrift. Berlin. 1, 1912- 42/43.

Our missions. London. 1-24, 1894-1917.

Outlook, a weekly review of politics, art, literature and finance. London. 1-61, 1898-
1928.

PA   Pacific affairs. Honolulu, n. y. 1, 1926-.

PW   Pacific world. Berkeley. 1-4, 1925-28.

Paideuma; mitteilungen zur kulturkunde. Bamberg. 1, 1938-.

Pakistan journal of science. See Pakistan journal of scientific research.

Pakistan journal of scientific research. Pakistan association for the advancement of science. Lahore. 1, 1949-.

Pakistan philosophical journal. Lahore. 1, 1957-.

JPTS   Pali text society. London. **Journal.** 1882-1924/27.

Pantheon; international zeitschrift für kunst. Munich. 1, 1928-.

ACF   Paris. Collège de france. **Annuaire.** 1, 1901-.

Paris. École pratique des hautes études. Bibliothèque. **Sciences religieuses.** 1, 1889-.

AMG   Paris. Musée guimet. **Annales.** 1-51, 1880-1935? **Bibliothèque de vulgarisation.**
BVAMG   1, 1889-.   **Conférences faites au musée guimet.** 1898/99-1914; 1902-16.
CMG

MIHEC   Paris. Université. Institut des hautes études chinoises. **Mélanges.** 1, 1957-.

Parnassus. N.Y. 1-13, 1929-41.

BCUP   Peking. Catholic university. **Bulletin.** 1-9, 1926-34.

JPOS   Peking oriental society. **Journal.** 1-4, 1885-98.

UPUMB   Pennsylvania. State university. University museum. **Museum journal.** 1-24, 1910-35.
Museum bulletin, 1-22, 1930-55.

Pennsylvania museum bulletin. See Philadelphia museum bulletin.

La pensée; revue du (bon) rationalisme moderne. Paris. 1939- ; n.s. no 1, oct/dec 1944-.

PC   **People's china.** Peking. 1, 1950-57.

PT   **People's tribune.** Peking. 1, 1931-1941(?)

Petermanns geographische mitteilungen. Gotha. 1, 1855-. Title varies.

Pharmazeutische industrie. Aulendorf. 1, 1933-.

PTP   **Phi theta papers.** Berkeley. 1, 1950-. 1950, 1954-55 titled **Phi theta annual.**

Philadalphia museum bulletin. Philadelphia. 1, 1903-. From 1920-38 titled **Pennsylvania museum bulletin.**

Philosophical magazine. London. 1, 1798-. Ser varies.

Philosophical quarterly. Calcutta. 1, 1925-.

Philosophical studies of japan. Comp by the Japanese national commission for UNESCO. Tokyo. 1, 1959-.

Philosophisches jahrbuch der görres-gesellschaft. Munich, etc. 1, 1888-. Suspended 1943-45 and 1952.

PEW   **Philosophy east and west.** Honolulu. 1, 1951-.

PS   **Popular science monthly.** N.Y. 1, 1872-.

Praxis der psychotherapie. Munich. 1, 1956- . 1-3 (1956-58) as **Psychotherapie.**

Proceedings of various societies and institutions are listed under the name or location of the organization in question.

Psyche. Heidelberg, stuttgart. 1, 1947-.

Psychoanalysis and the psychoanalytic review. N.Y. 1, 1913-. 1913-57, titled **Psychoanalytic review.**

Psychoanalytic review. See **Psychoanalysis and the psychoanalytic review.**

Psychotherapie. See **Praxis der psychotherapie.**

QJCA   **Quarterly journal of current acquisitions.** See under United States. Library of Congress.

QNCCR   **Quarterly notes on christianity and chinese religion.** See **Ching feng.**

Quarterly review. London. 1, 1809-.

Quest. London. 1-21, 1909-30.

Quiver. London. 1, 1861-. N.Y. 1-39, 1884-1926 is american ed of london publ.

Race. London. 1, 1959-.

Records of progress. See **Dokumente des fortschritte.**

Reforme sociale. See **Études sociales.**

RC   **Relations de chine (Kiang-nan)** Paris. 1, 1903-27 (?)

Religion in life; a christian quarterly. N.Y. 1, 1932-.

Religion und geisteskult. Gottingen. 1-8, 1907-14.

Religions. London. No 1-77, 1931-53.

Religious studies. London. 1, 1965-.

Rencontre orient-occident. Geneva. 1, 1954-.

RofR   **Review of religion.** N.Y. 1-22, 1936-58.

Review of religions. Punjab. 1, 1902-.

La revue. (Ancient revue des revues) Paris. 1, ? Vol 46, pt 3, 1903-. Title changes to **La revue mondiale.**

La revue; littérature, histoire, arts et sciences des deux mondes. Paris. 1948-. Supersedes **Revue des deux mondes.**

Le revue; littéraire et artistique. Paris. 1, 1882-.

Revue anthropologique. Paris. 1-50, 1891-1942; 1955-.

Revue apologétique. Paris. 1-68, 1905-39.

Revue apologétique. Brussels. 1-13, 1900-12.

RA   **Revue archéologique.** Paris. 1844-.

Revue blanche. Paris. 1-30, 1891-1903.

Revue bleue, politique et littéraire. Paris. 1863-1939. Title varies.

Revue britannique. Paris. 1-77, 1825-1901.

Revue catholique. Université catholique. Louvain. 1-61, 1843-98.

Revue critique. Paris. 1866-1935.

RE **Revue d'ethnographie.** Paris. 1-8, 1882-91.

Revue d'ethnographie et des traditions populaires. Paris 1-10, 1920-29. Supersedes **Revue des traditions populaires.**

Revue d'europe et d'amérique. Paris. 1-20, 1998-1908. Title varies.

Revue de l'art ancien et moderne. Paris. 1-71, 1897-1937.

REO **Revue de l'extrême-orient.** Paris. 1882-87.

Revue de la faculté de langues, d'histoire et de géographie. See under Ankara. Université.

RHR **Revue de l'histoire des religions.** Musée guimet. Paris. 1, 1880-.

ROA **Revue de l'orient et de l'algérie et des colonies.** Paris. 1843-65.

RMM **Revue de métaphysique et de morale.** Paris. 1, 1893-.

Revue de paris. Paris. 1, 1894-.

Revue de théologie et de philosophie. Genève. 1868-1911; 1913-.

RAA **Revue des arts asiatiques.** Paris. 1-13, 1924-42. Superseded by **Arts asiatiques.** See also Association française des amis de l'orient, **Bulletin.**

RDM **Revue des deux mondes.** Paris. 1829-1948.

Revue des études ethnographiques et sociologiques. Paris. 1-2, 1908-09. Superseded by **Revue d'ethnographie et de sociologie.** 1-5, 1910-14.

Revue des questions historiques. Paris. 1866-.

RR **Revue des religions.** Paris. 1-8, 1889-96.

Revue des revues. Paris. 1-50, 1876-1925.

Revue des traditions populaires. Paris. 1-34, 1886-1919. Superseded by **Revue d'ethnographie et des traditions populaires.**

Revue du clergé français. Paris. 1-103, 1895-1920.

Revue du monde catholique. Paris. 1-64, 1861-1925.

Revue du sud-est asiatique et de l'extrême-orient. Brussels. 1961-.

Revue encyclopédique. See **Revue universelle.** Paris.

Revue française de l'étranger et des colonies. Paris. 1885-1914.

Revue franco-chinoise. Association amicale franco-chinoise. Paris. 1, 1907- . 1907-15 as the association's **Bulletin.**

Revue de géographie commerciale. See Société de géographie commerciale de bordeaux.

RGI **Revue géographique internationale.** Paris. 1-28, no 1-326, 1876-1903.

Revue hebdomadaire. Paris. 1892-1939.

RIC **Revue indochinoise.** Hanoi. 1, 1893-.

Revue maritime et coloniale. Paris. no 1-202, 1861-1914; n.s. no 1-236, 1920-39.

Revue nationale chinoise. Shanghai. 1, 1929-. Suspended jan-june 1938.

Revue orientale et américaine. Paris. 1859-99. Title and ser vary.

Revue politique et parlementaire. Paris. 1, 1894-.

Revue scientifique. Paris. 1863-1954.

Revue universelle. Paris. 1891-1905. To 1900 as **Revue encyclopédique.**

Rheinische missionsgesellschaft. Barmen, germany. **Berichte.** 1, 1828/30- . Vol 1-8 (1828/30-36/37) as **Jahresbericht.**

Rider's review. London. 1, 1905- . Title varies as follows: 1-58.2 and 63-75.5 as **Occult review;** 58.3-62 as **London forum.**

RSO **Rivista degli studi orientali. Roma.** 1, 1907- .

Rocznik orjentalistyczny. Krakow. 1, 1914/15-.

SM Rome. Pontifica universita gregoriana. **Studia missionalia.** 1, 1943-.

Royal anthropological institute of great britain and ireland. London. **Journal.** 1, 1871-. **Proceedings.** 1965-.

Royal geographical society. London. **Proceedings.** 1-22, 1855/57-77/78; n.s. 1-14, 1879-92. See also **Geographical magazine** and **Geographical journal** publ by the society.

JRASB Royal asiatic society of bengal. See Asiatic society of bengal.

RAS Royal asiatic society of great britain and ireland. **Journal.** London. 1-20, 1834-63; n.s. 1-21, 1864-89; 1889-. **Transactions.** London. 1-3, 1827-33. Superseded by **Journal.** Publications of branches of the RAS are as follows:

JBBRAS Bombay branch. See under Asiatic society of bombay.

China branch. Shanghai. **Transactions.** 1-6, 1847-59. Journal, see North China branch.

JHKBRAS Hong kong branch. Hongkong. **Journal.** 1, 1960/61-.

JMBRAS Malayan branch. Singapore. **Journal.** 1, 1923- . Supersedes the Straits branch.

JNCBRAS   North China branch. Shanghai. **Journal.** 1-2, 1858-60; n.s. 1, 1864-. Vol 1 as
           Shanghai literary and scientific society journal. 1886-95 as the China branch, **Journal.**

JSBRAS   Straits branch. Singapore. **Journal.** 1-86, 1878-1922. Superseded by the
           Malayan branch.

BROMA   Royal ontario museum of archaeology. See under Toronto. Royal ontario museum.

           Royal society of new zealand. Wellington. **Transactions and proceedings.** 1, 1868-.

           Rupam. Calcutta. 1920-30. Superseded by the Indian society of oriental art. **Journal.**

           Rythmes du monde. Lyons. April, 1946-.

           S.E.T.; structure et évolution des techniques. Association pour l'étude des techniques.
           Paris. 1, 1949-.

           Saeculum; jahrbuch für universal geschichte. Freiburg, 1, 1950-.

           Saturday review of literature. N.Y. 1925-1973.

           Schweitzerische gesellschaft der freunde ostasiatische kultur. See Schweitzerische
           gesellschaft für asienkunde.

MSGFOK   Schweitzerische gesellschaft für asienkunde. Founded 1939 as above and changed to
           asienkunde in 1947. **Mitteilungen.** St. gall. No 1-8, 1937-46. Superseded by
           Asiatische studien.

           Science catholique. Paris. 1-20, 1886-1906.

           Sciences religieuses. See under Paris. École pratique des hautes études.

           'Scientia,' rivista di scienza. Bologna. 1, 1907- .

           Scientific monthly. Washington, etc. 1-85, 1915-1957. Merged into **Science.**

SCCM   **Selections from china mainland magazines.** Hongkong. No 1, 1955- .

           Seminarium kondakovianum. See under Belgrade.

           Seminars für orientalische sprachen. See under Berlin. Universität.

           Shanghae almanac for 1854 (1855) and miscellany. Shanghai. 1851-62. Subtitle varies.
           See also **Shanghai miscellany.**

           Shanghai literary and scientific society. **Journal.** 1, 1858. First vol of the **Journal** of the
           North china branch of the royal asiatic society.

           Shanghai miscellany. 1-2, 1834-57. 1853-56 included in **Shanghae almanac.**
           1857 publ sep.

           Siam respository. Bangkok. 1-6, 1869-74.

           Siam society. Bangkok. **Journal.** 1, 1904-.

BUA   Shanghai. Université de l'aurore. **Bulletin.** 1909-.

           Sinica; zeitschrift für chinakunde und china forschung. Frankfurt. 1-17, 1926-42.
           Suppl to **Chinesischer blätter für wissenschaft und kunst.**

           Sinica-sonderausgabe. Frankfurt a.m., 1934-.

SIJ   **Sino-indian journal.** Santiniketan, bengal. 1, 1947- .

SIS **Sino-indian studies.** Santiniketan, bengal. 1, 1944- .

Sino-indica. Calcutta university. Paris. 1, 1927- .

Sinologica. Basel. 1, 1947-.

SAWW **Sitzungsberichte der akademie der wissenschaften in wien.** See Akademie der wissenschaften. Vienna.

Social action. Boston, chicago. 1, 1935-.

Société d'acupuncture. Paris . **Bulletin.** 1, 1950-.

BMSAP Société d'anthropologie de paris. **Bulletins et mémoires.** 1860-.

Société d'émulation de roubaix. **Mémoires.** 1868-1931.

Société d'ethnographie. **Actes.** See **Ethnographie.**

BSEIS Société des études indochinoises de saigon. **Bulletin.** 1-71, 1883-1923; n.s. 1, 1926-.

Société de géographie. Paris. **Comptes rendus.** 1882-99. Continued in **Géographie.**

Société de géographie commerciale de bordeaux. **Bulletin.** 1874-1939. Title varies as **Revue de géographie commerciale.**

Société de géographie de l'est. Paris. **Bulletin.** 1-35, 1879-1914.

Société des études japonaises, chinois, tartares et indo-chinois. See Société sinico-japonaise. Paris.

Société finno-ougrienne. See Suomalais-ugrilanen seura.

Société française d'histoire de la médecine. Paris. **Bulletin,** 1902-42. Superseded by **Histoire de la médecine.**

BSAB Société royale belge d'anthropologie et de préhistoire de bruxelles. **Bulletin.** 1, 1882-.

ASAB Société royale d'archéologie de bruxelles. **Annales.** 1, 1887- .

Société sinico-japonaise. Paris. 1877 - ? as a section of the société d'ethnographie, Paris; also as Société des études japonaises, chinoises, tartares et indo-chinoises and Société sinico-japonaise et océanienne. Sometimes cited as Comité sinico-japonaise. **Annuaire.** 1873- . **Mémoires.** 1-10, 1873-91; n.s. 1-22, 1892-1901? Vol 5-9 of the first ser has title of **Lotus.**

Sociological bulletin. Bombay, delhi. 1, 1952-.

Sources orientales. Publisher's series. Paris. 1, 1959-. Irregularly publ; each vol has its own title.

SEAJT **South east asia journal of theology.** Singapore. 1, 1959-.

SWJA **Southwestern journal of anthropology.** Albuquerque. 1, 1945-.

BMFEA Stockholm. Ostasiatiska samlingarna (Museum of far eastern antiquities) **Bulletin.** 1, 1929-.

Structure et évolution des techniques. See **S.E.T.**

Studi e materiali di storia delle religioni. Rome universati. Rome. 1, 1925-.

SM   **Studia missionalia.** See under Rome.

SS   **Studia serica.** West china union university. Chinese cultural studies research institute. 1, 1940- . See also **Monograph** ser A, no 1, 1947- ; B, no 1, 1942- .

Studia taiwanica. Taipei. 1, 1956- . Catalogued under T'ai-wan yen-chiu.

Studien zur frühchinesischen kulturgeschichte. Antwerp. 1-2, 1941-43.

Studies on buddhism in japan. International buddhist society. Toyko. 1-3, 1939-41.

Studio; an illustrated magazine of fine and applied art. London. 1, 1893- . **London Studio.** N.Y. 1931-38, american ed.

Studium generale; zeitschrift für die einheit der wissenschaften zusammenhang ihrer begriftsbildungen und forschungs methoden. Berlin. 1, 1947-.

Sunday at home. London. 1854-1940.

Suomalais-ugrilainen seura. Helsingfors. **Aika kau skirja (Journal)** 1, 1886-.

SCMM   **Survey of China mainland magazines.** See **Selections from china. . .**

Symbolon; jahrbuch für symbolforschung. Basel. 1, 1960-.

Tamkang journal. See **Tan-chiang hsüeh-pao.**

Tan-chiang hsüeh-pao. Taipei. 1958-. Engl title **Tamkang journal.**

Technology review. M.I.T. boston. 1, 1899- .

TJR   **Tenri journal of religion.** Research institute for religion. Tenri, japan. 1, 1955- .

Theologische literaturzeitung. Leipzig, berlin. 1, 1876-.

Theosophical forum. N.Y, point loma, calif. 1-70, 1889-95; ser 2, 1, 1929-.

Theosophical path; illustrated monthly. Point loma, calif. 1-45, 1911-1935. Merged into Theosophical forum.

THM   **T'ien hsia monthly.** Shanghai. 1-12, 1935-41.

Tōhōgaku ronshu. Tokyo. 1, 1954-.

BMFJ   Tokyo. Maison franco-japonaise. **Bulletin.** 1-15, 1927/29-47; n.s. 1, 1951-. 1-5, titled Bulletin seri-française.

TBMRD   Tokyo. Tōyō bunko (oriental library). Research department. **Memoirs.** No 1, 1926- .

BROMA   Toronto. Royal ontario museum. Art and archaeology division. **Bulletin.** No 1-27, 1923-58. Supersedes the Royal ontario museum of archaeology which publ no 1-23.

TP   **T'oung pao.** Leiden. 1-10, 1890-99; ser 2, 1, 1900-.

TBMRD   Tōyō bunko, **memoirs of the research department.** See under Tokyo.

Tōyō gakuhō. Tokyo. 1, 1911-.

Tōyō University asian studies. Tokyo. 1, 1961-.

Transactions. See under the name or location of the organization.

Travel. N.Y. 1, 1901- . Title varies. Combined with **Holiday** in 1931.

TM   À travers le monde. Paris. 1-20, 1895-1914.

Tri-quarterly. Evanston, illinois. 1-6, 1958-64; n.s. no 1, 1964- .

Tribus; veroeffentlichungen des linden-museum. (Stuttgart. Museum für laend- und völker-kunde) Heidelberg. N.f. 1, 1951- . Vol 1 issued as **Jahrbuch des linden museum.**

TJ   **Tsinghua journal of chinese studies.** Peking, taipei. 1-12, 1924-37; n.s. 1, 1956- . Supersedes Tsing-hua journal. Peking. 1-4, 1919-? Chinese title, **Ch'ing-hua hsüeh-pao.**

NC   **Twentieth century.** London. 1, 1877- . Title varies as follows: 1877-1900 as **Nineteenth century; a monthly review;** 1901-50 as **Nineteenth century and after.**

United asia; international magazine of asian affairs. Bombay. 1, 1948- .

QJCA   United States. Library of congress. **Quarterly journal of current acquisitions.** 1, 1943- .

United States. National museum. **Bulletin.** 1, 1875- . **Proceedings.** 1, 1878- .

United states. National museum. Smithsonian institution. **Annual report of the board of regents.** 1, 1846- . From 1884, there are two ann vol, the second of which is **Report of the u.s. national museum.**

USJPRS   United states joint publications research service.

Universitas; zeitschrift für wissenschaft, kunst und literatur. Stuttgart. 1, 1946- .

University of ceylon review. Colombo. 1, 1943- .

University of madras. Madras. **Journal.** 1-14, 1928-42. Continued in two sections as follows: A-Humanities. 15-18, 1943-46; B-Science. 15, 1943- . **Annals of oriental research.** 1, 1936-

JOR   Vol 1 as **Journal of oriental research.**

UPUMB   **University of Pennsylvania museum bulletin.** See under Pennsylvania. State University. University museum.

Variétés sinologiques. Shanghai. 1-66, 1892-1938.

Verhandlungen. See under the name of the institution, organization, congress, etc.

Veröffentlichungen aus dem königlichen museum für völkerkunde. See under Berlin, Staatliche museem.

Visva-bharati bulletin. Calcutta. 1, 1924- .

VBA   **Visva-bharati annals.** Santiniketan, india. No. 1, 1945- .

VBQ   **Visva-bharati quarterly.** Calcutta. 1-8, 1923-32; n.s. 1, 1935- .

Voice of buddhism. Buddhist missionary society, Kuala lumpur. 1, 1964?-

Le voile d'isis. Paris. 1-?, 1890-?; 2e sér, 2, (?) 3e sér, 3, no 1-56, 1910-14.

Walters art gallery. Baltimore. **Journal.** 1, 1938- .

Warburg and courtauld institutes. **Journal.** See under London. University.

Welt des orients: wissenschaftliche beiträge zur kunde des morgenländes. Wuppertal. 1, 1947- .

Die weisse fahne. Pfullingen. 1-16, 1920-35; ?-.

Der weltkreis. Berlin. 1-3, 1929-33.

Der wendepunkt im leben und im leiden. Zürich, leipzig. 1, 1923-. Vol 1 lacks date.

WMM   Wesleyan Methodist magazine. See Methodist magazine.

West and East. Taipei. 1, 1956-. Also listed under chinese title Chung mei yüeh-k'an.

JWCBorder   West china border research society. Chengtu. Journal. 1-16, 1922/23-45. 12-16 issued in
ResS   two series, General and natural sciences, A and B respectively.

West china missionary news. Chengtu. 1, 1899- .

WBKKGA   Wiener beiträge zur kunst- und kulturgeschichte asiens. Verein der freunde asiatischen kunst
und kultur in wien. Vienna. 1-11, 1926-37?

Wiener völkerkundliche mitteilungen. Vienna. 1, 1953- . Issuing agent varies.

Wiener zeitschrift für die kunde des morgenländes. Orientalisches institut der universität wien.
Vienna. 1, 1887- .

Wiener zeitschrift für die kunde sud- und ostasiens und archiv für indische philosophie.
Indologische institut, universitaet wien. Vienna, 1, 1957- .

Wirkendes wort. Paedagogischen verlag schwann. Duesseldorf. 1, 1966- .

Wissen und leben. See Neue schweizer rundschau.

Wissenschaftliche annalen der gesammten heilkunde. Berlin. 1-30, 1825-34. 1-24 (1825-32)
as Litterarische annalen der gesemmten heilkunde. Superseded by the Neue
wissenschaftliche. . . .

Die woche, modern illustrierte zeitschrift. Berlin. 1, 1899- .

Worcester, mass. Art museum. Annual. 1, 1935/36- .

World mission. London. 1966- .

Worldmission. N.Y. 1, 1950- .

World's chinese students' journal. Shanghai. 1-8, 1906-14.

Yoga; international journal on the science of yoga. Bulsar, india. 1, 1933- .

Yoga; internationale zeitschrift für wissenschaftliche yoga-forschung. Harburg-wilhelmsburg.
1, 1931-?

Yoga series. Madanapalli, india. 1, 1956- .

YE   Young East. Tokyo. 1-8, 1925-41. Superseded by Young east; Japanese buddhist quarterly.

Young East. Tokyo. 1-15, 1952-66.

Zalmoxis, revue des études religieuses. Paris. 1, 1938.

Zeitschrift. See also the names or locations of issuing organization.

Zeitschrift für bauwesen. Berlin. 1-81, 1851-1931.

ZBK   Zeitschrift für bildende kunst. Leipzig. 1-65, 1866-1932.

Zeitschrift für buddhismus. Half-title for the following item: **Zeitschrift für buddhismus und vervandt gebiete.** Munich. 1-9, 1914-31.

Zeitschrift für die historische theologie. Leipzig. 1-45, 1831-75.

ZE   **Zeitschrift für ethnologie.** Berliner gesellschaft für anthropologie, ethnologie und urgeschichte. Berlin. 1, 1869- . May include **Verhandlugen** of the society.

Zeitschrift für geopolitik in gemeinschaft und politik. Bad godesberg, etc. 1, 1924- . 1924-55 as **Zeitschrift für geopolitik.**

Zeitschrift für menschenkunde und zentralblatt für graphologie. Heidelberg, vienna, etc. 1, may 1925- . Title varies. Cited in text as **Zeitschrift für menschenkunde.**

ZMK   **Zeitschrift für missionskunde and religionswissenschaft.** Allgemeiner evangelisch-protestantischen missionsverein. Berlin. 1-54, 1886-1939.

ZMR   **Zeitschrift für missionswissenschaft und religionswissenschaft.** Institut für missionswissen-schaftliche forschungen. Münster. 1, 1911- . Title varies.

Zeitschrift für religionspsychologie. Guterslah. 1-11, 1928-37.

Zeitschrift für religions-psychologie. Leipzig. 1-6, 1907-13.

Zeitschrift für religions und geistes geschichte. Marburg. 1, 1948- .

Zeitschrift für systematische theologie. Berlin. 1, 1923- .

Zeitschrift für theologie und kirche. Tübingen. 1891-1917; 1920-38; 1950- .

Zeitwende; die neue furche. Hamburg, etc. 1, 1925- .

Zinbun. Kyoto daigaku. Jimbun kagaku kenkyūjo. Kyoto. 1, 1957- .

Part One

Bibliography and
General Studies

1. BIBLIOGRAPHY

Barrow, John G. (comp) **A bibliography of bibliographies in religion.** Ann arbor, mich (1955) 489 p. See 4. Non-christian religions b. Buddhism; k. Taoism.

Beautrix, P. **Bibliographie du bouddhisme. I. Éditions de textes.** Bruxelles (1970) 210 p.

Beautrix, P. **Bibliographie du bouddhisme zen.** Bruxelles (1969) 114 p.

Benz, Ernst and Nambara Minoru (comp) **Das christentum und die nichtchristlichen hochreligionen. Begegnung und auseinandersetzung. Eine internationale bibliographie.** Leiden (1960) See 21-22, 46-51, 62, 79-82, 83-86.

Berkowitz, M. I. and Poon, Eddie K. K. (comp) **Hongkong studies: a bibliography.** Chin univ of hong kong (1969) 137 p.

Bibliographie bouddhique (various ed) Paris (1930-1937) t 1 - 7/8.

Chang, Lucy Gi Ding (comp) Acupuncture: a selected bibliography. **CC** 5.1 (1963) 156-160.

Chesneaux, Jean (ed) **Popular movements and secret societies in China 1840-1950.** Stanford univ (1972) Bibliography of works concerning secret societies, 279-288 (abbrev as **PMSSC**) Orig french ed: **Mouvements populaires et sociétés secrètes en chine aux xixe et xxe siècle,** paris (1970) (abbrev as **MPSSC**) Contents of the two versions are quite different.

Cordier, Henri (comp) **Bibliotheca sinica.** Paris (1904-24) 5 vol. Repr taipei (1966).

Diehl, Katherine Smith (comp) **Religions, mythologies, folklore: an annotated bibliography.** New brunswick, n.j. (1956) 2nd ed (1962)

Dobson, W. A. C. H. The religions of china (excepting buddhism) Being chap 2 in Charles J. Adams (ed) **A reader's guide to the great religions,** n.y. and london (1965) 31-44.

Eberhard, Wolfram. Neuere forschungen zur religion chinas 1920-1932. **ARW** 33 (1936) 304-344. Engl tsl: Studies of chinese religion 1920-1932, in **MSVC** (1971) 335-399.

Edmunds, Albert J. (comp) A buddhist bibliography, based upon the libraries of philadelphia. **JPTS** (1902-03) 1-60. Suppl in **LD** 4 (1904) 147-150, 193-198.

Erbacher, Hermann (comp) **Bibliographie der fest- und gedenkschriften für personlichkeiten aus evangelischer theologie und kirche 1881-1969.** Neustadt an der aisch (1971) See M: Religionswissenschaft 64: Religionsgeschichte: China (no 6334-6339)

Franke, O. Die religionswissenschaftliche literatur über china seit 1909. **ARW** 18 (1915) 394-479.

Genähr, J. New books on the religions and philosophy of china. **IRM** 3 (1914) 175-178.

Gotō, Kimpei. Studies on chinese religion in postwar japan. **MS** 15.2 (1956) 463-511.

Haas, Hans (comp) **Bibliographie zur frage nach den wechselbeziehungen zwischen buddhismus und christentum.** Berlin (1921) leipzig (1922) 47 p.

Haas, Hans. Neuer literatur über den buddhismus von china und japan. **OZ** 1 (1912-13) 238-245.

Hamilton, Clarence H. (comp) **Buddhism in india, ceylon, china and japan: a reading guide.** Univ chicago (1931) 107 p.

Hanayama, Shinsho (comp) **Shinsho hanayama bibliography on buddhism.** Commemoration committee for prof. shinsho hanayama's sixty-first birthday (ed) Tokyo (1961)

Harrassowitz, Otto (publishers) **Catalog 512: Buddhism.** Wiesbaden (1971) 48 p.

International bibliography of the history of religions. Bibliographie internationale de l'histoire des religions (various ed) Leiden (1954-1971) vol 1 - 15 (for years 1952-68)

Kramers, R. P. Religie in china: een selective bibliographie. **China informatie** 3.4 (1969) 4-13.

Lalou, Marcelle. Onze années de travaux européens sur le bouddhisme (mai 1936-mai 1947) **Muséon** 61 (1948) 245-276.

La Vallée Poussin, Louis de. Notes de bibliographie bouddhique. **MCB** 3 (1934-35) 355-407; 5 (1936-37) 243-304.

Lust, John (comp) **Index sinicus.** Cambridge, engl (1964) Periodical literature and collective works publ 1920-1955.

Marceron, Désiré J.-B. (comp) **Bibliographie du taoisme.** Paris (1898-1901) Forms pt 1 and 2 of t 15, Publications du comité sinico-japonais.

March, Arthur C. (comp) **A buddhist bibliography.** London (1935) xi + 257 p. Annual suppl 1 (1936) . . . 5 (1940)

Merkel, R. F. Zur geschichte der erforschung chinesisches religionen. **Studi e materiali di storia delle religioni** 15 (1939) 90-107.

Morgan, Kenneth W. **Asian religions. An introduction to the study of hinduism, buddhism, islam, confucianism and taoism.** N.Y. (1964) 30 p.

Needham, Joseph, with collaboration of Lu Gwei-djen. **Science and civilization in china.** Vol 5, **Chemistry and chemical technology, part II: spagyrical discovery and invention: magisteries of gold and immortality.** Cambridge univ (1974) Bibliog C, Books and journal articles in western languages, 387-469.

Religion of the chinese: a selective bibliography. **SM** 16 (1967) 117-132.

Répertoire générale de sciences religieuses. Bibliographie hors commerce . . . (various ed) Paris, publ annually (1950-68) covering years 1950-1959.

Revue bibliographique de sinologie (various ed) Paris (1957-1971) 9 vol covering years 1955-1963.

Richardson, Ernest Cushing (comp) **An alphabetical subject index and index encyclopaedia to periodical articles on religion 1890-1899.** N.Y. (1907) See China.

Robiou, F. Études récentes sur la première religion des chinois. **Revue des questions historiques** 52 (1892) 217-225.

Schloss, Oskar. **Verlags-katalog über die deutschsprachliche buddhistische und verwandte literatur.** München (1924) 110 p, 4 pl.

Skinner, G. William (ed) **Modern chinese society: an analytical bibliography.** Vol 1, **Publications in western languages, 1644-1972.** Stanford univ (1974) 880 p. See sec 13, 23, 32.2, 33, 36.3, 43, 63, 65.

Soymié, M. and Titsch, F. (comp) Bibliographie du taoisme études dans les langues occidentales. **Études taoistes** 3 (1968) 317-248 (sic) [publ in tokyo]

Taam, Cheuk-woon. On studies of confucius. **PEW** 3 (1953) 147-165.

Topley, Marjorie (comp) Published and unpublished materials on hong kong by overseas affiliated scholars. **JOS** 8.1 (1970) 219-225.

Yoo, Yushin. **Buddhism: a subject index to periodical articles in english, 1728-1971.** Metuchen, n.j. (1973) xxii + 162 p, author/ subj index, title index.

Yuan, T. L. (comp) **China in western literature.** Yale univ (1958) 'A continuation of cordier's bibliotheca sinica' for books only, publ 1921-57.

2. GENERAL STUDIES
(See also MODERN RELIGION)

Abel, Karl (tsl) **Arbeiten der kaiserlich russischen gerandschaft zu peking über china, sein volk, seine religion, seine institutionen, sozialen verhältnisse, etc. Aus dem russischen nach dem in st. petersburg 1852-57 veröffentlichten original von K. A. und F. A. Mecklenburg.** Berlin (1858)

Ansley, Delight. **The good ways.** N.Y. (1950) See chap 7, The road from china, 129-147.

Archer, John C. **Faiths men live by.** N.Y. (1934 et seq) See p 67-294.

Ayres, Lew. **Altars of the east.** N.Y. (1956) 284 p, illus.

B. J. La religion des chinois. **La Chine** 24 (1922) 1225-1233.

Ball, J. Dyer. **The celestial and his religions; or the religious aspect in china. Being a series of lectures on the religions of the chinese.** Hong kong (1906) xviii + 240 p.

Barthélemy, le Marquis de. Lettres de chine. 1. La chine religieuse . . . **RIC** n.s. 15/16 (aout 1911) 136-150.

Barton, George A. **The religions of the world.** Univ chicago (1917 et seq) See chap 11, The religion of china, 201-222.

Berle, A. A. The three religions of china. **Bibliotheca sacra** 52 (1895) 170-173.

Berry, Gerald L. **Religions of the world.** N.Y. (1947, 1956) See sec 8-9, p 47-53.

Bodde, Derk. **China's cultural tradition: what and whither?** N.Y. etc (1957) See sec B, The world of the supernatural, 20-30; sec G, The world of nature, 31-42.

Boerschmann, Ernst. Anhang. Einige beispiele für die gegenseitige durchdringung der drei chinesischen religionen. ZE 3/4 (1911) 429-435.

Bönner, Theodor. Vergleichende und kritisierende darstellung der chinesischen philosophie (mit anschluss der chinesischen religionen) Berlin-Steglitz (1909) (Besprochen von A. Forke, MSOS 13 [1910] 350-353)

Bouïnais, Albert M. A. La religion en chine. In author's De hanoi à pékin: notes sur la chine, paris (1892) 267-288.

Braden, Charles S. The world's religions. A short history. N.Y. and nashville (1939) rev ed (1954) See chap 10, Religions of china.

Browne, Lewis. This believing world. N.Y. (1926) See p 169-198.

Bunsen, C. C. J. Baron. God in history, or the progress of man's faith in the moral order of the world. Tsl fr german Susanna Winkworth. London (1868) See book 3, chap 5, The religious consciousness of the chinese, or sinism, 243-272.

Burder, William. The history of all religions of the world. N.Y. and springfield, mass (rev ed 1881) See Religious ceremonies and customs of the chinese, 678-700.

Burkhardt, Martha. Chinesische kultstätten und kultgebräuche. Erlenbach-Zürich (1920) 176 p.

Burtt, Edwin A. Man seeks the divine. N.Y. (1957) See chap 5, The native religions of china, 129-152.

Carus, Paul. Chinese life and customs. Illus by chinese artists. Chicago (1907) 114 p.

Castillon, J. Anecdotes chinoises, japonaises, siamoises, tonquinoises, etc.; dans lesquelles on s'est attaché princepalement aux moeurs, usages, coutumes et religions de ces différens peuples de l'asie. Paris (1774) 740 p. Comp fr works on japan and china, mainly by d'Entrecolles and Du Halde, jesuits.

Cave, Sydney. An introduction to the study of some living religions of the east. London (1921, 1947) See p 147-172.

Chan, Wing-tsit et al (comp). The great asian religions: an anthology. N.Y. etc (1969) See pt 2, Religions of china, 99-227. Textual excerpts.

Chavannes, Édouard. Compte rendu de j. j. m. de groot, religious system of china. RHR 37 (1898) 81-89.

Chavannes, Édouard. Compte rendu de r. dvorak, chinas religionen. RHR 32 (1895) 303-307; 48 (1903) 71-74.

Chen, Sophia H. What is the spiritual resort of a chinese? NRJ 7.3 (1947) 26-40.

Chêng, Tê-k'un. An introduction to chinese civilization. Religion and philosophy of the chinese. Orient 1.8 (mar 1951) 28-35.

Chêng, Tê-k'un. The religious outlook of the chinese. London, the china society, occasional papers no 9 (1956) 8 p.

Child, L. Maria. The progress of religious ideas, through successive ages. N.Y. (1855) See vol 1, chap 3, China, 199-221.

China's five religions. PT n.s. 15 (1936) 89-95.

Clennell, Walter J. The historical development of religion in china. London (2nd ed 1926) 262 p.

Cranston, Ruth. World faith. The story of the religions of the united nations. N.Y. (1949) See chap 3, The heavenly ways of the chinese sages, 53-76.

DeKorne, John C. Chinese altars to the unknown god. An account of the religions of china and the reactions to them of christian missions. Grand rapids, mich (1926) ix-xiii + 139 p, illus.

Dietrich. Die religionen chinas. AMZ 19 (1892) 419-424.

Dobbins, Frank S. assisted by S. Wells Williams and Isaac Hall. Error's chains: how forged and broken. N.Y. (1883) See chap 21-25, p 416-497. Same work publ under title: Story of the world's worship, chicago (1901) illus.

Doré, Henri. Manuel des superstitions chinoises. Shanghai, 2nd ed (1936) 221 p, table alphabétique with chin characters.

Doré, Henri. Recherches sur les superstitions en chine. Shanghai (1911-1938) 18 vol. Being Variétés Sinologiques no 32, 34, 36, 39, 42-42, 44-46, 48-49, 51, 57, 61-62, 66. Profusely illus. See next item.

Doré, Henri. Researches into chinese superstitions (Engl tsl of above). Vol 1 (1914) 2 (1915) 3 (1916) 4 (1917) 5 (1918) 6 (1920) 7 (1922) 8 (1926) tsl M. Kennelly, s.j. Vol 9 (1931) 10 (1933) tsl D. J. Finn, s.j. Vol. 13 (1938) tsl L. F. McGreal, s.j. Above engl vol all publ shanghai; republ taipei 1966-67. (7 vol remain untsl: 11, 12, 14, 15, 16, 17, 18)

DuBose, Hampton C. **The dragon, image and demon, or the religions of china: confucianism, buddhism, and taoism. Giving an account of the mythology, idolatry and demonolotry of the chinese.** London (1886) 463 p.

Duyvendak, J. J. L. Henri maspero, mélanges posthumes (etc.). (rev art) **TP** 40 (1951) 372-390.

Eder, Matthias. Die religion der chinesen. In Franz König (ed) **Christus und die religionen der erde. Handbuch der religions-geschichte.** Wien and freiburg (1961) vol 3, 319-391. Same title in **Die grossreligionen des fernen osten,** aschaffenburg (1961) ('Der christ in der welt, eine enzyklopädie,' XVII, Reihe die nichtchristlichen religionen, 7. band, p 5-66)

Edkins, Joseph. **Religion in china.** Boston (1859) rev and expanded ed (1878) 260 p.

Edkins, Joseph. **The religious condition of the chinese: with observations on the prospects of christian conversion among that people.** London (1859) viii + 288 p. (2nd ed 1878; 3rd ed 1884; french tsl paris 1882)

Edwards, Dwight W. The syncretic mind in chinese religions. **ChRec** 57 (1926) 400-413.

Eliot, Charles. The religion of china. **Quarterly review** 207 (1907) 351-376.

Endres, Franz Carl. **Die grossen religionen asiens; eine einführung in das verständnig ihrer grundlagen.** Zürich (1949) 186 p, pl.

Erkes, Eduard. Chinas religiöse entwicklung im zusammenhang mit seiner geschichte. **OZ** 4.1/2 (1915) 58-66.

Ermoni, V. Les religions de la chine. **Science catholique** 7 (mars 1892)

Faber, Ernst. **Introduction to a science of chinese religion. A critique of max müller and other authors.** Hong kong and shanghai (1879) xii + 154 p.

Feigl, Hermann. Die religion der chinesen. **Oesterreichische monatsschrift für den orient** 21 (1895) 41-51, 74-84, 101-112; 22 (1896) 1-12.

Fitch, Mary F. **Their search for god; ways of worship in the Orient.** N.Y. (1947).

Forlong, J. G. R. (ed) **Faiths of man. Encyclopedia of religions.** London (1906) republ n.y. (1964) See vol 1, China, 403-424.

Fradenburgh, J. N. **Living religions, or, the great religions of the orient, from sacred books and modern customs.** N.Y. (1888) 508 p.

Franke, O. Die chinesen. In Alfred Bertholet and Edvard Lehmann (ed) **Lehrbuch der religions-geschichte begründet von chantepie de la saussaye** [q.v.] **vierte, vollständig neuarbeitete auflage . . .** Tübingen (1925) See vol 1, 193-261.

Frazier, Allie M. (ed) **Readings in eastern religious thought.** Vol 3, **Chinese and japanese religions.** Philadelphia (1969) See 1-176, China.

Friess, Horace L. (ed) **Non-christian religions a to z. Based on the work of helmuth von glasenapp: Die nichtchristlichen religionen,** frankfurt-am-main (1957) q.v. N.Y. (1963) See Chinese universism, 52-69.

Genähr, J. Die religion der chinesen. **ZMR** 12 (1897) 79-92.

Giles, Herbert A. **Adversaria sinica.** Leyden (1905-08). See no 1-4, 6. (Rev of no 1 in **BEFEO** 6 [1906] 416-421, and no 3 in **TP** 7 [1906] 307-309) Abbrev **AdSin.**

Giles, Herbert A. **Confucianism and its rivals.** London (1915) ix + 271 p.

Glasenapp, Helmuth von. **Die fünf grossen religionen.** Düssendorf (1951-52) 2 vol. See vol 1, Die chinesische universismus, 152-221. French tsl Pierre Jundt: **Les cinq grandes religions du monde,** paris (1954) 558 p.

Glasenapp, Helmuth von. **Die grossen religionen der östlichen völker.** Zürich (1957) 48 p.

Gowen, Herbert H. **A history of religion.** Milwaukee, wisc (1934) See chap 14-15, The religions of china, 350-380.

Graham, Dorothy. Three faiths of china. **CW** 122 (mar 1926) 774-781.

Granet, Marcel. l'Esprit de la religion chinoise. **Scientia** 45 (1929) 329-337.

Granet, Marcel. **La religion des chinois.** Paris (1922) xi + 175 p,repr (1951)

Groot, J. J. M. de. **Religion in china. Universism: a key to the study of taoism and confucianism.** N.Y. and london (1912) xv + 327 p.

Groot, J. J. M. de. **The religion of the chinese.** N.Y. (1910) vii + 230 p.

Groot, J. J. M. de. Die religionen der chinesen. In P. von Hinneberg (ed) **Die kultur der gegenwort,** teil 1, abteilung 3, **Die orientalischen religionen,** berlin and leipzig (1906) 162-193.

Groot, J. J. M. de. **The religious system of china.** Leiden (1892-1910) repr taipei (1964) 6 vol. Vol 1-3: Disposal of the dead; vol 4-6: The soul and ancestral worship. (Compte rendu par Éd. Chavannes, **RHR** 37 [1898] 81-89)

Groot, J. J. M. de. **Universismus. Die grundlage d. religion u. ethik, d. staatswesens u. d. wissenschaften chinas.** Berlin (1918) viii + 404 p, 7 tafeln. (P. Pelliot rev in **JA** sér 11, 15/16 [juil/sept 1920] 158-165; E. Schmitt, in **OZ** 6.3/4 [1917-18] 279-289)

Grube, Wilhelm. **Religion und kultus der chinesen.** Leipzig (1910) vii + 220 p, 8 pl.

Grützmacher, Richard H. **Primitive und fernöstliche religionen: china und japan.** Leipzig (1937) 49 p.

Happel, Julius. Die religion in china. **ZMK** 5 (1890) 129-31, 191-201, 251-259; 6 (1891) 45-52.

Harding, D. E. **Religions of the world.** London 1966. See sec 4, p 51-67.

Hardwick, Charles. **Christ and other masters . . . Part III: Religions of china, america and oceania.** Cambridge (1858) See Religions of china, 272-346.

Hare, William L. **Chinese religion: a historical and literary sketch of ancestor worship, the teachings of kung fu tze and lao tze, and chinese natural philosophy.** London (1907) 62 p.

Harlez, Charles de. La religion en chine. À propos du dernier livre de m. a. réville. **Magasin littéraire et scientifique** (1889) 34 p.

Harlez, Charles de. The religion of the chinese people. **New world** 2 (1893-94) 646-676.

Harlez, Charles de. Les religions de la chine. **Muséon** 10 (1891-92) 145-176, 275-298, 523-548.

Harlez, Charles de. **Les religions de la chine. Aperçu historique et critique.** Leipzig (1891) 270 p.

Hartman, L. O. **Popular aspects of oriental religions.** N.Y. and cincinnati (1917) See chap 2, Fifty centuries of worship, 39-64, illus snapshots.

Hawkridge, Emma. **The wisdom tree.** Boston (1945) See pt 3, chap 3, Chinese, 403-466, illus.

Heiler, F. Die religion der chinesen. In **Die religionen der menschheit im vergangenheit und gegenwart.** Stuttgart (1959) p 108-134.

Henry, B. C. Feasts, pastimes, and folk-lore. Chap 8 in author's **CD** (1885) 152-172.

Horton, Walter M. Oriental religion: eastern asia, ii: The chinese national religion; iii: Buddhism in china, 74-88. In Henry N. Wieman and Walter M. Horton, **The growth of religion,** chicago and n.y. (1938)

Hsu, Francis L. K. **Americans and chinese. Reflections on two cultures and their people.** N.Y. (1953; 2nd ed 1970). See in 2nd ed, chap 9-10.

Hsu, Francis L. K. **Religion, science, and human crisis; a study of china in transition and its implications for the west.** London (1952) x + 142 p, illus.

Hu, Chang-tu et al. **China. Its people, its society, its culture.** New haven, conn. (1960) See chap 6, Religion, 110-139.

Hughes, E. R. and K. **Religion in china.** London (1950) 151 p.

Humphreys, Christmas. The religion of china. **MW** 18 (1943) 29-33.

Hurd, William. **A new universal history of the religious rites, ceremonies, and customs of the whole world: or, a complete and impartial view of all the religions in the various nations of the universe, both antient and modern, from the creation down to the present time . . .** London, n.d. (ca. 1780?) See The religion of the chinese, 58-66 (Taken from writings of Du Halde and Le Comte)

Hutchinson, John A. **Paths of faith.** N.Y. etc (1969) See chap 8, Chinese religion, 203-258.

Hutchinson, John A. and James A. Martin jr. **Ways of faith. An introduction to religion.** N.Y. (1953) See chap 2, Classical ways of china, 51-82.

Ingalls, Jeremy. Religions of asia in a world community. Part II: Worldviews in china. **Common cause** 3 (dec 1949-jan 1950) 253-261, 317-324.

James, E. O. **Teach yourself history of religions.** London (1956) See chap 4, Religion in china and japan, 89-114.

Jeremias, Alfred. **Allgemeine religions-geschichte.** München (1918) See 4, chap 2, Die religion in china, 170-197.

Johnson, Samuel. **Oriental religions and their relation to universal religion.** Vol. II: **China.** Boston (1877) 975 p.

Johnston, R. F. **Lion and dragon in northern china.** London (1910) See chap 8, Village customs, festivals and folk-lore, 155-194.

Jurji, Edward J. (ed) **The great religions of the modern world.** Princeton univ (1946) See sec on confucianism and taoism.

Kaltenmark, M. et O. Les religions de la chine. In Joseph Chaine et René Grousset (ed) **Littérature religieuse,** paris (1949) 719-815.

Kenny, P. D. Religion in unknown china. **Quiver** (1901) 508-515.

Kern, Maximilian. **Das licht des ostens: die weltanschauungen des mitteleren und fernen asiens, indien-china-japan, und ihr einfluss auf das religiöse und sittliche leben, auf kunst und wissenschaft dieser länder.** Stuttgart (1922) 597 p, 3 col pl (abbrev as **LO**)

Kitagawa, Joseph M. **Religions of the east.** Philadelphia, pa (1960). See chap 2, Chinese religions and the family system, 40-85.

Köster, Hermann. Was ist eigentlich universismus? **Sinologica** 9 (1967) 81-95.

Kraemer, H. **The christian message in a non-christian world.** Grand rapids, mich.(1938) 3rd ed (1956) See chap 6, sec on China, 182-191.

Kranz, P. Lichtstrahlen aus den in china herrschenden religion anschauungen. **ZMK** 8 (1893) 10-20, 65-70.

Krause, F. E. A. Die chinesischen religionen. In C. Clemen (ed) **Religionen der erde.** München (1927) 79-94. Engl tsl A. K. Dallas: **Religions of the world; their nature and their history,** n.y. and chicago (1931) illus; see 78-92.

Latourette, Kenneth Scott. **The chinese; their history and culture.** N.Y. (1934 et seq) 4th rev ed (1964) See vol 2, chap on Religion, with bibliog.

Lavollée, C. Sur la religion et les divinités de la chine. **Illustration** 4 (16 janv 1847) repr in **ROA** sér 2, 3 (1848) 349-352.

Legge, James. A fair and dispassionate discussion of the three doctrines accepted in china. From liu mi, a Buddhist writer. **Trans. ninth ICO.** London vol 2 (1893) 563-582.

Letourneau, Charles. l'**Évolution religieuse dans les diverses races humaines.** Paris (1898) See chap 10, B, La religion de la chine, 270-293.

Life Magazine Editorial Staff. Religion in the land of confucius. **Life** 38 (4 apr 1955) 64-84. Mostly illus, partly in col.

Life Magazine Editorial Staff. **The world's great religions.** N.Y. (1957) See The philosophy of china, 71-98; photos, many in col.

Life Magazine Editorial Staff. **The world's great religions. Vol One: Religions of the east.** N.Y. (1955) See: The philosophy of china, 83-110; photos, many in col.

Little, Archibald. (rev by Mrs A. Little) **Gleanings from fifty years in china.** London (1910) See chap 4, Religion and philosophy.

Lohmann, T. Religion im alten und neueren china. **Theologische literaturzeitung** 85 (1960) 805-806.

Lyon, Quinter M. **The great religions.** N.Y. (1957) See pt 4, Oriental religions of man and nature, chap 17-22, p 265-353.

Mao, W. E. The religion of the chinese. **CSM** 20 (1925) 12-15.

Martin, W. A. P. The san chiao, or three religions of china. In author's **Lore of cathay,** n.y. and chicago (1901) repr taipei (1971) 165-204.

Maspero, Henri. **Les religions chinoises.** (Mélanges posthumes sur les religions et l'histoire de la chine: I) Paris (1950) 255 p. Avant-propos par P. Demiéville. (Includes 3 unpubl and 2 re-issued studies) Abbrev as **HMRC.**

Masson-Oursel, Paul. La chine. In Maxime Gorce and Raoul Mortier (ed) **Histoire generale des religions,** paris (1944-51) t 4, 448-465. Abbrev as **HMRC.**

Matignon, J. J. **La chine hermétique; superstitions, crime et misère (souvenirs de biologie sociale)** . . . Paris (nouvelle ed 1936; orig ed Paris 1898, title sans **La chine hermétique**) 374 p, 42 pl.

McCarland, S. Vernon, Grace E. Cairns, and David C. Yu, **Religions of the world.** N.Y. (1969) See pt 5, Religions of east asia, chap 19-24, p 521-708.

Mémoires concernant l'histoire, les sciences, les arts, les moeurs et les usages des chinois par les missionaires de pékin (amyot, bourgeois, ko. poirot, gaubil) Paris (1776-1814) 16 vol. See passim (abbrev as **MCLC**)

Mensching, Gustav. **Soziologie der grossen religionen.** Bonn (1966) See 2, Soziologie des chinesischen universismus, 42-53.

Menzel. **Die religion der chinesen und die bisherigen missions-versuche in china.** Breslau (1898)

Menzies, Allan. **History of religion.** London (1905) See chap 8, China, 102-121.

Milloué, Léon de. **Catalogue du musée guimet. Pt. I: Inde, chine et japon.** Précédée d'un aperçu sur les religions de l'extrême-orient et suivie d'un index alphabétique des noms des divinités et des principaux termes techniques. Lyon (1883)

Moore, George F. **History of religions.** Vol 1: China, japan . . . etc. N.Y. (1913) See chap 1-5, China, 3-92.

Morgan, Kenneth W. **Asian religions. An introduction to the study of hinduism, buddhism, islam, confucianism, and taoism.** N.Y. (1964) 30 p.

Müller, F. Max. The religions of china. **NC** 48 (1900): 1. Confucianism (sept) 373-384; 2. Taoism (oct) 569-581; 3. Buddhism (nov) 730-742.

Murphy, John. **The origins and history of religions.** Manchester univ (1949) See chap 6-33, p 27-389.

Noss, John B. **Man's religions.** N.Y. (1949 et seq) 3rd rev ed (1963) See pt 3, chap 9, Chinese religion and the taoists, 327-368.

On the three principal religions in china. **The asiatic journal and monthly register,** 9 (1832) 302-316.

O'Neill, Frederick W. S. **The quest for god in china.** N.Y. and london (1925)

Orelli, Conrad von. **Allgemeine religionsgeschichte.** Bonn (1911) See vol 1, A, Turanische gruppe, 1, Religion der chinesen, 30-89.

Parker, Edward Harper. **China and religion.** London (1905) xxv + 317, illus. ("Popular ed" 1910)

Parker, E. H. The religion of the chinese. **New century review** 2 (1897) 179-190.

Parker, Edward Harper. **Studies in chinese religion.** London (1910) 308 p, index, photos. ". . . in the main . . . the original studies from which a summary was made and a popular work published, in 1905, called **China and religion.**"

Parrinder, Edward G. **An introduction to asian religions.** London (1957) vi + 138 p. See chap 5, Chinese religion, 87-115.

Parrinder, Geoffrey. **The faiths of mankind. A guide to the world's living religions.** N.Y. (1965) Original title: **The world's living religions,** london (1964) See chap 5, China's three ways, 89-110.

Parrish, Fred L. **History of religion: the destiny-determining factor in the world's cultures.** N.Y. (1965) See chap 11, The yinyang-tao religion of china (sixth century b.c. and after) 160-179.

Patai, R. Religion in middle eastern, far eastern, and western culture. **SWJA** 10 (1954) 233-254.

Paton, William. **Jesus christ and the world's religions.** London (1947) See chap 5, The message of christianity to china, 67-81.

Pavie, Théodore. Les trois religions de la chine, leur antagonisme, leur développement et leur influence. **RDM** sér 5, 9/12 (1 fevr 1845)

Peeters, Hermes. **The religions of china. Confucianism, taoism, buddhism, popular belief.** Peking (1941) 64 p. (Lectures delivered at the College of Chinese Studies)

Peisson, J. **Histoire des religions de l'extrême-orient.** Amiens (1888-89). 2 fasc: viii + 53; 53-127.

Pernitzsch, Max G. **Die religionen chinas.** Berlin (1940)

Petit, J. A. La chine philosophique et religieuse depuis l'antiquité jusqu'à l'établissement de la propagation de la foi. **Revue du monde catholique** 28 (juin-sept 1888)

Pfleiderer, Otto. **Religion and historic faiths.** Tsl fr german Daniel A. Huebsch. N.Y. (1907) See chap 5, The chinese religion, 89-102.

Price, Frank W. Religion in china. (Abstract) In Cheng Chi-pao (ed) **Symposium on chinese culture.** N.Y. (1964) 38-40.

Puech, H. C. (ed) **Histoire des religions.** Tome I: **Religions antiques. Religions de salut (inde et extrême-orient)** Paris (1970) 1,528 p, illus, cartes.

Rawlinson, Frank. Religion in china – many gods; no god! **MRW** n.s. 25.3 (1912) 177-182.

Rees, J. Lambert. The three religions and their bearing on chinese civilization. **ChRec** 27 (1896) 157-169, 222-231.

Reichelt, Karl Ludvig. **Meditation and piety in the far east. A religious-psychological study.** Tsl fr norwegian Sverre Holth. N.Y. and london (1954) 171 p.

Reichelt, Karl Ludvig. **Religion in chinese garment.** Tsl fr norwegian Joseph Tetlie. N.Y. and london (1951) 180 p.

Reischauer, August Karl. **The nature and truth of the great religions.** Tokyo (1966) See sec A:VI, The god-concept in chinese religion, 63-75; sec B:5, Chinese religion and the good life, 122-147; sec C:VI, Chinese religion and individual destiny, 171-173.

Religious glimpses of eastern asia. Being **SM** 16 (1967) Five art; four relevant ones are listed under appropriate headings in this bibliog.

Réville, Albert. **Histoire des religions.** Tome III: **La religion chinoise.** Paris (1889) Sec 1: jusqu'à la page 400; Sec 2: 401-710.

Réville, Albert. La religion chinoise. **Muséon** 12 (1893) 282f.

Réville, Albert. La religion chinoise à propos d'un ouvrage de m. de harlez [i.e. **Les religions de la chine,** q.v.] **RHR** 27.2 (1893) 226.

Ring, George C. **Religions of the far east: their history to the present day.** Milwaukee, wis (1950) x + 350 p, illus.

Rosny, Léon de. **Les religions de l'extrême-orient.** Paris (1886) 36 p.

Rowley, Harold H. **Submission and suffering, and other essays in eastern thought.** Cardiff, univ wales (1951) 170 p, index.

Sarkar, B. K. **Chinese religion through hindu eyes. A study in the tendencies of asiatic mentality.** Shanghai (1916) xxxii + 331 p.

Saussaye, P. D. Chantepie de la. **Lehrbuch der religionsgeschichte.** Freiburg (1887) See vol 1, Die chinesen, 232-261. Engl tsl Beatrice S. Colyer-Ferguson, **Manual of the science of religion,** london and n.y. (1891) See The chinese, 332-374. French tsl sous la direction de Henri Hubert et Isidore Lévy, **Manuel d'histoire des religions,** paris (1904) See chap 3, Les chinois (traduit par P. Bettelheim) 39-60.

Savage, Katherine. **The story of world religions.** N.Y. (1966) See chap 6, The religions of china, 89-103, illus. Juvenile level.

Schafer, Edward H. **Ancient china.** N.Y. (1967) Through T'ang dynasty. See chap 3-5; many relevant illus.

Schmitt, Erich. **Die chinesen.** No 6 in Alfred Bertholet (ed) **Religionsgeschichtliches lesebuch,** tübingen (1917) 110 p, index.

Schmitt, Erich. "Universismus." **OZ** 6.3/4 (1917-18) 279-289. Re book by J. J. M. de Groot.

Schoeps, Hans-Joachim. **An intelligent person's guide to the religions of mankind.** Tsl fr german Richard and Clara Winston. London (1967) See Religion in china, 181-196.

Smalley, Frank A. **Chinese philosophy and religion.** London (1947) 42 p, illus.

Smart, Ninian. **The religious experience of mankind.** N. Y. (1969) See sec Religions of the far east, 141-190.

Smith, D. Howard. **Chinese religions.** N.Y. etc (1968) 222 p. Historical treatment.

Smith, Mrs J. Gregory. **From dawn to sunrise: a review, historical and philosophical, of the religious ideas of mankind.** N.Y. (1880) See China and its religions, 180-199.

Smith, Stanley. Religion in china. **ChRec** 33 (1902) 334-343. (Extracted from **China from within**) See notice in **JRAS** (1904) 517-523.

Société des Études Japonaises, Chinoises, Tartares et Indo-Chinoises. **Chrestomathie religieuse de l'extrême-orient.** Paris (1887) 52 p.

Söderblom, N. **Die religionen der erde.** Halle a. saale (1905) 65 p.

Soothill, William E. **The three religions of china.** Oxford (1923) 271 p.

Soper, Edmund D. **The religions of mankind.** N.Y. and nashville (1921) 3rd rev ed (1951) See chap 8, The religion of china, 160-175.

Speer, Robert E. **The light of the world. A brief comparative study of christianity and non-christian religions.** West medford, mass (1911) See chap 3, Animism, confucianism and taoism, 121-176.

Spiegelberg, Frederic. **Living religions of the world.** Englewood cliffs, n.j. (1956) See chap 9-12, p 279-353.

Stange, H. O. H. Die religion des alten china (in anthropologisches hinsicht) In C. J. Bleeker (ed) **Anthropologie religieuse. l'Homme et sa destinée à la lumière de l'histoire des religions,** leiden (1955)

Stein, Rolf. Les religions de la chine. In l'Encyclopédie française. Paris (1957) See sec C, chap 4.

Stewart, James L. **Chinese culture and christianity. A review of china's religions and related systems from the christian standpoint.** N.Y. etc (1926) 316 p, bibliog, index.

Stronath, Alexander. A general view of what are regarded by the chinese as objects of worship. JIA 2 (1848) 349-352.

Stübe, R. Religion und kultus der chinesen. **Zeitschrift für religions-psychologie** 3 (1910) 346-350.

Tan, Yün-shan. What is chinese religion. **VBQ** n.s. 3 (1937-38) 152-163.

Thompson, Laurence G. **Chinese religion: an introduction.** Belmont, calif.(1969) 119 p, table, app, notes, index. 2nd rev ed Encino and belmont, calif.(1974)

Ting, W. Y. Konfuzianismus, taoismus und buddhismus. **CDA** (1933) p 24.

Tourchier, Louis. l'Esprit religieux des chinois. **Études** (20 dec 1910) 788-803.

Tscharner, Eduard Horst von. Ostasien. In **Mensch und gottheit in den religionen.** Herausgegeben von der universität bern. Bern-leipzig (1942) 91-119.

Tsukamoto, Zenryū and Makita Tairyō. China: history of religion. **Comité Japonais des sciences historiques** (1960) 324-329.

Underwood, Horace Grant. **The religions of eastern asia.** N.Y. and london (1910) 267 p.

Vail, Albert and Emily M. **Transforming light. The living heritage of world religions.** N.Y. etc (1970) See chap 7-8, 68-91.

Van der Sprenkel, O. B. Chinese religion (rev art) **British journal of sociology** 5 (1954) 272-275.

Variété. Relations de la chine (oct 1912) 529-546. Mostly on various popular deities.

Vinson, Julien. **Les religions actuelles.** Paris (1888) See chap 4, Les religions de la chine et du japon, 196-224.

Walshe, W. Gilbert. China. In **HERE** 3, 549-552.

Wei, Francis C. M. **The spirit of chinese culture.** N.Y. (1947) 186 p, index.

Wieger, Léon. Articles on the religions of china in A. d'Alès (ed) **Dictionnaire apologetique de la foi catholique,** paris (4th ed 1911)

Wieger, Léon. Histoire des croyances religieuses et des opinions philosophiques en chine depuis l'origine, jusqu'à nos jours. Sien-sien (2nd enl ed 1922) 796 p. Engl tsl E. T. C. Werner: **A history of the religious beliefs and philosophical opinions in china from the beginning to the present time.** Hsien-hsien (1927) 774 p, illus.

Wieger, Léon. La religion des chinois. In Joseph Huby et al, **Christus. Manuel d'histoire des religions.** Paris (1916) chap 4.

Wieger, Léon. **The religion of china.** London (1909) 32 p.

Wilhelm, Richard. **Die religion und philosophie chinas, aus den originalurkunden übersetzt und herausgegeben.** Tsingtau (1912?) See notice by P. Masson-Oursel in **JA** sér 11, 1 (mars-avril 1913) 491-494.

Wilhelm, Richard. Die seele chinas. Berlin (1926) 356 p, illus. Engl tsl John H. Reece: **The soul of china.** N.Y. (1928) 382 p.

Williams, S. Wells. Religion of the chinese. In author's **The middle kingdom.** N.Y. rev ed (1883) repr Taipei (1965) vol 2, 188-274.

Woog-Garry, Valentine. **Histoire, doctrine et rites des principales religions.** Paris (1959) See sec Les religions d'extrême-orient, 137-156.

Wyder, H. The religion of the chinese: an interpretation by a western missionary. **QNCCR** 5.2 (1961) 14-23.

Yang, C. K. **Religion in chinese society. A study of contemporary social functions of religion and some of their historical factors.** Univ california (1961) 473 p, notes, bibliog.

Yang, Yung-ch'ing. **China's religious heritage.** N.Y. and nashville, tenn.(1943) 196 p.

Yeates, T. The religion of the chinese, without altars, temples, priests, or any proper term to denote the true God. **ChRep** 15 (1846) 203-207.

Yeh, Theodore T. Y. **Confucianism, christianity and china.** N.Y. (1969) 249 p, notes, bibliog.

Zia, N. Z. The common ground of the three chinese religions. **CF** 9.2 (1966) 17-34.

Zur religiösen charakteristik der chinesen. **AMZ** 24 (1897) 283-300.

Part Two

Chinese Religion

Exclusive of Buddhism

1. TERMINOLOGY

Brandon, S. G. F. (ed) **A dictionary of comparative religions.** N.Y. (1970) See passim.

Chalmers, John. Tauist words and phrases. In **DV** (1872) vol 2, pt 3, no 7, p 229-237.

Chan, Wing-tsit. Chinese and buddhist religious terminology. In Vergilius Ferm (ed) **Encyclopedia of religion,** N.Y. (1945) passim. Repr as pamphlet, n.y. (1945) 36 p.

Chen, Chung-hwan. What does lao-tzu mean by the term "tao"? **TJ** n.s. 4.2 (1964) 150-161.

Havret, Henri. T'ien-tchou 'seigneur du ciel.' À propos d'une stèle bouddhique de tch'eng-tou. Shanghai (1901) 30 p. **(Variétés sinologiques** no 19)

Kaltenmark, Max. Ling-pao: note sur un terme du taoïsme religieuse. **MIHEC** 2 (1960) 559-588.

Ratchnevsky, Paul (unter mitarbeit von Johann Dill und Doris Heyde) **Historisch-terminologisches wörterbuch der yuan-zeit: medizinwesen.** Berlin (1967) xix + 118 p.

2. ANTIQUITY

Akatsuka, Kiyoshi. An attempt to restore the original state of how "shang-ti" was worshipped in the time of the yin dynasty. Tokyo, **Trans 11th ICO** (1966) 58-60.

Andersson, Johan Gunnar. On symbolism in the prehistoric painted ceramics of china. **BMFEA** 1 (1929) 65-69.

Bishop, Carl W. The worship of earth in ancient china. **JNCBRAS** 64 (1933) 24-43.

Bridgman, E. C. (tsl). Chinese sacrifices, illustrated by quotations from the shu king. **ChRep** 17 (1848) 97-101.

Buckens, F. Les antiquités funéraires du honan central et la conception de l'âme dans la chine primitive. **MCB** 8 (1946-47) 1-101.

Bunge, Martin L. **The story of religion, from caveman to superman.** Pasadena, calif.(1931) See chap 7, Chinese religion, 52-60.

Chang, Kwang-chih. Evidence for the ritual life in prehistoric china. **ASBIE** 9 (1960) engl summ 269-270.

Chang, Tsung-tung. **Der kult der shang-dynastie im spiegel der orakel-inschriften. Eine paläographische studie zur religion im archaischen china.** Frankfurt-am-main (1970) vi + 331 p.

Chavannes, Édouard. Le dieu du sol dans l'ancienne religion chinoise. **RHR** 43 (1901) 125-246. A rev version of this study forms Appendice to author's vol, **Le t'ai chan** q.v.

Chavannes, Édouard. La divination par l'écaille de tortue dans la haute antiquité chinoise (d'après un livre de m. lo tchen-yu) **JA** 10e sér, 17 (1911) 127-137.

Creel, Herrlee Glessner. **The birth of china. A study of the formative period of chinese civilization.** N.Y. (1937) See chap 12, The gods of shang; chap 13, Sacrifice; chap 25, Religion [of chou]

Danckert, Werner. Musikgötter und musikmythen altchinas. **ZE** 88 (1963) 1-48.

Dubs, Homer H. An ancient chinese mystery cult. **HTR** 35 (1942) 221-240.

Dubs, Homer H. The archaic royal jou religion. **TP** 46 (1958) 217-259.

Eberhard, Wolfram. **Lokalkulturen im alten china.** Leiden (1942) vol 1, passim. Vol 2, **Die lokalkulturen des südens und ostens.** Peiping (1942) "Greatly revised version" of vol 2, engl tsl Alide Eberhard: **The local cultures of south and east china.** Leiden (1968) 520 p, bibliog, index. See passim.

Edkins, Joseph. Astrology in ancient china. **ChRev** 14 (1885-86) 345-351.

Eichhorn, W. Zur religion im ältesten china (shang-zeit) **Wiener zeitschrift für die kunde süd- und ostasiens** 2 (1958) 33-53.

Erkes, E. The god of death in ancient china. **TP** 35 (1940) 185-210.

Erkes, E. A neolithic chinese idol? **AA** 3 (1928) 141-143.

Erkes, E. Zum altchinesischen orakelwesen. **TP** 35 (1940) 364-370.

Esbroek, A. van. Les cultes préhistoriques de la chine. **Nouvelle clio** 5 (1953) 195-196.

Everett, John R. **Religion in human experience.** London (1952) See chap 8, Pre-buddhist china, 150-162.

Gibson, H. E. Divination and ritual during the shang and chou dynasties. **CJ** 23 (1935) 22-25.

Giles, Herbert A. **Religions of ancient china.** London (1905) v + 65 p.

Giles, Lionel. Wizardry in ancient china. **AP** 13 (1942) 484-489.

Granet, Marcel. **La civilization chinoise.** Paris (1929) Engl tsl Kathleen E. Innes and Mabel R. Brailsford: **Chinese civilization.** London and n.y. (1930) See esp second pt, Chinese society, passim.

Granet, Marcel. **Danses et légendes de la chine ancienne.** Paris (1926) 2 vol.

Granet, Marcel. Le depôt de l'enfant sur le sol: rites anciens et ordalies mythiques. **RA** (1922) Repr **Études sociologiques sur la chine.** Paris (1953) 159-202.

Granet, Marcel. **Fêtes et chansons anciennes de la chine.** Paris (1919) 301 p. Notices: **BEFEO** 19 (1919) 65-75 by H. Maspero; **RHR** 83 (1921) 96-98 by P. Masson-Oursel. Engl tsl E. D. Edwards: **Festivals and songs of ancient china.** N.Y. (1932) 281 p.

Granet, Marcel. Programme d'études sur l'ancienne religion chinoise. **RHR** 69 (mars-avril 1914) 228-239.

Grube, W. Die religion der alten chinesen. In **Religionsgeschichtliches lesebuch in verbindung,** mit W. Grube . . . K. Geldner . . . et al, Tübingen (1908) 1-69.

Hager, Joseph. **Panthéon chinois, ou, parallèle entre le culte religieux des grecs et celui des chinois. Avec des nouvelles preuves que la chine a été connue des grecs, et que les sérès des auteurs classiques ont été des chinois.** Paris (1806)

Halbwachs, Maurice. Histoires dynastiques et légendes religieuses en chine, d'après un livre recent de m. granet. **RHR** 94 (1926) 1-16. Critique of Granet's **Danses et légendes de la chine ancienne,** q.v.

Harlez, Charles de. Les croyances religieuses des premiers chinois. **MCAM** t 41 (1888) 60 p.

Harlez, Charles de. La religion chinoise dans le tchün-tsiu de kong-tze et dans le tso-tchuen. **TP** 3.3 (1892) 211-237.

Hentze, Carl. **Bronzegerät Kultbauten; religion im ältesten china der shang-zeit.** Antwerpen (1951) xix + 273 p, 103 pl.

Hentze, Carl. **Chinese tomb figures: a study in the beliefs and folklore of ancient china.** London (1928) 112 p.

Hentze, Carl. **Les figurines de la céramique funéraire; matériaux pour l'étude des croyances et du folklore de la chine ancienne.** Dresden (1928) 2 vol, pl.

Hentze, Carl. **Frühchinesische bronzen und kultdarstellungen.** Antwerp (1937) 167 p + portfolio of pl.

Hentze, Carl. Gods and drinking serpents. **HR** 4.2 (1965) 179-208. 57 photo-illus.

Hentze, Carl. **Objets rituels, croyances et dieux de la chine antique et de l'amérique.** Antwerp (1936) 122 p.

Hentze, Carl. **Die sakralbronzen und ihre bedeutung in den früh-chinesischen kulturen.** Antwerpen (1941) 2 vol, pl.

Hentze, Carl. **Tod, auferstehung, weltordnung; das mythische bild im ältesten china, in den grossasiatischen und zirkumpazifischen kulturen.** Zürich (1955) 2 vol.

Hentze, Carl and Chewon Kim. Göttergestalten in der ältesten chinesischen schrift. **Studien zur früh-chinesischen kulturgeschichte** 2 (1943) 19-59, illus.

Hentze, Carl and Chewon Kim. **Ko- und Chi-waffen in china und in amerika. Göttergestalten in der ältesten chinesischen schrift.** Antwerpen (1943) 59 p, pl.

Hopkins, E. Washburn. **The history of religions.** N.Y. (1926) See chap 14, Religions of china. Pre-confucian religion, 224-248.

Hopkins, Lionel C. Working the oracle. **NCR** 1 (1919) 111-119, 249-261, pl. Re oracle bones.

Huang, Wen-shan. The artistic expression of totems in ancient chinese culture. **ASBIE** 21 (spring 1966) 1-13.

Huang, Wen-shan. The origins of chinese culture: a study of totemism. **Congrès internationale des sciences anthropologiques et ethnographiques Paris (1960)** vol 2 (1963) 139-143.

Huang Wen-shan. Totemism and the origin of chinese philosophy. **ASBIE** 9 (spring 1960) 51-66.

Ingram, J. H. The civilization and religion of the shang dynasty. **CJ** 3 (1925) 473-483, 536-545.

Karlgren, Bernhard. Legends and cults in ancient china. **BMFEA** 18 (1946) 199-365 (See rev by W. Eberhard in **AA**, 9)

Karlgren, Bernhard. Some fecundity symbols in ancient china. **BMFEA** 2 (1930) 1-54.

Karlgren, Bernhard. Some ritual objects of pre-historic china. **BMFEA** 14 (1942) 65-69.

Karlgren, Bernhard. Some sacrifices in chou china. **BMFEA** 40 (1968) 1-31.

Kiang, Chao-yuan. **Le voyage dans la chine ancienne, considéré principalement sous son aspect magique et religieux.** Trad du chin par Fan, Jen. Shanghai (1937) 375 p.

Koeppen, Georg von. Zwei träume aus dem tso-chuan und ihre interpretation. **ZDMG** 119 (1969) 133-156.

Köster, Hermann. Zur religion in der chinesischen vorgeschichte. **MS** 14 (1949-55) 188-214.

Kuo, P. C. Folkways in prehistoric china. **THM** 4 (1937) 115-135.

Kurz, H. Mémoire sur l'état politique et religieux de la chine, 2300 ans avant notre ère, selon le chou-king. **Nouv. JA** 5 (1830) 401-436; 6 (1830) 401-451.

Lanciotti, Lionello. On some religious beliefs in ancient china. **E&W** 4.2 (1953) 95-97.

Ling, Shun-sheng. Dog sacrifice in ancient china and the pacific area. **ASBIE** 3 (1957) engl summ 37-40, illus.

Ling, Shun-sheng. Origin of the she in ancient china. **ASBIE** 18 (1964) engl abrmt 36-44.

Lou, Dennis Wing-sou. Rain-worship among the ancient chinese and the nahua-maya indians. **ASBIE** 4 (1957) 31-108, illus.

Maspero, Henri. **La chine antique.** Paris (1927) rev ed (1955) See Book II, chap 2-5, p 130-231 in rev ed.

McCaffree, Joe E. **Divination and the historical and allegorical sources of the i ching, the chinese classic, or book of changes.** Los angeles (1967) 64 p, illus.

Milloué, L. de. La religion primitive de la chine. **CMG** (1907) 141-181.

Morgan, Evan. Sacrifices in ancient china. **JNCBRAS** 70 (1939) 30-36.

Morley, Arthur. A study in early chinese religion. **NCR** 1 (may 1919) 176-208; sec 2: (july 1919) 262-281; sec 3: (aug 1919) 372-384.

Mortier, F. Du sens primitif de l'antiquité et la célèbre figure divinatoire des taoistes chinois et japonais (sien t'ien) **BSAB** 59 (1948) 150-160.

Mullie, J. Les formules du serment dans le tso-tchouen. **TP** 38 (1948) 43-74.

Munsterberg, Hugo. An anthropomorphic deity from ancient china. **OA** 3.4 (1951) 147-152, illus.

Owen, G. The ancient cult of the chinese as found in the shu-ching. **JPOS** 1.5 (1887) 203-224.

Parker, E. H. Ancient chinese spiritualism. **AR** 19 (1923) 117-123.

Parrish, Fred L. **History of religion: the destiny-determining factor in the world's cultures.** N.Y. (1965) See chap 4 (B) In china: in the pre-confucian period (before the sixth century b.c.) 46-54.

Pichon, Jean-Charles. **Les cycles du retour éternel.** Paris (1963) See t 2, p 157-184.

Plath, J. H. **Die religion und der cultus der alten chinesen.** Abth. 1: **Die religion der alten chinesen.** München (1862) 108 p, 23 illus. Abth 2: **Der cultus der alten chinesen.** München (1863) 136 p. **Chinesische texte** (f. vol 2) München (1864) 46 pl.

R., S. C. B. The tuang [sic] fang sacrificial table. **BMMA** 19 (1924) 141-144, illus.

Die Religion der alten chinesen. **OstL** 7.27 (1893) 423-426.

Robiou, F. Études récentes sur la première religion des chinois. **Revue des questions historiques** 25 (1892) 217-225.

Ross, John. **The original religion of china.** Edinburgh and london (1909) 327 p.

Rotours, Robert des. La religion dans la chine antique. In Maurice Brillant and René Aigrain (ed) **Histoire des religions.** Paris (1953) t 2, 7-83.

Rousselle, Erwin. Konfuzius und das archaische weltbild der chinesischen frühzeit. **Saeculum** 5 (1954) 1-33.

Rowley, H. H. **Prophecy and religion in ancient china and israel.** Univ london (1956) 154 p.

Rydh, H. Seasonal fertility rites and the death cult in scandinavia and china. **BMFEA** 3 (1931) 69-98.

Schafer, Edward H. Ritual exposure in ancient china. **HJAS** 14 (1951) 130-184.

Schindler, Bruno. **Das priestertum im alten china.** Leipzig (1919)

Schindler, Bruno. On the travel, wayside and wind offerings in ancient china. **AM** 1 (1924) 624-656.

Shih, C. C. [Ching-ch'eng] Notes on a phrase in the tso chuan: 'The great affairs of a state are sacrifice and war.' **CC** 2.3 (1959) 31-47.

Sjöholm, Gunnar. The boundaries between religion and culture with a reference to the interpretation of ancient chinese religion. **CF** 13.4 (1970) 5-20.

Smith, D. H. Chinese religion in the shang dynasty. **Numen** 8 (1961) 142-150.

Smith, David Howard. Religious developments in ancient china prior to confucius. **Bulletin of the John Rylands Library,** manchester, engl 44 (1962) 432-454.

Söderblom, Nathan. **Das werden des gottesglaubens. Untersuchungen über die angänge der religion.** Deutsche bearbeitung, herausgegeben von Rudolf Stübe. Leipzig (1916) See 6, Chinesischen schang-ti [Notice by Bruno Schindler in **OZ** 4 (1916) 322-326]

Tiele, C. P. **Outlines of the history of religion to the spread of the universal religions.** Tsl fr dutch J. Estlin Carpenter. Preface (1877) 5th ed london (1892) See chap 2, Religion among the chinese, 25-38.

Tung, Tso-pin. **An interpretation of the ancient chinese civilization.** Taipei (1952) See esp sec 3, Religious beliefs, 18-21; repr in **CWayRel** (1973) 1-6.

Waidtlow, C. Ancient religions of china. **NCR** 4 (1922) 283-297, 373-387.

Warneck, Johann. Die urreligion chinas. **AMZ** 38 (1911) 393-413.

Wei Hwei-lin. Categories of totemism in ancient china. **ASBIE** 25 (1968) 25-34.

Weygandt, J. W. H. **Ritualfragmente zum schädelopfer in altchina.** Nurtingen (1953) 21 p, illus.

Wilhelm, Hellmut. Der sinn des geschehens nach dem buch der wandlung. **EJ** 26 (1957) 351-386.

Ymaizoumi, M. Des croyances et des superstitions des chinois avant confucius. Tsl M. Tomii. **CPOL** 1878, t 2, lyon (1880) 56-61.

Ymaizoumi, M. Du culte des ancêtres en chine sous la dynastie de tcheou, **CPOL** 1878, t 2, lyon (1880) 68-79.

3. MYTHOLOGY

Arlington, L. C. Chinese mythology. **ChRev** 25 (1900-01) 178-180.

Balfour, F. H. The peach and its legends. In author's **Chinese scrapbook** (1887) 145-148.

Ball, J. Dyer. Scraps from chinese mythology. **ChRev** 9 (1880-81) 195-212; 11 (1882-83) 69-86, 203-217, 282-297, 382-390; 12 (1883-84) 188-193, 324-331, 402-407; 13 (1884-85) 75-85.

Basset, B. E. Lecture on chinese mythology. **JWCBorderResS** 5 (1932) 92-101.

Bauer, Wolfgang. Der herr vom gelben stein (huang shih kung): wandlung einer chinesischer legenden figur. **OE** 3 (1956) 137-152, table.

Beauclair, Inez de. Appendix: comment: the place of the sun myth in the evaluation of chinese mythology. **ASBIE** 13 (1962) 123-132, bibliog.

Belpaire, B. Le folklore de la fondre en chine sous la dynastie des t'ang. **Muséon** 52 (1939) 163-172.

Birch, Cyril. **Chinese myths and fantasies, retold by cyril birch.** London (1961) 200 p, illus.

Bodde, Derk. Myths of ancient china. In Samuel N. Kramer (ed) **Mythologies of the ancient world,** n.y. (1961) 367-408.

Buschan, G. Tiergötter und fabeltiere bei den völkern des antike und des ostasiatischen kulturkreises. **Ciba zeitschrift** 8.86 (1942) 3005-3010.

Campbell, Joseph. **The masks of god: oriental mythology.** N.Y. (1962) See pt 3, chap 7, Chinese mythology, 371-460.

Chalmers, John. Chinese mythology. **ChRev** 14 (1885-86) 33-36.

Chan Ping-leung. An interpretation of two ancient chinese myths. **TJ** n.s. 7.2 (aug 1969) 206-232, engl summ.

Chang, Kwang-chih. Changing relationships of man and animal in shang and chou myths and art. **ASBIE** 16 (1963) 133-146, illus.

Chang, Kwang-chih. The chinese creation myths: a study in method. **ASBIE** 8 (1959) engl summ 77-79.

Chang, Kwang-chih. A classification of shang and chou myths. **ASBIE** 14 (1962) engl abrmt 75-94.

Charpentier, Léon. La mythologie populaire chez les chinois. **NR** (1 dec 1900) 359-372.

Christie, Anthony. **Chinese mythology.** Feltham, middlesex, engl (1968) 141 p, illus.

Clerke, E. M. Dragon myths of the east. **AQR** 4 (1887) 98-117.

Couchoud, Paul Louis (ed) **Mythologie asiatique illustrée.** Paris (1928) x + 431 p, illus.

Coyajee, Jehangir Cooverjee. **Cults and legends of ancient iran and china.** Bombay (1936) 308 p.

Duyvendak, J. J. L. The mythico-ritual pattern in chinese civilization. **Proceedings 7th ICHR** (1951) 137-138.

Dyson, Verne. **Forgotten tales of ancient china.** Shanghai (1927) xiii + 384 p, illus.

Eberhard, Wolfram. **Lokalkulturen im alten china.** Leiden (1942) vol 1, passim. Vol 2, **Die lokalkulturen des südens und ostens.** Peiping (1942) "Greatly expanded version" of vol 2, engl tsl Alide Eberhard: **The local cultures of south and east china.** Leiden (1968) 520 p, bibliog, index. See passim.

Erkes, E. Chinesisch-amerikanische mythen-parallelen. **TP** 24 (1926) 32-53. (See further E. von Zach: Einige bemerkungen zu Erkes's . . . **TP** 24 (1926) 382-383; Erkes: Zu E. von Zach's Bemerkungen . . . **TP** 25 (1928) 94-98.

Erkes, E. Eine p'an-ku-mythe der hsia-zeit? **TP** 36 (1942) 159-173.

Erkes, Eduard. Der pfau in religion und folklore. **JSMVL** 10 (1926-51 sic) 67-73.

Erkes, E. Spuren chinesischer weltschöpfungs-mythen. **TP** 28 (1931) 355-368.

Erkes, Eduard. Spuren einer kosmogonischen mythe bei laotse. **AA** 8 (1940) 16-38.

Erkes, Eduard. Ein taoistische schöpfungs-geschichte für kinder. **CDA** (1932) 14-15.

Feng, Han-yi and Shryock, J. K. Chinese mythology and dr. ferguson. **JAOS** 53 (1933) 53-65. (Criticism of ferguson's chinese mythology q.v.)

Ferguson, John C. Chinese mythology. In John A. MacCulloch (ed) **The mythology of all races,** vol 8: **Chinese, japanese.** Boston (1928) 3-203. See further author's rebuttal of Feng and Shryock's criticism, item above: Chinese mythology: a reply. **JAOS** 54 (1934) 85-87.

Forke, A. Mu wang und die königin von saba. **MSOS** 7 (1904) 117-172.

Forke, A. Se wang mu. **MSOS** 9 (1906) 409-417.

Franke, Herbert. Indogermanische mythen-parallelen zu einem chinesischen text der han zeit. In **MMDFL** (1963) 243-249.

Gieseler, G. Le mythe du dragon en chine. **RA** 5e sér, 6 (1917) 104-170.

Giles, Herbert A. Who was si wang mu? In author's **AdSin,** shanghai (1905) 1-19.

Grube, Wilhelm. **Taoistischer schöpfungsmythen nach dem sên-sien-kien, I.1.** Berlin (1896) 13 p.

Hentze, Carl. **Tod, auferstehung, weltordnung; das mythische bild im ältesten china, in den grossasiatischen und zirkumpazifischen kulturen.** Zürich (1955) 2 vol.

Humphreys, H. The horn of the unicorn. **Antiquity** 27 (1953) 15-19.

Izushi, Yoshihiko. A study of origin of the ch'i-lin and the feng-huang. **TBMRD** 9 (1937) 79-109.

James, E. O. **Creation and cosmology. A historical and comparative inquiry.** Leiden (1969) See chap 3, India and the far east.

Kaltenmark, Max. La naissance du monde en chine. In **La naissance du monde** ('Sources orientales' t 1) Paris (1959) 453-468.

Kim, Chewon. Han dynasty mythology and the korean legend of tan gun. **ACASA** 3 (1948-49) 43-48.

Kingsmill, T. W. Siwangmu and k'wenlun. **JNCBRAS** 37 (1906) 185-190.

Kingsmill, T. W. Some myths of the shiking. **JNCBRAS** 31 (1896) 182-192.

Krieg, Claus W. **Chinesische mythen und legenden.** Zürich (1946) 298 p, illus.

Kühnert, J. Entst. d. welt u. d. wesen d. menschen n. chin. anschauung. **Ausland** 66 (1893) 150-154.

Lacouperie, Terrien de. Le coco du roi de yueh et l'arbre aux enfants. Note de mythologie populaire en extrême-orient. **Trans ninth ICO, London 1892.** Vol 2 (1893) 897-905.

Lacouperie, Terrien de. On the ancient history of glass and coal and the legend of nü-kwa's coloured stones in china. **TP** 2 (1891) 234-243.

Lee, André. **Légendes chinoises.** Pékin (1937) 124 p, illus.

Ling, Jui-tang. The goddess of the moon. **CJ** 2 (1924) 497-502.

Ling, Shun-sheng. Kun lun chiu and hsi wang mu. **ASBIE** 22 (1966) engl abrmt 253-255.

MacKenzie, Donald A. **Myths of china and japan.** London (1923) 404 p.

Maspero, Henri. **Légendes mythologiques dans le chou-king. JA** 204 (1924) 1-100.

Maspero Henri. The mythology of modern china. In J. Hackin et al, **Asiatic mythology.** N.Y. (n.d.) 252-384, illus. Tsl fr french, **Mythologie asiatique illustrée,** paris (1928) by F. M. Atkinson.

Miao, D. F. The moon in chinese legend. **CJ** 19 (1933) 112-114.

Moor, de. **Essai sur les légendes chinoises concernant fo-hi, kong-kong, niuva, shin-nong et tchi-yeou. Précédé d'un coup d'oeil sur la religion primitive des chinois et sur l'introduction du christianisme en chine.** Paris (?) (1901) 58 p.

Morrison, John R. **Mythology of the various races and religions of china.** Publ in china (?) (ca. 1830) 100 drawings by chin artists.

O'Neill, John. **The night of the gods. An inquiry into cosmic and cosmogonic mythology and symbolism.** London, vol 1 (1893) 581 p, vol 2 (1897) Notices in **TP** 4.5 (1893) 444-452, 8 (1897) 231-232; necrologie in **ibid** 6.1 (1895) 77-78.

Ou-I-Tai. Chinese mythology. In Felix Guiran (ed) **New larousse encyclopedia of mythology,** tsl fr french Richard Aldington and Delano Ames. London, n.y. etc (1959) new ed (1968) 379-402, illus.

Perry, John W. **Lord of the four quarters. Myths of the royal father.** N.Y. (1966) See 5, The far east: china, 204-218. ('. . . we find in china the source and leading exponent of the sacral kingship.')

Riddel, W. H. Concerning unicorns. **Antiquity** 19 (1945) 194-202.

Rosenkranz, Gerhard. Das all und der mensch im chinesischen mythos. In **Festgabe für hans schomerus zum 65. geburstag am 20.3.1967,** karlsruhe-durlach (1967) 42-47.

Rousselle, Erwin. Dragon and mare, figures of primordial chinese mythology. In **The mystic vision: papers from the eranos yearbooks.** Princeton univ (1968) 103-119 (For german orig see following item)

Rousselle, E. Drahe und stute; gestalten der mythischen welt chinesischer urzeit. **EJ** 2 (1934) 11-33; **CDA** (1935) 6-17 (For engl version, see item above)

Sinensis. Chinese mythology. **ChRec** 3 (1870-71) 197-201, 234-239, 299-303, 310-315, 347-353.

Soymié, M. China: the struggle for power. In Pierre Grimal (ed) **Larousse world mythology** tsl fr french **Mythologies de la méditerranée au gange et Mythologies des steppes, des îles et des forêts** (1963) by Patricia Beardsworth, london, n.y. etc (l965) 271-292, illus.

Tan, J. M. **Légendes chinoises.** Louvain (1929) 126 p.

Vallerey, Gisèle. **Contes et légendes de chine.** Paris (1936 and 1946) 254 p, illus.

Werner, E. T. C. **A dictionary of chinese mythology.** Shanghai (1932) repr n.y. (1961) 627 p, bibliog.

Werner, E. T. C. **Myths and legends of china.** London (1922) 454 p, gloss, index, illus.

Yetts, W. Perceval. The chinese isles of the blest. **Folk-lore** 30 (mar 1919) 35-62.

4. ART AND SYMBOLISM

Alexander, Mary and Frances. **A handbook on chinese art symbols.** Photos by Dewey G. Mears. Austin, texas (1958) 77 p, illus, bibliog.

Andersson, J. G. Hunting magic in the animal style. **BMFEA** 4 (1932) 221-320.

Andersson, J. G. On symbolism in the prehistoric painted ceramics of china. **BMFEA** 1 (1929) 65-69.

Ayrton, W. E. and John Perry. Sur les miroirs magiques du japon. **ACP** 5e sér, 20 (1880) 110-142.

Ayscough, Florence. The symbolism of the forbidden city, peking. **JNCBRAS** 61 (1930) 111-126.

Balfour, F. H. The peach and its legends. In author's **Chinese scrapbook** (1887) 145-148.

Behrsing, S. Tou-mu, eine chinesische himmelsgöttin. **OZ** 27 (1941) 173-176.

Boerschmann, Ernst. **Die baukunst und religiöse kultur der chinesen.** Vol 1: **P'u t'o shan.** Berlin (1911) 203 p, 33 pl, fig.

Boerschmann, Ernst. **Die baukunst und religiöse kultur der chinesen.** Vol 2: **Gedächtnistempel; tzế tang.** Berlin (1914) xxiv + 288 p, illus.

Boerschmann, Ernst. K'uei-sing-türme und fengshui-säulen. **AM** 2 (1925) 503-530.

Brace, A. Unifying symbolism of chinese religions. **JWCBorderResS** 3 (1926-29) 154-155.

Brewster, D. Accounts of a curious chinese mirror, which reflects from its polished face the figures embossed upon its back. **Philosophical magazine** 1 (1832) 438-441.

Brodrick, A. H. The flight of the phoenix. **AR** 36 (1940) 758-772.

Bulling, A. The decoration of some mirrors of the chin and han periods. **AA** 18 (1955) 20-45.

Bulling, A. Die kunst der totenspiele in der östlichen han-zeit. **OE** 3 (1956) 28-56, illus.

Bulling, A. **The meaning of china's most ancient art; an interpretation of pottery patterns from kansu (ma ch'ang and panshan) and their development in the shang, chou, and han periods.** Leiden (1952) xx + 150 p, illus.

Bulling, A. Neolithic symbols and the purpose of art in china. **BM** 82/83 (1943) 91-101.

Bulling, A. Three popular motives in the art of the eastern han period. The lifting of the tripod. The crossing of a bridge. Divinities. **AAA** 20 (1966/67) 25-53, illus.

Cammann, Schuyler. Chinese mirrors and chinese civilization. **Archaeology** 2 (1949) 114-120.

Cammann, Schuyler. Cosmic symbolism of the dragon robes of the ch'ing dynasty. In **A&T** (1947) 125-129.

Cammann, Schuyler. Imperial dragon robes of the later ch'ing dynasty. **OA** 3 (1950) 7-16.

Cammann, Schuyler. The lion and grape patterns on chinese bronze mirrors. **AA** 16 (1953) 265-291.

Cammann, Schuyler. The magic square of three in old chinese philosophy and religion. **HR** 1 (1961) 37-80.

Cammann, Schuyler. A ming dynasty pantheon painting. **ACASA** 18 (1964) 38-46, illus.

Cammann, Schuyler. Ming festival symbols. **ACASA** 7 (1953) 66-70, pl.

Cammann, Schuyler. Old chinese magic squares. **Sinologica** 7 (1962) 14-53.

Cammann, Schuyler. On the decoration of modern temples in taiwan and hongkong. **JAOS** 88.4 (1968) 785-790. Reaction to W. Eberhard's art, Topics and moral values in chinese temple decorations, q.v.

Cammann, Schuyler. Origins of the court and official robes of the ch'ing dynasty. **AA** 12 (1949) 189-201.

Cammann, Schuyler. A rare t'ang mirror. **AQ** 9 (1946) 93-113.

Cammann, Schuyler. A robe of the ch'ien-lung emperor. **Journal of the walters art gallery** 10 (1947) 9-20.

Cammann, Schuyler. Significant patterns on chinese bronze mirrors. **ACASA** 9 (1955) 43-62.

Cammann, Schuyler. The symbolism in chinese mirror patterns. **JISOA** 9 (1952-53) 45-63.

Cammann, Schuyler. The symbolism of the cloud collar motif. **AB** 33 (1951) 1-9.

Cammann, Schuyler. The 'TLV' pattern on cosmic mirrors of the han dynasty. **JAOS** 68.4 (1948) 159-167.

Cammann, Schuyler. Types of symbols in chinese art. In **SCT** (1953) 195-231.

Carus, Paul. Kwan yin pictures and their artists. **OC** 27 (1913) 683.

Casey, E. T. Two chinese imperial robes. **EB** 26.3 (1938) 3-6.

Chang, Kwang-chih. Changing relationships of man and animal in shang and chou myths and art. **ASBIE** 16 (1963) 133-146, illus.

Chêng, Tê-k'un. Ch'ih yü: the god of war in han art. **OA** 4.2 (summer 1958) 45-54.

Chêng, Tê-k'un. Yin-yang wu-hsing and han art. **HJAS** 20 (1957) 162-186.

Chou, Tzu-ch'iang. Chinese phoenix and the bird of paradise: a new identification of the ancient chinese phoenix. **ASBIE** 24 (1967) engl summ 117-122 + 12 p pl.

Clutton-Brock, A. Chinese and european religious art. **BM** 20 (1922) 197-200, illus.

Cohn, W. The deities of the four cardinal points in chinese art. **TOCS** 18 (1940-41) 61-75.

Combaz, G. Masques et dragons en asie. **MCB** 7 (1939-45) 1-138.

Conrady, August. **Das älteste document zur chinesischen kunstgeschichte, t'ien-wen.** Leipzig (1931) vii + 266 p.

Conrady, G. Les huit immortels taoïstes dans l'art chinois pa-hien. **BSAB** 65 (1954) 167-170.

Croissant, Doris. Funktion und wanddekor der opferschreine von wu liang tz'u. Typologische und ikonographische untersuchen. **MS** 23 (1964) 88-162, pl.

Demiéville, Paul. La montagne dans l'art littéraire chinois. **FA** 20 (1965) 7-32, pl.

Dietz, E. Another branch of chinese painting. **Parnassus** 2.6 (1930) 35. On taoist paper scrolls.

Dieulafoy, Marcel. Les piliers funéraires et les lions de ya tcheou. **CRAIBL** (1910) 362-377.

Dubs, Homer H. Hill censers. In **SSBKD** (1959) 259-264.

Dye, D. S. Symbolism of the designs. **JWCBorder ResS** 2 (1924-25) 74-76.

Dye, Daniel S. **The yin yang dance of life and basic patterns, as seen in west china between december 1908 and april 1949.** Penfield downs, pa (1950) 26 p, illus.

Eberhard, Wolfram. Topics and moral values in chinese temple decorations. **JAOS** 87.1 (1967) 22-32. Further see Eberhard's Rejoinder to schuyler camman, **JAOS** 88.4 (1968) 790-792.

Ecke, Gustav. Zur architektur der gedächtnishalle. (Contribution to the study of sculpture and architecture – Der grabtempel des kang ping, aufgenommen von p. szongott) **MS** 5 (1940) 467-478.

Edkins, Joseph. **Ancient symbolism among the chinese.** London and shanghai (1889) 26 p.

Edkins, Joseph. The ju-i, or, sceptre of good fortune. **EA** 3 (1904) 238-240.

Éléments de decoration chinoise; motifs décoratifs relevés dans les temples et yamens. Pékin (1931) 60 col pl.

Erdberg-Consten, Eleanor von. A statue of lao tzu in the po-yün-kuan. **MS** 7 (1942) 235-241.

Erkes, E. Der ikonographische charakter einiger chou-bronzen. (I. Der tiger, II. Die eule) **AA** 6 (1936-37) 111-117; 7 (1937) 92-108.

Erkes, Eduard. Der pfau in religion und folklore. **JSMVL** 10 (1926-51 sic) 67-73.

Erkes, E. Some remarks on karlgren's "fecundity symbols in ancient china." **BMFEA** 3 (1931) 63-68.

Fairbank, Wilma. The offering shrines of 'wu liang tz'u.' **HJAS** 6 (1941) 1-36, 10 fig. Repr in author's **Adventures in retrieval,** harvard univ (1972) 41-86.

Fairbank, Wilma. A structural key to han mural art. **HJAS** 7 (1942) 52-88, illus. Comparison of offering shrines of chu wei at chin hsiang with hsiao-t'ang shan and wu liang tz'u shrines. Repr in author's **Adventures in retrieval,** harvard univ (1972) 87-140.

Ferguson, John C. Decorations of chinese bronzes. An interpretation. **JNCBRAS** 72 (1946) 1-6.

Ferguson, John C. Religious art in china. **THM** 1 (1935) 239-247.

Gieseler, G. Le mythe du dragon en chine. **RA** 5e sér, 6 (1917) 104-170.

Gieseler, G. Les symboles de jade dans le taoisme. **RHR** 105 (1932) 158-181.

Goette, J. Jade and man in life and death. **THM** 3 (1936) 34-44.

Govi, M. Les miroirs magiques des chinois. Tsl fr italian M. Pomonti. **ACP** 5e sér, 20 (1880) 99-105.

Govi, M. Nouvelles expériences sur les miroirs chinois. Tsl fr italian M. Pomonti. **ACP** 5e sér, 20 (1880) 106-110.

Gray, Basil. A great taoist painting. **OA** 11 (1965) 85-94, illus. On yen pien hsiang – "metamorphoses of heavenly being."

Hall, Ardelia R. The early significance of chinese mirrors. **JAOS** 55 (1935) 182-189.

Hall, Ardelia R. The wu ti mirrors. **OZ** 20 (1934) 16-23, pl.

Hansford, S. Howard. The disposition of ritual jades in royal burials of the chou dynasty. **JRAS** (1949) 138-142.

Hartner, Willy. Studien zur symbolik der frühchinesischen bronzen. **Paideuma** 3.6/7 (1949) 279-290.

Hayes, L. Newton. **The chinese dragon.** Shanghai (1922) xvi + 66 p, illus.

Hentze, Carl. Altchinesische kultbilder und ihre ausstrahlungen. **Sinologica** 8 (1965) 137-155, illus.

Hentze, Carl. **Chinese tomb figures. A study in the beliefs and folklore of ancient china.** London (1928) xii + 105 p, illus.

Hentze, Carl. Comment il faut lire l'iconographie d'un vase en bronze chinois de la période chang. **Conferenze tenute all'Is. M. E. O.** (1952) 49-108.

Hentze, Carl. **Funde in alt china: das welterleben im ältesten china.** Göttingen (1967) 300 p, 48 pl, many bl-and-wh photos, 92 text fig, characters, bibliog, maps.

Hentze, Carl. Gods and drinking serpents. **HR** 4 (1965) 179-208, pl.

Hentze, Carl. Les jades archaïques en chine. **AA** 3 (1928) 199-216; 4 (1930-32) 35-40. See P. Pelliot, Lettre ouverte à m. carl hentze, **RAA** 6 (1929-30) 103-122, 196; see further W. P. Yetts, À propos de la lettre ouverte, **ibid** 191.

Hentze, Carl. Mythologische bildsymbole im alten china. **Studium generale** 6 (1953) 264-277.

Hentze, Carl. Die regenbogenschlange: alt-china und alt-amerika. **Anthropos** 61 (1966) 258-266, illus.

Hentze, Carl. Le symbolisme des oiseaux dans la chine ancienne. **Sinologica** 5.2 (1957) 65-92; 5.3 (1958) 129-149, illus.

Hentze, Carl. Die wanderung der tiere um die heiligen berg. **Symbolon** 4 (1964) 9-104, pl.

Hermand, L. l'Art symbolique en chine. **RC** (juil 1907) 141-169.

Hirth, Friedrich. Chinese metallic mirrors with notes on some ancient specimens of the musée guimet, paris. In **BAV** n.y. (1907) 208-256.

Hodous, Lewis. The dragon. **JNCBRAS** 48 (1917) 29-41.

Hollis, H. C. Cranes and serpents. **BCMA** 25 (1938) 147-151.

Hopkins, L. C. The dragon terrestrial and the dragon celestial. A study of the lung and the ch'en. **JRAS** (1931) 791-806; (1932) 91-97.

Hopkins, L. C. Where the rainbow ends. An introduction to the dragon terrestrial and the dragon celestial. **JRAS** (1931) 603-612.

Hornblower, G. D. Early dragon-forms. **Man** 33 (1933) 79-87. See author's Additional notes on early dragon-forms, **ibid** 36 (1936) 22-24.

Howey, M. Oldfield. **The encircled serpent. A study of serpent symbolism in all countries and ages.** N.Y. (1955) See chap 26, Chinese serpent lore, 253-266.

Huang Wen-shan. The artistic expression of totems in ancient chinese culture. **ASBIE** 21 (1966) 1-13.

Ito, C. Architecture (Chinese). In **HERE** 1 (1908) 693-696.

Kaler, Grace. Chinese symbolism: the crane. **Hobbies** 71.12 (1967) 50. Chinese symbolism: the phoenix. **Ibid** 71.11 (1967) 50-57.

Kaler, Grace. Portrait in bronze: kuan ti, chinese god of war. **Hobbies** 72.1 (1967) 50, 47.

Karlgren, Bernhard. Some fecundity symbols in ancient china. **BMFEA** 2 (1930) 1-54 + 6 p pl.

Komor, Mathias. Chinese roof-figures. **THM** 2 (1936) 355-359.

Körner, Brunhild. Die brautkrone der chinesen. **Baessler archiv** 6 (1958) 81-98.

Köster, Hermann. **Symbolik des chinesischen universismus.** Stuttgart (1958) 104 p, kart.

Kung, Hsien-lan (ed) **The life of confucius. Reproduced from a book entitled sheng chi t'u, being rubbings from the stone "tablets of the holy shrine."** Shanghai (n.d.)

Laufer, Berthold. **Chinese pottery of the han dynasty.** Leiden (1909) repr tokyo and vermont (1962) illus. See esp chap 4, sec Tazzas or sacrificial vessels; sec Hill-censers; sec Hill-jars. Rev by Ed. Chavannes in **TP** 11 (1910) 300 et seq.

Laufer, Berthold. **The diamond. A study in chinese and hellenistic folk-lore.** Chicago (1915) 75 p.

Laufer, Berthold. **Jade. A study in chinese archaeology and religion.** Chicago (1912); repr south pasadena, calif (1946) 370 p, illus.

Lees, G. F. On the symbolism of jade. **Apollo** 29 (1939) 70-75.

Lessing, Ferdinand. Über die symbolsprache in der chinesischen kunst. **Sinica** 9 (1934) 121-155, 217-231, 237-269; 10 (1935) 31-42.

Lion, Lucien. **Les ivoires religieux et médicaux chinois d'après la collection lucien lion.** Texte de Henri Maspero, René Grousset, Lucien Lion. Paris (1939) 96 p, pl.

Loehr, Max. **Chinese art: symbols and images.** Wellesley, mass (1967) 63 p, illus.

Loewenstein, Prince John. **Swastika and yin-yang.** London (1942) 28 p, illus.

Lovelock, B. Dragon robes. **EW** 6.8 (1952) 34-35.

Marin, J. The chinese dragon — a myth and an emblem. **AP** 23 (1952) 103-115.

Maryon, Herbert. A note on magic mirrors. **ACASA** 17 (1963) 26-28.

Maspero, Henri. Les ivoires chinois et l'iconographie de chine. Text by Maspero from the Lucien Lion volume q.v.; repr in author's **Les religions chinoises**, paris (1950) 229-239 (**Mélanges posthumes sur les religions et l'histoire de la chine,** t l)

McFarlane, Sewell S. Stone figures in china. **Geographical journal** 22 (aug 1903) 210-211.

Meister, W. Eine datierte taoistische bronzeplastik. **OZ** 21 (1935) 93-95.

Miao, D. F. Some chinese paintings of deities. **CJ** 19 (1933) 6-8.

Millard, R. A. A taoist figure dated 607 a.d. **AA** 20 (1957) 45-49.

Milloué, Léon de. **Catalogue du musée guimet. Pt I: Inde, chine et japon.** Précédé d'un aperçu sur les religions de l'extrême-orient et suivie d'un index alphabétique des noms des divinités et des principaux termes techniques. Lyon (1883)

Mirrors, Japanese: brief notices. Atkinson, R. W. **Nature** 16 (1877) 62; Darbishire, R. D. **ibid** 142-143; Thompson, Sylvanus P. **ibid** 163; Parnell, J. **ibid** 227-228; T. C. A. **ibid** 31 (1884-85) 264.

Morgan, Harry T. **Chinese symbolism.** Los angeles (ca. 1941) 16 p, illus.

Morgan, Harry T. **Chinese symbolism and its associated beliefs.** Los angeles (1945) 20 p, illus.

Morgan, Harry T. **Chinese symbols and superstitions.** South pasadena, calif (1942) 192 p, illus, bibliog, index.

Munsterberg, Hugo. An anthropomorphic deity from ancient china. **OA** 3.4 (1951) 147-152, illus.

Munsterberg, Hugo. The symbolism of the four directions in chinese art. **AQ** 14 (1951) 33-44.

Musée Guimet. See various catalogues, from 1880 — .

Nance, F. N. Chinese symbolism. **CJ** 20 (1934) 5-24.

Nott, Charles Stanley. **Chinese culture in the arts.** N.Y. (1946) xx + 134, illus.

Nott, Charles Stanley. **Chinese jades in the stanley charles nott collection . . . exhaustively reviewing the symbolic ritualistic appurtenances of chinese jades and their various sacrificial usages . . .** St. augustine, fla.(1942) xvi + 536 p, 118 pl.

Pelliot, Paul. Lettre ouverte à m. carl hentze. **RAA** 6 (1929-30) 103-122, 196. See Hentze item, Les jades archaïques en chine.

Pelliot, Paul. Les plaques de l'empereur du ciel. **BMFEA** 4 (1932) 115-116.

Penniman, T. K. and Cohn, W. A steatite figure of the k'ang hsi period in the pitt rivers museum, oxford (god of longevity) **Man** 45 (1945) 73-74.

Petterson, Richard. The native arts of taiwan. **Claremont quarterly** 11.3 (1964) 49-58, 12 p of photos.

Pichon, Jean-Charles. **Les cycles du retour éternel.** Paris (1963) See t 2, p 157-184.

Plumer, James M. The chinese bronze mirrors: two instruments in one. **AQ** 7 (1944) 91-108.

Pommeranz-Liedtke, Gerhard. Bilder für jedes neue jahr. Zur wandlung des chinesischen neujahrbildes. **ZBK** 1 (1955)

Pommeranz-Liedtke, Gerhard. **Chinesische neujahrsbilder.** Dresden (1961) 202 p, illus, bibliog.

Priest, Alan. The exhibition of chinese court robes and accessories. **BMMA** 26 (1931) 283-288.

Priest, Alan. 'Li chung receives a mandate.' (Sung painting) **BMMA** 34 (1939) 254-257.

Priest, Alan. A note on kuan ti. **BMMA** n.s. 25 (1930) 271-272.

Priest, Alan. The owl in shang and chou bronzes. **BMMA** 33 (1938) 235-240.

Prinsep, James. Note on the magic mirrors of japan. **JRASB** 1 (1832) 242-245.

Przyluski, J. Dragon chinois et naga indien. **MS** 3 (1938) 602-610.

R., S. C. B. The tuang [sic] fang sacrificial table. **BMMA** 19 (1924) 141-144, illus.

Riddel, W. H. Tiger and dragon. **Antiquity** 19 (1945) 27-31.

Roberts, L. Chinese ancestral portraits. **Parnassus** 9.1 (1937) 28.

Rogers, Millard. A taoist figure dated 607 a.d. **AA** 20.1 (1957) 45-49, pl.

Rychterová, Eva. Commemorative ancestor portraits. **NO** 4 (1965) 176-177, illus.

Rydh, Hannah. Symbolism in mortuary ceramics. **BMFEA** 1 (1929) 71-120, 11 pl, 62 fig.

Salmony, Alfred. **Antler and tongue: an essay on ancient chinese symbolism and its implications.** Ascona (1954) 39 p, illus.

Salmony, Alfred. The magic bell and the golden fruit in ancient chinese art. In **A&T** (1947) 105-109.

Salmony, Alfred. Note on the iconography of the shang period. **RAA** 11 (1937) 102-104.

Salmony, Alfred. The owl as ornament in archaic chinese bronzes. **Parnassus** 6.2 (1934) 23-25.

Salmony, Alfred. A problem in the iconography of three early bird vessels. **ACASA** 1 (1945-46) 53-65.

Salmony, Alfred. The third early chinese owl with snake legs. **AA** 14 (1951) 277-282.

Salmony, Alfred. The three governors of taoism, an unusual chinese bronze sculpture. **GBA** 6e sér, 25 (1944) 315-317.

Saussure, Léopold de. Le cycle des douze animaux et le symbolisme cosmique des chinois. **JA** sér 11, 15/16, t 196/197 (1920) 55-58, fig.

Saussure, Léopold de. La tortue et le serpent. **TP** sér 2, 18/19 (1918-19) 247-248, fig.

Schultze, O. Der religiöse einfluss auf die chinesische kunst. **Mitt. geogr. comm. ges.** (1906) 1-11.

Schuster, C. A comparative study of motives in western chinese folk embroideries. **MS** 2 (1936-37) 21-80.

Schuster, C. A prehistoric symbol in modern chinese folk art. **Man** 36 (1936) 201-203.

Simmons, P. A chinese imperial robe. **BMMA** 24 (1929) 134-135.

Soon, Tan Tek. The chinese tree of life. **Monist** 10 (july 1900) 625.

Soothill, William E. **The hall of light; a study of early chinese kingship.** Ed Lady Hosie and G. F. Hudson. London (1951) xxii + 289, illus.

Soper, Alexander C. The dome of heaven in asia. **AB** 29 (1947) 225-248.

Soymié, Michel. La lune dans les religions chinoises. In **La lune: mythes et rites** ('Sources orientales' 5) paris (1962) 289-321.

Stein, Rolf A. Architecture et pensée religieuse en extrême-orient. **ArtsAs** 4.3 (1957) 163-186, illus.

Stein, Rolf. Jardins en miniature d'extrême-orient. **BEFEO** 42 (1942) 1-104, 5 pl.

Sullivan, Michael. The magic mountain. **Asian review** 51 (1955) 300-310.

Tomb jades of the chou period. **BMMA** 19 (1924) 121-123.

Tomita, Kojirō. A chinese sacrificial stone house of the sixth century a.d. **BMFA** 40 (1942) 98-110.

Tomita, Kojirō and A. Kaiming Chiu. Portraits of wu ch'üan-chieh (1269-1350) taoist pope in yüan dynasty. **BMFA** 44 (1946) 88-95.

Tredwell, Winifred Reed. **Chinese art motives interpreted.** N.Y. and london (1915) xiii + 110 p, illus.

Visser, M. W. de. **The dragon in china and japan.** Amsterdam (1913) xii + 242 p.

Vuilleumier, B. Tissus et tapisseries de soie dans la chine ancienne. Technique et symbolisme. **Revue de l'art ancien et moderne** 69 (1936) 197-216.

Vuilleumier, B. Vêtements rituels impériaux chinois et chasuble des premiers mandchous. **Revue de l'art ancien et moderne** 71 (1937) 243-245.

Waterbury, Florance. **Bird deities in china.** Ascona (1952) 191 p, bibliog, index.

Waterbury, Florance. An early chinese ritual vessel. **Worcester art museum annual** 4 (1941) 73-76.

Waterbury, Florance. **Early chinese symbols and literature: vestiges and speculations, with particular reference to the ritual bronzes of the shang dynasty.** N.Y. (1942) 164 p, pl.

Waterbury, Florance. The nedzu ho: chinese ritual vessels of the ho type. In **A&T** (1947) 110-115.

Waterbury, Florance. Speculations on the significance of a ho in the freer gallery. **AA** 15 (1952) 114-124.

Waterbury, Florance. The tiger and agriculture. **AA** 10.1 (1947) 55-56. Reply to a rev of her book **Early chinese symbols and literature,** q.v. by J. LeRoy Davidson in **AB** 25 (sept 1943)

Watson, William. A grave guardian from ch'angsha. **BMQ** 17.3 (1952) 52-56.

Wenley, A. G. **The grand empress dowager wen ming and the northern wei necropolis at fang shan.** Freer gallery. **Occasional papers** 1.1 (1947) 22 p, 7 pl.

Wenley, Archibald. The po-shan hsiang-lu. **ACASA** 3 (1948-49) 5-12.

White, William C. **Chinese temple frescoes. A study of three wall-paintings of the thirteenth century.** Univ toronto (1940) xvii + 230 p, illus. (Contains 2 pts: 1 – general intro, 11 chaps; 2 – the 3 frescoes ('the paradise of maitreya,'

'the lord of the northern dipper,' 'the lord of the southern dipper')

White, William C. The lord of the northern dipper. **BROMA** 13 (1945) 32 p, illus. See item above.

White, William C. The lord of the southern dipper. **BROMA** 14 (1946) 32 p, illus. See author's book, above.

Wilhelm II, German emperor. **Die chinesische monade; ihre geschichte und ihre dichtung.** Leipzig (1934) 66 p, illus.

Williams, C. A. S. **Outlines of chinese symbolism and art motives.** Shanghai, 2nd rev ed (1932) repr as **Encyclopedia of . . .,** N.Y. (1960) 467 p, illus.

Wong, K. C. The court robe and diadem of the ancient emperor of china. **CJ** 5 (1926) 281-286.

Yetts, W. P. À propos de la lettre ouverte à m. carl hentze. **RAA** 6 (1929-30) 191. Re P. Pelliot's Lettre, **ibid** 103-122, 196.

Yetts, W. P. Chinese tomb jade. **Folk-lore** 33 (1922) 319-321.

Yetts, W. Perceval. Notes on flower symbolism in china. **JRAS** (1941) 1-21, illus.

Yetts, W. P. Pictures of a chinese immortal. **BM** 39 (1921) 113-121.

Yetts, W. Perceval. **Symbolism in chinese art.** Leyden (1912) 28 p, illus.

5. RELIGION AND HISTORY (See also SECTS AND SECRET SOCIETIES)

Allen, C. F. R. (tsl) Proclamation against idol processions. In **DV** Vol 2, pt 3, no 61, p 516-518.

Allen, H. J. The connexion between taoism, confucianism and buddhism in early days. **Trans third ICHR,** oxford (1908) vol 1, 115-119.

Bielenstein, Hans. An interpretation of the portents in the ts'ien-han-shu. **BMFEA** 22 (1950) 127-143, diagr.

Boardman, Eugene P. Millenary aspects of the taiping rebellion, 1851-64. In Sylvia L. Thrupp (ed) **Millenial dreams in action; essays in comparative study,** the hague (1962) 70-79.

Bünger, Karl. Die rechtsidee in der chinesischen geschichte. **Saeculum** (1952) 192-217.

Bünger, Karl. Religiöse bindungen im chinesischen recht. In K. Bünger and Hermann Trimborn (ed) **Religiöse bindungen in frühen und in orient-alischen rechten,** wiesbaden (1952) 58-69.

Chan, Hok-lam. Liu ping-chung (1216-74), a buddhist-taoist statesman at the court of khubilai khan. **TP** 53.1/3 (1967) 98-146.

Chan, Wing-tsit. The historic chinese contribution to religious pluralism and world community. In E. J. Jurji (ed) **Religious pluralism and world community. Interfaith and intercultural communication,** leiden (1969)

Chavannes, Édouard. Inscriptions et pièces de chancellerie chinoises de l'époque mongole. **TP** 5 (1904) 366-404. Documents dealing with controversy betw buddhists and taoists under the mongols.

Ch'en, Kenneth K. S. Buddhist-taoist mixtures in the pa-shih-i-hua t'u. **HJAS** 9 (1945) 1-12.

Chia, Chung-yao. The church-state conflict in the t'ang dynasty. In E-tu Zen Sun and John DeFrancis (ed and tsl) **Chinese social history. Translations of selected studies,** washington, d.c. (1956) 197-206. Largely fr Ennin's **journal.**

Collis, Maurice. **The first holy one.** N.Y. (1948) 280 p, illus, index. On confucius and confucianism until triumph of confucianism in former han dynasty.

Coulborn, Rushton. The state and religion: iran, india and china. **CSSH** 1 (1958) 44-57.

Creel, H. G. **Religion as a political sanction in ancient china.** Far eastern leaflet (dec 1941)

Demiéville, Paul. La situation religieuse en chine au temps de marco polo. In **Oriente poliana,** rome (1957) 193-234.

Dien, Albert E. Yen chih-t'ui (531-591+): a buddho-confucian. In **CP** (1962) 43-64.

Dubs, Homer H. The victory of han confucianism. **JAOS** 58 (1938) 435-449. Same title in Dubs (tsl) **The history of the former han dynasty by pan ku,** baltimore, md, vol 2 (1944) chap 9, app 2, p 341-353.

Edkins, Joseph. **The early spread of religious ideas especially in the far east.** Oxford (1893) 144 p.

Edkins, Joseph. The introduction of astrology into china. **ChRev** 15 (1886-87) 126-128.

Edwards, E. D. Some aspects of the conflicts of religion in china during the six dynasties and t'ang periods. **BSOAS** 7.3 (1933-35) 799-808.

Eichhorn, Werner. Der aufstand der zauberin t'ang sai-êhr im jahre 1420. **OE** 1 (1954) 11-25.

Eichhorn, Werner. Bemerkungen zum aufstand des chang chio und zum staate des chang lu. **MIOF** 3.2 (1955) 291-327.

Eichhorn, Werner. Description of the rebellion of sun ên and earlier taoist rebellions. **MIOF** 2 (1954) 325-352.

Eichhorn, Werner. Nachträgliche bemerkungen zum aufstand des sun ên. **MIOF** 2 (1954) 463-476.

Enjoy, Paul d'. De la législation chinoise à l'égard des congregations religieuse. **BMSAP** 5e sér, 5 (1904) 154-157.

Erkes, Eduard. China's religiöse entwicklung in zusammenhang mit seiner geschichte. **OZ** 4.1/2 (1915) 58-66.

Gernet, Jacques. **La vie quotidienne en chine à la veille de l'invasion mongole 1250-1276.** Paris (1959) Engl tsl H. M. Wright: **Daily life in china on the eve of the mongol invasion 1250-1276.** See chap 5, The seasons and the universe: The seasons and days of the year — festivals — religion (p 179-218) The 3rd sec of this chap repr in **TC** (1970) 161-179.

Groot, J. J. M. de. Is there religious liberty in china? **MSOS** 5 (1902) 103-151.

Groot, J. J. M. de. **Sectarianism and religious persecution in china.** Leiden (1901) repr Taipei (1963) 2 vol, 595 p, index.

Harlez, Charles de. La religion des insurgés tchang-mao. **TP** 9.5 (1898) 397-401.

Harlez, Charles de. Le tien fu hia fan tchao shu, livre religieux des tai-ping. **TP** 10.3 (1899) 307-318.

Hu, Shih. Religion and philosophy in chinese history. In Sophia H. Chen Zen (ed) **Symposium on chinese culture,** shanghai (1931) 31-58.

Hughes, E. R. Chinese religion in the third century b.c. **AR** 31 (1935) 721-733.

Kaltenmark, Max. Religion et politique dans la chine de ts'in et des han. **Diogène** 34 (avr-juin 1961) 18-46.

Kao, Chü-hsün. The ching lu shen shrines of han sword worship in hsiung-nu religion. **Central asiatic journal** 5 (1960) 221-232.

Kimura, Eiichi. The new confucianism and taoism in china and japan from the fourth to the thirteenth centuries. **CHM** 5 (1960) 801-829.

Laufer, Berthold. Religiöse toleranz in china. **Globus** 86 (1904) 219-220.

Lay, W. T. (tsl) Another proclamation against idolatrous processions. **Missionary recorder** 1 (1867) 55-56. Chin text and tsl of proclamation by viceroy wu of fukien, 21 apr 1867.

Levenson, Joseph R. Confucian and taiping "heaven": the political implications of clashing religious concepts. **CSSH** 4 (1962) 436-453.

Levy, Howard S. The bifurcation of the yellow turbans in later han. **Oriens** 13-14 (1960-61) 251-255.

Levy, Howard S. Yellow turban religion and rebellion at the end of han. **JAOS** 76 (1956) 214-227.

Liu, Ts'un-yan. Lin chao-ên (1517-1598) the master of the three teachings. **TP** 53 (1967) 253-278.

Loewe, Michael. The case of witchcraft in 91 b.c.; its historical setting and effect on han dynastic history. **AM** 15.2 (1970) 159-196.

Maspero, Henri. Le ming-t'ang et la crise religieuse chinoise avant les han. **MCB** 9 (1948-51) 1-71.

Maspero, Henri. La religion chinoise dans son dévellopement historique. In author's **HMRC** (1950) 15-138.

Maspero, Henri. La société et la religion des chinois anciens et celles des tai modernes. In author's **HMRC** (1950) 139-194.

M'Clatchie, M. T. The chinese on the plain of shinar, or a connection established between the chinese and all other nations through their theology. **JRAS** 16 (1856) 368-435.

Mears, W. P. The religious history of china. **CMI** 47, n.s. 20 (1895) 321-334.

Medhurst, Dr. (tsl) The book of religious precepts of the t'haeping dynasty. **NCH** 147 (14 may 1853)

Michaud, Paul. The yellow turbans. **MS** 17 (1958) 47-127, bibliog.

Milne, W. C. The rebellion of the yellow caps, compiled from the history of the three states. **ChRep** 10 (1841) 98-103.

Nicolas-Vandier, Nicole. Les échanges entre le bouddhisme et le taoïsme des han aux t'ang. In **AC** t 1 (1959) 166-170.

Parsons, James B. Overtones of religion and superstition in the rebellion of chang hsien-chung. **Sinologica** 4.3 (1955) 170-177.

Peeters, Jan. **Eine stimme aus der sung-zeit über die heterodoxie: lun-yü, II, 16.** Breslau (1938) 83 p.

Rachewiltz, Igor de. The hsi-yu lu by yeh-lü ch'u-ts'ai. **MS** 21 (1962) 1-128. See for controversy betw buddhism and taoism in yuan dynasty.

Rachewiltz, Igor de. Yeh-lü ch'u-ts'ai (1189-1243): buddhist idealist and confucian statesman. In **CP** (1962) 189-216.

Religionen und religionspolitik im alten und neuen china. **China-analysen** 9 (july/aug 1970) 46-96.

Rule, Paul A. Jesuit and confucian? Chinese religion in the journals of matteo ricci, s.j., 1583-1610. **JRH** 5 (1968) 105-124.

Sargent, Galen E. Les débats personnels de tchou hi en matière de methodologie. **JA** 243 (1955) 213-228.

Stein, Rolf A. Remarques sur les mouvements du taoïsme politico-religieux au IIe siècle ap. j.-c. **TP** 50.1/3 (1963) 1-78.

Topley, Marjorie. Chinese religion and rural cohesion in the nineteenth century. **JHKBRAS** 8 (1968) 9-43.

Waidtlow, C. The imperial religions of ch'in and han. **ChRec** 58 (1927) 565-571, 698-703.

Waidtlow, C. The religion of emperor wu of the han. **ChRec** 55 (1924) 361-366, 460-464, 527-529.

Waidtlow, C. The religion of the first emperor (ch'in shih huang) **ChRec** 57 (1926) 413-416, 487-490.

Waley, Arthur. The heavenly horses of ferghana: a new view that the chinese expeditions of 102 b.c. had a magico-religious significance. **History today** 5 (feb 1955) 95-103, illus.

Waley, Arthur. History and religion. **PEW** 5 (1955-56) 75-78.

Walshe, W. G. Religious toleration in china. **CR** 85 (mar 1904) 442-447. On persecutions of buddhism.

Weber-Schäfer, Peter. **Oikumene und imperium. Studien zur zivil-theologie des chinesischen kaiserreichs.** München (1968) 317 p. Historical through period of han wu-ti.

Werner, E. T. C. The origin of the chinese priest-hood. **JNCBRAS** 59 (1928) 188-199.

Woodin, S. F. (tsl) A proclamation against certain idolatrous practices. **Missionary recorder** 1 (1867) 22-23. Chin text and tsl of proclamation by viceroy tso of fukien, 5 mar 1865.

Wright, Arthur F. The formation of sui ideology. In **CTI** (1957) 71-104.

Wright, H. K. The religious element in the tso chuan. **JNCBRAS** 48 (1917) 171-188.

Wright, Harrison K. Religious persecution in china: a historical study of the relations between church and state. **ChRec** 52 (1921) 233-249, 341-354, 397-411.

6. RELIGIOUS THOUGHT

A. L. Chinese notions as to the moment of death. **ChRev** 10 (1881-82) 431.

Antonini, P. Personne de l'éternel d'après la doctrine des chinois. **Compte rendu du congrès scientifique international des catholiques,** paris, t 1 (1897) 115-133.

Bertholet, R. l'Astrobiologie et l'état chinois. (l'Astrobiologie et la pensée d'asie: essai sur les origines des sciences et des théories morales II-III) **RMM** 40 (1933) 41-64, 457-479.

Bodde, Derk. The chinese view of immortality: its expression by chu hsi and its relationship to buddhist thought. **RofR** 6 (1942) 369-383.

Bodde, Derk. Evidence for 'laws of nature' in chinese thought. **HJAS** 20 (1957) 709-727.

Boone, W. J. and James Legge. **The notions of the chinese concerning god and spirits.** Hong kong (1852) repr taipei (1971)

Brandon, S. G. F. **The judgment of the dead. The idea of life after death in the major religions.** N.Y. (1967) See chap 9, The judgment of the dead bureaucratically organized, 178-188.

Bruce, J. P. The theistic import of the sung philosophy. **JNCBRAS** 49 (1918) 111-127.

Buckens, F. Les antiquités funéraires du honan central et la conception de l'âme dans la chine primitive. **MCB** 8 (1946-47) 1-101.

Chalmers, John. Chinese natural theology. **ChRev** 5 (1876-77) 271-281.

Chan, Wing-tsit. The individual in chinese religions. In Charles A. Moore (ed) with assistance of Aldyth V. Morris, **The status of the individual in east and west,** univ hawaii (1968) 181-198.

Chan, Wing-tsit. The neo-confucian solution of the problem of evil. **ASBIHP** 28 (1957) 773-791.

Chan, Wing-tsit. **A source book in chinese philosophy.** Princeton univ (1963) xxv + 856 p, chron of dynasties, chron of philosophers, app On trans-lating certain chinese philosophical terms, bibliog, gloss of chin characters, index. For religious thought see passim (table of contents as well as index give good indications)

Chan, Wing-tsit. Wang yang-ming's criticism of buddhism. In **WPDMD** (1968) 31-37.

Chang, Carsun. Buddhism as a stimulus to neo-confucianism. **OE** 2.2 (1955) 157-166.

Chau, Yick-fu. Religious thought in ancient china. Tsl fr chin F. P. Brandauer. **CF** 10.1 (1967) 20-33; 10.2 (1967) 20-33.

Chaudhuri, H. The concept of brahman in hindu philosophy (with a sec on brahman, tao and t'ai-chi) **PEW** 4 (1954) 47-66.

Ch'en, Kenneth. The buddhist contributions to neo-confucianism and taoism. In **TC** 155-160. Excerpt from author's **Buddhism in china: a historical survey** q.v. 471-476.

Chêng, Tê-k'un. Yin-yang, wu-hsing and han art. **HJAS** 20 (1957) 162-186.

Courant, Maurice. Sur le prétendu monothéisme des anciens chinois. **RHR** 41 (1900) 1-21.

Creel, Herrlee Glessner. **Sinism: a study of the evolution of the chinese world-view.** Chicago (1929) vii + 127 p.

Creel, H. G. Sinism — a clarification. **JHI** 10 (1949) 135-140.

Drake, F. S. The contribution of chinese religious thought. **ChRec** 72 (sept-oct 1941) 496-505, 537-545.

Dubs, Homer H. Theism and naturalism in ancient chinese philosophy. **PEW** 9 (1959-60) 163-172.

Duperray, E. La survie dans la tradition religieuse chinoise. **Bulletin de la société saint-jean-baptiste** 8.7 (1968)

Durme, J. van. **La notion primitive de 'dieu' en chine.** Bruges (1927) 16 p.

Eberhard, Wolfram. **Beiträge zur kosmologischen spekulation der chinesen der han-zeit.** Berlin (1933) 100 p, diagr.

Eberhard, Wolfram. Fatalism in the life of the common man in noncommunist china. **Anthropological quarterly** 39 (1966) 148-160. Repr in author's **MSVC** (1971)

Eberhard, Wolfram. **Guilt and sin in traditional china.** Univ california (1967) 141 p, gloss, bibliog, index.

Eliade, Mircea. **The sacred and the profane. The nature of religion** (German ed 1957) engl tsl Willard Trask, n.y. (1959) See sec Desacralization of nature (151-155) using 'miniature gardens' as example.

Erkes, Eduard. Ssu er pu wang [death without annihilation] **AM** 3.2 (1953) 156-161.

Erkes, E. Die totenbeigaben im alten china. **AA** 6 (1936-37) 17-36.

Forke, A. Chinesische und indianische philosophie. **ZDMG** 98 (1944) 195-237. Compares certain concepts: 1. Tao = brahman, das absolute; 2. Wu-wei = nivṛtti, passivität; 3. Wei-hsin lun = māyā, idealismus; 4. Chinesische anklänge an sāmkhya und yoga.

Forke, Alfred. Das unsterblichkeitsproblem in der chinesischen philosophie. **FF** 11 (1935) 114-115.

Forke, A. **The world-conception of the chinese.** London (1925) xiv + 300.

Frazier, Allie M. (ed) **Readings in eastern religious thought.** Vol 3, **Chinese and japanese religions.** Philadelphia (1969) See 1-176 for china.

Galpin, Francis W. Notes concerning the chinese belief of evil and evil spirits. **ChRec** 5.1 (jan-feb 1874) 42-50.

Graham, D. C. Mysterious potency in the chinese religion. **ChRec** 60 (1929) 235-237.

Granet, Marcel. **La pensée chinoise.** Paris (1934) xxiii + 611 p, bibliog, index.

Grava, Arnold. Tao: an age-old concept in its modern perspectives. **PEW** 13 (1963) 235-249.

Grison, P. Formes et formules traditionnelles, VIII. La voie du ciel. **FA** 106 (1955) 507-513.

Groot, J. J. M. de. **The religious system of china.** Leiden (1892-1910) Repr taipei (1964) 6 vol. 1-3: Disposal of the dead; 4-6: The soul and ancestral worship. Compte rendu par Éd. Chavannes, **RHR** 37 (1898) 81-89.

Hackmann, Heinrich F. **Chinesische philosophie.** München (1927) 406 p.

Hay, Eldon R. Religion and the death of god: hsün tzu and rubenstein. **SEAJT** 11 (spring 1970) 83-93.

Hoare, J. C. **God and man in the chinese classics, a short study of confucian theology.** Ningpo (1895) 52 p.

Hsiang, Paul S. God in ancient china. **Worldmission** 7 (1956) 224-232.

Hsiang, Paul S. The humanism in the religious thought of ancient china. **CC** 10 (sept 1969) 13-21.

Hu, Shih. The concept of immortality in chinese thought. **Harvard divinity school bulletin** (1946) 23-43.

Hu, Shih. The natural law in the chinese tradition. In **NLIP** 5 (1953) 119-153.

Hudson, W. H. Gods and demons: some current chinese conceptions. **ChRec** 51.8 (aug 1920) 550-556.

Ikeda, Suetoshi. Die eigentliche chinesische religion und yin-yang gedanke. **Journal of religious studies** 38.3 (1965)

Ikeda, Suetoshi. The origin and development of the wu-hsing (five elements) idea: a preliminary essay. **E&W** n.s. 16.3/4 (1966) 297-309.

J. W. Die ansichten der chinesen über die seelenwanderung. **OstL** 13 (1899) 341-342.

James, E. O. **Creation and cosmology. A historical and comparative inquiry.** Leiden (1969) See chap 3, India and the far east.

James, F. Huberty. The theism of china. **New world** 6 (1897) 307-323.

Katō, Jōken. **Religion and thought in ancient china.** Cambridge (1953) 44 p.

Katō, Jōken. Religion and thought in ancient china. **JSR:LPH** 8 (1957) 17-19.

Kühnert, J. Entst. d. welt u. d. wesen d. menschen n. china anschauung. **Ausland** 66 (1893) 150-154.

Lemaître, Solange. **Le mystère de la mort dans les religions d'asie.** Paris (1943) xi + 151 p.

Liebenthal, Walter. The immortality of the soul in chinese thought. **MN** 8 (1952) 327-397.

Liebenthal, W. On trends in chinese thought. In **SJV** (1954) 262-278.

Lübke, A. **Der himmel der chinesen.** (1931) 141 p.

Maclagan, Patrick J. **Chinese religious ideas: a christian valuation.** London (1926) 238 p.

Martin, W. A. P. The speculative philosophy of the chinese. **American journal of theology** 1 (1897) 289-297.

M'Clatchie, M. T. The chinese on the plain of shinar, or a connection between the chinese and all other nations through their theology. **JRAS** 16 (1856) 368-435.

M'Clatchie, Thomas. **Confucian cosmogony. A translation of section forty-nine of the 'complete works' of the philosopher choo-foo-tze, with explanatory notes.** Shanghai (1874) xviii + 161 p, incl chin text.

Moreau, J. La pensée de l'asie et l'astrobiologie d'après m. rené berthelot. **RMM** 48 (1941) 48-73.

Pauthier, G. **Lettre inédite du p. prémare sur le monothéisme des chinois** . . . Paris (1861) 54 p.

Pelliot, Paul. Die jenseitsvorstellung der chinesen. **Eranos** 7 (1939) 61-82.

Rawlinson, Frank J. **Chinese ideas of the supreme being.** Shanghai (1927) 57 p.

Reischauer, August Karl. **The nature and truth of the great religions.** Tokyo (1966) See sec A:VI, The god-concept in chinese religion, 63-75; sec B:V, Chinese religion and the good life, 122-147; sec C:VI, Chinese religion and individual destiny, 171-173.

Réveillère, le contre-admiral. Philosophie de la religion chinoise. **Revue d'europe** 9 (mars 1902) 194-197; **RIC** 5, no 187 (19 mai 1902) 448-449.

Ross, John. Chinese classical theology. **ChRec** 33.9 (1902) 436-438.

Rousselle, E. Konfuzius und das archaische weltbild der chinesischen frühzeit. **Saeculum** 5 (1954) 1-33.

Ruyer, R. Dieu-personne et dieu-tao. **RMM** 52 (1947) 141-157.

Saint Ina, Marie de. China's contribution to the spiritual foundation of humanity. **IPQ** 6.3 (sept 1966) 445-454. Mostly on i-ching theory.

Saussure, Léopold de. La cosmologie religieuse en chine, dans l'iran et chez les prophètes hébreux. **Actes du CIHR, 1923,** paris (1925)

Schindler, Bruno. The development of chinese conceptions of supreme beings. **AMHAV** (1923) 298-366.

Schmidt, P. Persian dualism in the far east. In **OSCEP** (1933) 405-406.

Shih, Joseph. The ancient chinese cosmogony. **SM** 18 (1969) 111-130.

Shih, Joseph. The notions of god in the ancient chinese religion. **Numen** 16 (1969) 99-138.

Shih, Joseph. The tao: its essence, its dynamism, and its fitness as a vehicle of christian revelation. **SM** 15 (1966) 117f.

Shih, Joseph. The two theological schools in the late chou china (722-221 b.c.) **SM** 16 'Religious glimpses of eastern asia' (1967) 9-35.

Shih, Vincent Y. C. A critique of motzu's religious views and related concepts. In Hong kong univ dept chin, **Symposium on chinese studies** . . . Hong kong (1968) vol 3, 1-17.

Simbriger, Heinrich. Betrachtungen über yang und yin. **Antaios** 7 (1965) 126-148.

Sjöholm, Gunnar. Observations on the chinese ideas of fate. In Helmer Ringgren (ed) **Fatalistic beliefs in religion, folklore and literature,** stockholm (1967) 126-132.

Smith, D. Howard. Chinese concepts of the soul. **Numen** 5 (1958) 165-179.

Smith, D. Howard. Saviour gods in chinese religion. In **SG** (1963) 174-190.

Smith, Huston. Transcendence in traditional china. **RS** 2 (1967) 185-196.

Smith, Wilfred C. **The faith of other men.** Toronto (1962) n.y. (1963) See chap 5, The chinese, 67-80.

The soul of an idol. **Our missions** 12 (1905) 30.

Steininger, Hans. Der heilige herrscher, sein tao und sein praktisches tun. In **SJFAW** (1956) 170-177.

Strausz und D. V. von Torney. **Der altchinesische monotheismus.** Heidelberg (1885)

Tien, Antoine Tcheu-kang. **l'Idée de dieu dans les huit premiers classiques chinois. Ses noms, son existence et sa nature étudiée à la lumière des découvertes archéologiques.** Fribourg (1942) 224 p.

Tscharner, E. H. von. Leben und tod im denken der grossen chinesischen weisen. **MSGFOK** 6 (1944) 69-95.

Tucci, G. The demoniacal in the far east. **E&W** 4 (1953) 3-11.

Voskamp, C. J. Die animistischen vorstellung im volksglauben der chinesen. **Religion und geisteskult** 7 (1913) 207-212.

Wei, Tat. Confucius and the i-ching. In Finley P. Dunne, jr (ed) **The world religions speak on 'the relevance of religion in the modern world',** the hague (1970) 64-71.

Werner, E. T. C. **The chinese idea of the second self.** Shanghai (1932) 49 p.

Werner, E. T. C. Rebuttal notes on chinese religion and dynastic tombs. **JNCBRAS** 56 (1925) 134-148. Rebuttal of F. Ayscough's critical comment in her Cult of the ch'eng huang lao yeh, **JNCBRAS** 55 (1924)

White, Hugh W. **Demonism verified and analyzed.** Shanghai (1922)

Wilhelm, Richard. Tod und erneuerung nach der ostasiatischen welt-auffassung. **CDA** (1929-30) 49-69.

Winance, Eleuthère. A forgotten chinese thinker: mo tzu. **IPQ** 1.4 (dec 1969) 593-619. Emphasizes religious aspects of his thought.

Wu, Joseph S. Some humanistic characteristics of chinese religious thought. **RS** 5 (1969) 99-103.

Yang, C. K. The functional relation between confucian thought and chinese religion. In **CTI** (1957) 269-290.

Yao Shan-yu. The cosmological and anthropological philosophy of tung chung-shu. **JNCBRAS** 73 (1948) 40-68.

Yü Ying-shih. Life and immortality in the mind of han china. **HJAS** 25 (1964-65) 80-122.

7. CONFUCIUS AND CONFUCIANISM (See also GENERAL STUDIES)

Allen, Herbert J. The connexion between taoism, confucianism and buddhism in early days. **Trans 3rd ICHR,** oxford (1908) vol 1, 115-119.

Amberley, Viscount. **An analysis of religious belief.** London (1876) See vol 1, pt 2: Means of communication downwards. V. Holy persons. Sec 1. Confucius.

Arlington, Lewis Charles. **Some remarks on the worship offered confucius in the confucian temple.** Peiping (1935) 8 + 20 p, pl. China chronicle 10.

Armstrong, Alexander. **Shantung (china): a general outline of the geography and history . . . and notes of a journey to the tomb of confucius.** Shanghai (1891) viii + 198.

Atkins, Gaius G. and Charles S. Braden. **Procession of the gods.** N.Y. and london (1930 et seq) 3rd rev ed (1948) See chap 11, Confucianism and the religion of heaven, 325-361.

Bach, Marcus. **Had you been born in another faith.** Englewood cliffs, n.j. (1961) See chap 4, Had you been born a confucianist, 63-82.

Bahm, Archie J. **The world's living religions.** Southern illinois univ (1964) See pt 2, Religions of china and japan; confucianism, p 175-198.

Baker, N. Confucianism. In J. N. D. Anderson (ed) **The world's religions,** london (1950)

Balazs, Étienne. Confucius. In **AC** t 1 (1959) 142-145.

Baldwin, S. L. Confucianism. In **DR** (1884) 378-419.

Ballou, Robert O. et al (ed) **The bible of the world.** N.Y. (1939) See sec Confucianist scriptures, 379-467.

Beach, Harlan P. The ethics of confucianism. In E. Hershey Sneath (ed) **The evolution of ethics as revealed in the great religions,** yale univ (1927) 39-74.

Biallas, Franz Xaver. **Konfuzius und sein kult. Ein beitrag zur kulturgeschichte chinas und ein führer zur heimatsstadt des konfuzius.** Peking (1928) 130 p, illus, plans.

Bishop, Carl W. Shantung: china's holy land. **UPUMB** 12.2 (june 1921) 85-115.

Bonsall, Bramwell S. **Confucianism and taoism.** London (1934) 127 p.

Braden, Charles S. **Jesus compared. Jesus and other great founders of religions.** Englewood cliffs, n.j. (1957) See Jesus and confucius, 108-131.

Braden, Charles S. (comp) **The scriptures of mankind: an introduction.** N.Y. (1952) See chap 9, The sacred literature of the chinese: Confucian, 236-273.

Bradley, David G. **A guide to the world's religions.** Englewood cliffs, n.j. (1963) See chap 15, Confucianism, 141-149.

Brou, Alexandre. Bulletin des missions chine: le défaite de confucius. **Études** (20 nov 1917) 493-506.

Brou, Alexandre. La nouvelle chine et le culte de confucius. **RC** (janv-avril 1918) 3-15, illus.

Brown, Brian. **The story of confucius, his life and sayings.** Philadelphia (1927) 265 p, pl.

Browne, Lewis (comp) **The world's great scriptures. An anthology of the sacred books of the ten principal religions.** N.Y. (1946) See sec The scriptures of confucianism, 209-291.

Burrell, David J. **The religions of the world.** Philadelphia (1902) See chap 8, Confucianism, 231-262.

Burrows, Millar. **Founders of the great religions. Being personal sketches of lao-tse, confucius, buddha, jesus, etc.** London and n.y. (1931) 243 p.

Burtt, Edwin A. **Man seeks the divine.** N.Y. (1957) See chap 6, Confucianism, 153-184.

Cauvin, le Dr. Excursion au Tai-chann et au tombeau de confucius. **RGI** 9 (août-sept-nov 1884) 10 (janv – nov 1885) 12 (janv 1887)

Cavin, Albert. **Le confucianisme.** Paris (1968) 295 p, illus.

Champion, Selwyn G. and Dorothy Short (comp) **Readings from world religions.** Boston (1951) See chap 7, Confucianism, 126-144.

Chan, Wing-tsit. Confucianism. In Vergilius Ferm (ed) **Religion in the twentieth century,** paterson, n.j. (1948) 95-111. Paperbk ed (1965) entitled **Living schools of religion.**

Chang, Ch'i-yun. **A life of confucius.** Tsl fr chin Shih, Chao-yin. Taipei (1954) 113 p.

Chang, Joseph. Confucius était-il agnostique ou croyant? **Mission bulletin** 6 (1954) 421-426, 547-551.

Chiu, Koon-noi. The religious elements in the teaching of confucius. **CSPSR** 12 (1928) 237-250; 431-450.

Chou, Chung-i. The common points in the opinion of chinese buddhists and confucianists. **West and East** 14 (apr 1969) 8-10.

Clarke, James F. **Ten great religions.** Boston and n.y. (1871) See chap 2, Confucius and the chinese, or the prose of asia, 32-76.

Clopin, Camille. Comparaison entre lao-tse, pythagore et confucius. Résultats définitifs pour la chine des deux doctrines examinées par m. milloué dans une conférence au musée guimet. **La géographie** 27.3 (1920) 60 p.

Confucianism. In Henry O. Dwight, H. Allen Tapper jr, and Edwin M. Bliss (ed) **The encyclopedia of missions,** n.y. and london (2nd ed 1910) 188-193.

Confucius. In Larousse, **Grande dictionnaire universel,** paris (préface 1865) t 4, p 919-921.

Cordier, Henri. Le confucianisme et le shinto. **Revue du clergé français** (1 fev 1911) 257-273.

Cordier, Henri. Confucius. In **La grande encyclopédie,** paris (n.d.) t 12, p 397-399.

Couchoud, Paul Louis (tsl) **Une visite au tombeau de confucius avec une note de lin tcheu et une préface de lou tseng-tsiang . . ..** Pékin (1920) 38 p, texte français et chin.

Creel, Herrlee G. **Confucius, the man and the myth.** N.Y. (1949) 363 p, app, notes, refs, bibliog, map, index.

Creel, H. G. Was confucius agnostic? **TP** 29 (1932) 55-99.

Crow, Carl. **Master kung. The story of confucius.** N.Y. and london (1938) 346 p, illus, end-paper map.

Dawson, Christopher. **Enquiries into religion and culture.** N.Y. (1934) See pt 2, chap The mystery of china, 128-138.

DeBary, William T. Confucianism. In Johnson E. Fairchild (ed) **Basic beliefs. The religious philosophies of mankind,** n.y. (1959) 92-113.

Delius, Rudolf von. **Kungfutse, seine persönlichkeit und seine lehre.** Leipzig (1930) 66 p.

Doré, Henri. Le confucéisme sous la republic. **La chine** 28 (1922) 1533-1543; 29 (1922) 1559-1571.

Doré, Henri. Le confucéisme sous la république, 1911-1922. **NCR** 4 (1922) 298-319.

Doré, Henri. Le culte de confucius sous la république chinoise (1911-1922) **Études** (20 août 1922) 433-448.

Douglas, Robert K. **Confucianism and taoism.** London (?) (1879)

DuBose, Hampden C. **The dragon, image and demon, or the religions of china: confucianism, buddhism, and taoism. Giving an account of the mythology, idolatry and demonolotry of the chinese.** London (1886) 463 p.

Dvorak, Rudolf. **Darstellungen aus dem gediete der nichtchristlichen religionsgeschichte** (12 Bd), **Chinas religionen.** Erste teil: **Confucius und seine lehre.** Münster (1895) vii + 244 p. Rev by Éd. Chavannes in **RHR** 32 (1895) 303-307; **ibid** 48 (1903) 71-74.

Eakin, Frank. **Revaluing scripture.** N.Y. (1928) See chap 16, The king and shu (confucian) 172-188.

Eastman, Max. **Seven kinds of goodness.** N.Y. (1967) See 2, The teacher of growth: confucius, 31-42.

Eberhard, Wolfram. Konfuzius als revolutionär und sittenkritiker. **Der weltkreis** 3 (1933) 1-7. Engl tsl in author's **MSVC** (1971) Confucius as a revolutionist and a critic of morals, 401-411.

Edkins, Joseph. A visit to the city of confucius. **JNCBRAS** n.s. 8 (1874) 79-92.

Edmunds, Charles K. Shantung: china's holy land. **NGM** 36.3 (sept 1919) 231-252.

Edwards, E. D. **Confucius.** London and glasgow (1940) xii + 146 p.

Étiemble, René. **Confucius.** Paris (1958) viii + 314.

Étiemble, René. Confucius et la chine contemporaine. **Évidences** (1954) 13-18.

Faber, Ernst. **Confucianism.** Shanghai (1895) 12 p. See same title in **CMH** (1896) 1-11; see also author's **China in the light of history** (tsl fr german E. M. H.) Shanghai (1897) app.

Faucett, Lawrence. **Six great teachers of morality.** Tokyo (1958) See chap 7, Seeking confucius in his sayings, 395-489, illus.

Finegan, Jack. **The archeology of world religions.** Princeton univ (1952) vol 2: **Buddhism, confucianism, taoism,** 234-599, illus.

Fingarette, Herbert. Human community as holy rite: an interpretation of confucius' analects. **HTR** 59 (1966) 53-67.

Ford, Eddy L. **A comparison of confucian and christian ideals.** Foochow (192 ?) 54 p.

Forlong, J. G. R. **Short studies in the science of comparative religions embracing all the religions of asia.** London (1897) chap 6, Confucius and his faith.

Franke, O. Die religiöse und politische bedeutung des konfuzianismus in vergangenheit und gegenwart. **Zeitschrift für systematische theologie** 8 (1931) 579-588.

Frost, S. E., jr (ed) **The sacred writings of the world's great religions.** N.Y.(?) (1943) See chap 4, Confucianism, 91-118.

Gaer, Joseph. **How the great religions began.** N.Y. (1929) rev ed (1956) See bk 2, pt 1, Confucianism, the teachings of a great sage, 113-145.

Gaer, Joseph (comp) **The wisdom of the living religions.** N.Y. (1956) See pt 3, The sayings of confucianism, 93-114.

Giles, Herbert A. **Confucianism and its rivals.** London (1915) ix + 271 p.

Giles, Herbert A. Le confucianisme au XIXe siècle. **Chine et sibérie** (dec 1900) 536-540, 555-559. Tsl fr **North-american review** 171 (july-dec 1900) 359-374. See also same title in engl: Confucianism in the nineteenth century, in, various authors, **Great religions of the world,** n.y. and london (1901) 3-30.

Giles, Lionel. Introduction to confucianism. In Selwyn G. Champion (ed) **The eleven religions and their proverbial lore. A comparative study,** n.y. (1954) 68-74 (the 'proverbial lore' on p 75-91)

Gobien, Charles le. Éclaircissement sur les honneurs que les chinois rendent à confucius et aux morts. In author's **Affaires de la chine,** paris (1700) vol 3, 217-332.

Graham, A. C. Confucianism. In **ZCE** (1959) 365-384.

Grant, C. M. **Religions of the world in relation to christianity.** London (1894) chap 3, Confucianism; chap 4, Sources of the strength and weakness of confucianism.

Gripenoven, Jeanne. **Confucius et son temps.** Neuchâtel, etc (1955) 116 p.

Groot, J. J. M. de. **Religion in china. Universism: a key to the study of taoism and confucianism.** N. Y. and london (1912) (see also author's **Universismus. . .**)

Grützmacher, Richard H. **Konfuzius, buddha, zarathustra, muhammed.** Leipzig (1921) 92 p.

Gundry, D. W. **Religions. A preliminary historical and theological study.** London and n.y. (1958) See 5, The monistic religions, confucianism, 78-84.

Haas, Hans. **Lao-tsze und konfuzius. Einleitung in ihr spruchgut.** Leipzig (1920) 60 p.

Haas, Hans. **Das spruchgut k'ung-tsze's und lao-tsze's in gedanklicher zusammenordnung.** Leipzig (1920) 244 p.

Hardon, John A. **Religions of the world.** N. Y. (1963) chap 6, Confucianism, 156-192.

Hardwick, Charles. **Christ and other masters.** Cambridge (1858) See Confucianism, 278-306.

Henry, B. C. Confucius and confucianism. Chap 4 in author's **CD** (1885) 62-79.

Herzer, Rudolf. Konfuzius in der volksrepublik. **ZDMG** 119.2 (1970) 302-331.

Hesse-Wartegg, Ernst von. China's 'holy land.' A visit to the tomb of confucius. With pictures from photographs taken by the author. **Century illustrated magazine** 60 (1900) 803-819.

Hesse-Wartegg, Ernst von. Zum grabe des confucius. In **Schantung** (1898) 168-175.

Hesse-Wartegg, Ernst von. Die vaterstadt des confucius. In **Schantung** (1898) 176-188.

Hirth, Friedrich. Confucius and the chinese. In J. Herman Randall, and J. L. Gardner Smith (ed) **The unity of religions,** n.y. (1910) 13-28.

Hoang, Tzu-yue. Lao-tseu, khong-tseu, mo-tseu. (Étude comparative sur les philosophies) **Annales de l'université de lyon** (1925) 37 p.

Hodous, Lewis. Confucianism. In Edward J. Jurji (ed) **The great religions of the modern world,** princeton univ (1946) 1-23.

Hopkins, E. Washburn. **The history of religions.** N.Y. (1926) See chap 15, Confucius, lao-tse, taoism, 249-274.

Hsiang, Paul S. Confucianism, raw material for christianity. **Worldmission** 5 (1955) 320-331.

Hsiao, Paul S. Y. Dschŭndz, das menschenideal der chinesen. **ZMR** 39 (1955) 269-283.

Hsieh, Tehyi. **Konfuzius. Eine einführung in das leben und werken des weisen und eine auswahl seiner gespräche und gedanken.** Übers von Ilse Kramer. Zürich (1954) 78 p.

Hubbard, Elbert. **Little journeys to the homes of great teachers,** vol 22.2 (feb 1908) Confucius.

Hume, Robert E. **The world's living religions. With special reference to their sacred scriptures and in comparison with christianity.** N.Y. (1924) rev ed (1959) See pt, Religions originating in east asia (china, japan): 6. Confucianism.

Johnston, Reginald F. **Confucianism and modern china.** London (1934) n.y. (1935) 272 p, illus.

Joos, G. Konfuzius und lao-tse. In **Geistige reiche und religiöse fragen der gegenwart** (1940) 14-24.

Jurji, Edward J. **The christian interpretation of religion. Christianity in its human and creative relationships with the world's cultures and faiths.** N.Y. (1952) See chap 8, The religion of humanism: confucianism, 172-191.

Kaizuka, Shigeki. **Confucius.** Tsl fr jap Geoffrey Bownas. London and n.y. (1956) 192 p, chron tables, maps, index.

Kaltenmark, Max. Le confucianisme. In **AC** t 1 (1959) 146-150.

Kellett, E. E. **A short history of religions.** N.Y. (1934) See p 428-443.

Kern, M. Konfuzianismus und taoismus. In **LO** (1922) 325-350.

Kimura, Eiichi. The new confucianism and taoism in china and japan from the fourth to the thirteenth centuries a.d. **CHM** 5 (1959-60) 801-829.

Klügmann, Karl. Aus dem religiösen leben der chinesen. Am grabe der konfuzius. Auf dem taishan. **Geist des ostens** 1 (1913) 284-295.

Koung-tsee, philosophe. In **MCLC** t 3 (1778) 41-43.

Kramers, R. P. Der konfuzianismus als religion. Versuche zur neubelebung eines konfuzianischen glaubens. **AS** 18/19 (1965) 143-166.

Krause, Friedrich E. A. **Ju-tao-fo. . . Die religiösen und philosophischen systeme ostasiens.** München (1924) 588 p.

Kung, Hsien-lan (ed) **The life of confucius. Repro-duced from a book entitled sheng chi t'u, being rubbings from the stone 'tablets of the holy shrine.'** Shanghai (n.d.) Cp Lair and Wang (tsl) **An illustrated life of confucius.**

Lair, H. P. and Wang, L. C. (tsl) **An illustrated life of confucius. from tablets in the temple at chufu, shantung, china.** n.p. (n.d.) repr taipei (1972) 113 p. Cp Kung, Hsien-lan (ed) **The life of confucius . . .**

Lancashire, Douglas. Confucianism in the twentieth century. In **China and its place in the world,** auckland (1967) 26-42.

Lee, H. T. Is confucianism a religion? **CSM** 21 (1926) 52-57.

Lee, Shao-chang. The attitude of confucius toward religion. **NRJ** 8 (july 1947) 43-50.

Lee, W. J. Heaven, earth and confucius. **FCR** 19 (sept 1969) 10-14.

Legge, James. **Christianity and confucianism compared in their teaching of the whole duty of man.** London (?) (1884) 36 p.

Legge, James. **Confucianism in relation to christianity.** Shanghai and london (1877) 12 p.

Legge, James. Confucius. In **EncyB,** 11th ed (1910-11) vol 6, p 907-912.

Legge, James. Confucius the sage, and the reli-gion of china. In **RSW** (1889 et seq) 61-75.

Legge, James. Imperial confucianism. **ChRev** 6.3 (nov-dec 1877) 147-158; 6.4 (jan-feb 1878) 223-235; 6.5 (mar-apr 1878) 299-310; 6.6 (may-june 1878) 363-374.

Legge, James. **The religions of china. Con-fucianism and taoism described and compared with christianity.** London (1880) 310 p.

Leslie, Daniel. **Confucius.** Paris (1962) 224 p.

Lessing, Ferdinand D. Bodhisattva confucius. **Oriens** 10.1 (1957) 110-113.

Liang, Si-ing. **La rencontre et le conflit entre les idées des missionaires chrétiens et les idées des chinois en chine depuis la fin de la dynastie des ming.** Paris (1940) 159 p.

Lillico, S. The tomb of confucius. **CJ** 21 (1934) 221-224.

Lim, Boon Keng. The confucian way of thinking of the world and god. Prepared for publ and annot David A. Wilson. **AR** ser 4, 7 (apr 1919) 168-178.

Liu, Wu-chi. **Confucius. His life and times.** N.Y. (1955) xv + 189 p.

Lyon, D. Willard (ed) **Religious values in con-fucianism. A source book of facts and opinions.** N.Y. and london (1927) 42 p.

Malebranche, Nicolas [1628-1715] **Entretien d'un philosoph chrétien et d'un philosoph chinois,** suivi de l'avis au lecteur. Avec une introduction et des notes par A. LeMoine. Marseille (1936) 11 + 119 p.

Martin, Alfred W. **Great religious teachers of the east.** N.Y. (1911) See chap 4, Confucius and lao-tze, 105-148.

Martin, Alfred W. (comp) **Seven great bibles.** N.Y. (1930) See chap 4, The bible of confucianism, 123-153.

Masdoosi, Ahmad Abdullah al. **Living religions of the world. A socio-political study.** Tsl fr urdu Zafar Ishaq Ansari. Karachi (1962) See chap 10, Confucianism, 214-257.

Matgioi (A. de Pourvoirville) **La chine des lettrés. . . leur religion. . .** Paris (1910)

McCartee, D. B. On a chinese tablet illustrating the religious opinions of the literary class. **JAOS** 9.2 (1851) lxi.

Messing, Otto. Confuzianismus. **ZE** 46 (1914) 754-772, fig.

Mou, Tseng-san. Confucianism as a religion. **QNCCR** 4.2 (july 1960) 1-12.

Müller, F. Max. The religions of china. Confucian-ism. **NC** 48 (sept 1900) 373-384.

Noss, John B. **Man's religions.** N.Y. (1949 et seq) 3rd rev ed (1963) See pt 3, chap 10, Confucius and confucianism: a study in optimistic humanism, 369-427.

Parker, E. H. Laocius and confucius as rival moralists. **AR** 20 (1924) 698-704; 21 (1925) 129-146.

Parrinder, E. G. **What world religions teach.** London etc (1963) See chap 8, Confucius and the social order, 72-79.

Peeters, Hermes. **The religions of china.** Confucianism, taoism, buddhism, popular belief. Peking (1941) 64 p.

Peisson, Z. Le confucianisme. **RR** 2 (1890)

Perrot, Albert. Le retour offensif de la vieille chine. Le confucianisme redevenu religion d'état. **Études** (20 mai 1914) 461-480; (juil 1914) 425-438, fig.

Planchat, Edmond. Le tombeau de confucius. **Le temps** (lundi 13 dec 1897)

Politella, Joseph. **Taoism and confucianism.** Iowa city (1967) 167 p.

The position and prospects of confucianism in china. **Chinese review** 1 (apr 1914) 50-51.

Potter, Charles F. **The great religious leaders.** N.Y. (1958) Rev ed of **The story of religion**, n.y. (1929) See chap 6, Confucius. . . The apostle of morality (including lao-tse of the divine way) 141-164.

La question du confucianisme et le gouvernement de pékin. **BAF** 16 (oct-dec 1916) 175-176.

Reid, Gilbert. **A christian's appreciation of other faiths.** Chicago and london (1921) See lecture on his appreciation of confucianism. . . 11-49.

Rosenkranz. Gerhard. **Der heilige in den chinesischen klassikern; eine untersuchung über die erlöser-erwartung in konfuzianismus und taoismus.** Leipzig (1935) vii + 188 p.

Ross, Floyd H. and Tynette Wilson Hills. **Questions that matter most, asked by the world's religions.** Boston (1954) See sec 3, Chinese religions, chap 11, Confucianism. Paperbk title: **The great religions by which men live.**

Ross, John. Religion of confucius. **Chinese review** 1 (july 1914) 125-133.

Rotours, Robert des. Confucianisme et christianisme. **Sinologica** 1 (1948) 231-245.

Rousselle, E. Konfuzius und das archaïsche weltbild der chinesischen frühzeit. **Saeculum** 5 (1954) 1-33.

Roy, A. T. Attacks upon confucianism in the 1911-1927 period. **CCJ** 4.1 (1964) 10-26.

Roy, A. T. Attacks upon confucianism in the 1911-1927 period: (2) and (3) From a taoist lawyer: wu yu. **CCJ** 4 (1965) 149-163; 5 (1965) 69-78.

Roy, A. T. Confucianism and social change. **CCJ** 3 (nov 1963) 88-104.

Rygaloff, Alexis. **Confucius.** Paris (1946) xii + 125 p.

Saint-Denys, le Marquis d'Hervey. Mémoire sur les doctrines religieuses de confucius et de l'école des lettrés. **MAIBL** t 32, 2e partie (1887) Publ sep paris (1887) 23 p.

Saint-Ina, [Marie de] Confucius: witness to being. **IPQ** 3.4 (dec 1963) 537-553.

Saitschick, Robert. Kungfutse, der 'meister' der religion chinas. **Hochland** 9 (1912) 15-38.

Schmidt, Charles. The 'wen miao,' commonly styled 'the confucian temple' in shanghai. **MDGNVO** (1877) 11-12, photo.

Schmitt, Erich. **Konfuzius; sein leben und seine lehre.** Berlin (1926) 216 p, pl.

Schneider, Laurence A. (tsl) A translation of ku chieh-kang's essay 'The confucius of the spring and autumn era and the confucius of the han era.' **PTP** (1965) 105-147.

Semenoff, Marc. **Confucius, sa vie, ses pensées, sa doctrine.** Paris (1951) 157 p, fig.

Sherley-Price, Lionel D. **Confucius and christ; a christian estimate of confucius.** Westminster, engl (1951) 248 p, illus.

Shih, Joseph. The place of confucianism in the history of chinese religion. **Gregorianum** 51 (1970) 485-508.

Shryock. J. K. Confucianism. In H. G. McNair (ed) **China**, univ california (1946) 245-253.

Sims, Bennett B. **Confucius.** N.Y. (1968) 139 p, illus, map.

Smart, Ninian. **The religious experience of mankind.** N.Y. (1969) See chap 4, Chinese and japanese religious experience; sec, Confucianism and taoism, 141-190.

Smith, Arthur H. Confucianism. In **The message of the world's religions**, n.y. (1898) Chap 3, 41-64. Repr fr **Outlook.**

Smith, Carl T. Radical theology and the confucian tradition. **CF** 10.4 (1967) 20-33.

Smith, Huston. **The religions of man.** N.Y. (1958) See chap 4, Confucianism, 142-174.

Soulié, Charles George de Morant. **La vie de confucius (kong tse)** Paris (1929) 213 p.

Spencer, Sidney. **Mysticism in world religion.** N.Y. (1963) london (1966) See sec 4, Taoist and confucianist mysticism, confucianism, 113-122.

Staiger, Brunhild. **Das konfuzius-bild im kommunistischen china; die neubewertung von konfuzius in der chinesisch-marxistische gesichtsschreibung.** Wiesbaden (1969) 143 p.

Stanley, Charles A. jr. T'ai shan and the tomb of confucius. **EA** 4 (1905) 301-309.

Starr, Frederick. **Confucianism; ethics, philosophy, religion.** N.Y. (1930) ix + 250, illus.

Storrs, Christopher. **Many creeds, one cross.** N.Y. (1945) See chap 5, Confucius and humanism, 101-126.

Stübe, R. **Das zeitalter des confucius.** Tübingen (1913) 54 p.

"The systems of buddha and confucius compared," extracted from the **ICG,** no 5, aout 1818 (p 149-157) **ChRep** 2 (1833-34) 265 f.

Taam, Cheuk-woon. On studies of confucius. **PEW** 3 (1953) 147-165.

Takeuchi, Teruo. A study of the meaning of jen advocated by confucius. **ActaA** 9 (1965) 57-77.

T'ang, Chun-i. Confucianism and chinese religions. In Moses Jung, Swami Nikhilanda and Herbert W. Schneider (ed) **Relations among religions today. A handbook of policies and principles,** leiden (1963), Chap 2.

T'ang, Chun-i. The development of ideas of spiritual value in chinese philosophy. In **PCEW** (1962) 227-235. Repr in **TC** (1970) 137-146, as: Spiritual values in confucian philosophy.

Thomas, Henry and Dana Lee. **Living biographies of religious leaders.** N.Y. (1942) See chap on Confucius, 57-68.

Thornberry, Mike. The encounter of christianity and confucianism: how modern confucianism views the encounter. **SEAJT** 10 (1968) 47-62.

Too-yu. The systems of foe and confucius compared, translated from the chinese. **ICG** no 5 (1818) 149-157.

Topley, Marjorie. Is confucius dead? **FEER** 58 (21 dec 1967) 561-563.

Trood, S.M.E. **The religions of mankind. An introductory survey.** London (1929) See chap 7, The native religions of china and japan--confucianism, 93-105.

Tsao, Wen-yen. Confucianism and religious tolerance. **CC** 9.2 (1968) 51-54.

Tschepe, A. **Heiligtümer des konfuzianismus im k'ü-fu und tschouhien.** Jentschou-fu (1906) viii + 132 p, 63 illus, 3 maps. Notices in **JNCBRAS** 39 (1908) 189-194; **AQR** ser 3,25 (apr 1908) 399-400.

Tschepe, A. The tomb of the holy yen-fu-tse. **FE** 1 (1906) 113-118.

Tschepe, A. Voyage au pays de confucius et de ses disciples. **RC** (avr 1910) 533-540, fig.

Turnbull, Grace H. (comp) **Tongues of fire. A bible of sacred scriptures of the pagan world.** N.Y. (1929) See The confucian canon, 121-156.

Valbert, G. Confucius et la morale chinoise. **RDM** 150 (1898) 673-684.

Van Buskirk, William R. **The saviors of mankind.** N.Y. (1929) See chap 2, Confucius, 25-61.

Waddell, N.A. (tsl) A selection from the ts'ai ken t'an ('vegetable-root discourses') **EB** 2.2 (nov 1919) 88-98.

Watts, Harold H. **The modern reader's guide to religions.** N.Y. (1964) See chap 19, Chinese and japanese religion, confucianism, 538-554.

Weber, Max. **Konfuzianismus und taoismus.** Tübingen (1922) (Author's Gesammelte aufsätze zur religionssoziologie, 1) Engl tsl Hans H. Gerth: **The religion of china: confucianism and taoism.** Glencoe, ill.(1951) london (1952) xi + 308 p.

Wei, Tat. Confucius and the i-ching. In Finley P. Dunne, jr (ed) **The world religions speak on 'the relevance of religion in the modern world,'** the hague (1970) 64-71.

Widgery, Alban G. **Living religions and modern thought.** N.Y. (1936) See chap 5, Confucianism and shinto, 108-134.

Wilhelm, Richard. In der heimat des konfuzius, eine reiseerrinerung. **CBWK** 1.1 (1925) 22-42.

Wilhelm, Richard. **Kung-tse, leben und werk.** Stuttgart (1925) 210 p.

Wilhelm, Richard. **K'ungtse und der konfuzianismus.** Berlin and leipzig (1928) 104 p. Engl tsl George H. and Annina P. Danton: **Confucius and confucianism.** N.Y. and london (1931) x + 181 p.

Williams, David Rhys. **World religions and the hope for peace.** Boston (1951) See chap 1, The reasonableness of confucius, 3-13.

Williams, E.T. Confucianism and the new china. **HTR** 9.3 (1916) 258-285.

Williams, E.T. Confucius and his teaching. Chap 11 in author's **CYT,** 223-248.

Wu, John C.H. The real confucius. The china academy, **Bulletin of the institute of pacific research** 1 (mar 1967) 77-89.

Wu, S. Confucianism and its significance to christianity in china. **CF** 12.1 (1969) 4-23.

Yang, Ming-che. Confucianism. **FCR** 17 (apr 1967) 22-28.

Yang, Ming-che. Confucianism vs. tao and buddha. **FCR** 19 (jan 1969) 21-29.

Yeh, George K.C. **The confucian conception of jen.** London (1943) 14 p. **China society occasional papers,** n.s. 3.

Yeh, Theodore T.Y. **Confucianism, christianity and china.** N.Y. (1969) 249 p, notes, bibliog.

Yetts, Walter Perceval. **The legend of confucius.** London (1943) **China society occasional papers,** n.s. 5.

Youn, Laurent Eulsu. **Confucius, sa vie, son oeuvre, sa doctrine.** Paris (1943) 126 p.

Yu, Pung Kwang. Confucianism. In **WPR** vol 1 (1893) 374-439.

Zia, Rosina C. The conception of "sage" in lao-tze and chuang-tze as distinguished from confucianism. **CCJ** 5 (may 1966) 150-157.

8. ETHICS AND MORALS
  (See also GENERAL STUDIES;
  CONFUCIUS AND CONFUCIANISM)

Bach, Marcus. **Major religions of the world.** N.Y. and nashville (1959) See chap 6, Confucianism and taoism–religion of good ethics, 74-84.

Baudens, G. Les doctrines morales de la chine. (extrait de la **china review.** Compte rendu analytique) **Revue maritime et coloniale** 41 (1874) 392-395.

Beach, Harlan P. The ethics of confucianism. In E. Hershey Sneath (ed) **The evolution of ethics as revealed in the great religions,** yale univ (1927) 39-74.

Bertholet, René. l'Astrobiologie et les moralistes chinois. **RMM** 40.4 (1933) 457-479.

Chan, Wing-tsit. The individual in chinese religions. In **SIEW** (1968) 181-198. Repr in **CM** (1967) 31-76.

Chan, Wing-tsit. K'ang yu-wei and the confucian doctrine of humanity (jen) In Jung-pang Lo (ed) **K'ang yu-wei: a biography and a symposium,** tucson, ariz.(1967) 355-374.

Chang, C. Essai d'une adaptation des exercises spirituels à l'âme chinoise. **SM** 6 (1950-51) 199-219.

Chavannes, Édouard. Les prix de vertu en chine. **CRAIBL** (1904) 667-691.

Chavannes, Édouard. De quelques idées morales des chinois. **BAF** (avr-juin 1917) 85-88. Idem: **Revue franco-étrangère** (juil-sept 1917) 230-235.

Chien, Wen-hsien. The confucian ethics. **The world's chinese students' journal** 6.7 (nov 1912) 95-98.

Chow, Bonaventura Shan-mou. **Ethica confucii.** Kohn (1957) 136 p.

David, Alexandra, La morale chinoise. **Les documents du progrès** Paris (?1913) See also author's Chinesische moral. **Dokumente des fortschritte,** Berlin 7.8 (1914) 216-219.

Eberhard, Wolfram. **Moral and social values of the chinese. Collected essays.** Taipei (1971) Pertinent art, all publ before 1970, are individually listed in this bibliog (Abbrev **MSVC**)

Eckardt, André. Die ethischen grundbegriffe bei laotse. **PJGG** 59.2 (1949) 200-207.

Edkins, Joseph. Ancient chinese thought, political and religious. **JNCBRAS** 31 (1896-97) 166-181.

Endres, Franz C. **Ethik des alltags.** Zürich, leipzig (1939) 135 p, pl.

Farjenel, Fernand. **La morale chinoise, fondement des sociétés d'extrême-orient.** Paris (1906) 258 p.

Faucett, Lawrence. **Six great teachers of morality.** Tokyo (1958) See chap 7, Seeking confucius in his sayings, 395-489, illus.

Forke, Alfred. Unbewusste und passive moral der taoisten. In **Handbuch der philosophie,** münchen (d?) abt 5, c 165-171.

Haenisch, Erich. Die heiligung des vater- und fürstennamens in china; ihre ethische begründung und ihre bedeutung in leben und schriftum. **Berichte über die verhandlungen der philologisch-historischen klasse der sächsischen akademie der wissenschaften zu leipzig** 84.4 (1932) 1-20.

Henke, Frederick G. Moral development of the chinese. **PS** (july 1915) 78-89.

Hsiang, Paul S. The humanism in the religious thought of ancient china. **CC** 10.3 (1969) 13-21.

Hsieh Yu-wei. The status of the individual in chinese ethics. In **SIEW** (1968) Repr in **CM** (1967) 307-322.

Hsü, Pao-chien. Ethical realism in neo-confucian thought. Columbia univ thesis (n.d. ca.1924) N.Y. and peking (1933) 165 p, illus.

Jung, Hwa Yol. Jen: an existential and phenomenological problem of intersubjectivity. **PEW** 16.3/4 (1966) 169-188.

Kiang, Kang-hu. The religious basis of everyday chinese life. **AP** 2 (1931) 200-203.

Ku, Hung-ming. The religion of a gentleman in china. **CSM** 17 (1922) 676-679.

Lee, Teng Hwee. The chinese idea of righteousness. **National review** 13 (may 1913) 459-460, 484-485.

Liu, Ts'un-yan. Yüan huang and his "four admonitions." **JOSA** 1/2 (1967) 108-132.

Martin, W.A.P. The ethical philosophy of the chinese. In author's **The lore of cathay,** n.y. (1901) repr taipei (1971) 205-233.

Nakamura, Hajime. The influence of confucian ethics on the chinese translations of buddhist sutras. **SIS** 5.3/4 (1957) 156-170.

Nakamura, Keijiro. The history and spirit of chinese ethics. **International journal of ethics** 8 (1897-98) 86-100.

Nivison, David S. Communist ethics and chinese tradition. **JAS** 16 (1956) 51-74.

Oehler, W. Sind die chinesen uns als volk moralisch überlegen? **EMM** n.s. vol 66 (feb 1922) 48-52.

Parker, E. H. Laocius and confucius as rival moralists. **AR** 20 (1924) 698-704; 21 (1925) 129-146.

Pike, E. Royston. **Ethics of the great religions.** London (1948) See chap 13, Confucianism, 215-228; chap 14, Taoism, 229-235.

Pohlman, W.J. (tsl) A confucian tract, exhorting mankind always to preserve their celestial principles and the good hearts. **ChRep** 15 (1846) 377-385, chin text and tsl.

Pott, William S.A. An approach to the study of confucian ethics. **NCR** 2 (1920) 448-455.

Pott, William S.A. The 'natural' basis of confucian ethics. **NCR** 3 (1921) 192-197.

Rawlinson, Frank J. **Chinese ethical ideals; a brief study of the ethical values in china's literary, social and religious life.** Shanghai (1934) x + 128 p.

Rawlinson, Frank J. The chinese sense of evil. **ChRec** 63.7 (july 1932) 428-434.

Rotermund, W. **Die ethik lao-tse's mit besonderer bezugnahme auf die buddhistische moral.** Gotha (1874) 26 p.

Rudd, H.F. **Chinese moral sentiments before confucius: a study in the origin of ethical valuations.** Shanghai (1916?) 220 p.

Schaefer, Thomas E. Perennial wisdom and the sayings of mencius. **IPQ** 3.3 (sept 1963) 428-444. On universality of moral wisdom.

Sheffield, D.Z. The ethics of christianity and of confucianism compared. **ChRec** 17 (1886) 365-379.

Shu, Seyuan. **Une conception du bien moral.** Paris (1941) 128 p.

Su, Jyun-hsyong. Menschenliebe und rechtschaffenheit im chinesischen rechtsleben. **Kairos** 9 (1967) 185-189.

Suppaner-Stanzel, Irene. Die ethischen ziele des taoismus und des existenzialismus. In festschrift: **Der mensch als persönlichkeit und als problem,** münchen (1963) 106-126.

Takeuchi, Teruo. A study in the meaning of jên advocated by confucius. **ActaA** 9 (1965) 57-77.

Tompkinson, Leonard. **Mysticism, ethics and service in chinese thought.** London (1956) 24 p.

Touan, Tchang-yuan. **La grande doctrine morale de dieu.** Trad en français par le colonel Tang-che. Pékin (1918) 97 p.

Tscharner, E.H. von. La pensée "métaphysique" et ethique de lao-tse. **Scientia** 72 (1942) 29-36.

Valbert, G. Confucius et la morale chinoise. **RDM** 150 (1898) 673-684.

Wieger, Léon. **Moeurs et usages populaires.** Ho-kien-fu (1905) 548 p. Engl tsl L. Davrout: **Moral tenets and customs in china.** Texts in chin. Ho-kien-fu (1913) 604 p, illus.

Yang, C.K. The functional relationship between confucian thought and chinese religion. In **CTI** (1957) 269-290.

Zenker, Ernst Victor. **Soziale moral in china und japan.** München, leipzig (1914) 42 p.

9. FILIAL PIETY

Bellah, Robert N. Father and son in christianity and confucianism. **Psychoanalytic review** 52 (1965) 92-114. Repr in author's collection: **Beyond belief: essays on religion in a post-traditional world,** n.y. (1970) 76-99.

Chen, Joseph. Les doctrines chrétienne et con-fucéene de la piété filiale. **Laval théologique et philosophique** 19 (1963) 335-349.

Ch'en, Kenneth. Filial piety in chinese buddhism. **HJAS** 28 (1968) 81-97.

Cordier, Henri. Bulletin critique des religions de la chine–(la piété filiale en chine) **RHR** 3.2 (1881) 218-227.

Cordier, Henri. La piété filiale et le culte des ancêtres en chine. **CMG** 35 (1910) 67-101. Also in **Bibliothèque de vulgarisation des BVAMG** 35 (1910)

Faber, Ernst. A critique of the chinese notions and practice of filial piety. **ChRec** 9 (1878) 329-343, 401-418; 10 (1879) 1-18, 83-96, 163-174, 243-253, 323-329, 416-428; 11 (1880) 1-12.

Giles, Herbert A. What is filial piety? In author's **AdSin** 1 (1905) 20-25.

Hoogers, Joseph. Théorie et pratique de la piété filiale chez les chinois. **Anthropos** 5 (1910) 1-15, 688-702, illus.

Hsieh Yu-wei. Filial piety and chinese society. In **PCEW** (1962) 411-427. Repr in **CM** (1967) 167-187.

Hsu, Francis L. K. **Clan, caste and club.** Princeton univ (1963) 335 p.

Koehn, Alfred (tsl) **Piété filiale en chine.** Peking (1943) 24 p. Engl ed: **Filial devotion in china.** Peking (1944) Tsl of Kuo, Chü-ching, **Erh-shih-ssu hsiao.**

Sachse, H. (tsl) Twenty-four examples of filial piety. **FE** 1 (1906) 181-186.

Stolberg, Baron. Filial affection as taught and practised by the chinese. **CW** 9 (1869) 416-421.

Thiersant, Dabry de. **La piété filiale en chine.** Paris (1877) 226 p.

What is filial piety? **JNCBRAS** 20 (1885) 115-144.

Williams, E.T. Confucianism in the home. Chap 12 in author's **CYT,** 249-262.

10. ANCESTRAL CULT

Addison, James Thayer. **Chinese ancestor worship. A study of its meaning and its relations with christianity.** n.p. (1925) 85 p.

Addison, James T. Chinese ancestor worship and protestant christianity. **JR** 5.2 (1925) 140-149.

Addison, J.T. The modern chinese cult of ancestors. **JR** 4 (1924) 492-503.

Aijmer, Göran. A structural approach to chinese ancestor worship. **BTLVK** 124.1 (1968) 91-98.

Amélineau, E. Les coutumes funéraires de l'égypte ancienne comparées avec celles de la chine. **Études critique et d'histoire par les membres de la section des sciences religieuses de l'école des hautes études.** Paris (1906) 2e sér, 1-34.

Ancestral worship. **ChRev** 7 (1878-79) 290-301, 355-364.

Arlington, L.C. The ceremony of disintering in china. **ChRev** 25.4 (1901) 176-178.

Baker, Hugh D. Burial, geomancy and ancestor worship. In **ASONT** (1965) 36-39.

Beyerhaus, Peter. The christian approach to ancestor worship. **Ministry** 6.4 (july 1966) 137-145.

Bidens. Mourning etiquette. **ChRev** 7 (1878-79) 351-352.

Blodget, H. Ancestral worship in the shu king. **JPOS** 3.2 (1892)

Boerschmann, Ernst. **Die baukunst und religiöse kultur der chinesen.** Vol 2; **Gedächtnistempel; tzé tang.** Berlin (1914) xxiv + 288 p, illus.

Boulinais, Lt.-Col. et A. Paulus. **Le culte des morts dans le céleste empire et l'annam comparé au culte des ancêtres dans l'antiquité occidentale.** Paris (1893) xxxiii + 267 p.

Burial societies. **ChRev** 13 (1884-85) 429-430.

Butcher, Charles H. Notes on the funeral rites performed at the obsequies of takee. **JNCBRAS** 2 (1865) 173-176.

Chen, Chung-min. Ancestor worship and clan organization in a rural village of taiwan. **ASBIE** 23 (1967) engl abrmt 21-24.

Chinese ancestral worship and its significance. **Biblical world** 7 (1896) 290-291.

Comber, Leon. **Chinese ancestor worship in malaya.** Singapore (1956) 41 p, 20 pl, chin index, bibliog.

Cordier, Henri. La piété filiale et le culte des ancêtres en chine. **CMG** 35 (1910) 67-101. Also publ in **BVAMG** 35 (1910)

Crémazy, L. Le culte des ancêtres en chine et dans l'annam. **RIC** 107 (1900) 1066-1068; 108 (1900) 1088-1089.

Davia, Jacques. La mort et les chinois. **TM** 5 (1899) 150-151.

Eatwell, W. On chinese burials. **Journal of the anthropological institute of great britain and ireland** 1.2 (1871) 207-208.

Edkins, Joseph. Literature of ancestral worship in china. **Academy** 28 (1885) 186-187.

Eigner, J. The significance of ancestor worship in china. **CJ** 26 (1937) 125-127.

Erkes, E. Ahnenbilder und buddhistische skulpturen aus altchina. **JSMVL** 5 (1913) 26-32, illus. Notice by Éd. Chavannes, **TP** (1914) 291-297.

Erkes, Eduard. Der schamanistische ursprung des chinesischen ahnenkultus. **Sinologica** 2 (1950) 253-262.

Erkes, E. Zum problem des chinesischen ahnenbildes. **AA** 8 (1945) 105-106; also in **Sinologica** 3 (1953) 240-241.

Faber, E. Seventeen paragraphs on ancestral worship. **Records of shanghai missionary conference** (1890)

Fabre, A. Avril au pays des aïeux. In **CCS** vol 8 (1935) Ancestor worship and burial practices re ch'ing ming, specifically in shun-te, kuangtung.

Farjenel, Fernand. Quelques particularités du culte des ancêtres en chine. **JA** 10e sér, 1 (1903) 85-86.

Farjenel, Fernand (tsl) Rites funéraires chinois; les funérailles impériales et celles des gens du peuple. Louvain (ca 1904) 63 p. Offprint fr **Le Muséon.**

Ferro, G. Vigna dal. l'Etiquette où la mort: moeurs d'extrême-orient. **TM** 4 (1898) 366-367.

Freedman, Maurice. Ancestor worship: two facets of the chinese case. In **SOERF** (1967) 85-103.

Freedman, Maurice. **Chinese lineage and society: fukien and kwangtung.** Univ london (1966) See esp chap 5, Geomancy and ancestor worship, 118-154, incl photos.

Freedman, Maurice. **Lineage organization in southeastern china.** London school of economics (1958) See chap 5, 10, 11.

Freedman, Maurice. Ritual aspects of chinese kinship and marriage. In **FKCS** (1970) 163-187.

Fung, Yu-lan. The confucianist theory of mourning, sacrificial and wedding rites. **CSPSR** 15 (1931) 335-345.

Galpin, F. China's tribute to the dead. **JMGS** 11 (1895) 209-216.

Gieseler, G. Le jade dans le culte et les rites funéraires en chine sous les dynasties tcheou et han. **RA** 5e sér, 4 (1916) 61-128, illus.

Gobien, Charles le. Éclaircissement sur les honneurs que les chinois rendent à confucius et aux morts. In author's **Affaires de la chine,** paris (1700) t3, 217-332.

Groot, J.J.M.de. The demise of an amoy gentleman. **ChRev** 19.5 (1891) 281-284.

Groot, J.J.M.de. **The religious system of china.** Leiden (1892-1910) repr taipei (1964) 6 vol. 1-3: Disposal of the dead; 4-6: The soul and ancestral worship. Compte rendu par Éd. Chavannes, **RHR** 37 (1898) 81-89.

Guimbretière, P. Les chinois et leurs morts. **RC** (janv 1906) 37-42.

Hardy, J. and C. Lenormand. l'Importance et l'agencement des tombeaux chinois. **TM** 12 (1906) 409-412, illus.

Henry, B.C. Ancestral worship and geomancy. Chap 7 in author's **CD** (1885) 123-151.

Hoogers, Joseph. Au sujet des sacrifices et offrandes chinoises pour les morts. **Anthropos** 4.2 (mars-avr 1909) 526.

Hsu, Francis L.K. **Clan, caste and club.** Princeton univ (1963)

Hu, Hsien-chin. **The common descent group in china and its function.** N.Y. (1948) See chap 2, Ancestor veneration, 31-40, illus.

J. Rites performed for the dead. **ChRev** 9 (1880-81) 397. See further D.G., same title, in **ibid** 10 (1881-82) 145-146.

Kalff, L. **Der totenkult in südschantung, ein beitrag zur volkskunde des landes.** Yenchowfu (1932) viii + 109 p, illus, diagr.

Kranz, P. The teaching of the chinese classics on ancestral worship. **ChRec** 35 (1904) 237-245.

Laufer, Berthold. The development of ancestral images in china. **Journal of religious psychology** 6 (1913) 111-123. Abrmt in W.A. Lessa and E.Z. Vogt (ed) **Reader in comparative religion,** evanston, ill. and white plains, n.y. (1958) 404-409.

Leong, Y. K. and L.K. Tao. **Village and town life in china.** London (1915) See The ancestral hall, 22-31.

Ling, Shun-sheng. Ancestral tablet and genital symbolism in ancient china. **ASBIE** 8 (1959) engl summ 39-46 + 14 p pl.

Ling, Shun-sheng. Origin of the ancestral temple in china. **ASBIE** 7 (1959) engl summ 177-184 + 6 p pl.

Mariage de morts au chan-si. **TM** 5 (1899) 191.

Martin, Ernest. Le culte des ancêtres, le culte des morts et le culte des funérailles chez les chinois. **Journal d'hygiène** 17 (1891) 313-320, 325-332.

Martin, Ernest. Les sépultures dans l'extrême-orient. **Revue scientifique** 31 (9 dec 1893) 753-756.

Martin, W.A.P. The worship of ancestors. How shall we deal with it? **ChRec** 35 (1904) 301-308.

Martin, W.A.P. The worship of ancestors in china. In author's **Hanlin papers,** london and shanghai (1880) repr in author's **The Lore of Cathay,** n.y. (1901) repr taipei (1971) 264-278.

Matignon, J.J. Un enterrement à pékin. In author's **l'Orient lointain. . .,** paris (?) (d?) 127-151.

Matignon, J.J. Les morts qui gouvernent. (À propos de l'immobilisme de la chine) **Archives d'anthropologie criminelle** 15 (1900) 457-484. See also author's **Superstitions, crime et misère. . .,** paris (1898) 337-374.

Matignon, J.J. Les préliminaires de l'enterrement en chine. **Bulletin société de géographie commerciale de bordeaux** 38e ann (1912) 244-249, illus.

Mayers, W.F. On the stone figures at chinese tombs and the offerings of living sacrifices. **JNCBRAS** 12 (1878) 1-17.

Mecquenem, J. de. Le faire-part de décès du général wou lou-tchen. **BAAFC** (janv 1914) 36-44, fig.

Mei, Y.P. Ancestor-worship: origin and value. **CSM** 21.6 (1926) 19-25.

Milloué, L. de. Culte et cérémonies en honneur des morts dans l'extrême-orient. **CMG** (1899-1900 et 1900-1901) 135-159.

Mitchell-Innes, Norman G. Birth, marriage and death rites of the chinese. **FLJ** 5 (1887) 221-245.

Moroto, Sojun. The idea of ancestor in chinese classics. In **RSJ** (1959) 192-201.

Munn, William. Ancestor-worship: its origins and results. **Church missionary review** 71 (dec 1920) 319-328.

Nitschkowsky. Der chinesische ahnenkultus. **AMZ** 22 (1895) 289-301, 360-374, 385-391.

Pacifique-Marie, P. d'Aingreville. Funérailles païennes en chine. **MC** 36 (1904) 406-408, 417-419, 429-431, 442-444.

Paléologue, Maurice. Sépultures chinoises. **RDM** 3e période, sér 9, t 83 (15 oct 1887) 918-932.

Parker, E.H. Animals at funerals. **ChRev** 17 (1888-89) 114.

Parker, E.H. Animals in funeral processions. **ChRev** 14 (1885-86) 171.

Parker, E.H. Funeral rites. **ChRev** 14 (1885-86) 225.

Parker, E.H. Phraseology of mourning. **ChRev** 15 (1886-87) 188.

Pitcher, P.W. Chinese 'ancestral worship.' **MRW** n.s. 7 (1894) 81-86.

Poore, Major R. Ancestral worship in china and 'family worth-ship' in england, as a practical basis of efficient state administration. **IAQR** ser 2,8 (july 1894) 141-149. See also Eugène Simon, 'Une imitation. . .' in **La reforme soziale** 25/26 (1893) 304-321.

Poseck, Helena von. Chinese customs connected with birth, marriages, deaths... III. Death and burial. **EA** 4 (1905) 24-32.

Potter, Jack M. Wind, water, bones and souls: the religious world of the cantonese peasant. **JOS** 8.1 (1970) 139-153. Repr in **C Way Rel** (1973) Study of ping shan, new territories, hong kong.

Price, P.F. The worship of ancestors. **ChRec** 33 (1902) 253-255.

Ravary, P. Les tablettes des ancêtres et leurs registres de la famille en chine. **ER** 18e ann, 5e sér, 6 (1874) 762-768.

Roberts, L. Chinese ancestral portraits. **Parnassus** 9.1 (1937) 28.

Rychterová, Eva. Commemorative ancestor portraits. **NO** 4 (1965) 176-177, illus.

Schalek, Alice. Chinesische sterbesitten. **Welt auf reisen** 14 (1914) 57-60.

Scott, A.C. Costumes of the chinese (Female mourning costume) **Orient** 2.2 (1951) 29.

Serebrennikov, J.J. Funeral money in china. **CJ** 18 (1933) 191-193.

Shih, C.C. A study of ancestor worship in ancient china. In **SW** (1964) 179-190.

Spiegel, H. Die architektur der gräber. **WBKKA** 7 (1932-33) 66-87.

Stanley, C.A. Ancestral worship. **ChRec** 33 (1902) 268-270.

Tavernier, E. Le culte des ancêtres. **BSEIS** n.s. 1 (1926) 133-173.

Tchang, Mathias. **Tombeau des liang, famille siao, lère partie: siao choen-tche.** Shanghai (1912) xiii + 108 p, illus (Variétés sinologiques no 33)

Thiel, Joseph. Doppelsprüche auf den torsäulen der grahaine. **Sinologica** 6 (1959) 25-56, 6 pl.

Tiberi, Fortunato. Der ahnenkult in china nach den kanonischen schriften. **AL** 27 (1963) 283-475.

Torrance, Thomas. Burial customs in sz-chuan. **JNCBRAS** 41 (1910) 57-75, illus.

Volpert, A. Gräber und steinskulpturen der alten chinesen. **Anthropos** 3 (1908) 14-18, illus.

W, Dr J. Totenkult in china. **Asien 6?** (dez 1906) 40-41.

Walker, J.E. Ancestral worship. **ChRec** 34 (1903) 199.

Walshe, W.G. Some chinese funeral customs. **JNCBRAS** 35 (1903-04) 26-64.

Waong, P.L. Les tablettes des ancêtres. **BUA** 3e sér, 2 (1941) 243-280.

Wei, Louis Tsing-sing. Das begräbnis im chinesischen konfuzianismus. **Concilium** 4 (feb 1968) 142-143.

Werner, E.T.C. Reform in chinese mourning rites. **NCR** 2 (1920) 223-247.

Wilhelm, Richard. Das altechinesische ahnenopfer. **Sinica** 5 (1930) 150-151.

Wilhelm [Richard]. Totenbräuche in schantung. **MDGNVO** 11.1 (1906) 33-45. See also R. Wilhelm, same title, in **ZMK** 23 (1908) 78-88, illus.

Williams, S. Wells. The worship of ancestors among the chinese: a notice of the ...kia li tieh-shih tsih-ching or collection of forms and cards used in family ceremonies. **ChRep** 18 (1849) 361-384.

Wilson, B.D. Chinese burial customs in hong kong. **JHKBRAS** 1 (1960-61) 115-123.

Wolf, Arthur P. Chinese kinship and mourning dress. In **FKCS** (1970) 189-208.

The worship of ancestors among the chinese. **ChRep** 18.7 (july 1849) 363-384.

Yang, Kun. **Recherches sur le culte des ancêtres comme principe ordonnateur de la famille chinoise; la succession au culte, la succession au patrimoine.** Univ lyon (1934) 174 p.

Yates, M.T. **Ancestral worship.** Shanghai (1877) 48 p.

Yates, M.T. Ancestral worship and fung-shuy. **ChRec** 1 (1868) 23, 37-43.

Ymaizoumi, M. Du culte des ancêtres en chine sous la dynastie de tcheou. **CPOL** t 2, lyon (1880) 68-79.

11. FENG-SHUI

Aijmer, Göran. Being caught by a fishnet: on fengshui in southeastern china. **JHKBRAS** 8 (1968) 74-81.

Baker, Hugh D. Burial, geomancy and ancestor worship. In **ASONT** (1965) 36-39.

Boerschmann, E. K'ueising türme und
fengshuisäulen. **AM** 2 (1925) 503-530.

Boxer, B. Space, change and feng-shui in tsuen
wan's urbanization. **JAAS** 3 (1968) 226-240.

Danielli, M. The geomancer in china, with some
reference to geomancy as observed in madagascar.
Folk-lore 63 (1952) 204-226.

Dukes, Edwin J. Feng-shui. In **HERE** vol 5
(1914) 833-835.

Edkins, Joseph. Fengshui. **ChRec** 4 (1871-72)
274-277, 291-298, 316-320. Repr **Shanghai
budget** (27 apr, 15 june, 6 and 13 july 1872)

Eitel, Ernest J. **Feng-shui: or, the rudiments of
natural science in china.** London (1873) 84 p.
French tsl L. de Milloué, **AMG** 1 (1880) 203-253.

Feng-shui. **Cornhill magazine** (mar 1874)

Freedman, Maurice. Ancestor worship: two facets
of the chinese case. **SOERF** (1967) 85-103.

Freedman, Maurice. **Chinese lineage and society:
fukien and kwangtung.** Univ london (1966) See esp
chap 5: Geomancy and ancestor worship,
118-154, incl photos.

Freedman, Maurice. Geomancy. **Proceedings of
the royal anthropological institute of great britain
and ireland for 1968,** 5-15. Presidential address.

Hayes, James W. Geomancy and the village. In
TICHK (1967) 22-30.

Hayes, James W. Movement of villages on lantau
island for fung shui reasons. **JHKBRAS** 3 (1963)
143-144.

Hayes, James W. Removal of villages for fung shui
reasons. Another example from lantau island,
hong kong. **JHKBRAS** 9 (1969) 156-158.

Hubrig. Fung schui oder chinesische geomantie.
**Verhandlungen berlin gesellschaft für
anthropologic ethnologie und urgeschichte**
(1879) 34-43.

Lapicque, P.A. Le fin du 'fong chouei' ou la
disparition des esprits des eaux et des airs.
RIC n.s. 16 (sept 1911) 299-301.

March, Andrew L. An appreciation of chinese
geomancy. **JAS** 27.2 (1968) 253-268, bibliog.

Potter, Jack. Wind, water, bones and souls: the
religious world of the cantonese peasant [Ping
shan, new territories of hong kong] **JOS** 8.1
(1970) 139-153. Repr in **CWayRel** (1973)

Regnault, Jules. Rôle du foung-choei et de la
sorcellerie dans la vie privée et publique des jaunes.
Revue politique et parlementaire (10 nov 1905)
353-373. (Étude extr. en grande partie d'un rapport présenté par le dr regnault au congrès colonial
de 1905, sous le titre: Hystérie, hypnose et sorcellerie en chine et en indo-chine)

Rousselle, E. Zum system der kaiserlichen
grabanlagen. **Sinica** 7 (1932) 155-160.

Sinensis. Chinese mythology: on the chinese
geomancy known as feng shui. **ChRec** 4 (1872)
19-23, 46-48, 93-96, 130-132, 217-222.

Stringer, H. Fengshui. **CJ** 3 (1925) 305-307.

Turner, F.S. Feng-shui. **Cornhill magazine** 29
(1874) 337-348.

Yates, M.T. Ancestral worship and fung-shuy.
ChRec 1.3 (1868) 23 et seq, 37-43.

12. STATE RELIGION

Amicus. The worship of confucius. **ICG** 11 (1820)
254-256.

Arlington, Lewis C. **Some remarks on the worship
offered confucius in the confucian temple.** Peiping
(1935) 8, 20 p, pl.

Ayscough, Florence. The chinese cult of ch'eng
huang lao yeh. **JNCBRAS** 55 (1924) 131-155.

Ayscough, Florence. The symbolism of the forbidden city, peking. **JNCBRAS** 61 (1930)
111-126.

Biallas, Franz Xaver. **Konfuzius und sein kult.**
Peking and leipzig (1928) 130 p, literaturnachweis,
anmerkungen, abbildungen, karten.

Blodget, Henry. Prayers of the emperor for snow
and rain. **ChRec** 15.4 (july-aug 1884) 249-253.

Blodget, Henry. The worship of heaven and earth
by the emperor of china. **JAOS** 20 (1899) 58-69.

Borch, A. von. The imperial tombs west of peking.
EA 1 (sept 1902) 181-191.

Bouillard, G. Environs de peking. iv. Tombeau pro-
prement dit. **La chine** 16 (1922) 569-578.

Bouillard, G. Le temple de la terre. **La chine** 34
(1923) 53-66.

Bouillard, G. Le temple de l'agriculture. **La chine**
33 (1922) 1833-1850.

Bouillard, G. Tombeaux des ming. **La chine** (all 1922) 19: 789-800; 20: 865-879; 21: 975-994; 22: 1051-1062.

Bouillard, G. Les tombeaux des ts'ing. **La chine** (all 1922) 23: 1137-1154; 24: 1187-1203; 25: 1273-1284.

Bouillard, G. **Tombeaux impériaux** (ming et ts'ing) Peking (1931) 225 p.

Bouillard, G. and Vaudescal. Les sépultures impériales des ming (che-san ling) **BEFEO** 20.3 (1920) 128 p. Rev in **TP** 21 (1922) 57-66 by Paul Pelliot.

Bourne, Frederick S.A. Notes of a journey to the imperial mausolea, east of peking. **Proceedings of the royal geographical society** n.s. 5 (1883) 23-31.

Brandt, M. von. **Die chinesische philosophie und der staats-confucianismus.** Stuttgart (1898) 121 p.

Brodrick, A.H. The sacrifices of the son of heaven. **AR** 36 (1940) 118-128.

Bünger, Karl. **Studien über religion und staat in china.** Tübingen (1949) vii + 179 p.

Chavannes, Édouard. Traité sur les sacrifices fong et chan de se ma t'sien. **JPOS** 3.1 (1890) xxxi + 95.

Combaz, Gilbert. Les sépultures impériales de la chine. **ASAB** 21 (1907) 381-462.

Combaz, Gilbert. Les temples impériaux de la chine. **ASAB** 26 (1912) 223-323.

Coulborn, Rushton. The state and religion: iran, india, and china. **CSSH** 1.1 (1958) 44-57.

Creel, Herrlee Glessner. **The birth of china. A study of the formative period of chinese civilization.** N.Y. (1937) See chap 28, The decree of heaven, 367-380.

Creel, Herrlee Glessner. **The origins of statecraft in china.** Vol 1: **The western chou empire.** Univ chicago (1970) See chap 5, The mandate of heaven, 81-100.

Dard, Émile. Au tombeau des mings. **Revue hebdomadaire** ann 18 (25 juin 1910) 512-520.

Devéria, Gabriel. Sépultures impériales de la dynastie ta ts'ing. **TP** 3 (1892) 418-421.

Dubs, Homer H. The victory of han confucianism. **JAOS** 58 (1938) 435-449. Rev version of this art in Dubs (ed) **The history of the former han dynasty by pan ku,** baltimore, md (1944) vol 2, app 2, 435-449.

Edkins, Joseph. The hall of light [ming t'ang] **ChRev** 15 (1886-87) 165-167.

Edkins, Joseph. **Religion in china.** Boston (1859; rev and enl ed 1878) See chap 2, Imperial worship.

Eichhorn, Werner. Die wiedereinrichtung der staatsreligion im anfang der sung-zeit. **MS** 23 (1964) 205-263.

Eisenstadt, S.N. Religious organizations and political process in centralized empires. **JAS** 21.3 (1962) 271-294.

Fabre, Maurice. **Pékin, ses palais, ses temples et ses environs, guide historique et descriptif.** Tien-tsin (ca.1937) xv + 347 p, illus. Illustré par Y. Darcy; compositions originales de J. Malval.

Farjenel, Fernand (tsl) Le culte impérial en chine. **JA** 10e sér, 8 (1906) 491-516. ('le sacrifice au grand dieu du ciel'; tsl fr ta ch'ing hui-tien)

Farjenel, F. (tsl) **Rites funéraires chinois; les funérailles impériales et celles des gens du peuple.** Louvain (ca.1904) 63 p. Offprint from **Le muséon.**

Ferguson, John C. The t'ai miao of peking. **THM** 6 (1938) 185-190.

Fischer, Emil S. A journey to the tung ling and a visit to the desecrated eastern mausolea of the ta tsing dynasty, in 1929. **JNCBRAS** 61 (1930) 20-39.

Fischer, Emil S. T'ai miao, a description of the supreme hall of sacrifices of the forbidden city. **JNCBRAS** 64 (1933) 72-76.

Fonssagrives, Eugène. **Si-ling. Étude sur les tombeaux de l'ouest de la dynastie des ts'ing.** Paris (1907) 180 p (AMG 31, pt 1)

Forrest, R.J. The ming tombs near nanking. **NCH** 571 (6 july 1861)

Franke, O. **Studien zur geschichte des konfuzianischen dogmas und der chinesischen staatsreligion; das problem des tsch'un-ts'iu und tung tschungschu's tsch'un-ts'iu fan lu.** Hamburg (1920) 329 p.

Funérailles de l'impératrice orientale de la chine. **MC** 14 (1882) 52-54.

Gausseron, Bernard H. Les tombeaux des ming. **Monde moderne** 74 (fev 1901) 225-228.

Gingell, W.R. (tsl) Chinese state mourning. **Siam repository** 2 (1870) 185-187.

Grantham, Alexandra E. **The ming tombs.** Peking (1926) 21 p, illus.

Grantham, Alexandra E. **The temple of heaven: a short study.** Peking (n.d.) 40 p.

Groot, J.J.M. de. **The religious system of china.** Leiden (1892-1910) repr taipei (1964) 6 vol. On ming imperial tombs see 3, 1177-1282; on ch'ing imperial tombs see 3, 1282-1373.

Hackenbroich, H. Die totengefolge der chinesischen kaiser. **Deutscher forschungsdienst** 52 (1958) 2-3.

Happel, Julius. **Die altchinesische reichsreligion vom standpunkte der vergleigenden religionsgeschichte.** Leipzig (1882) 46 p. French tsl in **RHR** 4.6 (1881) 257-298.

Happer, Andrew P. A visit to peking. **ChRec** 10.1 (jan-feb 1879) 23-47. Sep publ as **A visit to peking, with some notices of the imperial worship at the altars of heaven, earth, sun, moon and the gods of the grain and land,** shanghai (1879) 27 p.

Happer, Andrew P. The worship of heaven by the chinese emperor. **MRW** n.s. 7 (1894) 86-89.

Harlez, Ch. de (tsl) **Tà ts'īn̄g tsí lì. . .La religion et les cérémonies impériales de la chine moderne d'après le cérémonial et les décrets officiels.** Bruxelles (1893) 556 p.

Heigl, Ferdinand. **Die religion und kultur chinas.** Berlin (1900) 678 p. See teil 1, Die reichsreligion von china.

Herder, A.E. von. Einiges über die dung ling und die si ling. **Sinica** 7 (1932) 149-155.

Herzer, Rudolf. **Zur frage der ungesetzlichen opfer yin szu und ungesetzlichen errichtefen kultstätten yin-tz'u.** Hamburg (1963) 94 p.

Hsiao, Kung-ch'üan. **Rural china: imperial control in the nineteenth century.** Univ washington (1960) See 220-229, Tz'u-ssu: local sacrifices; 229-235, Heretical sects.

Hu, Shih. The establishment of confucianism as a state religion during the han dynasty. **JNCBRAS** 60 (1929) 20-41.

Huang, K'uei-yen and John K. Shryock (tsl) A collection of chinese prayers. Translated with notes. **JAOS** 49 (1929) 128-155. From a book used by officials in anhui.

Hubert, Ch. Les si-ling ou tombeaux de l'ouest. **Bulletin société de géographie de l'est** 33 (1912) 16-37.

Hubert, Ch. Les tombeaux des ming. **Bulletin société de géographie de l'est** 32 (1911) 107-115, plan.

Idols presented to the emperor of china, on his birth-day. **ICG** no 3 (1818) 54-55.

Imbault-Huart, Camille. Les tombeaux des ming près de peking. **TP** 4 (1893) 391-401, 3 photos.

Imbault-Huart, Camille. Une visite au temple de confucius à changhai. **JA** 7e sér, 16 (1880) 533-538.

Inquirer [Happer, A.P.] The state religion of china. **ChRec** 12.3 (1881) 149-192.

K. Das ming-grab bei nanking. **OstL** 13 (1899) 536.

Kobayashi, T. Some political aspects of the problem of confucian state religion. **JOSA** 7.1/2 (dec 1970) 46-69.

Krause, F.E.A. Zum konfuzianischen dogma und der chinesischen staatsreligion. **ARW** 21 (1922) 212-218.

Legge, James. Imperial confucianism. **ChRev** 6.3 (1877) 147-158; 6.4 (1878) 223-235; 6.5 (1878) 299-310; 6.6 (1878) 363-374.

Ling, Shun-sheng. A comparative study of the ancient chinese feng and shan [sacrifices] and the ziggurats of mesopotamia. **ASBIE** 19 (1965) engl abrmt 39-51 + 10 p pl.

Ling, Shun-sheng. The sacred enclosures and stepped pyramidal platforms of peiping. **ASBIE** 16 (1963) engl abrmt 83-100, pl.

Ling, Shun-sheng. The sacred places of chin and han periods. **ASBIE** 18 (1964) engl abrmt 136-142.

Liu, James T.C. Two forms of worshipping the heaven in sung china. **ASBIE** 18 (1964) engl summ 50f.

Lyall, A.C. Official polytheism in china. **NC** 28 (1890) 89-107.

Lyall, Alfred C. **Asiatic studies religious and social.** London (1882) 306 p. See chap 6, relations between the state and religion in china. French tsl: **Études sur les moeurs religieuses et sociales de l'extrême-orient.** Paris (1907)

J.M. Mourning days at the court of peking. **ChRev** 15 (1886-87) 181-182.

Martin, E. Les funérailles d'une impératrice de chine. **RE** 1 (1882) 230-234.

Meech, Samuel E. The imperial worship at the altar of heaven. **ChRec** 47.2 (feb 1916) 112-117.

Messing, Otto. Über die chinesische staatsreligion und ihren kultus. **ZE** 43.2 (1911) 348-375.

Meynard, A. Sacrifice to heaven and earth. **Asia** 28 (1928) 799-803.

Montuclat. Une visite aux tombeaux des ming. **La chine** (1921) 398-402.

Morrison, Robert. The state religion of china. . . **ChRep** 3 (1834) 49; repr **The cycle** (3 dec 1870)

Moule, G.E. Notes on the ting-chi or half-yearly sacrifice to confucius. **JNCBRAS** 33 (1900-01) 37-73 (as misprinted; actually 120-156) photos, drawings, plans, musical score.

Parker, E.H. Side lights on chinese religious ideas. **Gentleman's magazine** 282 (1897) 593-603.

Perrot, Albert. Le retour offensif de la vieille chine. Le confucianisme redevenu religion d'état. **Études** 139 (20 mai 1914) 461-480; 140 (juil 1914) 425-438, fig.

Perry, John W. **Lord of the four quarters. Myths of the royal father.** N.Y. (1966) See chap 5, The far east: china, 204-218. '. . .we find in china the source and leading exponent of the sacral kingship.'

Playfair, G.M.H. Days of official mourning in china. **ChRev** 17 (1888-89) 47-48.

Rousselle, Erwin. Zum system der kaiserlichen grabanlagen. **Sinica** 7 (1932) 155-160.

Schlegel, G. Ming graves. **TP** 2e sér, 2 (1901) 162.

Schupftabackdose. Worship of the emperor's tablet. **ChRev** 8 (1879-80) 61.

Schüler, Wilhelm. Die gründung des "amtes zur regelung der riten" in peking. **OR** 9.1 (2 jan 1928) 15-17.

Schüler, W. Die kultushandlungen der heutigen chinesischen staatsreligion. **ZMK** 26 (1911) 84-87.

Shryock, John K. **The origin and development of the state cult of confucius.** N.Y. and london (1932) 298 p, app, bibliog, index.

Soothill, William E. **The hall of light; a study of early chinese kingship.** Ed Lady Hosie and G.T. Hudson. London (1951) xxii + 289 p, illus.

Soothill, William E. Kingship in china. **JNCBRAS** 61 (1930) 92-99.

Steininger, Hans. Der heilige herrscher, sein tao und sein praktisches tun. In **SJFAW** (1956) 170-177.

Stuhr, P.F. **Die chinesische reichsreligion und die systeme der indischen philosophie in ihrem verhältsnisz zu offenbarungslehren mit rücksicht auf die anwichten von windischmann, schmitt und ritter, betrachtet von P.F. Stuhr.** Berlin (1835) vi + 109 p.

Swann, Peter C. **Chinese monumental art.** N.Y. (1963) See sec, The tombs of the ming emperors, 212-227 (pl 119-125) Chinese architecture. Peking and the forbidden city, 228-259 (pl 126-140) Photos Claude Arthaud and François Hébert-Stevens.

Tamura, Zitsuzo and Yukio Kubayashi. Tombs and murals of ch'ing-ling. Liao imperial mausoleums of the 11th century a.d. in eastern mongolia. **Japan quarterly** 1 (1954) 34-45.

Tran-Ham-Tan. Étude sur le van-mieu [wen miao] de ha-noi (temple de la littérature) **BEFEO** 45 (1951) 89-117, planche.

Waidtlow, C. The imperial religions of ch'in and han. **ChRec** 58 (1927) 565-571, 698-703.

Waidtlow, C. The religion of emperor wu of the han. **ChRec** 55 (1924) 361-366, 460-464, 527-529.

Waidtlow, C. The religion of the first emperor. **ChRec** 57 (1926) 413-416, 487-490.

Wang Ngen-jong. Cérémonial de la cour et coutumes du peuple de pékin. **BAAFC** 2.2 (avr 1910) 105-138; 2.3 (juil 1910) 215-237; 2.4 (oct 1910) 347-368; 3.2 (avr 1911) 134-155; 3.3 (juil 1911) 66-84.

Watters, Thomas. **A guide to the tablets in a temple of confucius.** Shanghai (1879) 259 p.

Weber-Schäfer, Peter. **Oikumene und imperium. Studien zur ziviltheologie des chinesischen kaiser-reichs.** München (1968) 317 p. Historical study through period of han wu-ti.

Wenley, A.G. **The grand empress dowager wen ming and the northern wei necropolis at fang shan.** Freer gallery. **Occasional papers** vol 1.1 (1947) 22 p, 7 pl.

Werner, E.T.C. Rebuttal notes on chinese religion and dynastic tombs. **JNCBRAS** 56 (1925) 134-148.

Wiethoff, Bodo. Der staatliche ma-tsu kult. ZDMG 116.2 (1966) 311-357, illus.

Williams, E.T. Agricultural rites in the religion of old china. JNCBRAS 67 (1936) 25-49.

Williams, E.T. Confucianism as a state religion. Chap 13 in author's CYT, 263-288.

Williams, E.T. The state religion of china during the manchu dynasty. JNCBRAS 44 (1913) 11-45.

Williams, E.T. The worship of lei tsu, patron saint of silk workers. JNCBRAS 66 (1935) 1-14.

Williams, E.T. Worshipping imperial ancestors in peking. JNCBRAS 70 (1939) 46-65.

13. TAOISM – GENERAL
(See also GENERAL STUDIES)

Ampère, J.J. La troisième religion de la chine, lao-tseu. RDM 4e sér, 31 (15 aout 1842) 521-539.

Bahm, Archie J. The world's living religions. Southern illinois univ (1964) See pt 2, Religions of china and japan; Taoism, p 151-174.

Balfour, Frederic H. Taoism. In RSW (1889 et seq) 76-91.

Block, Marguerite. Taoism. In Johnson E. Fairchild (ed) Basic beliefs. The religious philosophies of mankind, n.y. (1959) 114-134.

Bonsall, Bramwell S. Confucianism and taoism. London (1934) 127 p.

The Book of tao. A brief outline of the esoteric schools of buddhism and tao in china. Adyar (1933) 24 p.

Bradley, David G. A guide to the world's religion. Englewood cliffs, n.j. (1963) See chap 14, Taoism, 134-140.

Brémond, René. La sagesse chinoise selon le tao. Pensées choisies et traduites. . . Paris (1955) 208 p.

Burtt, Edwin A. Man seeks the divine. N.Y. (1957) See chap 7, Taoism, 185-201.

Carus, Paul. Taoism and buddhism. OC 20 (1906) 654-667, illus.

Chalmers, John. Tauism. ChRev 1.4 (1873) 209-220.

Chan, Wing-tsit. Taoism. EncyB (1960) vol 21, 796f.

Cordier, Henri. Taoism. Catholic encyclopédie. n.p. (n.d.) 446-448.

Couling, C.E. The oldest dress and the newest; or taoism in modern dress. HJ 22 (1924) 245-259.

Creel, H.G. What is taoism? JAOS 76.3 (1956) 139-152. Repr in author's collection: What is taoism and other studies in chinese cultural history, univ chicago (1970) 1-24.

Dobbins, Frank S. assisted by S. Wells Williams and Isaac Hall. Error's chains: how forged and broken. N.Y. (1883) Same work publ under title, Story of the world's worship, chicago (1901) See chap 21-22, 416-444, illus.

La Doctrine des tao-sse en chine. Actes de la société d'ethnographie 3 (1863) 229f.

Douglas, Robert K. Confucianism and taoism. London (1879)

DuBose, Hampden C. The dragon, image and demon, or the religions of china: confucianism, buddhism, and taoism. Giving an account of the mythology, idolatry and demonolotry of the chinese. London (1886) 463 p.

Dubs, Homer H. Taoism. In H.F. McNair (ed) China, univ california (1946) 266-289.

Duyvendak, J.J.L. Henri maspero, mélanges posthumes. . . TP 40 (1951) 372-390 (Rev)

Dvořák, Rudolf. Darstellungen aus dem gediete der nichtchristlichen religionsgeschichte (12 Bd): Chinas religionen. Zweiter teil: Lao tsï und seine lehre. Münster (1903) viii + 216 p.

Eichhorn, W. Taoism. In ZCE (1959) 385-401.

Erkes, E. Eine taoistische schöpfungsgeschichte für kinder. CDA (1932) 14-15.

Étiemble, René. Le mythe taoïste en france au XXe siecle. FA 17 (1960-61) 1834-1843.

Étiemble, René. Le vision taoïste. Nouvelle revue française n.s. 13 (aout 1965) 357-366.

Faber, Ernst. Der taoismus (1884)

Faber, Martin, et al. Taoism. CMH (1896) 23-31.

Finegan, Jack. The archeology of world religions. Princeton univ (1952) Vol 2: Buddhism, confucianism, taoism, 234-599, illus.

Forlong, J.G.R. Short studies in the science of comparative religions embracing all the religions of asia. London (1897) chap 5, Laotsze and tao-ism.

Franck, A. Le taoisme et son fondateur.
Bulletin de la société d'ethnographie 6 (1892)
5-59.

Gaer, Joseph. **How the great religions began.** N.Y.
(1929) rev ed (1956) See bk 2, pt 2, Taoism, the
religion few can understand, 149-175.

Gauchet, L. Contribution à l'étude du taoisme.
BUA 3e sér, 9 (1948) 1-38.

Giles, Lionel. Introduction to taoism. In Selwyn
G. Champion (ed) **The eleven religions and their
proverbial lore. A comparative study,** n.y. (1945)
272-277 (the 'proverbial lore' is on 278-287)

Goullart, Peter. **The monastery of jade mountain.** London (1961) 189 p, illus.

Groot, J.J.M. de. **Religion in china. Universism:
a key to the study of taoism and confucianism**
(see also author's **Universismus.** . .) N.Y. and
london (1912)

Grosier, l'Abbé. De la religion des chinois-sect
des tao-sée. In author's **Description générale de
la chine,** paris (1785) 2e pt chap 2.

Grube, W. Vorläufiges verzeichnis einer
taoistischen bildersammlung. **Mitteilungen aus der
ethnologischen abteilung der königlichen museen
zu berlin** 1.1 (1885) 16-38.

Gulik, R.H. van. The mango trick in china: an
essay on taoist magic. **TASJ** ser 3, 3 (1954)
117-175.

Gundry, D.W. **Religions. A preliminary historical
and theological study.** London and n.y. (1958)
See 5, The monistic religions: Taoism, 75-78.

Hackmann, Heinrich. China, religionen taoismus.
Jahresberichte der geschichtswissenschaft 34 (1911)

Hackman, Heinrich. Ein chinesisches urteil über den
taoismus von lung hu shan und shang ch'ing. **AO**
7 (1929) 293-304.

Hail, William J. Taoism. In Vergilius Ferm (ed)
Religion in the twentieth century, paterson, n.j.
(1948) 81-93. Paperbk ed (1965) entitled
Living schools of religion.

Hardon, John A. **Religions of the world.** N.Y.
(1963) chap 7: Taoism, 193-203.

Hardwick, Charles. **Christ and other masters.**
Cambridge (1858) See sec 2, Tao-ism or the
school of the fixed way, 307-321.

Hart, Virgil C. Taoism. In **DR** (1884) 285-339.

Henry, B.C. Taoism. Chap 6 in author's **CD** (1885)
100-122.

Herbert, Edward (pseud for Kenney, Edward H.)
A taoist notebook. London (1955) 80 p.

Hodous, Lewis. Taoism. In Edward J. Jurji (ed)
The great religions of the modern world, princeton
univ (1946) 24-43.

Hopkins, E. Washburn. **The history of religions.**
N.Y. (1926) See chap 15, Confucius, lao-tse,
taoism, 249-274.

Hsü Ti-shan. Taoism. In W.L. Hare (ed) **Religions
of the empire,** london (?) (1920) 245-271.

Hume, Robert E. **The world's living religions. With
special reference to their sacred scriptures and in
comparison with christianity.** N.Y. (1924) rev ed
(1959) See pt, Religions originating in east asia
(china, japan): 7. Taoism.

Jurji, Edward J. **The christian interpretation of
religion. Christianity in its human and creative
relationships with the world's cultures and faiths.**
N.Y. (1952) See chap 9, Mysticism and effortless
spontaneity: taoism, 192-198.

Kaltenmark, Maxime. **Lao tseu et le taoïsme.**
Paris (1965) Engl tsl Roger Greaves: **Lao tzu and
taoism.** Stanford univ (1969) In latter see chap 5,
The taoist religion, 107-143.

Kaltenmark, Max. Le maître spirituel dans la chine
ancienne. **Hermès** 4 (1967, no spécial: le maître
spirituel dans les grandes traditions d'occident et
d'orient) 219-225.

Kaltenmark, Max. La mystique taoïste. In **La
mystique et les mystiques,** paris (1965) 649-667.

Kaltenmark, Max. Le taoïsme. In **AC** t 1 (1959)
151-160.

Kenney, Edward H. See Herbert, Edward (pseud)

Kern, M. Konfuzianismus und taoismus. **LO** (1922)
325-350.

King, Winston L. The way of tao and the path to
nirvana. In **SA** (1963) 121-135.

Klaproth, Julius H. von. De la religion des tao-szu en
chine. **Nouvelles annales des voyages** 2 (1833) 129.

Krause, Friedrich E.A. **Ju-tao-fo.** . . **Die religiösen
und philosophischen systeme ostasiens.** München
(1924) 588 p.

Krone, Rudolf. Der taoismus in china. **Berichte des rheinischen missionsgesellschaft** 7 (1857) 102-111; 8 (1857) 114-119.

Legge, James. **The religions of china. Confucianism and taoism described and compared with christianity.** London (1880) 310 p.

Lin, T.C. The taoist in every chinese. **THM** 11 (1940-41) 211-225.

Mackintosh, Charles Henry. **Tao.** Chicago (1926)

Maclagan, P.J. Taoism. In **HERE** 12, 197-202.

Masdoosi, Ahmad Abdullah al. **Living religions of the world. A sociopolitical study.** Tsl fr urdu Zafar Ishaq Ansari. Karachi (1962) See chap 6, Taoism, 142-146.

Maspero, Henri. **Le taoïsme.** Paris (1950) 268 p **(HMRC** t 2)

l'Esprit des races jaune–le taoisme et les sociétés secrètes chinoises. Paris (1897) 32 p.

Matgioï [A. de Pourvoirville] Le taoïsme contemporain: sa hiérarchie, son enseignement, son rôle. **MCSJ** 19 (1889) 179-218.

Mead, G.R.S. **Quests old and new. (Taoism, buddhism, christianity. . .)** (1913)

Mears, W.P. The philosophy, ethics, and religion of taoism. Chiefly as developed by chwang-tsze. (A comparative sketch) **CR** 19.4 (1875-76) 225-242.

Miyahara, Mimpei. Taoism, the popular religion of china. **Contemporary japan** 9 (1940) 1140-1153.

Mortier, F. Le taoisme et ses variations doctrinales. **BSAB** 65 (1954) 161-166.

Müller, F. Max. The religions of china. 2: Taoism. **NC** 48 (oct 1900) 569-581.

Murphy, Gardner and Lois B. Murphy. Taoism. In authors' **Asian psychology,** n.y. and london (1968) 155-168.

Noss, John B. **Man's religions.** N.Y. (1949 et seq) 3rd rev ed (1963) See pt 3, chap 9, Chinese religion and the taoists, 327-368.

Pang Tzu-yau. Notes on popular taoism. **CF** 7.4 (1963) 9-16.

Parker, E.H. Taoism. **IAQR** ser 3, 22 (oct 1906) 311-333.

Parker, E.H. The taoist religion. **Dublin review** 133 (july-oct 1903) 128-162. Repr london (1904) 35 p, bibliog.

Pauthier, G. **Mémoire sur l'origine et la propagation de la doctrine du tao, fondée par lao-tseu; traduit du chinois, et accompagné d'un commentaire tiré des livres sanskrits et du tao-de-king de lao-tseu. . .** Paris (1831) 79 p. See further exchange of correspondence on this work betw author, J. Klaproth et al, **JA** 7 and 8.

Peeters, Hermes. **The religions of china. Confucianism, taoism, buddhism, popular belief.** Peking (1941) 64 p.

Politella, Joseph. **Taoism and confucianism.** Iowa city (1967) 167 p.

Préau, André. **La fleur d'or et le taoïsme sans tao.** Paris (1931) 62 p. 2 art orig in **Le voile d'isis** (fév et avr 1931)

Reid, Gilbert. **A christian's appreciation of other faiths.** Chicago and london (1921) See lectures 1 and 2 on his appreciations of confucianism and taoism, 11-49.

Rosenkranz, Gerhard. **Der heilige in den chinesischen klassikern; eine untersuchung über die erlösererwartung in konfuzianismus und taoismus.** Leipzig (1935) vii + 188 p.

Rosny, Léon de. **Le taoisme.** Paris (1892) xxvi + 179 p.

Rosny, Léon de. Le tao-sséime. In author's **Variétés orientales, historiques, géographiques, scientifiques, bibliographiques et littéraires,** paris, 3e éd (1872) 171-176.

Ross, Floyd H. and Tynette Wilson Hills. **Questions that matter most, asked by the world's religions.** Boston (1954) See sec 3, Chinese religions; chap 10, taoism. . . Paperbk title; **The great religions by which men live.**

Rousselle, Erwin. Der lebendige taoismus in heutigen china. **Sinica** 8 (1933) 122-131.

Saso, Michael R. The taoist tradition in taiwan. **CQ** 41 (jan-mar 1970) 83-102.

Smart, Ninian. **The religious experience of mankind.** N.Y. (1969) See chap 4, Chinese and japanese religious experience; sec, Confucianism and taoism, 141-190.

Smith, Huston. **The religions of man.** N.Y. (1958) chap 5, taoism, 175-192.

Spencer, Sidney. **Mysticism in world religion.** N.Y. (1963) london (1966) See 4, Taoist and confucianist mysticism, i. Taoism, 97-133.

Taoism. In Henry O. Dwight, H. Allen Tapper jr, and Edwin M. Bliss (ed) **Encyclopaedia of missions,** N.Y and london, 2nd ed (1910) 724-729.

Taoism. A prize essay. In **WPR** (1893) vol 2, 1355-1358.

The taou sect of china. **Asiatic journal** ser 2, 5 (1831) 97-104.

Trood, S.M.E. **The religions of mankind. An introductory survey.** London (1929) See chap 8. . . Taoism and shinto, 106-122.

Tsumaki, Naoyoshi. Dōkyō no kenkyū, études sur le taoïsme. **Tōyō Gakuhō** 1.1, 1-56; 1.2, 20-51; 2.1, 58-75.

Vandier-Nicolas, N. Pensée chinoise et taoïsme. **AS** 4 (1950) 64-89.

Vandier-Nicolas, Nicole. **Le taoïsme.** Paris (1965) 132 p.

Waddell, N.A. (tsl) A selection from the ts'ai ken t'an ('vegetable-root discourses') **EB** 2.2 (nov 1919) 88-98.

Walshe, W. Gilbert. Chinese mysticism. In **HERE** 9, 87-89.

Watts, Harold H. **The modern reader's guide to religions.** N.Y. (1964) See chap 19, Chinese and japanese religion: taoism, 554-565.

Weber, Max. **Konfuzianismus und taoismus.** Tübingen (1922) (Author's Gesammelte aufsätze zur religionssoziologie, 1) Engl tsl Hans H. Gerth: **The religion of china: confucianism and taoism.** Glencoe, ill.(1951); london (1952) xi + 308 p.

Welch, Holmes. **The parting of the way. Lao tzu and the taoist movement.** Boston and london (1957); slightly rev ed (1965) 204 p, app, bibliog, index.

Wilhelm, Richard. **Lao-tse und der taoismus.** (1925) repr stuttgart (1948) 164 p.

Williams, E.T. Taoism. Chap 15 in author's **CYT** (1928) 316-338.

Winter, H.J.J. Science, buddhism and taoism. **AP** 21 (may 1950) 206-208.

Yang, Ming-che. Confucianism vs. tao and buddha. **FCR** (jan 1969) 21-29.

Yang, Ming-che. Taoism. **FCR** 17 (july 1967) 20-26.

Yewdale, M.S. The wisdom of tao. **AP** 21 (1950) 365-368.

Zia, Rosina C. The conception of "sage" in lao-tze and chuang-tze as distinguished from confucianism. **CCJ** 5 (may 1966) 150-157.

14. LAO TZU AND TAO TE CHING*

Abel-Rémusat, J.P. Mémoire sur la vie et les opinions de lao-tseu, philosophe chinois du VIe siècle avant notre ère. **MAIBL** 7 (1820) 1-54. See also Extrait d'un mémoire. . . **JA** 3 (1823) 1-15.

Affinités des doctrines de lao-tse et du bouddha. Date incontestable de l'existence de lao-tse. Un savant prétend que lao-tse était un philosophe japonais. In **EM** (d?) t 26, 343f.

Alexander, G.G. Tao-ism. What lao-tze meant by tao. **IAQR** 3rd ser, 4 (1897) 387-396.

Amberley, John Russell, Viscount. **An analysis of religious belief.** London (1876) See vol 1, pt 2, Means of communication downwards. V. Holy persons. Sec 2. Lao-tse.

Anderson, A.E. The tao te king. A chinese mysticism. Univ calif, **University chronicle** 22 (1920) 395-402.

Baumann, C. Reflections prompted by lao-tse; a psychological approach. **Bulletin de la société suisse des amis de l'extrême-orient** 8 (1946) 49-62.

Benton, Richard P. Tennyson and lao tzu. **PEW** 13.2 (1962) 233-240.

Besse, J. (tsl) **Lao-tseu, notice historique (tirée des mémoires historiques de sse-ma-tsien)** Paris (1909) 167 p.

Bisson, T.A. Lao-tsu and the tao te ching. **CJ** 15 (1931) 120-127.

Bodde, Derk. Further remarks on the identification of lao tzu. **JAOS** 64 (1944) 24-27.

Bodde, Derk. The new identification of lao tzu proposed by professor dubs. **JAOS** 62 (1942) 8-13.

---

*No attempt is made to list the constantly increasing number of translations of the text (see our remarks in Foreword).

Bodde, Derk. Two new translations of lao tzu. **JAOS** 74 (1954) 211-217.

Borel, H. **Lao tzu's tao and wu-wei.** N.Y. (1919) thetford, vt.(1939) 139 p.

Borel, Henri. **The rhythm of life. Based on the philosophy of lao-tse.** Tsl fr dutch M.E. Reynolds. London (1921?) 89 p. Rev ed of author's **Wu wei** q.v.

Borel, Henri. **Wu wei. A phantasy based on the philosophy of lao tse.** Tsl fr dutch Meredith Ianson. London (1904 and 1907) vii + 69 p.

Braden, Charles S. **Jesus compared. Jesus and other great founders of religions.** Englewood cliffs, n.j. (1957) See Jesus and lao-tzu, 132-146.

Brecht, B. **Legende von der entstehung des buches taoteking auf dem weg des laotse in die emigration.** Zürich (1960)

Bucke, Richard M. Von komischen bewusstein: 1i-r = laotse. **Yoga** 5 (1958) 284-288.

Burrows, Millar. **Founders of the great religions. Being personal sketches of lao-tse, confucius, buddha, jesus, etc.** London and n.y. (1935) 243 p.

Carus, Paul. The authenticity of the tao-teh-king. **The monist** 11.3 (1900)

Chamberlain, Ida Hoyt. 'Magic writing' from ear to the east series. **China monthly** 2 (nov 1941) 9-12, 17-21. Account of recording music of tao-teh ching as chanted by priests.

Chavannes, Édouard. Lao-tseu. In **GE**(d?) t 21, 938-939.

Chen, Chung-hwan. What does lao-tzu mean by the term "tao"? **TJ** n.s. 4.2 (1964) 150-161.

Cheney, Sheldon. **Men who have walked with god.** N.Y. (1956) See 1, The golden age and the mystic poet lao-tse, 1-37.

Chiu, Moses. **Kritische betrachtung über lau-tsze und seine lehre.** Berlin (1911) 83 p.

Clopin, Camille. Comparaison entre lao-tse, pythagore et confucius. Résultats définitifs pour la chine des deux doctrines examinées par m. de milloué dans une conférence au musée guimet. **La géographie** 27.3 (1898) 285f.

Cordier, Henri Lao tseu. **BVAMG**, t 36. Paris (1911) 31-68.

Cornaby, W. Arthur. Lao tzu redivivus. **ChRec** 37 (1906) 67-74, 124-131.

Dahm, Annemarie. Welterkenntnis und lebensdeutung bei lao dsi. **Yoga** 6 (1961) 17-25; 7 (1961) 1-14; 8 (1961) 8-13.

Délétie, Henri. 'Tao te king' et son interpretation. **Rencontre orient-occident** 5 (jan-déc 1963-64) 9-12; (jan-june 1965) 11-15; (july-sept 1965) 12-14.

Dubs, Homer H. The date and circumstances of the philosopher lao-dz. **JAOS** 61 (1941) 215-221.

Dubs, Homer H. The identification of lao-tse. A reply to professor bodde. **JAOS** 62 (1942) 300-304.

Eckardt, André. Die ethischen grundbegriffe bei laotse. **PJGG** 59.2 (1949) 200-207.

Eckardt, André. Der gottesbegriff bei laotse. **PJGG** 58.2 (1948) 88-99; 58.3 (1948) 211-218.

Eckardt, André. Laotse und die philosophie des ostens. **Universitas** 12 (1957) 355-362.

Edkins, Joseph. The tau te ching. **ChRev** 13 (1884-85) 10-19.

Elwald, Oscar. **Laotse.** München (1928) 86 p.

Engler, Friedrich. Laotse, sein leben und seine persönlichkeit. **Das edle leben, zeitschrift für praktische philosophie** 12.11 (1963) 14-17.

Erdberg-Consten, Eleanor von. A statue of lao tzu in the po-yün-kuan. **MS** 7 (1942) 235-241.

Erkes, Eduard. Kumārajīvas laotse kommentar. **ZMR** 50 (1935) 49-53.

Erkes, Eduard. Ein märchenmotiv bei laotse. **Sinologica** 3 (1953) 100-105.

Erkes, Eduard. Spuren einer kosmogonischen mythe bei laotse. **AA** 8 (1940) 16-38.

Étiemble, René. En relisant lao-tseu. **Nouvelle revue française** n.s. 15 (mar 1967) 457-476.

Folberth, Otto. **Meister eckhart und laotse. Ein vergleich zweier mystiker.** Mainz (1925) 119 p.

Forke, A. Waley's tao-tê king. **ZDMG** 95 (1941) 36-45.

Gabelentz, Georg von der. The life and teachings of lao-tse. **ChRev** 17 (1888-89) 189-198. Tsl fr **Allegemeine real-encyclopädie der wissenschaft und kunst,** 2, sec xlii (1889)

Gaer, Joseph (comp) **The wisdom of the living religions.** N.Y. (1956) See pt 9, The sayings of taoism, 259-274.

Giles, Herbert A. Lao tzŭ and the tao tĕ king. In author's **Ad Sin** 3 (1906) 58-78.

Giles, Herbert A. The remains of lao tzŭ. **ChRev** 14 (1885-86) 231-280; 355-356. Separate work by same title, hong kong (1886) 50 p in 2 col; only in part identical with above art. See further various criticisms and rebuttals in later issues of **ChRev**; esp A critical notice of the Remains of lao tsze, retranslated, **ibid** 16 (1887-88) 195-214.

Griffith, Gwilym Oswald. **Interpreters of reality; a comment on heracleitus, lao tse and the christian faith.** London (1946) 106 p.

Guimet, E. Lao-tzeu et la brâhmanisme. **Actes** 2e **CIHR,**Bâle (1904) 16 p.

Haas, Hans. Lao-tsze und konfuzius. **Einleitung in ihr spruchgut.** Leipzig (1920) 60 p.

Haas, Hans. **Das spruchgut k'ung-tsze's und lao-tsze's in gedanklicher zusammenordnung.** Leipzig (1920) 244 p.

Haas, Hans. **Weisheitworte des lao-tsze.** Leipzig (1920) 36 p.

Harlez, Charles de. Lao-tze, le premier philosophe chinois ou un prédécesseur de schelling au VIe siècle avant notre ère. **MCAM** t 37 (1884) Sep publ, bruxelles (1885) 32 p.

Heiler, F. Weltabkehr und weltrückkehr ausserchristlicher mystiker. 1. teil: Laotse und bhagavadgita. **Eine heilige kirche** 22 (1941) 181-213.

Hesse, J. Laotze, ein vorchristlicher wahrheitszeuge. **Basler missionsstudien** 44 (1914) 64 p.

Hoang, Tzu-yue. Lao-tseu, khong-tseu, mo-tseu. (Étude comparative sur les philosophies) **Annales de l'université de lyon** (1925) 37 p.

Holzmann, Ferdinand. **Kleines laotse brevier. Zur stärkung und erleuchtung des herzens in der bedrängnis des tages zusammengestellt aus dem tao-te-king.** Heidelberg (1948) 8 p.

Hsiao, Paul. Laotse und die technik. **Die katholischen missionen** 75 (1956) 72-74.

Hsiung, Pin-ming. Non-quietist laotse. **Cina** 8 (1963) 39-41.

Hu, Shih. A criticism of some recent methods in dating lao tzu. Tsl Homer H. Dubs. **HJAS** 2 (1937) 373-397.

Hummel, Siegbert. **Zum ontologischen problem des dauismus (taoismus). Untersuchen an lau dsi, kap. 1 und 2.** Leipzig (1948) 45 p.

Hundhauser, Vincenz. **Lau dse: das tao als weltgesetz und vorbild.** Peking (1948) 83 p.

Hurvitz, Leon. A recent japanese study of lao-tzu: kimura eiichi's rōshi no shin-kenkyū. **MS** 20 (1961) 311-367.

Jang, Ching-schun. **Das chinesische philosoph lau-dze und seine lehre.** Übers von Gerhard Kahlenbach. [Ost] berlin (1955) 136 p.

Joos, G. Konfuzius und lao-tse. In **Geistige reiche und religiöse fragen der gegenwart** (1940) 14-24.

Kaltenmark, Max. Lao-tseu. In **Dictionnaire biographique des auteurs,** paris (1964) t 2, 61-63.

Kaltenmark, Max. Lao-tseu dans la religion taoiste. École pratique des hautes études, section des sciences religieuses, **Annuaire 1958-1959,** p 63f.

Kaltenmark, Max. **Lao tseu et le taoisme.** Paris (1965) Engl tsl Roger Greaves: **Lao tzu and taoism.** Stanford univ (1969) 158 p, bibliog·

Kimura, Eiichi. A new study on lao-tzu. **Philosophical studies in japan** 1 (1959) 85-104.

Kingsmill, T. W. Notes on the tao teh king. **JNCBRAS** n.s. 31.2 (1896) 206-209.

Kramers, R. P. Die lao-tsŭ–diskussionen in der chinesischen volksrepublik. **AS** 22 (1968) 31-67.

Lanczkowski, Günter. Neutestamentliche parallelen zu láo-tsés tao-te-king. In **Gott und die götter. Festgabe für emil fischer zum 60. geburstag,** berlin (1958) 7-15.

Lao-tseu. In Larousse, **Grande dictionnaire universel,** paris (préface 1865) t 10, 177-178.

La légende des taosséistes sur lao-tse. In **EM** (d?) t 26, p 171.

Legge, James. Lao-tsze. In **EncyB** 11th ed (1910-11) vol 16, 191-194.

152935

Liebenthal, Walter. Lord atman in the lao-tzu. **MS** 27 (1968) 374-380.

Lin, Yutang. A note on lao-tse. **EW** 3/4 (1949) 18f.

Lin, Yutang. The wisdom of lao-tse. **AP** 20 (1949) 2-5.

Lüth, Paul E. H. Weltgeheimnis und weltgefühl bei lao tse. In **Schule der freiheit, Uchtdorf im Pommern,** vol 9 (1941-42) 306-312.

Martin, Alfred W. **Great religious teachers of the east.** N.Y. (1911) See chap 4, Confucius and lao-tze, 105-148.

Martin, Alfred W. (comp) **Seven great bibles.** N.Y. (1930) See chap 5, An older contemporary of confucius and his book;–lao-tze and the tao teh-king.

Maspero, Henri. Études sur le taoisme. Le saint et la vie mystique chez lao-tseu et tchouang-tseu. **Bulletin de l'association française des amis de l'orient** 3 (1922) 69-89. Repr in author's **Le taoisme,** paris (1950) 225-242.

Maurer, Herrymon. **The old fellow.** N.Y. (1943) 296 p.

Medhurst, C. Spurgeon. The tao teh king. An appreciation. **ChRec** 30 (nov 1899) 540-551. (2) — . An analysis. **Ibid** 31 (jan 1900) 20-33.

Medhurst, C. Spurgeon. **The tao teh king. A short study in comparative religion.** Chicago (1905) xix + 134 p.

Mémoires concernant l'histoire, les sciences, les arts, les moeurs, les usages etc. des chinoise; par les missionaires de pékin. See t 3, paris (1778) Lao tsee, 38-41 (abbrev as **MCLC**)

Möller, N. De la métaphysique de lao-tseu. **Revue catholique** 4 (1849-50)

Müller, F. M. Die lehre des lao-tse. **Die woche** 44.3 (nov 1900)

Neef, Hans. **Die im tao-tsang erhaltenen kommentare zu tao-tê-ching kapitel vi.** Bochum (1938)

Noguier, A. **Lao-tse, un philosophe chinois du Vième siècle avant notre ère.** Montauban (1906) 79 p.

Opitz, Peter-Joachim. **Lao-tzu. Die ordnungsspek-ulation in tao-tê-ching.** München (1967) 202 p.

Osk, Ewald. **Lao-tse.** München (1928)

Osk, Ewald. **Von laotse bis tolstoi.** Berlin (1927)

Pachow, W. Laotzû and gautama buddha: an inquiry into the authenticity of laotzu's mission to india. In **PFV** (1966) 293-303.

Paravey, Charles-Hippolyte de. Explication du texte de lao-tseu sur la trinité. Le tao-te-king considéré non comme un livre historique mais comme un traité de philosophie. **APC** 4e sér, t 8 (1841) 246-258.

Parker, E. H. Laocius and confucius as rival moralists. **AR** 20 (1924) 698-704; 21 (1925) 129-146.

Parker, E. H. The tau teh king remains. **ChRev** 14 (1885-86) 323-333.

Parrinder, E. G. **What world religions teach.** London etc (1963) See chap 9, Lao tse and the way.

Pauthier, Georges. **Mémoire sur l'origine et la propagation de la doctrine du tao, fondée par lao-tseu; traduit du chinois et accompagné d'un commentaire tiré des livres sanscrits et du tao-te-king de lao-tseu, etablissant la conformité de certaines opinions philosophiques de la chine et de l'inde; orné d'un dessein chinois; suivi de deux oupanishads des vedas, avec le texte sanscrit et persan.** Paris (1831) 79 p. See critical rev by Anon [Stanislas Julien?] in **Nouveau JA** 7 (1831) 465-493; see further Pauthier's rebuttal in **ibid** 8 (1831) 129-158.

Pelliot, Paul. Autour d'une traduction sanscrite du tao tö king. **TP** n.s. 13 (1912) 351-430.

Potter, Charles Francis. **The great religious leaders.** N.Y. (1958) Rev ed of **The story of religion,** n.y. (1929) See chap 6, Confucius... (including lao-tse of the divine way) 141-164.

Rosny, Léon de. La philosophie du tao-teh king, leçon faite a l'école pratique des hautes-études. **Mémoires société des études japonaises** (janv 1887) 5-24.

Rosny, Léon de. **Le taoïsme.** Paris (1892) xxxvi + 179 p.

Rosny, Léon de. La texte du tao-teh-king et son histoire. Bibliothèque d'ećole des hautes études, **Sciences religieuses,** t 1 (1889) 323-340.

Rotermund, W. **Die ethik lao-tse's mit besonder-er bezugnahme auf die buddhistische moral.** Gotha (1874) 26 s.

Rousselle, Erwin. Lao-dsïs gang durch seele, geschichte und welt. Versuch einer deutung. **CDA** (1935) 24-41; also in **EJ** 3 (1935) 179-205.

Rousselle, Erwin. Lau-dsï und sein buch. (Über die tiergöttin, zu lao-tse, kap. 6) **Sinica** 16 (1941) 120-129.

Saitschick, Robert. Lao-tse. **Der wendepunkt im leben und im leiden** 13 (1936) 70-76.

Saitschick, Robert. **Schöpfer lebenswerte von lao-tse bis jésus.** Zürich (1945)

Schmidt, K. O. Künder des lichtes, III. Laotse. **Zu freien ufern** 13 (1963) 452-455.

Schulz, Bernard. Legende von der entstehung des buches tao te king auf dem weg des laotse in die emigration. **Wirkendes wort** 7 (dec 1956) 81-86.

Smith, Carl T. A heideggerian interpretation of the way of lao tzu. **CF** 10.2 (1967) 5-19.

Stübe, R. **Lao-tse. Seine persönlichkeit und seine lehre.** Tübingen (1912) 32 p.

Le Tao-teh-king. Identité des methodes de lao-tse et du bouddha. Commentaire bouddhique du tao-teh-king. Lao-tse sous le nom de lauthu. **CISE**, paris (1881) 765-771.

Trêve, Jacques. **l'Enseignement de lao-tsu.** Tunis (1934) 7 p.

Tröltsch, Charlotte Freifrau von. **Lao-tse; die bisher unbekannte lebensgeschichte des chinesischen weisen und sein wirken; aufgenommen durch besondere begabung eines dazu berufenen.** München (1935) 345 p.

Tscharner, E. H. von. Laotse und das innere licht. **Die weisse fahne** 28 (1955) 68-71.

Tscharner, E. H. von. La pensée "métaphysique" et éthique de lao-tse. **Scientia** 72 (1942) 29-36.

Turnbull, Grace H. (comp) **Tongues of fire. A bible of sacred scriptures of the pagan world.** N.Y. (1929) See The book of lao-tzu, 157-166.

Ular, Alexandre. Lao-tse le nietzschéen. À propos du livre de la voie et la ligne droite. **Revue blanche** 27 (1902) 161-167.

Van Buskirk, William R. **The saviors of mankind.** N.Y. (1929) See chap 1, Lao-tze, 1-24.

Watters, Thomas. **Lao-tzu. A study in chinese philosophy.** Hong kong (1870) 114 p. Most of this appeared first in **ChRec** 1 (1868) 31-32, 57-61, 82-86, 106-109, 128-132, 154-160, 209-214. The present book added 2 chap: 8, Lao tzu and confucius; 9, conclusion.

Weddingen. **La théodicée de lao-tze.** Louvain (1885)

Wilhelm, Richard. Laotse, der verborgene weise. **Sinica** 3 (1928) 26-31.

Williams, David Rhys. **World religions and the hope for peace.** Boston (1951) See chap 3, Lao-tse and the inner life, 22-32.

Yang, Ching-schun. **Der chinesische philosoph laudse und seine lehre.** Tsl fr russian G. Kahlenbach. Berlin (1955) 136 p.

Yewdale, M. S. Understanding the chinese through the tao teh king. **AP** 5 (1934) 582-584.

Ymaizoumi, M. Étude de m. ymaizoumi, sur le livre de la vertu et de la voie. **CPOL** t 2, lyon (1880) 82-88.

15. OTHER TAOIST TEXTS

Abel-Rémusat, J. P. (tsl) **Le livre des récompenses et des peines.** Paris (1816) (T'ai shang kan ying p'ien)

Balfour, F. H. (tsl) The book of purity and rest. **ChRev** 9 (1880-81) 83-85 (Ch'ing ching ching)

Balfour, Frederic Henry (tsl) The book of recompences [sic] **ChRev** 8 (1879-80) 341-352 (T'ai shang kan ying p'ien)

Balfour, Frederic H. The "su shu" or book of plain words. **ChRev** 9.3 (1880-81) 162-167.

Balfour, Frederic Henry (tsl) The 't'ai-hsi' king; or the respiration of the embryo. **ChRev** 9 (1880-81) 224-226 (T'ai hsi ching)

Balfour, Frederic Henry (tsl) **Taoist texts, ethical, political and speculative.** London and shanghai (1884) 118 p (Tao teh ching, Yin fu ching, T'ai hsi ching, Hsin yin ching, Ta t'ung ching, Ch'ih wen tung, Ch'ing ching ching, Hung lieh chuan ti yi tuan, Su shu, Kan ying p'ien)

Balfour, F. H. (tsl) Three brief essays. **ChRev** 9 (1880-81) 380-382 (Hsin yin ching, Ta t'ung ching, Ch'ih wen tung)

Balfour, Frederic Henry (tsl) The 'Yin-fu classic; or, clue to the unseen.' **ChRev** 10 (1881-82) 44-54.

Ballou, Robert O. et al (ed) **The bible of the world.** N.Y. (1939) See sec, Taoist scriptures, 471-558.

Belpaire, B. Note sur un traité taoïste. **Muséon** 59 (1946) 655-659.

Braden, Charles S. (comp) **The scriptures of mankind: an introduction.** N Y. (1952) See chap 9, The sacred literature of the chinese. . . taoist, 273-290.

Browne, Lewis (comp) **The world's great scriptures. An anthology of the sacred books of the ten principal religions.** N.Y. (1946) See sec, The scriptures of taoism, 295-358.

Champion, Selwyn G. and Dorothy Short, (comp) **Readings from world religions.** Boston (1951) See chap 6, Taoism, 103-125.

Chavannes, Édouard and Paul Pelliot. Au sujet du canon taoistes. Un traité manichéen retrouvé en chine, traduit et annoté . . **JA** (1911) 499-617; (1913) 99-199; 261-394, 325-329.

Dschi, Hiän-lin. Lieh tzu and buddhist sutras; a note on the author of lieh-tzu and the date of its composition. **SS** 9.1 (1950) 18-32. Tsl fr chin Chou, Ju-ch'ang.

Eichhorn, Werner. T'ai-p'ing und t'ai-p'ing religion. **MIOF** 5 (1957) 113-140. Re expression t'ai-p'ing, with tsl of 2 taoist texts.

Erkes, E. (tsl, ed, annot) The chao-yin-shi. 'Calling back the hidden scholar' by huai-nan-tzu. **AM** 1 (1924) 119-124.

Erkes, E. Der druck des taoistischen kanon. **Gutenberg jahrbuch** (1935) 326-327.

Frost, S E. jr. (ed) **The sacred writings of the world's great religions.** N.Y. (1943) See 3, Taoism, 79-90.

Gabelentz, Georg von der. Ueber das taoistische werk wên-tsi. **Berichte der k. sächs. ges. d. wiss phil. - hist. cl.** 39 (1887) 434-442.

Gaer, Joseph. **The wisdom of the living religions.** London (1958) chap 9, The sayings of taoism, 227-239.

Gauchet, L Contribution à l'étude du taoisme. **BUA** 3e sér, 9 (1948) 1-38.

Gauchet, L. En marge du 'canon taoiste.' **BUA** 2e sér, 36 (1937) 1-29.

Gauchet, L. Un livre taoique, le cheng-shen king, sur la génération des esprits dans l'homme. **BUA** 3e sér, 10 (1949) 63-72.

Gauchet, L. Le tou-jen king des taoïstes, son texte primitif et sa date probable. **BUA** 3e sér, 2 (1941) 511-534.

Gauchet, L. À travers le canon taoïque: quelque synonymes du tao. **BUA** 3e sér, 3 (1942) 303-319.

Giles, Lionel A t'ang manuscript of the sou shên chi . . . **NCR** 3 (1921) 378-385, 460-468. See also W. P. Yetts, **ibid** 65.

Harlez, Charles de. Le gan-shih-tang . . ou lampe de la salle obscure. **Actes onzième ICO** Paris (1897) 2e sec 37-48.

Harlez, Charles de (tsl) Ko-hiuen. Shang-ts'ing-tsing king, ou le livre de la pureté et du repos constant. Textes taoistes traduits des originaux chinois et commentés. **AMG** 20 (1891) 75-82.

Harlez, Charles de. La lampe de la salle obscure (gan-shih-tang). Traité de morale taoïste. La piété filiale, l'infanticide, le respect du ciel, les biens de la fortune. **RHR** 27 (1893) 294-314.

Harlez, Charles de. Le livre du principe lumineux et du principe passif shang thsing tsing king. **MCAM** 37 (1885)

Harlez, Charles de (tsl) **Textes tâoïstes traduits des originaux chinois et commentés.** Paris (1891) 391 p. (Préface; lao tze et le tao-te-king; ko-hiuen; wen-tze; han-fei-tze; hoei-nan-tze; tchuang-tze; lie-tze; hoang-ti nei-king; tchang-tze).

Huebotter, Franz (tsl) **Classic on the conformity of yin. Schrift von konformität der yin.** Tsingtao (1936) 12 p.

Julien, Stanislas (tsl) **Le livre des récompenses et des peines, en chinois et en francais; accompagné de quatre cents légendes, anecdotes et histoires, qui font connaître les doctrines les croyances, et les moeurs de la secte des tao-ssé.** Paris (1835) 531 p.

Julien, Stanislas (tsl) La visite du dieu du foyer à iu-kong **ROA** 2e sér, 16 (1854) 267-276. Previously publ in author's **Livre des récompenses et des peines** q.v. and in french ed of Sir John F. Davis: **Chine,** paris (1857) t 2.

Kaltenmark, Max (tsl) **Le lie-sien tchouan . . . Biographie légendaires des immortels taoiste de l'antiquité.** Pékin (1953) 204 p.

Legge, James. **The sacred books of china. The texts of taoism.** London (1891) 2 vol. F. Max Müller, ed. Sacred books of the east; vol 39 (pt 1) The tao teh king; the writings of kwang-sze [chuang-tzu] books 1-17; vol. 40 (pt 2) The writings of kwang-sze, books 18-33; the thâi-shang tractate of actions and their retributions; app 1-8 (Later repr as 2 vol in 1)

Liou, Tse Houa (tsl) **Lu yen. Le secret de la fleur d'or [par lu tsou]. Suivi du livre de la conscience et de la vie.** Paris (1969) 143 p, illus.

Liu, Hua-yang. Hui ming king. Das buch vom bewusstein und leben. **CBWK** 1.3 (1926) 104-114, 122-123.

Lu, K'uan-yü (Charles Luk) tsl. **Taoist yoga. Alchemy and immortality. A translation, with introduction and notes, of the secrets of cultivating essential nature and eternal life (hsin ming fa chueh ming chih) by the taoist master chao pi ch'en, born 1860.** London (1970) 206 p, illus.

Morgan, Evan. The operations and manifestations of the tao exemplified in history or the tao confirmed by history. 12th essay in huai nan tzû. **JNCBRAS** 52 (1921) 1-39.

Paravey, M. de. Explication du texte de lao-tseu sur la trinité. **APC** 4e sér, 8 (?1909)

Pelliot, Paul. Les premières éditions du canon bouddhique et du canon taoïque. In **Les débuts de l'imprimerie en chine,** paris (1953) **Oeuvres posthumes de paul pelliot,** 4, 88-93.

Pen tsi king (livre du termes originel). Ouvrage taoiste inédit du VIIe siècle. Manuscrits retrouvés à touen-houang reproduits en facsimilés. Introduction par Wu Chi-yü. Paris (1960) Mission paul pelliot, documents conservés à la bibliothèque nationale, 53 p + 208 facs.

Pfizmaier, A. Chinesische begründungen der taolehre. **SAWW** 111 (1885) bd 2, heft 5, s 801-867. Separately publ wien (1886) 69 p (T'ang text: Tao yen nei wai mi chüeh ch'üan shu –ch'uan tao chi by lü yen)

Pfizmaier, A. Ueber einige gegenstände des taoglaubens. **SAWW** 79; separately publ wien (1875) (T'ang text: Tao yen nei wai mi chüeh ch'üan shu by lü yen)

Philastre, P. L. F. Exégèse chinoise. **AMG** 1 (1880) 255-318. Tsl of Yin fu ching.

Rosny, Léon de (tsl) Le livre de la récompense des bienfaits secrets. **ROA** 2e sér, 16 (1854) 202-207; et **APC** t 53.

Schipper, Kristofer (ed) Concordance du pao-p'ou-tseu nei-p'ien. Paris (1965) xxxvii + 755 p.

Schubert, Renate. Das erste kapitel des pao-p'u-tzu wai-p'ien. **ZDMG** 119.2 (1970) 278-301.

Shastri, H. P. Hindu ideas and taoist texts. **AP** 10 (1939) 294-297.

Steininger, Hans. Der heilige herrscher -- sein tao und sein praktische tun (kuan yin tze traktat) In **Sino-japonica** (1956) 170-177.

Tonn W. (tsl) The book of eternal purity and rest. **CJ** 31 (1939) 112-117.

Wieger, Léon, **Taoïsme. T. 1: Bibliographie générale. I. Le canon (patrologie) II. Les index officiels et privés.** Ho-kien-fou (1911) 336 p.

Wieger, Léon. **Taoïsme. T. 2: Les pères du système taoïste, lao tzeu lie-tzeu, tchoang tzeu. Texte revu sur les anciennes éditions taoïstes, traduit d'après les commentaires et la tradition taoïstes.** Ho-kien-fou (1913) 521 p. Repr paris (1950)

Wilhelm, Richard. Dschuang dsï, der mystiker. **Sinica** 3 (1928) 73-80.

Wilhelm, Richard (tsl) **Das geheimnis der goldenen blüte, ein chinesisches lebensbuch.** München (1929) enl ed zürich and leipzig (1939) Engl tsl Cary F. Baynes: **The secret of the golden flower; a chinese book of life.** London (1931) enl ed n.y. (1962) Foreword and comm C. G. Jung (T'ai yi chin hua tsung chih; enl ed also has part of second text: hui ming ching) illus.

Yoshioka, Yoshitoyo. Historical study of taoist scriptures. **JSR:LPH** 8 (1957) 99-101.

16. TAOIST THEORY

Bagchi, P. C. The chinese mysticism. **CalR** 49 (1933) 66-69.

Chang, Chung-yüan. The concept of tao in chinese culture. **RofR** 17 (1952 53) 115-132.

Chang, Chung-yüan. **Creativity and taoism.** N.Y. (1963) 241 p, illus. See esp chap 2-4.

Chang, Chung-yüan. Creativity as process in taoism. **EJ** 25 (1956) 391-415.

Chang, Chung-yüan. Purification and taoism.
Proc 11th ICHR vol 2, leiden (1968) 139-140
(abstract)

Chang, Chung-yüan. Tao and the sympathy of all
things. **EJ** 24 (1955) 407-432.

Chang, Chung-yüan. Tao as inner experience.
Zeitschrift für religions und geistesgeschichte 10
(1958) 13-15.

Chen, Chung-hwan. What does lao-tzu mean by the
term "tao"? **TJ** n.s. 4.2 (1964) 150-161.

Davis, Tenney L. The dualistic cosmogony of huai-
nan-tzu and its relation to the background of chinese and european alchemy. **Isis** 25 (1936)
327-340.

Desai, Santosh. Taoism: its essential principles and
reflection in poetry and painting. **CC** 7.4 (dec 1966)
54-64.

Eichhorn, Werner. Die dauistische spekulation im
zweiten kapitel des dschuang dsi. **Sinica** 17 (1942)
140-162.

Eichhorn, Werner. T'ai-p'ing und t'ai-p'ing religion.
MIOF 5 (1957) 113-140. Re expression 't'ai-p'ing,'
with tsl of 2 taoist texts.

Erkes, Eduard. Ein taoistische schöpfungsgeschichte für kinder. **CDA** (1932) 14f.

Erkes, Eduard. Das weltbild des huai-nan-tze. Ein
beitrag zur ethnographie und kulturgeschichte des
alten china. **OZ** 5.1/4 (1917) 27-32.

Fitch, Robert F. A study of a taoist hell. **ChRec**
45.10 (1914) 603-606.

Forke, Alfred. **Chinesische mystik.** Berlin (1922)
32 p.

Fukunaga, Mitsuji. 'No-mind' in chuang-tzu and in
ch'an buddhism. **Zinbun** 12 (1969) 9-45.

Gillard, Jean-Louis. **Métaphysique taoïste et
acupuncture chinoise.** Bordeaux (1968) 51 p.

Grube, Wilhelm. **Taoistischer schöpfungsmythen
nach dem sen-sien-kien, I.1.** Berlin (1896) 13 p.

Hsiao, Paul S. Y. Schuld als spaltung vom tao.
Proc 11th ICHR vol 2, leiden (1968) 141-142
(abstract)

Hummel, Siegbert. **Zum ontologischen problem
des dauismus (taoismus) untersuchungen an lao
dsi, kapitel 1 und 42.** Leipzig (1948) 45 p.

Izutsu, Toshihiko. The absolute and the perfect
man in taoism. **EJ** 36 (1967) 379-441.

Kroker, Eduard Josef M. **Die realitäts idee bei
chuang chou. 3 parabeln, ein meditation.**
St. augustine/siegburg (1969) 31 p.

Möller, N. De la métaphysique de lao-tseu. **Revue
catholique** 4 (1849-50)

Morgan, Evan. An ancient chinese philosopher's
view on the perfect life (huai-nan tzu) **AR** 21
(1925) 449-464.

Morgan, Evan. The cosmic spirit. Its nature,
operations and influence. **JNCBRAS** 62 (1931)
153-171.

Morgan, Evan. The taoist superman. **JNCBRAS** 54
(1923) 229-245.

Murakami, Yoshimi. 'Nature' in lao-chuang
thought and 'no-mind' in ch'an buddhism.
KGUAS 14 (1965) 15-31.

Paravey, Charles-Hippolyte de. Explication du
texte de lao-tseu sur la trinité. Le tao-te-king
considéré non comme un livre historique mais
comme un traité de philosophie. **APC** 4e sér,
8 (1841) 246-258.

Reid, G.P. Revolution as taught by taoism.
International journal of ethics 35 (1924-25)
289-295.

Rousselle, Erwin. Seelische führung im lebenden
taoismus. **EJ** 1 (1933) 135-199. Same title in
CDA (1934) 21-44.

Rousselle, Erwin. **Zur seelischen führung im
taoismus.** Darmstadt (1962) Repr of 3 art,
without chin characters.

Shih, J. The tao: its essence, its dynamism, and
its fitness as a vehicle of christian revelation. **SM**
15 (1966) 117-133.

Solomon, Bernard S. Meditation on two concepts
of reality: biblical and taoist. **Tri-quarterly** no 8
(winter 1967) 125-131.

Suppaner-Stanzel, Irene. Die ethischen ziele des
taoismus und des existenzialismus. In festschrift:
Der mensch als persönlichkeit und als problem,
münchen (1963) 106-126.

Tomonobu, A. Imamichi. Das seinsproblem in der
philosophie des ostasiatischen altertums. Konfutse
und tschuang tschou. **Jahrbuch für psychologie
und psychotherapie** 6 (1958) 54-64.

Tscharner, E. H. von. La pensée "métaphysique" et éthique de lao-tse. **Scientia** 72 (1942) 29-36.

Vichert, Clarence G. Fundamental principles in chinese boxing. **JWCBorderResS** 7 (1935) 43-46.

Wang, Tch'ang-tche. Le mysticisme de tchoang-tse. **BUA** 3e sér, 2.3 (1941) 382-402.

Wilhelm, Richard. Dschuang dsï, der mystiker. **Sinica** 3 (1928) 73-80.

Woo, Kang. An exposition of the tao theory of chuang tze. **Atti del XII, congresso internazionale di filosofia**, 239-245.

Zenker, E. V. Der taoismus der frühzeit. Die alt- und gemeinchinesische weltanschauung. **SAWW** 222 (1945) 1-56.

17. TAOISM — HISTORY

Allen, Herbert J. The connexion between taoism, confucianism and buddhism in early days. **Trans. 3rd ICHR**, oxford (1908) vol 1, 115-119.

Allen, Herbert J. Similarity between buddhism and early taoism. **ChRev** 15 (1886-87) 96-99.

Amiot, P. Lettre du p. amiot, Peking, 16 oct 1787. **MCLC** 15 (1791) 208-392.

Belpaire, Bruno. Le taoisme et li t'ai-po. **MCB** 1 (1931-32) 1-14.

Brecht, B. **Legende von der entstehung des buches taoteking auf dem weg des laotse in die emigration.** Zürich (1960)

Chan, Hok-lam. Liu pin-chung (1216-1274), a buddhist-taoist statesman at the court of khubilai khan. **TP** 53.1/3 (1967) 98-146.

Chavannes, Édouard. Inscriptions et pièces de chancellerie chinoises de l'époque mongole. **TP** 5 (1904) 366-404. Documents dealing with contro- versy betw buddhists and taoists.

Ch'en, Kenneth. The buddhist contributions to neo-confucianism and taoism. In **TC** (1970) 155- 160. Excerpt from author's **Buddhism in china: a historical survey** q.v. 471-476.

Ch'en, Kenneth K.S. Buddhist-taoist mixtures in the pa-shih-i-hua t'u. **HJAS** 9 (1945-47) 1-12.

Ch'en, Kenneth. Neo-taoism and the prajña school during the wei and chin dynasties. **CC** 1 (oct 1957) 33-46, bibliog.

Cibot, Fr. Notice du cong-fou des bonzes tao- sée. **MCLC** 4 (1779) 441-451, illus.

Conrady, A. Die anfänge des taoismus. **Sinica** 3 (1928) 124-133.

Couling, C. E. The oldest dress and the newest, or taoism in modern china. **HJ** 22 (1924) 245-259.

Couling, C. The patriarch lu, reputed founder of the chih tan chiao. **JNCBRAS** 58 (1927) 157-171.

Creel, H. G. On two aspects of early taoism. In **SJV** (1954) 43-53. Repr in author's collection: **What is taoism and other studies in chinese cultural history,** univ chicago (1970) 37-47.

Duyvendak, J. J. L. Le taoisme sous les t'ang. **Actes 21e ICO,** paris (1949) 272.

Edkins, Joseph. Foreign origin of taoism. **ChRev** 19.6 (1890-91) 397-399.

Edkins, Joseph. Phases in the development of taoism. **JNCBRAS** 5 (1855) 83-99.

Edkins, Joseph. Steps in the growth of early taoism. **ChRec** 15 (1884) 176-190.

Edkins, Joseph. Taoism in ts'in and han dynasties. **ChRec** 15 (1884) 335-350.

Eichhorn, W. Bemerkungen zum aufstand des chang chio und zum staate des chang lu. **MIOF** 3 (1955) 291-327.

Eichhorn, Werner. Bemerkung zur einführung des zölibats für taoisten. **RSO** 30 (1955) 297-301.

Eichhorn, W. (tsl) **Ch'ing-yuan t'iao fa shih lei. Beitrag zur rechtlichen stellung des buddhismus und taoismus in sung-staat. Übersetzung der sek- tion taoismus und buddhismus aus dem ch'ing- yuan t'iao-fa shih-lei (ch. 50 und 51) Mit original text in faksimile.** Leiden (1968) 178 p.

Eichhorn, W. Description of the rebellion of sun ên and earlier taoist rebellions. **MIOF** 2 (1954) 325-352.

Eichhorn, Werner. Nachträgliche bemerkungen zum aufstand des sun ên. **MIOF** 2 (1954) 463-476.

Erkes, E. Die anfänge des taoismus. **Sinica** 3 (1928) 124-133.

Erkes, E. Ueber den heutigen taoismus und seine literatur. **Litterae orientales** 53 (1933) 1-5.

Faber, Ernst. The historical characteristics of taoism. ChRev 13 (1884-85) 231-247. A propos F. H. Balfour's Taoist texts q.v.

Franke, Otto. Ein dokument zur geistesgeschichte der han-zeit. SAWW (1924) 56-78.

Franke, O. Taoismus und buddhismus zur zeit der trennung von nord und süd. Sinica 9 (1934) 89-113.

Fukui, Kōjun. Fundamental problems regarding the schools of religious taoism. In RSJ (1959) 451-459.

Granet, Marcel. Remarques sur le taoïsme ancien. AM 2 (1925) 146-151. Repr in Études sociologiques sur la chine, paris (1953)

Groot, J. J. M. de. On the origin of the taoist church. Trans 3rd ICHR, vol 1, oxford (1908) 138-149.

Hackmann, H. Ein chinesisches urteil über den taoismus von lung hu shan und shang ch'ing. AO 7 (1929) 293-304.

Hart, V. C. The heavenly teachers. ChRec 10 (1879) 445-453. Author's report of his visit to lung-hu shan and interview with 61st chang t'ien-shih.

Imbault-Huart, Camille. La légende du premier pape des taoistes et l'histoire de la famille pontificale de tchang. JA 8e sér, 4 (nov-dec 1884) 389-461.

Kaltenmark, Max. Recherches sur l'histoire du taoisme religieux. École pratique des hautes études, section des sciences religieux, Annuaire (1959-60) 53f.

Kaltenmark, Max. Religion et politique dans la chine des ts'in et des han. Diogène 34 (1961) 18-46.

Kimura, Eiichi. The new confucianism and taoism in china and japan from the fourth to the thirteenth centuries a.d. CHM 5 (1959-60) 801-829.

Kopsch, H. The master of heaven. In DV vol 2, pt iii, 226-229.

Kubo, Noritada. Prolegomena on the study of the controversies between buddhists and taoists in the yüan period. TBMRD 26 (1968) 39-61.

Levy, Howard S. The bifurcation of the yellow turbans in later han. Oriens 13-14 (1960-61) 251-255.

Levy, Howard S. Yellow turban religion and rebellion at the end of han. JAOS 76 (1956) 214-227.

Link, Arthur E. Cheng-wu lun: the rectification of unjustified criticism. OE 8.2 (dec 1961) 136-165.

Mead, G. R. S. An historical note on taoism. In W. L. Hare (ed) Religions of the empire, london (1925) 243-244.

Michaud, Paul. The yellow turbans. MS 17 (1958) 47-127, bibliog.

Milne, W. C. The rebellion of the yellow caps, compiled from the history of the three states. ChRep 10 (1841) 98-103.

Morrison, Robert. Account of the sect tao-szu, from "The rise and progress of the three sects." In author's Horae sinicae, london (1812) Idem in Uhr-chih-tsze-teen-se-yin-pe-keaou, being a parallel dictionary between the two intended dictionaries by the rev. robert morrison and antionio montucci, 11.d., together with morrison's horae sinicae, a new edition, london (1817) 167-170.

Pachow, W. Laotzû and gautama buddha; an enquiry into the authenticity of laotzû's mission to india. In PFV Colombo (1966) 293-303.

Pauthier, Georges. Mémoire sur l'origine et la propagation de la doctrine du tao, fondée par lao-tseu; traduit du chinois et accompagné d'un commentaire tiré des livres sanscrits et du tao-te-king de lao-tseu, etablissant la conformité de certaines opinions philosophiques de la chine et de l'inde; orné d'un dessein chinois; suivi de deux oupanishads des vedas, avec la texte sanscrit et persan. Paris (1831) 79 p. See critical rev by Anon (Stanislas Julien?) in NouvJA 7 (1831) 465-493. See further Pauthier's rebuttal in ibid 8 (1831) 129-158.

Pauthier, M. Relation du voyage de k'hiéou, surnomme tchang-tch'un (long printemps), à l'ouest de la chine, au commencement du XIIIe siècle de notre ère. JA 6e sér, 9/10 (1867) 39-86.

Pelliot, Paul. Les mo-ni et le houa-hou-king. BEFEO 3 (1903) 318-327.

Pelliot. Paul. Les premières éditions du canon bouddhique et du canon taoïque. In Les débuts de l'imprimerie en chine, paris (1953) Oeuvres posthumes de paul pelliot, 4, 88-93.

Rosny, Léon de. Les origines du taoisme. RHR 22 (1890) 161f.

Saso, Michael. Red-head and black-head: the classification of the taoists of taiwan according to the documents of the 61st heavenly master. ASBIE 30 (aug 1970)

Schipper, Kristofer. l'Empereur wou des han dans le légende taoiste; han wou-ti nei tchouan. Paris (1965) Incl chin text.

Seidel, Anna K. La divinisation de lao tseu dans le taoisme des han. Paris (1969) 171 p, facs chin texts, bibliog, index.

Seidel, Anna K. The image of the perfect ruler in early taoist messianism: lao-tzu and li hung. HR 9.2/3 (nov. feb 1969-70) 216-247.

Stein, R.A. Remarques sur les mouvements du taoisme politico-religieux au IIe siècle ap. j.-c. TP 50 (1963) 1-78.

Ten Broek, Janet Rinaker and Yiu Tung. A taoist inscription of the yuan dynasty: the tao-chia pei. TP 40 (1950-51) 60-122. Tablet in the tung-yüeh miao, peking.

Thiel, Joseph. Der streit der buddhisten und taoisten zur mongolzeit. MS 20 (1961) 1-81.

Waley, Arthur (tsl) The travels of an alchemist: the journey of the taoist, chang-ch'un ... from china to the hindukush at the summons of chingiz khan, recorded by his disciple, li chih-ch'ang. London (1931) xi + 166 p, map.

Ware, James R. The wei shu and the sui shu on taoism. JAOS 53 (1933) 215-250; 54 (1934) 290-294.

Welch, Holmes. The chang t'ien shih and taoism in china. JOS 4 (1957-58) 188-212.

Welch, Holmes. Syncretism in the early taoist movement. Harvard univ Papers on china, 10 (1956) 1-54.

Wieger, Léon. The evolution of taoist doctrines. Engl tsl Lydia G. Robinson, from author's Taoïsme, t.1 q.v. under Taoist Texts. Chicago (1913)

Wieger, L. Taoïsme. Tome 1 -- Bibliographie générale. 1. Le canon (patrologie) 2. Les index officiels et privés. Ho-kien-fou (1911) 336 p.

Wilhelm, Richard. On the sources of chinese taoism. JNCBRAS 45 (1914) 1-12.

Zenker, E. V. Der taoismus des frühzeit. Die alt- und gemeinchinesische weltanschauung. SAWW 222.2 (1943) 1-56.

18. TAOIST IMMORTALS

Bauer, Wolfgang. Der herr vom gelben stein (chuang shih kung); wandlungen einer chinesischer legendenfigur. OE 3 (1956) 137-152.

Conrady, G. Les huit immortels taoïstes dans l'art chinois. Pa hien. BSAB 65 (1954) 167-170.

Couling, C. E. The patriarch lu, reputed founder of the chin tan chiao. JNCBRAS 58 (1927) 157-171.

Diez, E. Dauistische unsterbliche. Sinica 16 (1941) 48-53.

Edkins, Joseph. The eight genii. EA 2.3 (1903) 284-287.

Eichhorn, Werner. Eine erzählung aus dem wen-chien hou-lu. OE 2 (1955) 167-174.

Giles, Lionel (tsl) A gallery of chinese immortals. London (1948) 127 p.

Grube, W. (tsl) Taoistischer schöpfungsmythus nach dem sên-siên-kién. In Festschrift für adolf bastien au seimem 70. geburstag 26 jani 1896, berlin (1896) p 445-458.

Gützlaff, C. A general account of the gods and genii; in 22 vol. From a correspondent. ChRep 7 (1839) 505 et seq. (re shen hsien t'ung chien)

Harlez, Charles de. 'Shēn-siēn-shū.' Le livre des esprits et des immortels. Essai de mythologie chinoise d'après les textes originaux. Bruxelles (1893) 492 p.

Holzman, Donald. A chinese conception of the hero. Diogenes 36 (1961) 33-51. Re juan ch'i (210-263 a.d.) and his 'biography of master great man' - - a taoist immortal.

Jacquet, E. Légende de yê sou, selon le chin siên thoung kian [shen hsien t'ung chien] NouvJA 7 (1831) 223-228.

Kaltenmark, Max (tsl) Le lie-sien tchouan: biographies légendaires. Peking (1953) 204 p.

Laloy, Louis. Légendes des immortels (d'après les auteurs chinois) Paris (1922) 108 p.

Ling, Peter C. The eight immortals of the taoist religion. JNCBRAS 49 (1918) 53-75.

Morgan, Evan. The taoist superman. JNCBRAS 54 (1923) 229-245.

Parry, D. The eight immortals. EW 7.1 (1953) 26-27.

Pavie, Théodore. Yu-ki le magicien, légende chinoise. RDM (15 mars 1851) 1129-1144.

Pfitzmaier, August. Die lebensverlängerungen der männer des weges (tao shih) SAWW 68 (1871) 641f, 652f, 665f, 679f, 695f.

Seidel, Anna K. La divinisation de lao tseu dans le taoïsme des han. Paris (1969) 171 p, facs chin texts, bibliog, index.

Seidel, Anna. A taoist immortal of the ming dynasty: chang san-feng. In SSMT (1970) 483-531.

Tien, Tsung. The eight immortals. Orient 3.1 (1952) 50-52.

Yang, Richard F. S. A study of the origin of the legend of the eight immortals. OE 5.1 (1958) 1-22.

Yetts, W. Perceval. The chinese isles of the blessed. Folk-lore 30 (mar 1919) 35-62.

Yetts, W. Perceval. The eight immortals. JRAS (oct 1916) 773-807, illus.

Yetts, W. Perceval. More notes on the eight immortals. JRAS (1922) 397-426.

Yetts, W. P. Pictures of a chinese immortal. BM 39 (1921) 113-121.

Yetts, W. Perceval. Taoist tales. NCR 1 (mar 1919) 11-18, pl; (may 1919) 169-175. See further, same title, — A rejoinder, ibid 3 (feb 1921) 65-68.

19. TAOIST PANTHEON AND CULTS

Chavannes, Édouard. Le jet des dragons. Mémoires concernant l'asie orientale 3 (1919) 53-220, illus pl and reproductions of rubbings and texts.

Edkins, Joseph. Place of hwang-ti in early taoism. ChRev 15.4 (1886-87) 233-239.

Edkins, Joseph. A sketch of the tauist mythology in its modern form. JNCBRAS 1.3 (dec 1859) 45-49.

Edkins, Joseph. Titles of tauist gods. ChRev 24.4 (1895-96) 199.

Fêng, Han-chi. The origin of yü huang. HJAS 1 (1936) 242-250.

Gauchet, L. Recherches sur la triade taoïque. BUA 3e sér, 10 (1949) 326-366.

Maspero, Henri. Les dieux taoistes; comment on communique avec eux. CRAIBL (1937) 362-374.

Maspero, Henri. Le panthéon taoiste avant les t'ang. JA (1936) 483.

Mortier, F. Du sens primitif de l'antiquité et la célèbre figure divinatoire des taoistes chinois et japonais (sien t'ien) BSAB 59 (1948) 150-160.

Mueller, Herbert. Über das taoistische pantheon des chinesen, seine grundlagen und seine historische entwicklung. ZE 3-4 (1911) 393-428.

Natsume Ikken. Various phases of revelation in taoism. TJR 1 (mar 1955) 53-65, fig.

Soymié, Michel. Biography de chan tao-k'ai. MIHEC 1 (1957) 415-422. Patron saint of lo-fou shan.

20. TAOIST MONACHISM

Balfour, Frederic H. (1) Taoist hermits. In author's Leaves from my chinese scrapbook, london (1887) 135-139. (2) A taoist patriarch. In ibid, 140-144.

Bourne, F. S. The lo-fu mountains; an excursion. Shanghai (1895)

Drake, F. S. The taoists of lao-shan. ChRec 65 (1934) 238-245, 308-318.

Eichhorn, Werner. Bemerkung zur einführung des zölibats für taoisten. RSO 30 (1955) 297-301.

Erkes, Eduard. Die anfänge des dauistischen mönchtums. Sinica 11 (1936) 36-46.

Goullart, Peter. The monastery of jade mountain. London (1961) 189 p, photo illus.

Hackmann, H. Die dreihundert mönchsgebote des chinesischen taoismus. Amsterdam (1931) 60 p + 24 p chin text.

Hackmann, Heinrich. Die mönchsregeln des klöstertaoismus. OZ 8 (1919-20) 142-170.

Irving, E. A. A visit to the buddhist and tao-ist monasteries on the lo fau shan. BlM 157 (mar 1895) 453-467.

Schmitt, Erich. Taoistische klöster im licht des universismus. MSOS 19 (1916) 76-104.

Schüler, Wilhelm. Aus einem taoistischen kloster. ZMK 24 (1909) 265-269.

21. TAOIST YOGA AND ALCHEMY*

Amiot, J. J. M. Extrait d'une lettre . . . **MCLC** 15 (1791) v.

Amiot, J. J. M. Extrait d'une lettre sur la secte des tao-sée. **MCLC** 15 (1791) 208-259.

Balfour, Frederic (tsl) The "t'ai-hsi" king or the respiration of the embryo. **ChRev** 9 (1880) 224-226. Taoist text, Hsiu-chen pi-lu.

Barnes, W. H. The apparatus, preparations and methods of the ancient chinese alchemists. **JCE** 11 (1934) 655f.

Barnes, W. H. Chinese influence on western alchemy. **Nature** 135 (1935) 824f.

Barnes, W. H. Diagrams of chinese alchemical apparatus. **JCE** 13 (1936) 453.

Barnes, W. H. Possible references to chinese alchemy in the -4th or -3rd century. **CJ** 23 (1935) 75.

Barnes, W. H. and H.B. Yuan. T'ao the recluse (452-536 a.d.) ; chinese alchemist. **Ambix** 2 (1946) 138f.

Belpaire, B. Note sur un traité taoiste. **Muséon** 59 (1946) 655.

Beurdeley, M. (ed) **The clouds and the rain; the art of love in china.** With contributions by K. Schipper on Taoism and sexuality and other materials. London (1969)

Biroen, H. Taoismus: praktische system der wandlung und sublimation. **Yoga** 7.6 (1960) 27-31.

Bonmarchand, G. (tsl) Les notes de li yi-chan (yi-chan tsa tsouan) traduit du chinois; étude de littérature comparée. **BMFJ** n.s. 4.3 (1955) 1-84.

Chang, Chung-yüan. An introduction to taoist yoga. **RofR** 21 (1956) 131-148. Repr in **CWayRel** (1973) 63-76.

Chatley, Herbert. Alchemy in china. **National review** 14 (25 oct 1913) 456-457.

Chattopadhyaya, D. Needham on tantrism and taoism. **New age** 6.1 (1957) 43; 7.1 (1958) 32.

Ch'en, Kuo-fu and Tenney L. Davis (tsl) Inner chapters of pao-p'u-tzu. **PAAAS** 74.10 (dec 1941) 297f. Tsl chap 8 and 11; precis of remainder.

_____

*The exhaustive bibliography in this field is Joseph Needham, **Science and Civilization in China**, vol 5, pt 2, cambridge univ (1974) bibliog C, 387-469.

Chikashige, Masumi. **Alchemy and other chemical achievements of the ancient orient.** Engl tsl Nobuji Sasaki. Tokyo (1936) vii + 102 p, illus, pl.

Chou, Hsiang-kung. Taoismus und yoga. **Vivos voco: die weisse fahne ruft die legenden** 35 (1962) 156-158.

Chou, I-liang. Tantrism in china. **HJAS** 8 (1945) 241f.

Cibot, P. M. Notice sur le cong-fu, exercice superstitieux des taoche pour guérir le corps de ses infirmités et obtenir pour l'âme une certain immortalité. **MCLC** 4 (1779) 441-448.

Cowdry, E. V. Taoist ideas of anatomy. **AMH** 3 (1921) 301-309.

Coyaji, J. C. Some shahnamah legends and their chinese parallels. **JRASB** n.s. 24 (1928) 177f.

Coyaji, J. C. The shahnamah and the fêng shên yen i. **JRASB** n.s. 26 (1930) 491f.

Daumas, M. La naissance et le developpement de la chimie en chine. **S. E. T.; Structure et evolution des techniques** 6 (1949) 11f.

Davis, Tenney L. The chinese beginnings of alchemy. **Endeavour** 2 (1943) 154f.

Davis, Tenney L. The dualistic cosmogony of huai-nan-tzu and its relation to the background of chinese and european alchemy. **Isis** 25 (1936) 327-40.

Davis, Tenney L. Huang ti, legendary founder of alchemy. **JCE** 11 (1934) 635f.

Davis, Tenney L. The identity of chinese and european alchemical theory. **Journal of unified science** 9 (1929) 7f.

Davis, Tenney L. Ko hung (pao p'u tzu), chinese alchemist of the 4th century a.d. **JCE** 11 (1934) 517 f.

Davis, Tenney L. Liu an, prince of huai-nan. **JCE** 12 (1935) 1f.

Davis, Tenney L. The problem of the origins of alchemy. **Scientific monthly** 43 (1936) 551f.

Davis, Tenney L. Wei po-yang, father of alchemy. **JCE** 12 (1935) 51f.

Davis, Tenney L. and Chao Yün-ts'ung (tsl) An alchemical poem by kao hsiang-hsien. **Isis** 30 (1939) 236f.

Davis, Tenney L. and Chao Yun-ts'ung. Chang po-tuan, chinese alchemist of the 11th century a.d. **JCE** 16 (1939) 53f.

Davis, Tenney L. and Chao Yün-ts'ung (tsl) Chang po-tuan of t'ien-t'ai; his wu chen p'ien (essay on the understanding of the truth); a contribution to the study of chinese alchemy. **PAAAS** 73 (1940) 97f.

Davis, Tenney L. and Chao Yün-ts'ung. A fifteenth-century chinese encyclopaedia of alchemy. **PAAAS** 73 (1940) 391f.

Davis, Tenney L. & Chao Yün-ts'ung (tsl) The four-hundred word chin tan of chang po-tuan. **PAAAS** 73 (1940) 371f.

Davis, Tenney L. and Chao Yün-ts'ung. The secret papers in the jade box of ch'ing-hua. **PAAAS** 73 (1940) 385f.

Davis, Tenney L. and Chao Yün-ts'ung. Shih hsing-lin, disciple of chang po-tuan and hsieh tao-kuang, disciple of shih hsing-lin. **PAAAS** 73 (1940) 381f.

Davis, Tenney L. and Chao Yün-ts'ung (tsl) Three alchemical poems by chang po-tuan. **PAAAS** 73 (1940) 377f.

Davis, Tenney L. and Ch'en Kuo-fu. Shang yang tzu, taoist writer and commentator on alchemy. **HJAS** 7 (1942) 126f.

Davis, Tenney L. and Nakaseko Rokuro. The jofuku [hsü shen] shrine at shingu; a monument of earliest alchemy. **Nucleus** 15.3 (1937) 60-67.

Davis, Tenney L. and Nakaseko Rokuro. The tomb of jofuku [hsü fu] or joshi [hsü shih] ; the earliest alchemist of historical record. **Ambix** 1 (1937) 109, illus; **JCE** 24 (1947) 415.

Davis, Tenney L. and Wu Lu-ch'iang. The advice of wei po-yang to the worker in alchemy. **Nucleus** 8 (1931) 115-117; repr in **Double bond** 8 (1935) 13.

Davis, Tenney L. and Wu Lu-ch'iang. Chinese alchemy. **Scientific monthly** 31 (1930) 225f.

Davis, Tenney L. and Wu Lu-ch'iang. Ko hung on the gold medicine. **JCE** 9 (1932) 103-105.

Davis, Tenney L. and Wu Lu-ch'iang. Ko hung on the yellow and the white. **JCE** 13 (1936) 215-218.

Davis, Tenny L. and Wu Lu-ch'iang. The pill of immortality. **Technology review** 33 (1931) 383f.

Davis, Tenney L. and Wu Lu-ch'iang. T'ao hung-ch'ing. **JCE** 9 (1932) 859f.

Dubs, Homer H. The beginnings of alchemy. **Isis** 38.1/2 (1947) 62-86.

Dubs, Homer H. The origin of alchemy. **Ambix** 9 (1961) 23-36.

Dudgeon, J. "Kung-fu," or medical gymnastics. **JPOS** 3.3 (1893); 3.4 (1895) 341f.

Eliade, Mircea. The forge and the crucible: a post-script. **HR** 8.1 (1968) 74-88.

Eliade, Mircea. **Forgerons et alchimistes.** Paris (1956) Engl tsl Stephen Corrin: **The forge and the crucible,** london (1962) See chap 11, Chinese alchemy, 109-126.

Erkes, Eduard. Die taoistische meditation und ihre bedeutung für das chinesische geistesleben. **Psyche** 2.3 (1948-49) 371-379.

Feifel, E. (tsl) Pao-p'u-tzu nei-p'ien, translated and edited. **MS** 6 (1941) 113-311; 9 (1944) 1-33; 11 (1946) 1-32.

Fêng, Chia-lo and H.B. Collier. A sung-dynasty alchemical treatise; the "outline of alchemical preparations" [tan fang chien yuan] by tuku t'ao. **JWCBorderResS** 9 (1937) 199f.

Filliozat, J. Taoïsme et yoga. **Dan viêt nam** 3 (1949) 113-120.

Filliozat, J. Taoïsme et yoga. **JA** 257.1/2 (1969) 41-87.

Forke, A. Ko hung der philosoph und alchymist. **Archiv für die geschichte der philosophie** 41 (1932) 115f. See author's **Geschichte d. mittelälterlichen chinesischen philosophie,** hamburg (1934) 204f.

Gulik, R. H. van. Indian and chinese sexual mysticism. App 1 in author's **Sexual life in ancient china,** q.v. 339-359.

Gulik, R. H. van. **Sexual life in ancient china.** Leiden (1961) 392 p. See passim.

Hiordthal, T. Chinesische alchimie. In Paul Diergart (ed) **Beiträge aus der geschichte der chemie,** leipzig und wien (1909) 215-224. See comm by Éd. Chavannes in **TP** 2e sér, 10 (1909) 389.

Ho, Ping-yü and Ch'en T'ieh-fan. On the dating of the shun-yang lü chen-jen yao shih chih, a taoist pharmaceutical and alchemical manual. **JOS** 9 (1971) 181f.

Ho, Ping-yü and Joseph Needham. Elixir poisoning in medieval china. **Janus** 48 (1959) 221-251.

Ho, Ping-yü and Joseph Needham. The laboratory equipment of the early medieval chinese alchemist. **Ambix** 7 (1959) 57-115.

Ho, Ping-yü and Joseph Needham. Theories of categories in early medieval chinese alchemy. **Journal of the warburg and courtauld institutes** 22 (1959) 173-210.

Ho, Ping-yü and Ts'ao T'ien-ch'in. An early medieval chinese alchemical text on aqueous solutions. **Ambix** 7 (1959) 122-158.

Huang, Tzu-ch'ing. Über die alte chinesische alchemie und chemie. **Wissenchaftliche annalen** 6 (1957) 721f.

Johnson, Obed S. **A study of chinese alchemy.** Shanghai (1928) xi + 156 p.

Jung, C. G. **Alchemical studies.** Engl tsl R. F. C. Hull. London (1968) Collected works vol 8. See "European commentary" on the t'ai-i chin hua tsung chih, 1055; "Interpretation of the visions of zosimos," 57-108.

Kaltenmark, Max. Hygiène et mystique en chine. **Bulletin de la société d'acuponcture** 33.3 (1959) 21-30.

Kaltenmark, Max. Ling-pao: note sur un terme du taoisme religieux. **MIHEC** 2 (1960) 559-588.

Liu, Ts'un-yan. Lu hsi-hsing and his commentaries on the ts'an-t'ung ch'i. **TJ** 7.1 (1968) 71-98.

Liu, Ts'un-yan. Taoist self-cultivation in ming thought. In **SSMT** (1970) 291-330.

Lo, L. C. (tsl) Liu hua-yang; hui ming ching, das buch von bewusstsein und leben. **CBWK** 3.1.

Lu, K'uan-yü (Charles Luk) **The secrets of chinese meditation. Self-cultivation by mind control as taught in the ch'an, mahayana and taoist schools in china.** London (1964) 240 p, gloss, index, illus.

Lu, K'uan-yü (Charles Luk) **Taoist yoga. Alchemy and immortality. A translation, with introduction and notes, of the secrets of cultivating essential nature and eternal life (hsin ming fa chueh ming chih) by the taoist master chao pi ch'en, born 1860.** London (1970) 206 p, gloss, index, illus.

McGowan, D. J. The movement cure in china (taoist medical gymnastics) **Chinese imperial customs, medical report series** 29 (1885) 42f.

Mahdihassan, S. Alchemy a child of chinese dualism as illustrated by its symbolism. **IQB** 8 (1959) 15 f.

Mahdihassan, S. Alchemy and its chinese origin as revealed by its etymology, doctrines and symbols. **IQB** (1966) 22-58.

Mahdihassan, S. Alchemy and its connection with astrology, pharmacy, magic and metallurgy. **Janus** 46 (1956) 81-103.

Mahdihassan, S. Alchemy in its proper setting, with jinn, sufi, and suffa as loan-words from the chinese. **IQB** 7 (1959) 1f.

Mahdihassan, S. Alchemy in the light of jung's psychology and of dualism. **Pakistan philosophical journal** 5 (1962) 95f.

Mahdihassan, S. Chemistry a product of chinese culture. **Pakistan journal of science** 9 (1957) 26f.

Mahdihassan, S. The chinese origin of alchemy. **United asia** (India) 5.4 (1953) 241-244.

Mahdihassan, S. The chinese origin of the word chemistry. **Current science** 15 (1946) 136f. Another probable origin of the word chemistry from the chinese. **Ibid.**, 234.

Mahdihassan, S. Der chino-arabische ursprung des wortes chemikalie. **Pharmazeutische industrie** 23 (1961) 515f.

Mahdihassan, S. The early history of alchemy. **Journal of the university of bombay** 29 (1960) 173 f.

Mahdihassan, S. The genesis of alchemy. **Indian journal of the history of medicine** 5.2 (1960) 41f.

Mahdihassan, S. Das hermetische siegel in china. **Pharmazeutische industrie** 22 (1960) 92f.

Mahdihassan, S. Landmarks in the history of alchemy. **Scientia** 57 (1963) 1f.

Mahdihassan, S. The soma of the aryans and the chih of the chinese. **May and baker pharmaceutical bulletin** 21.3 (1972) 30f.

Mahdihassan, S. A triple approach to the problem of the origin of alchemy. **Scientia** 60 (1966) 444-455.

Martin, W. A. P. Alchemy in china. Abstract in **JAOS** 9 (1871) xlvi; **ChRev** 7 (1879) 242; repr in author's **Hanlin papers,** london and n.y. (1880) vol 1, p. 221, and **The lore of cathay,** n.y. and chicago (1901) p 44f.

Maspero, H. Les procédés de 'nourrir le principe vital' dans la religion taoiste ancienne. JA 229 (1937) 177-252, 353-430.

Maspero, H. Les dieux taoistes; comment on communique avec eux. CRAIBL (1937) 362-374.

Masson-Oursel, Paul. Tao et yoga. In AC t 1 (1959) 160-162.

Mély, F. de. l'Alchimie chez les chinois et l'alchimie grecque. JA 9e sér, 6 (1895) 314f.

Mortier, F. Les procédés taoistes en chine pour la prolongation de la vie humaine. BSAB 45 (1930) 118-129.

Needham, Joseph. The refiner's fire; the enigma of alchemy in east and west. A lecture given in london (1971) but apparently not publ in engl; french tsl, somewhat modified, Artisans et alchimistes en chine et dans le monde héllénistique, La pensée 152.3 (1970)

Pálos, István. Atem und meditation. Moderne chinesische atemtherapie als vorschule der meditation. Theorie, praxit, originaltexte.

Partington, J. R. An ancient chinese treatise on alchemy [ts'an t'ung t'ung ch'i of wei po-yang] Nature 136 (1935) 287f.

Partington, J. R. Chinese alchemy (a) Nature 119 (1927) 11; (b) Ibid, 120 (1927) 878; (c) Ibid, 128 (1931) 1074.

Partington, J. R. The relationship between chinese and arabic alchemy. Nature 120 (1928) 158f.

Pelliot, Paul. Notes sur quelques artistes des six dynasties et des t'ang. TP 22 (1923) 214f.

Pfizmaier, A. Die taolehre von den wahren menschen und den unsterblichen. SAWW 63 (1869) 217-280.

Pokora, T. An important crossroad of chinese thought. (Includes discussion of yogistic trends in ancient taoism) ArchOr 29 (1961) 64f.

Préau, André. La fleur d'or et le taoïsme sans tao. Paris (1931) 62 p ('Réunit deux articles parus en février et avril 1931 dans la revue Le voile d'isis')

Read, Bernard. Chinese alchemy. Nature 120 (1927) 877.

Roi, J. and Ou Yun-joei. Le taoïsme et les plantes d'immortalité. BUA 3e sér, 2 (1941) 535-546.

Rousselle, E. Seelische führung im lebenden taoismus. EJ 1 (1933) repr of art orig publ in CDA 21 (1934) together with author's Ne ging tu, "die tafel des inneren gewebes"; ein taoistisches meditationsbild mit beschriftung, orig publ in Sinica 8 (1933) 207. See further author's Zur seelischen führung im taoismus; ausgewählte aufsätze, darmstadt (1962)

Rousselle, E. Die typen der meditation in china. CDA (1932) 20-46.

Saso, Michael. The taoists who did not die. Afrasian (student journal, london institute of oriental and african studies) 3 (1970) 13f.

Scaligero, Massimo. Tao and grail: the search of earthly immortality. E&W 8 (1957) 67-72.

Schipper, K. M. (tsl) l'Empereur wou des han dans la légende taoiste; le 'han wou-ti nei-tchouan.' Paris (1965) index, chin text.

Seidel, Anna. La divinisation de lao tseu dans le taoisme des han. Paris (1969) 169 p, app, facs, bibliog, index.

Seidel, Anna. A taoist immortal of the ming dynasty: chang san-feng. In SSMT (1970) 483-526.

Sivin, Nathan. Chinese alchemy: preliminary studies. Harvard univ (1968) 339 p, app, index. Mainly a study of sun ssu-mo's tan ching yao chüeh, with critical ed of text.

Sivin, Nathan. Chinese alchemy as a science. In NCELYY (1970) 35-50.

Sivin, Nathan. On the pao p'u tzu (nei p'ien) and the life of ko hung (283-343 a.d.) Isis 60 (1969) 388f.

Sivin, Nathan. On the reconstruction of chinese alchemy. Japanese studies in the history of science 6 (1967) 60f.

Spooner, Roy C. Chang tao-ling, the first taoist pope. JCE 15 (1938) 503f.

Spooner, Roy C. Chinese alchemy. JWCBorderResS 12 (1940) 82.

Spooner, Roy C. and C. H. Wang. The divine nine-turn tan-sha method, a chinese alchemical recipe. Isis 28 (1948) 235-242.

Stadelmann, Heinrich. Biologie des laotse. Zeitschrift für menschenkunde 12 (1935) 207-225.

Stein, O. References to alchemy in buddhist scriptures. **BSOAS** 7 (1933) 263.

Stein, Rolf A. l'Habitat, le monde et le corps humain en extrême-orient et en haute-asie. **JA** 245 (1957) 37-74.

Stein, Rolf A. Spéculations mystiques et thèmes relatifs aux "cuisines" [ch'u] du taoisme. **ACF** 72 (1972) 489f.

Steininger, Hans. **Hauch- und körperseele und der dämon bei kuan-yin-tze. Untersuchungen zur chinesischen psychologie und ontologie.** Leipzig (1953) 93 p.

Strickmann, M. Notes on mushroom cults in ancient china. Rijksuniversiteit gent, gand (1966) (Paper to the 4e journée des orientalistes belge, brussels, 1966)

Ts'ao, T'ien-ch'in, Ho Ping-yü and Joseph Needham. An early medieval chinese alchemical text on aqueous solutions. **Ambix** 7 (1959) 122-158.

Waley, Arthur. Notes on chinese alchemy. **BSOAS** 6.1 (1930-32) 1-24.

Waley, Arthur. References to alchemy in buddhist scriptures. **BSOAS** 6.4 (1932) 1102-1103.

Waley, Arthur (tsl) **The travels of an alchemist; the journey of the taoist, ch'ang-ch'un . . . from china to the hindukush at the summons of chinghiz khan, recorded by his disciple, li chih-ch'ang.** London (1931) x + 166 p, map.

Ware, J. R. (tsl) **Alchemy, medicine, and religion in the china of a.d. 320. The nei p'ien of ko hung (pao-p'u tzu)** M. I. T. (1966) 388 p.

Wasson, R. G. **Soma. The divine mushroom of immortality.** Harcourt brace johanovich; printed in italy (1968) See chap 13, The marvelous herb [ling chih] 77-92, pl.

Wilhelm, Hellmut. Eine chou-inschrift über atemtechnik. **MS** 13 (1948) 385-388.

Wilhelm, Richard. (tsl) **The secret of the golden flower; a chinese book of life.** Engl tsl Cary F. Baynes. Foreword and comm by C. G. Jung. New, rev and augmented ed n.y. (1962) xvi + 149 p, app, illus. Tsl of two chin texts of two taoist sects.

Wilson, W. J. (ed) Alchemy in china. **Ciba symposia** 2.7 (1940) 594-624, bibliog.

Wu, Lu-ch'iang and Tenney L. Davis. An ancient chinese alchemical classic, ko hung on the gold medicine and on the yellow and the white. The fourth and sixteenth chapters of pao-p'u-tsu. **PAAAS** 70.6 (1935) 221-241.

Wu, Lu-ch'iang and Tenney L. Davis. An ancient chinese treatise on alchemy entitled ts'an t'ung ch'i written by wei po-yang about 142 a.d. **Isis** 18.2 (1932) 210-289.

Wu, Lu-ch'iang and Tenney L. Davis. (tsl) Translation of ko hung's biography in the lie-hsien-chuan. **JCE** (1934) 517-520.

Yewdale, M.S. The therapeutic power of taoism. **AP** 7 (1936) 271-274.

22. MEDITATION - GENERAL

Dumoulin, H. La mystique de l'orient et de l'occident. **BUA** 3e sér, 5 (1944) 152-202.

Lu, K'uan-yü (Charles Luk) **The secrets of chinese meditation. Self-cultivation by mind control as taught in the ch'an, mahāyāna and taoist schools in china.** London (1964) 240 p, gloss, index, illus.

Rousselle, Erwin. Die typen der meditation in china. **CDA** (1932) 20-46.

Wilhelm, Hellmut. Eine chou-inschrift über atemtechnik. **MS** 13 (1948) 385-388.

23. FOLK RELIGION - GENERAL

Bone, Charles. Chinese superstitions. **WMM** 120 (1897) 363-371.

Bredon, Juliet. Hell 'à la chinoise.' The several wards of the taoist inferno. **Asia** 25 (1925) 138-141.

A chapter of folklore. **JNCBRAS** 49 (1918) Four art listed in this bibliog sep by author: H. L. Harding, Lewis Hodous, James Hutson, H. A. Ottewill.

Clarke, G. W. The yü-li or precious records. **JNCBRAS** 28.2 (1893) 233-400. Deals with hells and punishments.

Davaranne, Theodor. **Chinas volksreligion; dargestellt nach einer rundfrage und verglichen mit den grundlehren des laotze, konfuzius und buddha.** Tübingen (1924) 48 p.

Day, Clarence Burton. **Chinese peasant cults. Being a study of chinese paper gods.** Shanghai (1940) repr taipei (1969) 243 p, bibliog, app 1 thru 10, lists of ma-chang (paper gods) illus.

Doré, Henri. **Recherches sur les superstitions en chine.** Shanghai (1911-1938) 18 vol. Being **Variétés sinologiques** no 32, 34, 36, 39, 41-42, 44-46, 48-49, 51, 57, 61-62, 66. Profusely illus. See next item.

Doré, Henri. **Researches into chinese superstitions** (engl tsl of above) Vol 1 (1914) 2 (1915) 3 (1916) 4 (1917) 5 (1918) 6 (1920) 7 (1922) 8 (1926) tsl M. Kennelly, s.j. Vol 9 (1931) 10 (1933) tsl D. J. Finn, s.j. Vol 13 (1938) tsl L. F. McGreal, s.j. Above engl vol all publ shanghai, repr taipei 1966-67. Seven vol remain untsl: 11, 12, 14, 15, 16, 17, 18.

Doré, Henri. **Superstitions chinoises pour les enfants.** RC (oct 1911) 247-253, fig.

Elvin, Arthur. Chinese superstitions. ChRec 21 (1890) 314-320.

Giles, Herbert A. (tsl) **Strange stories from a chinese studio.** Shanghai etc. 4th rev ed (1926) Tsl of liao chai chih yi. See app 1, on purgatory.

Grube, Wilhelm. Die chinesische volksreligion und ihre beeinflussung durch den buddhismus. **Globus** 63 (1893) 297-303.

Grube, W. Sammlung chinesischer volksgötter aus amoy. **Ethnologisches notizblatt** 1.2 (1895) 27-33.

Hefter, J. Über das regenbittopfer. **Zeitschrift für geopolitik** 62 (1930) 337-338.

Hodous, Lewis. Folk religion. In H. F. McNair (ed) **China,** univ california (1946) 231-244.

Hodous, Lewis. **Folkways in china.** London (1929) 248 p, illus. Mostly on foochow.

Hodous, Lewis. The kite festival in foochow. JNCBRAS 49 (1918) 76- 81. Art no 1 under heading: A chapter of folklore.

Horning, Emma. Values in rural chinese religion. ChRec 61 (1930) 39-42, 168-175, 234-238, 288-307, 775-781.

Kermadec, H. de. La religion populaire chinoise actuelle. **Rythmes du monde** 10.2 (1962) 13-36.

Körner, Brunhild. **Die religiöse welt der bäuerin in nord-china.** Stockholm (1959) 86 p, 12 pl.

Leong, Y. K. and L.K. Tao. **Village and town life in china.** London (1915) See The village temple, 32-39.

Mansfield, M. T. Chinese superstitions. **FLJ** 5 (1887) 127-129.

Maspero, Henri. The mythology of modern china. In J. Hackin et al, **Asiatic mythology.** Tsl fr french F. M. Atkinson. N.Y. (n.d.) 252-384, illus.

Nicouleau, M. Superstitions chinoises. **MC** (15 déc 1911) 595-597, fig (22 déc 1911) 610-611.

Oehler, W. Der buddhismus als volksreligion im heutigen china. **EMM** 55 (1911) 308-317.

Oehler, W. Die religion im chinesischen volksleben. In **LO** (1922) 411-454.

Parker, A. G. A study of the religious beliefs and practices of the common people of china. **ChRec** 53.8 (aug 1922) 503-512; 53.9 (sept 1922) 575-585.

Peeters, Hermes. **The religions of china. Confucianism, taoism, buddhism, popular belief.** Peking (1941) 64 p.

Pommeranz-Liedtke, Gerhard. Bilder für jedes neue jahr. Zur wandlung des chinesischen neujahrbildes. **ZBK** 1 (1955)

Pommeranz-Liedtke, Gerhard. **Chinesische neujahrsbilder.** Dresden (1961) 202 p, biblog, pl.

Ringgren, Helmer and Ake Ström. **Die religionen der völker. Grundriss der allgemeinen religionsgeschichte.** Stuttgart (1959) Tsl fr swedish Inga Ringgren and C. M. Schröder. See pt 4, Die ostasiatischen schriftkulturen: die chinesen, 419-436.

Schlegel, Gustave. Der todtenvogel bei den chinesen. **IAE** 11 (1898) 86-87.

Smith, Arthur H. **Village life in china. A study in sociology.** N.Y. (1899) See chap 11, Village temples and religious societies, 136-140; chap 12, Cooperation in religious observances, 141-145.

Stewart-Lockhart, J. H. Chinese folk-lore. **Folk-lore** 1 (1890) 359-368.

Topley, Marjorie. Paper charms, and prayer sheets as adjuncts to chinese worship. **JMBRAS** 26 (1953) 63-80, illus.

Vale, Joshua. **Chinese superstitions.** Shanghai (1904) 27 p, london (1906) 48 p.

Vandier-Nicolas, N. Le jugement des morts en chine. In **Le jugement des morts,** paris (1961) 231-254 ('Sources orientales' no 4)

Vleeschower, E. de. K'i yu [ch'i yü, praying for rain] **FS** 2 (1943) 39-50.

Willoughby-Meade, Gerald. **Chinese ghouls and goblins.** London (1928) xv + 431 p, illus.

Wright, A. R. Some chinese folk-lore. **Folk-lore** 14 (1903) 292-298.

24. LOCAL STUDIES – MAINLAND

Aijmer, Göran. **The dragon boat festival in the hunan and hupeh plains, central china: a study in the cere-monialism of the transplantation of rice.** Stockholm (1964) 135 p, bibliog.

Bodde, Derk (tsl) **Annual customs and festivals in peking, as recorded in the yen-ching sui-shih-chi by tun li-ch'en.** Peiping (1936) repr univ hong kong (1965) with new intro and corr; xxii + 147, 6 app, bibliog, index, illus, end-paper plan of peking.

Bone, C. The religious festivals of the cantonese. **ChRec** 20 (1889) 367-371, 391-393.

Bouillard, G. Calendrier chinois et européen à l'usage des residents de peking. **La chine** (all following 1922) 10: 69-76; 12: 282-284; 14: 453-460; 16: 603-608; 18: 721-723; 20: 881-882; 22: 1081-1086; 24: 1205-1209; 26: 1353-1356; 28: 1529-1532; 29: 1583-1586.

Bouillard, G. Usages et coutumes à pékin durant la (1) 2e lune. **La chine** 35 (1923) 117-136; (2) 3e lune: 37 (1923) 249-264; (3) 4e lune: 38 (1923) 299-311; (4) 5e lune: 18 (1922) 703-720; (5) 6e lune: 39 (1923) 391-405; (6) 7e lune: 40 (1923) 469-479; (7) 8e lune: 26 (1922) 1335-1355; (8) 9e lune: 29 (1922) 1573-1582; (9) 10e lune: 30 (1922) 1639-1651; (10) 11e lune: 32 (1922) 1791-1796.

Box, Ernest. Shanghai folk-lore. (1) **JNCBRAS** 34 (1901-02) 101-135 (2) **Ibid** 36 (1905) 130-156.

Brown, Frederick R. **Religion in tientsin.** Shanghai (1908) 62 p.

Brown, Frederick R. Superstitions common in kiangsi province. **NCR** 4.6 (1922) 493-504.

Brown, H. G. What the gods say in west china. **JWCBorderResS** 3 (1926-29) 134-150.

Chao, Wei-pang. The dragon-boat race in wu-ling, hunan. **FS** 2 (1943) 1-18.

Chao, Wei-pang. Games at the mid-autumnal festival in kuangtung. **FS** 3.1 (1944) 1-16.

Coffin, Edna, et al. Religion. In Far eastern and russian institute, univ washington (comp) **A regional handbook on northwest china.** HRAF 1 (1956) 324-363.

Cordier, G. Croyances populaires au yunnan. **RIC** (juin 1909) 597-601. Same title in **La chine** 36 (1923) 203-208 .

Culbertson, M. Simpson. **Darkness in the flowery land; or religious notions and popular superstitions in north china.** N.Y. (1857) 235 p.

Daudin, P. Deux amulettes du yunnan. **BSEIS** n.s. 21 (1946) 35-40.

Day, C. B. Shanghai invites the god of wealth. **CJ** 8 (1928) 289-294.

Dols, J. Fêtes et usages pendant le courant d'une année dans la province de kan-sou (chine) **AL** 1 (1937) 203-274.

Doré, Henri. **Manuel des superstitions chinoises.** Chang-hai [shanghai] 2e ed (1936) 221 p.

Eberhard, Wolfram. **The local cultures of south and east china.** Leiden (1968) 520 p. Tsl fr german Alide Eberhard. "A greatly revised version of the second volume of my **Lokalkulturen im alten china** in english translation." See passim.

Eberhard, Wolfram. **Studies in chinese folklore and related essays.** Indiana univ and the hague (1970) 329 p, notes, bibliog, index, illus. All but 3 studies are republ, and most are tsl fr german William Templer. See pt 1: Essays on the folklore of chekiang, china.

Eberhard, Wolfram. The supernatural in chinese folk-tales from chekiang. In Wayland D. Hand (ed) **Humaniora . . . essays honoring archer taylor . . .** Locust valley, n.y. and gluckstadt (1960) 335-341.

Eberhard, Wolfram. Zur volkskunde ven chêkiang. **ZE** 67 (1935) 248-265.

Edgar, J. H. Notes on litholatry on the western frontiers of china. **CJ** 4 (1926) 105-110.

Edgar, J. H. The sin bearer, a note on comparative religion. **JWCBorderResS** 3 (1926-29) p 151.

Eitel, E. J. The religion of the hakkas. **NQ** 1.12 (dec 1867) 161-163; 2.10 (oct 1868) 145-147; 2.11 (nov 1868) 167-169; 3.1 (jan 1869) 1-3.

Ethnographische beiträge aus der ch'ing hai provinz, zusammengest. von ch'ing hai missionären anlassl. des 75. jahrgen jubiläums der gesellschaft des göttlichen wortes. Catholic univ of peking (1952) [publ in japan] 354 p, 10 pl.

Ewer, F. H. Some accounts of festivals in canton. **ChRec** 3.7 (dec 1870) 185-188.

Ewer, F.H. and J. Doolittle. Native fete and natal days observed at canton and foochow. In **DV** 2, pt 3, no 30.

Fabre, A. Avril au pays des aïeux. **CCS** vol 8 (1935) Ancestor worship and burial practices re ch'ing ming, specifically in shun-tê, kuangtung.

Faulder, H. Croyier. The temples of shanghai. **CJ** 30.6 (june 1939) 340-345.

Fêng, Han-yi and John K. Shryock. Marriage customs in the vicinity of i-ch'ang. **HJAS** 13 (1950) 362-430.

Freedman, Maurice. **Chinese lineage and society: fukien and kwangtung.** Univ london (1966) See esp chap 5, Geomancy and ancestor worship, 118-154, incl photos.

Frick, Johann. How blood is used in magic and medicine in ch'inghai province. **Anthropos** 46 (1951) 964-979. Tsl fr german J. E. Mertz.

Frick, Johann. Magic remedies used on sick children in the western valley of sining. **Anthropos** 46 (1951) 175-186. German orig in **ibid** 45 (1950) 787-800.

Frick, Johannes. Die regenprozession in lungsi, nordwest china. In **Festschrift paul schebesta zum 75. geburstag,** vienna-mödling (1963) 385-400.

Frick, J. Der traum und seine deutung bei den chinesen in ch'inghai. **Anthropos** 49 (1954) 311-313.

Gamble, Sidney D. **North china villages. Social, political, and economic activities before 1933.** Univ california (1963) See 119-125 on community religion; 239-262 on history of a specific clan.

Graham, David Crockett. **Folk religion in southwest china.** Washington, d.c. (1961) 246 p, bibliog, index, illus. Folk religion in ssuch'uan.

Graham, David C. Notes on the primitive religion of the chinese in szechuan. **JWCBorderResS** 1 (1922-23) 53-55.

Graham, David C. **Religion in szechuan province china.** Washington, d.c. (1928) 83 p, 25 pl.

Graham, David C. Religion of the chinese in szechwan. **ChRec** 66.6 (june 1935) 363-369; 66.7 (july 1935) 421-428; 66.8 (aug 1935) 484-490; 66.9 (sept 1935) 547-555.

Graham, David C. Some strange customs in szechwan province (1) the 'human chicken' (2) human sacrifices in west china (3) uprisings of the boxers or red lantern society. **JWCBorderResS** 8 (1936) 141-144.

Graham, David C. The temples of suifu. **ChRec** 61 (1930) 108-120.

Graham, David C. Tree gods in szechwan province. **JWCBorderResS** 8 (1936) 59-61, 2 photos.

Groot, J. J. M. de. **Les fêtes annuellement célébrées à emoui (amoy). Étude concernant la religion populaire des chinois.** (Being **AMG** 11 and 12) Paris (1886) 2 vol. Tsl fr dutch C. G. Chavannes.

Grootaers, Willem A. The hagiography of the chinese god chen-wu. (The transmission of rural traditions in chahar) **FS** 11 (1952) 139-182.

Grootaers, Willem A. The hutu god of wan-ch'uan (chahar) **SS** 7 (1948) 41-53.

Grootaers, W. A. Rural temples around hsuan-hua (south chahar), their iconography and their history. **FS** 10 (1951) 1-116.

Grootaers, W. A. Les temples villageois de la région au sud de tat'ong (chansi nord), leurs inscriptions et leur histoire. **FS** 4 (1945) 161-212.

Grootaers, W.A., Li Shih-yü and Chang Chi-wen. Temples and history of wanch'üan (chahar). The geographical method applied to folklore. **MS** 13 (1948) 209-316.

Grube, Wilhelm. Pekinger todtengebräuche. **JPOS** 4 (1898) 79-142.

Grube, W. Sammlung chinesischer volksgötter aus amoy. **Ethnologisches notizblatt** 1.2 (1895) 27-33.

Gutzlaff, Charles. Temple of teen how [t'ien hou] at meichow. **ChRep** 2 (1834) 563-565.

Harding, H. L. On a method of divination practised at foochow. **JNCBRAS** 49 (1918) 82-85. Art no 2 under heading, A chapter of folklore.

Headland, Isaac T. Religion in peking. In **WPR** (1893) vol 2, 1019-1023.

Herrmann, F. Zur volkskunde der hakka in kuang-tung. **Sinica** 12 (1937) 18-38.

Hodous, Lewis. **Folkways in china.** London (1929) 248 p, illus. Mostly on foochow.

Hodous, Lewis, The great summer festival of china as observed in foochow: a study in popular religion. **JNCBRAS** 43 (1912) 69-80.

Hodous, Lewis. The reception of spring as observed in foochow, china. **JAOS** 42 (1922) 53-58.

Hsu, Francis L. K. **Magic and science in western yunnan.** N.Y. (1943) 53 p.

Hsu, Francis L. K. **Religion, science and human crisis.** London (1952) 142 p. West town, yunnan.

Hsu, Francis L. K. **Under the ancestors' shadow. Chinese culture and personality.** Columbia univ (1948) re-issued stanford univ (1967) with new chap (Re west town, yunnan) See 'The world of spirits,' 136-143; 'Man's relation with spiritual worlds,' 144-154.

James, F. H. North-china sects. **ChRec** 30 (1899) 74-76.

Johnston, R. F. **Lion and dragon in northern china.** London (1910) See chap 8-17, for religion in territory of weihaiwei, 155-425.

Körner, Brunhild. Nan-lao-ch'üan, eine flutsage aus westchina, und ihre auswirkung auf örtliches brauchtum. **Ethnos** 15.1/2 (jan-mar 1950) 46-56.

Körner, Brunhild. **Die reliöse welt der bäuerin in nordchina.** Stockholm (1959) 86 p, 12 pl.

Kulp, Daniel Harrison, II. **Country life in south china. The sociology of familism. Vol 1, Phenix village, kwangtung, china.** Columbia univ (1925) repr taipei (1966) See esp chap 10, Religion and the spiritual community, 284-314.

Laprairie, Père. Les religions du seutchouan. **Revue nationale chinoise** 41, no 134 (fev 1941) 125-142.

Leung, A. K. Peiping's happy new year. **NGM** 70 (1936) 749-792.

Li, Wei-tsu. On the cult of the four sacred animals (szu ta men) in the neighborhood of peking. **FS** 7 (1948) 1-94 (fox, weasel, hedge-hog, snake)

Liu, Chiang. Fukien folkways and religion. **ChRec** 64 (1933) 701-713. See also same title in **ACSS** (1957) 20-35.

Liu, Chiang. Religion, funeral rites, sacrifices and festivals in kirin. **ChRec** 65 (1934) 227-238. See also same title in **ACSS** (1958-59) 8-20.

Lutschewitz, W. Die religiösen sekten in nord-china, mit besonderer berücksichtigung d. sekten in shantung. **OstL** (1905) 1: 203-207, 247-251, 291-293, 337-340.

Macintyre, John. Roadside religion in manchuria. **JNCBRAS** n.s. 21.1 (1886) 43-66.

Maclagan, P. J. Folk-lore. Account of some customs observed in the first moon in the village of yü-lu-hsiang, ch'ao-chou-fu, chieh-yang hsien. **ChRev** 23 (1894-95) 120.

Martin, Ilse. Frühlingsdoppelsprüche (ch'un-lien) von 1942 an pekinger haustüren. **FS** 2 (1943) 89-174.

Murray, A. S. Religion in the villages of north china. **Religion** 16 (july 1936) 18-25.

Ng, Yong-sang. Fa-ti, land of flowers. Canton's new year pilgrimage to its garden suburb. **CJ** 20 (1934) 184-186.

Ng, Yong-sang. The temple of no sorrows. A cantonese santa claus story. **CJ** 19 (1933) 280-284.

Oberle, A. Der hundertkopfdämon im volksglauben des westtales und des chinesisch-tibetanischen kontaktgebietes im osttale von kuei-te in der provinz ch'ing-hai. In **Ethnographische beiträge aus der ch'inghai provinze (china)** Peking (1952) 222-233.

Osgood, Cornelius. **Village life in old china. A community study of kao yao, yunnan.** N.Y. (1963) Field work done 1938. See chap 18, Death and funerals, 288-300; chap 19, The shaman performs, 301-317; chap 20, Religious ideas, 320-327; chap 21 The ceremonial year, 328-345.

Palen, Lewis S. A guest of the empress of heaven. At home with gods and beggars in an ancient temple in manchuria. **Asia** 29 (1929) 50-53, 74-75, illus photos.

Porter, Henry D. A modern shantung prophet. **ChRec** 18 (1887) 12-21.

Potter, Jack M. Wind, water, bones and souls: the religious world of the cantonese peasant [ping shan, new territories of hong kong] **JOS** 8.1 (1970) 139-153. Repr in **CWayRel** (1973) 218-230.

Religion. In Stanford univ china project (comp) **East China, HRAF** 1 (1956) 344-387.

Religion. In Stanford univ china project (comp) **North china, HRAF** 1 (1956) 318-366.

Religion. In Stanford univ china project (comp) **Southwest china, HRAF** 1 (1956) 321-377.

Sadler, J. Chinese customs, and superstitions; or, what they do at amoy. **ChRev** 22 (1893-94) 755-758.

Schroeder, D. Das herbstdankopfer der t'ujen im sining-gebiet, nordwestchina. **Anthropos** 37-40 (1942-45) 867-873.

Shryock, John K. **The temples of anking and their cults. A study of modern chinese religion.** Paris (1931) 203 p, app, bibliog, index, illus.

Sowerby, A. de C. A monster procession in shanghai [kuan-yin] **CJ** 21 (1934) 6-7.

Spring festival in shanghai. **FEER** 51 (3 mar 1966) 413-415, illus.

Stenz, Georg M. **Beiträge zur volkskunde südschantungs.** Leipzig (1907) 1116p. Herausgegeben und eingeleitet von A.Conrady.

Swallow, Robert W. **Sidelights on peking life.** Peking (1927) xviii + 135 p, illus.

Tang, Peter S. H. Religion. In Far eastern and russian institute, univ washington (comp) **A regional handbook on northeast china, HRAF** 1 (1956) 227-243.

Thiel, Joseph. Der erdgeist-tempel als weiterentwicklung des alten eralters. (Aus eigener feldforschung in süd-shantung) **Sinologica** 5.3 (1958) 150-155, illus 10 photos.

Trippner, J. Der wandernde medizingott. **Anthropos** 46 (1951) 801-807. In ch'ing-hai.

Volpert, Ant. Volksgebräuche bei der neujahrsfeier in ost-schantung (china) **Anthropos** 12-13 (1917-18) 1118-1119.

Wen, Chung-i. The water gods and the dragon boats in south china. **ASBIE** 11 (1961) engl summ 121-124, 6 pl.

Wimsatt, G. B. Peking gate gods. **AArch** 26 (1928) 127-133.

Wong, C. M. The ancient customs of cantonese marriage. **ACSS** (1960-61) 60-65.

25. DEITIES AND IMAGES – GENERAL

Amicus. Demons. **ICG** 5 (1818) 144-145.

Buck, Samuel (pseud) The chinese spirit world. **Orient** 2.1 (1951) 31-34; 2.2 (1951) 21-24; 2.3 (1951) 31-34; 2.4 (1951) 22-25; 2.5 (1951) 26-28; 2.6 (1952) 32-35; 2.7 (1952) 39-42; 2.8 (1952) 31-33; 2.9 (1952) 31-34; 2.10 (1952) 28-30, 32; 2.11 (1952) 51-54; 2.12 (1952) 48-51.

Day, Clarence Burton. **Chinese peasant cults. Being a study of chinese paper gods.** Shanghai (1940) 243 p, bibliog, app 1-10, index, illus.

Day, C. B. Paper gods for sale. **CJ** 7 (1927) 277-284.

Dean, J. A. Consecrated images of china. **CJ** 21 (1934) 150-161.

Erkes, E. Gestaltwandel der götter in china. **FF** 21-22 (1947) 261-266.

Erkes, E. Idols in pre-buddhist china. **AA** 3 (1928) 5-12.

Frei, G. Zum chinesischen gottesbegriff. **NZM** 1 (1945) 221-228.

Graham, David C. Image worship in china. **ChRec** 60 (1929) 513-514.

Haydon, A. Eustace. **Biography of the gods.** N.Y. (1941) See chap 7, The gods of china, 166-198; see also chap 6, Buddhas and bodhisattvas, 126-165, passim.

Hayes, L. Newton. Gods of the chinese. **JNCBRAS** 55 (1924) 84-104.

Knodt, E. **Chinesische götter.** Berlin (1916)

Lanjuinais, J. D. Notice du panthéon-chinois du docteur hager. **Moniteur** (1807)

Maclagan, P. J. Demons and spirits (chinese) In **HERE** 4, 576-578.

Mong, Lee Siow. Chinese polytheism. **ACSS** (1962-63) 15-17.

Montell, G. The idol factory of peking. **Ethnos** 19 (1954) 143-156.

Perzynski, F. Von chinas göttern. **Neue orient** 6 (1920) 192-196.

The Soul of an idol. **Our missions** (1905) 30.

26. SPECIFIC DEITIES AND CULTS

Ayscough, Florence. The chinese cult of ch'eng huang lao yeh. **JNCBRAS** 55 (1924) 131-155.

Bedford, O. H. Kuan yü, china's god of war. **CJ** 27 (1937) 127-130.

Behrsing, S. Tou-mu, eine chinesische himmels-göttin. **OZ** 27 (1941) 173-176.

Blodget, Henry. The worship of the earth in china. **MRW** n.s. 10 (1897) 519-521.

Bridgman, J. G. (tsl) Mythological account of some chinese deities, chiefly those connected with the elements. Translated from the siú shin-ki [sou shen chi] **ChRep** 19 (1850) 312-317.

Buck, Samuel (pseud) Gods and goddesses of navigation. **Orient** (apr 1952) 25-27.

Buck, Samuel (pseud) Why chinese women worship kwan yin. **Orient** 2.8 (1952) 18-20, 22.

Chamberlayne, John H. The chinese earth-shrine. **Numen** 13 (oct 1966) 164-182.

Chamberlayne, John H. The development of kuan yin, chinese goddess of mercy. **Numen** 9 (1962) 45-62.

Chan, Ping-leung. Chinese popular water-god legends and the hsi yu chi. In **Essays in chinese studies presented to professor lo hsiang-lin,** univ hong kong (1970) 299-317.

Chavannes, Édouard. Le jet des dragons. **Mémoires concernant l'asie orientale** 3. Paris (1919) 53-220, pl + reproductions of rubbings and texts.

Chavannes, Édouard. **Le t'ai chan. Essai de monographie d'un culte chinois. Appendice: Le dieu du sol dans la chine antique.** Paris (1910) repr taipei (1970) 591 p, maps, pl, index.

Chêng, Tê-K'un. Ch'ih yü: the god of war in han art. **OA** 4.2 (summer 1958) 45-54.

D. G. The kitchen-god. **ChRev** 7 (1878-79) 418-422; 8 (1879-80) 388-390.

Day, Clarence B. Contemporary chinese cults. **FEQ** 6 (1947) 294-299.

Day, Clarence B. The cult of the hearth. **CJ** 10 (1929) 6-11.

Day, Clarence B. Kuan-yin: goddess of mercy. **CJ** 10 (1929) 288-295.

Day, Clarence B. Shanghai invites the god of wealth. **CJ** 8 (1928) 289-294.

Day, Clarence B. Studying the kitchen god. **ChRec** 57 (1926) 791-796.

Drake, F. S. The tao yüan, a new religious and spiritualistic movement. **ChRec** 54 (mar 1923) 133-144.

Dudgeon, John H. Medical divinities. In **DV** vol 2, pt 3, no 26, 318-319.

Dudgeon, John H. The worship of the moon. **ChRec** 13.2 (mar-apr 1882) 129-134.

Eastlake, F. Warrington. Equine deities. **TASJ** 11 (1883) 260-285.

Edgar, J. H. Notes on litholatry on the western frontiers of china. **CJ** 4 (1926) 105-110.

Edkins, Joseph. Account of kwan-ti, the god of war. **NCH** no 313 and 314, (26 july and 2 aug 1856) Repr in **Shanghai miscellany** (1857) no paging.

Edkins, Joseph. Place of hwang ti in early tauism. **ChRev** 15 (1886-87) 233-239.

Edkins, Joseph. Titles of tauist gods. **ChRev** 24.4 (1895-96) 199.

Edkins, Joseph. The use of the term . . . yu-hwang, addressed to mathetes. **ChRec** 25 (feb 1894) 91-92.

Edkins, Joseph. Worship of the god of fire. **ChRev** 18.2 (1889-90) 124-125.

Eitel, E. J. On dragon-worship. **NQ** 3.3 (mar 1869) 34-36.

Erkes, E. Zum problem der weiblichen kuanyin. **AA** 9 (1946) 316-320, illus.

Esbroek, A. van. Les cultes préhistoriques de la chine. **Nouvelle Clio** 5 (1953) 195-196.

Fêng, H. Y. The origin of yü huang. **HJAS** 1 (1936) 242-250.

Graham, David C. Original vows of the kitchen god. **ChRec** 61 (1930) 781-788; 62 (1931) 41-50, 110-116.

Graham, David C. Tree gods in szechwan province. **JWCBorderResS** 8 (1936) 59-61.

Groot, J. J. M. de. The idol kwoh shing wang. **ChRev** 7 (1878-79) 91-98.

Groot, J. J. M. de. Two gods of literature and a god of barbers. **ChRev** 9 (1880-81) 188-190.

Grootaers, Willem A. The hagiography of the chinese god chen-wu. (The transmission of rural traditions in chahar) **FS** 11 (1952) 139-182.

Grootaers, Willem A. The hutu god of wan-ch'üan (chahar) **SS** 7 (1948) 41-53.

Gutzlaff, Charles. Temple of teen how [t'ien hou] at meichow. **ChRep** 2 (1834) 563-565.

Hart, H. H. Kuan yin, the goddess of mercy. **AP** 11 (1940) 527-529.

Hodous, Lewis. The chinese church of the five religions. **JR** 4 (1924) 71-76.

Hodous, Lewis. The god of war. **ChRec** 44 (1913) 479-486.

Hommel, R. P. The idols of the thieves. **CJ** 10 (1929) 57-58.

Hsu, Shin-yi. The traditional ecology of the locust cult in traditional china. **Annals of the association of american geographers** 59.4 (dec 1969) 731-752.

Hudspeth, W. H. Tree worship. **CJ** 7 (1927) 206-208.

Huizenga, Lee S. Lü tsu and his relation to other medicine gods. **CMJ** 58 (1940) 275-283.

Hummel, Siegbert. Guan-yin in der unterwelt. **Sinologica** 2 (1950) 291-293, pl.

Hutson, James. Chia shen, the domestic altar. **JNCBRAS** 49 (1918) 93-100. Art 4 under heading: A chapter of folklore.

Johnston, R. F. The cult of military heroes in china. **NCR** 3 (feb 1921) 41-64; 3 (apr 1921) 79-91.

K. F. Die chinesische totencult. **OstL** 7.25 (1893) 548-549.

Kao, Chǔ-hsün. The ching lu shen shrines of han sword worship in hsiung-nu religion. **Central asiatic journal** 5 (1960) 221-232.

Koehn, Alfred. Harbingers of happiness, the door gods of china. Peiping (1948) 38 p, illus. Same title in **MN** 10 (1954) 81-106.

Lacouperie, Terrien de. The kitchen-god of china. **BOR** 8 (1895) 25-38.

Lacouperie, Terrien de. The silk goddess of china and her legend. **BOR** 4.12 (1890) 270-290; 5.1 (1891) 5-10.

Lecourt, H. Le dieu de l'âtre. **La chine** 70 (1924) 781-788.

Lee, Pi-cheng [Lǚ Pi-ch'eng] **Kwan yin's saving power; some remarkable examples of response to appeals for aid, made known to kwan yin by his devotees.** Oxford (1932) 39 p.

Lee, Tao. Ten celebrated physicians and their temple. **CMJ** 58 (1940) 267-274.

Li, Wei-tsu. On the cult of the four sacred animals (szu ta men) in the neighborhood of peking. **FS** 7 (1948) 1-94 (fox, weasel, hedgehog, snake)

Ling, Shun-sheng. The sacred places of chin and han periods. **ASBIE** 18 (1964) engl abrmt 136-142.

Liu, Chi-wan. The belief and practice of the wen-shen cult in south china and formosa. **PIAHA** (1963?) 715-722.

Liu, Chi-wan. The temple of the gods of epidemics in taiwan. **ASBIE** 22 (1966) 93-95.

Lou, Dennis Wing-sou. Rain worship among the ancient chinese and the nahua and maya indians **ASBIE** 4 (1957) 31-108.

Lyon, David N. Life and writings of the god of literature (wen ti ch'üan shu) **ChRec** 20 (1889) 411-420, 439-449.

Maspero, Henri. The mythology of modern china. In J. Hackin et al, **Asiatic mythology**, n.y. (n.d.) 252-384, illus. Tsl fr french F. M. Atkinson.

Mayers, William F. On wen-ch'ang, the god of literature: his history and worship. **JNCBRAS** n.s. 6 (1869/70) 31-44.

McCartee, D. B. (tsl) Translation of an inscription upon a stone tablet commemorating the repairs upon the ch'eng hwang miau or temple of the tutelary deity of the city . . . in the department of lai-chôu, in the province of shantung, a.d. 1752. **JNCBRAS** 6 (1869-70) 173-177.

M'Clatchie, T. Phallic worship. **ChRev** 4 (1875-76) 257-261.

Miao, D. F. Ho ho, the gods of marriage. **CJ** 16 (1932) 112-114.

Mortier, F. Le dragon chinois, son culte et ses fêtes. **BSAB** 62 (1951) 136-140.

Nagel, August. Die sieben schwestern. **OstL** 25.46 (17 nov 1911) 425-426.

Ng, Yong-sang, Lung mu, the dragon mother. The story of west river's own guardian angel. **CJ** 25 (1936) 18-20.

Ottewill, H. A. Note on the tu t'ien hui . . . held at chinkiang on the 31st may, 1917. **JNCBRAS** 49 (1918) 86-92. Art 3 under heading, A chapter of folklore.

Owen, G. Animal worship among the chinese. **ChRec** 18 (1887) 249-255, 334-346.

Parker, E. H. Medical deities. **ChRev** 17 (1888-89) 115.

Parker, E. H. Saints of literature. **ChRev** 15 (1886-87) 183-184.

Pfizmaier, A. Ueber die schriften des kaisers des wen-tschang. **SAWW** 73 (1873) 329-384. Also publ sep, wien (1873) 58 p.

Priest, Alan. A note on kuan ti. **BMMA** 25 (1930) 271-272.

Rostovtzeff, M. I. Le dieu équestre dans la russe méridionale, en indo-scythie et en chine. **Seminarium kondakovianum** 1 (1927) 141-146.

Rotours, Robert des. Le culte des cinq dragons sous la dynastie des t'ang (618-907) In **MSPD** (1966) t 1, 261-280, pl.

Rousselle, Erwin. Der kult der buddhistischen madonna kuan-yin. **NachrDGNVO** no 68 (1944) 17-23.

Rydh, H. Seasonal fertility rites and the death cult in scandinavia and china. **BMFEA** 3 (1931) 69-93.

Schlegel, G. Ma-tsu-po . . . koan-yin with the horse-head . . . **TP** 9.5 (1898) 402-406.

Schultze, O. Der chines. drache u. s. vereheung. **EMM** (1891) 13-27.

The seven lucky gods. **Orient** 2.8 (1952) 29-30.

S[huck] J. L. (tsl) Sketch of kwanyin, the chinese goddess of mercy. Translated from the sow shin ke [sou shen chi] **ChRep** 10 (1841) 185-191.

S[huck] J. L. (tsl) Sketch of teĕn fe [t'ien fei] or matsoo po, the goddess of chinese seamen. Translated from the sow shin ke [sou chen chi] **ChRep** 10 (1841) 84-87.

S[huck] J. L. (tsl) Sketch of yuhwang shangte, one of the highest deities of chinese mythology. Translated from the sow shin ke [sou chen chi] **ChRep** 10 (1841) 305-309.

Smith, D. Howard. Saviour gods in chinese religion. In **SG** (1963) 174-190.

Smith, G. Elliott. Dragons and rain gods. **Bulletin of the john ryland's library** 5 (1918-20) 317-380.

Spruyt, Dr. Les génies gardiens des portes. **Chine et sibérie** 2 (mai 1901) 193-195.

Suzuki, D. T. The kuan-yin cult in china. **EB** 6 (1935) 339-353.

Thiel, P. I. Der erdgeist-tempel als weiterentwicklung des alten erdalters. (Aus eigener feldforschung in süd-shantung) **Sinologica** 5.3 (1958) 150-155, 10 photos.

Tran-Ham-Tan. Étude sur le van-mien [wen-miao] de ha-noi (temple de la littérature) **BEFEO** 45 (1951) 89-117, planche.

Trippner, J. Der wandernde medizingott. **Anthropos** 46 (1951) 801-807.

Volpert, P. A. Tsch'ŏng huang [ch'eng huang] **Anthropos** 5.5/6 (sept-dec 1910) 991-1026.

Wen, Chung-i. The water gods and the dragon-boats in south china. **ASBIE** 11 (1961) engl summ 121-124,6 pl.

Werner, E. T. C. Chinese composite deities. **JNCBRAS** 54 (1923) 250-267.

Wiethoff, Bodo. Der staatliche ma-tsu kult. **ZDMG** 116.2 (1966) 311-357.

Williams, E. T. The worship of lei tsu, patron saint of silk workers. **JNCBRAS** 66 (1935) 1-14.

Williams, S. Wells. Mythological account of hiuen-tien shangti, the high ruler of the sombre heavens, with notices of the worship of shangti among the chinese. **ChRep** 18 (1849) 102 et seq.

Wimsatt, G. B. Peking gate gods. **AArch** 26 (1928) 127-133.

Wong, K. Chimin. Hua t'o, the god of surgery. **CMJ** 41 (1927)

Wright, A. R. Chinese tree-worship and trial by ordeal. **Folk-lore** 22 (1911) 233-234.

Wright, A. R. Tree worship in china. **Folklore** 17 (1906) 190.

Wu ti. Die kriegsgott d. chinesen. **OstL** 13 (1899) 50.

27. FESTIVALS - CUSTOMS - RELIGIOUS CALENDAR

Adam, Maurice. Us et coutumes de la région de pékin, d'après le je sia sieou wen k'ao, ch. 146-147-148. Pékin (1930) viii + 48 p, pl.

Aijmer, Göran. **The dragon boat festival in the hunan and hupeh plains, central china; a study in the ceremonialism of the transplantation of rice.** Stockholm (1964) 135 p, bibliog.

Allen, G. W. New year decorations in china. **Discovery** 3 (1922) 188-190.

Bateson, Joseph H. Festivals and fasts (chinese) In **HERE** 5, p 843.

Bell of antermony. Fêtes données à la cour à l'occasion de la nouvelle année, 1721. **La Chine** 12 (1922) 215-220.

Bodde, Derk. **Annual customs and festivals in peking, as recorded in the yen-ching sui-shih-chi by tun li-ch'en.** Peiping (1936) repr univ hong kong (1965) xxii + 147, 6 app, bibliog, index, illus.

Bone, C. The chinese moon festival. **EA** 5 (1906) 29-32.

Bone, C. The religious festivals of the cantonese. **ChRec** 20 (1889) 367-371, 391-393.

Bouillard, G. Calendrier chinois et européen à l'usage des residents de pékin. **La chine** (all 1922) 10: 69-76; 12: 282-284; 14: 453-460; 16: 603-608; 18: 721-723; 20: 881-882; 22: 1081-1086; 24: 1205-1209; 26: 1353-1356; 28: 1529-1532; 29: 1583-1586.

Bouillard, G. La nouvelle année chinoise, usages et coutumes. **La chine** 11 (1922) 127-181.

Bouillard, G. Les pèlerinages de la première quinzaine de la première lune. **La chine** 12 (15 fev 1922) 193-213.

Bouillard, G. Usages et coutumes à pékin durant la (1) 2e lune. **La chine** 35 (1923) 117-136; (2) 3e lune: 37 (1923) 249-264; (4) 4e lune: 38 (1923) 229-311; (5) 5e lune: 18 (1922) 703-720; (6) 6e lune: 39 (1923) 391-405; (7) 7e lune: 40 (1923) 469-479; (8) 8e lune: 26 (1922) 1335-1355; (9) 9e lune: 29 (1922) 1573-1582; (10) 10e lune: 30 (1922) 1639-1651; (11) 11e lune: 32 (1922) 1791-1796.

Bredon, Juliet. **Chinese new year festivals: a picturesque monograph of the rites, ceremonies and observances in relation thereto.** Shanghai (1930) 29 p.

Bredon, Juliet and Igor Mitrophanow. **The moon year. A record of chinese customs and festivals.** Shanghai (1927) 508 p, bibliog, chart, index, illus.

Buck, Samuel (pseud) (a series in **Orient**) The chinese first moon – new year,1.7 (feb 1951) 22-24; The chinese second moon – earth spirits,1.8 (mar 1951) 22-24; The chinese third moon – ch'ing ming,1.9 (apr 1951) 22-24; The chinese fourth moon – buddhism,1.10 (may 1951) 17-19; The chinese fifth moon – dragon boat festival,1.11 (june 1951) 20-22; The chinese sixth moon – china's methuselah,1.12 (july 1951) 17-20; The chinese eighth moon – mid-autumn,1.2 (sept 1950) 18-20; The chinese ninth moon – the double ninth, 1.2 (sept 1950) 20-23; The chinese tenth moon,1.4 (nov 1950) 20-22; The chinese eleventh moon – astrological influences,1.5 (dec 1950) 20-22; The chinese twelfth moon – oracles,1.6 (jan 1951) 20-22.

Buck, Samuel (pseud) Origin of the dragon boat. **Orient** 2.11 (1952) 37-40.

Burkhardt, Valentine R. **Chinese creeds and customs.** Hong kong. Vol 1 (1953) 181 p; vol 2 (1955) 201 p; vol 3 (1958) 164 p; each vol with index, illus.

Chao, Wei-pang. The dragon-boat race in wu-ling, hunan. **FS** 2 (1943) 1-18.

Chao, Wei-pang. Games at the mid-autumnal festival in kuangtung. **FS** 3.1 (1944) 1-16.

Charpentier, Léon. Les fêtes du nouvel an et du renouveau en chine. **NR** n.s. 8 (1901) 161-176.

Cheng, Homer Hui-ming. **Chinese religious festivals in singapore.** Singapore, china society annual publication (1949)

Chinese customs and superstitions. **EA** 4 (1905) 298-300. See further same title in **ibid**, 5 (1906) 99-100.

Das Chinesische neujahr und seine feier. **OstL** 18 (1904) 267-269.

Chu, Liang-cheng. New year and gods. **FCR** 11.2 (1961) 13-16.

Cormack, Annie. **Chinese birthday, wedding, funeral, and other customs.** Peking (1922) 220 p, pl.

Cormack, Annie. **Chinese births, weddings and deaths.** Peking (1923) 35 p, pl.

Cormack, Annie. **Everyday customs in china.** Edinburgh and london (1935) 264 p, illus.

Daudin, P. Coutumes du nouvel an chinois. **FA** 6 (1950) 864-867.

Davis, A. R. The double ninth festival in chinese poetry: a study of variations upon a theme. In **Wen-lin** (1968) 45-64.

Day, Clarence B. The new year ceremonials of chow-wang-miao. **CJ** 32 (1940) 6-12.

Dols, J. Fêtes et usages pendant le courant d'une année dans la province de kan-sou (chine) **AL** 1 (1937) 203-274.

Doré, Henri. **Manuel des superstitions chinoises.** Shanghai, 2e ed (1936) 221 p.

Dymond, F. J. The feast of the seventh moon. **EA** 2.4 (dec 1903) 376-378.

Eberhard, Wolfram. **Chinese festivals.** N.Y. (1952) new ed taipei (1972) 152 p, illus.

Eder, Matthias. Spielgeräte und spiele im chinesischen neujahrsbrauchtum, mit aufzeigung magischer bedeutungen. **FS** 6.1 (1947) 1-207.

Eigner, J. Celebrating the ancient dragon boat festival. **CJ** 27 (1937) 8-10.

Eitel, E. J. (comp) **Eastern religious kalendar for** ...**1882.** Hong kong (1881)

Ewer, F. H. and J. Doolittle. Native fete and natal days observed at canton and foochow. In **DV** vol 2, pt 3, no 30.

Fabre, A. Avril au pays des aïeux. **CCS** 8 (1935) Ancestor worship and burial practices at ch'ing ming, specifically in shun-te, kuangtung.

Fêng, Han-yi and J. K. Shryock. Marriage customs in the vicinity of i-ch'ang. **HJAS** 13 (1950) 362-430.

Goodwin, P. Dragon boat festival. **GM** 33 (1961) 479-485.

Graham, Dorothy. The first day of the first moon [in peking] **CW** 122 (jan 1926) 487-492.

Groot, J. J. M. de. **Les fêtes annuellement célébrées à émoui (amoy) Étude concernant la religion populaire des chinois.** Being **AMG** 1 and 2, paris (1886) 2 vol. Tsl fr dutch C. G. Chavannes.

Hell, H. (E. de T.) Une fête chinoise. **RIC** 14 (dec 1910) 607-609.

Highbaugh, Irma. **Family life in west china.** N.Y. (1948) xi + 240 p.

Hodous, Lewis. The ch'ing ming festival. **JNCBRAS** 46 (1915) 58-60.

Hodous, Lewis. The feast of cold food. **NCR** 4 (1922) 470-473.

Hodous, Lewis. **Folkways in china.** London (1929) 248 p, illus, list of works consulted, list of chin names, index.

Hodous, Lewis. The great summer festival of china as observed in foochow: a study in popular religion. **JNCBRAS** 43 (1912) 69-80.

Hodous, Lewis. The kite festival in foochow. **JNCBRAS** 49 (1918) 76-81. Being art 1 under heading, A chapter of folklore.

Hodous, Lewis. The reception of spring observed in foochow, china. **JAOS** 42 (1922) 53-58.

Hooyman and Vogelaar. Relation abrégée du tien-bing, vulgairement appelé la fête de morts, chez les chinois de batavia. **JA** 2 (1823) 236-243. Tirée des **Mémoires de la société de batavia** 6 (1792) et trad du hollandais.

Hummel, Margaret G. **Fun and festival from china.** N.Y. (1948) 48 p, illus.

Imbault-Huart, Camille. La fête de la mi-automne et du lapin lunaire. **JA** 8e sér, 5 (jan 1885) 71-73.

Imbault-Huart, Camille. Origine de la fête du double-neuf. **JA** 8e sér, 3 (jan 1884)

Imbert, Henri. **Poésies chinoises sur les fêtes annuelles.** Pekin (1924) 34 p, illus.

Lanöe, F. Tsing ming. **La chine** 65 (1924) 313-314.

Leung, A. K. Peiping's happy new year. **NGM** 70 (1936) 749-792.

Lin Yueh-hwa. **The golden wing. A sociological study of chinese familism.** London (1948) repr westport, conn. (1974) On betrothal and wedding see chap 4, 36-48; on major festivals see loc. cit.

Liu, Chiang. The mid-autumn festival. **ACSS** (1956) 2-8.

Liu, Chiang. Religion, funeral rites, sacrifices and festivals in kirin. **ChRec** 65 (1934) 227-238. Same title in **ACSS** (1958-59) 8-20.

Lo, Dorothy and Leon Comber. **Chinese festivals in malaya.** Singapore (1958) 66 p, bibliog, indexes, illus.

Lum, Peter. **Great day in china: the holiday moon.** London and n.y. (1964) 32 p, illus.

Maclagan, P. J. Folk-lore. Account of some customs observed in the first moon in the village of yŭ-lu-hsiang, ch'ao-chou-fu, chieh-yang-hsien. **ChRev** 23 (1894-95) 120.

Martin, Ilse. Frühlingsdoppelsprüche . . . von 1942 an pekinger haustüren. **FS** 2 (1943) 89-174.

McOmber, Douglas. Considering the festival of the fifth day of the fifth month. **Journal of the society for asian studies** 3 (apr 1970) 17-29.

Montuclat. l'Année du rat. **La chine** 58 (1924) 147-156.

Morgan, Harry T. **Chinese festivals.** Los angeles (1941) 16 p, illus.

Mori, S. The festivals of the 15th of the first month in the chinese calendar. **Journal of the oriental society of kyoto** 22 (1954) 168-180.

Nagel, August. Die sieben schwestern. **OstL** 25.46 (17 nov 1911) 425-426.

Ng, Yong-sang. Fa-ti, land of flowers. Canton's new year pilgrimage to its garden suburb. **CJ** 20 (1934) 184-186.

Ottewill, H. A. Notes on the tu t'ien hui, held at chinkiang on the 31st may 1917. **JNCBRAS** 49 (1918) 86-92.

Otto, P. Some notes on chinese festivals and their observances. **EA** 2 (1903) 81-94.

Richard, Timothy. **Calendar of the gods in china.** Shanghai (1916) 37 p.

Rousselle, Erwin. Chinesische neujahrsbräuche. **Sinica** 12 (1937) 1-17.

Saso, Michael. **Taiwan feasts and customs. A handbook of the principal feasts and customs of the lunar calendar on taiwan.** Hsinchu (1965) 95 p.

Schlegel, G. La fête de fouler le feu célébrée en chine et par les chinois à java, le treize du troisième mois, anniversaire du 'grand dieu protecteur de la vie' (pao chîng [sheng] ta ti) **IAE** 9 (1896) 193-195, 1 pl.

Schröder, Dominik. Ying-hsi, die bewillkommnung der freude. **Anthropos** 41/44.1/3 (1946-49) 185-192.

Scidmore, E. R. The moon's birthday. **Asia** 21 (1921) 251-254, 262, 264.

Shen, Ting-su. The chinese new year. **FCR** 11.2 (1961) 5-12.

Sowerby, Arthur de C. The chinese yuletide. **CJ** 7 (1927) 271-273.

Sowerby, Arthur de C. Crossing the year. **CJ** 3 (1925) 53-57.

Sowerby, Arthur de C. The dragon boat festival. **CJ** 20 (1934) 305-306.

Splitter, Henry W. The chinese feast of lanterns. **JAFL** 63 (oct-dec 1950) 438-443.

Spring festival in shanghai. **FEER** 51 (3 mar 1966) 413-415, illus.

Stuart, J. Leighton. A glance at chinese worshippers. **MRW** n.s. 4 (1891) 531-533.

Sun, Chan-ko. The spring festival. **PC** 5 (1953) 19-20.

Sung, H. C. Der 7.7 – ein chinesischer festag. **Sinologica** 3.1 (1951) 50-51.

Superstitions and customs of the chinese. **JIA** n.s. 2 (1888) 349-363.

Swallow, Robert W. **Sidelights on peking life.** Peking (1927) xviii + 135 p, illus.

Tao, Frank. The spring festival. **China magazine** 18 (feb 1948) 29-32.

Tien, Tsung. A diabolical almanac (new type almanac) **Orient** 3.8 (1953) 22-23.

Tien, Tsung. The year of the dragon. **Orient** 2.7 (1952) 24-26.

Tien, Tsung. Year of the water snake. **Orient** 3.7 (1953) 18-19, 36.

Tonn, W. Y. Chinese new year. **CJ** 34 (1941) 6-7.

Volpert, Ant. Volksgebräuche bei der neujahrsfeier in ost-schantung (china) **Anthropos** 12-13 (1917-18) 1118-1119.

Wei, T. F. Chinese festivals. **CJ** 34 (1941) 106-111.

Wen, Ch'ung-i. The water gods and the dragon-boats in south china. **ASBIE** 11 (1961) engl summ 121-124, 6 pl.

Williams, E. T. The calendar and its festivals. Chap 10 in author's **CYT** (1928) 205-222.

Wolfers, M. Spring festivals in china. **CR** 169 (may 1946) 299-302.

Wong, C. S. **A cycle of chinese festivities.** Singapore (1967) xv + 204 p, notes, bibliog, index, illus.

Worcester, G. R. F. The origin and observance of the dragon boat festival in china. **Mariner's mirror** 42 (1956) 127-131, illus.

Young, W. The feast of lanterns at padang (sumatra) **ChRev** 9 (1880-81) 320-321.

Yu, Feng. New year pictures. **PC** 5 (1953) 12-14.

28. TEMPLES AND MOUNTAINS

Allen, C. F. R. (tsl) Fifty-six temple oracles or stanzas. From a tauist temple at foochow. In **DV** vol 2, pt 3, no 58, p 507-512.

Allen, C. F. R. (tsl) Twenty-eight temple oracles or stanzas. From a temple at foochow. In **DV** vol 2, pt 3, no 57, p 504-507.

Alley, Rewi. Some temples in the western hills [near peking] **EH** 3.9 27-30, illus.

Alley, Rewi. Sung shan, the central peak [hunan] **EH** 4.7 (1965) 33-36, illus.

Ayscough, Florence. Shrines of history. Peak of the east − t'ai shan. **JNCBRAS** 48 (1917) 57-70.

Baker, Dwight C. **T'ai shan. An account of the sacred eastern peak of china.** Shanghai (1925) repr taipei (1971) xx + 225 p, app, index, map, illus.

Bouillard, Georges. **Pékin et ses environs, cinquième série, le temple de la terre, les temples du soleil et de la lune, le temple de l'agriculture.** Peking (1923) [44 p] repr fr **la chine** 33, 34.

Bouillard, Georges. **Pékin et ses environs, huitième série, les temples autour du hsiang shan: tien t'ai sze, wo fo sze.** Peking (1924) repr fr **la chine** 48, 49, 51.

Bouillard, Georges. **Pékin et ses environs, première série, le yang shan et ses temples.** Peking (1921) [44 p] repr fr **la chine** 3-6.

Bouillard, Georges. **Pékin et ses environs, quatorzième série, environs sud-ouest: she king shan, yün kiü sze, tung yu sze, si yü sze.** Peking (1924) [74 p] repr fr **la chine** (1923)

Bouillard, Georges. **Pékin et ses environs, quatrième série, le temple du ciel.** Peking (1923) [100 p] repr fr **la chine** 27, 28, 31.

Bouillard, Georges. **Pékin et ses environs, quinzième série, environs sud-ouest: tien k'ai shan, ku shan, shang fang shan, tow shuai sze et les grottes de yün shui t'ung.** Peking (1924) [54 p] repr fr **la chine** 56-59.

Bouillard, Georges. **Pékin et ses environs, sixième série, le temple de pi yün sze.** Peking (1923) [22 p] repr fr **la chine** 44.

Bourne, F. S. A. **The lo-fou mountains: an excursion.** Hong kong (1895) 48 p.

Bretschneider, Emil. Celebrated mountains of china. **JNCBRAS** 16 (1882) 223-228.

Cammann, Schuyler. On the decoration of modern temples in taiwan and hongkong. **JAOS** 88.4 (1968) 785-790. Criticism of W. Eberhard: Topics and moral values in chinese temple decorations q.v.

Cauvin, Dr. Excursion au tai-chann et au tombeau de confucius. **RGI** (août-nov 1884; janv-nov 1885; janv 1887)

Chambers, William. **Designs of chinese buildings.** London (1757) Facsimile repr farnborough, engl (1969) See: Of the temples of the chinese, 1-5; Of the towers [taa = t'a, or pagodas] 5-6; pl 1-5.

Chavannes, Édouard. **Le t'ai chan. Essai de monographie d'un culte chinois.** Appendice: **Le dieu du sol dans la chine antique.** Paris (1910) repr taipei (1970) 591 p, maps, pl, index.

Comber, Leon. **Chinese temples in singapore.** Singapore (1958) 110 p, illus.

Day, Clarence B. The new year ceremonials of chow-wang-miao. **CJ** 32 (1940) 6-12.

Demiéville, Paul. La montagne dans l'art littéraire chinois. **FA** 20 (1965-66) 7-32, pl.

Drake, F. S. The taoists of lao-shan. **ChRec** 65 (1934) 238-245; 308-318.

Dunlap, Eva Wyman. The chin shan tsui temple: peitaiho. **JNCBRAS** 71 (1940) 67-71.

Eberhard, Wolfram. Temple-building activities in medieval and modern china -- an experimental study. **MS** 23 (1964) 264-318. Repr in author's **MSVC**, taipei (1971)

Eberhard, Wolfram. Topics and moral values in chinese temple decorations. **JAOS** 87 (1967) 22-32. Repr in author's **MSVC**, taipei (1971) See above item by Schuyler Cammann: On the decoration of modern temples in taiwan and hongkong which is a criticism of Eberhard's art; and further, Eberhard's rejoinder in **JAOS** 88.4 (1968) 790-792.

Edkins, Joseph. T'ai shan, the legendary centre of tauist belief in a future state. **ChRev** 18 (1889-90) 61-62.

Faulder, H. Croyier. The temples of shanghai. **CJ** 30.6 (june 1939) 340-345, 12 illus.

Frey, H. **Les temples egyptiens primitifs identifiés avec les temples actuels chinois.** Paris (1909)

Goodrich, Anne Swann. **The peking temple of the eastern peak. The tung-yüeh miao in peking and its lore.** **MS** monograph, nagoya (1964) 326 p, app, bibliog, 20 pl.

Grootaers, W. A. Rural temples around hsüan-hua (south chahar), their iconography and their history. **FS** 10 (1951) 1-116.

Grootaers, W. A. Les temples villageois de la région au sud de tat'ong (chansi nord), leurs inscriptions et leur histoire. **FS** 4 (1945) 161-212.

Grootaers, W. A., Li Shih-yü and Chang Chi-wen. Temples and history of wanch'üan (chahar). The geographical method applied to folklore. **MS** 13 (1948) 209-316.

Gutzlaff, Charles. Temple of teen how [t'ien hou] at meichow. **ChRep** 2 (1834) 563-565.

Happer, A. P. Visit to two celebrated peking temples. **ChRec** 12 (1881) 363-372.

Hayes, James W. Chinese temples in the local setting. In **TICHK** (1967) 86-95.

Hayes, James W. A list of temples in the southern district of the new territories and new kowloon, 1899-1967. In **TICHK** (1967) 96-98.

Hubbard, Gilbert E. **The temples of the western hills [near peking].** Peking and tientsin (1923) 76 p, illus.

Hudson, B. W. Mokanshan [chekiang] **EA** 4 (1905) 285-297.

Ildephonse, Dom Prior. A visit to the t'ai shan. **BCUP** 6 (1931) 98-118.

Imbault-Huart, Camille. Une visite au temple de confucius à changhai. **JA** 7e sér, 16 (oct-dec 1880) 533-538.

Irving, E. A. A visit to the buddhist and tao-ist monasteries on the lo fau shan. **BIM** 157 (mar 1895) 453-467.

Klügmann, Karl. Aus dem religiösen leben der chinese. Am grabe des konfuzius. Auf dem taishan. **Geist des ostens** 1 (1913) 284-295.

Krone, R. Der lofau-berg . . . in china. **Petermanns geographische mitteilungen** (1864) 283-292.

Kupfer, Carl F. Kiu hua shan, or, the nine-lotus-flower mountain. **EA** 4 (1905) 45-56.

Kupfer, Carl F. **Sacred places in china.** Cincinnati, ohio (1911) 111 p. Five of the 7 papers orig publ in **EA**.

Lee, Tao. Ten celebrated physicians and their temple. **CMJ** 58 (1940) 267-274.

Leprince-Ringuet, M. F. En chine. Ascension de la montagne sainte de t'aè-houa-chan. **Annuaire club alpin français** 27 (1900) 356-382, illus.

Liu, Chi-wan. The temple of the gods of epidemics in taiwan. **ASBIE** 22 (1966) engl summ 93-95.

Lu, Hung-nien. A visit to yunglokung. **EH** 1.9 (1961) 29-31.

Mateer, Calvin W. T'ai shan temples. **ChRec** 10 (1879) 361-369, 399-415.

McCartee, D. B. (tsl). Translation of an inscription upon a stone tablet commemorating the repairs upon the ch'eng hwang miau or temple of the tutelary deity of the city . . . in the department of lai-chôu, in the province of shantung, a.d. 1752. **JNCBRAS** 6 (1869-70) 173 et seq.

Morrison, Mrs. H. M. In the holy places of hua shan: a dance; a legend; and an offering. **Illustrated london news** 211 (30 aug 1947) 247-249, illus.

Moule, A. C. Le t'ai chan par prof. éd. chavannes. (Note de m. chavannes) **TP** (1911) 425-429.

Moule, A. C. T'ai shan. **JNCBRAS** 43 (1912) 3-31, pl.

Mullikin, Mary Augusta. Tai shan, sacred mountain of the east. **NGM** 87.6 (june 1945) 699-719, illus.

O'Hara, Albert R. A factual survey of taipei's temples and their functions. **JSS** 17 (1967) 323-337. Repr in author's collection; RCCS (1971)

Preston, John (tsl) Tablet mottoes from temples. Collected at foochow. In **DV** vol 2, pt 3, no 12, p 258-262.

Roussel, Romain. **Les pèlerinages à travers les siècles.** Paris (1954) See Bouddhistes . . . Taoïstes.

S. v. F. The bells of mokanshan. **FE** 1 (1906) 187-192.

Savage-Landor, A. Henry. A journey to the sacred mountain of siao-outai-shan, in china. **Fortnightly review** (sept 1894) 393-409. Repr in **Eclectic magazine** 123 (july-dec 1894) 596 et seq. Also repr in **Littel's living age** 203 (oct-dec 1894) 143 et seq.

Scarborough, W. Notes of a visit to the famous wu-tang shan. **ChRec** 5 (1874) 77-82.

Schipper, Kristofer. Les pèlerinages en chine: montagnes et pistes. In **Les pèlerinages**, paris (1960) 303-342 ('Sources orientales,' 3).

Schmidt, Charles. The 'wen miao,' commonly styled 'the confucian temple' in shanghai. (?) **MDGNVO** (1877) 11-12, photo.

Shryock, John K. **The temples of anking and their cults. A study of modern chinese religion.** Paris (1931) 203 p, app, bibliog, index, illus.

Soymié, Michel. Le lo-feou chan. Étude de géographie religieuse. **BEFEO** 48.1 (1956) 1-139, app, bibliog, index, illus, map.

Stanley, Charles A. jr. T'ai shan and the tomb of confucius. **EA** 4 (1905) 301-309.

Sullivan, Michael. The magic mountain. **AR** 50 (1955) 300-310.

Thiel, P. I. Der erdgeist-tempel als weiterent-wicklung des alten erdalters. (Aus eigener feldforschung in süd-shantung) **Sinologica** 5.3 (1958) 150-155, 10 photos.

Topley, Marjorie and James Hayes. Notes on shrines and temples of tai ping shan street area. In **TICHK** (1967) 123-141.

Tran-Ham-Tan. Étude sur le van-mieu [wen-miao] de ha-noi (temple de la littérature) **BEFEO** 45 (1951) 89-117, planche.

Tschepe, A. The hsin-fu-sze temple [kiangsu] **FE** 1 (1906) 238-240.

Tschepe, A. **Der t'ai-schan und seine kulturstätten.** Jentschoufu (1906) 124 p, 35 illus. Notice in **JNCBRAS** 40 (1909) 119-122.

Wales, H. G. Quaritch. The sacred mountain in the old asiatic religion. **JRAS** (1953) 23-30.

Woodbridge, Samuel I. Kuling. **EA** 2 (1903) 327-336. [in kiangsi].

Yao, Ruth. Temples of taiwan. **FCR** 14.4 (apr 1964) 13-20, illus.

The Yeang-tai mountains and spirit-writing in china. **BIM** 93 (apr 1863) 499-520.

Zacher, J. Die tempelanlagen am südabhang des richthofengebirges, erläutert am beispiel von yen-hu-chai-tzu. **FS** 8 (1949) 270-276.

29. RITES AND CEREMONIES

Aijmer, Göran. **The dragon boat festival in the hunan and hupeh plains, central china; a study in the ceremonialism of the transplantation of rice.** Stockholm (1964) 135 p, bibliog.

Arlington, L. C. The ceremony of disintering in china. **ChRev** 25.4 (1901) 176-178.

Armstrong, E. A. Chinese bull ritual and its affinities. **Folk-lore** 56 (1945) 200-207.

Bennett, Miss M. I. [Procession to propitiate evil spirits] **CMI** 56 (1905) 58.

Bishop, Carl W. The ritual bull-fight. **CJ** 3 (1925) 630-637.

Dols, J. l'Usage du sang dans les cérémonies chinoises. **BSAB** 54 (1939) 123-128.

Duyvendak, J. J. L. The mythico-ritual pattern in chinese civilization. **Proc. 7th ICHR, amsterdam 1950** (1951) 137-138.

Eichhorn, W. Über die abergläubischen gebräuche im kreise ting. **Sinica-sonderausgabe forke festschrift** 1 (1937) 43-52.

Farjenel, F. (tsl) **Rites funéraires chinois, les funérailles impériales et celles des gens du peuple** Louvain (ca 1904) 63 p offpr fr **Le muséon.**

Freedman, Maurice. Ritual aspects of kinship and marriage. In **FKCS** (1970) 163-188.

Frick, Johannes. Die regensprozession in lungsi (nordwest china) In **Festschrift paul schebesta zum 75. geburstag,** wien-mödling (1963) 385-400.

Frick, Johannes, Wiederversöhnung der verletzten ergeister. (Ein brauch im chinesischttibetischen grenzgebiet) **Wiener völkerkundliche mitteilungen** 2 (1954) 39-43.

Fung, Yu-lan. The confucianist theory of mourning, sacrificial and wedding rites. **CSPSR** 15 (1931) 335-345.

Gibson, H. E. Divination and ritual during the shang and chou dynasties. **CJ** 23 (1935) 22-25.

Graham, David C. **The ancient caves of szechuan province, china.** Washington, d.c. (1932) 29 p, illus. Burial customs.

J. Rites performed for the dead. **ChRev** 9 (1880-81) 397. See also D. G., same title, **ibid** 10 (1881-82) 145-146.

Johnston, R. F. Worship (chinese) In **HERE** 12, p 759.

Kaltenmark, Max. Les danses sacrées en chine. In **Les danses sacrées,** 'Sources orientales', 6, paris (1963) 411-450.

Klaproth, Julius H. Über religiöse zeremonien der chinesen. **Asiatisches magazin** 2 (1802) 76-78.

Lanöe, F. La danse des diables au temple de hei seu. **La chine** 15 (1 avr 1922) 557-558.

Lavollée, C. Prières chinoises. **ROA** 6 (1849) 100-104.

Lin, Yueh-hwa. **The golden wing. A sociological study of chinese familism.** London (1948) repr westport, conn (1974) On death and its rituals see chap 10, 103-112.

Liu, Chiang. Religion, funeral rites, sacrifices and festivals in kirin. **ChRec** 65 (1934) 227-238. Same title in **ACSS** (1958-59) 8-20.

Mayers, W. F. On the stone figures at chinese tombs and the offering of living sacrifices. **JNCBRAS** 12 (1878) 1-17.

Milloué, L. de. Culte et cérémonies en honneur des morts dans l'extrême-orient. **CMG** (1899-1900 et 1900-01) 135-159.

Mitchell-Innes, Norman G. Birth, marriage, and death rites of the chinese. **FLJ** 5 (1887) 221-245.

Mollard, Sidney G. jr. Confucius and music. **EWCR** 3.3 (feb 1967) 31-39.

Morisse, Lucien. Les éclipses et les rites chinois. **Asie française** 2.17 (aout 1902) 367-372.

Newell, William H. The sociology of ritual in early china. **Sociological bulletin** 6 (1957) 1-13.

Palatre, Père. Une procession païenne en chine. **MC** 2 (1869) 386-387, 395-397, 405-406. Cortège de se-siang-kong.

Parker, E. H. Funeral rites. **ChRev** 14 (1885-86) 225.

Pfizmaier, A. Die lösung der leichname und schwerter. Ein beitrag zur kenntniss des taoglaubens. **SAWW** 64 (1870) 25-92; also publ sep, wien (1870) 70 p.

Propitiating evil spirits. **Annual report of the church missionary society,** london (1905) 351.

Rydh. H. Seasonal fertility rites and the death cult in scandinavia and china. **BMFEA** 3 (1931) 69-93.

Sampson, Theos. Burial in china. **NQ** 2 (1868) 109-111.

Schafer, Edward H. Ritual exposure in ancient china. **HJAS** 14 (1951) 130-184.

Schmeltz, J.D.E. Das pflugfest in china. **IAE** 11 (1898) 72-81.

Schüler, W. Ein tempeleinweihungsfest in china. **ZMK** 21 (1906) 110-115.

Thiel, J. Stellvertretende gelübdeerfüllung. **FS** 1 (1942) 28-32.

Torrance, Thomas. Burial customs in sz-chuan. **JNCBRAS** 41 (1910)

Tran-Ham-Tan. Étude sur le van-mieu [wen-miao] de ha-noi (temple de la littérature) **BEFEO** 45 (1951) 89-117, planche.

Vleeschower, E. de. K'i yu (Rain ceremony) **FS** 2 (1943) 39-50.

Volpert, A. Chinesische volksgebräuche beim t'chi jü, regenbitten. **Anthropos** 12-13 (1917-18) 144-151.

Werner, E.T.C. Reform in chinese mourning rites. **NCR** 2 (1920) 223-247.

Wolf, Arthur P. Chinese kinship and mourning dress. In **FKCS** (1970) 189-208.

30. DIVINATION

Arlington, L.C. Chinese versus western chiromancy. **CJ** 7 (1927) 67-76, 170-175, 228-235; 8 (1928) 67-76.

Balfour, F.H. A chinese 'planchette' seance. **ChRev** 9 (1880-81) 362-370.

Balfour, F.H. Portents. In author's **Leaves from my chinese scrapbook** (1887) 158-162.

Bielenstein, Hans. An interpretation of the portents in the ts'ien-han-shu. **BMFEA** 22 (1950) 127-143, diagr.

Brown, H.G. What the gods say in west china. **JWCBorderResS** 3 (1926-29) 134-150.

Buck, Samuel (pseud) Chinese fortune telling. **Orient** 2.10 (1952) 39-42.

Chao, Wei-pang. The chinese science of fate-calculation. **FS** 5 (1946) 279-315.

Chao, Wei-pang. The origin and growth of the fu chi [planchette] **FS** 1 (1942) 9-27.

Chavannes, Édouard. La divination par l'écaille de tortue dans la haute antiquité chinoise (d'après un livre de m. lo tchen-yu) **JA** 10e sér,17 (1911) 127-137.

Cohen, Alvin P. An example of word-divination in the tarng shu. **PTP** 11 (dec 1968) 68-75.

Cordier, Georges. (tsl) La divination chinoise: clef des songes. **RIC** n.s. 12 (oct 1909) 1033-1041; n.s. 12 (nov 1909) 1135-1140; n.s. 12 (dec 1909) 1241-1243; n.s. 16 (dec 1911) 638-653; n.s. 17 (mai 1912) 484-491.

Divination in china. **ICG** no 12 (1820) 318-320.

Edkins, Joseph. Astrology in ancient china. **ChRev** 14 (1885-86) 345-351.

Edkins, Joseph. The introduction of astrology into china. **ChRev** 15 (1886-87) 126-128.

Frick, J. Der traum und seine deutung bei den chinesen in ch'inghai. **Anthropos** 49 (1954) 311-313.

Gibson, H.E. Divination and ritual during the shang and chou dynasties. **CJ** 23 (1935) 22-25.

Giles, Herbert A. Mesmerism, planchette and spiritualism in china. **Fraser's magazine** ser 2, 19 (feb 1879) 238-245.

Giles, Herbert A. Palmistry in china. **Nineteenth century and after** (dec 1904) 985-988.

Giles, Herbert A. Phrenology, physiognomy and palmistry. In author's **AdSin** no 6 (1908) 178-184.

Groot, J.J.M. de. On chinese divination by dissecting written characters. **TP** 1 (1890) 239-247.

Harding, H.L. On a method of divination practised at foochow. **JNCBRAS** 49 (1918) 82-85. Art 2 under heading, A chapter of folklore.

Harlez, C. de. **Miscellanées chinois. 1–Le rêve dans les croyances chinoises.** Paris? (d?) 22 p.

Hopkins, Lionel C. Working the oracle [re oracle bones] **NCR** (1919) 111-119, 249-261, pl.

Koeppen, Georg von. Zwei träume aus dem tso-chuan und ihre interpretation. **ZDMG** 119 (1969) 133-156.

Lee, Charles L. (pseud for Yen P'u-sheng) tsl and annot. **The great prophecies of china, by li chung-feng [602-670] and yuan tien-kang.** N.Y. (1950) 64 p.

Lessa, William A. Chinese body divination. In **FRWVSP** (1968) 85-96.

Lessa, William A. **Chinese body divination. Its forms, affinities, and functions.** Los angeles (1968) 220 p, bibliog, index, illus.

Lum, Chung Park. **Chinese fortune telling.** N.Y. (1930) 15 p, illus.

Macgowan, D.J. Table-moving and spiritual mani-festations in china. **NCH** 196 (29 apr 1854) repr **Shanghae almanac for 1855 and Miscellany**; also repr in **China mail** 484 (25 may 1854)

McCaffree, Joe E. **Divination and the historical and allegorical sources of the i ching, the chinese classic, or book of changes.** Los angeles (1967) 64 p, illus.

Mégroz, R.L. Dream interpretation, chinese--greek--islamic. **AP** 6 (1935) 28-31.

Milloué, L. de. l'Astrologie et les différentes formes de la divination dans l'inde, en chine et au tibet. **CMG** (1899-1900 et 1900-01) 179-205.

Miyazaki, Ichisada. Le dévelopement de l'idée de divination en chine. In **MSPD**, t 1 (1966) 161-165.

Moebius, P. Die grundlagen der chinesischen divinations-lehren. **OZ** 17 (1931) 215-218.

Mortier, F. Les animaux dans la divination et la médicine populaire chinoise. **BSAB** 51 (1936) 268-275.

Mortier, F. Du sens primitif de l'antiquité et la célèbre figure divinatoire des taoistes chinois et japonais (sien t'ien) **BSAB** 59 (1948) 150-160.

N., L.M. Modes of consulting the oracles. **ChRev** 7 (1878-79) 134.

Nakayama, Shigeru. Characteristics of chinese astrology. **Isis** 57 (winter 1966) 442-454.

Natsume, Ikken. Various phases of revelation in taoism. **TJR** 1 (mar 1955) 53-65, fig.

Ohlinger, Franklin. Studies in chinese dreamlore. **EA** 4 (1905) 381-389; 5 (1906) 16-28, 256-267.

Parker, A.P. The chinese almanac. **ChRec** 19.2 (feb 1888) 61-74.

Parker, A.P. Review of the imperial guide to astrology. . . hieh ki pien fang shú. **ChRec** 19 (1888) 493-499, 547-554.

Przyluski, Jean. La divination par l'aiguille flottante et par l'araignée dans la chine méridionale. **TP** n.s. 15 (1914) 214-224.

Schafer, Edward H. Li kang: a rhapsody on the banyan tree. **Orient** 6 (1953) 344-353.

Soymié, Michel. Les songes et leur interpretation en chine. In **Les songes et leur interpretation**, paris (1959) 275-305 ('Sources orientales' 2).

Stiassny, M. Quelques formes de la divination des chinois. **Archives suisses d'anthropologie générale** 12 (1946) 159-163.

Stirling, W.G. Chinese divining blocks and the 'pat kwa' or eight-sided diagram with text figures. **JMBRAS** 2 (1924) 72-73.

Ting, Su. Fortune telling. **Asia** 3 (1953) 428-437.

Tseung, F.I. Some aspects of fortune-telling in hong kong. In **TICHK** (1967) 60-72.

Wilhelm, Hellmut. Der sinn des geschehens nach dem buch der wandlung. **EJ** 26 (1957) 351-386.

31. SHAMANISM AND MEDIUMS

Eitel, E.J. Spirit-rapping in china. **NQ** 1.12 (dec 1867) 164-165.

Eliade, Mircea. **Le chamanisme et les techniques archaïques de l'extase.** Paris (1951) Engl tsl Willard R. Trask: **Shamanism; archaic techniques of ecstacy.** Princeton univ (1964) bibliog, index. For china, see index.

Eliade, Mircea. Einführende betrachtungen über den schamanismus. **Paideuma** 5 (1951) 87-97.

Eliade, Mircea. Le problème de chamanisme. **RHR** 131 (1946) 5-52.

Eliade, Mircea. Smiths, shamans and mystagogues. **E&W** 6 (1955) 206-215.

Elliott, Alan J.A. **Chinese spirit-medium cults in singapore.** London school of economics and political science (1955) 179 p, illus.

Enjoy, Paul d'. Le spiritisme en chine. **BMSAP** 5e sér, 7 (1906) 87-100.

Erkes, E. The god of death in ancient china. **TP** 35 (1940) 185-210.

Erkes, E. Mystik und schamanismus. **AA** 8 (1945) 197-215.

Erkes, Eduard. Der schamanistische ursprung des chinesischen ahnenkultus. **Sinologica** 2 (1950) 253-262.

Giles, Herbert A. Mesmerism, planchette and spiritualism in china. **Fraser's magazine** ser 2, 19 (feb 1879) 238-245.

Goltz, Freiherrn von der. Zauberei und hexenkünste, spiritismus und schamanismus in china. **MDGNVO** bd 6, heft 51 (1893) 1-50.

Grootaers, Willem A. Une séance de spiritisme dans une religion secrète à péking en 1948. **MCB** 9 (1948-51) 92-98.

Harvey, E.D. Shamanism in china. In **Studies in the science of society presented to a. g. keller** (1937) 247-266.

Hentze, Carl. Le culte de l'ours et du tigre et le t'ao-t'ié. **Zalmoxis** 1 (1938) 50-68.

Hentze, Carl. Eine schamanen-darstellung auf einem han-relief. **AM** n.s. 1.1 (1944) 74-77.

Hentze, Carl. Eine schamanentracht in ihrer bedeutung für die altchinesische kunst und religion. **Jahrbuch für prähistorische ethnographische kunst** 20 (1960-63) 55-61.

Hentze, Carl. Zur ursprünglichen bedeutung des chinesischen zeichens t'ou = kopf. **Anthropos** 45 (1950) 801-820.

Hopkins, L.C. The bearskin, another pictographic reconnaissance from primitive prophylactice to present-day panache: a chinese epigraphic puzzle. **JRAS** (1943) 110-117.

Hopkins, L.C. The shaman or chinese wu: his inspired dancing and versatile character. **JRAS** (1945) 3-16.

Hopkins, L.C. The shaman or wu. A study in graphic camouflage. **NCR** 2 (1920) 423-439.

König, H. Schamane und medizinmann. **Ciba zeitschrift** 4.38 (1936) 1294-1301.

Körner, Theo. Das zurückrufen der seele in kuei-chou. **Ethnos** 3.4/5 (july-sept 1938) 108-112.

Kremsmayer, Heimo. Schamanismus und seelenvorstellung im alten china. **AV** 9 (1954) 66-78.

Lanciotti, Lionello. Sword casting and related legends in china. **E&W** (1) 6.2 (july 1955) 106-114; (2) 6.4 (jan 1956) 316-322.

Laufer, Berthold. Origin of the word shaman. **American anthropologist** n.s. 19.3 (1917) 361-371.

Metzger, Emil. Zauber und zauberjungen bei den chinesen. **Globus** 42.7 (feb 1882) 110-112; 42.8 (feb 1882) 119-121.

Minnaert, P. Le chamanisme. **BSAB** 51 (1936) 216-234.

Minnaert, P. Magie ou thaumaturgie et chamanisme. **BSAB** 48 (1933) 19-34.

Mironov, N.D. and S. M. Shirokogoroff. S'ramana-shaman (Etymology of the word 'shaman') **JNCBRAS** 55 (1924) 105-130.

Parker, E.H. Ancient chinese spiritualism. **AR** 19 (jan 1923) 117-123.

Rock, J.F. Contribution to the shamanism of the tibetan-chinese borderland. **Anthropos** 54.5/6 (1959) 796-816, 4 pl.

Schang, Tscheng-tsu. **Der schamanismus in china: eine untersuchung zur geschichte der chinesischen 'wu'.** Hamburg (1934) 83 p.

Thiel, Jos. Schamanismus im alten china. **Sinologica** 10.2/3 (1968) 149-204.

Vichert, C.G. A study of the growth of a legend. **JWCBorderResS** 8 (1936) 173-174.

Waley, Arthur. **The nine songs. A study of shamanism in ancient china.** London (1955) 64 p, index.

32. MAGIC AND SORCERY

Andersson, J.G. Hunting magic in the animal style. **BMFEA** 4 (1932) 221-320.

Black, W.H. On chinese charms. **Journal of the ethnological society.** n.s. 1 (1868-69) 38-39.

Blanchard, Raphael and Bui Van Quy. Sur une collection d'amulettes chinoises. **Revue anthropologique** 28 (mai-juin 1918) 131-172 fig (dessins de mlle Gilberte Zaborowska)

Bodde, Derk. The chinese cosmic magic known as watching for the ethers. In **SSBKD** (1959) 14-35.

Bodde, Derk. Sexual sympathetic magic in han china. **HR** 3 (1964) 292-299.

Böttger, Walter. Jagdmagie im alten china. In **SJFAW** (1956) 9-14.

Brace, A.J. Spirits and magic in chinese religion. **JWCBorderResS** 5 (1932) 133-148.

Cammann, Schuyler. Magical and medicinal woods in old chinese carvings. **JAFL** 74, no 292 (apr-june 1961) 116-125.

Charpentier, Léon. La magie chez les chinois. **NR** n.s. 9 (1901) 523-536.

Chatley, Herbert. Magical practice in china. **JNCBRAS** 48 (1917) 16-28.

Ch'en,Hsiang-ch'un. Examples of charm against epidemics with short explanations. **FS** 1 (1942) 37-54, 15 cuts of charms.

Chochod, Louis. **Occultisme et magie en extrême-orient: inde, indochine, chine.** Paris (1949) 404 p, illus.

Comber, Leon. **Chinese magic and superstitions in malaya.** Singapore (1957) 80 p, illus.

Daudin, P. Deux amulettes du yunnan. **BSEIS** n.s. 21 (1946) 35-40.

Day, Clarence B. Celestial insurance limited (Popular charms) **Asia** 33 (1933) 113-115.

Dember, H. Ostasiatische zaubespiegel. **OZ** 19 (1933) 203-207.

Dunstheimer, **G.G.** Religion et magie dans le mouvement des boxeurs d'après les textes chinois. **TP** 47.3/5 (1959) 322-267.

Eberhard, Wolfram. Chinesischer bauzauber. **ZE** 71 (1939) 87-99.

Eder, Matthias. Spielgeräte und spiele im chinesischen neujahrsbrauchtum, mit aufzeigung magischer bedeutungen. **FS** 6.1 (1947) 1-207.

Elwin, Arthur. A strange scene. **ChRec** 12.1 (jan-feb 1881) 16-19. On exorcism.

Fêng, Han-yi and John K. Shryock. The black magic in china known as ku. **JAOS** 55 (1935) 1-30.

Fischer, C. Chuan-chou. Die magie der umkreisung. **AA** 4 (1930-32) 213-220.

Frick, J. How blood is used in magic and medicine in ch'inghai province. Tsl fr german James E. Mertz. **Anthropos** 46 (1951) 964-979.

Frick, J. Magic remedies used on sick children in the western valley of sining. Tsl James E. Mertz. **Anthropos** 46 (1951) 175-186. German orig in **ibid** 45 (1950) 787-800.

Giles, Lionel. Wizardry in ancient china. **AP** 13 (1942) 484-489.

Goltz, Freiherrn von der. Zauberei und hexenkünste, spiritismus und schamanismus in china. **MDGNVO** bd 6, heft 51 (1893) 1-50.

Groot, J.J.M.de. **The religious system of china.** Leiden (1892-1910) repr taipei (1964) 6 vol. 1-3: Disposal of the dead; 4-6 The soul and ancestor worship. See passim, esp vol 4-6.

Gulik, R.H. van. The mango trick in china: an essay on taoist magic. **TASJ** ser 3, 3 (1954) 117-175.

Henry, Victor. **La magie dans l'inde antique.** Paris (1909) xl + 286 p.

Herrmann, F. Chinesischer schutz und gluckszauber. **Sinica-Sonderausgabe** (1935) 24-28.

Hsu, Francis L.K. **Magic and science in western yunnan.** N.Y. (1943) 53 p.

Hsu, Francis L.K. **Religion, science and human crisis.** London (1952) 142 p.

Johnston, R.F. Magic (chinese) In **HERE** 8, p 259.

Julien, Stanislas. Notice sur les miroirs magiques des chinois et leur fabrication. . . **Comptes rendus de l'académie des science** 24 (1847) 999-1009.

Kiang,Chao-yuan. **Le voyage dans la chine ancienne, considéré principalement sous son aspect magique et religieux.** Shanghai (1937) 375 p. Trad du chin par Fan, Jen.

Manabe, Shunsho. The expression of elimination of devils in the iconographic texts of the t'ang period and its background. **JIBS** 15.2 (mar 1967) 907-914, illus.

Minnaert, P. Magie ou thaumaturgie et chamanisme. **BSAB** 48 (1933) 19-34.

Morgan, Harry T. **Chinese astrology.** Los angeles (ca. 1945) 20 p, illus.

Morrison, John Robert. Some account of charms, and felicitous appendages worn about the person, or hung up in houses, &c., used by the chinese. **Trans RAS** 3 (1833) 285-290; **ChRep** 14 (1845) 229-234.

Mortier, Florent. La magie en chine. **BSAB** 47 (1932) 353-360.

Palatre, le père. La magie et le nénuphar blanc au kiangnan. **MC** 10 (1878) 434-441, 446-450, 458-465.

Preston, John. Charms and spells in use amongst the chinese. **ChRev** 2.3 (nov-dec 1873) 164-169.

Regnault, Jules. Rôle du foung-choei et de la sorcellerie dans la vie privée et publique des jaunes. **Revue politique et parlementaire** (10 nov 1905) 353-373. Étude extr. en grande partie d'un rapport présenté par le dr. regnault au congrès colonial de 1905, sous le titre: Hystérie, hypnose et sorcellerie en chine et en indo-chine.

Soulié, Charles G. **Sciences occult en chine. Le main.** Paris (1932) 136 p, illus.

Stirling, W.G. Chinese exorcists. **JMBRAS** 2 (1924) 41-47.

Tao, Pung-fai. Blick auf die welt der mystik und des aberglaubens in china. **OR** 16.4 (16 feb 1935) 105-108; 16.5 (1 märz 1935) 129-133.

Thiel, Josef. (Aufnahmen von Matthias Eder) Stellvertretende [t'i shen] gelübdeerfüllung. **FS** 1 (1942) 28-36, 6 photos.

Topley, Marjorie. Paper charms and prayer sheets as adjuncts to chinese worship. **JMBRAS** 26.1 (1953) 63-80.

Trying to tempt back the soul of an unconscious invalid. **Annual report of the church missionary society,** london (1906) 319.

Vichert, C.G. A study of the growth of a legend. **JWCBorderResS** 8 (1936) 173-174.

Waley, Arthur. Magical use of phallic representations. Its late survival in china and japan. **BMFEA** 3 (1931) 61-62. À propos B. Karlgren: Some fecundity symbols in ancient china, **ibid** 2 (1930)

Williams, E.T. Witchcraft in the chinese penal code. **JNCBRAS** 38 (1907) 61-96.

33. MEDICINE AND RELIGION

Arlington, L.C. The mystic art of pulse feeling in china. **CJ** 7 (1927) 67-76, 170-175, 228-235; 8 (1928) 67-76.

Beau,Georges. **Le médicine chinoise.** Paris (1965) 190 p, illus.

Bowers, John Z. Chinese traditional medicine. **Asia** 5 (spring 1966) 62-69.

Breitenstein, H. **Gerichtliche medezin der chinesen von wang-in-hoai.** Nach der holländischen übers des herrn C.P.M. de Grys. Leipzig (1908)

Bridgman, R.F. La médecine dans la chine antique. **MCB** 10 (1955)

Cammann, Schuyler. Magic and medicinal wood in old chinese carvings. **JAFL** 74.292 (apr-june 1961) 116-125.

Chamfrault, A. **Traité de médicine chinoise. . . d'après les textes chinois anciens et modernes.** Angoulème, coquemart (1964) 986 p, diagr.

Chang,Chen-yun. **The history and methods of physical diagnosis in classical chinese medicine.** Tsl Ronald Chen. N.Y. (1969) 72 p, illus.

Choa, Gerald. Chinese traditional medicine and contemporary hong kong. In **TICHK** (1967) 31-35.

Chinese medicine. **Lancet** 182 (1912) 1006-1007.

Cowdry, E.V. Taoist ideas of anatomy. **AMH** 3 (1921) 301-309.

Criqui, Fernand. **Le médecine chinoise.** Monte-carlo (1967) 96 p, illus.

Diagnostic des médecins chinois. **RC** (1921) 509-513, fig.

Dudgeon, John. Kung-fu, or medical gymnastics. **JPOS** 3.3 (1893); 3.4 (1895)

Dudgeon, John. Medical divinities. In **DV**, vol 2, pt 3, no 26, 318-319.

Filliozat, Jean. Le médecine indienne et l'expansion bouddhique en extrême-orient. **JA** 224 (1934) 301-307.

Frick, Johann. How blood is used in magic and medicine in ch'inghai province. Tsl fr german James E. Mertz. **Anthropos** 46 (1951) 964-979.

Frick, Johann. Magic remedies used on sick children in the western valley of sining. Tsl James E. Mertz. **Anthropos** 46 (1951) 175-186. German orig in ibid 45 (1950) 787-800.

Gillard, Jean-Louis. **Métaphysique taoïste et acupuncture chinoise.** Bordeaux (1968) 51 p.

Gruenhagen. Die grundlagen der chinesischen medizin. **Janus** 13 (1908) 1-14, 121-137, 191-205, 268-278, 328-337.

Guillemet, Dr. La médecine et les médecins en chine. **Annales d'hygiène et de médecine coloniales** 15 (1912) 152-175, 234-254.

Hackmann, Heinrich. Aus die heilsmethode des buddhismus. **ZMK** 17 (1902) 360-367.

Harlez, Charles de (tsl) Le livre de hoang-ti (hoang-ti nei king) Textes taoistes traduits des originaux chinois et commentés. **AMG** 20 (1891) 343-368.

Hartner, Willy. Heilkunde im alten china. **Sinica** 16 (1941) 217-265; 17 (1942) 266-328.

Hsieh, E.T. A review of ancient chinese anatomy. **Anatomical record** 20 (1921)

Hsu, Francis L.K. **Religion, science and human crisis.** London (1952) 142 p, illus.

Huard, Pierre and Wong Ming. Évolution de la matière médicale chinoise. **Janus** 47 (1958) 3-67.

Huard, Pierre and Wong Ming. Quelques aspects de la doctrine classique de la médecine chinoise. **Biologie médicale** 46 (1957) 3-119.

Huebotter, Franz. **Die chinesische medizin zu beginn des jahrhundert und ihr historisches entwicklungsgang.** Leipzig (1929)

Huebotter, Franz. **Zwei berühmte chinesische ärzte des altertums, chouen-yü i. . . und hoa t'ouo. . .** Tokyo (1927) 48 p.

Huizenga, Lee S. Lü tsu and his relation to other medicine gods. **CMJ** 58 (1940) 275-283.

Hume, Edward H. **The chinese way in medicine.** Baltimore (1940) ref, index, illus. See esp lecture 1, The universe and man in chinese medicine.

Hume, Edward H. The square kettle. **BIHM** 2 (1934) 547-557 (On one of the three isles of the immortals)

Kaltenmark, Max. Hygiène et mystique en chine. **Bulletin de la société d'acupuncture** 33.3 (1959) 21-30.

Kervyn, Joseph. **Medecine chinoise. Choses vues.** Bruxelles (1947) 15 p.

Laird, P.J. [Exorcism of an evil spirit as a cure in china] **CMI** 57 (1906) 540.

Lee, T'ao. Achievements of chinese medicine in the sui (589-617 a.d.) and t'ang (618-907 a.d.) dynasties. **CMJ** 71 (1953) 301-320.

Lee, T'ao. Ten celebrated physicians and their temple. **CMJ** 58 (1940) 267-274.

Li, Huan-hsin. Chinese medicine. **CC** 10.1 (1969) 67-79.

Liétord. Le pèlerin bouddhiste chinois i-tsing et la médecine de l'inde au IIIe siècle. **Bulletin de la société française d'histoire de la médecine** 1 (1903) 472-487.

Lion, Lucien. **Les ivoires religieux et médicaux chinois d'après la collection lucien lion. Texte de henri maspero, rené grousset, lucien lion.** Paris (1939) 96 p, pl.

Martinie, J.A. Essai sur la médecine chinoise. Saigon, **Education** 1 (1948) 15-23.

Martinie, Jean. La medecine chinoise. **FA** 4 (fevr 1949) 549-569.

La Médecine chinoise. **TM** 6 (1900) 397-398.

Morse, William R. **Chinese medicine.** N.Y. (1934) xxiii + 185 p, illus.

Morse, W.R. A memorandum on the chinese procedure of acupuncture. **JWCBorderResS** 5 (1932) 153-196, illus.

Morse, W.R. The practices and principles of chinese medicine. **JWCBorderResS** 3 (1926-1929) 82-104, charts.

Mortier, F. Les animaux dans la divination et la médecine populaire chinoise. **BSAB** 51 (1936) 268-275.

Nakayama, T. **Acupuncture et medecine chinoise vérifées au japon.** Paris (1934) 90 p, illus.

Needham, Joseph and Lu Gwei-djen. Hygiene and preventive medicine in ancient china. **JHMAS** 17 (1962) 429-478.

Nguyen-Van-Quan. **Acupuncture chinoise pratique; sur quelque recherches touchant la medecine traditionnelle sino-japonaise.** Paris (1936) 126 p, illus.

Oshawa, Georg. **Lehrbriefe der fernöstlichen philosophie und medizin in theorie und praxis.** Übers von Winifried Eggert. Heidelberg (1958) 22 p.

Otto, Johann H. **Das dau, tao, in der chinesischen heilkunst.** Hamburg (1954) 10 p.

Pálos, István. **Atem und meditation. Moderne chinesische atemtherapie als vorschule der meditation. Theorie. Praxis. Originaltexte.** Weilheim (1968) 225 p, illus.

Pálos, István. **Chinesische heilkunst. Rückbesinnung auf eine grosse tradition.** Aus dem ungarischen in deutsche übertragen von Wilhelm Kronfuss. München (1966) 205 p, illus. Engl tsl [unnamed]: Stephan Palos, **The chinese art of healing,** london (1971) 237 p, illus.

Parker, E.H. Medical deities. **ChRev** 17 (1888-89) 115.

Porkett, Manfred. Die energetische terminologie in den chinesischen medizinklassikern. **Sinologica** 8 (1965) 184-210.

Rall, Jutta. Über das ch'ao-shih chu-ping yüan-hou lun, ein werk der chinesischen medizin aus dem 7 jahrhundert. **OE** 14 (1967) 143-178, tables.

Rall, Jutta. Uber die wärmekrankheiten. **OE** 9 (1962) 139-153. Tsl of ch'ao yüan-fang: chu-ping yüan-hou lun, On the origins and symptoms of diseases, 610 a.d.; modern ed peking (1955)

Rall, Jutta. **Die vier grossen medizinschulen der mongolenzeit. Stand und entwicklung der chinesischen medizin in der chin und yüan zeit.** Wiesbaden (1970) 114 p.

Read, Bernard E. Ancient chinese medicine and its modern interpretation. **THM** 8 (1939) 221-234, illus.

Sen, Satiranjan. Two medical texts in chinese translation [in tripitaka] **VBA** 1 (1945) 70-95.

Sivin, Nathan A. A seventh-century chinese medical case history. **BHM** 41 (1967) 76-78, illus.

Soulié, George de Morant. **l'Acupunture chinoise.** Paris (1939-41) 2 t, illus. See further same title, paris (1957) 1,000 p, illus.

Soulié, George de Morant. **Précis de la vraie acuponture chinoise. Doctrine, diagnostic, therapeutique.** Paris (1936) 6e éd, 199 p, illus; (1947) éd, 201 p, illus; (1964) éd, 209 p, pl, figs.

Topley, Marjorie. Chinese traditional ideas and the treatment of disease: two examples from hong kong. **Man** n.s. 5 (1970) 421-437.

Trippner, P.J. Der wandernde medizingott. **Anthropos** 46 (1951) 801-807. Re ch'inghai.

Tschen, Yin-ko. Buddhistischer in den biographien von tsan tschung und hua to im san guo dschï. **TJ** 6 (1930) 17-20.

Veith, Ilza. Some philosophical concepts of early chinese medicine. Basavangudi, bangalore, Indian institute of culture, **Transactions** 4 (dec 1950) 15 p.

Veith, Ilza. The supernatural in far eastern concepts of mental disease. **BHM** 37.2 (1963) 139-158.

Veith, Ilza. **The yellow emperor's classic of internal medicine.** Univ california (1949) new [but not rev] ed (1966) 260 p, illus. See esp Introduction, passim.

Wieger, Leon. La médecine chinoise. Historique. **Bulletin médical franco-chinois, pékin** 1 (1920) 1-3.

Wong, K. Chimin. Chinese medical superstition. **National medical journal** 2 (1916)

Wong, K. Chimin. Hua t'o, the god of surgery. **CMJ** 41 (1927)

Wong, K. Chimin and Wu Lien-teh. **History of chinese medicine.** Tientsin (1932) 2nd ed shanghai (1936) xxviii + 906 p, illus.

Yewdale, M.S. The therapeutic power of taoism. **AP** 7 (1936) 271-274.

Zimmerman, Werner and Leung Tit-sang. **Chinesische weisheit und heilkunst.** München (1954) 51 p, illus.

Zwaan, J.P. Kleiweg de. **Völkerkundliches und geschichtliches über die heilkunde der china und japaner mit bes. berücksichtigung holländscher einflüssen.** Haarlem (1917) 656 p, illus.

34. RELIGION IN FOLKLORE, TRACT, LITERATURE AND DRAMA

Abel-Rémusat, J.P. (tsl) **Le livre des récompenses et des peines, ouvrage taoiste traduit du chinois avec des notes et des éclaircissements.** Paris (1816) 79 p, repr paris (1939) 113 p.

Basset, R. Contes et légendes de l'extrême-orient. **RE** 1 (1920) 60-61.

Beck, L. Adams. Chinese pilgrim's progress. **HJ** 20 (1921) 5-19. Contents derived from T. Richards' tsl A mission to heaven.

Belpaire, Bruno. Le taoisme et li t'ai-po. **MCB** 1 (1931-32) 1-14.

Bodde, Derk. Again some chinese tales of the supernatural. Further remarks on kan pao and his sou-shen chi. **JAOS** 62.4 (1942) 293-299.

Bodde, Derk. Some chinese tales of the supernatural. Kan pao and his sou-shen chi. **HJAS** 6 (1941-42) 338-357.

Chan, Ping-leung. Chinese popular water-god legends and the hsi yu chi. In **Essays in chinese studies presented to professor lo hsiang-lin,** univ hong kong (1970) 299-317.

Chiang, Alpha C. Religion, proverbs, and economic mentality. **American journal of economics and sociology** 20.3 (apr 1961) 253-264.

Clayton, George A. Where the river-god lies buried. A chinese nature study. **EA** 3 (1904) 87-91.

Cornaby, W. Arthur. Sir diamond, the demon-vanquisher. **WMM** 122 (1899) 260-266. Same title in **EA** 4 (1905) 227-236.

Cornaby, W. Arthur. Theology and eschatology of the chinese novel. **ChRec** 51 (1920) 166-170, 254-265, 331-342.

Davis, A.R. The double-ninth festival in chinese poetry: a study of variations upon a theme. In **Wen-lin** (1968) 45-64.

Demiéville, Paul. La montagne dans l'art littéraire chinois. **FA** 20 (1965-66) 7-32, pl.

Dennys, N.B. The folklore of china. **ChRev** 3.5–5.2 (mar-apr 1875–sept-oct 1876) Sep publ as **The folklore of china,** hong kong (1876) 156 p, repr detroit (1971)

Dien, Albert E. The yan-hun chih (accounts of ghosts with grievances): a sixth-century collection of stories. In **Wen-lin** (1968) 211-228.

Duyvendak, J.J.L. A chinese 'divina commedia'. **TP** 41 (1952) 255-316. On Lo Mao-teng: San-pao ta-chien hsia hsi-yang chi (1597) a fictitious and fantastic account of the voyages of cheng ho.

Eberhard, Wolfram. Orakel und theater in china. **AS** 18/19 (1965) 11-30.

Eberhard, Wolfram. **Studies in chinese folklore and related essays.** Indiana univ and the hague (1970) 329 p, notes, bibliog, index, illus. All but 2 are republ, and most are tsl fr german William Templer. See pt 1, Essays on the folklore of chekiang, china, 17-144; pt 2, Essays on the folklore of china, 145-230. (Abbrev **SCFRE)**

Eberhard, Wolfram. **Studies in taiwanese folktales.** Taipei (1970) 193 p.

Eberhard, Wolfram. Volkspoesie an tempelwänden. **Sinica** 11.3/4 (mai-juli 1936) 127-130, repr in author's **SCFRE** (1970)

Eder, Matthias. Das jahr im chinesischen volkslied. **FS** 4 (1945) 1-160.

Edkins, Joseph. The books of the modern religious sects in north china. **ChRec** 19 (1888) 261-268, 302-310.

Eichler, E.R. The k'uen shih wan [ch'üan shih wen] or, the practical theology of the chinese. **ChRev** 11 (1882) 93-101, 146-161. Popular moral and religious tracts.

Eichler, E.R. Die religiöse tractliteratur der chinesen. **AMZ** 19 (1892) 499-511.

Erkes, Eduard. Der pfau in religion und folklore. **JSMVL** 10 (1926-51 sic) 67-73.

Erkes, Eduard (tsl) Das 'zurückrufen der seele' (chao hun) des sung-yüh. Text, übers und erläuterungen. Leipzig (1914)

Fujino, Iwatomo. On chinese soul-inviting and firefly-catching songs: a study on chinese folklore. **ActaA** [tokyo] 19 (dec 1970) 40-57.

Garritt, J.C. Popular account of the canonization of the gods, illustrated. **ChRec** 30 (1899) 162-174. Feng shen yen-i.

Giles, Lionel. A t'ang manuscript of the sou shen chi. **NCR** 3 (1921) 378-385, 460-468.

Grube, Wilhelm (tsl) **Fêng-shên-yen-i. Die metamorphosen der goetter.** Leiden (1912) bd 1, xxiv + 304; bd 2, 305-657.

Grube, Wilhelm. Die huldigungsfeier der acht genien für den gott des langen lebens, ein chinesischer schattenspieltext. In **BMV** (1906) 1-4.

Grube, Wilhelm. Zur pekinger volkskunde. **Veröffentlichungen aus dem königlichen museum für völkerkunde** 7.1/4 (1901) 1-160.

Haden, R.A. (tsl) The kan ying pien. . . The tractate on rewards and punishments by the great exalted. **EA** 3 (1904) 172-182.

Hawkes, David. The quest of the goddess. **AM** n.s. 13 (1967) 71-94. On the ch'u tz'u, Songs of the south.

Hawkes, David. The supernatural in chinese poetry. In D. Grant and M. Maclure (ed) **The far east: china and japan,** univ toronto (1961) 311-324.

Imbault-Huart, C. (tsl) Trois contes de fées traduits du chinois. **REO** 2 (1883) 281-286 (Extr du shen-nü chuan)

Jameson, R.D. **Three lectures on chinese folklore.** Peking (1932) ix + 13 + 164 p.

Julien, Stanislas (tsl) **Livre des récompenses et des peines.** Paris (1835) (T'ai-shang kan-ying p'ien)

Kalvodová, Dana. Wang k'uei in hell: the metamorphosis of a chinese play. **Dodder** 2 (jan 1970) 46-48.

Ling, Shun-sheng. Kuo shang and li hun of the nine songs and the ceremonies of head-hunting and head-feast. **ASBIE** 9 (1960) engl abrmt 451-461.

Liu, Ts'un-yan. **Buddhist and taoist influences on chinese novels. Volume 1: The authorship of the fêng shen yen i.** Wiesbaden (1962) viii + 326 p, index, pl.

Macgowan, John. **Chinese folk-lore tales.** N.Y. (1910) 197 p.

Mansfield, M.T. Chinese legends. **FLJ** 5 (1887) 124-127.

Martin, W.A.P. **The lore of cathay.** N.Y. (1901) repr taipei (1971) See Native tracts. . . 148-162.

Mitsunori, Okuno. Chinese superstition in fiction and folklore. **Contemporary japan** 9 (1940) 1567-1577.

Moule, G.E. (tsl) A guide to true vacuity. By yuen-yang-tsze. **JNCBRAS** 23 (1889) 9-22. A popular philosophical-religious tract on one sheet, from hangchow.

Ng, Yong-sang. Pai ngo t'an. The legend of the maçao passage. **CJ** 24 (1936) 202-204.

Ng, Yong-sang. The temple of no sorrows. A cantonese santa claus story. **CJ** 19 (1933) 280-284.

Oberle, A. Der hundertkopfdämon im volks-glauben des westtales und des chinesisch-tibetanischen kontaktgebietes im osttale von kuei-te in der provinz ch'ing-hai. In **Ethnographische beiträge aus der ch'inghai provinz,** peking (1952) 222-233.

Odontius, L. Chinesische märchen. (Nemesis, gleichgesinnte seelen, seelenwanderung, o-ha) **OstL** 17 (1903) 798-799.

Pavie, Théodore. Yu-ki le magicien, légende chinoise. **RDM** 6e sér, 9 (15 mars 1851) 1129-1144.

Plopper, Clifford H. **Chinese religion seen through the proverb.** Shanghai (1926) 381 p, illus.

Porkert, Manfred. Die zweispältige rolle des chiang tzu-ya, der zentralfigur in feng-shen yen-i. **Sinologica** 11 (1970) 135-143.

Poseck, Helena von. Why the city god of yench'en has no skin on his face. **EA** 3 (1904) 169-171.

Richard, Timothy (tsl) **One of the world's literary masterpieces, hsi yu chi, a mission to heaven. A great chinese epic and allegory by ch'iu ch'ang ch'un, a taoist gamaliel who became a prophet and advisor to the chinese court.** Shanghai (1913) xxxix + 362 + viii p, illus.

Richard, Timothy (tsl) One of the world's literary masterpieces. Introduction to a great chinese epic or religious allegory by ch'iu ch'ang ch'un born a.d. 1148. . . **JNCBRAS** 44 (1913) 3-10. Re hsi yu chi.

Scarborough, William. The popular religious litera-ture of the chinese. **ChRec** 13.4 (july-aug 1882) 13.5 (sept-oct 1882) 337-355.

Schipper, K.M. The divine jester, some remarks on the gods of the chinese marionette theater. **ASBIE** 21 (1966) 81-94.

Schüler, W. Das chinesische volkstheater in religiöses bedeutung. **ZMK** 25 (1910) 27-38.

Steininger, Hans. **Hauch- und körperseele und der dämon bei kuan yin tze; untersuchungen zur chinesischen psychologie und ontologie.** Leipzig (1953) 93 p.

Suzuki, Teitaro and Paul Carus (tsl) **T'ai-shang kan-ying p'ien.** Chicago (1906) repr la salle, ill (1950) Popular tract.

Suzuki, Teitaro and Paul Carus (tsl) **Yin wen chih.** Chicago (1906) repr la salle, ill (1950) Popular tract.

Turrettini, François (tsl) **Le livre des récompenses et des peines.** Génève (1889) T'ai-shang kan-ying p'ien.

Watters, T. Chinese fox-myths. **JNCBRAS** 8 (1873) 45-65.

Webster, James (tsl) **The kan ying pien. . . with full introduction, the text, translation, and notes.** Shanghai (1918)

Wen, Ch'ung-i. A study of the river god of the nine songs. **ASBIE** 9 (1960) engl summ 161-162.

Wen, Ch'ung-i. The supreme being and the natural gods in the nine songs. **ASBIE** 17 (1964) engl summ 70-71.

Wetterwald, Albert. Le diable sonneur de cloches. RC (1906) 24-41.

Whitaker, K.P.K. Tsaur jyr's 'luoshern fu.' (On the goddess of the luoh river) AM ser 3, 4 (1954) 36-56.

Wieger, Léon. Catéchisms taoïste (t'ai-shang kan-ying p'ien) In author's Rudiments, 4. Morale et usages, ho-kien-fou, 2nd ed (1905) 231-299.

Williams, Mrs E.T. Some popular religious literature of the chinese. JNCBRAS 33 (1900-01) 11-29.

Williams, F. Wells. Chinese folklore and some western analogies. Annual report of the board of regents of the smithsonian institution (1900) 575-600.

Willoughby-Meade, G. Ghost and vampire tales of china. AR 21 (1925) 690-700; 22 (1926) 113-148.

Yetts, W.P. Taoist tales. NCR 2 (1920) 290-297.

35. SECTS AND SECRET SOCIETIES

Alabaster, Chaloner. The antiquity of freemasonry in china. NCH (5 feb 1860) 100-101.

Bach, A.H. Die triasgesellschaft. FO 2 (1903) 268-283.

Balfour, Frederic. Secret societies and their political significance. In author's Waifs and strays, london and shanghai (1876) 23-38.

Balfour, Frederic H. Secret societies in china. JMGS 7 (1891) 40-56. Same title in Goldthwaite's geographical magazine 4 (1892) 775-782.

Baynes, Herbert. Secret societies in china. IAQR 3rd ser, 6 (1898) 318-321.

Blake, Lady. The triad society and the restoration of the ming dynasty. NC 71 (1912) 667-687.

Blythe, Wilfred. The impact of chinese secret societies in malaya. London (1970) 14 + 566 p, bibliog.

Boyle, F. Chinese secret societies. Harper's new monthly magazine 83 (june-nov 1891) 595-602.

Brace, A.J. Some secret societies in szechwan. JWCBorderResS 8 (1936) 177-180.

Candlin, George F. The associated fists. The society which caused the riots, and led to war in china. OC 14 (sept 1900) 551-561. About the boxers.

Castellane, le comte Boni de. Boxeurs et sociétés secrètes en chine. RDM 10e sér, 160 (1 aout 1900) 689-700.

Chan, Hok-lam. The white lotus-maitreya doctrine and popular uprisings in ming and ch'ing china. Sinologica 10 (1969) 211-233.

Chao, Wei-pang. Secret religious societies in north china in the ming dynasty. FS 7 (1948) 95-115.

Chavannes, Édouard. La société des boxeurs en chine au commencement du XIXe siècle. JA 9e sér, 17 (1901) 164-168.

Ch'en, Jerome. Secret societies. Ch'ing-shih wen-t'i 1.3 (feb 1966) 13-16.

Chesneaux, Jean. Chinese secret societies in the XIX-XX centuries. Ch'ing-shih wen-t'i 1.1 (may 1965) 5-8.

Chesneaux, Jean (ed) MPSSC. Paris (1970) PMSSC. Stanford univ (1972) 328 p, notes, bibliog, gloss, index. The 2 versions are not same in contents; 9 papers of french version are not in engl; 1 art in engl ed was not in french; many substantially rev in engl.

Chesneaux, Jean. Les sociétés secrètes en chine (XIXe et XXe siècles) Paris (1965) 277 p, illus. Avec la collaboration de Marianne Rochline. Engl tsl Gillian Nettle: Secret societies in china in the 19th and 20th centuries. Hong kong and univ michigan (1971) 210 p, bibliog, chin character index, index, illus.

A chinese secret society: the rise and growth of the 'ch'ing pang.' China review [london] 3 (1934) 35-37.

Comber, Leon. An introduction to chinese secret societies in malaya. Singapore (1957) 77 p, map, 12 pl.

Comber, Leon. The traditional mysteries of chinese secret societies in malaya. Singapore (1961) xii + 113 p, illus.

Cordier, Henri. Les sociétés secrètes chinoises. RE 7.1/2 (1888) 52-72. Same title in Revue bleue, ann 39 (23 mars 1901) 365-369.

Culin, Stewart. The i hing or 'patriotic rising.' A secret society among the chinese in america. Proc numismatic and antiquarian society of philadelphia (1887-89)

Culin, Stewart. Chinese secret societies in the u.s. JAFL 3.8 (feb-mar 1890) 39-43.

DeKorne, John C. **The fellowship of goodness. T'ung shan she. . . A study in contemporary chinese religion.** Grand rapids, mich (1941) vi + 109 p (publ by author in mimeo)

Dubarbier, Georges. Les sociétés secrètes en chine. NR 4e sér, 49 (1928) 31 et seq.

Dunstheimer, Guillaume. Quelques aspects religieux des sociétés secrètes. MPSSC (1970) 69-73. Engl tsl, Some religious aspects of secret societies, in PMSSC (1972) 23-28.

Dunstheimer, G.G. Religion et magie dans le mouvement des boxeurs d'après lex textes chinois. TP 47 (1959) 322-367.

Edkins, Joseph. The books of the modern religious sects in north china. ChRec 19.6 (1888) 261-268; 19.7 (1888) 302-310.

Enjoy, Paul d'. Associations, congrégations et sociétés secrètes chinoises. RIC 7 (15 avr 1907) 440-452.

Enjoy, Paul d'. Congrégations et sociétés secrètes chinoises. La revue 52 (1 nov 1904) 75-89.

Fang, Fu-an. Almost everybody has his secret society in china. CWR (14 june 1930) 60.

Favre, Benoit. Les sociétés de frères jures en chine. TP 19 (1918-19) 1-40.

Favre, Benoit. **Les sociétés secrètes en china; origine–rôle historique–situation actuel.** Paris (1933) 222 p.

Floris, George A. Chinese secret societies. CR 193 (june 1958) 319-322.

G.M.C. The origin of the t'ien ti hwui. NQ 1 (1867) 55-58.

Gambo, Charles. Chinese associations in singapore. JMBRAS 39.2 (1966) 123-168.

Genähr, G. Gottsucher unter den chinesen (lung-hwa-sekte) AMZ 33 (1906) 38-44, 72-77, 117-129.

Geoffrey, C.C. Red spears in china. CSM 22.4 (1927) 27-29.

Giles, Herbert A. **Freemasonry in china.** Amoy (1880) 34 p; 2nd ed shanghai (1890) 38 p with add.

Glick, Carl and Hong Sheng-hwa. **Swords of silence. Chinese secret societies, past and present.** N.Y. (1947) 292 p.

Grootaers, Willem A. Une séance de spiritisme dans une religion secrète à péking en 1948. MCB 9 (1948-51) 92-98.

Grootaers, Willem A. Une société secrète moderne, i-koan-tao. FS 5 (1946) 316-352.

Gutzlaff, Charles. On the secret triad society of china, chiefly from papers belonging to the society found at hong kong. JRAS 8 (1846) 361-367.

Heckethorn, Charles W. **The secret societies of all ages and countries.** London (1875) See vol 1, chap 6, 87 et seq; vol 2, 328.

Hodous, Lewis. The tao tê hsüeh shê, a modern syncretistic sect in china. Actes 18e ICO, Leiden, 1931 (1932) 122-123.

Hoffman, Johann J. Oath taken by members of the triad society, and notices of its origin. ChRep 18.6 (june 1849) 281-295.

Hsiao, Kung-ch'üan. **Rural china: imperial control in the nineteenth century.** Univ washington (1960) See 229-235: Heretical sects.

Hugh, Albert Y. Significance of secret societies in chinese life. CWR 42 (10 sept 1927) 38-39.

Hutson, James (tsl) History of chinese secret societies. CJ 9 (1928) 164-170, 215-221, 276-282; 10 (1929) 12-16. Tsl fr chin tsl of jap work by Hirayama Amane.

Initiation ceremonies of the 'red spears.' PT n.s. 6 (1934) 147-151.

James, F.H. North-china sects. ChRec 30 (1899) 74-76.

James, F.H. Secret societies in shantung. In Records of the 1890 missionary conference, shanghai (1890)

Katschen, Leopold. Chinesische geheimgesell-schaften. Deutsche rundschau für geographie und statistik 22 (1899-1900) 250-254.

Labadie-Lagrave, G. Les sociétés secrètes en chine. TM 6 (1900) 222-223, 230.

Leboucq, P. **Associations de la chine. Lettres du p. leboucq, missionaire au tché-ly-sud-est, publiées par un de ses amis.** Paris (ca 1875?) xiii + 312.

Leboucq, P. Les sociétés religieuses en chine. Tche-ly sud-est, village de iam-kia-sé, ler mars 1875. ER 19e ann, 5e sér, 8 (1875) 641-664.

Leboucq, P. Les sociétés secrètes en chine. District de X. . ., province de tche-ly, 27 février 1875. **ER** 19e ann, 5e sér, 8 (1875) 197-220.

Liao, T'ai-ch'u. The ko lao hui in szechuan. **PA** 20 (1947) 161-173.

Llewellyn, Bernard. Secret societies of china. **CR** 181 (apr 1952) 217-220.

Lutschewitz, W. Die religiösen sekten in nordchina, mit besonderer berücksichtigung d. sekten in shantung. **OstL** 19 (1905) 203-207, 247-251, 291-293, 337-340.

Lyman, Stanford M. Chinese secret societies in the occident: notes and suggestions for research in the sociology of secrecy. **Canadian review of sociology and anthropology** 1 (may 1964) 79-102.

Lyman, Stanford, W.E. Willmott, and Ho Berching. Rules of a chinese secret society in british columbia. **BSOAS** 27.3 (1964) 530-539, illus.

Mangrin, Ignace. Les boxeurs dans le tché-li sud-est. Tchang-kia-tchouang, 25 mars 1900. **Études** 84 (5 aout 1900) 366-399.

Masters, Frederic J. Among the highbinders. An account of chinese secret societies. **ChRec** 23 (1892) 268-273, 305-315.

Matgioï (A. de Pourvoirville) l'**Esprit des races jaune – le taoïsme et les sociétés secrètes chinoises.** Paris (1897) 32 p.

Matgioï (E.A.P. de Pourvoirville) **Le taoïsme et les sociétés secrètes chinoises.** Paris (1897) 32 p.

Miles, George. Vegetarian sects. **ChRec** 33 (1902) 1-10.

Millican, Frank R. (tsl) Religious elements in the esoteric societies of china. **ChRec** 58 (1927) 757-766. Tsl of art by Wang, Chao-hsiang: Chung-kuo pi-mi she-hui chung ti tsung-chiao, in **Wen-she yüeh-k'an** 2 (jan 1927) 41-54.

Milne, Dr. Communicated by Robert Morrison. Some account of a secret society in china entitled 'the triad society.' **Trans RAS** 1 (1827) 240-250.

Morgan, W.P. **Triad societies in hong kong.** Hong kong (1960) 306 p, app, illus.

Morrison, Robert. A transcript in roman characters, with a translation, of a manifesto in the chinese language, issued by the triad society. **JRAS** 1 (1834) 93-95.

Muramatsu, Yuji. Some themes in chinese rebel ideologies. In A.F. Wright (ed) **The confucian persuasion,** stanford univ (1960) 241-267.

Mury, Francis. Les sociétés secrètes et le gouvernement chinois. **Revue des revues** 25 (15 juil 1900) 117-134, 17 gravures.

Newbold, Lt. and Maj.-Gen. Wilson. The chinese secret triad-society tien-ti-huih. **JRAS** 6 (1840-41) 120-158.

Of the tea sect, translated from the peking gazette. **ICG** 1 (may 1817) 19-22. Re ch'ing-ch'a men chiao.

Origine des boxeurs [avec une lettre de mgr favier] **Revue française de l'étranger et des colonies** (août 1900) 464-471.

Palatre, P. La magie et le nénuphar blanc au kiangnan. **MC** 10 (1878) 434-441, 446-450, 458-465.

Pelliot, Paul. La secte du lotus blanc et la secte du nuage blanc. **BEFEO** 3.2 (1903) 304-317. See further: Notes additionelles sur. . .in **ibid** 4 (1904) 436-440.

Pickering, W.A. Chinese secret societies and their origin. **JSBRAS** pt 1 no 1 (july 1878) 63-84; pt 2 no 3 (july 1879) 1-18.

Playfair, G.M.H. The lolao. . . secret society. **ChRev** 15 (1886-87) 129-130.

Porter, H.D. Secret sects in shantung. **ChRec** 17 (1886) 1-10, 64-73.

Pourvoirville, Albert de. La révolution et les sociétés secrètes en chine. **Revue de paris** (1 mars 1912) 119-132.

Rankin, Mary L.B. The ku-t'ien incident (1895): christians versus the ts'ai-hui. **PC** 15 (dec 1961) 30-61.

Rape, C.B. Buddhistic brotherhood of the sacred army and the adventures of an american ship on the upper yangtsze. **CWR** 44 (17 mar 1928) 62-63.

Rawlinson, Frank. A study of the rebellions of china. **ChRec** 36 (1905) 107-117.

Richard, Timothy. The secret sects of china. **CMH** (1896) 41-45.

Rué, M. Sociétés secrètes en chine – la secte des trois-points au kouang-si. **MC** 38 (1906) 190-191.

Saglio, Charles. Les sociétés secrètes en chine. **Revue encyclopédique (larousse)** (1 sept 1900) 686-689.

Schlegel, Gustave. **Thian ti hwui. The hung league or heaven-earth-league. A secret society with the chinese in china and india.** Batavia (1866) x1 + 253, tables, illus. Repr N.Y. (1973)

Schram, Stuart R. Mao tse-tung and secret societies. **CQ** 27 (1966) 1-13.

Secret associations. **ICG** no 4 (1818) 87-88.

Les Sectes chinoises. **RIC** no 118 (21 janv 1901) 66-67.

Shih, Vincent. Some chinese rebel ideologies. **TP** 44.1/3 (1956) 150-226.

La Société des boxeurs en chine au commencement du XIXe siècle. **JA** 9e sér, 17 (1901) 164-168.

Les Sociétés secrètes en chine. **AEO** 6 (1883-84) 209-211.

Sparling, G.W. China's new religious sects. **West china missionary news** 26 (1924) 17-22.

Speed, John G. Chinese secret societies of new york city. **Harper's weekly** 44 (july 1900) 658.

Stanton, William. The triad society, or heaven and earth association. **ChRev** 21 (1892-93) 159-181, 217-230, 311-335, 378-399; 22 (1893-94) 429-447. See further same title publ as book, hong kong (1900) 124 p.

Stirling, W.G. The coffin breakers society. **JMBRAS** 4.1 (1926) 129-132.

Stirling, W.G. The red and white flag societies. **JMBRAS** 3.1 (1925) 57-61.

T'ang, Leang-li. The historical significance of the chinese secret societies. **PT** n.s. 3 (1932-33) 222-228.

Tien, Tsung. Chinese secret societies. **Orient** 3.2 (1952) 23-26; 3.3 (1952) 48-50; 3.4 (1952) 56-58; 3.5 (1952) 39-41; 3.6 (1953) 47-50.

Topley, Marjorie. The great way of former heaven; a group of chinese secret religious sects. **BSOAS** 26 (1963) 362-392, tables.

Topley, Marjorie. Notes on some vegetarian halls in hong kong belonging to the sect of hsien-t'ien tao (the way of former heaven) **JHKBRAS** 8 (1968) 135-148.

Twinem, P. de W. Modern syncretic religious societies in china. **JR** 5 (1925) 463-482, 595-606.

Wakeman, Frederic jr. The secret societies of kwangtung, 1800-1856. In **NCELYY** (1970) 127-160.

Ward, Barbara E. Chinese secret societies. In Norman MacKenzie (ed) **Secret societies,** london (1967) 174-203.

Ward, John S.M. and W. G. Stirling. **The hung society, or, the society of heaven and earth.** London (1925-26) 3 vol, diagr, illus.

Williams, S. Wells. Oath taken by members of the triad society, and notices of its origin. **ChRep** 18 (1849) 280-295.

Wylie, Alexander. Secret societies in china. **NCH** 165 (24 sept 1853) repr in **Shanghae almanac for 1854 and miscel.** Also repr in author's **Chinese researches** (1897) 110-146.

Yu, Shih-yu. **Religions secrètes contemporaines dans le nord de la chine.** Chengtu (1948) viii + 175 p, illus.

36. MODERN (PRE-1949) RELIGION

The anti-religion movement, symposium **CSPSR** 7.2 (1923) 103-113.

Bellah, Robert N. The religious situation in the far east. **CRJ** 4 (june 1963) 95-117.

Braden, Charles S. **Modern tendencies in world religions.** N.Y. (1933) See chap 3, Modern tendencies in china, 87-135.

Brou, Alexandre. Bulletin des missions chine: la défaite de confucius. **Études** 153 (20 nov 1917) 493-506.

Brou, Alexandre. La nouvelle chine et le culte de confucius. **RC** (janv-avril 1918) 3-15, illus.

Buck, John Lossing, Peasant movement. **CCY** (1928) 265-282.

Chan, Wing-tsit. **Religious trends in modern china.** Columbia univ (1953) xiii + 327 p, bibliog, gloss, chin character list, index.

Chang, Neander S. The anti-religion movement. **ChRec** 54.8 (aug 1923) 459-467.

Couling, C.E. The oldest dress and the newest; or taoism in modern dress. **HJ** 22 (1924) 245-259.

Cressy, Earl H. A study in indigenous religions. In Orville A. Petty (ed) **Laymen's foreign missions inquiry,** supplementary series pt 2, **fact-finders' reports,** vol 5, **china,** n.y. and london (1933) 655-716.

Day, Clarence B. Contemporary chinese cults. **FEQ** 6 (1947) 294-299.

Day, Clarence B. Current values in peasant religion. **ChRec** 63 (1932) 419-427.

DeKorne, John C. **The fellowship of goodness. T'ung shan she. . . A study in contemporary chinese religion.** Grand rapids, mich (1941) vi + 109 p (publ by author in mimeo)

Doré, Henri. Le confucéisme sous la république. **La chine** 28 (1922) 1533-1543; 29 (1922) 1559-1571.

Doré, Henri. Le confucéisme sous la république, 1911-1922. **NCR** 4 (1922) 298-319. See also same author's Le culte de confucius sous la république chinoise (1911-1922) **Études** 172 (20 août 1922) 433-448.

Drake, F.S. The tao yüan, a new religious and spiritualistic movement. **ChRec** 54 (1923) 133-144.

Eberhard, Wolfram. Neuere forschungen zur religion chinas 1920-1932. **ARW** 33 (1933) 304-344. Engl tsl: Studies of chinese religion 1920-1932, in author's **MSVC** (1971) 335-399.

Edkins, Joseph. The books of the modern religious sects in north china. **ChRec** 19 (1888) 261-268, 302-310.

Edwards, E.D. Religion in modern china. **PA** 28 (mar 1955) 79-81. Rev of W.T. Chan, **Religious trends in modern china** q.v.

Elia, Pascal M. d' La religion et les religions d'après un des plus grands lettrés contemporains [liang ch'i-ch'ao] **RC** (janv-avril 1920) 278-287, illus.

Erkes, E. Ueber den heutigen taoismus und seine literatur. **Litterae orientales** 53 (1933) 1-5. Offpr publ sep, leipzig (1933) 10 p.

Franke, Otto. **Geistige strömungen im heutigen china.** Berlin (1903-04) 29 p.

Franke, O. Das religiöse problem in china. **ARW** 17 (1914) Offpr publ sep, leipzig and berlin (1914) 32 p.

Hamilton, C.H. Religion and the new culture movement in china. **JR** 1 (1921) 225-232.

Hodous, Lewis. The chinese church of the five religions. **JR** 4 (1924) 71-76.

Hodous, Lewis. A chinese premillenarian. **JR** 4 (1924) 592-599. Re t'ang huan-chang and the cult of the amalgamation of the 6 true religions; study of an 1822 manifesto by t'ang.

Hodous, Lewis. The ministry of chinese religions. **IRM** 25 (1936) 329-341.

Hodous, Lewis. Non-christian religious movements in china. In M.T. Stauffer (ed) **The christian occupation of china,** shanghai (1922) 27-31.

Hodous, Lewis. The tao tê hsüeh shê, a modern syncretistic sect in china. **Actes 18e ICO, Leiden 1931** 18 (1932) 122-123.

Johnston, Charles. A chinese statesman's view of religion. **HJ** 7 (oct 1908) 19-26. Statesman is k'ang yu-wei.

Johnston, R.F. The religious future of china. **NC** 65 (nov 1913) 908-923.

Ku, Hung-ming. The religion of a gentleman in china. **CSM** 17 (1922) 676-679.

Lancashire, Douglas. Confucianism in the twentieth century. In Nicholas Tarling (ed) **China and its place in the world,** univ auckland (1967) 26-42.

Löwenthal, Rudolf. **The religious periodical press in china.** Peking (1940) 294 p.

Matgioï (E.A.P. de Pourvoirville) Le taoisme contemporain: sa hiérarchie, son enseignement, son rôle. **MCSJ** 19 (1889) 179-218.

Millican, Frank R. Philosophical and religious thought in china. **CCY** (1926) 423-469.

Moore, Frederick. President yuan shih-kai at the altar of heaven. **Far eastern review** 11 (feb 1915) 349-354, 14 fig.

Perrot, Albert. Le retour offensif de la vieille chine. Le confucianisme redevenu religion d'état. **Études** (20 mai 1914) 461-480 (juil 1914) 425-438, fig.

The Position and prospects of confucianism in china. **Chinese review** 1 (apr 1914) 50-51.

Rawlinson, Frank.J. Modern revolution and religion in china [1911-1927] **IRM** 18 (1929) 161-178.

Rawlinson, Frank J. **Revolution and religion in modern china. A brief study of the effects of modern revolutionary movements in china on its religious life.** Shanghai (1929) 97 p. 'Modern' refers to period 1911-1927.

Reid, Gilbert. Recent religious movements in china. **China mission year book** (1924) 59-66.

Reid, Gilbert. Trends in china's religious life. **CCY** (1926) 71-79.

Rousselle, Erwin. Der lebendige taoismus im heutigen china. **Sinica** 8 (1933) 122-131.

Rousselle, Erwin. Modern welt- und lebensanschauung in china. **Sinica** 6 (1931) 212-214.

Roy, A.T. Attacks upon confucianism in the 1911-1927 period. **CCJ** 4.1 (nov 1964) 10-26.

Roy, A.T. Attacks upon confucianism in the 1911-1927 period (2) and (3) From a taoist lawyer: wu yü. **CCJ** 4 (may 1965) 149-163; 5 (nov 1965) 67-78.

Slater, N.B. Religion in china today. **Religions** 44 (july 1943) 15-17.

La Suppression des processions en chine. **TM** 15 (1909) 14.

Ts'ai Yuan-pei. On religion and aesthetics. **PT** n.s. 4 (1933) 180.

Tsu Yu-yue. Trends of thought and religion in china. **NO** (1933)

Twinem, P. de W. Modern syncretic religious societies in china. **JR** 5 (1925) 463-482, 595-606.

Vargas, P. de. The religious problem in the chinese renaissance. **IRM** 15 (1926) 3-20.

Welch, Holmes. The chang t'ien shih and taoism in china. **JOS** 4 (1957-58) 188-212.

Werner, E.T.C. Reform in chinese mourning rites. **NCR** 2 (1920) 223-247.

Williams, E.T. Confucianism and the new china. **HTR** 9.3 (july 1916) 258-285.

Youan chi kai, grand prêtre de ciel. **BAF** 15 (avr-juin 1915) 75-77.

Yu Shih-yu. **Religions secrètes contemporaines dans le nord de la chine.** Chengtu (1948) viii + 175 p, illus.

37. RELIGION UNDER COMMUNISM

Bellah, Robert N. The religious situation in the far east. **CRJ** 4 (june 1963) 95-117.

Bush, Richard C. The impact of communism on religions in china. In **Proc 11th ICHR, claremont, calif (1965)** vol 3 (1968) 57-72.

Bush, Richard C. jr. **Religion in communist china.** Nashville and n.y. (1970) 432 p, index.

Chan, W.T. Modern trends in chinese philosophy and religion. In Joseph Kitagawa (ed) **Modern trends in world religions,** la salle, ill (1959) 193-220.

Chen, Chung-kuei. Respect for religious beliefs [in communist china] **CB** 449 (11 apr 1957) 6-10.

Chen, Kenneth K.S. Religious changes in communist china. **CC** 11.4 (1970) 56-62.

China notes. (Periodical dealing mainly with religion and related topics on mainland china; many tsl) East asia dept, national council of churches, n.y. (sept-dec 1962 –)

Croizier, Ralph C. (ed) **China's cultural legacy and communism.** N.Y. (1970) See chap 2 sec 3, Ting Chung: Repair of temples and preservation of cultural objects; chap 5, Religion, art by Holmes Welch, Ch'u Chung, and Joseph R. Levenson.

Eitner, Hans-Jürgen. "Sie ziehen es vor, sich an gott zu wenden": das kommunistische china im kampf mit der volksreligion. **Zeitwende; die neue furche** 32.5 (mai 1961) 320-326.

Erkes, Eduard. Die heutige stellung der religionen in china. **Numen** 3 (1956) 28-35.

Étiemble, René. Confucius et la chine contemporaine. **Évidences** (1954) 13-18.

Faure, Edgar. **The serpent and the tortoise. Problems of the new china.** N.Y. (1958) Tsl fr french Lovett F. Edwards. See chap 15, The regime and the cults; chap 16, The regime and the cults (continued – the other cults) 129-156.

Firzgerald, C.P. Les communistes chinois et la religion jusqu'à la révolution culturelle. **Problèmes politiques et sociaux** 21 (22 mai 1970) 17-20.

Fitzgerald, C.P. Religion and china's cultural revolution. **PA** 40 (1967) 124-129.

Franke, Wolfgang. Der kampf der chinesischen revolution gegen den konfuzianismus. **NachrDGNVO** 74 (1953) 3-9.

Glüer, Winfried. Religion in the people's republic of china. A survey of the official chinese press 1964-1967. **CF** 10.3 (1967) 34-57.

Graf, O. Religion und 'religion' im china von heute. **NZM** 10 (1954) 96-108.

Herzer, Rudolf. Konfuzius in der volksrepublik china. **ZDMG** 119.2 (1970) 302-331.

Hinton, Harold C. Religion in china since 1949. In S. Chandrasekhar (ed) **A decade of mao's china**, bombay (1960)

Ho, Wellington. Religion versus atheism. **FCR** 14.12 (dec 1964) 45-49, illus.

Huang, Lucy Jen. The role of religion in communist chinese society. **AsSur** 11.7 (july 1971) 693-708. Abrmt repr in **CWayRel** (1973) 239-241.

Kramers, R.P. Die lao-tsû-diskussionen in der chinesischen volksrepublik. **AS** 22 (1968) 31-67.

LaDany, L. Religious trends in china. **Social action** 19 (oct-dec 1969) 316-322.

LaDany, Ladislao. The tortuous history of the cult of mao. **CNA** 743 (7 feb 1969) 1-7.

Lee, Rensselaer W. III. General aspects of chinese communist religious policy, with soviet comparisons. **CQ** 19 (july-sept 1964) 161-173. Partially repr in **CWayRel** (1973) 232-235.

Lee, W.J. Religion's mainland ordeal. **FCR** 15 (july 1965) 15-20.

Levenson, Joseph R. The communist attitude toward religion. In Werner Klatt (ed) **The china model**, hong kong (1965)

Life and religion. **CNA** 717 (19 july 1968) 1-7.

Lohmann, T. Religion im alten und neueren china. **Theologische literaturzeitung** 85 (1960) 805-806.

London, Ivan D. and Mariam B. Attitudes of mainland youth toward traditional chinese customs and beliefs. **CC** 11.4 (dec 1970) 46-55.

MacInnis, Donald E. Maoism and religion in china today. In Donald R. Cutler (ed) **The religious situation: 1969**, boston (1969) 3-24.

MacInnis, Donald E. Maoism: the religious analogy. **Christian century** 85 (10 jan 1968) 39-42.

Maoism and religion in china today. N.Y. Missionary research library **Occasional bulletin** 19.9 (sept 1968) 1-12.

Matthias, Leo L. Religionen im neuen china. **Merkur; deutsche zeitung für europäisches denken** 11.2 (feb 1957) 168-184.

Michael, Franz H. Ideology and the cult of mao. In Frank N. Trager and William Henderson (ed) **Communist china, 1949-1969: a twenty-year appraisal**, n.y. (1970) 27-44.

Nivison, David S. Communist ethics and chinese tradition. **JAS** 16 (1956) 51-74.

O'Connor, Patrick. 'Freedom of religion' in yenan. **China magazine** 17.4 (apr 1947) 25-28.

La Question du confucianisme et le gouvernement de pékin. **BAF** 16 (oct-dec 1916) 175-176.

Ravenholt, Albert. **The gods must go!** AUFS: Far east (china) **AR-9-58** (1958) 7 p.

Religionen und religionspolitik im alten und neuen china. Frankfurt a.m. **China-analysen** 9 (1970) 46-96.

Roll, Christian. Die religionen im kommunistischen china. **Aussenpolitik** 15 (july 1964) 483-491.

Schram, Stuart R. Mao tse-tung and secret societies. **CQ** 27 (1966) 1-13.

Sohier, A. La religion en chine populaire. In Centre d'étude des pays de l'est, institut de sociologie solvay, univ libre de bruxelles et centre national pour l'étude des pays à régime communiste (ed) **Le régime et les institutions de la république populaire chinoise**, brussels (1960) 138-151.

Some recent articles on religion in communist china. **CB** 510 (15 june 1958) 30 p.

Staiger, Brunhild. **Das konfuzius-bild im kommunistischen china; die neubewertung von konfuzius in der chinesisch-marxistischen gesichtsschreibung.** Wiesbaden (1969) 143 p.

Sumiya, Kazuhiko. The long march and the exodus: "the thought of mao tse-tung" and the contemporary significance of "emissary prophecy." Tsl fr jap Pharis Harvey, Hiroshi Shinmi and Tadashi Miyabe. In Bruce Douglass and Ross Terrill (ed) **China and ourselves; explorations and revisions by a new generation**, boston (1969) 189-223.

Taussig, H.C. Religion and state in china. **EW** 11 (feb 1957) 12-14.

Thomas, M.M. and M. Abel. Religion, state, and ideologies in china. In **Religion, state, and ideologies in east asia**, bangalore (1965) 15-30.

USJPRS reports:
Religion in communist china. NY-59/1
(19 apr 1958)
Selected translations on religions in china.
DC-513-D (3 feb 1959) 4 p.
Selected translations of religious articles on communist china from **T'ien feng** nos 6 and 7.
NY-1313-N (5 mar 1959) 51 p.
Selected articles [on religion in communist china]
NY-1348 (11 mar 1959) 21 p.
Newspaper articles on activities of religious
circles (communist china) NY-1454
(7 apr 1959) 25 p.
Articles [on religion in communist china] DC-828
(24 july 1959) 9 p.
Religious persecution in communist china.
DC-952 (10 oct 1959) 9 p.
Translations of religious articles from chinese
communist publications. NY-1184-N
(1959) 43 p.
Translations of selected articles on religious
theory and activity in communist china.
NY-1210-N (1959) 23 p.
Translations of chinese communist articles on
religion. DC-1150, 3192, 5108, 5474 (feb-
sept 1960) 23, 8, 26, 12 p.

Varma, S.C. Religion under communism.
Indian journal of social research 7.1 (apr 1966)
37-40.

Welch, Holmes. Changing attitudes toward
religion in modern china. In **China in
perspective**, wellesley, mass. (1967) 79-97.

Welch, Holmes. Facades of religion in china.
AsSur 10.7 (1970) 614-626.

Wu, Yao-tsung. Problems of religious policy
[in communist china] **CB** 449 (11 apr 1957) 1-5.

Wu, Yao-tsung. Religion is free in china.
CRecon 1.6 (nov-dec 1952) 33-37.

Ya Han-chang. On the difference between the
theist idea, religion, and feudal superstitions;
incidentally, a reply to comrades yu hsiang
and liu chün-wang. **SCMM** 413 (20 apr 1964)
1-7.

Ya, Han-zhang. Les options idéologiques de la
liberté des croyances religieuses. **Problèmes
politiques et sociaux** 21 (22 mai 1970) 4-9.

Yang, C.K. **The chinese family in the communist
revolution**. M.I.T. (1959) repr in author's
**Chinese communist society: the family and the
village**, m.i.t. (1965) See chap 10, Secularization of the family institution, 183-190.

Yu, Hsiang and Liu Chün-wang. The correct
recognition and handling of the problem of
religion. **SCMM** 410 (31 mar 1964) 41-49.

38. TAIWAN

Albrecht, Ardon and Go Sin-gi (tsl fr taiwanese)
**A guidebook for christians on taiwanese customs and
superstitions.** Taipei (1965) Tsl of a romanized bk
written by taiwanese lutheran pastor.

Cammann, Schuyler. On the decoration of modern
temples in taiwan and hongkong. **JAOS** 88.4
(1968) 785-790. Criticism of W. Eberhard: Topics
and moral values in chinese temple decorations q.v.

Chen, Chi-lu. An annual procession of tai-chion-
ya-bio (a taoist temple) of hsin-chuang, taipei
prefecture. **Studia taiwanica** 1 (1956) i-iv, illus.

Chen, Chung-min. Ancestor worship and clan
organization in a rural village of taiwan. **ASBIE** 23
(1967) engl summ 192-193.

Diamond, Norma. **K'un shen. A taiwan village.**
N.Y. etc. (1969) See esp chap 6, The religious
life in k'un shen, 84-107; but also passim.

Eberhard, Wolfram. Religious activities and religious
books in modern china. **ZMR** 49 (1965) Repr in
author's **MSVC** (1971) 161-176.

Eberhard, Wolfram. **Studies in taiwanese folktales.**
Taipei (1970) 193 p.

Eberhard, Wolfram. Topics and moral values in
chinese temple decorations. **JAOS** 87.1 (1967)
22-32. Further see Eberhard's Rejoinder to
schuyler cammann,**ibid** 88.4 (1968) 790-792.

Freytag, Justus. **The church in villages of taiwan.
The impact of modern society and folk-religion on
rural churches.** Tainan (1969) 117 p, bibliog.

Gallin, Bernard. **Hsin hsing, taiwan: a chinese
village in change.** Univ california (1966) See
chap 8, Religion and magic in hsin hsing village,
231-269.

Hang, T. and J. Masson. Une enquête religieuse chez
des étudiants de tainan (taiwan) **SM** 16 (1967)
99-115.

Hwang, Teh-shih. An important characteristic of
taiwan folk belief. **JCS** 6 (1969) 79-85.

Kramer, Gerald P. and George Wu. **An introduction to taiwanese folk religions.** Taipei (1970)
71 p, tables, illus.

Lévesque, Léonard. **Hakka beliefs and customs.**
Tsl fr french Maynard Murphy. Taichung (1969)
113 p. Refers esp to hsinchu county.

Li Yih-yuan. Ghost marriage, shamanism and kinship
behavior in rural taiwan. In **FRWVSP** (1968) 97-99.

Lighting the way for the spirits. **FCR** 20.3
(mar 1970) 37-44.

Liu, Chi-wan. The belief and practice of the wen-
shen cult in south china and formosa. **PIAHA**
(1963?) 715-722.

Liu, Chi-wan. The temple of the god of epidemics
in taiwan. **ASBIE** 22 (1966) engl summ 93-95.

Mollard, Sidney G. jr. Confucius and music.
EWCR 3.3 (feb 1967) 31-39.

O'Hara, Albert. Attitudes toward religion in the
university-world of free china. **SM** 16 (1967)
75-98. Repr in author's collection: **RCCS**
(1971) 111-134.

O'Hara, Albert R. A factual survey of taipei's
temples and their functions. **JSS** 17 (1967)
323-337. Repr in author's collection: **RCCS**
(1971) 91-109.

Petterson, Richard. The native arts of taiwan.
Claremont quarterly 11.3 (spring 1964) 49-58
+ 12 p photos.

Religion. In Stanford univ china project (comp)
Taiwan (formosa) HRAF 1 (1956) 193-206.

Saso, Michael. **Taiwan feasts and customs. A
handbook of the principal feasts and customs
of the lunar calendar on taiwan.** Hsinchu (1965)
3rd ed (1968) 95 p (mimeo)

Saso, Michael. The taoist tradition in taiwan.
CQ 41 (jan-mar 1970) 83-102.

Schipper, K.M. The divine jester; some remarks
on the gods of the chinese marionette theater.
ASBIE 21 (1966) 81-94, 2 p pl.

Social values, patterns of living, and folk beliefs.
In Stanford univ china project (comp) **Taiwan
(formosa)** HRAF 1 (1956) 149-162.

Sung, Lung-fei. Decorative art of the 'chiao tan'
structure of sungshan. **ASBIE** 25 (1968)
engl abrmt 219-224 + 18 p pl, illus.

Thelin, Mark and Lin Wen-lang. Religion in two
taiwanese villages. **JCS** 3 (1963) 44-57.

Thompson, Laurence G. Notes on religious trends
in taiwan. **MS** 23 (1964) 319-350, map.

Welch, Holmes. The chang t'ien shih and taoism in
china. **JOS** 4 (1957-58) 188-212, illus.

Yao, Ruth. Temples of taiwan. **FCR** 14.4
(apr 1964) 13-20, illus.

39. OVERSEAS CHINESE (INCLUDING HONG KONG)

Anderson, Eugene N. jr. Sacred fish. **Man** n.s. 4
(1969) 443-449. Repr in author's collection:
Essays on south china's boat people, taipei (1972)

Baker, Hugh D. Burial, geomancy and ancestor
worship. In **ASONT** (1965) 36-39.

Baker, Hugh D.R. **A chinese lineage village. Sheung
shui** [new territories, hong kong] Stanford univ
(1968) 237 p, bibliog, gloss, index, photos. See
passim.

Berkowitz, Morris I., Frederick P. Brandauer and
John H. Reed. **Folk religion in an urban setting.
A study of hakka villagers in transition.** Hong
kong (1969) 167 p, maps, table, illus. Also publ in
CF 12.3/4 (1969) 1-167.

Berkowitz, Morris I., Frederick P. Brandauer, and
John H. Reed. Study program on chinese religious
practices in hong kong -- a progress report. **CF**
11.3 (1968) 5-19.

Blythe, Wilfred. **The impact of chinese secret
societies in malaya.** London (1970) 14 + 566 p,
bibliog.

Boxer, Baruch. Space, change and feng-shui in tsuen
wan's urbanization. **JAAS** 3 (1968) 226-240.

Buck, Samuel (pseud) Chinese temples in hong
kong. **Orient** 2.7 (1952) 27-29.

Burkhardt, Valentine R. **Chinese creeds and
customs.** Hong kong, vol 1 (1953) 181 p; vol 2
(1955) 201 p; vol 3 (1958) 164 p; each vol with
index, illus.

Cheng, Homer Hui-ming. **Chinese religious
festivals in singapore.** Singapore (1949)

Choa, Gerald. Chinese traditional medicine and
contemporary hong kong. In **TICHK** (1967) 31-35.

Comber, Leon. **Chinese ancestor worship in
malaya.** Singapore (1956) 41 p, illus.

Comber, Leon. **Chinese magic and superstitions in
malaya.** Singapore (1957) 50 p, illus.

Comber, Leon. **Chinese temples in singapore.**
Singapore (1958) 110 p, illus.

Comber, Leon. **An introduction to chinese secret
societies in malaya.** Singapore (1957) 77 p, map,
illus.

Comber, Leon. **The traditional mysteries of chinese secret societies in malaya.** Singapore (1961) xii + 113 p, illus.

Culin, Stewart. Customs of the chinese in america. **JAFL** 3 (july-sept 1890) 191-200.

Culin, Stewart. **The religious ceremonies of the chinese in the eastern cities of the united states.** Philadelphia (1887) 23 p, illus.

Edmonds, Juliet. Religion, intermarriage and assimilation: the chinese in malaya. **Race** 10 (july 1968) 57-67.

Elliott, Alan J.A. **Chinese spirit-medium cults in singapore.** Dept of anthropology, london school of economics and political science (1955) 179 p, illus.

Finn, D.J. Cult-objects from aberdeen (hong kong, china) in the lateran museum. **AL** 1 (1937) 35-68.

Gambo, Charles. Chinese associations in singapore. **JMBRAS** 39.2 (1966) 123-168.

Hayes, James W. A ceremony to propitiate the gods at tong fuk, lantau, 1958. **JHKBRAS** 5 (1965) 122-124.

Hayes, James W. Chinese temples in the local setting. In **TICHK** (1967) 86-95.

Hayes, James W. Geomancy and the village. In **TICHK** (1967) 22-30.

Hayes, James W. A list of temples in the southern district of the new territories and new kowloon, 1899-1967. In **TICHK** (1967) 96-98.

Hayes, James W. Movement of villages on lantau island for fung shui reasons. **JHKBRAS** 3 (1963) 143-144.

Hayes, James W. Removal of villages for fung shui reasons. Another example from lantau island, hong kong. **JHKBRAS** 9 (1969) 156-158.

Hooyman and Vogelaar. Relation abrégée du tien-bing, vulgairement appelé la fête de morts, chez les chinois de batavia. **JA** 2 (1923) 236-243. Tirée des **Mémoires de la société de batavia** 6 (1792) et trad du hollandais.

Kung, Chan-yuen. The development of the islet fu-t'ang men (fu tong mun) and the temples in various parts of the region. In Lo Hsiang-lin (ed) **Hong kong and its external communications before 1842,** hong kong (1963) 119-132.

Lo, Dorothy and Comber, Leon. **Chinese festivals in malaya.** Singapore (1958) 66 p, bibliog, indexes, illus.

Lombard-Salmon, Claudine. La communauté chinoise de makasar, vie religieuse. **TP** 55 (1969) 241-297.

Lyman, Stanford M. Chinese secret societies in the occident: notes and suggestions for research in the sociology of secrecy. **Canadian review of sociology and anthropology** 1 (1964) 79-102.

Lyman, Stanford, Willmott, W.E. and Ho, Berching. Rules of a chinese secret society in british columbia. **BSOAS** 27.3 (1964) 530-539, illus.

Mollard, Sidney G. jr. Confucius and music. **EWCR** 3.3 (feb 1967) 31-39.

Morgan, W.P. **Triad societies in hong kong.** Hong kong (1960) 306 p, illus.

Schlegel, G. La fête de fouler le feu célébrée en chine et par les chinois à java, le treize du troisième mois, anniversaire du 'grande dieu protecteur de la vie (pao chîng [sheng] ta ti) **IAE** 9 (1896) 193-195, 1 pl.

Schlegel, Gustave. **Thian ti hwui. The hung-league or heaven-earth-league. A secret society with the chinese in china and india.** Batavia (1866) x1 + 253, 16 tables, illus.

Speed, John G. Chinese secret societies of new york city. **Harper's weekly** 44 (july 1900) 658.

Stirling, W.G. Chinese exorcists. **JMBRAS** 2 (1924) 41-47.

Stirling, W.G. The coffin breakers society. **JMBRAS** 4.1 (1926) 129-132.

Stirling, W.G. The red and white flag societies. **JMBRAS** 3.1 (1925) 57-61.

The Sian Giap. Religion and overseas chinese assimilation in southeast asian countries. **Revue du sud-est asiatique** 2 (1965) 67-83.

Topley, Marjorie. Chinese occasional rites in hong kong. In **TICHK** (1967) 99-117.

Topley, Marjorie. Chinese religion and religious institutions in singapore. **JMBRAS** 29 (1956) 70-118.

Topley, Marjorie. Chinese women's vegetarian houses in singapore. **JMBRAS** 27.1 (1954) 51-67.

Topley, Marjorie. The emergence and social function of chinese religious associations in singapore. **CSSH** 3.3 (1961) 289-314. Same title in Lloyd A. Fallers (ed) **Immigrants and associations,** the hague (1967) 49-82.

Topley, Marjorie. Ghost marriages among the singapore chinese. **Man** 55 (1955) 29-30. See further same title + A further note, in **Ibid** 56 (1956) 71-72.

Topley, Marjorie. Is confucius dead? **FEER** 58 (21 dec 1967) 561-563.

Topley, Marjorie. Paper charms, and prayer sheets as adjuncts to chinese worship. **JMBRAS** 26 (1953) 63-80, illus.

Topley, Marjorie. Some basic conceptions and their traditional relationship to society. In **TICHK** (1967) 7-21.

Topley, Marjorie. Some occasional rites performed by the singapore cantonese. **JMBRAS** 24 (1951) 120-144.

Topley, Marjorie (ed) **Some traditional chinese ideas and conceptions in hong kong social life today.** Hong kong (1967) 145 p (Abbrev as **TICHK**)

Topley, Marjorie and James W. Hayes. Notes on shrines and temples of tai ping shan street area. In **TICHK** (1967) 123-141.

Topley, Marjorie and James W. Hayes. Notes on some vegetarian halls in hong kong belonging to the sect of hsien-t'ien tao (the way of former heaven) **JHKBRAS** 8 (1968) 135-148.

Tseung, F.I. Some aspects of fortune-telling in hong kong. In **TICHK** (1967) 60-72.

Vaughan, J.D. **The manners and customs of the chinese of the straits settlements.** Singapore (1879) repr taipei (1971) See index, passim.

Ward, John S.M. and W.G. Stirling. **The hung society, or, the society of heaven and earth.** London (1925-26) 3 vol, diagr, illus.

Wilson, B.D. Chinese burial customs in hong kong. **JHKBRAS** 1 (1960-61) 115-123.

Wong, C.S. **A cycle of chinese festivities.** Singapore (1967) xv + 204 p, notes, bibliog, index, illus. Chinese in malaysia.

Wynne, M.L. **Triad and tabur: a survey of the origin of chinese and mohammedan secret societies in the malay peninsula 1800-1935.** Singapore (1941)

Young, W. The feast of lanterns at padang (sumatra) **ChRev** 9 (1880-81) 320-321.

40. COMPARATIVE STUDIES

Addison, James Thayer. **Chinese ancestor worship. A study of its meaning and its relations with christianity.** n.p. (1925) 85 p.

Addison, James T. Chinese ancestor worship and protestant christianity. **JR** 5.2 (1925) 140-149.

Affinités des doctrines de lao-tse et du bouddha. Date incontestable de l'existence de lao-tse. Un savant prétend que lao-tse était un philosoph japonais. In **EM** 26 (d?) 343-344.

Amélineau, E. Les coutumes funéraires de l'égypte ancienne comparées avec celles de la chine. Dans **Études de critique et d'histoire, par les membres de la section des sciences religieuses de l'école des hautes études,** paris, 2e sér (1896) 1-34.

Arlington, L.C. Chinese versus western chiromancy. **CJ** 7 (1927) 67-76, 170-175, 228-235; 8 (1928) 67-76.

Barnes, W.H. Chinese influence on western alchemy. **Nature** 135 (1935) 824f.

Bellah, Robert N. Father and son in christianity and confucianism. **Psychoanalytic review** 52 (1965) 92-114. Repr in author's collection: **Beyond belief: essays on religion in a post-traditional world,** n.y. (1970) 76-99.

Benton, Richard P. Tennyson and lao tzu. **PEW** 13.3 (1962) 233-240.

Benz, Ernst and Nambara Minoru (comp) **Das christentum und die nicht-christlichen hochreligionen. Begegnung und auseinandersetzung. Eine internationale bibliographie.** Leiden (1960) See 21-22, 46-51, 62, 79-82, 83-86.

Beyerhaus, Peter. The christian approach to ancestor worship. **Ministry** 6.4 (july 1966) 137-145.

Boüinais, Lt-Col. and A. Paulus. **Le culte des morts dans le céleste empire et l'annam comparé au culte des ancêtres dans l'antiquité occidentale.** Paris (1893) xxxiii + 267 p.

Braden, Charles S. **Jesus compared. Jesus and other great founders of religions.** Englewood cliffs, n.j. (1957) See Jesus and confucius, 108-131; Jesus and lao-tzu, 132-146.

Chang, C. Essai d'une adaptation des exercices spirituels à l'âme chinoise. **SM** 7 (1950-51) 199-219.

Chaudhuri, H. The concept of brahman in hindu philosophy [with a section on brahman, tao and t'ai-chi] **PEW** 4 (1954) 47-66.

Chen, Ivan. A comparative study of english and chinese customs and superstitions. **London and china express** 49 (14 nov 1907)

Chen, Joseph. Les doctrines chrétienne et confucéene de la piété filiale. **Laval théologique et philosophique** 19 (1963) 335-349.

Chochod, Louis. **Occultisme et magie en extrême-orient: inde, indochine, chine.** Paris (1949) 404 p, illus.

Clopin, Camille. Comparaison entre lao-tse, pythagore et confucius. Résultats définitif pour la chine des deux doctrines examinées par m. de milloué dans une conférence au musée guimet. **La géographie** 27.3 (1898) 285f.

Combaz, G. Masques et dragons en asie. **MCB** 7 (1939-45) 1-328.

Cordier, Henri. Le confucianisme et le shinto. **Revue de clergé français** 65 (1 fev 1911) 257-273.

Coulborn, Rushton. The state and religion: iran, india, and china. **CSSH** 1.1 (1958) 44-57.

Coyajee, Jehangir Cooverjee. **Cults and legends of ancient iran and china.** Bombay (1936) 308 p.

Crémazy, L. Le culte des ancêtres en chine et dans l'annam. **RIC** no 107 (1900) 1066-1068; no 108 (1900) 1088-1089.

Danielli, M. The geomancer in china, with some reference to geomancy as observed in madagascar. **Folk-lore** 63 (1952) 204-226.

Dawson, Christopher. **Enquiries into religion and culture.** N.Y. (1934) See pt 2, chap The mystery of china.

DeKorne, John C. **Chinese altars to the unknown god. An account of the religions of china and the reactions to them of christian missions.** Grand rapids, mich.(1926) ix-xiii + 139 p, illus (publ by author in mimeo)

Dumoulin, Heinrich. La mystique de l'orient et de l'occident. **BUA** 3e sér, 5 (1944) 152-202.

Duyvendak. J.J.L. A chinese 'divina commedia.' **TP** 41 (1952) 255-316. On lo mao-teng: san-pao ta-chien hsia hsi-yang chi [1597] a fictitious and fantastic account of the voyages of cheng ho.

Edgar, J.H. The sin bearer, a note on comparative religion. **JWCBorderResS** 3 (1926-29) 151.

Erkes, Eduard. Chinesisch-amerikanische mythen-parallelen. **TP** 24 (1926) 32-53. See further E. von Sach: Einige bemerkungen zu Erker's. . . **ibid** 382-383; Erkes: Zu E. von Sach's bemerkungen. . . **ibid** 25 (1928) 94-98.

Folberth, Otto. **Meister eckhart und lao-tse. Ein vergleich zweier mystiker.** Mainz (1925) 119 p.

Ford, Eddy L. **A comparison of confucian and christian ideals.** Foochow (192?) 54 p.

Forke, A. Chinesische und indianische philosophie. **ZDMG** 98 (1944) 195-237 (Compares certain concepts: 1. Tao = brahman, das absolute; 2. Wu-wei = nivṛtti, passivität; 3. Wei-hsin lun = mâyā, idealismus; 4. Chinesische anklänge an sāmkhya und yoga)

Franke, Herbert. Indogermanische mythenparallelen zu einem chinesischen text der han zeit. In **MMDFL** (1963) 243-249.

Frey, H. **Les temples égyptiens primitifs identifiés avec les temples actuels chinois.** Paris (1909)

Fukunaga, Mitsuji. 'No-mind' in chuang-tzu and in ch'an buddhism. **Zinbun** 12 (1969) 9-45.

Garvie, A.E. Mutual sharing. **IRM** 24 (1935) 181-192.

Glasenapp, Helmuth von. **Die fünf grossen religionen.** Düsseldorf/köln (1951) See Schlussbetrachtung, indische und chinesische religiosität, 221-228.

Grant, C.M. **Religions of the world in relation to christianity.** London (1894) Chap 3 and 4 deal with confucianism.

Griffith, Gwilym O. **Interpreters of reality: a comment on heracleitus, lao tse and the christian faith.** London (1946) 106 p.

Guignes, Joseph de. Observations sur quelques points concernant la religion et la philosophie des égyptiens et des chinois. **MAI** 40 (1780) 163-186.

Guimet, E. Lao-tzeu et la brâhmanisme. **Verhandlungen 2 CIHR, Basel, 1904,**bâle (1905) 168-183.

Gulik, R.H. van. Indian and chinese sexual mysticism. App I in author's **Sexual life in ancient china,** leiden (1961) 339-359.

Haar, Hans. **Bibliographie zur frage nach den wechselbeziehungen zwischen buddhismus und christentum.** Berlin (1921) leipzig (1922) 47 p.

Hager, Joseph. **Panthéon chinois, ou, parallèle entre le culte religieux des grecs et celui des chinois. Avec de nouvelles preuves que la chine a été connue des grecs, et que les sérès des auteurs classiques ont été des chinois.** Paris (1806) 175 p, illus.

Hardon, John A. **Religions of the orient. A christian view.** Chicago (1970) See: Confucianism, 77-106.

Harlez, Ch. de. **La religion nationale des tartares orientaux, mandchous et mongols, comparée à la religion des anciens chinois, d'après les textes indigènes, avec le rituel tartare de l'empereur k'ien-long, traduit par la première fois.** MCAM 40 (1887) 216 p.

Heiler, F. Weltabkehr und weltrückkehr ausserchristlicher mystiker. 1. teil: Laotse und bhagavadgita. **Eine heilige kirche** 22 (1941) 181-213.

Hentze, Carl. **Objets rituels, croyances et dieux de la chine antique et de l'amérique.** Antwerp (1936)

Hentze, Carl. **Die regenbogenschlange:** alt-china und alt-amerika. **Anthropos** 61 (1966) 258-266, illus.

Hentze, Carl. **Tod, auferstehung, weltordnung; das mythische bild in ältesten china, in den grossasiatischen und zirkumpazifischen kulturen.** Zürich (1955) 2 vol.

Hentze, Carl and Kim Chewon. **Ko- und chi-waffen in china und in amerika. Göttergestalten in der ältesten chinesischen schrift.** Antwerpen (1943) 59 p, pl.

Howe, P.W.H. The bible and the chinese book of changes. **AP** 39 (aug 1968) 360-363.

Hsu, Francis L. K. **Americans and chinese. Reflections on two cultures and their people.** N.Y. (1953) 2nd ed (1970) See, in 2nd ed, chap 9 and 10.

Hsu, Francis L.K. **Clan, caste and club.** Princeton univ (1963) 335 p.

Hume, Robert E. **The world's living religions. With special reference to their sacred scriptures and in comparison with christianity.** N.Y. (1924) rev ed (1959) See chap 6 and 7.

James, Edwin O. **The comparative study of religions of the east (excluding christianity and judaism)** Cambridge univ (1959) 32 p.

King, Winston L. The way of tao and the path to nirvana. In **SA** (1963) 121-135.

Kuong-hoa (Joseph Li) Die 'pietät' bei den völkern im orient und okzident. **Ecclesia apostolica** (1951) 40-56.

Lanczkowski, Günter. Neutestamentaliche parallelen zu láo-tse's tao-te-king. **In Gott und die götter. Festgabe für erich fascher zum 60.** geburstag, berlin (1958) 7-15.

Legge, James. **Christianity and confucianism compared in the teaching of the whole duty of man.** London (1884) 36 p.

Legge, James. **Confucianism in relation to christianity.** Shanghai (1877) 12 p.

Legge, James. **The religions of china. Confucianism and taoism described and compared with christianity.** London (1880) 310 p.

Liebenthal, Walter. Lord atman in the lao-tzu. **MS** 27 (1968) 374-380.

Ling, Shun-sheng. Comparative study of the ancient chinese feng-shan and the ziggurat of mesopotamia. **ASBIE** 19 (1965) engl abrmt 39-51 + 10 p pl.

Ling, Shun-sheng. Dog sacrifice in ancient china and the pacific area. **ASBIE** 3 (1957) engl summ 37-40, illus.

Lou, Dennis Wing-sou. Rain worship among the ancient chinese and the nahua and maya indians. **ASBIE** 4 (1957) 31-108, illus.

MacLagan, Patrick J. **Chinese religious ideas: a christian valuation.** London (1926) 238 p.

Malan, Saloman C. **A letter on the pantheistic and on the buddhistic tendency of the chinese and of the mongolian versions of the bible.** London (1856) 38 p.

Maspero, Henri. La société et la religion des chinois anciens et celles des tai modernes. In author's **HMRC** t 1, paris (1950) 139-194.

M'Clatchie M. T. The chinese on the plain of shinar, or a connection between the chinese and all other nations through their theology. **JRAS** 16 (1856) 368-435.

Mears, W. P. The philosophy, ethics, and religion of taoism. Chiefly as developed by chwang-tsze (a comparative sketch) **ChRev** 19 (1890-91) 225-242.

Medhurst, C. Spurgeon. **The tao teh king. A short study in comparative religion.** Chicago (1905) xix + 134.

Mégroz, R. L. Dream interpretation: chinese–greek–islamic. **AP** 6 (1935) 28-31.

Milloué, L. de. l'Astrologie et les différentes formes de la divination dans l'inde, en chine et au tibet. **CMG** (1899-1900 et 1900-01) 179-205.

Murakami, Yoshimi. 'Nature' in lao-chuang thought and 'no-mind' in ch'an buddhism. **KGUAS** 14 (1965) 15-31.

Pachow, W. Laotzû and gautama buddha; an enquiry into the authenticity of laotzû's mission to india. In **PFV** (1966) 293-303.

Patai, R. Religion in middle eastern, far eastern, and western culture. **SWJA** 10 (1954) 233-254.

Pauthier, Georges. **Mémoire sur l'origine et propagation de la doctrine du tao, fondée par lao-tseu; traduit du chinois et accompagné d'un commentaire tiré des livres sancrits et du tao-te-king de lao-tseu; établissant la conformité de certaines opinions philosophiques de la chine et de l'inde; orné d'un dessein chinois; suivi de deux oupanishads des vedas, avec le texte sanscrit et persan.** Paris (1831) 79 p.

Poore, R. Ancestral worship in china and 'family worth-ship' in england, as a practical basis of efficient state administration. **IAQR** (july 1894) 141-149. See also Eugène Simon, Une imitation . . . **La Réforme sociale** 2e sér, 8 (1893) 304-321.

Przyluski, J. Dragon chinois et naga indien. **MS** 3 (1938) 602-610.

Rosenkranz, G. Der geist europos und die religionen des ostens. **Zeitschrift für theologie und kirche** n.f. 47 (1950) 106-144.

Rotours, Robert des. Confucianisme et christianisme. **Sinologica** 1 (1948) 231-245.

Rowley, Harold H. **Submission in suffering, and other essays in eastern thought.** Cardiff, univ wales (1951) 170 p, index.

Rule, Paul A. Jesuit and confucian? Chinese religion in the journals of matteo ricci, s.j. 1538-1610. **JRH** 5 (1968) 105-124.

Sarkar, B. K. **Chinese religion through hindu eyes. A study in the tendencies of asiatic mentality.** Shanghai (1916) xxxii + 331 p.

Sarkar, B. F. Confucianism, buddhism, and christianity. **OC** 33 (1919) 661-673.

Saussure, Léopold de. La cosmologie religieuse en chine, dans l'iran et chez les prophètes hébreux. **Actes CIHR, Paris, 1923,** paris (1925)

Scaligero, Massimo. Tao and grail: the search of earthly immortality. **E&W** 8 (apr 1957) 67-72.

Schmidt, P. Persian dualism in the far east. In **OSCEP** (1933) 405-406.

Schuster, C. A comparative study of motives in western chinese folk embroideries. **MS** 2 (1936-37) 21-80.

Shastri, H. P. Hindu ideas and taoist texts. **AP** 10 (1939) 294-297.

Sheffield, D. Z. The ethics of christianity and of confucianism compared. **ChRec** 17 (1886) 365-379.

Sherley-Price, Lionel D. **Confucius and christ: a christian estimate of confucius.** Westminster, engl (1951) 248 p, illus.

Shih, J. The tao: its essence, its dynamism, and its fitness as a vehicle of christian revelation. **SM** 15 (1966) 117-133.

Simon, Eugène. Une imitation de la famille chinoise. Le major poore et les villages du wiltshire. **La réforme sociale** (16 aout - 1 sept 1893) 304-321. See Poore, R. Ancestral worship in china and . . . .

Smith, Carl T. A heideggerian interpretation of the way of lao tzu. **CF** 10.2 (1967) 5-19.

Smith, Carl T. Radical theology and the confucian tradition. **CF** 10. 4 (1967) 20-33.

Smith, D. Howard. Saviour gods in chinese religion. In **SG** (1963) 174-190.

Smith, Huston, Man and his fulfillment: china, india, and the west. **CF** 9.1 (1965) 19-23.

Söderblom, N. Die religionen der erde. Halle a. saale (1905) 65 p.

Solomon, Bernard S. Meditation on two concepts of reality: biblical and taoist. **Tri-quarterly** 8 (winter 1967) 125-131.

Sparham, Charles G. **Christianity and the religions of china. A brief study in comparative religions.** London (1896) 24 p.

Speer, Robert E. **The light of the world. A brief comparative study of christianity and non-christian religions.** West bedford, mass (1911) See chap 3, Animism, confucianism and taoism, 121-176.

Stewart, James Livingstone. **Chinese culture and christianity. A review of china's religions and related systems from the christian standpoint.** N.Y. etc (1926) 316 p, bibliog, index.

Sumiya, Kazuhiko. The long march and the exodus: "the thought of mao tse-tung" and the contemporary significance of "emissary prophecy." Tsl fr jap Pharis Harvey, Hiroshi Shinmi and Tadashi Miyabe. In Bruce Douglass and Ross Terrill (ed) **China and ourselves; explorations and revisions by a new generation,** boston (1969) 189-223.

Suppaner-Stanzel, Irene. Die ethischen ziele des taoismus und des existenzialismus. In festschrift, **Der mensch als persönlichkeit und als problem,** münchen (1963) 106-126.

T'an Yün-shan. **The universal mother in sino-indian culture and chinese universalism.** Santiniketan (1960) 19 p.

T'ang, Chün-i. Confucianism and chinese religions. In Moses Jung, Swami Nikhilanda, and Herbert W. Schneider (ed) **Relations among religions today. A handbook of policies and principles,** leiden (1963) 39-44.

Le Tao-teh-king. Identité des méthodes de lao-tse et du bouddha. Commentaire bouddhique du tao-teh-king. Lao-tse sous le nom de lauthu. **CISE** (1881) 765-771.

Thornberry, Mike. The encounter of christianity and confucianism: how modern confucianism views the encounter. **SEAJT** 10 (1968) 47-62.

Too-yu. The systems of foe and confucius compared, translated from the chinese. **ICG** no 5 (1818) 149-157.

Uno, T. The influence of chinese confucianism upon the spiritual life of japan. **YE** 3 (1927) 69-74; **PW** 3 (1927) 69-74.

Vlar, Alexandre. Lao-tse le nietzchéen. À propos du livre de la voie et la ligne droite. **Revue blanche** 27 (1902) 161-167.

Wickersham, James. The religion of china and mexico compared. **American antiquarian and oriental journal** 19 (1897) 319-320.

Winter, H.J.J. Science, buddhism and taoism. **AP** 21 (may 1950) 206-208.

Wu, John C.H. **Chinese humanism and christian spirituality. Essays of john c. h. wu.** St. john's univ (1965) 227 p.

Wyman, Mary. Chinese mysticism and wordsworth. **JHI** 10 (1949) 517-538.

Yeh, Theodore T.Y. **Confucianism, christianity and china.** N.Y. (1969) 249 p, notes, bibliog.

Zia, N.Z. The common ground of the three chinese religions. **CF** 9.2 (1966) 17-34.

Zia, Rosina C. The conception of 'sage' in lao-tze and chuang-tze as distinguished from confucianism. **CCJ** 5 (may 1966) 150-157.

41. MISCELLANEOUS

Bach, A.H. Glauben und aberglauben in china. **OstL** 2 (d?) 1087-1089, 1112-1113.

C.C. Suttee in china. **All the year round** 6 (sept 1861) 538-541. Repr in **Chinese and japanese repository** (may 1862?) 457-461.

Chan, Wing-tsit. The historic chinese contribution to religious pluralism and world community. In Edward J. Jurji (ed) **Religious pluralism and world community; interfaith and intercultural communication,** leiden (1969) 113-130.

Chan, Wing-tsit. The individual in chinese religions. In **SIEW** (1968) 181-198.

Douglas, R.K. Social and religious ideas of the chinese, illustrated in language. **Journal of the anthropological institute of great britain and ireland** 22 (1893-94) 159-173.

Erkes, Eduard. Die profanisierung sakraler zeichen in der chinesischen schrift. **Wissenchaftliche zeitschrift der universität leipzig** 3 (1954) 413-416.

Ho, Lien-kwei. The cultural status of tortoise. **ASBIE** 16 (1963) engl summ 111-114.

Hodous, Lewis. The ministry of chinese religions. **IRM** 25 (july 1936) 329-341.

Hopkins, J. Castell. Chinese religious and national characteristics. **Canadian magazine of politics, science, art and literature** 5 (1895) 528-535.

Hutson, James. The domestic altar. **JNCBRAS** 49 (1918) 93-100.

Johnston, Reginald F. The religious future of china. **Nineteenth century and after** 74 (nov 1913) 908-923.

Kaltenmark, Maxime. Religions de la chine. In **Problèmes et méthodes d'histoire des religions. Mélanges publiés par la section des sciences religieuses à l'occasion du centenaire de l'école pratique des hautes études,** paris (1968) 53-56.

Kuong-Hoa (Joseph Li) Die 'pietät' bei den völkern im orient und okzident. **Ecclesia apostolica** (1951) 40-56.

Levy, Marion J. jr. **The family revolution in modern china.** Harvard univ (1949) See chap 7, The kinship structure of integration and expression: integration, 247-257.

Martin, W.A.P. The religious attitude of the chinese mind. **MRW** n.s. 4 (1891) 296-301.

Murphy, Gardner, and Lois B. Murphy (ed) **Asian psychology.** N.Y. and london (1968) See pt 2, The psychology of china, 127-177.

Niida, Noboru. The industrial and commercial guilds of peking and religion and fellow-countrymanship as elements of their coherence. **FS** 9 (1950) 179-206.

Religion and poverty in china. **Methodist review** 77 (1895) 141-142.

Rowley, Harold H. **Submission in suffering, and other essays in eastern thought.** Cardiff, univ wales (1951) 170 p, index.

Sjöholm, Gunnar. The boundaries between religion and culture with a reference to the interpretation of ancient chinese religion. **CF** 13.4 (1970) 5-20.

Sumiya, Kazuhiko. The long march and the exodus: "the thought of mao tse-tung" and the contemporary significance of "emissary prophecy." Tsl fr jap Pharis Harvey, Hiroshi Shinmi and Tadashi Miyabe. In Bruce Douglass and Ross Terrill (ed) **China and ourselves; explorations and revisions by a new generation,** boston (1969) 189-223.

Tompkinson, Leonard. **Mysticism, ethics and service in chinese thought.** London (1956) 24 p.

Wasson, R. Gordon. **Soma. The divine mushroom of immortality.** Harcourt brace johanovich: printed in italy (1968) See chap 13, The marvelous herb [ling chih] 77-92, pl.

Williams, David Rhys. **World religions and the hope for peace.** Boston (1951) See chap 2, Mo ti and the will to peace.

Wolcott, Leonard and Carolyn. **Religions around the world.** Nashville and n.y. (1967) See chap 5, Chinese religions, 71-88. Juvenile level.

Wurm, Paul. Religiöser eifer bei chines. buddhisten. **AMZ** 10 (1883) 501-503.

Yang, C.K. **The chinese family in the communist revolution.** M.I.T. (1959) repr in author's **Chinese communist society: the family and the village,** m.i.t. (1965) See chap 10, Secularization of the family institution, 183-190.

Part Three

Chinese Buddhism

1. REFERENCE WORKS

Akanuma, Chizen. **The comparative catalogue of chinese āgamas and pali nikāyas (kan-pa shi-bu shi-agon gosho-roku)** Nagoya (1929) 2nd ed tokyo (1958) xvi + 424 p.

Anesaki, Masaharu. **The four buddhist āgamas in chinese, a concordance of their parts and of the corresponding counterparts in the pali nikāyas.** TASJ 35.3 (1908) 149 p.

Bagchi, P. C. **Le canon bouddhique en chine, les traducteurs et les traductions.** Univ calcutta (publ in paris) vol 1 (1927) vol 2 (1938) lii + 436 p.

Bagchi, P. C. **Deux lexiques sanskrit-chinois.** Univ calcutta (publ in paris) vol 1 : **Fan yu tsa ming,** attributed to li-yen; **Fan yu ts'ien tsen wen,** attributed to yi-tsing (1929) 336 p; vol 2 : **Étude critique des deux lexiques** (1937) 204 p.

Beal, Samuel. **The buddhist tripitaka as it is known in china and japan. A catalogue and a compendious report.** Printed for the india office. Devonport (1876) 117 p.

Beal, Samuel. Results of an examination of chinese buddhist books in the library of the india office. **Trans 2nd ICO london 1874,** london (1876) 132-162. See also author's art, The buddhist works in chinese in the india office library, **IA** 4 (1875) 90-101.

Brandon, S.G.F. (ed) **A dictionary of comparative religions.** N.Y. (1970) See buddhist entries passim.

Chan, Wing-tsit. Chinese and buddhist religious terminology. In Vergilius Ferm (ed) **Encyclopedia of religion,** n.y. (1945) passim. Repr as pamphlet, n.y. (1945) 36 p.

Demiéville, Paul (redacteur en chef) **Hôbogirin. Dictionnaire encyclopédique du bouddhisme d'après les sources chinoises et japonaises.** Publié sous la direction de S. Levi et J. Takakusu. Fascicles i-iii (a-chi) with fascicle annexe (tables de taisho issaikyo) In 4 pt (all publ) tokyo (1929-37)

Demiéville, Paul. Manuscrits chinois de touen-houang à leningrad. TP 51.4 (1964) 355-376.

Demiéville, Paul. **Récents travaux sur touen-houang. Aperçu bibliographique et notes critiques.** Leiden (1970) vi + 94 p.

Demiéville, Paul. Sur les éditions imprimées du canon chinois. **BEFEO** 24 (1924) 181-218.

Edkins, Joseph. Buddhist words and phrases. In DV vol 2, pt 3, no 6, 221-229.

Eitel, E. J. **Handbook for the student of chinese buddhism.** Hong kong (1870) viii + 224 p.

Eitel, Ernest J. **Hand-book of chinese buddhism, being a sanskrit chinese dictionary with vocabularies of buddhist terms in pali, singhalese, siamese, burmese, tibetan, mongolian and japanese.** Hong kong, 2nd ed rev and enl (1888) 231 p in 2 col.

Feer, Henri L. Introduction au catalogue spécial des ouvrages bouddhiques du fonds chinois de la bibliothèque nationale. **TP** 9 (1898) 201-214.

Forke, A. **Katalog des pekinger tripitaka der königlichen bibliothek au berlin.** Berlin (1916) 216 p.

Fou Si-hoa. Catalogue des pao-kiuan. Mélanges sinologiques 2 (1951) 41-103.

Fujishima, Ryauon. Index des mots sanscrits-chinois contenus dans les deux chapitres d'i-tsing. JA 8e sér, 13 (1889) 490-496.

Giles, Lionel. **Descriptive catalogue of the chinese manuscripts from tun-huang in the british museum.** London (1957) xxv + 334 p.

Giles, Lionel. **Six centuries at tun-huang. A short account of the stein collection of chinese mss in the british museum.** London (1944) 50 p, facs.

Grinstead E. D. **Title index to the descriptive catalogue of chinese manuscripts from tunhuang in the british museum** London (1963) 41 p.

Gutzlaff, Charles. List of the principal buddhistical works from the pali, in chinese characters. **JRAS** 9 (1848) 207-213.

Hackmann, Heinrich. Alphabetisches verzeichnis zum kao sêng ch'uan. **AO** 2 (1923) 81-112.

Hackmann, Heinrich. **Erklärendes worterbuch zum chinesischen buddhismus. Chinesisch-sanskrit-deutsch.** Von Heinrich Hackmann nach seinem handschriftlichen nachlass überarbeitet von Johannes Nobel. Leiden (1951-54) 1fg 1-6 (voranstlicher gesamtungfang 12 lieferungen)

Haneda, T. and P. Pelliot. **Manuscrits de touen-houang, conservés à la bibliothèque nationale de paris et pub. par le toa-kokyukwai de changhai.** Kyoto (1926) 2 vol.

Julien, Stanislas. Concordance sinico-samskrite d'un nombre considérable de titres d'ouvrages bouddhiques, recueillie dans un catalogue chinois de l'an 1306, et publiée, après le déchiffrement et la restitution des mots indiens. JA 4e sér, 14 (1849) 353-446. Réimpr dans les **Mélanges de géographie asiatique et de philologie sinico-indienne,** paris (1864)

Julien, Stanislas. **Méthode pour déchiffrer et transcrire les noms sanscrits, qui se rencontrent dans les livres chinois.** Paris (1861)

Julien, Stanislas. Renseignements bibliographiques sur les relations des voyages dans l'inde et les descriptions du si-yu, qui ont été composées en chinois entre le Ve et le XVIIIe siècle de notre ère. JA sér 4, 10 (1847) 265-269.

Krueger, R. and E. D. Francis. **Index to lessing's lamaist iconography of the peking temple, yung-ho-kung.** Bloomington, ind (1966) 31 p.

Lalou, Marcelle. Onze années de travaux européens sur le bouddhisme (mai 1936-mai 1947) Muséon 61 (1948) 245-276.

La Vallée Poussin, L. de. **Catalogue of the tibetan manuscripts from tun-huang in the india office library. With an appendix on the chinese ms. by kazuo enoki.** Ed S. C. Sutton. London (1962) 318 p, 4 pl.

La Vallée Poussin, Louis de. Notes de bibliographie bouddhique. MCB 3 (1934-35) 355-407; 5 (1936-37) 243-304.

Mizuno, Kogen. An index to the pali texts translated into chinese. **Proceedings of the okurayama oriental research institute** 1 (1956) 14-26.

Nanjio, Bunyiu. **A catalogue of japanese and chinese books and manuscripts lately added to the bodleian library.** Oxford (1881) 28 col in 15 p.

Nanjio, Bunyiu [Nanjō, Bunyū] **A catalogue of the chinese translation of the buddhist tripiṭaka, the sacred canon of the buddhists in china and japan.** Oxford (1883) repr tokyo (1929) [ix] + xxxvi + 480 col.

Pelliot, Paul. Hôbogirin (etc) Deuxième fascicule. (rev) TP 28 (1931) 95-104.

Rahder, Johannes. **Glossary of the sanskrit, tibetan, mongolian and chinese versions of the dašabhümika-sütra.** Paris (1928) 210 p.

Rosenberg, Otto. **Introduction to the study of buddhism according to material preserved in japan and china. Part 1: Vocabulary. A survey of buddhist terms and names arranged according to radicals with japanese reading and sanscrit equivalents** . . . Tokyo (1916) x + 527 + 17 p.

Rosny, Léon de. Extraits d'un glossaire bouddhique sanscrit-chinois. **Lotus** 9 (juil 1890) 129-192.

Ross, E. D. **Alphabetical list of the titles of works in the chinese buddhist tripitaka. Being an index to bunyiu nanjio's catalogue and to the 1905 kioto reprint of the buddhist canon.** Calcutta (1910) xcvii + 97 p.

Ross, E. Denison (tsl) The preface to the fan-i-ming-i, a sanscrit chinese glossary. TP 11 (1910) 405-409.

Schlegel, Gustave. **Catalogue of all buddhist books contained in the pitaka collection in japan and china. With an alphabetical index by S. Fujii.** Kyoto (1898)

Soothill, William E. and Lewis Hodous. **A dictionary of chinese buddhist terms.** London (1937) Same title, with add by Shih Sheng-kang, Liu Wu-long and Tseng Lai-ting, taipei (1962)

Suzuki, D. T. **An index to the lankavatara sutra (nanjio edition). Sanskrit-chinese-tibetan, chinese-sanskrit, and tibetan-sanskrit, with a tabulated list of parallel pages of the nanjio sanskrit text and the three chinese translations (sung, wei, and t'ang) in the taisho edition of the tripitaka.** Kyoto, 2nd ed (1934) 503 p.

Sykes, William H. On a catalogue of chinese buddhistical works. JRAS 9 (1848) 199-213.

Wogihara [or Wogiwara or Ogiwara] Unrai. On the proposed supplement to the 'catalogue of the chinese translations of the tripitaka' by bunyiu nanjio. **Verh. 13th ICO** (1903) 62.

2. GENERAL STUDIES
(See also Pt 1: 2: GENERAL STUDIES)

Abel-Rémusat, J. P. Observations sur la religion samanéene. In author's **Mélanges posthumes d'histoire et de littérature orientales** . . . paris (1843) 1-64.

Abel-Rémusat, J. P. Observations sur trois mémoires de m. deguignes insérés dans le tome xl de la collection de l'académie des inscriptions et belles-lettres, et relatifs à la religion samanéenne. NouvJA 7 (1831) 241 et seq.

Ampère, J. J. De la chine et les travaux de m. rémusat. RDM lère sér, 8 (1832) 373-405; 2e sér, 4 (1833) 249-275; ibid 561-595. Repr in author's work, **La science et les lettres en orient,** paris (?) (1865)

Bahm, Archie J. **The world's living religions.** Southern illinois univ (1964) See pt 2, religions of china and japan . . . buddhism 199-231.

Balfour, Frederic. A superficial view of buddhism.
In author's **Waifs and strays** (1876) 134-142.

Ball, J. Dyer. **Is buddhism a preparation or a
hindrance to christianity in china?** Hong kong
(1907) 31 p.

Bazin, M. Recherches sur l'origine, l'histoire, et la
constitution des ordres religieux dans l'empire
chinois. **JA** 5e sér, 8 (1856) 105-174; also publ
sep, paris (1861) 70 p.

Beal, Samuel. Buddhism in china. In **RSW**,
(1889 et seq) 166-179.

Beal, Samuel. **Non-christian religious systems. –
buddhism in china.** London and n.y. (1884)
viii + 263 p.

Benton, Warren G. Chinese buddhism. **PS** 38
(1890-91) 530-537.

Chambeau, Gabriel. Le bouddhisme chinois.
Études 127 (5 juin 1911) 697-707. À propos du
L. Wieger, **Bouddhisme chinois** q.v.

Ch'en, Kenneth K. S. **Buddhism: the light of asia.**
N.Y. (1968) See chap 4, 7, 10-13.

Chou, Chung-i. The common points in the opinion of chinese buddhists and confucianists. **West
and East** 14 (apr 1969) 8-10.

Clarke, James Freeman. Buddhism; or the
protestantism of the east. **Atlantic monthly** 23
(1869) 713-728.

Dás, Baboo Sarat Chandra. Contributions on the
religion, history, &c. of tibet. **JRASB** 50.1
(1881) See 8, Rise and progress of jin or buddhism
in china, 87-99; 9, Ancient china, its sacred literature, philosophy and religion as known to the
tibetans, 99-114.

Davrout, L. Le bouddhisme d'après un livre recent.
Revue apologetique 1 (16 mai 1911) sep publ
bruxelles (1911) 15 p. À propos de l'ouvrage
du p. L. Wieger, **Bouddhisme chinois** q.v.

Demiéville, Paul. Le bouddhisme chinois. In **AC** 1
(1959) 162-166.

Deshautesrayes. Recherches sur la religion de fo,
professée par les bonzes ho-chang de la chine. **JA** 7
(1825) 150-173, 228-243, 311-317; 8 (1826)
40-49, 74-88, 179-188, 219-223.

DuBose, Hampden C. **The dragon, image and
demon, or the religions of china: confucianism,
buddhism, and taoism. Giving an account of the
mythology, idolatry and demonolotry of the
chinese.** London (1886) 463 p.

Dumoulin, Heinrich. Mahayana-buddhismus in
ostasien und tibet. **Saeculum** 20 (1969) 253-258.

Dutt, Sukumar (ed) **Buddhism in east asia.** See
under Lahiri, Miss Latika.

Edkins, Joseph. **Chinese buddhism. A volume of
sketches, historical, descriptive, and critical.**
London, 2nd ed (1879) 453 p, index.

Edkins, Joseph. Notices of chinese buddhism (all
in **NCH** (29 apr 1854 to 20 oct 1855) The various
art collected and repr in **The shanghae miscellany**
for 1855 and 1856.

Eitel, Ernest J. **Buddhism: its historical, theo-
retical, and popular aspects. In three lectures.**
Hong kong, 2nd ed (1873) 130 p; 3rd ed (1884)
145 p.

Eitel, Ernest J. **Three lectures on buddhism.**
Hong kong and london (1871) 38 p.

Everett, John R. **Religion in human experience.**
London (1952) See chap 9, Chinese buddhism,
163-173.

Finegan, Jack. **The archeology of world religions.**
Vol 2: **Buddhism, confucianism, taoism.** Princeton univ (1952) 234-599, illus.

Foucaux, Philippe Édouard. Notices bouddhiques
– 1. Le tripitaka des chinois et des japonais.
2. Le bouddhisme du nord et du sud. 3 Défini-
tion du nirvana par subhadra bhikshu. **Lotus** 9
(janv 1890) 50-61.

Friess, Horace L. and Herbert W. Schneider.
Religion in various cultures. N.Y. (1932) See
chap 5, Buddhism; sec 6, Chinese buddhism,
179-197.

Fung, Yu-lan. **A history of chinese philosophy.**
Tsl fr chin Derk Bodde. Princeton univ, vol 2
(1953) See chap 7-10.

Grison, P. Le bouddhisme d'inde en chine.
FA 16, no 158-159 (july-aug 1959) 1093-1103.

Groot, J. J. M. de. Der buddhismus [in china] In
P. D. Chantepie de la Saussaye, **Lehrbuch der
religionsgeschichte** bd 1, tübingen (1905) 104-114.

Groot, J. J. M. de. Der buddhismus der chinesen.
In **Kultur der gegenwart** tl 1, abtlg 3, 1, Die
orientalische religionen, berlin and leipzig (1906)
184-192.

Groot, J. J. M. de China. (Buddhism in) In
HERE 3, 552-556.

Grootaers, W. A. Bouddhisme et christianisme en chine. **Bulletin des missions** (1951) 1-5.

Guignes, Joseph de. **Recherches historiques sur la religion indienne et sur les livres fondamenteux de cette religion, qui ont été tr. de l'indien en chinois.** Paris (1773) 167 p.

Guignes, Joseph de. Recherches sur les philosophes appelés samanéens. **MAI** 26 (1759) 770-804.

Gutzlaff, C. Remarks on the present state of buddhism in china. **JRAS** 16 (1856) 73-92.

Hackmann, Heinrich F. **Buddhism as a religion: its historical development and its present conditions.** London (1910) 315 p. Tsl fr german, rev and enl.

Hackmann, Heinrich. **Der buddhismus.** Tübingen (1906) See chap 3, Der buddhismus in china, korea und japan.

Hackmann, Heinrich. Chinese buddhism and buddhist china. **ChRec** 41 (1910) 770-780.

Hackmann, Heinrich. Zum chinesischen buddhismus, hinterlassenes fragment. **AS** 5 (1951) 81-112.

Hamilton, C. H. Buddhism. In H. F. McNair (ed) **China,** univ california (1946) 290-300.

Hardwick, Charles. Fo-ism or chinese buddhism. Pt 3 sec 3 in author's **Christ and other masters,** cambridge (1858) 321-346.

Harlez, Charles de. Le bouddhisme en chine. **La controverse et la contemporain** 4e sér, 2 (1884) 624-637; 5e sér, 4 (1885) 589-602.

Henry, B. C. Buddhism in china. Chap 5 in author's **CD** (1885) 80-99.

Hodgson, B. H. **Illustrations of the literature and religion of the buddhists.** Serampore (1841) 220 p. Collection of 15 art orig publ in **JRASB.**

Horton, Walter M. Oriental religion: eastern asia, 3, buddhism in china. In Henry N. Wieman and Walter M. Horton, **The growth of religion,** chicago and n.y. (1938) 74-88.

Huang, Chia-cheng [François Houang] **Le bouddhisme de l'inde à la chine.** Paris (1963) 126 p.

Inglis, James W. The christian element in chinese buddhism. **IRM** 5 (oct 1916) 587-602.

Johnston, Reginald F. The buddhism of china. **OC** 28 (1914) 697-706.

Johnston, Reginald Fleming. **Buddhist china.** London (1913) 403 p, map, index, photos.

King, Winston L. The way of tao and the path to nirvana. In **SA** (1963) 121-135.

Klaproth, J. von. Ueber die fo-religion in china. **Asiatisches magazin** 1/2 (1802) 149-169.

Krause, Friedrich E. A. **Ju-tao-fo. Die religiösen und philosophischen systeme ostasiens.** München (1924) 588 p.

Krone, Rudolf. Der buddhismus in china. **Berichte der rheinischen missionsgesellschaft** 16 (1855) 241-255.

Lahiri, Miss Latika. China. Chap 9 in Sukumar Dutt, **Buddhism in east asia,** new delhi (1966) 127-158.

Lamairesse, E. l'empire chinois. – **Le bouddhisme en chine et en thibet.** Paris (1894) 440 p.

Liebenthal, Walter. The problem of chinese buddhism. **VBQ** ser 2, 18.3 (1953) 233-246.

Liebenthal, Walter. Was ist chinesischer buddhismus? **AS** 6 (1952) 116-129.

Martin, W. A. P. On reformed buddhism in china and japan. **IA** 11 (1882) 294-295.

Martinie, J. A. Chinese buddhism **Asia** 1 (mar 1951) 85-93.

McGovern, William M. **An introduction to mahayana buddhism, with especial reference to chinese and japanese phases.** London and n.y. (1922) 233 p, diagr.

Mead, G. R. S. **Quests old and new.** London (1913) 338 p.

Migot, André. Le bouddhisme en chine. **FA:BPB** (1959) 697-716.

Milloué, L. de. **Le bouddhisme. Son histoire, ses dogmas, son extension et son influence sur les peuples chez lesquels il s'est répandu.** Lyon (1882) 23 p.

Milloué, Léon de. **Catalogue du musée guimet. Pt 1, Inde, chine et japon. Precédé d'un aperçu sur les religions de l'extrême-orient et suivie d'un index alphabétique des noms des divinités et des principaux termes techniques.** Paris and lyon (1883) lxviii + 323 p.

Minayeff, I. P. **Recherches sur la bouddhisme.** Tsl fr russian R. H. Assier de Pompignan. Paris (1894) 315 p.

Morgan, Kenneth W. (ed) **The path of the buddha. Buddhism interpreted by buddhists.** N.Y. (1956) 432 p, bibliog, gloss, index. See chap 4 and 5.

Morrison, Robert (tsl) Account of foe. Tr. from the san-kiao-yuen-liew, 'the rise and progress of the three sects.' In author's **Horae sinicae**, London, new ed (1817) 160-165. Orig ed london (1812)

Müller, F. Max. The religions of china. 3. Buddhism and christianity. **NC** 48 (nov 1900) 730-742.

Murakami, S. Mahāyāna buddhism. **EB** 1 (1921) 95-108.

Ōchō, Enichi. Studies in chinese buddhism. **JSR:HS** 11 (1960) 45-48.

Parker, E. H. **Buddhism in china.** London (1905)

Parker, E. H. Chinese buddhism. **IAQR** ser 3, 14 (july-oct 1902) 372-390. French tsl Louis de la Vallée Poussin: Le bouddhisme chinois, **Muséon** n.s. 4 (1903) 135-158.

Parrinder, E. G. **What world religions teach.** London etc (1963) See chap 7, Northern buddhism: salvation by faith, 64-71.

Parrinder, Geoffrey. **Worship in the world's religions.** London (1961) See chap 7, Mahāyāna buddhism, 117-137.

Peeters, Hermes. **The religions of china. Confucianism, taoism, buddhism, popular belief.** Peking (1941) 64 p.

Piton, Charles. **Der buddhismus in china. Eine religionsgeschichtliche studie.** Bâsle (1902) 32 s.

Pratt, James Bissett. **The pilgrimage of buddhism and a buddhist pilgrimage.** N.Y. (1928) 758 p. See chap 11-20.

Reichelt, Karl L. **Meditation and piety in the far east.** London (1953) 170 p.

Reichelt, Karl L. **Religion in chinese garment.** London (1951) See chap 5, which is essentially a digest of author's **Truth and tradition** q.v.

Reichelt, Karl L. **The transformed abbott.** London (1954) 157 p.

Reichelt, Karl L. **Truth and tradition in chinese buddhism. A study of chinese mahayana buddhism.** Shanghai (1927) repr n.y. (1968) 330 p, index, illus.

Richard, Timothy. Chinese buddhism; its rise and progress; Edkins, Joseph. Chinese buddhism; its excellencies and defects. Two art under heading: Buddhism a preparation for christianity, in **CMH** (1896) 12-22.

Robinson, Richard H. Buddhism: in china and japan. In **ZCE** (1959) 321-347.

Rosenkranz, Gerhard. **Der weg des buddha. Werden und wesen der buddhismus als weltreligion.** Stuttgart (1960)

Rosny, Léon de. Le bouddhisme dans l'extrême-orient. **Revue scientifique** 2e sér, 17 (20 dec 1879) 581-585.

Schott, Wilhelm. **Über den buddhismus in hochasien und in china. Akademie der wissenschaft zur berlin, philologische und historische abhandlungen 1844,** Berlin (1846) 161-288.

Stroup, Herbert. **Four religions of asia.** N.Y. (1968) See Buddhism, 115-168.

Tan Yun-shan. **Some aspects of chinese buddhism.** Santiniketan, india (1963) 22 p.

Too-yu. The systems of foe and confucius compared, translated from the chinese. **ICG** no 5 (1818) 149-157.

Tsukamoto, Zenryū. Buddhism in china and korea. In Kenneth Morgan (ed) **The path of the buddha** q.v. 182-236.

Ward, C. H. S. **Buddhism.** Vol 2: Mahāyāna. London (1952) See Contents for several pertinent sec.

Watters, Thomas. Buddhism in china. **ChRec** 2 (1869) 1-6, 38-43, 64-68, 81-88, 117-122, 145-150.

Wei, Francis C.-M. Buddhism as a chinese christian sees it. **IRM** 17 (1928) 455-463.

Wentworth, Erastus. Buddhism. In J. M. Reid (ed) **DR** (1884) 243-284.

Wieger, Léon. **Bouddhisme chinois.** 2 vol (1910-1913) repr (1940) (See entry under Texts in Translation)

Williams, E. T. Chinese buddhism. Chap 14 in author's **CYT** (1928) 289-315.

Winter, H. T. J. Science, buddhism and taoism. **AP** 21 (may 1950) 206-208.

Yang, Ming-che. Confucianism vs.tao and buddha. **FCR** 19 (jan 1969) 21-29.

Yule, Henry. Northern buddhism. **JRAS** n.s. 6 (1873) 275-277.

Zürcher, Erik. Buddhism in china. In Raymond Dawson (ed) **The legacy of china**, oxford (1964) 56-79.

3. TEXTS IN TRANSLATION

Bailey, D. R. Shackleton (tsl) **Mātṛceta. Śatapañcāśatka. Sanskrit text, tibetan translation and commentary, and chinese translation.** London (1951) xi + 237 p.

Bapat, P. V. in collaboration with A. Hirakawa (tsl) **Shan-chien-p'i p'o-sha. A chinese version by sanghabhadra of samantapasadika commentary on pali vinaya.** (1970) lxiii + 588 p.

Beal, Samuel. Brief prefatory remarks to the translation of the amitābha sūtra from chinese. **JRAS** n.s. 2.1 (1866) 136-144.

Beal, Samuel (comp and tsl) **A catena of buddhist scriptures from the chinese.** London (1871) 436 p. Repr taipei (1970)

Beal, Samuel (tsl) Confessional of kwan-yin. An attempt to translate from the chinese a work known as the confessional service of the great compassionate kwan yin, possessing 1000 hands and 1000 eyes. **JRAS** n.s. 2.2 (1866) 403-425.

Beal, Samuel (tsl) **The fo-sho-hing-tsan-king. A life of buddha by asvaghosha bodhisattva translated from sanskrit into chinese by dharmaraksha, a.d. 420 and from chinese into english by samuel beal.** Oxford (1883) xxxvii + 380 p. Vol 19 of F. Max Muller (ed) 'Sacred books of the east.'

Beal, Samuel (tsl) The legend of dipaṅkara buddha. Translated from the chinese (and intended to illustrate plates xxix and 1., 'tree and serpent worship.') **JRAS** n.s. 6 (1873) 377-395.

Beal, Samuel (tsl) A life of the buddha: translated from the p'u yao king . . . (suite) **BOR** 3.12 (nov 1889) 265-274; 4.1 (dec 1889) 12-15.

Beal, Samuel (tsl) The páramitá-hridaya sútra, or, the great páramitá heart sutra. **JRAS** n.s. 1.2 (1864) 25-28.

Beal, Samuel (tsl) **The romantic legend of sâkya buddha: from the chinese-sanskrit . . .** London (1875) xii + 395 p.

Beal, Samuel (tsl) **Suh-ki li-lih-kiu. The suhrilleicha or 'friendly letter,' written by lung shu (nâgârjuna), and addressed to king sadvaha. Translated from the chinese edition of i-tsing.** London (1892) 51 p + 13 p chin text.

Beal, Samuel (tsl) The sutra of the forty-two sections, from the chinese. **JRAS** 19 (1862) 337-349.

Beal, Samuel (tsl) Text and commentary of the memorial of sakya buddha tathagata. By wong puh . . . with prefatory remarks by the rev. spence hardy. **JRAS** 20 (1863) 135-220.

Beal, Samuel (tsl) **Texts from the buddhist canon, commonly known as dhammapada, with accompanying narratives. Translated from the chinese** . . . London (1878) viii + 176 p.

Beal, Samuel. Two chinese-buddhist inscriptions found at buddha-gayâ. **JRAS** n.s. 13 (oct 1881) 552-572.

Beal, Samuel (tsl) Vajra-chhediká, the 'kin kong king' or 'diamond sutra.' **JRAS** n.s. 1.1 (1864) 1-24.

Beal, Samuel and D. J. Gogerly. Comparative arrangements of two translations of the buddhist ritual for the priesthood, known as the prátimoksha, or pátimokshan. By the rev. s. beal from the chinese, and the rev. d. j. gogerly from the pali. **JRAS** 19 (1862) 407-480.

Behrsing, S. Das chung-tsi-king des chinesischen dirghâgama. Über. und mit anmerkungen versehen. **AM** 7 (1932) 1-149, 483; 8 (1933) 277. See also Weitere nachträge u. verbesserungen zu S. Behrsing, Das chung-tsi-king . . . **ibid** 8 (1933) 277.

Bischoff, F. A. (ed, tsl, comm) **Ārya mahābala-nāma-mahāyānasūtra. Tibétain (mss de touen-houang) et chinois. Contribution à l'étude des divinités mineures du bouddhisme tantrique.** Paris (1956) 138 p, 4 facs.

Chan, Wing-tsit (comp and tsl) **A source book in chinese philosophy.** Princeton univ (1963) See chap 20-26 for tsl buddhist texts, 336-449.

Chavannes, Édouard (tsl) **Cinq centes contes et apologues extraits du tripitaka chinois et traduit en français** . . . Paris, 3 vol (1910-11) Repr paris (1962) 4 vol in 3 (vol 4 is vol 1 of series: 'Bibliothèque de l'institut des hautes études chinoises') Orig ed, vol 1: xx + 428, vol 2: 449, vol 3: 395 p.

Chavannes, Édouard and S. Lévi (tsl) La notation de tréfonds (âlaya vijñâna) Extraits du fan yi min yi tsi, tok. 36, 11, 85a; chap. 16. In S. Lévi, Un système de philosophie bouddhique: matériaux pour l'étude du système vijñâptimâtra, paris (1932) 125-173.

Chédel, A. (tsl) Le dhammapada, recueil de sentences bouddhiques. Extraits de versions chinoises. MSGFOK 5 (1934) 55-61.

Ch'en, Kenneth K. S. A study of the svāgata story in the divāvadāna in its sanskrit, pali, tibetan and chinese versions. HJAS 9 (1945-47) 207-314.

Chou, Ta-fu. Three buddhist hymns. SIS 1 (1944) 85-98.

Chu, Ch'an (pseud for John Blofeld) (tsl) The sutra of 42 sections and two other scriptures of the mahayana school. London (1947) (The other two scriptures: The sutra of the doctrine bequeathed by the buddha; the sutra of the eight awakenings of the great ones)

Csongor, B. Some chinese texts in tibetan script from tun-huang. Acta orientalia academiae scientiarum hungaricae 10 (1960) 97-140.

Davidson, J. LeRoy. The lotus sutra in chinese art. A study in buddhist art to the year 1000. Yale univ (1954) 105 p, bibliog, pl.

DeBary, William Theodore, with collab of Yoshito Hakeda and Philip Yampolsky (comp) The buddhist tradition in india, china and japan. N.Y. (1969) xxii + 417 p. Largely taken from the 3 vol: Sources of indian, chinese, and japanese tradition, columbia univ (1958, 1960, 1958) See chap 5-7 for tsl chin budd texts, 125-251.

DeBary, William T., W. T. Chan, and Burton Watson (comp and tsl) Sources of chinese tradition. Columbia univ (1960) See chap 15-17 for tsl buddhist texts, 306-408.

Demiéville, Paul. Le concile de lhasa; une controverse sur le quiétisme entre bouddhistes de l'inde et de la chine au VIII. siècle de l'ère chrétienne. Paris (1952) viii + 398 p, facs.

Dumoulin, H. (tsl) Genninron [yüan-jen-lun] Tsung-mi's traktat vom ursprung der menschen. Aus die chinesischen übers., erlautet u. eingeleitet in zusammenarbeit mit S. Furuta u. T. Ibara. MN 1 (1938) 178-221.

Edkins, Joseph (tsl) A buddhist shastra, translated from the chinese; with an analysis and notes. Journal of the shanghai literary and scientific society 1 (june 1858)*107-128. Text is i-lung-lu-ka lun. *The only vol publ under this title, which was changed to JNCBRAS.

Finot, Louis (tsl) La marche à la lumière (bodhičaryāvatāra) Paris (1920) 166 p.

Fischer, J. and Y. Takezo (tsl) Vimalakīrti-nirdeśa. Wei-ma-ch'ih so-shuo-ching. Das sutra vimalakīrti. (Nach einem japanischen ms. von kawase kōzyun übers.) Tokyo (1969) 166 p.

Gauthiot, R. et P. Pelliot (tsl) Le sutra des causes et des effets, texte sogdien de touen-houang, publié en facsimilé, avec transcription, traduction et commentaire par r. gauthiot, accompagné du facsimilé et de la traduction de la version chinoise par p. pelliot, et un glossaire sogdien-français-chinois par r. gauthiot et p. pelliot. Paris (1914-1923) Mission pelliot en asie centrale; série linguistique, t 1.

Gemmell, W. (tsl) The diamond sutra (chin-kang-ching) or prajña-paramitā. London (1912) xxxii + 117 p.

Goddard, Dwight (ed) A buddhist bible. N.Y. (1932) 2nd ed, rev and enl (1938) 677 p.

Groot, J. J. M. de. Le code du mahayana en chine, son influence sur la vie monacal et sur le monde laïque. Amsterdam (1893) 271 p. Includes tsl of the 58 vows of the fan wang ching.

Guignes, Joseph de (tsl) Das buch des fo aus der chinesischen sprache. In's deutsche übersetzt (aus de guignes' histoire des huns) Zürich (1791)

Hackmann, Heinrich (tsl) Laien-buddhismus in china. Das lung shu ching t'u wên des wang jih hsiu. Aus dem chin. über., erläutert und beurteilt. Gotha and stuttgart (1924) xvi + 347 s.

Hackmann, Heinrich (tsl) Die textgestalt des sutra der 42 abschnitt. AO 5 (1927) 197-237.

Hakeda, Yoshita S. (tsl) The awakening of faith attributed to aśvaghosha. Columbia univ (1967) 128 p, notes, selected bibliog, index.

Hamilton, Clarence H. (tsl) Wei shih er shih lun . . . or, the treatise in twenty stanzas on representation-only, by vasubandhu. Translated from the chinese version of hsüan tsang, tripitaka master of the t'ang dynasty. New haven, conn. (1938) 82 p.

Harlez, Charles de (ed and tsl) **Les quarante-deux leçons de bouddha, ou le king des xlii sections (sze-shi-erh-tchang-king). Texte chinois avec trad., introd. et notes.** Bruxelles (1899) 68 p. Being **MCAM** vol 59.

Harlez, Charles de. A sanskrit-chinese lexicon: mahāvyutpattiḥ (pt 1) Tokyo (1901) **Rep. of the society for oriental research** 1-18.

Harlez, Ch. de (tsl) Vajracchedikā (prajñāpâramitâ). Traduite du texte sanscrit avec comparaison des versions chinoise et mandchoue. **JA** 8e sér, 18 (nov-dec 1891) 440-509.

Harlez, Ch. de. Vocabulaire bouddhique sanscrit-chinois . . . han-fan tsih-yao. Précis de doctrine bouddhique. **TP** 7 (1896) 356-396; 8 (1897) 129-154.

Humphreys, Christmas (ed) **The wisdom of buddhism.** N.Y. and evanston (1960) See chap, The new wisdom schools: china and japan, 156-210.

Idumi, Hokei (tsl) Vimalakirti's discourse on emancipation. (Tsl fr chin vimalakirtī-nirdeśa) **EB** 2 (1923) 358-366; 3 (1924) 138-153, 224-242, 336-349; 4 (1926) 48-55, 177-190, 348-366.

Iwamoto, Yutaka (tsl) **Sumāgadhāvadāna** (incl chin version in transcription) Kyoto (1968) 262 p.

Jaworski, J. (tsl) l'Avalambanasūtra de la terre pure. **MS** 1 (1935-36) 82-107. With chin text.

Johnston, E. H. (tsl) The buddha's mission and last journey; **buddhacarati,** xv to xxviii. (tsl of the tibetan and chin versions) **AO** 15 (1937) 26-62, 85-111, 231-292.

Lamotte, Étienne (tsl) **La concentration de la marche héroïque (sūramgamasamādhisūtra)** Bruxelles (1965) xiii + 308 p. Being **MCB** vol 13.

Lamotte, É. (tsl) Le traité de l'acte de vasubandhu, karmasiddhi-prakana: traduction, versions tibétaine et chinoises; avec une introduction et un appendice, la traduction du chapitre XVII de la madhamakavrtti. **MCB** 4 (1935-36) 151-288.

Lamotte, É. (tsl) **Vimalakīrtinirdeśa. l'Enseigne-ment de vimalakīrti.** Louvain (1962) 503 p. Tsl fr tibetan of kandjur with the chin variants of hsüan chuang.

La Vallée Poussin, L. de (tsl) Documents d'abhidharma traduits et annotés. **BEFEO** 30 (1930) 1-28, 247-298. Same title in **MCB** 5 (1936-37) 1-187.

La Vallée Poussin, L. de (tsl) Documents madhyamaka. **MCB** 2 (1932-33) 1-146.

La Vallée Poussin, L. de (tsl) **Vijnaptimātratāsiddhi. La siddhi de hiuan-tsang.** Paris, 3 vol (1928-48) 873 p, index.

Lévi, S. La légende de rama dans un avadâna chinois. In **MSL** (1937) 271-274.

Lévi, Sylvain (ed and tsl) **Mahākarmavibhaṅga (la grande classification des actes) et karmavibhaṅgagopadeśa (discussion sur le mahākarmavibhaṅga).** Textes sanscrits rapportés du nepal, édités et traduits avec les textes paralleles en sanscrit, en pali, en tibétain, en chinois et en koutcheen. Ouvrage illustré de 4 pl: le karmavibhaṅgagopadeśa sur les bas-reliefs de boro-boudour, à java. Paris (1932) 272 p, 4 pl.

Lévi, S. (tsl) Une poésie inconnue du roi harṣa çilâditya. In **MSL** (1937) 244-256.

Liebenthal, Walter (tsl) **The book of chao.** Peking (1948) 2nd rev ed hong kong (1968) 152 p. The **chao-lun** by seng-chao.

Lin, Li-kouang (tsl) **Avalokitasimha. Dharma-samuccaya. Compendium de la loi. Recueil de stances. Extraites du saddharma-smrty-upasthāna-sūtra.** (le partie: ch. i-v. Texte sanscrit éd. avec la version tibétaine et les versions chinoises et trad. en français) (2e partie: ch. vi a xii. Texte sanscrit éd. avec la version tibétaine et les versions chinoises et trad. en français) Paris (1946-69) 292; 424, 27 p. Révision de A. Bareau, J. W. de Jong et P. Demiéville. Avec des appen-dices par J. W. de Jong.

Luk, Charles [Lu, K'uan-yu] (tsl) **The surangama sutra (leng yen ching)** London (1966) 262 p.

Masson-Oursel, Paul. Le yuan jen louen. **JA** 11e sér, 5 (mars-avr 1915) 299-354.

Masuda, J. (tsl) Origin and doctrines of early indian buddhist schools. A translation of the hsüan-chwang version of vasumitra's treatise. **AM** 2 (1925) 1-78.

Masuda, Jiryo (ed) Saptaśatika-prajñāpāramitā. Text and hsüan-chwang's chinese version with notes. **Journal of taisho university,** vol 6-7 **(wogihara commemoration volume)** pt 2 (1930) 185-242, 1 pl.

Meynard. La marche à la lumière. **La chine** 35 (1923) 153-158. Rev with summ of Louis Finot (tsl) **Bodhičaryāvatāra** q.v.

Monumenta Serindica: Vol 1: **Chinese buddhist texts from tunhuang.** Kyoto (1958) Ed by the research society of central asian culture.

Müller, F. Max and Nanjio Bunyiu (ed and tsl) **Sukhāvati-vyūha. Description of sukhāvati the land of bliss.** (With two appendixes: 1, Text and translation of sanghavarman's chinese version of the poetical versions of the sukhāvati-vyūha; 2, Sanskrit text of the smaller sukhāvati-vyūha) Oxford (1883)

Naitō, Torajirō. Trois manuscrits de l'époque des t'ang récemment publiés au japon. **BEFEO** 2 (1902) 315-340.

Neumann, Charles F. (tsl) **The catechisms of the shamans; or, the laws and regulations of the priesthood of buddha, in china.** London (1831) 152 p. Tsl of treatise on the vinaya by chu-hung; it 'is very likely the earliest rendering into english of a chinese buddhist text,' acc.to Kenneth K. S. Ch'en: **Buddhism in china** q.v. p 544. German version, Der katechismus der schamanen . . . In **Zeitschrift f. d. historische theologie** 4 (1834) Publ sep, leipzig (1834) 70 p.

Nobel, J. (tsl) **Suvarnaprabhāsottamasūtra. I-tsing's chinesische version und ihre tibetische übersetzung.** Bd 1, I-tsing's chinesische version; bd 2, Die tibetische übersetzung. Leiden (1958)

O'Brien, Paul W. (tsl) A chapter on reality from the madhyānta-vibhāgaçastra. **MN** 9 (1953) 277-303; 10 (1954) 227-269.

Ohara, Masatoshi. Questions of pe-suh, the brahman landlord. **HZ** 14.6 (1899) 38-44. Tsl fr chin text.

Ohara, Masatoshi. Vimalakīrti-nirdeśa-sūtra. **HZ** 13 (1898)

Okakura, Kakuso (tsl) Chi ki (chik i) [sic] i.e. founder of japanese tendai chiso daishi: on the method of practising concentration and contemplation. Pref note by William Sturgis Bigelow. **HTR** 16.2 (1923) 109-141.

Pachow, W. (tsl) A buddhist discourse on meditation from tun huang. **University of ceylon review** 21.1 (apr 1963) 47-62. Tsl of discourse of hung-jen.

Price, A. T. (tsl) **The diamond sutra or the jewel of transcendental wisdom.** London, 2nd ed (1955) 75 p.

Radloff, W. (tsl) **Kuan-si-im pusar.** Eine türkische übersetzung des xxv kapitels der chinesischen ausgabe des saddharmapuṇḍarīka. St petersbourg (1911) viii + 119 p.

Rahder, J. Daśabhūmika-sūtra seventh stage. (With comparisons with the tibetan and chinese versions.) **AO** 4 (1926) 214-256.

Ramanan, K. Venkata (tsl) **Nagarjuna's philosophy as presented in the mahā-prajñāparamitā-śāstra.** Rutland, vt.etc (1966) 409 p, bibliog, notes, index.

Reuter, J. N. Some buddhist fragments from chinese turkestan in sanskrit and 'khotanese.' **Journal société finno-ougrienne** 30 (1913-18) 37 p, 9 pl.

Richard, Timothy (tsl) **The awakening of faith in the mahayana doctrine: the new buddhism, by patriarch ashvagosha.** Shanghai (1907) xxv + 45 p engl tsl; 46 p chin text. See further author's **New testament of higher buddhism.**

Richard, Timothy (tsl) **Guide to buddhahood. Being a standard manual of chinese buddhism.** Shanghai (1907) xxiii + 108 p. Manual is hsüan fo p'u.

Richard, Timothy (tsl) **The new testament of higher buddhism.** Edinburgh (1910) 275 p. Expanded version of author's **Awakening of faith in the mahayana doctrine** q.v.

Richard, Timothy. Synopsis of 'how to awaken faith in the mahayana school' by ma ming (died 100 a.d.) **JNCBRAS** 27 (1892-93) 263-278.

Robinson, Richard (tsl) **Chinese buddhist verse.** London (1954) 85 p, bibliog, notes, index of chin texts tsl.

Schaeffer, Phil. (ed and tsl) **Nagarjuna, yukti-ṣaṣṭika. Die 60 sätze des negativismus. Nach der chinesischen version übers. Mit photographischer reproduktion des chinesischen und tibetischen textes.** Heidelberg (1923)

Suzuki, [Daisetz] Teitaro (tsl) **Açvaghosha's discourse on the awakening of faith in the mahāyāna. Translated for the first time from the chinese version.** Chicago (1900) xvi + 160 p.

Suzuki, D. T. (tsl) Sutra in 42 sections. In Soyen Shoku (ed) **Sermons of a buddhist abbott,** chicago (1906) 3-21.

Takakusu, Junjirō (tsl) Pāli elements in chinese buddhism: a translation of buddhaghosa's samantapāsādikā, a commentary on the vinaya, found in the chinese tripiṭaka. **JRAS** (july 1896) 415-439.

Thomas, F. W., S. Miyamoto, and G. L. M. Clauson (tsl) A chinese mahāyāna catechism in tibetan and chinese characters. **JRAS** (1929) 37-76.

Tucci, Guiseppe (tsl) **The nyâyamukha of dignāga. The oldest buddhist text on logic. After chinese and tibetan materials.** Heidelberg (1930) 72 p.

Tucci, Guiseppe (tsl) **Pre-dignāga buddhist text on logic from chinese sources.** Baroda (1929)

Ui, H. (tsl) **The vaisesika philosophy according to the dasapadartha-sastra: chinese text, with introduction, translation, and notes.** Ed F. W. Thomas. London (1917) xii + 265 p.

Utsuki, Nishū (tsl) **Buddhabhāṣita-amitāyuḥ-sūtra (the smaller sukhāvatī-vyūha). Translated from the chinese version of kumārajīva.** Kyoto (1924) 43 p.

Vandier-Nicolas, Nicole (tsl) **Sariputra et les six maîtres d'erreur; facsimilé du manuscrit chinois 4524 de la bibliothèque nationale, présenté par nicole vandier-nicolas avec traduction et commentaire du texte.** Paris (1954) 3 p, 1, 32 p (Mission pelliot en asie centrale)

Waldschmidt, Ernst (tsl) **Die legende von leben des buddha. In auszügen aus den heiligen texten. Aus dem sanskrit, pali und chinesischen übers. u. eingeführt. Mit vielen zum teil farbigen illus. wiedergegeben nach tibetischen tempelbildern aus dem besitz des berliner museums für völkerkunde.** Berlin (1929) 248 p, 21 illus.

Waldschmidt, Ernst (tsl) **Das mahāvadānasūtra. Ein kanonischer text über die sieben letzten buddhas. Sanskrit, verglichen mit dem pali, nebst einer analyse der in chinesischer übers. überlieferten parallelversionen. T 2, Die textbearbeitung.** Berlin (1956)

Waley, Arthur (tsl) [Buddhist] texts originating in china and japan. In Edward Conze (ed) **Buddhist texts through the ages,** oxford (1954) 287-306.

Walleser, Max. **Prajñā pāramitā – die vollkommenheit der erkenntnis. Nach indischen, tibetischen und chinesischen quellen.** Göttingen (1914) 164 p.

Ware, J. R. (tsl) The preamble to the samgharakṣitavadana. **HJAS** 3 (1938) 47-67.

Weller, Friedrich (tsl) Buddhas letzte wanderung. **MS** 4 (1939-40) 40-84, 406-440; 5 (1940) 141-207.

Weller, Friedrich (tsl) Kāśyapaparivarta nach der djin-fassung verdeutscht. **MIOF** 12.4 (1966) 379-462.

Weller, Friedrich (tsl) Die sung-fassung des kāśyapaparivarta. Versuch einer verdeutschung. **MS** 25 (1966) 207-361.

Weller, Friedrich (tsl) Über den aufban des pāṭikasuttanta. I: Der pali-text (d. n. xxiv). II: Übers. des chines. textes. **AMHAV** (1923) 620-639; **AM** 5 (1928) 104-140.

Wieger, Léon (tsl) **Bouddhisme chinois. Extraits du tripitaka, des commentaires, tracts, etc.** Mission de sienhsien, tientsin, 2 vol (1910-13) Repr peking (1940) 2 vol in 1. T 1: **Vinaya, monachisme et discipline. (Hinayana, véhicule inferieur)** 479 p; t 2: **Les vies chinoises du buddha,** 453 p. Chin texts with french tsl facing, illus.

Wong, Mow-lam (tsl) **Buddhabhashitamitayus sutra (the smaller sukhavativyuha). Chinese text and english translation.** Shanghai (1932)

Wong, Mow-lam (tsl) Vijñaptimâtratâ siddhi śâstra (nanjio no. 1197). Chapter I. Translated from the sanskrit into chinese by yuen chwang, and into english by wong mow-lam. **Chinese buddhist** 2 (1932) 1-57.

Yamaguchi, Susumu (tsl) Dignāga; examen de l'objet de la connaissance (ālambana-parīkṣā). Textes tibétain et chinois et trad. des stances et du commentaire, éclaircissements et notes d'après le commentaire tibétain de vinītadeva en collaboration avec henriette meyer. **JA** 220 (janv-mars 1929) 1-65.

Ymaïzoumi, Y. et Yamata (tsl) O-mi-to-king ou soukhavati-vyouha-soutra d'après la version chinoise de koumarajiva. **AMG** 2 (1881) 39-64.

Zach, E. von Notiz zu de harlez' vocabulaire bouddhique sanscrit-chinois [q.v.] (This rev followed by F. Weller: Bemerkungen zur vorstehenden notiz) **AM** 3 (1926) 569-573.

4. STUDIES OF TEXTS AND TERMS

Abel-Rémusat, J. P. Note sur quelques epithètes descriptives de bouddha. **Journal des savants** 2e sér, 4 (oct 1819) 625-633.

Anesaki, Masaharu. The four buddhist āgamas and their pāli counterparts. **TASJ** 35 (1908) 1-149.

Anesaki, Masaharu. On the relation of the chinese āgamas to the pāli nikāyas. **JRAS** (1901) 895-900.

Anesaki, Masaharu. Der sagâtha-vagga des samytta-nikâya und seine chinesische versionen. **Verhandlung 13 ICO Hamburg (1902)** Leiden (1904) s 61. See also french version: Le sagâtha-vagga du samyutta-nikâya et ses versions chinoises, in **Muséon** n.s. 6 (1905) 23-37.

Anesaki, Masaharu. Sutta-nipāta in chinese. **JPTS** (1906-07) 51.

Bagchi, P. C. Buddhist studies in japan and the taisho edition of the chinese tripitaka. **New asia** 1.1 (1939) 16-20.

Bagchi, P. C. A fragment of the kāśyapa-samhitā in chinese. **Indian culture** 9 (1942) 53-64.

Banerjee, A. C. Vinaya texts in chinese. **IHQ** 25 (1949) 87-94.

Bareau, André. À propos de deux traductions chinoises de brahma-jālasūtra du dīrghāgama. **MIHEC** 2 (1960) 1-4.

Bareau, A. Une confusion entre mahāsanghika et vātsīputrīya. **JA** 241 (1953) 399-406.

Bareau, André. l'Origine du dirgha-āgama traduit en chinois par buddhayaśas. In U. Ba Shin et al (ed) **Essays offered to g. h. luce in honour of his seventy-fifth birthday**, ascona (1966) vol 1, 49-58.

Bareau, André. The superhuman personality of buddha and its symbolism in the mahāparinirvāṇa-sūtra of the dharmaguptaka [from chinese text] In Joseph M. Kitagawa and Charles H. Long (ed) **Myths and symbols; studies in honor of mircea eliade**, univ chicago (1969) 9-21.

Bareau, A. Trois traités sur les sectes bouddhiques. **JA** 242 (1954) 229-233.

Beal, Samuel. **Abstract of four lectures on buddhist literature in china, delivered at university college, london.** London (1882) xvi + 185 p, 5 pl.

Beal, Samuel. The age and writings of nagarjuna-bodhisattva. **IA** 15 (1886) 353-356.

Beal, Samuel. **The buddhist tripitaka as it is known in china and japan. A catalogue and compendious report.** Printed for the india office . . . devonport (1876) 117 p.

Beal, Samuel. On a chinese version of the sánkhya kárikā, etc., found among the buddhist books comprising the tripitaka, and two other works. **JRAS** n.s. 10 (1878) 355-360.

Beal, Samuel. Results of an examination of chinese buddhist books in the library of the india office. **Trans 2nd ICO, London (1874)** London (1876) 132-162. See also author's art: The buddhist works in chinese in the india office library, in **IA** 4 (1875) 90-101.

Beal, Samuel. Some remarks on the suhrillekha or 'friendly communication' of nagarjuna-bodhisattva to king shatopohanna. **IA** 16 (1887) 169-172.

Bendall, C. C. (ed) **Contributions to the study of the śiksāsamuccaya derived from chinese sources.** St petersburg (1897-1902)

Bennett, A. G. Chinese translations of sanskrit buddhist literature during the 5th and 6th centuries. **MB** 66.1 (jan 1958) 2-10.

Bennett, A. G. Translations of sanskrit buddhist literature in china previous to the 5th century. **MB** 65 (1957) 77-82.

Cerbu, A. Zigmund. A tun-huang version of the āśrayaparāvrtti. **Adyar library bulletin** 25 (1961) 40-48.

Chan, Wing-tsit. The lotus sutra. In W. T. DeBary (ed) **Approaches to the oriental classics**, columbia univ (1959) 143-165.

Châu, Thích-minh. **The chinese madhayama agama and the pali majhima nikaya; a comparative study.** Saigon (1964) 388 p.

Châu, Thích-minh. **Milindapanha and nagasenabhikshusutra: a comparative study through pali and chinese sources.** Calcutta (1964) 127 p.

Ch'en, Kenneth K. S. A propos the feng-fa-yao of hsi ch'ao. **TP** 50 (1963) 79-92.

Ch'en, Kenneth K. S. A propos the mendhaka story. **HJAS** 16 (1953) 374-403.

Ch'en, Kenneth K. S. Notes on the sung and yüan tripitaka. **HJAS** 14 (1951) 208-214.

Ch'en, Kenneth K. S. Some problems in the translation of the chinese buddhist canon. **TJ** n.s. 2.1 (1960) 178-188.

Chi, Richard See Yee. **Buddhist formal logic. Part 1: a study of dignaga's 'hetucakra' and k'uei-chi's 'great commentary on the 'nyayapravesa.'** London (1969) 222 p, illus.

Chou, Ta-fu and P. C. Bagchi. New lights on the chinese inscriptions of bodhganā. **SIS** 1 (1944) 111-114.

Clark, Walter E. Some problems in the criticism of the sources for early buddhist history. **HTR** 23 (1930) 121-147.

Demiéville, Paul. Apocryphes bouddhiques en chine. **ACF** 54 (1954) 246-249; 55 (1955) 237-241.

Demiéville, Paul. Le chapitre de la bodhisattvabhumi sur la perfection du dhyana. **Rocznik orientalistyczny** 21 (1957) 109-128.

Demiéville, Paul. Deux documents de touen-houang sur le dhyâna chinois. In EZT (1961) 1-27.

Demiéville, Paul. Manuscrits chinois de touen-houang à leningrad. TP 51.4/5 (1964) 355-376.

Demiéville, Paul. l'Origine des sectes bouddhiques d'après paramârtha. MCB 1 (1931-32) 15-64.

Demiéville, Paul. Sur l'authenticité du ta tch'ing k'i sin louen. BMFJ 2.2 (1929) 1-78.

Demiéville, Paul. Sur la mémoire des existences antérieures. BEFEO 27 (1927) 283-298.

Demiéville, Paul. Sur les éditions imprimées du canon chinois. BEFEO 24 (1924) 181-218. A pt of following art.

Demiéville, Paul. Les versions chinoises du milindapanha. Being BEFEO 24 (1924) 258 p, pl, tables.

Demiéville, Paul. La yogâcârabhūmi de sangharaksa. BEFEO 44 (1947-50) 339-436.

Dschi, Hiän-lin. On the oldest chinese trans-literations of the name buddha. SIS 3 (1947) 1-9.

Edkins, Joseph. Notes of a correspondence with sir john bowring on buddhist literature in china. By prof. wilson. With notices of chinese buddhist works translated from the sanskrit. JRAS 16 (1856) 316-339.

Edmunds, Albert J. The chinese âgamas. With appeal to the japanese buddhists. LD 2 (1903) 21-23, 43-46.

Edmunds, Albert J. The chinese itivuttakam and its proof of the pali additions. LD 5 (1905) 85-86.

Fachow. Chuan tsi pai yuan king and the avadānaśataka. VBA no 1 (1945) 35-55.

Fachow. Comparative studies in the mahâparinibbânasutta and its chinese versions. SIS 1 (1944) 167-210; 2 (1945) 1-41.

Fachow. Development of tripitaka-translations in china. In BCL pt [vol] 1 (1945) 66-74.

Feer, Léon. Introduction au catalogue spécial du fonds chinois de la bibliothèque nationale. TP 9.3 (1898) 201-214.

Finot, L. Manuscrits sanskrits de sāhana's retrouvé en chine. JA 225 (1934) 1-86.

Franks, A. W. On some chinese rolls with buddhist legends and representations. Communicated to the society of antiquarians by a. w. franks. Westminster (1892) 6 p, 1 pl. Same title in Archaeologie 53, 2 sér, no 3, pt 1 (1892) 239-244, 1 taf.

Friese, Heinz. Das tao-yǔ-lu . . . des yao kuang-hsiao (1335-1418) OE 8 (1961) 42-58, 177-187.

Fuchs, Walter. Eine buddhistische tun-huang-rolle v.j. 673. In Asiatica (1954) 155-160, illus.

Fuchs, Walter. Zur technischen organisation der übersetzungen buddhistischer schriften ins chinesiche. AM 6 (1930) 84-103.

Fujieda, Akira. The tunhuang manuscripts: a general description. Zinbun 9 (1966) 1-32; pt 2 ibid 10 (1969) 17-39, fig, tables.

Gard, Richard A. On the authenticity of the chung-lun. JIBS 3.1 (1954) 7-13.

Giles, Lionel. Descriptive catalogue of the chinese manuscripts from tun-huang in the british museum. London (1957) xxv + 334 p.

Giles, Lionel. An illustrated buddhist sūtra. BMQ 11 (1936) 29.

Giles, Lionel. Six centuries at tun-huang. A short account of the stein collection of chinese mss in the british museum. London (1944) 50 p, facs.

Goodrich, Luther Carrington. Earliest printed editions of the tripitaka. VBQ 19.3 (1953-54) 215-220.

Gulik, Robert Hans von. Siddham: an essay on the history of sanskrit studies in china and japan. Nagpur (1956) 2 vol, pl.

Haas, Hans. Tsungmi's yuen-zan-lun. Eine abhandlung über den ursprung des menschen aus dem kanon des chinesischen buddhismus. ARW 12 (1909) 491-532.

Hamilton, Clarence H. Buddhist idealism in wei shih er shih lwen. EP (1929) 99-115.

Hamilton, Clarence H. K'uei chi's commentary on wei-shih-er-shih-lun. JAOS 53 (1933) 144-151.

Harlez, Charles de. Man-han-si-fan-tsyeh-yao, a buddhist repertory in sanscrit, tibetan, mandchu, mongol, and chinese. BOR 2 (1887) 8-14, 49-55; 3 (1889) 69-72, 116-118, 143-144, 210-215, 232-239, 275-282; 4 (1890) 59-63, 112-116, 164-168, 188-192, 213-216, 238-240.

Havret, Henri. **T'ien-tchou, 'seigneur du ciel.'**
À propos d'une stèle bouddhique de tch'eng-tou.
Shanghai (1901) 30 p. (Variétés sinologiques
no 19)

Hoernle, A. F. R. **Manuscript remains of buddhist
literature found in eastern turkestan. Facsimiles
of mss. in sanskrit, khotanese, kuchean, tibetan
and chinese with transcriptions, translations and
notes, critical introductions and vocabularies.**
Oxford (1916) vol 1 (all publ) 446 p, 22 pl.

Huber, Éd. Études de littérature bouddhique.
BEFEO 4 (1904) 698-726; continued in **ibid** 6
(1906) 1-43, 335-340. Re certain chin tsl of
indian texts; some tsl.

Hummel, A. W. An ancient chinese manuscript.
(Mahāparinirvāna sūtra chuan 1-2) **QJCA** 3.4
(1946) 6.

Hurvitz, Leon. Additional observations on the
'defense of the faith.' In **EZT** (1961) 28-40.

Ivanovski, A. O. Sur une traduction chinoise du
recueil bouddhique 'jātakamālā.' **RHR** 47 (1903)
298-335. Tsl fr russian M. Duchesne.

Iwai, Hirosato. The compilers of the ching-tu-
pao-chu-chi. **TBMRD** 13 (1951) 47-86.

Jan, Yün-hua. The fo-tsu-t'ung-chi, a biographical
and bibliographical study. **OE** 10 (1963) 61-82.

Jong, J. W. de. **Buddha's word in china.**
Australian national univ (1968) 26 p (28th
george ernest morrison lecture)

Karlgren, Bernhard. Prononciation ancienne de
caractères chinois figurant dans les transcriptions
bouddhiques. **TP** 2e sér, 19 (1918-19) 104-121.

Kielhorn, F. Sanskrit manuscripts in china. **JRAS**
(1894) 835-838. Repr in **Academy** 45 (16 june
1894) 498-499.

Kimm, Chung Se. Ein chinesisches fragment des
prātimokṣa aus turfan. **AM** 2 (1925) 597-608.

Kimura, Mitsutaka. One aspect of the
saddharmapundarīka sūtra śāstra. **Studies on
buddhism in japan** 3 (1941) 71-80.

Kuroda, C. A note on the lankavatara sutra. **TJR**
no 1 (1955) 91-94.

Lacouperie, Albert J. B. Terrien de. On hiuen-
tsiang instead of yüan chwang, and the necessity
of avoiding the pekinese sounds in the quotations
of ancient proper names in chinese. **JRAS** (1892)
835-840.

Lamotte, Étienne. l'Ālayavijñana (le receptacle)
dans le mahāyānasamgraha (chapitre II). Asanga
et ses commentateurs. **MCB** 3 (1934-35) 169-255.

Lancaster, Lewis R. The chinese translation of
the aṣṭasāhasrikā-prajñāpāramitā-sutra attributed
to chih ch'ien. **MS** 28 (1969) 246-257.

Laufer, Berthold. Origin of the word shaman.
American anthropologist n.s. 19.3 (1917) 361-371.

La Vallée Poussin, Louis de. Brahma-jāla suttanta
in chinese. **JRAS** (1903) 583.

La Vallée Poussin, Louis de. Les neuf kalpas qu'à
franchi sākyamuni pour devancer maitreya.
TP 26 (1929) 17-24.

La Vallée Poussin, L. de. Notes de bibliographie
bouddhique. **MCB** 3 (1934-35) 355-407;
5 (1936-37) 243-304.

Lee, Shao-chang. The prajnaparamita hridaya
sutra or 'Essence of transcendental wisdom' (after
hsuan chang, a.d. VIIth cent.) **JNCBRAS** 65 (1934)
150-151. Same title in **Orient et occident** (geneva)
1.11 (1935) 55.

Lévi, S. Bilanga-dutiya. In **MSL** (1937) 405-412.

Lévi, Sylvain. Les éléments de formation du
divyāvadāna. **TP** 8 (1907) 105-122.

Lévi, Sylvain. La légende de râma dans un avadâna
chinois. In **MSL** (1937) 271-274.

Lévi, S. Un nouveau document sur le milinda-
praçna. In **MSL** (1937) 214-217.

Lévi, S. l'Original chinois du sutra tibétain sur la
grande-ourse. **TP** 2e sér, 9 (1908) 453-454.

Lévi, Sylvain. Les saintes écritures du bouddhisme.
Comment s'est constituée le canon sacré. **CMG** 31
(d?) 105-129.

Liebenthal, Walter. New light on the mahāyāna-
śraddhotpāda śāstra. **TP** 46 (1958) 155-216.

Liebenthal, Walter. Notes on the vajrasāmadhi.
TP 44 (1954) 347-386.

Liebenthal, Walter. "One-mind-dharma." In
**Tsukamoto hakase shōju kinen bukkyōshigaku
ronshu [essays on buddhist history presented to
professor z. tsukamoto]** kyoto univ (1961) 41-47.

Lin, Li-kouang. **l'Aide-mémoire de la vraie loi
(saddharmasmrtyupashtanasutra). Recherches sur
un sutra développé du petit véhicle.** Paris (1949)
xv + 383 p. Introduction de P. Demiéville.

Link, Arthur E. Shyh daw-an's preface to saṅgharakṣa's yogācarabhūmisūtra and the problem of buddho-taoist terminology in early chinese buddhism. **JAOS** 77 (1957) 1-14.

Maître, Ch. E. Une nouvelle édition du tripitaka chinois. **BEFEO** 2 (1902) 341-351.

Maki, Itsu. On the chinese dhammapada with special reference to the preface attached thereto. **Hitotsubashi academy annals** 9 (1958) 109-121.

Maspero, Henri. **Sur la date et l'authenticité du fou fa tsang yin yuan tchouan.** Angers (n.d.) 21 p.

Mather, Richard B. Wang chin's 'dhuta temple stele inscriptions' as an example of buddhist parallel prose. **JAOS** 83 (1963) 338-359.

Meier, F. J. Neuerscheinungen zur buddhistischen geistesgeschichte. **Saeculum** 3 (1952) 319-340.

Mironov, N. D. Buddhist miscellanea. **JRAS** (1927) 241-279. Re name kuan-yin.

Mironov, N. D. Nyāyāpraveśa. **TP** 28 (1931) 1-24.

Mori, Sodō. On the fēn-bie-gŏng-dé-lùn. **JIBS** 19.1 (dec 1970) 32-38.

Mukherji, Probhat Kumar [Mukhopādhyāya, Prabhāta-Kumārā] **Indian literature in china and the far east.** Calcutta (1932) 334 p.

Müller, F. Max. Chinese translations of sanskrit texts. **IA** 10 (1881) 121-122. Same title in author's **Chips from a german workshop,** 1 2nd ed (1868) 292-304.

Müller, F. W. K. Die 'persischen' kalendarausdrücke im chines. tripitaka. **SAWW** 155, pt 1 (1907) 458-465.

Mus, Paul. **La lumière sur les six voies. Tableau de la transmigration bouddhique d'après des sources sanskrites, pāli, tibétaines et chinoises en majeure partie inédites.** T 1: **Introduction et critique des textes.** Paris (1939) 360 p, 6 pl.

Nagao, Gadjin M. An interpretation of the term samvriti (convention) in buddhism. In **SJV** (1951) 550-561.

Nakamura, Hajime. The influence of confucian ethics on the chinese translations of buddhist sutras. **SIS** 5.3/4 (1957) (Liebenthal festschrift) 156-170.

Najio, Buniyu [sic] Les versions chinoises du saddharmapuṇḍarīka. **PCIEEO** (1903) 110-112.

Pachow, W. A comparative study of the pratimoksa. **SIS** 4 (1953) 18-193; 5 (1955) 1-45.

Pai, Hui. On the word 'cittavarana' in the prajñāparamitā-hdrayasūtra. **SIS** 3 (1947) 131-139.

Parker, E. H. The diamond sutra (chin-kang-ching) **AQR** n.s. (ser 4) 2 (1913) 428-429.

Pelliot, Paul. Encore un mot à propos du sutra des causes et des effets et de l'expression siang-kiao. **TP** 26 (1929) 51-52.

Pelliot, Paul. The kāçyapaparivarta. (Rev of 3 art publ by Stäel-Holstein and F. Weller) **TP** 32 (1936) 68-76.

Pelliot, Paul. Les noms propres dans les traductions chinoises du milindapañha. **JA** 11e sér, 4 (sept-oct 1914) 374-419.

Pelliot, Paul. Quelques transcriptions apparentées à çambhala dans les textes chinois. **TP** 20.2 (1920-21) 73-85.

Pelliot, Paul. Les stances d'introduction de l'abhidharmahrdayaśāstra de dharmatrāta. **JA** 217 (1930) 267-273.

Pelliot, Paul. Le terme siang-kiao comme designation du bouddhisme. **TP** 25 (1928) 92-94.

Pelliot, Paul. Textes chinois sur pāṇḍuraṅga. **BEFEO** 3 (1903) 649-654.

Pelliot, Paul. Trois termes de mémoires de hiuantsang. In **EORL** (1932) t 2, p 423-431.

Petzold, Bruno. The completion of the new edition of the chinese tripitaka. **YE** 4 (1929) 193-196; **PW** 4 (1929) 521-524.

Petzold, Bruno. Die neuausgabe des chinesischen tripitaka. **NachrDGNVO** ?18 (1929) 13-18.

Pruden, Leo M. Some notes on the fan-wangching. **JIBS** 15.2 (1967) 915-925.

Przyluski, J. **The legend of emperor aśoka in indian and chinese texts.** Calcutta (1967) Tsl fr french with add notes and comments by D. K. Biswas.

Przyluski, J. and M. Lalou. Notes de mythologie bouddhique. 1. Yakṣa et gandharva dans le mahāsamayasuttanta. 2. Les rgynd sum-pa manuscrits de touen-houang. 3. Les fils de brahmâ. **HJAS** 3 (1938) 40-46, 128-136; 4 (1939) 69-76.

Przyluski, J. Le parinirvāna et les funérailles du buddha. Examen comparatif des textes. **JA** 11e sér, 11 (mai-juin 1918) 485-526; 11e sér, 12 (nov-dec 1918) 401-456. II: Vêtements de religieux et vêtements de rois, **ibid** 11e sér, 13 (mai-juin 1919) 365-430. [III] Les éléments rituels dans les funérailles du buddha, **ibid** 11e sér, 15 (janv-mars 1920) 5-54. Idem: Première partie, extrait du **JA** (1918-20) Paris (1920) 216 p.

Przyluski, J. Le partage des reliques du buddha. **MCB** 4 (1935-36) 341-367.

Richard, Timothy. How to awaken faith in the mahayana school. **JNCBRAS** 27.2 (1892) 263-272. Synopsis.

Sastri, S. S. Suryanarayana. The chinese suvarṇa-saptati and the maṭharavriti. **JOR** 5 (1932) 34-40.

Schlegel, G. Le terme bouddhique tu-p'i. **TP** 9 (1898) 269-271.

Schlegel, G. Les termes yü-lan-p'en et yü-lan-p'o. **TP** 2e sér, 2.2 (mai 1901) 146-148.

Schott, Wilhelm. Zur litteratur des chinesischen buddhismus. **Akademie der wissenschaft zur berlin, philologische und historische klasse, Abhandlungen 1873.** Berlin (1874) 37-65.

Sedgwick, Ellery. A chinese printed scroll of the lotus sutra. **QJCA** 6.2 (feb 1949) 6-9, pl, facs. With a note by Arthur W. Hummel.

Sen, Satiranjan. Two medical texts in chinese translation (In tripitaka) **VBA** 1 (1945) 70-95.

Smith, Helmer. En marge du vocabulaire sanskrit des bouddhistes. **Orientalia suecana** 2 (1953) 119-128; 3 (1954) 31-35; 4 (1955) 109-113.

Specht, Édouard. **Deux traductions chinoises du milindapañha.** Paris (1893) 25 p. Sub-title: Mélanges sinologiques ii. Introduction de Sylvain Lévi.

Stäel-Holstein, A. von. On a peking, a st. petersburg, and a kyoto reconstruction of a sanskrit stanza transcribed with chinese charac-ters under the northern sung dynasty. In **Studies presented to ts'ai yüan-p'ei on his 65th birthday,** peking, vol 1 (1933) 175-187.

Suzuki, D. T. An introduction to the study of the lankavatara sutra. **EB** 5 (1929) 1-79.

Sykes, William H. On a catalogue of chinese buddhistical works. **JRAS** 9 (1848) 199-213.

Takakusu, Junjirō. Buddhaghosa's samantapāsādikā in chinese. **JRAS** (1897) 113-114.

Takakusu, Junjirō. Chinese translations of the milinda pañho. **JRAS** (1896) 1-21.

Takakusu, Junjirō. The name of 'messiah' found in a buddhist book; the nestorian missionary adam, presbyter, papas of china, translating a buddhist sutra. **TP** 7.5 (1896) 589-591.

Takakusu, Junjirō. Notes on buddhist books. **JRAS** (1903) 181-183.

Takakusu, Junjirō. On the abhidharma literature of the sarvāstivādins. **JPTS** (1905) 67-146. See also author's art, The abhidharma literature, pali and chinese, **JRAS** (1905) 160-162.

Takakusu, Junjirō. **A pali chrestomathy; with notes and glossary giving sanskrit and chinese equivalents.** Tokyo (1900) 94 + 6 + 272 p.

Takakusu, Junjirō. Pali elements in chinese buddhism. A translation of buddhaghosa's samantapasadika, a commentary on the vinaya, found in the chinese tripitaka. **JRAS** 28 (1896) 415-439.

Takakusu, Junjirō. La sāmkhyakārikā étudiée à la lumière de sa version chinoise. **BEFEO** 4 (1904) 1-65, 978-1064. See further next item.

Takakusu, Junjirō. La sāmkhyakārikā étudiee à la lumière de sa version chinoise. **PCIEEO** (1902) 39-41. Same title in engl, in **Journal of the madras univ** 4.1 suppl (1932) 1-51; 5 (1933) 81-114. See preceding item.

Takakusu, Junjirō. A study of paramartha's life of vasu-bandhu; and the date of vasu-bandhu. **JRAS** (1905) 33-53.

Takakusu, Junjirō. The works of samgha-bhadra, an opponent of vasu-bandhu. **JRAS** (1905) 158-159.

Takasaki, Jikido. Structure of the anuttarāsrayasūtra (wu-shang-i-ching) **JIBS** 8.2 (mar 1960) 30-37.

Takasaki, Jikido. **A study on the ratnagotravibhāga (uttaratantra). Being a treatise on the tathāgata-garbha theory of mahāyāna buddhism.** Rome (1966) 452 p, app, indices. Incl tsl fr sanskrit text and comparison with tibetan and chin versions.

T'ang, Yung-t'ung. On ko-yi, the earliest method by which indian buddhism and chinese thought were synthesized. In W. R. Inge (ed) **Radhakrishnan: comparative studies in philosophy presented in honour of his 60th birthday,** london (1951) 276-286.

T'ang, Yung-t'ung. The editions of the ssu-shih-erh chang-ching. **HJAS** 1 (1936) 147-155.

Thomas, F. W. A buddhist chinese text in brāhmī script. **ZDMG** 91 (1937) 1-48.

Thomas, F. W. Paramartha's life of vasubandhu and the date of kaniska. **JRAS** (1914) 748-751.

Thomas, F. W. and G. L. M. Clauson. A chinese buddhist text in tibetan writing. **JRAS** (1926) 508-526.

Thomas, F. W. and G. L. M. Clauson. A second chinese buddhist text in tibetan characters. **JRAS** (1927) 281-306. See further: Note supplementary to the article, 'A second chinese . . .' in **ibid** 858-860.

Thomas, F. W., S. Miyamoto and G. L. M. Clauson. A chinese mahāyāna catechism in tibetan and chinese characters. **JRAS** (1929) 37-76.

Thomas, F. W. and H. Ui. 'The hand treatise,' a work of aryadeva. **JRAS** (1918) 267-310.

Tomomatsu, E. Sûtralamkâra et kalpanâmaṇḍitikâ. **JA** 219 (1931) 135-174, 245-337.

Tubyansky, M. On the authorship of nyāyapraveça. **Izvestiya akademiya nauk** ser 6, vol 20 (1926) 975-982.

Tucci, G. Is the nyayapravesa by dinnaga? **JRAS** (1928) 7-13.

Tucci, G. Un traité d'āryadeva sur le 'nirvana' des hérétiques. **TP** 24 (1926) 16-31.

Vassiliev, Boris. 'Ju-shih lun' – a logical treatise ascribed to vasubandhu. **BSOAS** 8.4 (1937) 1013-1037.

Ventakasubbiah, A. On the grammatical work si-t'an-chang. **JOR** 10 (1936) 11-26.

Visser, Marinus Willem de. The canon of chinese buddhism. **Museum** 11.1 (1903) col 1-5.

Ware, J. R. Notes on the fan wang ching. **HJAS** 1 (1936) 156-161.

Ware, J. R. Studies in the divyāvadāna. **JAOS** 48 (1928) 159-165; 49 (1929) 40-51.

Ware, J. R. Transliteration of the names of chinese buddhist monks. **JAOS** 52 (1932) 159-162.

Watanabe, K. Aśvaghoṣa and the great epics. **JRAS** (1907) 664-665.

Watanabe, Kaikioku (or Kaikyoku) A chinese text corresponding to parts of bower manuscript. **JRAS** (1907) 261-266.

Watanabe, Kaikioku (or Kaikyoku) The nepalese nava dharmas and their chinese translations. **JRAS** (1907) 663-664.

Watanabe, Kaikioku (or Kaikyoku) The oldest record of the rāmāyana in a chinese buddhist writing (mahāvibhāṣa) **JRAS** (1907) 99-103.

Watters, Thomas. The a-mi-t'o ching. **ChRev** 10 (1881-82) 225-240.

Watters, Thomas. Notes on the miao-fa-lien-hua-ching, a buddhist sutra in chinese. **JNCBRAS** n.s. 9 (1874) 89.

Watters, Thomas. The ta-yun-lun-ch'ing-yu-ching. **ChRev** 10 (1881-82) 384-395.

Weinstein, Stanley. On the authorship of the hsi-fang-yao-chüeh. **Trans ICfO Japan** 4 (1959) 12-25.

Weller, F. Über den aufbau des patikasuttanta. ii. Übersetzung des chinesischen textes. **AM** 5 (1930) 104-140.

Wogihara (or Wogiwara or Ogiwara) Unrai. Contributions to the study of the śikṣa-samuccaya derived from chinese sources. **Muséon** n.s. 5 (1904) 96-103, 209-215; 7 (1906) 255-261.

Wohlgemuth, Else. Über die chinesische version von aśvaghoṣas buddhacarita . . . fo-so-hing-tsan. **MSOS** 19 (1916) 1-75.

Wu, K. T. Chinese printing under four alien dynasties. **HJAS** 13 (1950) 441-457, 515-516. Re buddhist texts.

Zach, E. von. Einige bemerkungen zu pelliot's sūtra des causes et des effets. **TP** 25 (1928) 403-413.

5. THEORY AND DOCTRINE

Abel-Rémusat, J. P. Essai sur la cosmographie et la cosmogonie des bouddhistes, d'après les auteurs chinois. **Journal des savants** 2e sér, 16 (oct 1831) 597-610; 2e sér, 16 (nov 1831) 668-674; 2e sér, 16 (déc 1831) 716-731. See also author's **Mélanges posthumes d'histoire et de littérature orientales,** paris (1843) 65-131.

Abel-Rémusat, J. P. **Observations sur quelques points de la doctrine samanéenne, et en particulier sur les noms de la triade suprême chez les différents peuples bouddhistes.** Paris (1831) 67 p.

Bertholet, R. l'Astrobiologie et la pensée bouddhique. (l'Astrobiologie et la pensée d'asie: essai sur les origines des sciences et des théories morales) **RMM** 41 (1931) 509-529.

Bloom, Alfred. The sense of sin and guilt and the last age [mappo] in chinese and japanese buddhism. **Numen** 14 (1967) 144-149.

Bodde, Derk. The chinese view of immortality; its expression by chu hsi and its relationship to buddhist thought. **RofR** 6 (1942) 369-383.

Chang, Carsun. Buddhism as a stimulus to neo-confucianism. **OE** 2.2 (1955) 157-166.

Chung, Albert C. The mysticism of the buddhists. **CC** 5.1 (1963) 99-121.

Day, Clarence B. **The philosophers of china.** N.Y. (1962) See chap 8, The inner development of chinese buddhism, 111-180.

Edkins, Joseph. The buddhist doctrine of future punishment. **Sunday at home** (july 1879)

Edkins, Joseph. The four elements. **ChRev** 16 (1888) 369-370.

Edkins, Joseph. The nirvana of the northern buddhists. **JRAS** n.s. 13 (jan 1881) 59-79. See also author's The nirvana according to northern buddhism, **Atti 4th ICO Florence, 1878,** vol 2, Florence (1881) 295-308.

Edkins, Joseph. Paradise of the western heaven. **ChRev** 17 (1888-89) 175-176.

Eitel, E. J. Amita and the paradise of the west. **NQ** 2 (1868) 35-38.

Eitel, E. J. A buddhist purgatory for women. **NQ** 2 (1868) 66-68, 82-85.

Eitel, E. J. The nirvana of chinese buddhists. **ChRec** 3 (1870-71) 1-6.

Fung, Yu-lan. **A history of chinese philosophy.** Tsl fr chin Derk Bodde. Princeton univ, vol 2, (1953) See chap 7-10.

Fung, Yu-lan. **A short history of chinese philosophy.** Ed Derk Bodde. N.Y. (1948) See chap 21, The foundation of chinese buddhism, 241-254.

Gurij, P. Der buddhismus des mahāyāna . . . aus dem russischen übersetzt mit einer einleitung . . . von w. a. unkrig. **Anthropos** 16-17 (1921-22) 343-359, 801-818; 18-19 (1923-34) 267-277.

Hackmann, Heinrich. **Chinesische philosophie. Mit einem bilde bodhidharmas.** München (1927) 406 s. See p 237-311.

Hamilton, Clarence H. Buddhist idealism in wei shih er shih lun. In **EP** (1929) 99-115.

Hamilton, Clarence H. Hsüan chuang and the wei shih philosophy. **JAOS** 51 (1931) 291-308.

Hamilton, Clarence H. The idea of compassion in mahāyāna buddhism. **JAOS** 70 (1950) 145-151.

Harlez, Charles J. de. Tathāgatha. **JRAS** (1899) 131.

Hurvitz, Leon. Chih tun's notions of prajñā. **JAOS** 88 (1968) 243-261.

Hurvitz, Leon. Road to buddhist salvation as described by vasubhadra. **JAOS** 87 (1967) 434-486.

Kung, Tien-min. Some buddhist and christian doctrines compared. **QNCCR** 5.2 (1961) 34-37.

La Vallée Poussin, Louis de. Staupikam. **HJAS** 2 (1937) 276-289. Theory of stupa and its evolution.

La Vallée Poussin, Louis de. Studies in buddhist dogma: the three bodies of a buddha. **JRAS** (1906) 943 f.

Lee, Pi-cheng [Lü Pi-ch'eng] (ed and tsl) **An outline of karma.** N.p. [publ by tsl] (1941?) 97 p.

Liang Ch'i-ch'ao. Kurzer überblick über die buddhistische psychologie . . . Tsl fr chin R. Wilhelm. **Sinica** 4 (1929) 18-27, 68-83.

Liebenthal, Walter. The immortality of the soul in chinese thought. **MN** 8 (1952) 327-397.

Matsunaga, Alicia. **The buddhist philosophy of assimilation. The historical development of the honji-suijaku theory.** Tokyo (1969) See chap 3, Buddhist assimilation in china, 97-138.

McGovern, William M. Buddhist metaphysics in china and japan. **Proc aristotelian society** n.s. 20 (1920) 157-166.

Meister, Peter Wilhelm. Buddhistische planetendarstellungen. **OE** 1 (1954) 1-5, pl.

Mortier, F. Le bouddhisme et des variations doctrinales. **BSAB** 65 (1954) 197-202.

Mus, Paul. **La lumière sur les six voies. Tableau de la transmigration bouddhique d'après des sources sanskrites, pāli, tibétaines et chinoises en majeure partie inédites.** T 1: **Introduction et critique des textes.** Paris (1939) 360 p, 6 pl.

Petzold, B. Mahāyāna. OL 41 (1938) col 600-607.

Pratt, J. B. Buddhism and scientific thinking. JR 14 (1934) 13-24.

Rotermund, W. **Die ethik lao-tse's mit besonderer bezugnahme auf die buddhistische moral.** Gotha (1874) 26 p.

Sakamoto, Yukio. The development of the theories on the buddhata in china. In RSJ (1959) 350-358.

Schott, Wilhelm. Die moral der buddh. chinesen. MLA 18 (1840) 445-451.

Schott, Wilhelm. Die verklärte welt des buddha amitabha. MLA 18 (1840) 321-322.

Ščuckij, J. Ein dauist im chinesischen buddhismus. Sinica 15 (1940) 114-129.

Selby, T. G. Yan kwo, yuk lik, or the purgatories of popular buddhism. ChRev 1 (1872-73) 301-311.

Servus. The paradise of fuh. ICG no 6 (1818) 194-200.

Shen, C. T. The five eyes: a study of buddhism. CC 10.3 (1969) 22-32.

Suzuki, Beatrice Lane. What is mahāyāna buddhism? EB 1 (1921) 61-69.

Suzuki, D. T. Buddha in mahāyāna buddhism. EB 1 (1921) 109-122.

Suzuki, Daisetz T. Freedom of knowledge in chinese buddhism. MW 31 (1906) 12-18.

Suzuki, D. T. The natural law in the buddhist tradition. NLIP 5 (1953) 91-115.

'The systems of buddha and confucius compared' extracted from the ICG no 5, aout 1818, 149-157. ChRep 2 (1833-34) 265 et seq.

Tai-hü. Über das nichtvorhandensein eines objectiven geistes. Sinica 4 (1929) 206-215.

Takakusu, Junjiro. **The essentials of buddhist philosophy.** Ed W. T. Chan and Charles A. Moore. n.p. [Honolulu] 1st ed (1947) 2nd ed (1949) 221 p, charts, index.

Takata, Ninkaku. The relations between esotericism and the tathāgatagarbha theory as seen in the shou-hu-kuo-chieh-chu-dhāranī-ching. JIBS 9.2 (mar 1961) 34-39.

Tamaki, Koshiro. The development of the thought of tathāgatagarbha from india to china. JIBS 9.1 (jan 1961) 25-33.

Ui, H. **The vaiśesika philosophy.** London (1917)

Unno, Taisetsu. The buddhatā theory of fa-tsang. Trans ICfO Japan 8 (1963) 34-41.

Waley, Arthur. References to alchemy in buddhist scriptures. BSOAS 6.4 (1932) 1102-1103.

Wilhelm, Richard. Einige probleme der buddhistischen psychologie. Sinica 4 (1929) 120-130.

Wogihara (or Wogiwara, or Ogiwara) Unrai. Bemerkungen über die nordbuddhistische terminologie im hinblick auf die bodhisattvabhūmi. ZDMG 58 (1904) 451-454.

6. HISTORY

Allen, Herbert J. The connexion between taoism, confucianism and buddhism in early days. Trans 3rd ICHR, Oxford (1908) vol 1, 115-119.

Allen, H. J. The first introduction of buddhism into china. Academy 40 (1891) 221.

Allen, Herbert J. Similarity between buddhism and early taoism. ChRev 15 (1886-87) 96-99.

Ampère, J. J. Histoire du bouddhisme: relation des royaumes bouddhiques, tr. du chinois par abel rémusat. RDM 4e sér, 9 (15 janv 1837) 736-751. See also what is apparently german tsl: Zur geschichte des buddhismus. Aus der reise des chinesischen priester fa-hian. In MLA 12 (d?) 349-350, 354-355.

Aurousseau, L. Paul pelliot — 'meou-tseu ou les doutes levés' (etc.) BEFEO 22 (1922) 276-298.

Bagchi, P. C. The beginnings of buddhism in china. SIS 1 (1944) 1-17.

Bagchi, Prabodh Chandra. **India and china: a thousand years of cultural relations.** Bombay, 2nd rev and enl ed (1950) n.y. (1951) 234 p, map, app, bibliog, index.

Bagchi, P. C. On foreign element in the tantra. IHQ 7 (1931) 1-16.

Bagchi, P. C. On the original buddhism, its canon and language. **SIS** 2 (1945) 107-135.

Bagchi, P. C. Some early buddhist missionaries of persia in china. **CalR** ser 3, vol 24 (1927) 60-64.

Balazs, Stefan. Der philosoph fan dschen und sein traktat gegen den buddhismus. **Sinica** 7 (1932) 220-234. Engl tsl H. M. Wright: The first chinese materialist, in Arthur F. Wright (ed) **Chinese civilization and bureaucracy. Variations on a theme** [collection of essays by Etienne Balazs, in engl tsl] yale univ (1964) 255-276.

Bareau, André. Indian and ancient chinese buddhism: institutions analogous to the jisa. **CSSH** 3 (1961) 443-451 ('Jisa' is tibetan for the principal land of the monastery)

Beal, Samuel. The buddhist inscription at keu-yung-kwan. **IA** 9 (1880) 195-196.

Beal, Samuel. Early buddhist missionaries in china. **Academy** 33 (28 jan 1888) 65.

Berval, René de. l'Expansion du bouddhisme en asie. **FA:BPB** (1959) 685-693.

Blofeld, John. Lamaism and its influence on chinese buddhism. **THM** 7 (1938) 151-160.

Bloom, Alfred. The sense of sin and guilt and the last age (mappo) in chinese and japanese buddhism. **Numen** 14 (1967) 144-149.

Bose, Phanindra Nath. **The indian teachers in china.** Triplicane, madras (1923) 148 p.

Brandauer, Frederick P. The encounter between christianity and chinese buddhism from the four-teenth century through the twentieth century. **CF** 11.3 (1968) 30-38.

Bras, Gabriel le. Quelques problèmes sociolog-iques de l'histoire du bouddhisme. **Archives de sociologie des religions** 11.21 (jan-june 1966) 119-124.

Brough, John. Gāndhārā, shan-shan, and early chinese buddhist translations. **Tôhôgaku** 32 (1966) 164-172.

Carter, Thomas F. **The invention of printing in china and its spread westward.** Columbia univ (1925) rev ed (1931) 3rd rev ed (1955) See esp chap 4, The dynamic force that created the demand for printing, the advance of buddhism; chap 6, The beginnings of block printing in the buddhist monasteries of china; chap 8, The first printed book. The diamond sutra of 868.

Chan, David B. The role of the monk tao-yen in the usurpation of the prince of yen (1398-1402) **Sinologica** 6.2 (1959) 83-100.

Chan, Hok-lam. The white lotus-maitreya doctrine and popular uprisings in ming and ch'ing china. **Sinologica** 10.4 (1969) 211-233.

Chan, Wing-tsit. Transformation of buddhism in china. **PEW** 7.3/4 (oct 1957-jan 1958) 17-116. Repr in Charles K. H. Chen (ed) **Neo-confucianism, etc.: essays by wing-tsit chan,** hong kong (1969) 422-437.

Chan, Wing-tsit. Wang yang-ming's criticism of buddhism. In **WPDMD** (1968) 31-37.

Châu, Thích-minh. Some chinese contributions to buddhism. **MB** 69 (1961) 113-117.

Chavannes, Édouard. Communication sur l'inscription de kiu-yong-koan. **Actes 10e ICO Geneva, 1894,** 5e sec, Leiden (1897) 89-93.

Chavannes, Édouard. Inscriptions et pièces de chancellerie chinoises de l'époque mongole. **TP** n.s. 5 (1904) 366-404. Documents dealing with controversy between buddhists and taoists.

Chavannes, Édouard. Les pays d'occident d'après le wei lio. **TP** n.s. 6 (1905) 519-571. Re intro of buddhism into china. See rev by P. Pelliot in **BEFEO** 6 (1906) 361-400; he also discusses various aspects of han buddhism.

Chavannes, Édouard. Le sūtra de la pario occi-dentale de l'inscription de kiu-yong-koan. In **Mélanges charles de harlez,** leiden (1869) 60-81.

Chavannes, Édouard et Sylvain Lévi. Note pré-liminaire sur l'inscription de kiu-yong koan. Première partie, Les inscriptions chinoises et mongoles, par E. C. Deuxième partie. Les inscriptions tibétaines, par S. L. **JA** 9e sér, 4 (sept-oct 1894) 354-373.

Ch'en, Kenneth K. S. Anti-buddhist propaganda during the nan-ch'ao. **HJAS** 15 (1952) 166-192.

Ch'en, Kenneth K. S. **Buddhism in china. A historical survey.** Princeton univ (1964) 560 p, bibliog, gloss, list of chin names, index.

Ch'en, Kenneth K. S. The buddhist contributions to neo-confucianism and taoism. In **TC** (1970) 155-160 (Excerpt from author's **Buddhism in china** q.v. 471-476).

Ch'en, Kenneth K. S. Buddhist-taoist mixtures in the pa-shih-i-hua t'u. **HJAS** 9 (1945) 1-12.

Ch'en, Kenneth K. S. Chinese communist attitudes towards buddhism in chinese history. **CQ** 22 (1965) 14-30.

Ch'en, Kenneth K. S. Economic background of the hui-ch'ang persecution. **HJAS** 19 (1956) 67-105.

Ch'en, Kenneth K. S. Neo-taoism and the prajña school during the wei and chin dynasties. **CC** 1 (oct 1957) 33-46, bibliog.

Ch'en, Kenneth K. S. On some factors responsible for the anti-buddhist persecution under the pei-ch'ao. **HJAS** 17.1/2 (1954) 261-273.

Ch'en, Kenneth K. S. The sale of monk certificates during the sung dynasty. **HTR** 49.4 (1956) 307-327.

Chia Chung-yao. The church-state conflict in the t'ang dynasty. In E-tu Zen Sun and John DeFrancis (ed) **Chinese social history; translations of selected studies,** washington d.c. (1956) 197-206. Art largely excerpted from diary of japanese monk ennin.

China institute. Ancient cultural contacts between china and india. **China institute bulletin** 6 (mar-apr 1942) 4-8, map.

Chou, Hsiang-kuang. **A history of chinese buddhism.** Allahabad (1955) 264 p.

Chuan, T. K. Some notes on kao seng chuan. **THM** 7 (1938) 452-468.

Clemen, K. Christliche einflüsse auf den chinesischen und japanischen buddhismus. **OZ** 9 (1920-22) 10-37, 185-200.

Conrady, August. Indisches einfluss in china im 4. jahrhundert v. chr. **ZDMG** 60 (1906) 335-351.

Cutts, Elmer H. Chinese-indian contacts prior to the latter half of the first century. **IHQ** 14 (1938) 486-502.

Daudin, Pierre. l'Idéalisme bouddhique chez wang wei. **BSEIS** 43.2 (1968) 1-152.

Davidson, J. LeRoy. Buddhist paradise cults in sixth century china. **JISOA** 17 (1949) 112-124.

Demiéville, Paul. À propos du concile de vaiśāti. **TP** 40 (1951) 239-296. Review art.

Demiéville, Paul. Le bouddhisme sous les t'ang. **ACF** 52 (1952) 212-215; 53 (1953) 218-221. See also same title in **AC** t 1 (1959) 171-175.

Demiéville, Paul. **Le concile de lhasa. Une controverse sur le quiétisme entre bouddhistes de l'inde et de la chine au VIII-ème siècle de l'ère chrétien.** Paris (1952) viii + 398 p, facs.

Demiéville, Paul. l'Origine des sectes bouddhiques d'après paramãrtha. **MCB** 1 (1931-32) 15-64.

Drake, F. S. The shên-t'ung monastery and the beginning of buddhism in shantung. **MS** 4 (1939-40) 1-39.

Dubs, Homer H. The 'golden man' of former han times. **TP** 33 (1937) 1-14. See also idem, Postscript to dubs, The golden idol of former han times, in **ibid** 191-192.

Dubs, Homer H. Han yü and the buddha's relic: an episode in medieval chinese religion. **RofR** 9.1 (1946) 5-17.

Dutt, S. Migrations of buddhism over asia. In **Studies in asian history** (Proceedings of the asian history congress, new delhi, 1961) london (1969) 40-44.

Duyvendak, J. J. L. The dreams of the emperor hsüan-tsung. In **India antiqua** (1947) 102-108.

Eberhard, Wolfram. Die buddhistische kirche in der toba-zeit [Université d'ankara] **Revue de la faculté de langues, d'histoire et de géographie** 4 (1946) 308-311.

Edkins, Joseph. **The early spread of religious ideas especially in the far east.** Oxford (1893) 144 p.

Eichhorn, W. (tsl) **Ch'ing-yüan t'iao-fa shih-lei. Beitrag zur rechtlichen stellung des buddhismus und taoismus in sung-staat.** Übersetzung der secktion taoismus und buddhismus aus dem ch'ing yüan t'iao-fa shih-lei (ch. 50 und 51). Mit original text in faksimile. Leiden (1968) 178 p.

Eliot, Charles. **Hinduism and buddhism. An historical sketch.** London (1921) repr (1954) 3 vol. See vol 2, bk 4: The mahayana; vol 3, chap 41-46.

Filliozat, Jean. Emigration of indian buddhists to indo-china c. a.d. 1200. In **Studies in asian history** (proceedings of the asian history congress, new delhi, 1961) london (1969) 45-48.

Filliozat, Jean. Le médecine indienne et l'expansion bouddhique en extrême-orient. **JA** 224 (1934) 301-307.

Finot, L. Kālidãsa in china. **IHQ** 9 (1933) 829-834.

Franke, O. Die ausbreitung der buddhismus von indien nach turkestan und china. **ARW** 12 (1909) 207-220.

Franke, Otto. **Eine chinesische tempelinschrift au idikutšahri bei turfan (turkistan) üb. u. erklärt.** Berlin (1907) 92 s, 1 taf.

Franke, Otto. Das datum der chinesischen tempelinschrift von turfan. **TP** 2e sér, 10 (1909) 222-228.

Franke, Otto. Skt. mss. in china. **ChRev** 21 (1894) 204.

Franke, O. Taoismus und buddhismus zur zeit der trennung von nord und süd. **Sinica** 9 (1934) 89-113.

Franke, O. Zur frage der einführung des buddhismus in china. **MSOS** 13 (1910) 295-305. See rev by H. Maspero in **BEFEO** 10 (1910) 629-636.

Friese, Heinz. Der mönch yao kuang-hsiao . . . und seine zeit. **OE** 7.2 (1960) 158-184.

Fuchs, Walter. Zur technischen organization der übersetzungen buddhistischen schriften in chinesische. **AM** 6 (1930) 84-103.

Fukui, Fumimasa-Bunga. Buddhism and the structure of ch'ing-t'an. — A note on sino-indian intercourse. **CC** 10.2 (june 1969) 25-30.

Gard, Richard A. Why did the mādhyamika decline? **JIBS** 5.2 (1957) 10-14.

Gaspardone, E. Bonzes des ming réfugiés en annam. **Sinologica** 2 (1950) 12-30.

Gernet, Jacques. **Les aspects économiques du bouddhisme dans la société chinoise du Ve au Xe siècle.** Saigon (1956) See also rev by A. F. Wright, **JAS** 16.3 (1957) 408-414; D. C. Twitchett, **BSOAS** 19.3 (1957) 526-549; K. Ch'en, **HJAS** 20 (1957) 733-740.

Glüer, Winfried. The encounter between christianity and chinese buddhism during the nineteenth century and the first half of the twentieth century. **CF** 11.3 (1968) 39-57.

Goodrich, L. Carrington. Earliest printed editions of the tripitaka. **VBQ** ser 2 vol 19 (1953-54) 215-220.

Goodrich, L. Carrington. The revolving bookcase in china. **HJAS** 7 (1942-43) 130-161. Re invention and history of case for tripitaka.

Groot, J. J. M. de. **Sectarianism and religious persecution in china.** Amsterdam, vol 1 (1903) vol 2 (1904) repr taipei (1963) 2 vol in 1, 595 p.

Groot, J. J. M. de. Wu tsung's persecution of buddhism. **ARW** 7 (1904) 157-168.

Grünwedel, Albert. **Altbuddhistische kultstätten in chinesisch-turkistan. Bericht über archäologische arbeiten von 1906 bis 1907 bei kuća qarašahr und in der oase turfan.** Berlin (1912) 371 p.

Guelny, A. À propos d'une préface. Aperçu critique sur le bouddhisme en chine au 7e siècle. **Muséon** 13 (1894) 437-449; 14 (1895) 85.

Guignes, Joseph de. Recherches historiques sur la religion indienne, et sur les livres fondamentaux de cette religion; qui ont été traduits de l'indien en chinois. Première mémoire. Établissement de la religion indienne dans l'inde, la tartarie, le thibet & les isles. Second mémoire. Établissement de la religion indienne dans la chine, et son histoire jusqu'en 531 de jésus christ. Troisième mémoire. Suite de l'histoire de la religion indienne à la chine. **MAI** (1773-76) repr in **Histoire et mémoires AIBL** 40 (1780) 187-355.

Gundert, Wilhelm. Bodhidharma und wu-di von liang. **SJFAW** (1956) 48-66.

Haas, Hans. Ein wenig bekannter buddhistisches autor des alten china und sein werk. **Orientalische archiv** 1 (1910-11) 25-33.

Haenisch, Erich (ed and tsl) **Die viersprachige gründungsinschrift des tempels an-yüan-miao in jehol v. jahre 1765.** Wiesbaden (1951) 22 p, pl.

Haneda, A. Les conquérants tartares et le bouddhisme. **CHM** 1 (1954) 922-926.

Havret, Henri. T'ien-tchou 'seigneur de ciel.' À propos d'une stèle bouddhique de tch'eng-tou. Shanghai (1901) 30 p. (Variétés sinologiques no 19) Same title in **Études** 89 (1901) 398-409, 546-553.

Hée, L. von. Le bouddha et les premiers missionaires en chine. **AM** 10 (1934) 365-372.

Hodgson, B. H. (tsl) Introductions of buddhism in china. Translated from the 'tae-ping-kuang-ke.' **Asiatic journal and monthly register** no 5 (1831) 71.

Hodous, Lewis. The introduction of buddhism into china. In **The macdonald presentation volume,** princeton univ (1933) 223-235.

Holth, Sverre. The encounter between christianity and chinese buddhism during the nestorian period. **CF** 11.3 (1968) 20-29.

Hrdličková, V. The first translations of buddhist sutras in chinese literature and their place in the development of storytelling. **ArchOr** 26.1 (1958) 114-144.

Hu, Shih. The indianization of china. In **Independence, convergence, and borrowing in institutions, thought and art,** harvard univ (1937) 239-246.

Huang Chia-cheng. **Le bouddhisme de l'inde à la chine.** Paris (1963) 126 p.

Hulsewé, A. F. P. Sidelights on popular buddhism in china in the fifth century. **Proc 7th ICHR Amsterdam, 1950,** Amsterdam (1951) 139-141.

Hurvitz, Leon. 'Render unto caesar' in early chinese buddhism: hui-yüan's treatise on the exemption of the buddhist clergy from the requirements of civil etiquette. **SIS** 5.3/4 (1957) (Liebenthal festschrift) 80-114.

Hurvitz, Leon. Toward a comprehensive history of chinese buddhism. **JAOS** 89 (1969) 763-773.

Hurvitz, Leon (tsl) **Treatise on buddhism and taoism: an english translation of the original chinese text of wei-shu CXIV and the japanese annotation of tsukamoto zenryū.** Kyoto univ (1956) 25-103 p. See rev by L. S. Yang and K. Ch'en in **HJAS** 20 (1957) 362-382.

I, Ying-ki. The secularization decree of emperor wu-tsung. **BCUP** 6 (1929) 119-124 (Refers to buddhists and nestorians)

Imbault-Huart, Camille. Note sur l'inscription bouddhique et la passe de kiu-young-kouan près de la grande muraille. **REO** 2.4 (1884) 486-493.

Jan Yün-hua. Buddhist historiography in sung china. **ZDMG** 114 (1964) 360-381.

Jan, Yün-hua. Buddhist relations between india and sung china. **HR** 6.1 (1966) 24-42.

Jan, Yün-hua. Buddhist self-immolation in medieval china. **HR** 4 (1965) 243-268.

Jan, Yün-hua (tsl) **Chih-p'an. A chronicle of buddhism in china, 581-960 a.d.; translations from monk chih-p'an's fo-tsu t'ung-chi.** Santiniketan, visva-bharati (1966) 189 p.

Jan, Yün-hua. Kashmir's contribution to the expansion of buddhism in the far east. **IHQ** 37 (1961) 93-104.

Jan, Yün-hua. Some new light on kuśinagara from 'the memoir of hui-ch'ao.' **OE** 12.1 (1965) 55-63.

Kamstra, J. H. **Encounter or syncretism. The initial growth of japanese buddhism.** Leiden (1967) See chap 3.a, pt 1, China and buddhism, 142-185.

Kasugai, Shinya. The historical background of kumarajiva and his historical influence on chinese buddhism. **Philosophical quarterly** 31 (1958-59) 121-125.

Kennedy, J. The secret of kanishka. **JRAS** (1912) 665-688, 981-1019.

Kennedy, J. Sidelights on kanishka. The introduction of buddhism into china . . . **JRAS** (1913) 369-378.

Kimura, Ryūkan. **A historical study of hinayāna and mahāyāna and the origin of mahāyāna buddhism.** Calcutta univ (1927)

Konow, S. Kālidāsa in china. **IHQ** 10 (1934) 566-570.

Kubo, Noritada. Prolegomena on the study of the controversies between buddhists and taoists in the yüan period. **TBMRD** 26 (1968) 39-61.

Lacouperie, Terrien de. How in 219 b.c. buddhism entered china. **BOR** 5.5 (1891) 97-105.

Lacouperie, Terrien de. The introduction of buddhism into china. **Academy** 40 (3 oct 1891) 389-390.

Lacouperie, Terrien de. The yueh-ti and the early buddhist missionaries in china. **Academy** (?) (31 dec 1897) 443-444.

Lamotte, É. Les premières missions bouddhiques en chine. **Académie royale belge bulletin, classe des lettres** 5e sér, 39 (1953) 220-231.

Lamotte, É. Sur la formation du mahāyāna. In **Asiatica** (1954) 377-396.

Lancashire, Douglas. Buddhist reaction to christianity in late ming china. **JOSA** 6.1/2 (1968-69) 82-103.

Lee, Peter H. Fa-tsang and uisang. **JAOS** 82.1 (1962) 56-59 + chin text 60-62.

Lévi, S. Les missions de wang hiuen ts'e dans l'inde. **JA** 9e sér, 15 (1900) 401-468. Re introduction of buddhism into china.

Lévi, Sylvain et Édouard Chavannes. Quelques titres énigmatiques dans la hiérarchie ecclésiastique du bouddhisme indien. **JA** 9e sér, 5 (1915) 193-223. Add et rectifications in **ibid** 6 (1915) 307-310.

Lévi, Sylvain et Édouard Chavannes. Les seize arhat protecteurs de la loi. **JA** 11e sér, 8 (juil-aout 1916) 5-50; **ibid** (sept-oct 1916) 189-304.

Liang, Ch'i-ch'ao. **China's debt to buddhist india.** N.Y. (?1927) 15 p. With a biographical note by Herbert A. Giles.

Liebenthal, Walter. Chinese buddhism during the fourth and fifth centuries. **MN** 11.1 (1955) 44-83.

Liebenthal, Walter. **Sanskrit inscriptions from yünnan, and the dates of the foundation of the main pagodas in the province.** Peiping (1947) 40 p. See author's art, Sanskrit inscriptions from yünnan, **SIS** 5 (1955) 46-48.

Liebenthal, Walter. Shih hui-yüan's buddhism as set forth in his writings. **JAOS** 70 (1950) 243-259.

Link, Arthur E. Cheng-wu lun: the rectification of unjustified criticism. **OE** 8.2 (dec 1961) 136-165.

Link, Arthur E. Professor tang yong-torng's 'various traditions concerning the entry of buddhism into china.' **PTA** 4 (1953) 31-93.

Link, Arthur E. Shyh daw-an's preface to saṅgharakṣa's yogācarabhūmi-sūtra and the problem of buddho-taoist terminology in early chinese buddhism. **JAOS** 77 (1957) 1-14.

Link, Arthur E. and Tim Lee. Sun cho's yü-tao-lun: a clarification of the way. **MS** 25 (1966) 169-196.

Lo, Hsiang-lin. Sino-indian relations over the chiao-kwang route and new discoveries on buddhism and its art in the kwangtung-kwangsi areas in the tang dynasty. **CC** 1.3 (1958) 181-203.

MacGowan, D. J. An inscription from a tablet in a buddhist monastery at ningpo in china. **JRASB** 13 (1844) 113-114, pl.

Maejima, Shinji. The travels of a japanese buddhist priest in 13th century to yüan china. **JSR:HS** 10 (1959) 97-101.

Masaki, Haruhiko. The practice of buddhist austerities and its popularization in shan-tao and prince shotoku — in connection with śrīmālā and vaidehī. **JIBS** 16.2 (1968) 943-955.

Maspero, Henri. Comment le bouddhisme s'est introduit en chine. In author's **HMRC** Paris (1950) 195-211.

Maspero, Henri. Communautés et moines bouddhistes chinois au IIe et IIIe siècles. **BEFEO** 10 (janv-mars 1910) 222-232.

Maspero, Henri. Les origines de la communauté bouddhique de loyang. **JA** 225 (1934) 87-107.

Maspero, Henri. Le songe et l'ambassade de l'empereur ming. Étude critique des sources. **BEFEO** 10 (1910) 95-130.

Masunaga, Reiho. The place of dōgen in zen buddhism. In **RSJ** (1959) 339-349.

Mather, Richard The conflict of buddhism with native chinese ideologies. **RofR** 20 (1955-56) 25-37; repr in **CWayRel** (1973) 77-86.

Mather, Richard B. Vimalakīrti and gentry buddhism. **HR** 8 (1968) 60-73.

Mayers, William Frederick. Chinese views respecting the date of introduction of buddhism. **NQ** 1 (1867) 52.

Meunié, Jacques. Le couvent des otages chinois de kanīska au kāpiśa. **JA** 234 (1943-45) 151-162.

Michihata, Ryoshu. A study of chinese buddhism in t'ang dynasty. **JSR:HS** 10 (1959) 54-56.

Modi, J. J. An iranian prince of the parthian dynasty as the first promulgator of buddhism in china. In **Jha commemoration volume,** poona (1937) 249-258.

Mukherjee, Probhat Kumar [Mukhopādhyāya, Prabhātā-Kumārā] **Indian literature abroad (china)** Calcutta (1928) 98 p.

Mukherji, Probhat K. [Mukhopādhyāya, Prabhātā-Kumārā] **Indian literature in china and the far east.** Calcutta (pref 1931) iv + 2 + 334 + 18 + 4.

Mukhopādhyāya, Sujit. Sino-indian relations of old. **SIJ** 1 (july 1947) 77-94.

Murata, J. (ed) **Chü-yung-kuan. The buddhist arch of the 14th century a.d at the pass of the great wall northwest of peking.** Kyoto (1958) 2 vol, 360 p, 110 pl, 34 illus, 4 charts. Text in 6 languages: sanskrit, tibetan, mongol, uighur, hsi-hsia, chin, and synopsis in engl.

Needham, Joseph. Buddhism and chinese science. In Louis Schneider (ed) **Religion, culture and society,** n.y. etc (1964) 353-358. Excerpted from Needham's **Science and civilization in china,** cambridge univ, vol 2 (1956) 417-422, 430-431.

Nicolas-Vandier, Nicole. Les échanges entre le bouddhisme et le taoïsme des han aux t'ang. In **AC** t 1 (1959) 166-170.

Ohashi, Kaishun. Die spuren des buddhismus in china vor kaiser ming. **EB** 6 (1934) 247-278, 432-477; 7 (1937) 214-226.

Olschki, L. Manichaeism, buddhism and christianity in marco polo's china. **AS** 5 (1951) 1-21.

Palatin, W. von. Kaiser t'ai-tsung's edikt gegen die bonzen und ihre klöster. **FO** 2 (1903) 181-183.

Parker, E. H. Early buddhism in china. **ChRec** 25 (1894) 224-234, 282-288, 343-347.

Parker, E. H. Notes on the history of buddhism in china. **JNCBRAS** 37 (1906) 198.

Pelliot, Paul. Deux titres bouddhiques portés par les religieux nestoriens. **TP** 2e sér, 12 (1911) 664-670.

Pelliot, Paul. Les kouo-che ou 'maîtres du royaume' dans le bouddhisme chinois. **TP** 2e sér, 12 (1911) 671-676.

Pelliot, Paul (tsl) Meou-tseu, ou les doutes levés. **TP** 19 (1918-19) 255-433. See rev by L. Aurousseau, **BEFEO** 22 (1922) 276-298.

Pelliot, Paul. Les mo-ni et le houa-hou-king. **BEFEO** 3 (1903) 318-327.

Pillai, A. Balakrishna. The 'kalpa' chronology in ancient china. **SIJ** 1 (july 1947) 117-146.

Piton, Charles. Der buddhismus in china und was wir von ihm für die christ. missionstätigkeit lernen können. **AMZ** 19 (1892) 118-126.

Pokora, Timoteus. An important crossroad of the chinese thought. **ArchOr** 29.1 (1961) 64-76. Re intro of buddhism.

Rachewiltz, Igor de. The hsi-yu lu by yeh-lü ch'u-ts'ai. **MS** 21 (1962) 1-128. Re controversy betw buddhists and taoists in yüan times.

Raguin, Yves E. Father ricci's presentation of some fundamental theories of buddhism. **CC** 10.1 (mar 1969) 37-43.

Reischauer, Edwin O. (tsl) **Ennin's diary. The record of a pilgrimage to china in search of the law.** N.Y. (1955) xvi + 454 p, character gloss, index, end-paper maps.

Reischauer Edwin O. **Ennin's travels in t'ang china.** N.Y. (1955) xii + 341 p, notes, index, end-paper maps.

Saha Kshanika. Some buddhist monks of central asian china. **MB** 77 (oct 1969) 341-342.

Sargent, G. E. The intellectual atmosphere in lingan at the time of the introduction of buddhism. In **HKS** (1967) 161-171.

Sargent Galen E. **Tchou hi contre le bouddhisme.** Paris (1955) 158 p.

Saunders, Kenneth J Buddhism in china – a historical sketch. **JR** 3 (1923) 157-169, 256-275.

Schlegel, G. Names of the 33 first buddhist patriarchs. **TP** 8.3 (1897) 341-342.

Schubert J. Die viersprachige inschrift des buddhistischen klosters fa lun szŭ in mukden (im originaltext herausgegeben, übersetzt und erläutert) **AA** 5 (1935) 71-75, 251-255.

Seu, Kshtiti Mohan. India and china. Their union through buddhism. **VBQ** n.s. 1 (1935-36) 35-45.

Shih, Robert (tsl and annot) **Biographies des moines éminents (kao seng tchouan) de houei-kiao. Première partie: Biographies des premiers traducteurs.** Louvain (1968) xi + 177 p, followed by chin text.

Staël-Holstein, A. A. von. The emperor ch'ien-lung and the larger śūrangama-sūtra. **HJAS** 1 (1936) 136-146.

Steininger, Hans. Der buddhismus in der chinesischen geschichte (zu den arbeiten von e. zürcher, j. gernet und a. f. wright). **Saeculum** 13.2 (1962) 132-165.

Stevenson, J. Buddhist antiquities in china. **JBBRAS** 5 (1855) 408 et seq.

Suzuki, D. T. The recovery of a lost ms. on the history of zen in china. **EB** 6.1 (apr 1932) 107-110.

Tai-hü. Buddhistische studien. Der buddhismus in geschichte und gegenwort. **Sinica** 3 (1928) 189-196.

Takakusu, Junjirō. A study of chinese inscriptions. 1. Notes on the earliest chinese inscription found at buddhagayâ in india. **HZ** 12.5 (1897) 20-29.

Takakusu, Junjirō (tsl) Le voyage de kanshin en orient 742-754, par aomi-no mabito genkai, 779. **BEFEO** 28 (1928) 1-41, 441-472; 29 (1929) 47-62.

Thiel, Joseph. Der streit der buddhisten und taoisten zur mongolenzeit. **MS** 20 (1961) 1-81.

Thomas, F. W. Three letters from buddhist kings to the chinese court in the fifth century. **JRAS** (1933) 897-905.

Todo, Kyoshun. The critical views, or the sense of uneasiness, in chinese buddhism and their relief — especially in the first half of the 6th century a.d. **JIBS** 10 (mar 1962) 1-6.

Tsukamoto, Zenryū. The buddha-image made by king udayana in china and japan. In **RSJ** (1959) 359-367.

Tsukamoto, Zenryū. The dates of kumārajīva and seng-chao re-examined. In **SJV** (1954) 568-584.

Tsukamoto, Zenryū. The early stages in the introduction of buddhism into china. **CHM** 5 (1960) 546-572.

Tucci, Giuseppe. A tibetan history of buddhism in china. In **Eduard erkes in memoriam 1891-1958,** leipzig (1962) 230.

Twitchett, D. C. The monasteries and china's economy in medieval times. **BSOAS** 19 (1957) 526-549.

Twitchett, D. C. Monastic estates in t'ang china. **AM** n.s. 5 (1956) 123-146.

Waley, Arthur. Did buddha die of eating pork? With a note on buddha's image. **MCB** 1 (1931-32) 343-354.

Waley, Arthur. New light on buddhism in medieval india. **MCB** 1 (1931-32) 355-376.

Ware, James R. Once more the 'golden man.' **TP** 34 (1938) 174-178.

Ware, James R. (tsl) Wei shou on buddhism. **TP** 30 (1933) 100-181.

Weller, F. Die überlieferung des älteren buddhistischen schrifttums. **AM** 5 (1930) 149-182.

Witte, Johannes. **Das buch des marco polo als quelle für den buddhismus.** Berlin (1915) 71 p.

Wittfogel, Karl A. and Fêng Chia-shêng. **History of chinese society: liao.** Philadelphia (1949) See 291-309 on buddhism.

Wittfogel, Karl A. and Fêng Chia-shêng. Religion under the liao dynasty, 907-1125. **RofR** 12 (1948) 355-374.

Wright, Arthur F. **Buddhism in chinese history.** Stanford univ (1959) 144 p, selection of further readings, index, illus.

Wright, Arthur F. The economic role of buddhism in china. **JAS** 16 (1957) 408-414. A rev art on J. Gernet's **Les aspects économiques du bouddhisme** . . . q.v.

Wright Arthur F. The formation of sui ideology In **CTI** (1957) 71-104.

Wright, Arthur F. Fu i and the rejection of buddhism. **JHI** 12 (1951) 33-47.

Wright, Arthur F. Hui-chiao as a chinese historian. **JIBS** 3.1 (1954) 1-6.

Wu, K. T. Chinese printing under four alien dynasties. **HJAS** 13 (1950) 451-457, 515-516. Re buddhist texts.

Wylie, Alexander. On an ancient buddhist inscription at keu-yung-kwan, in north china. **JNCBRAS** 5 (1870) 14-44.

Wylie Alexander. Remarks on some impressions from a lapidary inscription at keu-yung kwan on the great wall near peking. **JNCBRAS** n.s. 1 (1864) 133-136, 163-166.

Yamazake, Hiroshi. The study on buddhist policy of the sui dynasty. **JSR:LPH** 4 (1953) 231-233.

Yang, Lien-sheng. Buddhist monasteries and four money-raising institutions in chinese history. **HJAS** 13 (1950) 174-191. Repr in author's collection, **Studies in chinese institutional history,** cambridge, mass.(1963) 198-215.

Yang, Ming-che. China reinterprets buddhism. **FCR** 18 (dec 1968) 27-32.

Ying, Ignatius. The secularization decree of wu tsung. **BCUP** 6 (1931) 119-124.

Zach, E. von. Einige bemerkungen zur tempelinschrift von idikutśahri (im museum für völkerkunde, berlin) **AM** 2 (1925) 345-347. Re inscription in maitreya temple, turfan.

Zürcher, Erik. **The buddhist conquest of china. The spread and adaptation of buddhism in early medieval china.** Leiden (1959) vol 1: Text; vol 2: Notes, bibliog, indexes.

Zürcher, Erik. Zum verhältnis von kirche und staat in china während der frühzeit des buddhismus. **Saeculum** 10 (1959) 73-81.

7. SCHOOLS (EXCEPT CH'AN)

Armstrong, R. C. The doctrine of the tendai school. **EB** 3 (1924) 32-54.

Blofeld, John Calthorpe. Lamaism and its influence on chinese buddhism. **THM** 7.2 (1938) 151-160, photos.

Bloom, Alfred. **Shinran's gospel of pure grace.** Univ arizona (1965) On chin pure land patriarchs see 7-17.

The Book of tao. A brief outline of the esoteric schools of buddhist [sic] and tao in china. Theosophical publ house, adyar (1933) 24 p.

Chou, Yi-liang. Tantrism in china. **HJAS** 8 (1945) 241-332.

Demiéville, Paul. l'Origine des sectes bouddhiques d'après paramārtha. **MCB** 1 (1931-32) 15-64.

Dutt, S. The ten schools of chinese buddhism. In **HPEW** (1952) vol 1, 590-595.

Edkins, Joseph. Notice of the wu-wei-kiau . . . a reformed buddhist sect. **Trans China branch RAS** 6 (1858) 63-69.

Hackmann, Heinrich. Die schulen des chinesischen buddhismus. **MSOS** 14.1 (1912) 232-266.

Hurvitz, Leon. Chu-hung's one mind of pure land and ch'an buddhism. In **SSMT** (1970) 451-482.

Julien, Stanislas. Listes diverses des noms des dix-huit écoles schismatiques qui sont sorties du bouddhisme. **JA** 5e sér, 14 (1859) 327-361.

Liebenthal, Walter. The world conception of chu tao-sheng. **MN** 12.1/2 (1956) 65-103; 12.3/4 (1957) 241-268.

Lo, Hsiang-lin. Transmission of the she-lun school of buddhism. **JOS** 1 (1954) 313-326.

Luk, Charles (Lu K'uan-yü) **The secrets of chinese meditation.** London (1964) 240 p. Self-cultivation according to several buddhist as well as taoist schools.

Okakura, Kakuzo (tsl) Chi ki (chik i) [sic] i.e. founder of japanese tendai: chisho daishi: on the method of practising concentration and contemplation. Pref note by William Sturgis Bigelow. **HTR** 16.2 (1923) 109-141.

Ono, G. A note on tz'u-min's works and some points of his religious teaching. **PIAJ** 2.8 (1926) 361-363. Ching-t'u school.

Ono, Gemmyō. On the pure land doctrine of tz'u-min. **EB** 5 (1930) 200-213.

Petzold, Bruno. The chinese tendai teachings. **EB** 4 (1927-28) 299-347.

Petzold, Bruno. Tendai buddhism as modern world-view (chinese tendai) **YE** 4 (oct 1929) 281-304.

Robinson, Richard H. **Early mādhyamika in india and china.** Univ wisconsin (1967) 347 p, documents, notes, bibliog, index.

Rousselle, Erwin. Die typen der meditation in china. **CDA** (1932) 20-46.

Sasaki G. What is the true sect of the pure land? **EB** 1 (1921) 167-179.

Sasaki, Genjun H. Hinayana schools in china and japan. **FA:BPB** (1959) 499-514.

Suzuki, D T. The development of the pure land doctrine. **EB** 3 (1924) 285-327.

Suzuki D. T The mādhyamika school in china. **Journal of the buddhist text society** 6 (1898) 23-30.

Wieger, Léon. **Amidisme chinois et japonais.** Hien-hien (1928) 51 p, illus.

8. BUDDHIST INDIVIDUALS (EXCEPT CH'AN)

Broomhall, Marshall. **In quest of god. The life story of pastors chang and ch'u, buddhist priest and chinese scholar.** London etc (pref 1921) xiii + 190 p.

Callahan, Paul E. T'ai hsü and the new buddhist movement. Harvard univ, **Papers on china** 6 (1952) 149-188.

Chan, Hok-lam. Liu pin-chung (1216-1274), a buddhist-taoist statesman at the court of khubilai khan. **TP** 53.1/3 (1967) 98-146.

Chavannes, Édouard. Seng-houei . . . +280 p.c. **TP** 10 (mai 1909) 199-212.

Chou, Hsiang-kuang. **T'ai hsu. His life and teachings.** Allahabad (1957) 74 p.

Chuan, T. K. Some notes on kao seng chuan. **THM** 7 (1938) 452-468.

Dien, Albert E. Yen chih-t'ui (531-591+): a buddho-confucian. In **CP** (1962) 43-64.

Franke, Herbert. Zur biographie des pa-ta shan-jen. In **Asiatica** (1954) 119-130.

Friese, Heinz. Der mönch yao kuang-hsiao. . . und seine zeit. **OE** 7.2 (1960) 158-184.

Gundert, W. Die nonne liu bei we-schan. In **Asiatica** (1954) 184-197.

Haas, Hans. Ein wenig bekannter buddhistischer autor des alten china und sein werk. **Orientalisches archiv** 1 (1910-11) 25-33.

Hackmann, Heinrich. Ein heiliger des chinesischen buddhismus und seine spüren im heutigen china (tsi k'ae) **ZMK** 18 (1903) 65.

Hamilton, Clarence H. Hsüan chuang and the wei shih philosophy. **JAOS** 51 (1931) 291-308.

Harlez, Charles de. The buddhist schools. **Dublin review** no 105, 3rd ser, vol 22 (july 1889) 47-71. See also author's article: Les écoles bouddhistes, in **Science catholique** 5 (mai-juil 1890)

Hurvitz, Leon. **Chih-i (538-597). An introduction to the life and ideas of a chinese buddhist monk.** Comprises **MCB** vol 12 (1962) 372 p.

Hurvitz, Leon. Chu-hung's one mind of pure land and ch'an buddhism. In **SSMT** (1970) 451-482.

Jan, Yün-hua. Hui-ch'ao and his works: a reassessment. **IAC** 12 (1964)

Johnston, Reginald. A poet monk of modern china [su man-shu] **JNCBRAS** 63 (1932) 14-30.

Julien, Stanislas. Listes diverses des noms des dix-huit écoles schismatiques qui sont sorties du bouddhisme. **JA** 5e sér, 14 (1859) 327-364.

Laufer, Berthold. Zum bildnis des pilges hsüan tsang. **Globus** 88 (1905) 257-258.

Lee, Peter H. Fa-tsang and uisang. **JAOS** 82.1 (1962) 56-59 + chin text 60-62.

Liebenthal, Walter. A biography of chu tao-sheng. **MN** 11.3 (1955) 64-96.

Liebenthal, Walter. Shih hui-yüan's buddhism as set forth in his writings. **JAOS** 70 (1950) 243-259.

Liebenthal, Walter. The world conception of chu tao-sheng. **MN** 12.1/2 (1956) 65-104; 12.3/4 (1957) 241-268.

Lin, Li-kouang. Punyodaya (na-t'i), un propagateur du tantrisme en chine et au camboge à l'époque de huian tsang. **JA** 227 (1935) 83-100.

Link Arthur (tsl) Biography of tao an. **TP** 46 (1958) 1-48.

Link, Arthur E. Hui-chiao's 'critical essay on the exegetes of the doctrine' in the kao seng chuan (lives of eminent monks) In **NCELYY** (1970) 51-80.

Link, Arthur E. Remarks on shih seng-yu's ch'u san tsang chi-chi as a source for hui-chiao's kao-seng chuan as evidenced in two versions of the biography of tao-an. **Oriens** 10.2 (1957) 292-295.

Luk, Charles (Lu K'uan-yü) (tsl) The 300th patriarch: great master seng-ts'an. **MB** 67 (1959) 22-23.

Makita, Tairyō. Hui-yüan — his life and times. Tsl fr jap Philip Yampolsky. **Zinbun** 6 (1962) 1-28.

McAleavy, Henry. **Su man-shu, a sino-japanese genius.** London (1960) 51 p.

Millican, Frank R. T'ai-hsü and modern buddhism. **ChRec** 54.6 (1923) 326-334.

Monestier, Alphonse. The monk lu cheng-hsiang **BCUP** 5 (1930) 11-21.

Ono Gemmyō. A note on tz'u-min's works and some points of his religious teachings. **PIAJ** 2.8 (1926) 361-363.

Onò, Gemmyō. On the pure land doctrine of tz'u-min. **EB** 5 (1930) 200-213.

Rachewiltz, Igor de. Yeh-lü ch'u-ts'ai (1189-1243): buddhist idealist and confucian statesman. In **CP** (1962) 189-216.

Robinson, Richard H. Mysticism and logic in seng-chao's thought. **PEW** 8 (1958-59) 99-120.

Rousselle, Erwin. Das leben des patriarchen hui-neng. **Sinica** 5 (1930) 174-191.

Sargent, Galen E. (tsl) T'an-yao and his times. **MS** 16 (1957) 363-396. A chap fr Tsukamoto Zenryū's book, **Shina bukkyōshi kenkyū hokugi-ken,** tokyo (1942)

Shih, Robert (tsl) **Hui-chiao. Biographies des moines éminents de houei-kiao. Kao seng tchouan, 1 partie. Biographies des premiers traducteurs.** Louvain (1968) xi + 177. Chin text and french tsl.

Soymié, Michel. Biographie de chan tao-k'ai. **MIHEC** 1 (1957) 415-422.

Takakusu, Junjirō. K'uei-chi's version of a controversy between the buddhist and the sāmkhya philosophers. — An appendix to the translation of paramārtha's 'life of vasu-bandhu.' **TP** 2e sér, 5 (1904) 461-466.

Takakusu, Junjirō (tsl) The life of vasu-bandhu by paramārtha (a.d. 499-569) **TP** 2e sér, 5 (1904) 269-296.

Takakusu, Junjirō (tsl) Le voyage de kanshin en orient, 742-754, par aomi-no mabito kenkai, 779. **BEFEO** 28 (1928) 1-41, 441-472; 29 (1929) 47-62.

Tamaki, Koshiro. The ultimate enlightenment of hui-yŭan in lu-shan. **JIBS** 12.2 (1964) 1-12.

Tschen, Yin-ko. Buddhistischer in den biographien von tsan tschung und hua to im san guo dschi. **TJ** 6 (1930) 17-20.

Tsukamoto, Zenryū. The dates of kumarajiva . . . and seng-chao . . . reexamined. Tsl fr jap Leon Hurvitz. In **SJV** (1954) 568-584.

Ui, Hakuju. Maitreya as an historical personage. In **Indian studies in honor of charles rockwell lanman,** cambridge, mass (1929) 95-101.

Unno, Taisetsu. The buddhatā theory of fa-tsang. **Trans 8th ICfO Japan** (1963) 34-41.

Walleser, Max. The life of nāgārjuna from tibetan and chinese sources. In **AMHAV** (1923) 421-455.

Weinstein, Stanley. A biographical study of tz'u-ên. **MN** 15.1/2 (1959) 119-149.

Wilhelm, Richard. Der grossabt schi tai hŭ. **Sinica** 4 (1929) 16.

Wright, A. F. Biography and hagiography. Hui-chiao's lives of eminent monks. In **SJV** (1954) 383-432.

Wright, Arthur F. Biography of the nun an-ling-shou. **HJAS** 15 (1952) 193-196.

Wright, Arthur F. Fo t'u teng . . . a biography. **HJAS** 11 (1948) 322-370.

Wright, Arthur F. Seng-jui alias hui-jui: a biographical bisection in the kao-seng chuan. **SIS** 5.3/4 (1957) (Liebenthal festschrift) 272-294.

9. CH'AN

Baumann, C. A few psychological aspects of ch'an buddhism. **AA** 8 (1940-45) 216-237.

Benl, Oscar. Der zen-meister dōgen in china. **NachrDGNVO** no 79-80 (1956) 67-77.

Blofeld, John. Ch'an, zen or dhyana. **EH** 1.3 (nov 1960) 22-27.

Blofeld, John (tsl) **The path to sudden attainment. A treatise of the ch'an (zen) school of chinese buddhism by hui hai of the t'ang dynasty.** London (1948) 51 p.

Blofeld, John (tsl) **The zen teaching of huang po on the transmission of mind. Being the teaching of the zen master huang po as recorded by the scholar p'ei hsiu of the t'ang dynasty.** N.Y. (1959) 136 p, index. Rev and enl ed of tsl entitled **The huang po doctrine . . .** q.v. under Chu Ch'an below.

Chan, Wing-tsit (tsl) **The platform scripture.** N.Y. (1963) 193 p, notes, index.

Chang, C. C. Ch'an and madamudra. **CC** 2.1 (1959) 10-16.

Chang, Chen-chi. The nature of ch'an (zen) buddhism. **PEW** 6 (1957) 333-355.

Chang, Chen-chi. **The practice of zen.** London (1960) 256 p, notes, bibliog, app, index.

Chang, Chung-yüan. Ch'an buddhism: logical and illogical. **PEW** 17 (1967) 37-59.

Chang, Chung-yŭan. Ch'an master niu-t'ou fa-yung and his teachings on prajñāparamitā. **CC** 7.1 (mar 1966) 32-50.

Chang, Chung-yüan. Ch'an teachings of fa-yen school. **CC** 6.3 (june 1965) 55-80.

Chang Chung-yüan. Ch'an teachings of kuei-yang school. **CC** 7.4 (dec 1966) 12-53.

Chang, Chung-yüan. Ch'an teachings of the yŭn-mên school. **CC** 5.4 (june 1964) 14-39.

Chang, Chung-yüan. **Original teachings of ch'an buddhism, selected from the transmission of the lamp.** N.Y. (1969) 333 p, chart of eminent ch'an masters (594-990) bibliog, index.

Chang, Chung-yüan. Ts'ao-tung ch'an and its metaphysical background, with translations of the dialogues of the founders. **TJ** n.s. 5 (1965) 33-65.

Chang, Chung-yüan. Ways of experiencing ch'an. **Main currents in modern thought** 20 (jan-feb 1964) 57-61.

Chapin, Helen B. The ch'an master pu-tai. **JAOS** 53 (1933) 47-52.

Chapin, Helen B. Three early portraits of bodhidharma. **ACASA** 1 (1945-46) 66-98.

Chen, C. M. Comment on śamatha, samāpatti, and dhyāna in ch'an (zen) **PEW** 16.1/2 (1966) 84-87.

Ch'en, Jen-dao. **The three patriarchs of the southern school in chinese paintings.** Hong kong (1955) 8 p.

Chi, R. S. Y. (tsl) Dialogue on zen by nan-ch'üan (nansen) **MW** 34 (1959) 117-123.

Chou, H. K. **Buddhism and the chan school of china.** Allahabad ? (1965) 24 p.

Chou, Hsiang-kuang. **Dhyana buddhism in china; its history and teaching.** Allahabad (1960) xii + 216 p, illus.

Chu, Ch'an [pseud for John Blofeld] **The huang po doctrine of universal mind, being the teaching of dhyana master hsi yün as recorded by p'ei hsiu, a noted scholar of the t'ang dynasty.** London (1947) 52 p. French tsl Y. Laurence: **Le mental cosmique selon la doctrine de huang po. Selon les annales de p'ei hsiu erudit bien connu sous la dynastie t'ang.** Adyar (1954) 144 p. See, for enlarged ed of engl work, under Blofeld, John, **The zen teaching of huang po . . .**

Chung, Albert Chi-lu. The chinese mind and zen buddhism. **CC** 3.4 (oct 1961) 64-73.

Demiéville, Paul. Le miroir spirituel. **Sinologica** 1.2 (1948) 112-137.

Demiéville, Paul. Le recueil de la salle des patriarches (tsou-t'ang tsi) **TP** 56.4/5 (1970) 262-286.

Dumoulin, Heinrich. Bodhidharma und die anfänge des ch'an buddhismus. **MS** 10 (1945) 222-238. Same title in **MN** 7 (1951) 67-83.

Dumoulin, Heinrich. **The development of chinese zen after the sixth patriarch [hui-neng] in the light of mumonkan [wu men kuan]** N.Y. (1953) xxii + 146 p, tables. Tsl fr german art, Die entwicklung des chinesischen ch'an . . . q.v. with add notes and app by Ruth Fuller Sasaki.

Dumoulin, Heinrich. The encounter between zen buddhism and christianity. **JCS** 7 (1970) 53-63.

Dumoulin, Heinrich. Die entwicklung des chinesischen ch'an nach hui-neng im lichte des wu-men-kuan. **MS** 6 (1941) 40-72. For engl tsl see **The development of chinese zen . . .**

Dumoulin, Heinrich. Das wu-men-kuan. 'Der pass ohne tor.' **MS** 8 (1943) 41-102.

Dumoulin, Heinrich. **Wu-men-kuan, der pass ohne tor.** Tokyo (1953) x + 64 p.

Dumoulin, Heinrich. **Zen. Geschichte und gestalt.** Bern (1959) 332 p, 16 pl. Engl tsl Paul Peachey: **A history of zen buddhism,** n.y. (1963) viii + 335 p, notes, bibliog, index.

Ecke, G. Concerning ch'an in painting. **ArtsAs** 3 (1956) 296-306, illus.

Evola, J. Zen and the west. **E&W** 6 (1955) 115-119.

Fontein, Jan and Money L. Hickman. **Zen painting and calligraphy.** Boston (1970) liv + 173 p, illus.

Fukunaga, Mitsuji. 'No-mind' in chuang-tzu and in ch'an buddhism. **Zinbun** 12 (1968) 9-45.

Fung, Paul F. and George D. (tsl) **The sutra of the sixth patriarch [hui neng] on the pristine orthodox dharma.** San francisco (1964) 187 p.

Fung, Yu-lan. Ch'anism, the philosophy of silence. Being chap 6 in author's **A short history of chinese philosophy,** ed Derk Bodde, n.y. (1948)

Fung, Yu-lan. The inner-light school (ch'an tsung) of buddhism. Being chap 7 in author's **The spirit of chinese philosophy,** tsl fr chin E. R. Hughes, london (1947) 156-174.

Gernet, J. Biographie de maître chen-houei du ho-tsö. **JA** 239 (1951) 29-68.

Gernet, Jacques. Complément aux 'entretiens du maître de dhyâna chen-houei (668-760)' **BEFEO** 44.2 (1947-50) 453-466.

Gernet, Jacques. **Entretiens du maître de dhyâna chen-houei du ho-tsö (668-760)** Hanoi (1949) x + 126 p.

Gernet, Jacques. Les entretiens du maître ling-yeou du kouei-chau (771-853) **BEFEO** 45.1 (1951) 65-70.

Giles, Herbert A. Liao-yüan fo-yin. **NCR** 4 (1922) 36-37.

Gray, Terence. A metaphysical interpretation of takuan's letter to tajima no kami. **MW** 35 (1960) 103-106.

Gundert, W. (tsl) Bi-yän-lu. In **Meister yüan-wu's niederschrift von der smaragdenen felswand.** Munich (1960) chap 1-33.

Gundert, Wilhelm. Bodhidharma und wu-di von liang. In **SJFAW** (1956) 48-66.

Gundert, Wilhelm (tsl) Das 35. kapitel des bi-yän-lu, übersetzt und erläutet. **MDGNVO** 44 teil 3 (1964) 1-25.

Gundert, Wilhelm (tsl) Fěng-hsüan's eiserner stier. Das 38. beispiel des bi-yän-lu. **OE** 12.2 (1965) 129-160.

Gundert, Wilhelm (tsl) Das neunte beispiel des bi-yän-lu. **NachrDGNVO** no 79-80 (1956) 8-14.

Gundert, Wilhelm (tsl) Die nonne liu bei we-schan; das 24. kapitel des bi-yän-lu, eingeleitet, übersetzt und erläutert. In **Asiatica** (1954) 184-197.

Gundert, Wilhelm (tsl) Pang's, des privatstudierten, schöne schneeflocken; das 42. beispiel des bi-yän-lu. **NachrDGNVO** 97 (1965) 13-28.

Gundert, Wilhelm (tsl) Das 47. kapitel des bi-yän-lu. **OE** 11 (1964) 127-141.

Gundert, Wilhelm (tsl) Yang-schan's fünfalten-hörner; das 34. beispiel des bi-yän-lu. **OE** 9 (1962) 200-219.

Houlné, Lucien (tsl) **Houeï-neng, sixième patriarche du bouddhisme zen, discours et sermons d'après le sûtra de l'estrade sur les pierres précieuses de la loi fa-pao-t'an-king.** Paris (1963) 185 p.

Hu, Shih. Ch'an (zen) buddhism in china, its history and method. Is ch'an (zen) beyond our understanding? **PEW** 3.1 (1953) 3-24.

Hu, Shih. The development of zen buddhism in china. **CSPSR** 15 (1932) 475-505. Repr in **SIS** 3 (1949)

Hurvitz, Leon. Chu-hung's one mind of pure land and ch'an buddhism. In **SSMT** (1970) 451-482.

Kaiten, Nukariya. **The religion of the samurai. A study of zen philosophy and discipline in china and japan.** London (1913) xxii + 253.

Lanciotti, Lionello. New historic contribution to the person of bodhidharma. **AA** 12.1/2 (1949) 141-144.

Liebenthal, Walter. The sermon of shen-hui. **AM** n.s. 3.2 (1952) 132-155.

Liebenthal, Walter (tsl) Yung-chia cheng-tao-ko or yung-chia's song of experiencing the tao. **MS** 6 (1941) 1-39.

Liu, Guan-ying (tsl) **Der heilige als eulenspiegel (chi-kung-chuan, ausz.dt.) 12 abenteuer e. zenmeisters.** Basel and stuttgart (1958) 167 s, mit abb.

Lu, K'uan-yü (Charles Luk) **Ch'an and zen teaching.** London, ser 1 (1960) 225 p; ser 2 (1961) 254 p; ser 3 (1962) 306 p.

Luk, Charles (Lu K'uan-yü) **The secrets of chinese meditation.** London (1964) 240 p. Deals with both taoist and several schools of buddhist techniques incl ch'an.

Masunaga, Reiho. The gist of sōtō zen. **JIBS** 7.2 (1959) 19-35.

Merton, Thomas. A christian looks at zen. Being the intro to John C. H. Wu: **The golden age of zen,** q.v. 1-28.

Merton, Thomas. Mystics and zen masters. **CC** 6.2 (mar 1965) 1-18. Same title incl in author's collection (which is itself also entitled **Mystics and zen masters)** n.y. (1961 et seq)

Murakami, Yoshimi. 'Nature' in lao-chuang thought and 'no-mind' in ch'an buddhism. **KGUAS** 14 (1965) 15-31.

Muralt, Raoul von (ed and tsl) **Wei lang. Das sutra des sechsten patriarchen.** Zürich (1958) 149 p.

Petzold, B. Was ist zen? **OL** 45 (1942) col 89-102.

Rousselle, E. (tsl) Buddhistische studien: das sūtra des sechsten patriarchen. **Sinica** 2 (1936) 202-210.

Rousselle, E. Buddhistische wesenschau nach der lehre der meditationssekte. **CDA** (1931) 76-86.

Rousselle, E. (tsl) Das leben des patriarchen hui neng. **Sinica** 5 (1930) 174-191.

Rousselle, E. Die typen der meditation in china. **CDA** (1932) 20-46.

Rousselle, E. Vergeistigte religion. Nach der lehre der meditationssekte. (Buddhistische studien) **Sinica** 6 (1931) 26-34.

Sakamaki, Shunzo. Zen and intuited knowledge. **Etc.** 16 (1959) 203-207.

Seckel, Dietrich. Mu-hsi: sechs kaki-fruchte; interpretation eines zen-bildes. **NachrDGNVO** 77 (1955) 44-55, pl.

Shaw, R. D. M. (tsl) **The blue cliff records; hekigan roku, containing 100 stories of zen masters of ancient china.** London (1961) 299 p.

Shibata, Masumi. Le dialogue dans le zen chinois. **RMM** 64 (1959) 310-319.

Shibata, Masumi (tsl) **Wu-men-kouan. Passe sans porte. Texte essentiel zen.** Paris (1968) 2e éd rev and corr, 166 p.

Siren, Osvald. Ch'an (zen) buddhism and its relation to art. **Theosophical path** 44 (oct 1934) 159-176.

Spiegelberg, Frederic. **Living religions of the world.** Englewood cliffs, n.j. (1956) See chap 12, Zen buddhism, 328-353.

Suzuki, D. T. The awakening of a new consciousness in zen. **EJ** 23 (1954) 275-304.

Suzuki, Daisetz Teitaro. **Essays in zen buddhism.** London, first ser (1927) 388 p, index, illus; second ser (1933) 367 p, index, illus; third ser (1934) 396 p, index, illus. See all 3 vol passim.

Suzuki, Daisetz Teitaro. **Introduction to zen buddhism.** Kyoto (1934) 152 p, illus. See passim.

Suzuki, D. T. The lankavatara sutra as a mahayana text in especial relation to the teaching of zen buddhism. **EB** 4 (1927-28) 199-298.

Suzuki, Daisetz Teitaro. **Living by zen.** Tokyo (1949) 235 p. See passim.

Suzuki, Daisetz Teitaro. **Manual of zen buddhism.** Kyoto (1935) 192 p, illus. See passim.

Suzuki, D. T. The recovery of a lost ms. on the history of zen in china. **EB** 6.1 (apr 1932) 107-110.

Suzuki, Daisetz Teitaro. **The training of the zen buddhist monk.** Kyoto (1934) 161 p, illus.

Suzuki, D. T. Zen: a reply to hu shih. **PEW** 3 (1953) 25-46. Re Hu's art: Ch'an (zen) buddhism in china . . . **ibid** 3-24 q.v.

Suzuki, D. T. Zen and pragmatism – a reply. **PEW** 4 (1954) 167-174.

Suzuki, D. T. **Zen buddhism. Selected writings of d. t. suzuki.** Ed William Barrett. N.Y. (1956) See passim.

Suzuki, D. T. Zen buddhism as chinese interpretation of the doctrine of enlightenment. **EB** 2 (1923) 293-347.

Suzuki, D. T. **The zen doctrine of no-mind. The significance of the sūtra of hui-neng.** Ed Christmas Humphreys. London (1969) 160 p.

Tsujimura, Koichi and Hartmar Buchner (tsl) **Der ochs und sein hirte (kuo-an-shih-niu-tu, dt.) Eine altchines. zen-geschichte.** Erl. von daizohkutsu rekidoh ohtsu. Pfullingen (1958) 132 s, mit jap bildern aus d. 15. jahrhundert. Engl tsl M. H. Trevor: **The ox and his herdsman. A chinese zen text. With commentaries and pointers by master d. r. otsu and japanese illustrations of the fifteenth century,** tokyo (1969) 96 p, illus.

Waddell, N. A. (tsl) A selection from the t'sao ken t'an ('vegetable-root discourses') **EB** 2.2 (nov 1919) 88-98.

Wai-dau and Dwight Goddard (tsl) **Buddhist practice of concentration; dhyana for beginners [by chih-i]** Santa barbara, calif (1934) 59 p. French tsl G. Constant Lounsberry: **Dhyana pour les débutants . . .,** paris (1944) 104 p.

Waley, Arthur. History and religion. **PEW** 5 (1955) 75-78. Re debate between hu shih and d. t. suzuki.

Waley, Arthur. **Zen buddhism and its relation to art.** London (1922) 31 p.

Watts, Harold H. **The modern reader's guide to religions.** N.Y. (1964) See Chinese and japanese religion: zen buddhism, 565-576.

Weller, Friedrich. Neues vom ch'an buddhismus und zwei worte dazu. **OL** 59 (july-aug 1964) 325-338.

Wong, Mou-lam (tsl) **Sutra spoken by the sixth patriarch, wei lang [hui neng] . . .** Shanghai (pref 1930) 76 p. New ed rev Christmas Humphreys: **The sutra of wei lang (or hui neng)** london (1944) further rev ed (1953) 128 p.

Wu, John C. H. **The golden age of zen.** Taipei (1967) 332 p, notes, index; app: My reminescences [sic] of dr. daisetz t. suzuki. With intro by Thomas Merton: A christian looks at zen, 1-28.

Wu, John C. H. Hui-neng's fundamental insights. **CC** 6.4 (oct 1965) 42-55.

Wu, John C. H. Little sparks of zen. **CC** 8 (mar 1967) 1-31.

Wu, John C. H. Zen: its origin and its significance. **JCS** 6 (1969) 87-95.

Yampolsky, Philip (tsl) **The platform sutra of the sixth patriarch (hui-neng). The text of the tun-huang manuscript with translation, introduction and notes.** Columbia univ (1967) 212 p. facs.

Yung, Hsi. **Buddhism and the chan school of china.** Tsl fr chin Chou, Hsiang-kuang. Allahabad (1965) 24 p.

10. SANGHA – MONACHISM – MONASTERIES

Aufhauser, Johannes B. Ein blick in buddhistische heiligtümer des fernen ostens. **Zeitschrift für buddhismus und vervandte gebiete** 6 (1924-25) 243-258.

Ball, J. Dyer. Tonsure (chinese) – 2. Buddhist. In **HERE** 12 (1921) 38-39.

Bazin, M. Recherches sur l'origine, l'histoire et la constitution des ordres religieux dans l'empire chinois. **JA** 5e sér, 8 (1856) 105f; publ sep, paris (1861) 70 p.

Bleichsteiner, R. **Die gelbe kirche. Mysterien der buddhistischen klöster in indien, tibet, mongolei und china.** Wien (1937) 272 p, 83 pl.

Blofeld, John. Life in a chinese buddhist monastery. **THM** 8 (1939) 145-154.

la Bonzerie de kou-chan, près de fou-tcheou-fou (fokien). Par un dominicain, du couvent de lyon, ancien miss. en chine, 3 janvier 1870. **MC** 10 (1878) 81-83.

Chambeau, Gabriel. Une visite aux monastères bouddhiques de kieou-hoa-chan. **Études** 130 (20 mars 1912) 785-798; 131 (5 avril 1912) 34-52.

Chu, Ch'an (pseud for John Blofeld) Life in a ch'an monastery. **Buddhism in england** 16 (1941) 10-11.

Chü Tsan. A buddhist monk's life. **CRecon** 3.1 (1954) 42-44.

Cumming, C. F. Gordon. Ningpo and the buddhist temples. **Century magazine** 24, n.s. 4 (may-oct 1882) 726-739, illus.

Curzon, George N. The cloister in cathay. **Fortnightly review** 49 (1888) 752-767.

Drake, F. S. The shên-t'ung monastery and the beginning of buddhism in shantung. **MS** 4 (1939-40) 1-39.

Dukes, J. and A. Fielde. Ein buddhist kloster in china. **EMM** n.s. 36 (1892) 57-71.

Edkins, Joseph. The monasteries at pu-to. **NCH** 345 (7 mar 1856)

Edkins, Joseph. Visit to the chan-t'an-sï – monastery of the sandal-wood buddha. **ChRec** 7 (1876-77) 431-435.

Eigner, J. Life in buddhist monasteries. **CJ** 28 (1938) 275-279.

Fitch, D. F. In the 'monastery of the soul's retreat.' **Asia** 24 (1924) 524-527.

Goodrich, G. Nuns of north china. **Asia** 37 (1937) 90-93.

Graham, Dorothy. Pools for the preservation of life. **CW** 147 (1938) 536-542.

Groot, J. J. M. de. **Le code du mahayana en chine, son influence sur la vie monacale et sur le monde laïque.** Amsterdam (1893) 271 p.

Groot, J. J. M. de. Militant spirit of the buddhist clergy in china. **TP** sér 1, 2.2 (juin 1891) 127-139. Same title in **JNCBRAS** 26 (1894) 108-120.

Gundert, Wilhelm. Die nonne liu bei we-schan. In **Asiatica** (1954) 184-197.

Hackmann, Heinrich. Buddhist monastery life in china. **EA** 1.3 (sept 1902) 239-261. German version: Buddhistisches klosterleben in china, **FO** 1 (1902) 235-256.

Hackmann, Heinrich. Das buddhisten-kloster tien-dong in der chinesischen provinz che-kiang. **ZMK** 17 (1902) 173-178.

Hackmann, Heinrich. 'Pai chang ch'ing kuei.' The rules of buddhist monastic life in china. **TP** n.s. 9 (1908) 651-662. Same title in **Trans. 3rd ICHR Oxford, 1908**, vol 1, oxford (1908) p 137.

Hackmann, Heinrich. Die schulen des chinesischen buddhismus. **MSOS** 14 (1911) 232-266.

Hardy, Jacques and Ch. Lenormaud. Le monastère du kou-chan [fukien] **Monde moderne** 29 (déc 1906) 206-214.

Harlez, Charles de. Une visite au monastère bouddhique de wu-tchin par pe-k'iu-yi. **Muséon** 12 (1893) 99-107, 197-212.

Hecken, Joseph van. Les lamaseries d'oto (ordos) **MS** 22 (1963) 121-168, illus, map.

Hsü, Vivian. Monks and nuns as comic figures in yüan drama. **Dodder** 2 (jan 1970) 10-12.

Initiation of buddhist priests. **ChRec** 9.3 (may-june 1878) 181-184.

Irving, E. A. A visit to the buddhist and tao-ist monasteries on the lo fau shan. **BIM** 157 (mar 1895) 453-467.

Kiang, Alfred. A new life begins in the [buddhist] temples. **CWR** 116 (11 feb 1950) 173-174.

Little, Alicia Bewicke. Among chinese monasteries. **MacMillan's magazine** 81 (jan 1900) 201-208.

Loi. Der mönch des klosters kilungsan. **OstL** 18 (1904) 163-165, 202-203, 243-247.

Maspero, Henri. Communautés et moines bouddhistes chinois au IIe et IIIe siècles. **BEFEO** 10 (1910) 222-232.

Maspero, Henri. Les origines de la communauté bouddhiste de loyang. **JA** 225 (1934) 87-107.

Matignon, J. J. l'Auto-crémation des prêtres bouddhistes. **Archives d'anthropologie criminelle** 13 (15 janv 1898); also in author's book, **Crime, superstition et misère,** lyon (1899) q.v. 143-156

Peri, N. and H. Maspero. Le monastère de la kouan-yin qui ne vent pas s'en aller. **BEFEO** 9 (1909) 797-807 (P'u-t'o shan)

Prip-Møller, Johannes. **About buddhist temples.** Peiping (1931) 33 p, illus.

Prip-Møller, Johannes. **Chinese buddhist monasteries. Their plan and its function as a setting for buddhist monastic life.** Copenhagen and oxford univ (1937) repr univ hong kong (1967) 396 p, index, sketches, plans, elevations, photos.

Prip-Møller, Johannes. Streiflichter auf die entwicklung des bauplans chinesischer buddhistischer klöster in ihrem verhältnis zum buddhistischem kultus. **OZ** 24 (1938) 156-166.

Sato, Mitso. The ceremony of the ordination and its understanding in chinese terms of the vinaya. **JIBS** 11 (1963) 1-8.

Saunders, Kenneth J. Buddhist monasticism and its fruits. **AP** 10 (1939) 229-234.

Tsu, Y. Y. (tsl) A diary of a buddhist nun. **JR** 7.5/6 (oct 1927) 612-618. From **Hai ch'ao yin** 3.11/12 (feb 1923) Repr in **CWayRel** (1973) 120-124.

Twitchett, D. C. The monasteries and china's economy in medieval times. **BSOAS** 19 (1957) 526-549.

Twitchett, D. C. Monastic estates in t'ang china. **AM** n.s. 5 (1956) 123-146.

Verdeille, Maurice (tsl) Le monastère de la montagne 'ou-tai' en révolution. **BSEIS** 70 (1919) 21-37, 2 pl. Extr par l'éditeur des 'siao-siao chouo' du livre intitulé 'liang shan po.'

Welch, Holmes. The buddhist career. **JHKBRAS** 2 (1962) 37-48.

Welch, Holmes. The chinese sangha, the good and the bad. **The buddhist annual** (Colombo) 1 (1964) 23-26.

Yang, Lien-sheng. Buddhist monasteries and four money-raising institutions in chinese history. **HJAS** 13 (1950) 174-191. Repr in author's collection: **Studies in chinese institutional history,** cambridge, mass (1963) 198-215.

11. PILGRIMS

Abegg, Emil. Chinesische buddhapilger in indien. 2. Huan-tsang. **AS** 1-2 (1948) 56-79.

Abel-Rémusat, J. P. **Foĕ kouĕ ki ou relation des royaumes bouddhiques: voyage dans la tartarie, dans l'afghanistan et dans l'inde, exécuté, à la fin du IVe siècle, par chỹ fǎ hian. Traduit du chinois et commenté par m. abel-rémusat. Ouvrage posthume revu, complété, et augmenté d'éclaircissements nouveaux par mm. klaproth et landresse.** Paris (1836) lxviii + 424 p. See item by H. H. Wilson, Account of the foe kúe ki . . .

Abel-Rémusat, J. P. Mémoire sur un voyage dans l'asie centrale, dans le pays des afghans et des beloutches, et dans l'inde, exécuté à la fin du IVe siècle de notre ère, par plusieurs samanéens de la chine. **MAIBL** n.s. 13 (1831) 345 et seq. See also author's art: Voyage dans la tartarie, dans l'afghanistan et dans l'inde, exécuté à la fin du IVe siècle par plusieurs samanéens de la chine. **RDM** (1 janv 1832)

Allan, C. W. The priest hsuan tsang and the sian monuments. **ChRec** 39 (oct 1908) 576-577.

Bagchi, P. C. (tsl) **She-kia-fang-che.** Santiniketan (1959) 151 p.

Beal, Samuel. Indian travels of chinese buddhists. **IA** 10 (1881) 109-111, 192-199, 246-248.

Beal, Samuel (tsl) **The life of hiuen-tsiang. By the shaman hwui li. With an introduction containing an account of the works of i-tsing.** London (1911) xlvii + 218 p.

Beal, Samuel (tsl) **Si-yu-ki. Buddhist records of the western world. Translated from the chinese of hiuen tsiang (a.d. 629)** London (1884) vol 1, cviii + 242 p; vol 2, vii + 368 p. Beal's **Travels of fahhian and sung yun** q.v. is incorporated in this work. Repr as **Travels of hiouen-thsang,** calcutta (1957-58) 4 vol.

Beal, Samuel. Some remarks on the narrative of fâ-hien. **JRAS** n.s. 19 (1887) 191-206.

Beal, Samuel (tsl) **Travels of fah-hian and sung-yun, buddhist pilgrims, from china to india (400 a.d.-518 a.d.)** London (1896) lxxiii + 208 p.

Beal, Samuel. Two chinese-buddhist inscriptions found at buddha gaya. **JRAS** n.s. 13 (1881) 552-572.

Bodh-Gayā inscriptions: See a ser of art and responses by Édouard Chavannes and Gustave Schlegel, the former publ in **RHR**, the latter in **TP**:
    E.C. – Les inscriptions chinoises de B.-G.
        RHR 34.1 (1896)
    G.S. – (same title) **TP** 7.5 (1896)
    E.C. – La première inscr. chin. de B.-G.
        RHR 36.1 (1897)
    G.S. – (same title) **TP** 8.5 (1897)
    G.S. – Les inscriptions chin. de B.-G.
        ii. Première partie. **TP** 8.1 (1897)
    G.S. – Les inscr. chin. de B.-G. ii. Deuxième
        partie. **TP** 8.2 (1897)
    G.S. – Les inscr. chin. de B.-G. iii-iv. **TP** 8.3
        (1897)

Boulting, William. **Four pilgrims: (1) hiuen tsiang . . .** London and n.y. (1920) viii + 256 p.

Chang, Kuei-sheng. The travels of hsüan chuang. **CC** 1.3 (1958) 86-123.

Châu, Thích-minh. **Hsuan tsang, the pilgrim and scholar.** Nha-trang (1963) 139 p.

Chavannes, Édouard. Gunavarman. **TP** n.s. 5 (1904) 193-206.

Chavannes, Édouard. l'Itinéraire de ki-ye. **BEFEO** 4 (1904) 75-81.

Chavannes, Édouard. I-tsing. In **La grande encyclopédie,** paris, vol 20 (1894) 1137.

Chavannes, Édouard. Voyage de song-yun dans l'udyāna et le gandhāra (518-522 apr j.-c.) **BEFEO** 3 (1903) 379-441. Note additionelle par Paul Pelliot, p 442.

Chavannes, Édouard (tsl) **Voyages des pèlerins bouddhistes. – Les religieux éminents qui allerent chercher la loi dans les pays d'occident, mémoire composé à l'époque de la grand dynastie t'ang par i-tsing.** Paris (1894) xxi + 218 p.

Ch'en, Kenneth K. S. Hsüan tsang. In **EncyB** vol 11 (1970)

Cunningham, Alexander. Verification of the itinerary of hwan thsang through ariana and india. With reference to major anderson's hypothesis of its modern compilation. **JRASB** 17 (1848) 476-488.

Cunningham, Alexander. Verification of the itinerary of the chinese pilgrim, hwan thsang, through afghanistan and india during the first half of the seventh century of the christian era. **JRASB** 17 (1848) 13-60.

Doré, H. Le grand pèlerinage bouddhique de langchan et les cinq montagnes de tong-tcheou. **NCR** 1.1 (mar 1919) 41-56; 1.2 (may 1919) 120-144; 1.3 (july 1919) 282-298; 1.5 (oct 1919) 457-479; 1.6 (dec 1919) 580-603; 2.1 (feb 1920) 44-46.

Douglas, Robert K. Fa-hien's description of the image of maitreya buddha (bodhisattva) **Athenaeum** (12 mar 1887) 359. Also see J. Legge's art on the image, **ibid** 390, 454.

Edgar, J. H. Did hsüan tsang visit the west of china after his return from india? **JWCBorderResS** 3 (1926-29) 106.

Fa Hsien. Record of early buddhist countries. **CL** 3 (1956) 153-181, map.

Feer, Henri L. Les jatakas dans les mémoires de hiouen-thsang. **Actes du 11e ICO, Paris 1897,** t 1, sec 1, paris (1898) 151-169.

Finot, Louis. Hiuan-tsang and the far east. **JRAS**
(jan 1920) 447-452.

Fujishima, Ryauon (tsl) Deux chapitres extraits
des mémoires d'i-tsing sur son voyage dans l'inde.
JA 8e sér, 12 (1888) 411-439.

Fujishima, Ryauon. Index des mots sanscrits-
chinois contenus dans les deux chapitres d'i-tsing.
JA 8e sér, 13 (1889) 490-496.

Giles, Herbert A. (tsl) **Record of the buddhist
kingdoms.** London (1877) Retsl as **The travels of
fa-hsien (399-414 a.d.), or, record of the buddhist
kingdoms.** Cambridge univ (1923) xvi + 96 p.
Repr london (1956)

Gowen, Herbert H. The travels of a buddhist
pilgrim, a.d. 399-414. **American antiquarian and
oriental journal** 21 (1899) 3-13. Re fa hsien.

Grimes, A. The journey of fa-hsien from ceylon
to canton. **JMBRAS** 19 (1941) 76-92, 4 charts.

Grousset, René. **Sur les traces du bouddha.** Paris
(1929) 329 p, map, illus. Engl tsl Mariette Leon:
In the footsteps of the buddha, london (1932)
352 p, map, indexes, illus (Hsüan chuang and
yi-ching)

Guignes, Joseph de. Recherches historiques sur la
religion indienne. Second mémoire . . . **MAIBL**
40 (1780) 247-306.

Harlez, Charles de. Un pèlerin-missionaire
bouddhiste au IVe siècle de notre ère. **La controverse et la contemporain** 11 (1887) 5-33.

Huber, É. l'Itinéraire de pèlerin ki-ye dans
l'inde. **BEFEO** 2 (1902) 256-259.

Introduction to the buddhist library of huen
chwang. By the emperor tai tsung a.d. 627-649.
JNCBRAS 48 (1917) 115-117.

Jan, Yün-hua. Hui ch'ao and his works: a reassessment. **IAC** 12 (jan 1964) 177-190.

Julien, Stanislas (tsl) **Histoire de la vie d'hiouen
thsang, et de ses voyages dans l'inde entre les
années 629 et 645 de notre ère.** Paris (1851) 72 p.
See further next item.

Julien, Stanislas (tsl) **Histoire de la vie de hiouen-
thsang et de ses voyages dans l'inde depuis l'an
629 jusq'en 645, par hoëi-li et yen thsong; suivi de
documents et d'éclaircissements géographique
tirés de la relation originale de hiouen-thsang.**
Paris (1853) lxxxiv + 472 p.

Julien, Stanislas (tsl) **Mémoires sur les contrées
occidentales, traduits du sanscrit en chinois, en
l'an 648, par hiouen-thsang, et du chinois en
français, par S. J.** Paris, vol 1 (1857) lxxviii + 493;
vol 2 (1858) xix + 576.

Julien, Stanislas. Renseignements bibliographiques
sur les relations des voyages dans l'inde et les
descriptions du si-yu, qui ont été composées en
chinois entre le Ve et le XVIIIe siècle de notre ère.
JA 4e sér, 10 (1847) 265-269.

Julien, Stanislas (tsl) **Voyages des pèlerins
bouddhistes.** Paris (1853-58) t 1: **Histoire de la
vie de hiouen thsang et de ses voyages dans l'inde;**
t 2 et 3: **Mémoires sur les contrées occidentales.**
See foregoing items.

Klaproth, J. Reise des chinesischen buddha-
priesters hiüan thsang durch mittel-asien und
indien. **Sitzung der berliner geog. gesel.** (15 nov
1834) 8 p.

Lacouperie, Albert J. B. Terrien de. On hiuen-
tsiang instead of yüan chwang, and the necessity of
avoiding the pekinese sounds in the quotations of
ancient proper names in chinese. **JRAS** (1892)
835-840.

Laidlay, J. W. **The pilgrimage of fa hian; from the
french edition of the foe koue ki of mm. remusat,
klaproth, and landresse with additional notes and
illustrations.** Calcutta (1848) viii + 373 p.

Lamiot, Louis (tsl) **Ta-t'ang-hsi-yu-chi. Esquisse
du sy-yu, ou des pays à l'ouest de la chine.** Paris,
2 pt (1832)

Laufer, Berthold. Ein buddhistisches pilgerbild.
Globus 86 (1904) 386-388.

Laufer, Berthold. Zum bildnis des pilgers hsüan
tsang. **Globus** 88 (1905) 257-258.

Legge, James. The image of maitreya. **Athenaeum**
(12 mar 1887) 390, 454. See art by R. K. Douglas
above.

Legge, James (tsl) **A record of buddhistic kingdoms. Being an account by the chinese monk
fa-hien of his travels in india and ceylon (a.d. 399-
414) in search of the buddhist books of discipline.**
Oxford univ (1886) repr (1964) index, illus, chin
text in corean rescension.

Legge, James. Sur un passage de la préface du. . .
hsi yü ki. **Mémoires société études japonaises etc.**
5 (nov 1886) 263-266.

Lévi, Sylvain. Hiouen-tsang. In **La grande encyclopédie**, paris, vol 20 (1894) 105-106.

Lévi, Sylvain (tsl) **l'Itinéraire d'ou-k'ong (751-790)** Paris (repr 1895) 48 p.

Lévi, Sylvain. Les missions de wang hiuen-ts'e dans l'inde. **JA** (1900) 297-341, 401-468.

Lévi, Sylvain. Wang hiuan-ts'ö et kaniska. **TP** 2e sér, 13 (1912) 307-309.

Lévi, Sylvain et Édouard Chavannes (tsl) Voyages des pèlerins bouddhistes. – l'Itinéraire d'ou-k'ong (751-790) **JA** 9e sér, 6 (1895) 341-384.

Levy, Paul. Les pèlerins chinois en inde. In **FA:BPB** (1959) 375-436.

Li, Hsin-tsung. Hsuan chuang and chinese buddhism. **China today** 10.6 (june 1967) 13-17.

Li, Yung-hsi (tsl) **Monk hui-li: the life of hsuan tsang, the tripitaka-master of the great tzu-en monastery.** Peking (1959) 274 p.

Li, Yung-hsi (tsl) **A record of the buddhist countries by fa-hsien.** Peking (1957) 94 p, map.

Liétord. Le pèlerin bouddhiste chinois i-tsing et la médecine de l'inde au IIIe siècle. **Bulletin de la société française d'histoire de la médecine** 1 (1903) 472-487.

Meuwese, C. **l'Inde du bouddha. Vue par les pèlerins chinois sous la dynastie tang (VIIe siècle)** Paris (1968) 319 p, illus, map.

Neumann, Carl F. Pilgerfahrten buddhistischer priester von china nach indien. – aus dem chinesischen übersetzt, mit einer einleitung und mit anmerkungen versehen . . . **Zeitschrift für die historische theologie** 3 (1833) 66 p.

Nilakantasastri, K. A. The chinese pilgrims. In **FA:BPB** (1959) 437-448.

Pelliot, Paul. Deux itinéraires de chine en inde à la fin du VIIIe siècle. **BEFEO** 4 (1904) 131-413.

Pelliot, Paul. Note sur le récit de hiuan-tsang relatif à la légende de sou-ta-na. **BEFEO** 3 (1903) 334.

Pelliot, Paul. Trois termes de mémoires de hiuan-tsang. In **EORL** (1932) t 2, 423-431.

Raja, C. K. I-tsing and bhartthari's vakyapadiya. In **Dr. s. krishnaswami aiyangar commemoration volume**, madras (1936) 285-298.

Rosthorn, A. V. Letter on hiouen-tsang's 'twelve chang.' **Wiener zeitschrift für die kunde des morgenländes** 10 (1896) 280-284.

Roussel, Romain. **Les pèlerinages à travers les siècles.** Paris (1954) 326 p. See . . . Bouddhistes . . . Taoïstes . . .

Schlegel, G. Itinerary to the western countries of wang-nieh in a.d. 964. **MCSJ** 21 (1893) 35-64.

Seu, A. C. Chinese pilgrims in ancient india. **IAC** 6 (1958) 271-275.

Silabhadra, Bhikkhu. Fa-hien's indian travel. **MB** 49 (1941) 436-448.

Staël-Holstein, A von. Hsüan-tsang and modern research. **JNCBRAS** 54 (1923) 16-24.

Stein, Mark Aurel. The desert crossing of hsüan-tsang, 630 a.d. **Geographical journal** 54.5 (nov 1919) 265-277.

Stein, Mark Aurel. La traversée du desert par hiuan-tsang en 630 ap. j.-c. **TP** 20 (1921) 332-354.

Takakusu, Junjirō. Discovery of hiuen tsang's memorials. **YE** 2 (8 aug 1926) 75-77.

Takakusu, Junjirō. Fa-hian. In **HERE** 5 (1912) 678.

Takakusu, Junjirō. Hiuen tsang. A great traveller in india. **HZ** 12.11 (1897) 24-25.

Takakusu, Junjirō. **Kanshin's (chien-chên's) voyage to the east, a.d. 742-54, by aomi-no-mabito genkai (a.d. 779)** London (1925)

Takakusu, Junjirō (tsl) **A record of the buddhist religion as practised in india and the malay archipelago (a.d. 671-695) by i-tsing.** Oxford univ (1896) repr taipei (1970) lxiv + 240 p, map, notes, index.

Takakusu, Junjirō. Th. Watters: On yuan chwang's travels in india. **JRAS** (1905) 412-417. Review art.

Takakusu, Junjirō. Le voyage de kanshin au japon (742-754) **PCIEEO** (1902) 56-60.

Takakusu, Junjirō. Yuan-chwang, fa-hian and i-tsing. In **HERE** 12 (1921) 841-843.

Taylor, G. The marvelous genealogy of hsuen tseng. **ChRev** 17 (1889) 258-265.

Thomas, F. W. A chinese buddhist pilgrim's letters of introduction. **JRAS** (1927) 546-558.

Valentino, Henri. **Le voyage d'un pèlerin chinois dans l'inde des bouddhas** . . . Paris (1932) 243 p, map.

Waley, Arthur. **The real tripitaka and other pieces.** London (1952) See pt one, 9-130, on hsüan chuang; pt two, 131-168, on ennin and ensai.

Watters, Thomas. Fa-hsien and his english translators. **ChRev** 8 (1879-80) 107-116, 131-140, 217-230, 277-284, 323-341.

Watters, Thomas. **On yuan chwang's travels in india, 629-645 a.d.** Ed T. W. Rhys David and S. W. Bushell. London (1904) vol 1, 401 p; vol 2, 357 p; indexes, maps.

Watters, Thomas. The shadow of a pilgrim, or, notes on the ta-t'ang hsi-yü-chi of yuan-chwang. **ChRev** 18 (1889-90) 327-347; 19 (1890-91) 107-126, 182-189, 201-224, 376-383; 20 (1891-92) 29-32.

Weller, Friedrich. Kleine beiträge zur erklärung fa-hsiens. In **AMHAV** (1923) 560-574.

Wethered, H. Newton. **The four paths of pilgrimage.** London (1947) See chap 4 sec 5-6 on hsuan-tsang, 182-191.

Wilson, H. H. Account of the foe kúe ki, or travels of fa hian in india, translated from the chinese by m. remusat. **JRAS** 5 (1839) 108-140. Repr in **ChRep** 9 (1840) 334-366.

Wilson, H. H. Summary review of the travels of hiouen thsang, from the translation of the si-yu-ki by m. julien, and the mémoire analytique of m. vivien de saint-martin. **JRAS** 17 (1860) 106-137.

Yule, Henry. Hwen t'sang [hsuan chuang] In **EncyB** 9th ed (1881) vol 12, 418-419.

12. RITES – PRACTICES – CULTS – INSTRUMENTS

Chinese rosary. **ICG** no 9 (1819) 138-139.

Davidson, J. LeRoy. Buddhist paradise cults in sixth century china. **JISOA** 17 (1949) 112-124.

Day, Clarence B. The cult of amitabha. **CJ** 33 (1940) 235-249.

Devéria, G. Liturgie bouddhique. **REO** 1.2 (1882)

Duyvendak, J. J. L. The buddhistic festival of all-souls in china and japan. **AO** 5 (1927) 39-48.

Edkins, Joseph. Earnestness in chinese buddhism. **IA** 12 (1883) 104-110.

Edkins, Joseph. Mandal. **ChRev** 16 (1888) 369.

Edkins, Joseph. Religious devotion among buddhists. **Sunday at home** (may 1882)

Edkins, Joseph. Wooden fish as a buddhist implement. **ChRev** 16 (1888) 375.

Eurius, O. Die gelübde der buddhisten und die ceremonie ihrer ablegung bei den chinesen. In Karl Abel (tsl) **Arbeiten der kaiserlich russischen gerandschaft zu peking** . . . [q.v. in Part One: General Studies] (1858) 315-419.

Gernet, Jacques. Les suicides par le feu chez les bouddhistes chinois du Ve au Xe siècle. **MIHEC** 2 (1960) 527-558.

Graham, Dorothy. Dance of the whirling devils; huang ssu monastery, peking. **CW** 122 (feb 1926) 594-599.

Groot, J. J. M. de. Buddhist masses for the dead at amoy. **Actes, 6eICO Leide, 1883** leiden (1885) 1-120.

Groot, J. J. M. de. Miséricorde envers les animaux dans le bouddhism chinois. **TP** 3 (1892) 466-489.

Gulik, Robert Hans van. **Hayagrīva. The mantrayānic aspect of the horse-cult in china and japan.** Leiden (1935) 103 p, illus.

Imbault-Huart, Camille. Une cérémonie bouddhiste en chine: scène de la vie intime chinoise. **JA** 7e sér, 16 (oct-dec 1880) 526-533.

Iwai, Hirosato. The buddhist priest and the ceremony of attaining womanhood during the yüan dynasty. **TBMRD** 7 (1935) 105-161.

Jan, Yün-hua. Buddhist self-immolation in medieval china. **HR** 4.2 (1964-65) 243-268.

Jan, Yün-hua. Der buddhistische begräbnisritus. **Concilium** 4 (feb 1968) 144-146.

Johnston, R. F. Purification (chinese) In **HERE** 10, p. 470.

Johnston, R. F. Vows (chinese) In **HERE** 12, p 646.

Karutz, Richard. Von buddhas heiliger fuss-spur. **Globus** 89 (jan 1906) 21-25, 45-49.

Landon, Perceval. A remnant of buddha's body. **NC** 50 (aug 1901) 236-243.

La Vallée Poussin, Louis de. Staupikam. **HJAS** 2 (1937) 276-289. Theory of stupa and its origin.

Lessing, Ferdinand D. Structure and meaning of the rite called the bath of the buddha according to tibetan and chinese sources. In **SSBKD** (1959) 159-171.

Lessing, Ferdinand D. The thirteen visions of a yogācārya. A preliminary study. **Ethnos** 15 (1950) 108-130.

Lessing, Ferdinand D. Wu-liang-shou . . . a comparative study of tibetan and chinese longevity rites. **ASBIHP** 28 (1957) 794-824.

Lucius. A bone of fuh. **ICG** no 12 (1820) 305-308.

MacGowan, D. J. Self-immolation by fire. **ChRec** 19 (1888) 445-451, 508-521.

MacLagan, P. J. Celibacy (chinese) In **HERE** 3, p 271.

Masaki, Haruhiko. The practice of buddhist austerities and its popularization in shan-tao and prince shotoku – in connection with śrimālā and vaidehī. **JIBS** 16.2 (mar 1968) 943-955.

Matignon, J. J. l'Auto-crémation des prêtres bouddhistes. **Archives d'anthropologie criminelle** 13 (15 janv 1898) also in author's **Crime, superstition et misère** q.v. 143-156.

Matignon, J. J. La transformation assise (tso-hua) **TP** 9.3 (1898) 230-232.

Mayers, W. F. The buddhist rosary and its place in chinese official costume. **NQ** 3 (1869) 26-28.

Orcet, G. d'. Les moulins à prières dans l'inde, en chine et au japon. **Revue britannique** n.s. 1 (1882) 31-62.

Prip-Møller, J. Buddhist meditation ritual. **ChRec** 66.12 (dec 1935) 713-718.

Przyluski, J. Les rites d'avalambana. **MCB** 1 (1931-32) 221-225.

Reichelt, Karl L. (tsl) Extracts from the buddhist ritual. **ChRec** 59 (mar 1928) 160-170. Passages from ch'ang meng er sung.

Rousselle, E. Ein abhiṣeka-ritus im mantra-buddhismus. **Sinica-Sonderausgabe** (1934) 58-90; (1935) 1-23.

Rousselle, E. Der kult der buddhistischen madonna kuan-yin. **NachrDGNVO** 68 (1944) 17-23.

Saintyves, P. Le culte de la croix dans le bouddhisme en chine, au nepal et au tibet. **RHR** 75 (janv-févr 1917) 1-52, fig.

Simpson, William. **The buddhist praying-wheel. A collection of material bearing upon the symbolism of the wheel and circular movements in custom and religious ritual.** London (1896) viii + 303 p.

Suzuki, D. T. The kuan-yin cult in china. **EB** 6 (1935) 339-353.

Trautz, F. M. Eine erhebende musikaufführung am 'fünffachen stupa' (des wu-t'a-ssŭ bei peking) **AM** 2 (1925) 581-596.

Wiese, J. Selbstrerbrennung buddhistischer priester in china. **Asien** 7 (1909) 68-70.

Yetts, W. Perceval. Note on the disposal of buddhist dead in china. **JRAS** (july 1911) 699-725, pl.

13. ART AND ICONOGRAPHY

A. GENERAL

Binyon, Laurence. Chinese art and buddhism. **Proc british academy** 22 (1936) 157-175. Also publ sep london (1936) 21 p, 9 illus.

Buddhistische kunst ostasiens. Ausstellung der museums für ostasiatische kunst der stadt köln, vom 11. april-13. oktober 1968. Museum für ostiatische kunst, köln (1968) 86 s, illus.

Burland, Cottie A. Buddhism in art at the berkeley galleries, nov. 1948-jan. 1949. **Asian horizon** 1.4 (winter 1948) 53-57.

Chavannes, Édouard. l'Exposition d'art bouddhique au musée cernuschi. **TP** (1913) 261-286, pl.

Chinese buddhist bronzes: a loan exhibition under the joint auspices of department of fine arts, freer fund, and museum of art, april 13-may 7, 1950. Univ michigan (1950) 15 p, 23 pl.

Corbet, R. G. Buddhism and art. **IAQR** (july-oct 1902) 114-120.

Focillon, Henri. **Art et religion – l'art bouddhique.** Paris (1921) xvi + 164 p, 24 pl.

Hackin, J., O. Sirén, L. Warner, and P. Pelliot. **Studies in chinese art and some indian influences.** London (1938) vii + 63 p, pl. Lectures at royal academy of arts in connection with the burlington exhibition of chinese art.

Ludwig, Ernst. Lama temples in peking. 1. Yung-hô-kung. **EA** 1 (1902) 81-103. See also Pekinger lamaserails (yung-hô-kung) in **FO** 1 (1902) 105-125.

Milloué, Léon de. **Catalogue du musée guimet. Pt 1: Inde, chine et japon.** Précédé d'un aperçu sur les religions de l'extrême-orient et suivie d'un index alphabétique des noms des divinités et des principaux termes techniques. Paris (1883) lxviii + 323 p.

Petrucci, R. l'Art bouddhique, en extrême-orient d'après les découvertes récentes. **GBA** (sept 1911) 193-213.

Petrucci, Raphael. Buddhist art in the far east and the documents from chinese turkestan. **BM** 18 (1910-11) 138-144.

Petrucci, R. l'Exposition d'art bouddhique au musée cernuschi. **BAAFC** 5 (1913) 223-229.

Scott, Alexander. Buddhistic art. **Museum journal** 5 (1914) 58-61.

Seckel, Dietrich. **Buddhistische kunst ostasiens.** Stuttgart (1957) 383 s, 204 abh, 2 ktn.

Seckel, Dietrich. **Kunst des buddhismus. Werden, wanderung und wandlung.** Baden-baden (1964) Engl tsl Ann E. Keep: **The art of buddhism,** n.y. (1964) 331 p, app, maps, bibliog, index, illus.

Segalen, Victor. Bouddhisme chinois. **RAA** 3 (1926) 119-122.

Sickman, Laurence. Notes on later chinese buddhist art. **Parnassus** 11.4 (1939) 12-17.

Sirén, Osvald. Ch'an (zen) buddhism and its relation to art. **Theosophical path** (oct 1934) 159-176.

Soper, Alexander C. Literary evidence for early buddhist art in china, 1. **OA** 2.1 (1949) 28-35. Same title, 2. in **AA** 16 (1953) 83-110.

Soper, Alexander C. **Literary evidence for early buddhist art in china.** Ascona (1959) 296 p, indexes.

Swann, Peter C. **Chinese monumental art.** N.Y. (1963) also french ed (1963) 276 p, 157 pl, maps and fig, bibliog, index. Photos Claude Arthaud and François Hébert-Stevens.

Warner, Langdon. A chinese exhibition at cleveland museum of art. **BM** 56 (apr 1930) 205-211, 2 pl.

B. ICONOGRAPHY – MOTIFS

Behrsing, S. Der heiligenschein in ostasien. **ZDMG** 103 (1953) 156-192.

Bouillard, G. **Notes divers sur les cultes en chine: les attitudes des buddhas.** Pékin (1924) 28 p, pl.

Bouillard, G. Notes diverses sur les cultes en chine. **La chine** 60 (1924) 239-247; 65 (1924) 227-232.

Bunker, Emma C. Early chinese representations of vimalakirti. **AA** 30.1 (1968) 28-52.

Cammann, Schuyler. The four great kings of heaven – part 2. **JWCBorderResS** 11 (1939) 78-84.

Chapin, Helen B. A study in buddhist iconography. **OZ** 18 (1932) 29-43, 111-129; 21 (1935) 125-134, 195-210.

Chapin, Helen B. Yunnanese images of avalokiteśvara. **HJAS** 8 (1944) 131-186, 16 pl, bibliog.

Clapp, F. M. Arhats in art. **Art studies** 3 (1925) 95-130.

Cohn, W. **Buddha in der kunst ostasiens.** Leipzig (1925) 5 + lxiv + 253 p illus.

Davidson, J. LeRoy. The origin and early use of the ju-i. **AA** 13.4 (1950) 239-249.

Davidson, J. LeRoy. A problem in skulls. **Parnassus** 11.1 (1939) 33-35. Iconography.

Dumoutier, Gustave. Le swastika et la roue solaire dans les symboles et dans les caractères chinois. **RE** 4.4 (1885) 319-350.

Erkes, Eduard. Zum problem der weiblichen kuanyin. **AA** 9 (1946) 316-320, illus.

Fontein, J. **The pilgrimage of sudhana. Study of gandavyūha illustrations in china, japan and java.** The hague (1967) 237 p, 64 pl.

Franks, A. W. On some chinese rolls with buddhist legends and representations. **Archaeologia** 2nd ser, pt 3.1 (1892) 239-244.

Gaillard, Louis. **Croix et swastika en chine.** Shanghai (1893) 282 p (Variétés sinologiques no 3)

Getty, Alice. **The gods of northern buddhism.** Oxford univ 1st ed (1914) 2nd ed (1928) repr of 2nd ed (1962) liv + 220 p, bibliog, index, 67 pl. See rev by Kanaoka Shuyu, **CRJ** 5.3 (sept 1964) 207-220.

Hée, Louis van. Le témoignage de l'occident. **AA** 1 (1925) 217-226.

Lessing, Ferdinand D. **Yung-ho-kung. An iconography of the lamaist cathedral in peking with notes on lamaist mythology and cult.** Stockholm (1942) 179 p, fig, plan, app, notes, bibliog, pl.

Lim, K. W. Studies in later buddhist iconography. **BTLVK** 120.3 (1964) 327-341.

Mallman, Marie Thérèse de. À propos d'une coiffure et d'un collier d'avalokiteśvara. **OA** 1 (spring 1949) 168-176, illus.

Mallman, Marie Thérèse de. **Étude iconographique sur mañjuśri.** Paris (1964) 284 p, 16 pl.

Mallman, Marie Thérèse de. Notes sur les bronzes du yunnan représentant avalokiteśvara. **HJAS** 14 (1951) 567-601, illus.

Manabe, Shunshō. The expression of elimination of devils in the iconographic texts of the t'ang period and its background. **JIBS** 15.2 (mar 1967) 907-914, pl.

Marchal, H. The flying (quivering) flame in the decorations of the far east. In **New IA**, extra ser 1 (1939): **A volume of eastern and indian studies, presented to f. w. thomas,** 148-151.

Meister, P. W. Buddhistische planetendarstellungen in china. **OE** 1 (1954) 1-5.

Milloué, L. de. Le svastika. **CMG** 31 (d?) 83-103.

Minamoto, H. l'Iconographie de la 'descente d'amida.' Tsl fr jap R. Linossier. In **EORL** (1932) 99-130.

Przyluski, J. Études indiennes et chinoises. **MCB** 2 (1932-33) 307-332; 4 (1935-36) 289-339.

Przyluski, J. (tsl) La roue de la vie à ajanta. **JA** 11e sér, 16 (1920) 313-331. Tsl of vinaya of mūla-sarvāstivādin by yi-tsing.

Rowland, Benjamin, jr. **The evolution of the buddha image.** N.Y. (1963) 140 p, 68 pl.

Rowland, Benjamin, jr. The iconography of the flame halo. **BFoggMA** 11 (june 1949) 10-16, illus.

Saunders, E. Dale. **Mudrā. A study of symbolic gestures in japanese buddhist sculpture.** N.Y. (1960) 296 p, notes, bibliog, index, fig, pl.

Saunders, E. Dale. Symbolic gestures in buddhism. **AA** 21 (1958) 47-63.

Scherman, L. Sanskrit letters as mystical symbols in later buddhism outside india. In **A&T** (1947) 55-62.

Schmidt, H. Die buddha des fernöstlichen mahâyâna. **AA** 1 (1925) 6-31, 98-120, 176-190, 245-258; 2 (1927) 11-29, 123-132, 165-179, 265-277.

Seckel, Dietrich. Die beiden dvârapâla-figuren im museum rietburg, zürich. **AA** 25 (1962) 23-44, pl.

Soper, Alexander C. Japanese evidence for the history of architecture and iconography of chinese buddhism. **MS** 4.2 (1940) 638-678.

Soymié, Michel. Notes d'iconographie chinoise: les acolytes de ti-tsang. **ArtsAs** 14 (1966) 45-78, pl.

Stiassny, M. Einiges zur 'buddhistischen madonna.' **JAK** 1 (1924) 112-119.

Tucci, G. Buddhist notes. **MCB** 9 (1948-51) 173-220. Re evolution of kuan-yin in art and texts.

Ward, W. E. The lotus symbol: its meaning in buddhist art and philosophy. **JEAC** 11 (1952-53) 135-146.

Watters, Thomas. The eighteen lohan of chinese buddhist temples. **JRAS** (apr 1898) 329-347; repr separately shanghai (1925) 45 p, portraits of the lohan.

Wegner, M. Ikonographie des chinesischen maitreya. **OZ** 15 (1929) 156-178, 216-229, 252-270, illus.

Wilson, Thomas. The swastika, the earliest known symbol, and its migrations . . . **U.S. national museum report for 1894** (smithsonian institution) 757-1011, pl 1-25, fig 1-374. Issued sep washington, d.c. (1896)

Wu, Feng-p'ei. The conch-shell trumpet of the esoteric buddhism. **NPMB** 3.5 (nov-dec 1968) 1-2, illus.

C. SPECIFIC TEMPLES

Abraham, A. Art treasures of a hangchow pagoda. **CJ** 26 (1937) 12-13.

Art treasures rediscovered (Ping-ling ssû, monastery in kansu) **CRecon** 2.4 (1953) 25-27.

Bouillard, Georges. **Le temple des lamas. Temple lamaïste de yung ho kung à pékin: description, plans, photos, cérémonies.** Peiping (1931) 127 p.

Bridgman, E. C. A picture of the precious porcelain pagoda in the recompensing favor monastery of kiangnan (commonly known as the porcelain tower) **ChRep** 13 (1844) 261-265.

Burn, D. C. **A guide to lunghwa temple. With brief notes on chinese buddhism.** Shanghai (1926) 62 p, illus.

Cook, T. The great buddha of kiating. **JWCBorderResS** 7 (1935) 36-39.

Dahlmann, Joseph. In den pagoden pekings. **OstL** 18 (1904) 782-785.

Drake, F. S. The shên-t'ung monastery and the beginning of buddhism in shantung. **MS** 4 (1939-40) 1-39.

Dumoutier, Gustave. Les bouddhas des pagodes de quan-am et de chuan-dê. **RGI** 17 (1892) 219-220.

Ecke, G. Ergänzungen und erläuterungen zu professor boerschmanns kritik von 'the twin pagodas of zayton' [q.v.] **MS** 2 (1936-37) 208-217.

Ecke, G. Once more, shen-t'ung ssu and ling-yen ssu. **MS** 7 (1942) 295-311.

Hildebrand, Heinrich. **Der tempel ta-chüeh-sy (tempel des grossen erkenntnis) bei peking.** Berlin (1897) 36 s, 87 text-abb, 12 taf.

Hurst, R. W. The chao chung temple at pagoda anchorage. **ChRev** 16 (1887-88) 177-179.

Lartigue, J. Le sanctuaire bouddhique du long-hong-sseu à kiating. **RAA** 5 (1928) 35-38.

Latham, A. Le temple de fa-hai-sse. **GBA** 6e sér, 18.2 (1937) 253-257.

Liang, Ssu-ch'eng. China's oldest wooden structure: fo-kuang ssu, the temple of buddha's light. **Asia** 41 (july 1941) 384-387, illus.

Lovegren, L. A. Measurements of the kiating big buddha. **JWCBorderResS** 5 (1932) 102-103.

Ludwig, Ernst. Lama temples in peking. 1. Yung-hô-kung. **EA** 1 (1902) 81-103. See also Pekinger lamaserails (yung-hô-kung) in **FO** 1 (1902) 105-125.

Melchers, Bernd. **China. Der tempelbau. Die lochan von ling-yän-sï; ein hauptwerk buddhistischer plastik.** Hagen i.w. (1921) 47 p text, 73 p photos of temple, 45 p photos of sculpture, 37 p drawings, photos and arch plans of temple.

Pantoussoff, N. Le temple chinois 'bei-iun-djuan,' dans la passe d'ak-su, province d'ili (vièrny, turkestan russe) **Revue des études ethnographiques et sociologiques** 1 (août 1908) 398-403, 2 pl.

Sirén, Osvald. A chinese temple and its plastic decoration of the 12th century. In **EORL** (1932) t 2, 499-505, pl lvi-lxiv.

Soper, Alexander C. Hsiang-kuo-ssû, an imperial temple of northern sung. **JAOS** 68.1 (1948) 19-45.

Sprague, Roger. The most remarkable monument in western china. **PS** 83 (1913) 557-566. Re temple and great buddha in kiating.

Tschepe, A. Der tempel hsing-fu-sze. **FO** 3 (1904?) 257-259.

Wong, C. S. **Kek lok si, temple of paradise.** Singapore (1963) 131 p. On a famous temple, chi-lo ssu, in penang.

Yang, Yu. Art treasures of the ping-ling-ssu temple. **PC** 15 (1953) 28-30.

D. ARCHITECTURE (EXCEPT PAGODAS)

Beylié, L. de. **l'Architecture hindoue en extrême-orient.** Paris (1907) 416 p. Illus de Tournois et Doumenq.

Boerschmann, Ernst. **Die baukunst und religiöse kultur der chinesen.** Vol 1, **P'u t'o shan.** Berlin (1911) 203 p, 33 pl, fig.

Boerschmann, Ernst. Chinese architecture and its relation to chinese culture. **Annual reports of the smithsonian institution** (1911) Tsl fr **ZE** 42 (1910)

Boerschmann, Ernst. **Chinesische architektur.** Berlin (1925) 2 vol.

Bulling, A. Buddhist temples in the t'ang period. **OA** n.s. 1 (1955) 79-86, 115-122.

Chambers, William. **Designs of chinese buildings.** London (1757) facs repr farnborough, engl (1969) See, Of the temples of the chinese, 1-5; Of the towers [taa = t'a, or pagodas] 5-6, pl 1-5.

Ito, C. Architecture (chinese) In **HERE** vol 1 (1908) 693-696.

Liang, Ssu-ch'eng. China's oldest wooden structure. **Asia** 41 (july 1941) 384-387, illus. T'ang temple on wu-t'ai shan, shensi.

Parmentier, H. Origine commune des architectures hindoues dans l'inde et en extrême-orient. **Études asiatiques** 2 (1925) 199-242.

Prip-Møller, Johannes. **Chinese buddhist monasteries. Their plan and its function as a setting for buddhist monastic life.** Copenhagen and oxford univ (1937) repr univ hong kong (1967) 396 p, index, sketches, plans, elevations, photos.

Prip-Møller, Johannes. The hall of ling ku ssu, nanking. **Artes** (copenhagen) 3 (1934)

Prip-Møller, Johannes. Streiflichter auf die entwicklung des bauplans chinesischer buddhistischer klöster in ihrem verhältnis zum buddhistischem kultus. **OZ** 24 (1938) 156-166.

Soper, Alexander C. Architecture. Being pt 2 of Laurence Sickman and Alexander Soper, **The art and architecture of china**, harmondsworth, middlesex, engl (1956) 2nd ed with add (1960) 205-288; notes 307-310; gloss 313; bibliog, index, fig, pl.

Soper, Alexander C. Four columns from a chinese temple. **Honolulu academy of arts, special studies** 1 (apr 1947) illus.

Soper, Alexander C. Japanese evidence for the history of architecture and iconography of chinese buddhism. **MS** 4.2 (1939-40) 638-678.

Stein, Rolf. Architecture et pensée religieuse en extrême-orient. **ArtsAs** 4.3 (1957) 163-186, illus.

E. PAGODAS

Abraham, A. Art treasures of a hangchow pagoda. **CJ** 26 (1937) 12-13.

Alley, Rewi. Pagodas and towers in china. **EH** 2 (may 1962) 20-28, illus.

Boerschmann, Ernst. **Die baukunst und religiöse kultur der chinesen.** Vol 3: **Pagoden; pao-t'a.** Berlin and leipzig (1931) 288 p, illus.

Boerschmann, Ernst. Eisen- und bronzepagoden in china. **JAK** 1 (1924) 223-235.

Boerschmann, E. K'ueising türme und fengshuisäulen. **AM** 2 (1925) 503-530.

Boerschmann, Ernst. Pagoden der sui- und frühen t'angzeit. **OZ** n.f. 11 (1924) 195-221.

Boerschmann, Ernst. Pagoden im nördlichen china unter fremden dynastien. In Hans H. Schaeder (ed) **Der orient in deutscher forschung,** leipzig (1944) 182-204.

Boerschmann, Ernst. Die pai t'a von suiyüan: eine nebenform der t'ienningpagoden. **OZ** n.f. 14,24 (1939) 185-208.

Bouchot, J. La grande pitié des pagodes en chine. **La chine** 2 (1922) 97-106; 12 (1922) 250-264.

Bowen, A. J. 'The porcelain tower' (Description in engl bk of 1698) **CJ** 5 (1926) 77-81.

Bridgman, E. C. A picture of the precious porcelain pagoda in the recompensing favor monastery of kiangnan (commonly known as the porcelain tower) **ChRep** 13 (1844) 261-265.

Brousse, Jean de la. Les t'a, tours chinoises après l'introduction du bouddhisme. **RC** (avr 1922) 110-123, illus; (juil 1922) 169-176; (oct 1922) 223-230, fig.

Buhot, J. l'Origine des pagodes sur plan hexagonal. **RAA** 13 (1939-42) 36-41.

Buhot, J. Stupa et pagode: une hypothèse. **RAA** 11 (1937) 235-239.

Chambers, William. **Designs of chinese buildings.** London (1757) facs repr farnborough, engl (1969) See Of the towers [taa = t'a, or pagodas] 5-6, pl 1-5.

Chen, Tsung-chou. Pagodas. **China pictorial** no 5 (may 1963) 28-31, illus.

Chinese pagodas. **JNCBRAS** 46 (1915) 45-57.

Combaz, G. l'Évolution du stūpa en asie. Contributions nouvelles et vue d'ensemble. **MCB** 3 (1934-35) 93-144.

Combaz, G. l'Évolution du stūpa en asie: étude d'architecture bouddhique. **MCB** 2 (1932-33) 163-305.

Combaz, G. l'Évolution du stūpa en asie: les symbolismes du stūpa. **MCB** 4 (1935-36) 1-125.

Cumine, E. B. The chinese pagoda. **CJ** 31 (1939) 160-163.

Ecke, G. Ergänzungen und erläuterungen zu professor boerschmanns kritik von 'the twin pagodas of zayton' [q.v.] **MS** 2 (1936-37) 208-217.

Ecke, Gustav. Structural features of the stone-built t'ing pagoda. A preliminary study. Chapter ii: Brick pagodas in the liao style. **MS** 1 (1935-36) 253-276; 13 (1948) 331-365.

Ecke, Gustav. Two ashlar pagodas at fu-ching in southern fu-chien. **BCUP** 8 (1933) 49-66.

Ecke, G. and P. Demiéville. **The twin pagodas of zayton. A study of later buddhist sculpture in china.** Harvard univ (1935) viii + 95 p, maps, pl. Photographs and intro G. Ecke; iconography and history P. Demiéville.

Finot, L. and V. Goloubew. Le fan-tseu t'a de yunnan fou. **BEFEO** 25 (1925) 435-448.

Groot, J. J. M. de **Der thupa, das heiligste heiligtum des buddhismus in china.** Berlin (1919) viii + 96 s, 6 taf.

Hobson, H. E. (tsl) The porcelain pagoda of nanking. Translation of the historical portion of a pictorial sheet engraved and published by the buddhist high priest in charge of the pao-en temple. Tsl of the devotional portion by W. A. P. Martin. **JNCBRAS** 23 (1888) 31-38.

Hoech, G. T. Der ursprung der pagoden, topen und zwiebelkuppeln. **Zeitschrift für bauwesen** 44 (1914) hft 7-9, col 524-542.

Liang, Ssu-ch'eng. Five early chinese pagodas. **Asia** 41 (aug 1941) 450-453, 7 illus.

March, Benjamin. The lintsing pagoda. **CJ** 5 (1926) 250-252.

Meurs, H. van. Alter und symbolische bedeutung der stupa. **OZ** 27 (1941) 32-45.

Milne, William C. Pagodas in china. A general description of the pagodas in china. **(?)Trans china branch RAS** 5 (1854) 17-63.

Moule, A. C. The lei feng ta. **JRAS** (1925) 285-288.

Oelmann, F. Der ursprung der pagode. **Sinica** 6 (1931) 196-199.

Prip-Møller, Johannes. On the building history of pao shu t'a, hangchow. **JNCBRAS** 67 (1936) 50-57.

Sawamura, Sentarō. Die stupa im bezirk des shao-lin-ssu. **OZ** 12 (1925) 265-272.

Soper, Alexander C. Two stelae and a pagoda on the central peak, mt. sung. **ACASA** 16 (1962) 41-48.

Williams, S. Wells. Pagodas in and near canton; their names and time of their erection. **ChRep** 19 (1850) 535-543.

F. SCULPTURE

Adams, P. R. A sui dynasty bodhisatva. **AQ** 15 (1952) 85-86.

Ashton, Leigh. **An introduction to the study of chinese sculpture.** London (1924) xvii + 108, 63 pl.

Bachhofer, Ludwig. Die anfänge der buddhistischen plastik in china. **OZ** n.s. 10 (1934) 1-15, 107-126, bibliog.

Bachhofer, Ludwig. Zur geschichte der chinesischen plastik vom bis 14. jhd. **OZ** n.s. 14 (1938) 65-82, 113-136.

Bell, Hamilton. An early bronze buddha. **BM** 25 (1914) 144-153, 2 pl.

The Buddha of measureless light and the land of bliss. A chinese buddhist group in bronze. **BMFA** 24 (1926) 2-10.

Bunker, Emma C. The spirit kings in sixth century chinese buddhist sculpture. **ACASA** 18 (1964) 26-37, illus.

Chavannes, Édouard. **Mission archéologique dans la chine septentrionale.** T 1: Première partie: **La sculpture à l'époque des han,** paris (1913) 290 p, pl. T 2: Deuxième partie: **La sculpture bouddhique,** paris (1915) 291-614, pl. There are 2 add vol pl: Première partie, pl i-cclxxxvi, paris (1909); Deuxième partie, pl cclxxxvii-cccclxxxviii, paris (1909) See also: Note sur les 488 planches de sa mission, **TP** 10 (1909) 538-547 (There is a small literature on this famous mission, which we do not list)

Cook, T. The great buddha of kiating. **JWCBorderResS** 7 (1935) 36-39. See also **ibid** 5, 102-103, art by L. A. Lovegren, Measurements of the kiating big buddha.

Davidson, Martha. Great chinese sculpture in america. **ANA** (1939) 71-74, 174-176.

Ecke, G. Ananda and vakula in early chinese carvings. **SIS** 5.3/4 (1957) (Liebenthal festschrift) 40-46, illus.

Ecke, G. On some buddhist images at the honolulu academy of arts. **AS** 21 (1967) 24-30, pl.

Ecke, G. A throning sakyamuni of the early t'ang period. **OA** 5 (1959) 165-169.

Ecke, G. and P. Demiéville. **The twin pagodas of zayton. A study of later buddhist sculpture in china.** Harvard univ (1935) viii + 95 p, maps, pl. Photographs and intro G. Ecke; iconography and history P. Demiéville.

Erkes, E. Ahnenbilder und buddhistische skulpturen aus altchina. **JSMVL** 5 (1913) 26-32, illus.

Fernald, Helen E. A buddhist stone sculpture from t'ien-lung shan, shansi, 8th century a.d. **BROMA** 22 (sept 1954) 1-3, illus facing p 12.

Fernald, Helen E. A chinese buddhistic statue in dry lacquer (late yuan-early ming) **MJ** 18.3 (1927) 284-294. Offpr, univ pennsylvania, univ museum (1927) 10 p.

Fischer, O. Chinesische buddh- und bodhisatvaköpfe. **JAK** 1 (1924) 159-164.

Fischer, O. **Chinesische plastik.** München (1948) 200 p, 136 pl.

From maitreya to sakyamuni; the gilt-bronze buddha of the wei dynasty. **ACASA** 19 (1965) 63-65, illus.

Fu, Tien-chou. The sculptured maidens of the tsin temple. **CL** 4 (apr 1962) 92-98.

Gangoly, O. C. A fragment of chinese buddhist sculpture. **Rupam** 33-34 (jan-apr 1928) 1, 1 pl.

Griswold, A. B. Prolegomena to the study of the buddha's dress in chinese sculpture. With particular reference to the rietberg museum's collection. **AA** 26 (1963) 85-131, pl 1-28. See further pt ii, **ibid** 27 (1964-65) 335-348, pl 29a-40.

Grünwald, Michael. Geistige und stilistische konvergenzen zwischen frühbuddhistischen skulpturen und religiöser plastik des frühen mittelalters in europa. **AA** 9 (1946) 34-67, illus.

Ho, Wai-kam. Notes on chinese sculpture from northern ch'i to sui. Part 1: Two seated stone buddhas in the cleveland museum. **AAA** 22 (1968-69) 6-55.

Ho, Wai-kam. Three seated stone buddhas. **BCMA** 53.4 (apr 1966) 83-102, illus.

Hollis, Howard C. A head from the lung men caves. **BCMA** 35 (sept 1948) 159-161, illus.

Jayne, H. H. F. Early chinese stone sculpture. **Pennsylvania museum bulletin** 214 (jan 1929) 15-25.

Jayne, H. H. F. Maitreya and guardians. **UPUMB** 9 (jan 1941) 2-8, 4 illus.

Jayne, H. H. F. A tile relief of a bodhisattva. **Pennsylvania museum bulletin** 214 (jan 1929) 25-29.

Joyce, T. A. A chinese bodhisattva. **BM** 42 (1923) p 130, photo on p 110.

Joyce, T. A. Note on a gilt bronze figure of padmapani in the british museum. **Man** 22 (1922) 33.

Kelley, Charles F. A buddhist triad of the t'ang dynasty. **BAIC** 24 (may 1930) 60-63.

Kingman, S. More precious than rubies; bodhisattva head from the caves of t'ien lung shan, china. **Asia** 34 (aug 1934) 498-499.

Klee, Th. Die plastik in den höhlen von yün-kang, lung-mên und kung-hsien. **OZ** 7 (1918-19) 31-56.

Lao, Kan. Six tusked elephants on a han bas-relief. **HJAS** 17 (dec 1954) 366-369.

Lee, Sherman E. Five early gilt bronzes. **AA** 12.1/2 (1949) 5-22.

Lee, Sherman E. The golden image of the new-born buddha. **AA** 18.3/4 (1955) 225-237, illus.

Leuridan, Thre. Sur une statuette chinoise du musée de roubaix, la déese pou-ssa. **Mémoires de la société d'émulation de roubaix,** t 5.

Liebenthal, Walter. An early buddhist statue from yünnan. **IHQ** 32 (1956) 352-353.

Lindsay, J. H. The makara in early buddhist sculpture. **JRAS** (1951) 134-138, pl. Re a monster fish.

Little, D. B. A chinese stone lion from lung-mên datable to a.d. 680-1. **BMFA** 38 (1940) 52-53.

Lobsiger-Dellenbach, W. Statuaire des song méridionaux (chine) **AS** 10 (1956) 105-113.

March, Benjamin. Detroit's bronze maitreya. **Art in america** 18 (1930) 144-150. See also: Maitreya (n. wei bronze) **BDetIA** 12 (nov 1930) 14-16.

March, Benjamin. New chinese sculptures. **BDetIA** 11 (nov 1929) 20-25.

Melchers, Bernd. **China. Der tempelbau. Die lochan von ling-yan-si; ein hauptwerk buddhistischer plastik.** Hagen i. w. (1922) 47 p text, 73 p photos of temple, 45 p photos of sculpture, 37 p drawings, photos and plans of temple.

Migéon, Gaston. Une sculpture chinoise classique, collection rockefeller à new york. **Revue de l'art** 55 (1929) 57-62, 5 illus, 1 pl.

Mizuno, S. **Bronze and stone sculpture of china.** Tokyo (1960)

Mizuno, S. **Chinese stone sculpture.** Tokyo (1950) 33 p, pl, maps.

Munsterberg, Hugo. **The art of the chinese sculptor.** Tokyo and rutland, vt (1960) 32 p, 12 col pl.

Munsterberg, Hugo. Buddhist bronzes of the six dynasties period. **AA** 9.4 (1946) 275-315.

Munsterberg, Hugo. Chinese bronzes of the t'ang-period. **AA** 11.1/2 (1948) 27-45.

Munsterberg, Hugo. **Chinese buddhist bronzes.** Rutland, vt (1967) 192 p, illus.

Munsterberg, Hugo. Chinese buddhist bronzes of the kamakura museum. **AA** 19 (1956) 101-110.

Murdoch, W. G. B. Buddhist sculpture of china. **American magazine of art** 18 (sept 1927) 461-470.

A Note on two chinese buddhist dedicatory groups. **BMFA** 26 (1928) 57-60.

Pelliot, Paul. Un bronze bouddhique de 518 au musée du louvre. **TP** 24 (1926) 381-382.

Pelliot, Paul. Une statue de maitreya de 705. **TP** 28 (1931) 381-382.

Plumer, James M. China's ancient cave temples. Early buddhist sculpture in the northwest. **CJ** 22 (1935) 52-57, 104-109, illus.

Poor, Robert. Chinese-buddhist sculpture: a figure of kuan-shih-yin. Minneapolis institute of arts, **Bulletin** 58 (1969) 19-28.

Priest, Alan. **Chinese sculpture in the metropolitan museum of art.** N.Y. (1944) 81 p, pl. Photos by Tet Borsig.

Priest, Alan. A collection of buddhist votive tablets. **BMMA** 26 (1931) 209-213.

Priest, Alan. A note on kuan ti. **BMMA** 25 (1930) 271-272, illus.

Priest, Alan. A stone fragment from lung mên. **BMMA** 36 (1941) 114-116.

Priest, Alan. Two buddhist masterpieces of the wei dynasty. **BMMA** 34 (1939) 32-38.

Rao, M. Basava. A buddhist image from china. Maharaja sayajirao univ of baroda, **Journal** 16 (mar 1967) 249-250, illus.

Reitz, S. C. B. A bronze-gilt statue of the wei period. **BMMA** 21 (1926) 236-240.

Reitz, S. C. B. A chinese lacquered lohan statue. **BMMA** 22 (1927) 134-136.

Rhie, Marylin M. Aspects of sui k'ai-huang and t'ang t'ien-pao buddhist images. **E&W** n.s. 17.1/2 (mar-june 1967) 96-114, illus pl.

Rowland, Benjamin. Chinese sculpture of the pilgrimage road. **BFoggMA** 4.2 (mar 1935)

Rowland, Benjamin. Indian images in chinese sculpture. **AA** 10.1 (1947) 5-20.

Rowland, Benjamin. Notes on the dated statues of the northern wei dynasty and the beginning of buddhist sculpture in china. **AB** 19.1 (1937) 92-107.

Salmony, Alfred. **Chinese sculpture: han to sung. The j. klijkamp and e. monroe collections.** N.Y. (1944) 57 p, 28 pl.

Scherman, Lucian. **Frühbuddhistische steinskulpturen in china.** München (1921) 11 p mit abb.

Seckel, Dietrich. Die beiden dvârapâla-figuren im museum rietburg, zürich. **AA** 25 (1962) 23-44, pl.

Sickman, Laurence. Painting and sculpture. Being pt 1 of Laurence Sickman and Alexander Soper, **The art and architecture of china,** harmondsworth, middlesex, engl (1956) 2nd ed with add (1960) See chap 8-10, 12, 14; notes, gloss, bibliog, index, fig, pl.

Sirén, Osvald. **Chinese sculpture from the fifth to the fourteenth centuries.** London (1925) 4 vol. French ed paris (1925)

Sirén, Osvald. Chinese sculpture of the sung, liao, and chin dynasties. **BMFEA** 14 (1942) 45-64.

Sirén, Osvald. Chinese sculpture of the transition period. **BMFEA** 12 (1940)

Sirén, Osvald. A chinese temple and its plastic decoration of the 12th century. In **EORL** (1932) t 2, 499-505, pl lvi-lxiv.

Sirén, Osvald. **A history of early chinese art.** Vol 3: **Sculpture.** London (1930) French ed paris and bruxelles (1930)

Sirén, Osvald. Studien zur chinesischen plastik der post-t'ang-zeit. **OZ** n.f. 4 (1927-28) 1-2, 16 taf.

Soper, Alexander. Chinese sculptures. **Apollo** 84 (aug 1966) 103-112, illus. From avery brundage collection.

Soper, Alexander C. Some late chinese bronze images (eighth to fourteenth centuries) in the avery brundage collection, m. h. deyoung museum, san francisco. **AA** 31 (1969) 32-54.

Sprague, R. Most remarkable monument in western china. **PS** 83 (dec 1913) 557-566. Great buddha at yung hsien, kiating, ssuchuan.

The Statue of a bodhisattva from yün-kang. **BMMA** 17 (1922) 252-255.

Stone carvings at ta-tsu. Peking (1958) 228 p, 205 pl.

Sudzuki, Osamu. Chinese stone lions in tenri museum. **TJR** 7 (dec 1965) 8-24, illus.

Swann, Peter C. **Chinese monumental art.** N.Y. (1963) French ed (1963) 276 p, 157 pl, maps, fig, bibliog, index. Photos by Claude Arthaud and François Hébert-Stevens.

Tani, Nobukazu. On the stone images of buddha from the pao-ch'ing-ssu temple. **Kokka** 499 and 501 (jun and aug 1932) 161-164, 239-245, pl.

Tizac, H. d'Ardenne de. **La sculpture chinoise.** Paris (1931) 49 p, 64 pl.

Tokiwa, D. Buddhist monuments in china. **PIAJ** 2 (1926) 93-95.

Tomita, Kojirō. The chinese bronze buddhist group of a.d. 593 and its original arrangement. **BMFA** 43 (june 1945) 14-19, 5 illus.

Tomita, Kojirō. The tuan fang altarpiece and the accessories dated a.d. 523. **BM** 87 (1945) 160-164.

Tomita, Kojirō. Two chinese sculptures from lung-mên. **BMFA** 35 (1937) 2-4.

Trubner, H. A bodhisattva from yün-kang. **AQ** 11 (1948) 93-105.

Trubner, H. Three important buddhist images of the t'ang dynasty. **AA** 20.2/3 (1957) 102-110.

Vogel, J. Ph. Études de sculpture bouddhique. **BEFEO** 8 (1908) 487-500, illus.

Warner, Langdon. An introduction to the bronze statuettes of the far east. **Parnassus** 9.1 (1937) 18-20.

Wegner, M. Eine chinesische maitreya-gruppe vom jahre 529. **OZ** 15 (1929) 1-4.

Welch, William. Notes on some bronze buddhas from pekin. **Transactions and proceedings of the new zealand institute** 37 (1905) 208-211.

Willetts, William. **Chinese art.** Harmondsworth, middlesex, engl (1958) See vol 1, chap 5, Sculpture, 293-391 and pl.

Willetts, William. **Foundations of chinese art from neolithic pottery to modern architecture.** London (1965) See chap 5, Sculpture: six dynasties and early t'ang, 173-228, incl pl 119-151.

Yetts, W. P. **The george eumorfopoulos collection: Catalogue . . .** vol 3: **Buddhist sculpture.** London (1929)

G. STELAE

Böttger, Walter. Weitere buddhistische votivstelen aus dem alten china im besitz der museum für völkerkunde zu leipzig. **JSMVL** 25 (1968) 92-102.

Chicago art institute. **A chinese buddhist stele of the wei dynasty in the collection of the art institute of chicago.** Chicago (1927) 5 p, pl.

Fernald, Helen. An early chinese sculptured stela of 575 a.d. **EArt** 3 (1931) 73-111.

Gatling, E. I. A dated buddhist stele of 461 a.d. and its connections with yün kang and kansu province. **AA** 20 (1957) 241-250.

Havret, Henri. **T'ien-tchou 'seigneur du ciel.' À propos d'une stèle bouddhique de tch'eng-tou.** Shanghai (1901) 30 p, (Variétés sinologiques no 19) Same title in **Études** 89 (1901) 398-409, 546-553.

Kuntze, Hertha. Eine votif-stele aus dem jahre 538. **Tribus** 11 (1962) 85-87, illus.

Mather, Richard B. Wang chin's 'dhuta temple stele inscriptions' as an example of buddhist parallel prose. **JAOS** 83 (1963) 338-359.

Pal, Pratapaditya. Notes on a so-called t'ang dynasty votive tablet. **AAA** 20 (1966-67) 71-75.

Peat, Wilbur D. A chinese buddhist stele. **Bulletin of the john herron institute,** 39 (oct 1952) 31-34.

Roberts, Laurance P. A stele of the north wei dynasty. **Parnassus** 7.2 (1935) 13-15.

Soper, Alexander C. Two stelae and a pagoda on the central peak, mt. sung. **ACASA** 16 (1962) 41-48.

H. PAINTING (INCLUDING WOODCUTS AND FRESCOES)

Andrews, F. H. **Wall paintings from ancient shrines in central asia recovered by sir aurel stein.** Oxford univ (1948) xxiv + 128 p, illus, folding map, portfolio of 32 pl.

Awakawa, Yasuichi. **Zen painting.** Tsl fr jap John Bester. Tokyo (1970) 184 p, 139 illus. German tsl Dorothea Javorsky: **Die malerei des zen-buddhismus. Pinselstriche des unendlichen,** münchen (1970) 184 p.

Bachhofer, Ludwig. 'Maitreya in ketumati' by chu hao-ku. In **India antiqua** (1947) 1-7, pl.

Boston museum of fine arts. Dept of asiatic art. **Catalogue of a special exhibition of ancient chinese buddhist paintings, etc.** Boston (1894) 37 p. Intro Ernest Fenollosa.

Brasch, K. **Zenga (zen-malerei)** Tokyo (1961) 192 s, 108 taf.

Chapin, Helen. A long roll of buddhist images. **JISOA** 6 (1938) 26-67. See further same title as revised by Alexander C. Soper, with his Foreword and excursus on the text of the nan chao t'u chuan, in **AA** 32 (1970) 5-41 and 33 (1971) 75-142, 157-199, 259-306; sep publ ascona (1971) 142 p text, 58 pl-pages.

Chapin, Helen B. Three early portraits of bodhidharma. **ACASA** 1 (1945-46) 66-98.

Ch'en,Jen-dao. **The three patriarchs of the southern school in chinese painting.** Hong kong (1955) 8 p.

Cohn, W. Amida-bilder in der ostasiatischen kunstsammlung. **Berliner museum** 54 (1933) 75-80.

Cohn, W. Ein chinesisches kuanyin-bild. **Berliner museum** 49 (1928) 70-74.

Coq, Albert von le. Peintures chinoises authentiques de l'époque t'ang provenant du turkestan chinois. **RAA** 5 (1928) 1-5, illus.

Dietz, E. Sino-mongolian temple painting and its influence on persian illumination. **Ars islamica** 1 (1934) 160-170.

Eastman, A. C. A chinese fresco of kuan yin. **BDetIA** 9 (apr 1928) 81-83.

Ecke, G. Concerning ch'an in painting. **ArtsAs** 3 (1956) 296-306, illus.

Fernald, Helen E. Another fresco from moon hill monastery (honan) **MJ** 19 (1928) 109-129.

Fernald, Helen E. Chinese frescoes of the t'ang dynasty in the [toronto] museum (from a honan monastery: moon hill) **MJ** 17 (1926) 229-244.

Fernald, Helen E. Two sections of a chinese fresco newly acquired, belonging to the great kuan yin wall. **MJ** 20 (june 1929) 119-129.

Fong, Wen. **The lohans and a bridge to heaven.** Freer gallery. **Occasional papers** 3.1 (1958) xii + 64 p, illus.

Franke, Herbert. Zur biographie des pa-ta shan-jen. In **Asiatica** (1954) 119-130.

Giles, Lionel. An illustrated buddhist sutra. **BMQ** 11 (1936) 29.

Grimm, Martin (ed) **Das leben buddhas: ein chinesisches holzschnitt fragment.** Frankfurt-ammain (1968) 58 p. Re a chin col woodcut collection of the life of buddha, d 1793.

Hadl, Richard. Langdon warner's: Buddhist wall-paintings. **AA** 9 (1946) 160-164.

Hummel, Siegbert. Guan-yin in der unterwelt. **Sinologica** 2 (1950) 291-293. Description of a scroll.

Hummel, Siegbert. Vom wesen der chinesischen tuschmalereien aus des sung-zeit. **JSMVL** 11 (1953) 12-22, 5 fig.

Hummel, S. Zur frage der aufstellung buddhistischer bildwerke zentral- und ostasiens. **JSMVL** 10 (1926-51 sic) 50-57.

Jenyns, Soame. **A background to chinese painting.** London (1935) See chap 2, The influence of religion, 35-88.

Kelley, Charles F. A chinese buddhist fresco. **BAIC** 25 (nov 1931) 110-111.

Lalou, M. Trois aspects de la peinture bouddhique. **AIPHO** 3 (1935) 245-261.

Laufer, Berthold. Zum bildnis des pilgers hsüan tsang. **Globus** 88 (1905) 257-258.

Lessing, Ferdinand. The eighteen worthies crossing the sea. Stockholm [**reports of the sino-swedish expedition,** viii. **ethnography 6]** (1954) 109-128, 6 pl.

Loehr, Max. **Chinese landscape woodcuts from an imperial commentary to the tenth-century printed edition of the buddhist canon.** Cambridge, mass. (1968) 114 p, notes, chin characters, bibliog, index, 41 pl.

March, Benjamin. A tun-huang buddhist painting. **BDetIA** 10 (may 1929) 109-111.

Matsumoto, Yeiichi. On some amulet pictures from tun-huang. **Kokka** 482 (1931) 3-6; 488 (1931) 249-254, illus.

Nagahiro, T. On wei-ch'ih i-sêng – a painter of the early t'ang dynasty. **OA** n.s. 1 (1955) 70-74.

Pelliot, Paul. Les déplacements de fresques sous les t'ang et le song. **RAA** 8 (1934) 201-228.

Pelliot, Paul. Les fresques de touen-houang et les fresques de m. eumorfopolous. **RAA** 5 (1928) 143-163, 193-214, illus.

Petrucci, Raphaël. Les peintures bouddhiques de touen-houang (mission stein) **AMG** (1916) 115-150, illus.

Pommeranz-Liedtke, Gerhard (hrsg) **Kuan-hsiu: Die sechzehn lohans; eine berühmte bildnisreihe der chinesisch-buddhistischen kunst.** Leipzig (1961) 51 p (chiefly illus)

Rousselle, E. Buddhistische studien. Die typischen bildwerke des buddhistischen tempels in china. **Sinica** 7 (1932) 62-71, 106-116; 8 (1933) 62-77; 9 (1934) 203-217; 10 (1935) 120-165. Publ sep as: **Von sinn der buddhistischen bildwerke in china,** darmstadt (1958)

Schnitzer, Joseph. Chinesisch-buddhistische höllenbilder. **Wissen und leben** 2 (1909) 379-384.

Seckel, D. Grundzüge der buddhistischen malerei. **MDGNVO** 36,teil c (1945) 1-115.

Seckel, Dietrich. Mu-hsi: sechs kaki-fruchte; interpretation eines zen-bildes. **NachrDGNVO** no 77 (1955) 44-55, pl.

Sickman, Laurence. Painting and sculpture. Being pt 1 of Laurence Sickman and Alexander Soper, **The art and architecture of china,** harmondsworth, middlesex, engl (1956) 2nd ed with add (1960) See esp chap 13, 20-21; notes, gloss, bibliog, index, fig, pl.

Sickman, Laurence. Wall paintings of the yuan period in kuang-shêng-ssû, shansi. **RAA** 11 (1937) 53-67.

Sirén, Osvald. Three chinese buddhist paintings. **Parnassus** 9.3 (1937) 25-28.

Soper, Alexander C. Early buddhist attitudes toward the art of painting. **AB** 32.2 (1950) 147-155.

Stein, Marc Aurel. Specimens from a collection of ancient buddhist pictures and embroideries discovered at tun-huang. **Journal of indian art and industries** n.s. 15 (1912) 60-66, 4 pl.

Tomita, Kojirō. Two chinese paintings depicting the infant buddha and mahāprajapati. **BMFA** 42 (feb 1944) 13-20, 7 illus.

Tomita, Kojirō. Two more dated buddhist paintings from tun-huang. **BMFA** 26 (1928) 11.

Waley, Arthur. Chinese temple paintings. **BM** 41 (1922) 228-231. Paintings in ch'ang-an and lo-yang temples mentioned and described in chang yen-yuan's records of painting in successive ages (a.d. 847)

White, William Charles. **Chinese temple frescoes. A study of three wall-paintings of the thirteenth century.** Univ toronto (1940) xvii + 230 p, pl, illus.

White, William Charles. Chinese temple frescoes. Number one. Constituting **BROMA** no 12 (july 1937) 32 p, illus. Included in author's book, above, chap 12.

Yetts, W. P. Some buddhist frescoes from china. **BM** 51 (1927) 121-128.

I. HISTORICAL EMPHASIS

Davidson, J. LeRoy. Buddhist paradise cults in sixth century china. **JISOA** 17 (1949) 112-124.

Davidson, J. LeRoy. **The lotus sutra in chinese art. A study in buddhist art to the year 1000.** Yale univ (1954) 105 p, bibliog, 40 pl.

Davidson, J. LeRoy. Traces of buddhist evangelism in early chinese art. **AA** 11.4 (1948) 251-265, illus.

Coq, A.von le. **Die buddhistische spätantike in mittelasien.** Berlin (1922-33) 7 vol.

Ghose, Hemendra Prasad. Indian art in the far east. **CalR** (oct 1903) 287-313.

Liang, Ssu-ch'eng. China's oldest wooden structure. **Asia** 41 (july 1941) 384-387, illus. Re t'ang temple on wu-t'ai shan.

Lo, Hsiang-lin. Sino-indian relations over the chiao-kwang route and new discoveries on buddhism and its art in the kwangtung-kwangsi areas in the tang dynasty. **CC** 1.3 (1958) 181-203.

Soper, Alexander C. South chinese influence on the buddhist art of the six dynasties period. **BMFEA** 32 (1960) 47-112, 18 pl.

Waley, Arthur. **Zen buddhism and its relation to art.** London (1922) 31 p.

With, K. Suiko. Über den beginn der buddhistischen kunst in ostasien. **Zeitschrift für buddhismus und verwandte gebiete** 4 (1922) 190-196.

J. MISCELLANEOUS

A Chinese priest of the t'ang dynasty. **EB** 10 (1922) 23-24. Pottery grave figure.

Coomaraswamy, Ananda K. and F. S. Kershaw A chinese buddhist water vessel and its indian prototype. **AA** 3 (1928) 122-141.

Hobson, R. L. Two pottery lokapalas. **BMQ** 7 (1933) 83. T'ang grave figures.

Kopf des mönchs ki-tsi besser bekannt unter dem namen pu-tai. **Sinologica** 8.1 (1964) 10, pl. Bronze.

A Large pottery lohan of the t'ang period. **BMMA** 16 (1921) 15-16, 120.

Lerner, Martin. A seventh-century chinese buddhist ivory. **BCMA** 55 (nov 1968) 294-302, illus.

Munsterberg, Hugo. A buddhist reliquary in the musée guimet. **OA** 12 (1966) 231-233, illus.

Polonyi, P. Chinese sutra covers in the collection of the ferenc hopp museum of eastern asiatic arts in budapest. **AO** 23.1 (1970) 85-106.

Pope, John. A chinese buddhist pewter with a ming date. **ACASA** 16 (1962) 88-91, illus.

Sarre, F. Eine chinesische pilgerflasche der t'angzeit. **Pantheon** 14 (1934) 273-276.

Simmons, P. An eighteenth century priest robe. **BMMA** 29 (1934) 7-8.

Soper, Alexander C. A buddhist travelling shrine in an international style. **E&W** 15 (1965) 211-225, pl.

Turner, Gerald. A magic mirror of buddhist significance. **OA** 12 (1966) 94-98, illus.

Wolf, Marion. The lohans from i-chou. **OA** n.s. 15.1 (1969) 51-57, illus.

14. CAVES AND MOUNTAINS

A. GENERAL

Akiyama, Terukazu and Matsubara Saburo. **Arts of china. Buddhist cave temples; new researches.** Tsl fr jap Alexander C. Soper. Tokyo and palo alto, calif.(1969) 248 p, chron, bibliog, map, col and bl-&-wh pl.

Brankston, A. D. Buddhist cave temples from china to ellora. **AR** 34 (1938) 497-509.

Doré, Henri. Le grand pèlerinage bouddhique de lang-chan et les cinq montagnes de tung-tcheou. **NCR** 1 (1919) 41-56, 120-144, 282-298, 457-479, 588-603; 2 (1920) 44-68, pl.

Klee, Th. Die plastik in den höhlen von yün-kang, lung-mên, und kung-hsien. **OZ** 7 (1918) 31-56.

Soper, Alexander C. Imperial cave-chapels of the northern dynasties. **AA** 28 (1966) 241-270, illus, fig.

Swann, Peter C. **Chinese monumental art.** N.Y. (1963) french ed (1963) 276 p, 15 maps and fig, bibliog, index, 157 pl. Photos Claude Arthaud and François Hébert-Stevens.

Tokiwa, Daijo and Sekino Tadashi. **Buddhist monuments in china.** Tokyo (1926-28) 6 vol text; 6 vol pl.

B. YÜN-KANG

Adam, M. Les grottes de yün kang. **La chine** 66 (1924) 350-364.

Boode, P. A visit to the yün kang caves. **TOCS** (1937-38) 55-62.

Chang, Y. H. (photog) The yunkang caves. **EH** 5.4 (1966) 8 p photos betw 12-21.

Cox, Leonard B. **The buddhist cave temples of yün-kang and lung-mên.** Australian national univ (1957) 14 p, 5 pl (george e. morrison lecture in anthropology no 18)

Crane, L. Buddhist treasures in the shansi mountains. **Asia** 31 (1931) 434-438.

Drake, F. S. Yün-kang: the buddhist caves of the fifth century a.d. in north china . . . report of the archaeological survey . . . of the tōhō bunka kenkyūsho (rev art) **JOS** 2 (1955) 324-337.

Eigner, J. The grandeur of the yun kang caves. **CJ** 25 (1936) 315-317.

Gabain, Annemarie v. Die fliegenden genien von yün-kang, verkörperung geistiger freude. **NachrDGNVO** no 97 (june 1965) 7-12, pl.

Geelmuyden, N. The yun-kan [sic] caves, one of buddhism's earliest manifestations in china. **Journal of the siam society** 46.1 (1958) 37-45.

Giles, W. R. Cave temples in china. Exquisite sculpture revealed in mountain caves. **Asia** 18 (mar 1918) 234-236, illus.

Les grottes de yün-kang. l'Art des wei. Pékin (192?) 6 p, pl.

Hansford, S. Howard. The stone buddhas of yünkang. **GM** 14 (jan 1942) 134-141, illus, map.

Kaul, T. N. The caves of yun kang. **United asia** 5 (1953) 313-314.

King, Gordon. **The buddhist cave temples at yünkang.** Peiping (1935) 12 p, illus.

Klee, Th. Die plastik in den höhlen von yün-kang, lung-mên und kung-hsien. **OZ** 7 (1918-19) 31-36.

Krueger, H. E. The caves at tatung. **CJ** 31 (1939) 91-94.

Mizuno, Seiichi. Archaeological survey of the yün-kang grottoes. **ACASA** 4 (1950) 39-60.

Mizuno, Seiichi and Nagahiro Toshio. **Yün-kang: the buddhist cave-temples of the fifth century a.d. in north china. Detailed report of the archaeological survey carried out by the mission of the tōhōbunka kenkyūsho, 1938-45.** Kyoto (1951-56) 16 vol text, 16 vol pl, engl and jap text.

Mullikan, Mary Augusta. **Buddhist sculptures at the yun kang caves. Text and illustrations by mary augusta mullikan, with additional illustrations by anna h. hotchkiss.** Peiping (1935) 66 p, illus. See same title in **Studio** 108 (1934) 65-70.

Mullikan, Mary Augusta. China's great wall of sculpture. Man-hewn caves and countless images form a colossal art wonder of early buddhism. **NGM** 73 (mar 1938) 313-348, illus.

Musée cernuschi. **Yun-kang et nara. Documents photographiques sur l'art bouddhique.** Paris (1952) 34 p, illus.

Read, B. E. Yun kan [sic]; buddhist temple-caves. **Orient** 1.8 (mar 1951) 19-21.

Shinkai, Taketarō and Nakagawa Tadayori. **Rock-carvings from the yun-kang caves, selected by shinkai taketarō and nakagawa takayori.** Photos Yamamoto Akira and Kishi Masakatsu. Tokyo (1921) 16 p, 200 pl. Intro in jap and engl.

Yashiro, Yukio. The present state of the yünkang caves. **BEA** no 15 (1941) 3-12.

C. LUNG-MEN

Chavannes, Édouard. Le défilé de long-men dans la province de ho-nan. **JA** 9e sér, 20 (1902) 133-158, 6 fig.

Cox, Leonard B. **The buddhist cave temples of yün-kang and lung-mên.** Australian national univ (1957) 14 p, 5 pl (george e. morrison lecture in anthropology no 18)

Fu Tien-chou. The rock sculptures of lungmen. **CL** 5 (may 1962) 65-71.

Giles, W. R. Cave temples in china. Exquisite sculpture revealed in mountain caverns. **Asia** 18 (mar 1918) 234-236, ill.

Klee, Th. Die plastik in den höhlen von yün-kang, lung-mên und kung-hsien. **OZ** 7 (1918-19) 31-36.

Mizuno, S. and T. Nagahiro. **A study of the buddhist cave-temples at lung-mên, honan.** Tokyo (1941) 482 p, jap and engl. App 1: Z. Tsukamoto's Buddhism under the northern wei dynasty.

Spruyt, A. Reminiscences of the édouard chavannes expedition. Evidences of early buddhism in china. The sacred mountain of lung-men. **Indian art and letters** 5.2 (1931) 103-110, 4 pl.

Spruyt, A. Souvenir d'un voyage à la montagne sacrée de long men. **MCB** 1 (1932) 241-262, 18 photos, 1 carte.

D. T'IEN-LUNG SHAN

Boerschmann, E. Die kultstätte des t'ien lung shan. **AA** 1 (1925) 262-279.

Lartigue, J. Le sanctuaire bouddhique de t'ien-long-chan. **RAA** 1 (1924) 3-9.

Vanderstappen, Harry and Marylin Rhie. The sculpture of t'ien lung shan: reconstruction and dating. **AA** 27 (1964-65) 189-220, 81 pl.

E. O-MEI SHAN

Bonin, Charles-Eudes. Le mont omei. **Bulletin de géographie historique et descriptive** 1 (1899) 64-75.

Cammann, Schuyler. Temples in the clouds, mount omei. **Travel** 78 (1942) 4-10.

Hart, Virgil C. **Western china. A journey to the great buddhist centre of mount omei.** Boston (1888) 306 p.

Johnston, R. F. **From peking to mandalay.** N.Y. (1908) See chap 6, Mount omei and chinese buddhism, 54-81; chap 7, Mount omei, 82-111.

Little, Archibald J. **Mount omi and beyond. A record of travel on the thibetan border.** London (1901) xiv + 272 p, map. Same title in **NCH** (26 may 1893) 76-78, 809, 881, 926, 964 (5 jan 1894) 19-20.

Madrolle, Claudius. **Le mont omei, lieu de pèlerinage bouddhique.** Paris (1914) 16 p, cartes.

Migot, A. Les temples bouddhiques de mont o-mei (o-mei chan) **ArtsAs** 4 (1957) 20-34, 131-142.

Phelps, Dryden L. (tsl) **Omei illustrated guide book. A new edition of the omei illustrated guide book, by huang shou-fu and t'an chung-yo, a.d. 1887-1891. Pictures redrawn from the original plates by yü tzu-tan.** Chengtu (1936) 353 p, text in chin and engl, illus.

Phelps, Dryden L. A sung dynasty document of mount omei. **JWCBorderResS** 11 (1939) 66-77. Intro, with 2 photos, and tsl of travel account by fan ch'en of sung dynasty.

Shields, E. T. Omei shan: the sacred mountain of west china. **JNCBRAS** 44 (1913) 100-109.

F. WU-T'AI SHAN

David-Neel, A. The manjushri of wu t'ai shan. **JWCBorderResS** ser A.14 (1942) 25-30.

Irving, Christopher. Wu-t'ai-shan and the dalai lama. **NCR** 1 (may 1919) 151-163.

Lamotte, Étienne. Mañjuśrī. **TP** 48 (1960) 54-96. On mañjuśrī and wu-t'ai shan.

Limpricht, W. Eine durchwanderung der wutaischan-ketten. **MSOS** 16 (1913) 141-176, fig.

Rockhill, William W. A pilgrimage to the great buddhist sanctuary of north china [wu-t'ai shan] **Atlantic monthly** 75 (june 1895) 758-769.

Savage-Landor, A. Henry. A journey to the sacred mountain of siao-outai-shan, in china. **Fortnightly review** (sept 1894) 393-409. Repr in **Eclectic magazine** 123 (july-dec 1894) also repr in **Littel's living age** 203 (oct-dec 1894)

Swallow, R. W. A journey to wu tai shan, one of the meccas of buddhism. **JMGS** (1903) 173-182.

Verdeille, Maurice (tsl) Le monastère de la montagne 'ou-tai' en révolution. Extrait par l'éditeur des 'siao-siao chuou' du livre intitulé 'liang-shan-po.' **BSEIS** 70 (1919) 21-37, 2 pl.

G. P'U-T'O SHAN

Arène, Jules. Excursion a l'île sacré de pou tou. **l'Explorateur** no 20.1 (1875)

Ein ausflug nach der heiligen insel putu. **Das ausland** 31 (1876)

Bock, Carl. l'Île sacrée de pouto (archipel de tchou-san ou chusan, chine) **Comptes rendus société géographie** (1891) 483-485.

Boerschmann, Ernst. **Die baukunst und religiöse kultur der chinesen; vol 1: P'u t'o shan.** Berlin (1911) 203 p.

Crane, L. Honoring the goddess of mercy; pootoo, the island sanctuary of kuan yin. **Travel** 56 (mar) 1931) 22-26.

Edkins, Joseph. The monasteries at pu-to. **NCH** 345 (7 mar 1856)

Fitch, Robert F. **Pootoo itineraries.** Shanghai (1929) 90 p.

Fitch, Robert F. Puto, the enchanted island. **NGM** 89 (mar 1946) 373-384, illus.

Franke, O. Die heilige insel pu-to. **Globus** 63 (1893) 117-122.

Fryer, J. Gleanings about poo-too. **NCH** (8 aug 1868)

Gundry, R. S. **Sketches of excursions to chusan, poo-too . . . Nanking and kioto.** Shanghai (1876) ix + 116 p.

Gützlaff, C. ['Philosinensis'] Remarks on buddhism; together with brief notices of the island of poo-to, and of the numerous priests who inhabit it. **ChRep** 2 (1833-34) 214 et seq.

H. [a letter about p'u-t'o shan] **NCH** 734 (1864)

Inveen, Emma. Pootoo: china's sacred island (ii) **EA** 3 (1904) 357-362.

Krieger. Putu, chinas heilige insel. **Koloniale rundschau** 1 (1909) 762-770.

Kupfer, Carl F. Pootoo: china's sacred island (i) **EA** 3 (1904) 264-281.

Mizande, François. Dans l'archipel des chu-san: pu-tu, l'île des pagodes ou la terre de bouddha. **TM** 18 (1912) 265-268, 273-276, carte et illus.

Natz, Marie. Eine pilgerfahrt nach pu-to. **OstL** vol 28 no 23 (1914) 21-23.

Peri, N. and H. Maspero. Le monastère de la kouan-yin qui ne veut pas s'en aller [in p'u-t'o shan] **BEFEO** 9 (1909) 797-807.

Rondot, Natalis. **Excursion a l'île de pou-tou (province de tché-kiang)** 7 et 8 octobre, **1845.** Reims (1846) 40 p, 2 lith.

Stanley, Arthur. Putoshan. A draught at the well-springs of chinese buddhist art. **JNCBRAS** 46 (1915) 1-18, illus.

H. TUN-HUANG

Bonin, Charles-Eudes. Les grottes de mille bouddhas. **CRAIBL** pt 1 (mar-avr 1901) 209-217.

Chang, Shu-hung. The art treasures of tunhuang. **China pictorial** no 1 (jan 1956) 19-21, illus.

Chavannes, Édouard. Présentation du touen-houang che che yi chou. **CRAIBL** (juin 1910) 245-246.

Chen Tsu-lung. **La vie et les oeuvres de wou-tchen (816-895). Contribution à l'histoire culturelle de touen-houang.** Paris (1966) 165 p, bibliog, indexes, map.

Chêng, Tê-k'un. **Tun-huang studies in china.** Chengtu (1947) 14 p.

Chou, Shao-miao and Wu Mi-feng (copyists) **Designs from the tunhuang caves.** Intro Wang Hsun. Peking (1956) 20 leaves in portfolio.

Demiéville, Paul. Récente travaux sur touen-houang. Aperçu bibliographique et notes critiques. **TP** 56.1/3 (1970) 1-94.

Fontein, Jan and Money L. Hickman. **Zen painting and calligraphy.** Boston (1970) liv + 173 p, illus.

Fourcade, François. **Le peinture murale de touenhouang.** Paris (1962) 134 p, illus, maps, plans, table.

Gray, Basil. **Buddhist cave paintings at tun-huang.** Photos J. B. Vincent; preface Arthur Waley. Univ chicago (1959) 83 p, 70 pl, notes on pl, bibliog.

Hadl, R. Langdon warner's buddhist wall paintings. **AA** 9 (1946) 160-164.

Hejzlar, Josef. Recollections of tunhuang. **NO** 5 (feb 1966) 15-16, 4 p illus.

Lao, Kan. The art of tunhuang. Tsl fr chin Ho Chien. **CC** 1 (oct 1957) 47-74.

March, Benjamin. A tun-huang buddhist painting. **BDetIA** 10 (may 1929) 109-111.

Matsumoto, Yeiichi. On some amulet pictures from tun-huang. **Kokka** 482 (1931) 3-6; 488 (1931) 249-254, illus.

Mizuno, S. **Wall paintings of tun-huang.** Tokyo (1958)

Musée Cernuschi. **Relevés de touen-houang et peintures anciennes de la collection tchang ta-ts'ien.** Paris (1956) 25 p, 29 pl.

Pelliot, Paul. Arthur waley: A catalogue of paintings recovered from tun-huang (etc) (rev art) **TP** 28 (1931) 383-413.

Pelliot, Paul. Une bibliothèque médiévale retrouvé au kan-sou. **BEFEO** 8 (1908) 501-529.

Pelliot, Paul. Les fresques de touen-houang et les fresques de m. eumorfopoulos. **RAA** 5 (1928) 143-163, 193-214, illus.

Pelliot, Paul. Les grottes des mille bouddhas. **JRAS** (1914) 421-426.

Pelliot, Paul. **Mission pelliot en asie centrale: les grottes de touen houang.** Paris (1914-24) 6 vol pl (no text)

Petrucci, R. Les peintures bouddhiques de touen-houang (mission stein) **AMG** (1916) 115-140, illus.

Plumer, James M. Tun huang: vision of buddhist glory as seen in irene vincent's photographs. **AQ** 14 (spring 1951) 56-57, illus.

Riboud, Mme Krishna and Gabriel Vial, avec le concours de Mlle. M. Hallade. **Tissus de touen-houang. Conservés au musée guimet et à la bibliothèque nationale.** Paris (1970) 443 p, 103 pl, charts (Mission paul pelliot no 13)

Shor, Franc and Jean. The caves of the thousand buddhas. **NGM** 99 (mar 1951) 383-415, illus.

Silva-Vigrier, Anil de. **Chinese landscape painting in the caves of tun-huang.** London (1967) 240 p, maps, tables, illus.

Soper, Alexander C. Representations of famous images at tun-huang. **AA** 27 (1965) 349-364, pl.

Stein, Aurel. **Serindia: detailed report of explorations in central asia and westernmost china.** Oxford univ (1921) 5 vol, pl.

Stein, Marc Aurel. Specimens from a collection of ancient buddhist pictures and embroideries discovered at tun-huang. **Journal of indian art and industries** n.s. 15 (1912) 60-66, 4 pl.

Stein, Aurel. **The thousand buddhas: ancient buddhist paintings from the cave-temples of tun-huang on the western frontier of china.** London (1921) 3 vol, pl.

Su, Ying-hui. The buddhist art of wei, tsin, and southern and northern dynasties at tunhuang in china. **CC** 11.2 (june 1970) 55-61.

Su, Ying-hui. **A collection of articles on tunhuang.** Taipei (1969) 80 p. Most of art in chin; 3 art in engl and abstracts of the others.

Su, Ying-hui. On the tunhuang science. **West and East** 9.6 (june 1964) 7-10; 9.7 (july 1964) 5-7, illus.

Su, Ying-hui. The tun huang stone cave and the thousand buddha caves. **CC** 5.2 (oct 1963) 32-46, illus.

Tomita, Kojirō. A dated buddhist painting from tun-huang. **BMFA** 25 (1927)

Tomita, Kojirō. Two more dated buddhist paintings from tun-huang. **BMFA** 26 (1928) 11.

Tunhuang, Kansu, National Art Institute. The sacred grottoes of tunhuang. **China magazine** 19 (jan 1949) 28-42, illus.

Vincent, Irene Vongehr. **The sacred oasis. Caves of the thousand buddhas, tun huang.** London (1953) 114 p, map, bibliog, index, photos.

Waite, Arthur E. The shrine of a thousand buddhas. **Occult review** 15 (1912) 195-203.

Waley, Arthur. **A catalogue of paintings recovered from tun-huang by sir aurel stein, k.c.i.e., preserved in the british museum and in the museum of central asian antiquities, delhi.** London (1931) lii + 328 p, diagr. Rev Paul Pelliot, q.v. above.

Warner, Langdon. **Buddhist wall-paintings. A study of a ninth-century grotto at wan fo hsia.** Harvard univ (1938) xv + 33 p, map, pl.

Warner, Langdon. **The long old road in china. Descriptive of a journey into the far west of china to discover and bring back famous buddhist frescoes and statuary.** N.Y. (1926) 176 p, illus.

Wright, Harrison K. The thousand buddhas of the tun-huang caves. **NCR** 4 (oct 1922) 401-407.

I. MISCELLANEOUS

Chambeau, Gabriel. Une visite aux monastères bouddhiques de kieou-hoa-chan. **Études** 130 (20 mars 1912) 785-798; 131 (5 avr 1912) 34-52.

Doré, H. Le grand pèlerinage bouddhique de lang-chan et les cinq montagnes de tong-tcheou. **NCR** 1.1 (mar 1919) 41-56; 1.2 (may 1919) 120-144; 1.3 (july 1919) 282-298; 1.5 (oct 1919) 457-479; 1.6 (dec 1919) 580-603; 2.1 (feb 1920) 44-46, pl.

Edwards, R. The cave reliefs of ma hao (szechuan) **AA** 17 (1954) 5-28, 103-129.

Imbault-Huart, Camille. Le pèlerinage de la montagne du pic mystérieux près de péking. **JA** 8e sér, 5 (jan 1885) 62-71. Re miaô-foung-chan and temple de fées.

Jayne, H. H. F. The buddhist caves of the ching ho valley. **EArt** 1 (1928-29) 157-173, 243-261, illus.

King, Gordon. Wondrous cave temples of wu chou shan. **Illustrated london news** (10 oct 1931) 553.

Klee, Th. Die plastik in den höhlen von yün-kang, lung-mên und kung-hsien. **OZ** 7 (1918-19) 31-36.

Mather, Richard. The mystical ascent of the t'ien-t'ai mountains: sun cho's yu-t'ien-t'ai-shan fu. **MS** 20 (1961) 226-245.

Meech, S. E. A recent visit to the yün-shui tung [on shang-fang shan, about 140 li southeast of peking] **ChRec** 5 (1874) 339-347.

Mizuno, S. and T. Nagahiro. **The buddhist cave-temples of hsiang t'ang-ssû.** Kyoto (1937) 48 illus, 66 pl.

Mullikan, Mary Augusta. China's ancient cave temples, sui dynasty cliff and cave sculptures in shantung. **CJ** 22 (1935) 304-306.

Plumer, James M. China's ancient cave temples. Early buddhist sculpture in the northwest. **CJ** 22 (1935) 52-57, 104-109, illus.

Soymié, Michel. Le lo-feou chan. Étude de géographie religieuse. **BEFEO** 48.1 (1956) 1-139, 2 app, bibliog, index, map, illus.

Stein, Aurel. **Ruins of desert cathay: personal narrative of explorations in central asia and westernmost china.** London (1912) 2 vol.

Sullivan, Michael. **The cave temples of maichishan.** Photos Dominique Darbois. With an account of the 1958 expedition to maichishan by Anil de Silva. Univ california (1969) 77 p text, 104 p photos [southern kansu]

Tao-chün (pseud for Martin Steinkirk) **Buddha and china: tsi-hia-schan.** Potsdam (1940) 30 p.

Teng, Chien-wu. The cave-temples of chingyang [kansu] **EH** 4.6 (1965) 6-15, 4 p photos.

Wu Tso-jen. Grottoes of maichishan [southern kansu] **E&W** 5 (1954) 210-212. See same title in **CRecon** 3.3 (1954) 25-27.

Wu, Tso-jen. **The rock grottoes of maichishan.** (1954) 161 pl.

15. SPECIFIC DEITIES

Abegg, E. **Der buddha maitreya. MSGFOK** 7 (1945) 7-37.

Aufhauser, Johannes B. Avalokitesvara − kuan yin (kwannon) − maria. **OR** 10.13 (1929) 366-367.

Bischoff, F. A. (tsl) Ārya mahābala-nāma-mahāyānasūtra. Tibétain (mss. de touen-houang) et chinois. Contribution à l'étude des divinités mineurs du bouddhisme tantrique. Paris (1956) 138 p, 4 facs.

Borel, Henri. **Kwan yin. die göttin der gnade.** Tsl fr dutch Alfred Reuss. (1912) 72 p.

Carus, Paul. **Amitabha. A story of buddhist theology.** Chicago (1906) 121 p.

David-Neel, Alexandra. The manjushri of wu t'ai shan. **JWCBorderResS** ser A, 14 (1942) 25-30.

Day, Clarence B. The cult of amitabha. **CJ** 33 (1940) 235-249.

Eitel, E. J. Amita and the paradise of the west. **NQ** 2 (1868) 35-38.

Eitel, E. J. The trinity of the buddhists in china. **NQ** 2 (1868) 115-117.

Erkes, Eduard. Zum problem der weiblichen kuanyin. **AA** 9 (1946) 316-320, illus.

Fuchs, Walter. **Der wille der kwan-yin. Eine chinesische legende.** Zürich and stuttgart (1955) 46 p, pl.

Hummel, Siegbert. Der pfauenbuddha. **Sinologica** 2 (1950) 234-241, pl.

Inglis, J. W. The vows of amida. A comparative study. **JNCBRAS** 48 (1917) 1-11.

Karutz, Richard. **Maria im fernen osten; das problem der kuan yin.** Leipzig (1925) 99 p, illus.

Koerber, Hans Nordewin von. Kuan yin, the buddhist madonna. **Theosophical forum** 19 (1941) 6-16.

Lamotte, Étienne. Mañjuśrī. **TP** 48 (1960) 54-96. On mañjuśrī and wu-t'ai shan.

Laufer, Berthold. Defender of the faith: statue of the god, wei-t'o. **Asia** 34 (may 1934) 290-291. See also Defender of the faith and his miracles, **OC** 46 (oct 1932) 665-667.

Lee, Pi-cheng [Lü Pi-ch'eng] **Kwan yin's saving power; some remarkable examples of response to appeals for aid, made known to kwan yin by his devotees. Collected, translated and edited by lee pi-cheng.** Oxford (1932) 39 p.

Lévi, S. Maitreya le consolateur. In **EORL** (1932) 355-402.

Mallman, Marie Thérèse de. **Étude iconographique sur mañjuśrī.** Paris (1964) 284 p, 16 pl.

Mallman, Marie Thérèse de. **Introduction à l'étude d'avalokiteśvara.** Paris (1948) 384 p, 32 pl.

Mironov, N. D. Buddhist miscellanea. **JRAS** (1927) 241-252. Re the name avalokiteśvara and kuan-yin.

Mus, Paul. Thousand-armed kwannon: a mystery or a problem? **JIBS** 12 (1964) 1-33.

Pelliot, Paul. Le bhaisajyaguru. **BEFEO** 3.1 (1903) 33-37.

Pelliot, Paul. Une statue de maitreya de 705. **TP** 28 (1931) 381-382.

Peri, Noël. Le dieu wei-t'o. **BEFEO** 16.3 (1916) 41-56.

Pohlman, W. J. Translation of a buddhist print descriptive of the one thousand hands, one thousand eyes, the all-prevalent and most merciful to-lo-ni (goddess of mercy) **ChRep** 15 (1846) 351-354.

Poor, Robert. Chinese-buddhist sculpture: a figure of kuan-shih-yin. Minneapolis institute of art, **Bulletin** 58 (1969) 19-28.

Rousselle, E. Der kult der buddhistischen madonna kuan-yin. **NachrDGNVO** 68 (1944) 17-23.

Schlegel, G. Ma-tsu-po . . . or koan-yin with the horsehead . . . **TP** 9.5 (dec 1898) 402-406.

Staël-Holstein, A. von. Avalokita and apalokita. **HJAS** 1 (1936) 350-362.

Suzuki, Beatrice Lane. The bodhisattvas. **EB** 1 (1921) 131-139.

Suzuki, D. T. The kuan-yin cult in china. **EB** 6 (1935) 339-353.

Takakusu, Junjirō. Kwan-yin. In **HERE** 7, p 763-765.

Tucci, G. Buddhist notes. **MCB** 9 (1948-51) 173-220. Re evolution of kuan-yin in art and texts.

Visser, Marinus Willem de. The arhats in china and japan. **OZ** 7.1/2 (1918) 87-102; 9 (1920-22) 116-144. Same title publ sep, berlin (1923) 215 p, pl.

Visser, Marinus Willem de. **The bodhisattva akāśagarbha (kokūzō) in china and japan.** Amsterdam (1931) 47 p.

Visser, Marinus Willem de. The boddhisattva ti tsang (jizo) in china and japan. **OZ** 2 (1913) 179-192, 266-305; 3 (1914) 61-92, 326-327.

Visser, Marinus Willem de. Die pfauenkönig (k'ung-tsioh ming wang, kujaku myō-ō) in china and japan. **OZ** 8 (1919-20) 370-387.

Watters, Thomas. The eighteen lohan of chinese buddhist temples. **JRAS** (apr 1898) 329-347. Same title publ sep, shanghai (1925) 45 p, illus.

Wegner, M. Ikonographie des chinesischen maitreya. **OZ** n.s. 5 (1929) 156-178, 216-229, 252-270.

16. POPULAR BUDDHISM — BUDDHIST STORIES

Allan, C. Wilfrid. Chinese picture tracts. **EA** 5 (1906) 94-98.

Basset, René. Les contes indiens et orientaux dans la littérature chinoise. **Revue des traditions populaires** 27 (sept 1912) 441-448. À propos des **Cinq cents contes** . . . de É. Chavannes, q.v.

Bassett, Beulah E. Lecture on chinese mythology. **JWCBorderResS** 5 (1932) 92-101. On hsi-yu-chi.

Belpaire, B. Un conte chinois d'inspiration bouddhique du IXe siècle a.d. **Muséon** 67 (1954) 373-395.

Chavannes, Édouard (tsl) **Cinq cents contes et apologues extraits du tripiṭaka chinois et traduit en français.** Paris (1910-11) 3 t: 428, 449, 395 p. Repr paris (1962) 3 t.

Chavannes, Édouard (tsl) **Contes et légendes du bouddhisme chinois.** Paris (1921) 220 p, table, illus. Préface et vocabulaire de Sylvain Lévi.

Chavannes, Édouard (tsl) Fables et contes de l'inde extraits du tripiṭaka chinois. **Actes 14eICO Algiers, 1905,** paris (1905) 84-145. Same title publ sep, paris (1905) 63 p.

Chavannes, Édouard. Une version chinoise du conte bouddhique de kalyânamkara et pâpaṃkara. **TP** 15 (oct 1914) 469-500.

Chavannes, Mme Édouard. **Fables chinoises du IIIe au VIIIe siècle de notre ère (d'origine hindoue) traduit par édouard chavannes . . . versifiées par mme. édouard chavannes.** Paris (1921) 95 p. Tiré des **Cinq cents contes** . . .

Chinese tables of merits and errors. **ICG** no 3 (1821) 154-165, 205-206; repr **JIA** n.s. 2 (1858) 210-220.

Eder, M. Buddhistische legenden aus yünnan und kueichou. **FS** 1 (1942) 91-99.

Edkins, Joseph. Paradise of the western heaven. **ChRev** 17 (1888-89) 175-176.

Eitel, E. J. Amita and the paradise of the west. **NQ** 2 (1868) 35-38.

Eitel, E. J. A buddhist purgatory for women. **NQ** 2 (1868) 66-68, 82-85.

Ferguson, J. C. The miraculous pagoda of pa li chuang. **CJ** 9 (1928) 230.

Grube, Wilhelm. Die chinesische volksreligion und ihre beeinflussung durch den buddhismus. **Globus** 63 (1893) 297-303.

Hackmann, Heinrich (tsl) **Laien-buddhismus in china. Das lung shu ching t'u wen des wang jih hsiu, übers.** Gotha and stuttgart (1924)

Hayes, Helen M. **The buddhist pilgrim's progress. From the shi yeu ki, 'the record of the journey to the western paradise,' by wu ch'eng-en.** London (1930) 105 p.

Hrdličková, V. The first translations of buddhist sutras in chinese literature and their place in the development of story telling. **ArchOr** 26.1 (1958) 114-144.

Hulsewé, A. F. P. Sidelights on popular buddhism in china in the fifth century. **Proc. 7th ICHR Amsterdam, 1950,** amsterdam (1951) 139-141.

Julien, Stanislas (tsl) Apologues indiens traduits sur une ancienne version chinoise. **Revue orientale et américaine** 4 (1860) 461-403; 5 (1861) 306-308.

Julien, Stanislas (tsl) **Les avadânas contes et apologues indiennes inconnus jusqu'à ce jour suivis de fables, de poésies et de nouvelles chinoises.** Paris (1859) 3 t: xx + 240, viii + 251, 272 p.

Julien, Stanislas. Fables indiennes, traduites pour la première fois sur une ancienne version chinoise. **Revue orientale et américaine** 1 (1859) 20.

Lee, Shao Chang (tsl) **Popular buddhism in china.** Shanghai (1939) engl text 52 p; chin text 22 p. Contains tsl 10 buddhist poems, 32 proverbs, hsüan chuang's Essence of wisdom sutra (hsin ching), Diamond sutra (chin kang pan-jo po-lo-mi ching)

Leong, Y. K. and L. K. Tao. **Village and town life in china.** London (1915) See The popular aspect of chinese buddhism, 115-155.

Mok, P. R. Tragic mountain. **Asia** 32 (1932) 503-507, 521-523; 37 (1937) 227-230, 240. Story of a monk's life and thought.

Moule, G. E. (tsl) A buddhist sheet-tract, containing an apologue of human life. Translated with notes. **JNCBRAS** n.s. 19 (1884) 94-102.

Odontius, L. (tsl) Zwei buddhistische märchen. **OstL** (1901) 599-601.

The Paradise of fuh. 'An exhortation to worship fuh, and seek to live in the land of joy, situated in the west.' **ICG** no 6 (1818) 194-200.

Pavie, Théodore. Étude sur le sy-yeóu-tchin-tsuen, roman bouddhique chinois. **JA** 5e sér, 9 (1857) 357-392; 10 (1857) 308-374.

Richard, Timothy. **One of the world's literary masterpieces, hsi-yu-chi, a mission to heaven. A great chinese epic and allegory by ch'iu ch'ang ch'un a taoist gamaliel who became a prophet and advisor to the chinese court.** Shanghai (1913) xxxix + 363 + viii p, illus.

Schnitzer, Joseph. Chinesisch-buddhistische höllenbilder. **Wissen und leben** 2 (1909) 379-384.

Selby, T. G. Yan kwo; yuk lik, or the purgatories of popular buddhism. **ChRev** 1 (1872-73) 301-311.

Sokei-an (Sasaki, Shigetsu) **The story of the giant disciples of buddha, ānanda and mahākaśyapa. From the chinese version of the sūtras of buddhism.** N.Y. (1931) 32 p.

Takakusu, Junjirō. Tales of the wise man and the fool, in tibetan and chinese. **JRAS** (1901) 447-460.

Verdeille, Maurice (tsl) Le monastère de la montagne 'ou-tai' en révolution. Extr par l'éditeur des 'siao-siao chuou' . . . du livre intitulé 'liang-shan-po.' **BSEIS** 70 (1919) 21-37, 2 pl.

Waley, Arthur (tsl) **Ballads and stories from tun-huang: an anthology.** London (1960) See 10, The buddhist pieces, 202-215; 11, Mu-lien rescues his mother, 216-235.

Waley, Arthur D. Hymns to kuan-yin. **BSOAS** 1 (1920) 145-146.

Whitaker, K. P. K. Tsaur jyr and the introduction of fannbay into china. **BSOAS** 20 (1957) 585-597.

Wood, C. F. Some studies in the buddhism of szechwan. **JWCBorderResS** 9 (1937) 160-179.

17. BUDDHISM AND CHINESE CULTURE

Bagchi, P. C. Indian influence on chinese thought. In **HPEW** (1952) vol 1, 573-589.

Belpaire, B. Un conte chinois d'inspiration bouddhique du IXe siècle a.d. **Muséon** 67 (1954) 373-395.

Chang, Carsun. Buddhism as a stimulus to neo-confucianism. **OE** 2 (1955) 157-166.

Ch'en, Kenneth K. S. Buddhist-taoist mixtures in the pa-shih-i-hua t'u. **HJAS** 9 (1945-47) 1-12.

Ch'en, Kenneth K. S. Filial piety in chinese buddhism. **HJAS** 28 (1968) 81-97.

Ch'en, Kenneth K. S. Mahayana buddhism and chinese culture. **Asia** 10 (winter 1968) 11-32.

Chi, Hsien-lin. Lieh-tzu and buddhist sutras. **SS** 9.1 (1950) 18-32.

Chou, Hsiang-kuang. Buddhist studies in china and its impact on chinese literature and thought. **CC** 4.4 (mar 1963) 43-59.

DeBary, William T. Buddhism and the chinese tradition. **Diogenes** no 47 (fall 1964) 102-124.

Demiéville, Paul. La pénétration du bouddhisme dans la tradition philosophique chinoise. **CHM** 3.1 (1956) 19-38.

Frodsham, J. D. Hsieh ling-yün's contribution to medieval chinese buddhism. **PIAHA** (1963) 27-55.

Grube, W. Chin. volksreligion u. i. beeinflussung durch d. buddhismus. **Globus** 63 (1893) 297-303.

Hrdličková, V. The first translations of buddhist sūtras in chinese literature and their place in the development of story-telling. **ArchOr** 26 (1958) 114-144.

Hsü, Vivian. Monks and nuns as comic figures in yüan drama. **Dodder** 2 (jan 1970) 10-12.

Hu, Shih. Buddhistic influence on chinese religious life. **CSPSR** 9 (1925) 142-150.

Huard, Pierre. Le bouddhisme et la médecine chinoise. **HM** 8.1 (1958) 5-51, illus.

Huber, E. Termes persans dans l'astrologie bouddhique chinoise. **BEFEO** 6 (1906) 39-43.

Johnston, Reginald F. Han-shan (kanzan) and shih-tê (jittoku) in chinese and japanese literature and art. **TPJS** 34 (1936-37) 133-137.

Lee, Siow Mong. Chinese culture and religion. **Voice of buddhism** 6 (mar 1969) 6-10.

Lessing, Ferdinand D. Bodhisattva confucius. **Oriens** 10.1 (1957) 110-113.

Liebenthal, Walter. The problem of chinese buddhism. **VQB** 18 (1952-53) 233-246.

Liu, Ts'un-yan. **Buddhist and taoist influences on chinese novels.** Vol 1: **The authorship of the fêng shên yen i.** Wiesbaden (1962) viii + 326 p, index, illus.

Lo, Ch'ang-p'ei. Indian influence on the study of chinese phonology. **SIS** 1.3 (1944) 117-124.

Maspero, Henri. Le dialecte de tch'ang-ngan sous les t'ang. **BEFEO** 20 (1920) 1-124. Influence of buddhism on language.

Mather, Richard. The conflict of buddhism with native chinese ideologies. **RofR** 20 (1955-56) 25-37; repr in **CWayRel** (1973) 77-86.

Mather, Richard. The landscape buddhism of the fifth-century poet hsieh ling-yün. **JAS** 18 (nov 1958) 67-79. Same title in **Trans ICfO** 2 (1957) 34-36 (summ)

Müller, F. W. K. Die persischen kalendarsdrücke im chinesischen tripitaka. **SAWW** 155 (1907) 458-465.

Needham, Joseph. Buddhism and chinese science. In Louis Schneider (ed) **Religion, culture and society,** n.y. etc (1964) 353-358. Excerpted fr Needham's **Science and civilization in china,** cambridge univ, vol 2 (1956) 417-422 430-431.

Průšek, Jaroslav. Narrators of buddhist scriptures and religious tales in the sung period. **ArchOr** 10 (1938) 375-389; repr in author's collection: **Chinese history and literature; collection of studies,** dordrecht (1970) 214-227.

Przyluski, J. Les rites d'avalambala. **MCB** 1 (1931-32) 221-235.

Rees, J. Lambert. The three religions and their bearing on chinese civilization. **ChRec** 27 (1896) 157-169, 222-231.

Richard, Timothy. The influence of buddhism in china. **ChRec** 21.2 (feb 1890) 49-64.

Watters, Thomas. **Essays on the chinese language.** Shanghai (1889) See esp chap 8 and 9, The influence of buddhism on the chinese language.

Wright, Arthur F. Buddhism and chinese culture: phases of interaction. **JAS** 17 (nov 1957) 17-42.

18. MODERN (PRE-1949) BUDDHISM

Aufhauser, Johannes B. Ein blick in buddhistische heiligtümer des fernen ostens. **Zeitschrift für buddhismus und verwandt gebiete** 6 (1924-25) 243-258.

Aufhauser, Johannes B. Christentum und buddhismus in ringen am fernasien. **Bücherei der kultur und geschichte** 25 (1922)

Benz, Ernst. **Buddhism or communism. Which holds the future of asia?** Tsl fr german Richard and Clara Winston. N.Y. (1965) 234 p. Orig german ed: **Buddhas wiederkehr, und die zukunft asiens,** münchen (1963) 274 p.

Blanchet, C. Le congrès bouddhiste de shanghai. **RHR** 67 (mai-juin 1913) 397-398.

Blanchet, C. Une nouvelle édition du tripiṭaka chinois. **TP** n.s. 11 (mai 1910) 315-318.

Blofeld, John. **The jewel in the lotus. An outline of present day buddhism in china.** London (1948) 193 p.

Blofeld, John. **The wheel of life. The auto-biography of a western buddhist.** London (1959) 263 p, index, illus.

Callahan, Paul E. T'ai hsü and the new buddhist movement. Harvard univ, **papers on china** 6 (1952) 149-188.

Chan, Wing-tsit. **Religious trends in modern china.** Columbia univ (1953) See chap 2-3.

Chou, Hsiang-kuang. **T'ai hsu: his life and teachings.** Allahabad (1957) 74 p.

Demiéville, Paul. Le bouddhisme et la guerre. Postscriptum à l'histoire des moines guerriers de japon de G. Renondeau. **MIHEC** 1 (1957) 347-385.

Edkins, Joseph. The recent visit of a chinese buddhist monk to india. **JNCBRAS** 31 (1896-97) 203.

Franke, Otto. Ein buddhistischer reformversuch in china. **TP** n.s. 10 (1909) 567-602.

Franke, Otto. Eine neue buddhistische propaganda. **TP** 5 (1894) 299-310.

Franke, Otto. Die propaganda des japanischen buddhismus in china. In author's **Ostasiatische neubildungen,** hamburg (1911) 158-165.

Fürrer, Arnold. Der buddhismus in seiner bedeutung für die gegenwärtige religiöse krisis in china. **ZMK** 29 (1914) 264-281.

Galetzki, Th. von. Buddhistische missionen japans in china und nordamerika. **Dokumente des fortschritte** 1.2 (1908) 1155-1160.

Glüer, Winfried. The encounter between christianity and chinese buddhism during the nineteenth century and the first half of the twentieth century. **CF** 11.3 (1968) 39-57.

Gutzlaff, Charles. Remarks on the present state of buddhism in china. Communicated by lieut. col. w. h. sykes. **JRAS** 16 (1856) 73-92.

Hackmann, Heinrich. Ein heiliger des chinesischen buddhismus und seine spüren im heutigen china (Tsi k'ae) **ZMK** 18 (1903) 65.

Hamilton, Clarence H. Buddhism resurgent. **JR** 17 (1937) 30-36.

Hodous, Lewis. **Buddhism and buddhists in china.** N.Y. (1924) 84 p.

Hodous, Lewis. The buddhist outlook in china. **CSM** 21.6 (1926) 9-11.

Johnston, Reginald F. A poet monk of modern china [su man-shu] **JNCBRAS** 43 (1932) 14-30.

Kuan, Chiung. Buddhism. In **The chinese year book, 1935-36,** shanghai (1935) 1510-16; **ibid, 1936-37,** shanghai (1936) 1445-50; **ibid, 1937,** shanghai (1937) 70-75.

Kupfer, Carl F. Buddhism in hwang mei. **EA** 2 (1903) 185-194.

McDaniel, C. Yates. Buddhism makes its peace with the new order. **Asia** 35.9 (sept 1935) 536-541.

Millican, Frank R. Buddhist activities in shanghai. **ChRec** 65.4 (apr 1934) 221-227.

Millican, Frank R. T'ai-hsü and modern buddhism. **ChRec** 54.6 (1923) 326-334.

Oehler, W. Der buddhismus als volksreligion im heutigen china. **EMM** n.s. 55 (1911) 308-317.

Pratt, James Bissett. **The pilgrimage of buddhism and a buddhist pilgrimage.** N.Y. (1928) 758 p. See chap 11-20 for mahāyāna and chin buddhism.

Pratt, James Bissett. A report on the present condition of buddhism. **CSPSR** 8.3 (1924) 1-32.

Reichelt, Karl L. Buddhism in china at the present time and the new challenge to the christian church. **IRM** 26 (1937) 153-166.

Reichelt, Karl L. A conference of chinese buddhist leaders. **ChRec** 54.11 (1923) 667-669.

Reichelt, Karl L. Special work among chinese buddhists. **ChRec** 51.7 (1920) 491-497.

Rosenberg, Otto. **Die weltanschauung des modernen buddhismus im fernen osten. (Ein vortr. geh. in d. ersten buddh. ausstell. zu st. petersburg 1919 von prof. dr. o. rosenberg.) Aus d. russ. übers. v. Ph. Schaeffer** . . . Heidelberg (1924) 47 s.

Roussel, Alfred. **Religions orientales. Première série. – Le bouddhisme contemporain.** Paris (1916) ix + 520 p.

Saunders, Kenneth J. Sketches of buddhism as a living religion. **JR** 2 (1922) 418-431.

Tai-Hü. Buddhistische studien. Der buddhismus in geschichte und gegenwart. **Sinica** 3 (1928) 189-196.

T'ai Hsü. **Lectures in buddhism.** Paris (1928) 92 p, illus.

Tsu, Y. Y. Buddhism and modern social-economic problems. **JR** 14 (1934) 35-43.

Tsu, Yu-yue. Present tendencies in chinese buddhism. **JR** 1.5 (1921) 497-512.

Tsukamoto, Zenryū. Japanese and chinese buddhism in the twentieth century. **CHM** 6.3 (1961) 572-602.

Wei-huan. Buddhism in modern china. **THM** 9.2 (sept 1939) 140-155.

Welch, Holmes. Buddhismus in china. **Saeculum** 20 (1969) 259-270. See same title in H. Dumoulin (hrsg) **Buddhismus der gegenwart,** freiburg (1970) 95-106.

Welch, Holmes. **The buddhist revival in china.** Harvard univ (1968) 385 p, app, notes, bibliog, gloss-index. With a section of photos by Henri Cartier-Bresson.

Welch, Holmes. Case histories of motivation: two modern chinese monks. **ZMR** 54.2 (apr 1970) 112-123.

Welch, Holmes. The foreign relations of buddhism in modern china. **JHKBRAS** 6 (1966) 73-99.

Welch, Holmes. **The practice of chinese buddhism, 1900-1950.** Harvard univ (1967) notes, bibliog, gloss, index, app, illus.

Wilhelm, Richard. Der grossabt schī tai hü. **Sinica** 4 (1929) 16.

Wilhelm, Richard. The influence of the revolution on religion in china. **IRM** 2.8 (oct 1913) 625-642.

Witte, H. Die wirkung der umwälzung in china auf den chinesischen buddhismus. **ZMK** 29 (1914) 19-22.

Witte, Johannes. Neues leben im ostasiatischen buddhismus. **ZMK** 41 (1926) 33-41.

Witte, Johannes. Die rede des führers der chinesischen vertreter auf dem buddhistenkongress in tokyo im nov. 1925. **ZMK** 41 (1926) 257-263.

Witte, Johannes. Zur propaganda des japanischen buddhismus in china und zur propaganda der religionen überhaupt. **Christliche welt** 27 (1915)

19. BUDDHISM UNDER COMMUNISM

Amritananda, Bhikku. **Buddhist activities in socialist countries.** Peking (1961) 89 p, illus.

Bapat, P. V. A glimpse of buddhist china today. **MB** 64 (1956) 388-392.

Benz, Ernst. **Buddhism or communism. Which holds the future of asia?** Tsl fr german Richard and Clara Winston. N.Y. (1965)

Bräker, Hans. Kommunismus und buddhismus. Zur religions und asienpolitik der sowjetunion und chinas. **Moderne welt** 8 (1967) 50-64.

Buddhists in peking. **FEER** (21 nov 1963) 381-382.

Chao, P'u-ch'u. **Buddhism in china.** Peking (1957) 55 p, illus; rev ed (1960) 51 p, illus. See same title as art in **FA:BPB** (1959) 717-732.

Chao, P'u-ch'u. New ties among buddhists. **CRecon** 5 (apr 1956) 12-17, illus.

Chao, P'u-ch'u. The story of the buddha's tooth-relic. **CRecon** 8 (sept 1959) 36-37, illus.

Ch'en, Kenneth, K. S. Chinese communist attitudes towards buddhism in chinese history. **CQ** 22 (apr-june 1965) 14-30.

Ch'en, Kenneth, K. S. Religious changes in communist china. **CC** 11.4 (dec 1970) 56-62. Mostly on buddhism.

Chih, Sung. Chinese buddhism yesterday and today. **PC** 22 (16 nov 1956) 31-35.

Chinese Buddhist Association, Peking, publications:
  a) **Buddhism in china** (1955) 4 p text, 24 col pl
     in portfolio.
  b) **Statues and pictures of gautama buddha**
     (1956) 8 p, pl.
  c) **Buddhists in china** (1956) 177 p.
  d) **Buddhists in new china** (1957) 189 p,
     chiefly illus.
  e) **The friendship of buddhism** (1957) 160 p.
  f) **The buddha tooth relic in china** (1961) 10 p,
     pl.

Chü Tsan. A buddhist monk's life. **CRecon** 3
(jan-feb 1954) 42-44.

Gard, Richard A. Buddhist trends and perspectives
in asia. In **FA:BPB** (1959) 561-568.

Hsu, William. **Buddhism in china.** Hong kong
(1964) 72 p, illus.

Jaltso, Shirob. New appearance of buddhism in
china. **CB** 627 (18 july 1960) 26-30.

Kiang, Alfred. A new life begins in the [buddhist]
temples. **CWR** 116 (11 feb 1950) 172-174.

Langerhans, Heinz. Die buddhistische renaissance. 2. In ceylon, burma, kambodscha – und
china. **Frankfurter** 20 (nov 1965) 763-774.

Migot, André. Situation des religions en chine
populaire: bouddhisme et marxisme. In Centre
d'étude des pays de l'est, institut de sociologie
solvay, univ libre de bruxelles and centre national
pour l'étude des pays à régime communiste (ed)
**Le régime et les institutions de la république
populaire chinoise**, brussels (1960) 39-55.

Price, Frank W. Communist china (buddhism in
china) **Religion in life** 25 (fall 1956) 512-515.

Raguin, Yves. Nouvelle attitude des jeunes
bouddhistes. **CMBA** 2 (dec 1950)

USJPRS reports:
   Articles on buddhist activities. DC-613
      (24 mar 1959) 1, a-b, 63 p.
   Articles on chinese buddhist theory and activ-
      ity. NY-1461 (9 apr 1959) 1, a, 55 p.
   Translations from hsien-tai-fo-hsüeh (modern
      buddhism) JPRS-2638 (25 may 1960) 1, a,
      19 p.

Welch, Holmes. Asian buddhists and china.
FEER 40 (4 apr 1963) 15-21.

Welch, Holmes. Buddhism after the seventh
[world federation of buddhists conference]
FEER 47.10 (12 mar 1965) 433-435.

Welch, Holmes. Buddhism since the cultural revolution. **CQ** 40 (oct-dec 1969) 127-136.

Welch, Holmes. Buddhism under the communists.
CQ 6 (apr-june 1961) 1-14.

Welch, Holmes. Buddhismus in china. **Saeculum**
20 (1969) 259-270.

Welch, Holmes. Buddhists in the cold war. **FEER**
35.10 (8 mar 1962) 555-563, photos. Author's
report on 6th world federation of buddhists conference that he attended nov 1961 in phnom penh.

Welch, Holmes. The deification of mao. **Saturday
review** (19 sept 1970) 25, 50.

Welch, Holmes. Facades of religion in china.
AsSur 10.7 (july 1970) 614-626.

Welch, Holmes. The reinterpretation of chinese
buddhism. **CQ** 22 (apr-june 1965) 143-153.

Yang, I-fan. **Buddhism in china.** Hong kong
(1956) 98 p.

20. TAIWAN AND OVERSEAS (INCLUDING HONG KONG)

Bodhedrum Publications: **Buddhism in taiwan.**
Taichung (n.d., ca 1959) 44 p, chiefly photos.

Chien, S. C. Buddhism: the chinese version.
FCR 13 (may 1963) 37-43, illus.

Chu, Pao-t'ang. Buddhist organizations in taiwan.
CC 10.2 (june 1969) 98-132, tables.

Kitagawa, Joseph M. Buddhism in taiwan today.
FA 18 (1962) 439-444.

Kuo, Huo-lieh. Buddhism in taiwan today: attitudes toward changing society. **QNCCR** 5.2
(1961) 24-33. Same title in **SEAJT** 3.2 (oct 1961)
43-58.

Lee, H. T. New horizons of universe and life in
buddhism. **Tamkang journal** 6 (nov 1967)
267-289.

Raguin, Yves. Buddhismus auf taiwan. **Saeculum**
20 (1969) 277-280. See same title in H. Dumoulin
(hrsg) **Buddhismus der gegenwart**, freiburg (1970)
113-116.

Topley, Marjorie. Chinese women's vegetarian
houses in singapore. **JMBRAS** 27.1 (may 1954)
51-67.

Trippner, J. Formosa's buddhismus und die
rückkehr zum festland china. **NZM** 14 (1958)
304-305.

Wei Wu Wei. The passing away of a buddhist sage
in taiwan. **MW** 38 (1964) 156-158.

Welch, Holmes. Buddhist organizations in hong
kong. **JHKBRAS** 1 (1960-61) 98-114.

Wong, C. S. **Kek lok si – temple of paradise.**
Singapore (1963) 131 p. On a famous temple,
chi-lo ssu, in penang.

Yang, Ming-che. China reinterprets buddhism.
FCR 18 (dec 1968) 27-32.

21. COMPARATIVE STUDIES RELATED TO BUDDHISM

Affinités des doctrines de lao-tse et du bouddha.
Date incontestable de l'existence de lao-tse. Un
savant prétend que lao-tse était un philosophe
japonais. In **EM** 26 (d?) 343f.

Aufhauser, Johannes B. Christentum und
buddhismus in ringen am fernasien. **Bücherei der
kultur und geschichte** 25 (1922)

Bagchi, P. C. Indian influence on chinese thought.
In **HPEW** (1952) vol 1, 573-589.

Ball, J. Dyer. **Is buddhism a preparation or a
hindrance to christianity in china?** Hong kong
(1907) 31 p.

Bareau, André. Indian and ancient chinese buddhism: institutions analogous to the jisa. **CSSH** 3
(1961) 443-451 ('Jisa' is tibetan for the principal
land of the monastery)

Bernard-Maître, Henri. La découverte du
bouddhisme. (La découverte spirituelle de
l'extrême-asie par l'humanisme européen)
FA 10.2 (1954) 1141-1153.

Brandauer, Frederick P. The encounter between
christianity and chinese buddhism from the four-
teenth century through the seventeenth century.
CF 11.3 (1968) 30-38.

Chang, Chung-yüan. Concept of tao in chinese
culture. **RofR** 17.3/4 (1953) 115-132.

Châu, Thích-minh. **The chinese madhayama
agama and the pali majhima nikaya; a comparative
study.** Saigon (1964) 388 p.

Châu, Thích-minh. **Milindapañha and nagasenabhikshusutra: a comparative study through pali and
chinese sources.** Calcutta (1964) 127 p.

Clemen, K. Christliche einflüsse auf den chinesischen und japanischen buddhismus. **OZ** 9 (1920-
22) 10-37, 185-200.

Demiéville, Paul. l'État actuel des études
bouddhiques. **Revue de théologie et de philosophie**
14 (1927) 43-65.

Dietz, E. Sino-mongolian temple painting and its
influence on persian illumination. **Ars islamica** 1
(1934) 160-170.

Dschi, Hiän-lin. Lieh-tzu and buddhist sutras.
A note on the author of lieh-tzu and the date of
its composition. **SS** 9.1 (1950) 18-32.

Dumoulin, Heinrich. The encounter between zen
buddhism and christianity. **JCS** 7 (1970) 53-63.

Dumoulin, Heinrich. **Östliche meditation und
christliche mystik.** München (1966) 340 p.

Edmunds, Albert J. **Buddhist and christian gospels.
Being gospel parallels from pali texts. Now first
compared from the originals by albert j. edmunds.
Third and complete edition – Edited with parallels
and notes from the chinese buddhist tripitaka by
m. anesaki.** Tokyo (1905) philadelphia (1902;
1908; 1935) vol 2 (all publ?) 341 p, xiii + 230 p.

Eitel, E. J. Buddhism versus romanism. **ChRec** 3
(1870-71) 142-143, 181-183.

Erkes, Eduard. Kumārajīvas laotse kommentar.
ZMR 50 (1935) 49-53.

Evola, J. Zen and the west. **E&W** 6 (1955)
115-119.

Fachow. Comparative studies in the mahāparinib-
bānasutta and its chinese versions. **SIS** 1 (1944)
167-210; 2 (1945) 1-41.

Fukunaga, Mitsuji. 'No-mind' in chuang-tzu and
in ch'an buddhism. **Zinbun** 12 (1969) 9-45.

Galetzki, Th. von. Buddhistische missionen
japans in china und nordamerika. **Dokumente des
fortschritte** 1.2 (1908) 1155-1160.

Glüer, Winfried. The encounter between christianity and chinese buddhism during the nineteenth
century and the first half of the twentieth century.
CF 11.3 (1968) 39-57.

Grootaers, W. A. Bouddhisme et christianisme en
chine. **Bulletin des missions** (1951) 1-5.

Gulik, R. H. van. Indian and chinese sexual
mysticism. App I in author's **Sexual life in
ancient china,** leiden (1961) 339-359.

Hackmann, Heinrich. Aufgabe des christentums gegen über dem buddhismus. **Christliche welt** 19 (1905) 565.

Holth, Sverre. The encounter between christianity and chinese buddhism during the nestorian period. **CF** 11.3 (1968) 20-29.

Inglis, James W. The christian element in chinese buddhism. **IRM** 5.20 (oct 1916) 587-602.

Inglis, James W. The vows of amida. A comparative study. **JNCBRAS** 48 (1917) 1-11.

Johnston, Reginald F. Buddhist and christian origins. An appreciation and a protest. **Quest** 4 (oct 1912) 137-163.

King, Winston L. The way of tao and the path to nirvana. In **SA** (1963) 121-135.

Kung, Tien-min. Some buddhist and christian doctrines compared. **QNCCR** 5.2 (1961) 34-37.

Lancashire, Douglas. Buddhist reaction to christianity in late ming china. **JOSA** 6.1/2 (1968-69) 82-103.

Malan, Salomon C. **A letter on the pantheistic and on the buddhistic tendency of the chinese and of the mongol versions of the bible.** London (1856) 38 p.

Merton, Thomas. A christian looks at zen. Being the intro to John C. H. Wu: **The golden age of zen,** taipei (1967) 1-28.

Murakami, Yoshimi. 'Nature' in lao-chuang thought and 'no-mind' in ch'an buddhism. **KGUAS** 14 (1965) 15-31.

Olschki, L. Manichaeism, buddhism and christianity in marco polo's china. **AS** 5 (1951) 1-21.

Pachow, W. A comparative study of the pratimoksa. **SIS** 4 (1953) 18-193; 5 (1955) 1-45.

Parker, E. H. Buddhism and christianity in china. **ChRev** 16 (1887) 188.

Pauthier, Georges. **Mémoire sur l'origine et la propagation de la doctrine du tao, fondée par lao-tseu; traduit du chinois et accompagné d'un commentaire tiré des livres sanscrits et du tao-te-king de lao-tseu, établissant la conformité de certaines opinions philosophiques de la chine et de l'inde; orné d'un dessein chinois; suivi de deux oupanishads des vedas, avec le texte sanscrit et persan.** Paris (1831) 79 p. See critical rev by Anon [Stanislas Julien?] in **NouvJA** 7 (1831) 465-493; further Pauthier's rebuttal in **ibid** 8 (1831) 129-158.

Przyluski, J. Études indiennes et chinoises. **MCB** 2 (1932-33) 307-332; 4 (1935-36) 289-339.

Re, Arundel del. Amidism and christianity. **Marco polo** 3 (apr 1941) 68-81.

Sarkar, B. F. Confucianism, buddhism, and christianity. **OC** 33 (1919) 661-673.

Stuhr, P. F. **Die chinesische reichsreligion und die systeme der indischen philosophie in ihrem verhältnis zu offenbarungslehren. Mit rücksicht auf die ansichten von windischmann, schmitt und ritter.** Berlin (1835) vi + 109.

Takakusu, Junjirō. Tales of the wise man and the fool, in tibetan and chinese. **JRAS** (1901) 447-460.

Tamaki, Kōshirō. The development of the thought of tathāgatagarbha from india to china. **JIBS** 9.1 (jan 1961) 25-33.

Thurn, E. Buddhism in the pacific. **Nature** 105 (1920) 407.

Too-yu. The systems of foe and confucius compared, translated from the chinese. **ICG** no 5 (1818) 149-157.

Visser, Marinus W. de. The arhats in china and japan. **OZ** 7 (1918) 87-102; 9 (1920-22) 116-144. Same title publ sep, berlin (1923) 215 p, pl.

Visser, Marinus Willem de. **The bodhisattva akāśagarbha (kokūzō) in china and japan.** Amsterdam (1931) 47 p.

Visser, Marinus Willem de. The bodhisattva ti tsang (jizo) in china and japan. **OZ** 2 (1913) 179-192, 266-305; 3 (1914) 61-92, 326-327.

Visser, Marinus Willem de. Die pfauenkönig (k'ung-tsioh ming wang, kujaku myō-ō) in china and japan. **OZ** 8 (1919-20) 370-387.

Wei, Francis C. M. Buddhism as a chinese christian sees it. **IRM** 17 (1928) 455-463.

Witte, Johannes. Zur propaganda des japanischen buddhismus in china and zur propaganda der religion überhaupt. **Christliche welt** 29 (1915) 535-541, 609-663, 679-683, 705-706, 725-727.

22. MISCELLANEOUS

Rape, C. B. Buddhistic brotherhood of the sacred army and the adventures of an american ship on the upper yangtsze. **CWR** 44 (17 mar 1928) 62-63.

Index of Authors, Editors, Compilers, Translators, Photographers, Illustrators

A.L. 26L
Abegg, Emil 140R, 161L
Abel, Karl 3R, 144R
Abel, M. 97R
Abel-Rémusat, J.P. 49R, 53R, 88R, 109R, 117R, 123R, 125R, 140R, 141L, 142R, 144L
Abraham, A. 147R, 149L
Adam, Maurice 74R, 156R
Adams, Charles J. 2L
Adams, P.R. 150L
Addison, James Thayer 38R, 101R
Aigran, René 14R
Aijmer, Göran 38R, 41R, 67L, 74R, 81L
Akanuma, Chizen 108L
Akatsuka, Kiyoshi 12L
Akiyama, Terukazu 156R
Alabaster, Chaloner 91L
Albrecht, Ardon 98R
Aldington, Richard 17L
Alès, A.d' 10R
Alexander, Frances 17R
Alexander, G.G. 49R
Alexander, Mary 17R
Allan, C. Wilfrid 141L, 162R
Allen, C.F.R. 23R, 78L
Allen, G.W. 74R
Allen, Herbert J. 23R, 29R, 57L, 125R
Alley, Rewi 78L, 149L
Amberley, Viscount John Russell 29R, 49R
Amélineau, E. 38R, 101R
Ames, Delano 17L
Amicus 42R, 70R
Amiot, J.J.M. [Amyot] 7R, 57L, 61L
Ampère, J.J. 46L, 109R, 125R
Amritananda, Bhikku 166R
Anderson, A.E. 49R
Anderson, Eugene N. jr. 99R
Anderson, J.N.D. 29R
Andersson, J.G. 12L, 17R, 84R
Andrews, F.H. 154L
Anesaki, Masaharu 108L, 117R, 168R
Ansari, Zafar Ishaq 33R, 48L
Ansley, Delight 3R
Antonini, P. 26L
Archer, John C. 3R
Arène, Jules 158R
Arlington, L.C. 15R, 29R, 38R, 42R, 81L, 82L, 86R, 101R
Armstrong, Alexander 29R
Armstrong, E.A. 81L
Armstrong, R.C. 133L
Arthaud, Claude 45R, 146L, 153L, 156R
Ashton, Leigh 150R
Atkins, Gaius G. 29R
Atkinson, F.M. 17L, 66R, 73L
Atkinson, R.W. 21R
Aufhauser, Johannes B. 139L, 161L, 164R, 165L, 168L

Aurousseau, L. 125R, 131L
Awakawa, Yasuichi 154L
Ayres, Lew 3R
Ayrton, W.E. 3R, 17R
Ayscough, Florence 18L, 29L, 42R, 71L, 78L

B.J. 3R
Ba shin, U. 118L
Bach, A.H. 91L, 105R
Bach, Marcus 29R, 36L
Bachhofer, Ludwig 150R, 154L
Bagchi, Prabodh Chandra 55R, 108L, 118L, 118R, 125R, 126L, 141L, 163R, 168L
Bahm, Archie J. 29R, 46L, 109R
Bailey, D.R. Shackleton 113L
Baker, Dwight C. 78L
Baker, Hugh D.R. 38R, 41R, 99R
Baker, N. 29R
Balazs, Étienne (or Stefan) 29R, 126L
Baldwin, S.L. 29R
Balfour, Frederic H. 15R, 18L, 46L, 53L, 54L, 58L, 60R, 61L, 82L, 91L, 110L
Ball, J. Dyer 3R, 15R, 110L, 139L, 168L
Ballou, Robert O. 29R, 54L
Banerjee, A.C. 118L
Bapat, P.V. 113L, 166R
Bareau, André 115R, 118L, 126L, 168L
Barnes, W.H. 61L, 101R
Barrett, William 138R
Barrow, John G. 2L
Barthélemy, le Marquis de (Saint-Hillaire, J. Barthélemy) 3R
Barton, George A. 3R
Basset, René 88R, 162R
Bassett, Beulah E. 15R, 162R
Bateson, Joseph H. 74R
Baudens, G. 36L
Bauer, Wolfgang 15R, 59R
Baumann, C. 49R, 135R
Baynes, Cary F. 55R, 65L
Baynes, Herbert 91L
Bazin, M. 110L, 139L
Beach, Harlan P. 29R, 36L
Beal, Samuel 108L, 110L, 113L, 113R, 118L, 126L, 141L
Beardsworth, Patricia 17R
Beau, Georges 86R
Beauclair, Inez de 15R
Beautrix, P. 2L
Beck, L. Adams 88R
Bedford, O.H. 71R
Behrsing, S. 18L, 71R, 113R, 146R
Bell, Hamilton 150R
Bellah, Robert N. 38L, 94R, 96L, 101R
Belpaire, Bruno 15R, 54L, 57L, 61L, 88R, 162R, 163R
Bendall, C.C. 118R
Benl, Oscar 135R

Bennett, A.G. 118R
Bennett, Miss M.I. 81L
Benton, Richard P. 49R, 101R
Benton, Warren G. 110L
Benz, Ernst 2L, 101R, 165L, 166R
Berkowitz, M.I. 2L, 99R
Berle, A.A. 3R
Bernard-Maître, Henri 168L
Berry, Gerald L. 3R
Bertholet, Alfred 5R, 9R, 26L
Bertholet, René 28L, 36R, 124L
Berval, René de 126L
Besse, J. 49R
Bester, John 154L
Bettelheim, P. 9L
Beurdeley, M. 61L
Beyerhaus, Peter 38R, 101R
Beylié, L. de 148R
Biallas, Franz Xaver 29R, 42R
Bidens 38R
Bielenstein, Hans 23R, 82L
Bigelow, William Sturgis 116L, 133R
Binyon, Laurence 145R
Birch, Cyril 15R
Biroen, H. 61L
Bischoff, F.A. 113R, 161L
Bishop, Carl W. 12L, 29R, 81L
Bisson, T.A. 49R
Biswas, D.K. 121R
Black, W.H. 84R
Blake, Lady 91L
Blanchard, Raphael 84R
Blanchet, C. 165L
Bleeker, C.J. 9R
Bleichsteiner, R. 139L
Bliss, Edwin Munsell 30R, 49L
Block, Marguerite 46L
Blodget, Henry 38R, 42R, 71R
Blofeld, John C. (see also Chu Ch'an) 114L, 126L,
     133L, 135R, 136L, 139L, 165L
Bloom, Alfred 124L, 126L, 133L
Blythe, Wilfred 91L, 99R
Boardman, Eugene P. 23R
Bock, Carl 158R
Bodde, Derk 3R, 15R, 26L, 49L, 50L, 50R, 67L,
     74R, 84R, 85L, 89L, 110R, 124L, 136R
Boerschmann, Ernst 4L, 18L, 38R, 42L, 148L,
     148R, 149L, 149R, 157R, 158R
Bone, Charles 65R, 67L, 75L
Bonin, Charles-Eudes 158L, 159L
Bonmarchand, G. 61L
Bönner, Theodor 4L
Bonsall, Bramwell S. 29R, 46L
Boode P. 156R
Boone, W.J. 26L
Borch, A. von 42R
Borel, Henri 50L, 161L
Borsig, Tet 152L
Bose, Phanindra Nath 126L
Böttger, Walter 85L, 153R

Bouchot, J. 149R
Bouillard, Georges 42R, 43L, 67L, 75L, 78L,
     78R, 146R, 147R
Botlinais, Lt-Col Albert M.A. 4L, 39L, 101R
Boulting, William 141L
Bourgeois 7R
Bourne, Frederick S.A. 43L, 60R, 78R
Bowen, A.J. 149R
Bowers, John Z. 86R
Bownas, Geoffrey 32R
Box, Ernest 67R
Boxer, Baruch 42L, 99R
Boyle, F. 91L
Brace, A.J. 18L, 85L, 91L
Braden, Charles S. 4L, 29R, 30L, 50L, 54L,
     94R, 101R
Bradley, David G. 30L, 46L
Brailsford, Mabel R. 13L
Bräker, Hans 166R
Brandauer, Frederick P. 26R, 99R, 126L, 168L
Brandon, Samuel G.F. 12L, 26L, 108L
Brandt, M. von 43L
Brankston, A.D. 156R
Bras, Gabriel le 126L
Brasch, K. 154L
Brecht, B. 50L, 57L
Bredon, Juliet 65R, 75L
Breitenstein, H. 86R
Brémond, René 46L
Bretschneider, Emil 78R
Brewster, D. 18L
Bridgman, Elijah Coleman 12L, 148L, 149R
Bridgman [Eliza] J. Gillet 71R
Bridgman, R.F. 86R
Brillant, Maurice 14R
Brodrick, A.H. 18L, 43L
Broomhall, Marshall 133R
Brou, Alexandre 30L, 94R
Brough, John 126L
Brousse, Jean de la 149R
Brown, Brian 30L
Brown, Frederick R. 67R
Brown, H.G. 67R, 82R
Browne, Lewis 4L, 30L, 54L
Bruce, J. Percy 26L
Buchner, Hartmar 138R
Buck, John Lossing 94R
Buck, Samuel (pseud) 70R, 71R, 75L, 75R, 82R,
     99R
Bucke, Richard M. 50L
Buckens, F. 12L, 26R
Buhot, Jean 149R
Bui, Van Quy 84R
Bulling, A. 18L, 148R
Bunge, Martin L. 12L
Bünger, Karl 23R, 24L, 43L
Bunker, Emma C. 146R, 150R
Bunsen, C.C.J. 4L
Burder, William 4L
Burckhardt, Martha 4L

Burkhardt, Valentine R. 75R, 99R
Burland, Cottie A. 145R
Burn, D.C. 148L
Burrell, David J. 30L
Burrows, Millar 30L, 50L
Burtt, Edwin A. 4L, 30L, 46L
Buschan, G. 15R
Bush, Richard C. jr. 96R
Bushell, S.W. 144L
Butcher, Charles H. 39L

C.C. 105R
Cairns, Grace E. 7R
Callahan, Paul E. 133R, 165L
Cammann, Schuyler 18L, 18R, 19L, 78R, 79L,
    85L, 86R, 98R, 146R, 158L
Campbell, Joseph 15R
Candlin, George F. 91L
Carpenter, J. Estlin 15L
Carter, Thomas F. 126L
Cartier-Bresson, Henri 166L
Carus, Paul 4L, 18R, 46L, 50L, 90R, 161L
Casey, E.T. 18R
Castellane, le Comte Boni de 91R
Castillon, J. 4L
Cauvin, Dr 30L, 78R
Cave, Sydney 4L
Cavin, Albert 30L
Cerbu, A. Zigmund 118R
Chaine, Joseph 7L
Chalmers, John 12L, 15R, 26R, 46L
Chambeau, Gabriel 110L, 139L, 160R
Chamberlain, Ida Hoyt 50L
Chamberlayne, John H. 71R
Chambers, William 78R, 148R, 149R
Chamfrault, A. 86R
Champion, Selwyn G. 30L, 31R, 47L, 54L
Chan, David B. 126R
Chan, Hok-lam 24L, 57L, 91R, 126R, 133R
Chan, Ping-leung 15R, 71R, 89L
Chan, Wing-tsit 4L, 12L, 24L, 26R, 30L, 36R,
    46L, 94R, 95L, 96R, 105R, 108L, 113R,
    114L, 118R, 125L, 126R, 135R, 165L
Chandrasekhar, S. 97L
Chantepie (see Saussaye, P.D. Chantepie de la)
Chang, C. 36R, 101R
Chang, Carsun 26R, 124L, 164L
Chang, Chen-chi 135R
Chang Chen-yun 86R
Chang, Chi-wen 69L, 79L
Chang, Ch'i-yün 30L
Chang, Chung-yuan 55R, 56L, 61L, 135R,
    136L, 168L
Chang, Joseph 30L
Chang, Kuei-sheng 141R
Chang, Kwang-chih 12L, 16L, 18R
Chang, Lucy Gi Ding 2L
Chang, Neander S. 94R
Chang, Shu-hung 159L
Chang, Tsung-tung 12R

Chang, Y.H. 156R
Chao, P'u-ch'u 166R
Chao, Wei-pang 67R, 75R, 82R, 91R
Chao, Yün-ts'ung 61R, 62L
Chapin, Helen B. 136R, 146R, 154L
Charpentier, Léon 16R, 75R, 85L
Chatley, Herbert 61L, 85L
Chattopadhyaya, D. 61L
Châu, Thích-minh 118R, 126R, 141R, 168L
Chau, Yick-fu 26R
Chaudhuri, H. 26R, 101L
Chavannes, C.G. 68R, 76L
Chavannes, Édouard 4L, 4R, 6L, 12R, 21L, 24L,
    27R, 31L, 36R, 39L, 39R, 43L, 50L, 54L, 57L,
    60L, 62R, 71R, 78R, 80L, 82R, 91R, 113R,
    114L, 126R, 130L, 133R, 141L, 141R, 143L,
    145R, 150R, 157R, 159L, 162R
Chavannes, Mme Édouard 162R
Chédel, A. 114L
Chen, Charles K.H. 126R
Chen, Chi-lu 98R
Chen, Chung-hwan 12L, 50L, 56L
Chen, Chung-kuei 96R
Chen, Chung-min 39L, 98R, 136L
Ch'en, Hsiang-ch'un 85L
Chen, Ivan 102L
Ch'en, Jen-dao 136L, 154L
Ch'en, Jerome 91R
Chen, Joseph 38L, 102L
Ch'en, Kenneth K.S. 24L, 26R, 38L, 57L, 96R,
    110L, 114L, 116L, 118R, 126R, 127L, 128L,
    129L, 141R, 164L, 166R
Ch'en, Kuo-fu 61L, 62L
Chen, Ronald 86R
Chen, Sophia H. 4R
Ch'en, T'ieh-fan 62R
Chen, Tsu-lung 159L
Chen, Tsung-chou 149R
Cheney, Sheldon 50L
Cheng, Chi-pao 8R
Cheng, Homer Hui-ming 75R, 99R
Chêng, Tê-k'un 4R, 19L, 26R, 71R, 159L
Chesneaux, Jean 2L, 91R
Chi, Hsien-lin 164L
Chi, Richard See Yee 118R, 136L
Chia, Chung-yao 24L, 127L
Chiang, Alpha C. 89L
Chien, S.C. 167R
Chien, Wen-hsien 36R
Chih, Sung 166R
Chikashige, Masumi 61L
Child, L. Maria 4R
Chiu, A. Kaiming 23L
Chiu, Koon-noi 30R
Chiu, Moses 50L
Choa, Gerald 86R, 99R
Chochod, Louis 85L, 102L
Chou, Chung-i 30R, 110L
Chou, Hsiang-kuang 127L, 134L, 136L, 139L,
    164L, 165L

Chou, Hsiang-kung 61L
Chou, I-liang 61L, 133L
Chou, Ju-ch'ang 54L
Chou, Shao-miao 159L
Chou, Ta-fu 114L, 118R
Chou, Tzu-ch'iang 19L
Chou, Yi-liang 133L
Chow, Bonaventura Shan-mou 36R
Christie, Anthony 16L
Chu, Ch'an (pseud of Blofeld, John C. q.v.)
    114L, 136L, 139L
Ch'u, Chung 96R
Chu, Liang-cheng 75R
Chu, Pao-t'ang 167R
Chü, Tsan 139R, 167L
Chuan, T.K. 127L, 134L
Chung, Albert Chi-lu 124L, 136L
Cibot, Père M. 57R, 61L
Clapp, F.M. 146R
Clark, Walter E. 118R
Clarke, G.W. 65R
Clarke, James Freeman 30R, 110L
Clauson, G.L.M. 116R, 123L
Clayton, George A. 89L
Clemen, C. 7L
Clemen, K. 127L, 168R
Clennell, Walter J. 4R
Clerke, E.M. 16L
Clopin, Camille 30R, 50L, 102L
Clutton-Brock, A. 19L
Coffin, Edna 67R
Cohen, Alvin P. 82R
Cohn, William 19L, 21R, 146R, 154L
Collier, H.B. 62R
Collis, Maurice 24L
Colyer-Ferguson, Beatrice S. 9L
Combaz, Gilbert 19L, 43L, 102L, 149R
Comber, Leon 39L, 76R, 78R, 85L, 91R, 99R,
    100L
Compte, L. le 6R
Conrady, August 19L, 57R, 70R, 127L
Conrady, G. 19L, 59R
Conze, Edward 117L
Cook, T. 148L, 150R
Coomaraswamy, Ananda K. 156L
Coq, Albert von le 154L, 155R
Corbet, R.G. 145R
Cordier, Georges 67R, 82R
Cordier, Henri 2L, 30R, 38L, 39L, 46R, 50L,
    91R, 102L
Cormack, Annie 75R
Cornaby, W. Arthur 50R, 89L
Corrin, Stephen 62R
Couchoud, Paul Louis 16L, 30R
Coulborn, Rushton 24L, 43L, 102L
Couling, C.E. 46R, 57R, 59R, 94R
Courant, Maurice 26R
Cowdry, E.V. 61L, 86R
Cox, Leonard B. 156R, 157R
Coyajee [also Coyaji], Jehangir Cooverjee
    16L, 61L, 102L

Crane, Louise 156R, 158R
Cranston, Ruth 4R
Creel, Herrlee Glessner 12R, 24L, 26R, 30R, 43L,
    46R, 57R
Crémazy, L. 39L, 102L
Cressy, Earl H. 94R
Criqui, Fernand 86R
Croissant, Doris 19L
Croizier, Ralph C. 96R
Crow, Carl 30R
Csonger, B. 114L
Culbertson, M. Simpson 67R
Culin, Stewart 91R, 100L
Cumine, E.B. 149R
Cumming, C.F. Gordon 139R
Cunningham, Alexander 141R
Curzon, George N. 139R
Cutler, Donald R. 97L
Cutts, Elmer H. 127L

D.G. 40L, 71R, 81R
Dahlmann, Joseph 148L
Dahm, Annemarie 50R
Dallas, A.K. 7L
Danckert, Werner 12R
Danielli, M. 42L, 102L
Danton, George H. 35R
Danton, Annina P. 35R
Darbishire, R.D. 21R
Darbois, Domonique 161L
Darcy, Y. 43R
Dard, Emile 43L
Dás, Baboo Sarat Chandra 110L
Daudin, Pierre 67R, 75R, 85L, 127L
Daumas, M. 61L
Davaranne, Theodor 66L
Davia, Jacques 39L
David-Neel, Alexandra 36R, 158L, 161L
Davidson, J. LeRoy 23L, 114L, 127L, 144L,
    146R, 155R
Davidson, Martha 150R
Davis, A.R. 75R, 89L
Davis, John F. 54R
Davis, Tenney L. 56L, 61L, 61R, 62L, 65R
Davrout, L. 38L, 110L
Dawson, Christopher 30R, 102L
Day, Clarence Burton 66L, 67R 71L, 71R, 72L,
    75R, 78R, 85L, 95L 124L, 144L, 161L
Dean, J.A. 71L
DeBary, William Theodore 30R, 114L, 118R,
    164L
DeFrancis, John 24L, 127L
DeKorne, John C. 4R, 92L, 95L, 102L
Délétie, Henri 50R
Delius, Rudolf von 30R
Dember, H. 85L
Demiéville, Paul 7R, 19L, 24L, 79L, 89L, 108L,
    110L, 114L, 115R, 118R, 119L, 120R, 127L,
    127R, 133L, 136L, 150L, 150R, 159L, 164L,
    165L, 168R
Dennys, N.B. 89L
Desai, Santosh 56L

Deshautesrayes 110L
Devéria, Gabriel 43L, 144L
Diamond, Norma 98R
Diehl, Katherine Smith 2L
Dien, Albert E. 24L, 89L, 134L
Diergart, Paul 62R
Dietrich 4R
Dietz, E. 19L, 154L, 168R
Dieulafoy, Marcel 19L
Diez, Ernst 59R
Dill, Johann 12L
Dobbins, Frank S. 4R, 46R
Dobson, W.A.C.H. 2L
Dols, J. 67R, 75R, 81L
Doolittle, Justus 68L, 76L
Doré, Henri 4R, 30R, 31L, 66L, 67R, 76L, 95L,
    141R, 156R, 160R
Douglas, Robert K. 31L, 46R, 105R, 141R, 142R
Douglass, Bruce 97R, 105L, 106L
Doumenq 148R
Drake, F.S. 26R, 60R, 72L, 79L, 95L, 127R,
    139R, 148L, 156R
Dschi, Hiän-lin 54L, 119L, 168R
DuBose, Hampden C. 5L, 31L, 46R, 110L
Dubarbier, Georges 92L
Dubs, Homer H. 12R, 19L, 24L, 26R, 43L, 46R,
    49R, 50R, 51R, 62R, 127R
Duchesne, M. 120L
Dudgeon, John 62R, 72L, 86R
Du Halde 4L, 6R
Dukes, J. 139R
Dukes, Edwin J. 42L
Dumoulin, Heinrich 65R, 102L, 110R, 114L,
    136L, 136R, 166L, 167R, 168R
Dumoutier, Gustave 146R, 148L
Dunlap, Eva Wyman 79L
Dunne, Finley P. jr 29L, 35R
Dunstheimer, Guillaume G. 85L, 92L
Duperray, E. 27L
Durme, J. van 27L
Dutt, Sukumar 110R, 111R, 127R, 133L
Duyvendak, J.J.L. 5L, 16L, 46L, 57L, 81L, 89L,
    102L, 127R, 144L
Dvorák, Rudolf 4R, 31L, 46R
Dwight, Henry Otis 30R, 49L
Dye, Daniel S. 19L
Dymond, F.J. 76L
Dyson, Verne 16L

E.M.H. 31L
Eakin, Frank 31L
Eastlake, F. Warrington 72L
Eastman, A.C. 154L
Eastman, Max 31L
Eatwell, W. 39L
Eberhard, Alide 12R, 16L, 67R
Eberhard, Wolfram 2L, 12R, 14L, 16L, 18R, 19L,
    27L, 31L, 36R, 67R, 68L, 76L, 78R, 79L,
    85L, 89L, 89R, 95L, 98L, 127R
Eckardt, André 36R, 50R
Ecke, Gustav 19L, 136R, 148L, 149R, 150L,
    150R, 154L

Eder, Matthias [see also Thiel, Joseph] 5L, 76L,
    85L, 89R, 162R
Edgar, J.H. 68L, 72L, 102R, 141R
Edkins, Joseph 5L, 12R, 19R, 24L, 31L, 36R,
    39L, 42L, 43R, 50R, 57R, 59R, 60L, 72L,
    79L, 82R, 89R, 92L, 95L, 108L, 110R, 112R,
    114R, 119L, 124L, 127R, 133L, 139R, 144R,
    158R, 162R, 165L
Edmonds, Juliet 100L
Edmunds, Albert J. 2L, 119L, 168R
Edmunds, Charles K. 31L
Edwards, Dwight W. 5L
Edwards, Evangeline D. 13L, 24R, 31L, 95L
Edwards, Lovett F. 96R
Edwards, R. 160R
Eggert, Winifried 88L
Eichhorn, Werner 12R, 24R, 43R, 46R, 54L,
    56L, 57L, 59L, 60R, 81L, 127R
Eichler, E.R. 89R
Eigner, J. 39L, 76L, 139R, 156R
Eisenstadt, S.N. 43R
Eitel, Ernest J. 42L, 68L, 72L, 76L, 83R, 108R,
    110R, 124L, 161L, 162R, 168R
Eitner, Hans-Jürgen 96R
Elia, Pascal M. d' 95L
Eliade, Mircea 27L, 62R, 83R
Eliot, Charles 5L, 127L
Elliott, Alan J.A. 83R, 100L
Elwald, Oscar 50R
Elwin, Arthur 66L, 85L
Endres, Franz Carl 5L, 36R
Engler, Friedrich 50R
Enjoy, Paul d' 24R, 84L, 92L
Entrecolles, d' 4L
Erbacher, Hermann 2R
Erdberg-Consten, Eleanor von 19R, 50R
Erkes, Eduard 5L, 12R, 16L, 19R, 24R, 27L,
    39L, 46R, 50R, 54L, 56L, 57L, 60R, 62R,
    71L, 72L, 84L, 89R, 95L, 96R, 102R, 105R,
    146R, 150R, 161R, 168R
Ermoni, V. 5L
Esbroek, A. van 12R, 72L
Étiemble, René 31L, 46R, 50R, 96R
Eurius, O. 144R
Everett, John R. 12R, 110R
Evola, J. 136R, 168R
Ewer, F.H. 68L, 76L

Faber, Ernst 5L, 31L, 38L, 39L, 46R, 58L
Faber, Martin 46R
Fabre, A. 39L, 68L, 76L
Fabre, Maurice 43R
Fachow 119L, 168R
Fairbank, Wilma 19R
Fairchild, Johnson E. 30R, 46L
Fallers, Lloyd A. 100R
Fan, Jen 14L, 85R
Fang, Fu-an 92L
Farjenal, Fernand 36R, 39R, 43R, 81L

Faucett, Lawrence 31L, 36R
Faulder, H. Croyier 68L, 79L
Faure, Edgar 96R
Favier, Msgr, 93R
Favre, Benoit 92L
Feer, Henri L. 108R, 141R
Feer, Léon 119L
Feifel, Eugen 62R
Feigl, Hermann 5L
Fêng, Chia-lo 62R
Feng, Chia-sheng 132R
Feng, Han-yi [Han-chi]   16R, 60L, 68L, 72L, 76L, 85L
Fenollosa, Ernest 154L
Ferguson, John C. 16R, 19R, 43R, 163L
Ferm, Vergilius 12L, 30L, 47L, 108L
Fernald, Helen E. 151L, 153R, 154R
Ferro, G. Vigna dal 39R
Fielde, Adele 139R
Filliozat, Jean 62R, 86R, 127R
Finegan, Jack 31R, 46R, 110R
Fingarette, Herbert 31R
Finn, D.J. 4R, 66L, 100L
Finot, Louis 114R, 115R, 119L, 127R, 142L, 150L
Fischer, C. 85L
Fischer, Emil S. 43R
Fischer, J. 114R
Fischer, O. 151L
Fitch, D.F. 139R
Fitch, Mary F. 5L
Fitch, Robert F. 56L, 158R
Fitzgerald, C.P. 96R
Floris, George A. 92L
Focillon, Henri 145R
Folberth, Otto 50R, 102R
Fong, Wen 154R
Fonssagrives, Eugène J.P.M. 43R
Fontein, Jan 136R, 146R, 159L
Ford, Eddy L. 31R, 102R
Forke, Alfred 4L, 16R, 27L, 36R, 50R, 56L, 62R, 102R, 108R
Forlong, J.G.R. 5L, 31R, 46R
Forrest, R.J. 43R
Fou, Si-hoa 108R
Foucaux, Philippe Edouard 110R
Fourcade, Francois 159L
Fradenburgh, J.N. 5R
Francis, E.D. 109L
Franck, A. 47L
Franke, Herbert 16R, 102R, 134L, 154R
Franke, Otto 2R, 5R, 31R, 43R, 58L, 95L, 128L, 158R, 165L
Franke, Wolfgang 96R
Franks, A.W. 119R, 146R
Frazier, Allie M. 5R, 27L
Freedman, Maurice 39R, 42L, 68L, 81L
Frei, G. 71L
Frey H. 79L, 102R
Freytag, Justus 98R
Frick, Johann[es] 68L, 68R, 81L, 82R, 85R, 86R, 87L

Friese, Heinz 119R, 128L, 134L
Friess, Horace L. 5R, 110R
Frodsham, J.D. 164L
Frost, S.E. jr. 31R, 54L
Fryer, John 158R
Fu, Tien-chou 151L, 157R
Fuchs, Walter 119R, 128L, 161R
Fujieda, Akira 119R
Fujii, S. 109R
Fujino, Iwamoto 89R
Fujishima, Ryauon 108R, 142L
Fukui, Fumimasa-Bunga 128L
Fukui, Kōjun 58L
Fukunaga, Mitsuji 56L, 102R, 136R, 168R
Fung, George D. 136R
Fung, Paul F. 136R
Fung, Yu-lan 39R, 81L, 110R, 124L, 136R
Fürrer, Arnold 165L
Furuta, S. 114L

G.M.C. 92L
Gabain, Annemarie von 157L
Gabelentz, George von der 51L, 54L
Gaer, Joseph 31R, 47L, 51L, 54L
Gaillard, Louis 146R
Galetzki, Th. von 165L, 168R
Gallin, Bernard 98R
Galpin, Francis W. 27L, 39R
Gamble, Sidney D. 68R
Gambo, Charles 92L, 100L
Gangoly, O.C. 151L
Gard, Richard A. 119R, 128L, 167L
Garritt, J.C. 89R
Garvie, A.E. 102R
Gaspardone, E. 128L
Gatling, E.I. 153R
Gaubil 7R
Gauchet, L. 47L, 54R, 60L
Gausseron, Bernard H. 43R
Gauthiot, R. 114R
Geelmuyden, N. 157L
Geldner, K. 13L
Gemmell, W. 114R
Genähr, G. 92L
Genähr, J. 2R, 5R
Geoffrey, C.C. 92L
Gernet, Jacques 24R, 128L, 131R, 132R, 136R, 137L, 144R
Gerth, Hans H. 35R, 49L
Getty, Alice 146R
Ghose, Hemendra Prasad 155R
Gibson, H.E. 13L, 81L, 82R
Gieseler, G. 16R, 19R, 39R
Giles, Herbert A. 5R, 13L, 16R, 31R, 38L, 51L, 66L, 82R, 84L, 92L, 130L, 137L, 142L
Giles, Lionel 13L, 31R, 47L, 54L, 59R, 85R, 89R, 108R, 119R, 154R
Giles, W.R. 157L, 157R
Gillard, Jean-Louis 56L, 87L
Gingell, W.R. 43R

Glasenapp, Helmuth von 5R, 102R
Glick, Carl 92L
Glüer, Winfried 96R, 128L, 165R, 168R
Go, Sin-gi 98R
Gobien, Charles le 31R, 39R
Goddard, Dwight 114R, 138R
Goette, J. 19R
Gogerly, D.J. 113R
Goloubew, V. 150L
Goltz, Freiherrn von der 84L, 85R
Goodrich, Anne Swann 79L
Goodrich, G. 139R
Goodrich, L. Carrington 119R, 128L
Goodwin, P. 76L
Gorce, Maxime 7R
Goto, Kimpei 2R
Goullart, Peter 47L, 60R
Govi, M. 19R
Gowen, Herbert H. 5R, 142L
Graf, 0. 97L
Graham, A.C. 31R
Graham, David C. 27L, 68R, 71L, 72L, 72R, 81L
Graham, Dorothy 5R, 76L, 139R, 144R
Granet, Marcel 5R, 13L, 27L, 58L
Grant, C.M. 31R, 102R
Grant, D. 89R
Grantham, Alexandra E. 43R, 44L
Grava, Arnold 27L
Gray, Basil 19R, 159R
Gray, Terence 137L
Greaves, Roger 47R, 51R
Griffith, Gwilym Oswald 51L, 102R
Grimal, Pierre 17R
Grimes, A. 142L
Grimm, Martin 154R
Grinstead, E.D. 108R
Gripenoven, Jeanne 32L
Grison, P. 27R, 110R
Griswold, A.B. 151L
Groot, J.J.M.de 4L, 5R, 6L, 9R, 24R, 27L, 32L, 39R, 44L, 47L, 58L, 68R, 72L, 76L, 82R, 85R, 110R, 114R, 128L, 139R, 144R, 150L
Grootaers, Willem A. 68R, 69L, 72L, 79L, 84L, 92R, 111L, 168R
Grosier, l'Abbé 47L
Grousset, René 7L, 21L, 87R, 142L
Grube, Wilhelm 6L, 13L, 16R, 47L, 56L, 59R, 66L, 69L, 89R, 163L, 164L
Gruenhagen 87L
Grünwald, Michael 151L
Grünwedel, Albert 128R
Grützmacher, Richard H. 6L, 32L
Grys, C.P.M. de 86R
Guelny, A. 128L
Guignes, Joseph de 102R, 109R, 111L, 114R, 128R, 142L
Guillemet, Dr 87L
Guimbretière, P. 39R
Guimet, E. 51L, 102R

Guiran, Félix 17L
Gulik, Robert Hans van 47L, 62R, 85R, 102R, 119R, 144R, 168R
Gundert, Wilhelm 128R, 134L, 137L, 139R
Gundry, D.W. 32L, 47L
Gundry, R.S. 158R
Gurij, P. 124L
Gützlaff, Charles (see also Philosinensis, pseud) 59R, 69L, 72R, 79L, 92R, 108R, 111L, 158R, 165R

H. 158R
Haar, Hans 102R
Haas, Hans 2R, 32L, 51L, 119R, 128R, 134L
Hackenbroich, H. 44L
Hacken, J. 17L, 66R, 73L, 145R
Hackmann, Heinrich F. 27R, 47L, 58L, 60R, 87L, 108R, 111L, 114R, 124R, 133L, 134L, 139R, 140L, 163L, 165R, 169L
Haden, R.A. 89R
Hadl, Richard 154R, 159R
Haenisch, Erich 37L, 128R
Hager, Joseph 13L, 71L, 103L
Hail, William J. 47L
Hakeda, Yoshito S. 114L, 114R
Halbwachs, Maurice 13L
Hall, Ardelia R. 20L
Hall, Isaac 4R, 46R
Hallade, Mlle M. 159R
Hamilton, Clarence H. 2R, 95L, 111L, 114R, 119R, 124R, 134L, 165R
Hanayama, Shinsho 2R
Hand, Wayland D. 68L
Haneda, A. 128R
Haneda, T. 108R
Hang, T. 98R
Hansford, S. Howard 20L, 157L
Happel, Julius 6L, 44L
Happer, A.P. (see also Inquirer, pseud) 44L, 79L
Harding, D.E 6L
Harding, H.L. 65R, 69L, 82R
Hardon, John A. 32L, 47L, 103L
Hardwick, Charles 6L, 32L, 47L, 111L
Hardy, Jacques 39R, 140L
Hardy, Spence 113R
Hare, William L. 6L, 47R, 58R
Harlez, Charles de 6L, 9L, 13L, 24R, 44L, 51L, 54R, 59R, 82R, 87L, 103L, 111L, 115L, 117R, 119R, 124R, 134L, 140L, 142L
Harrassowitz, Otto (publisher) 2R
Hart, Henry H. 72R
Hart, Virgil C. 47L, 58L, 158L
Hartman, L.O. 6L
Hartner, Willy 20L, 87L
Harvey, E.D. 84L
Harvey, Pharis 97R, 105L, 106L
Havret, Henri 12L, 120L, 128R, 153R
Hawkes, David 89R
Hawkridge, Emma 6L
Hay, Eldon R. 27R
Haydon, A. Eustace 71L

Hayes, Helen M. 163L
Hayes, James W. 42L, 79R, 80R, 100L, 101L
Hayes, L. Newton 20L, 71L
Headland, Isaac T. 69L
Hébert-Stevens, François 45R, 146L, 153L, 156R
Hecken, Joseph van 140L
Heckethorn, Charles W. 92R
Hée, Louis van 128R, 147L
Hefter, J. 66L
Heigl, Ferdinand 44L
Heiler, F. 6R, 51L, 103L
Hejzlar, Josef 159R
Hell, H. (E. de T.) 76L
Henderson, William 97R
Henke, Frederick G. 37L
Henry, B.C. 6R, 32L, 39R, 47R, 111L
Henry, Victor 85R
Hentze, Carl 13L, 13R, 16R, 20L, 21R, 23R, 84L,
    103L
Herbert, Edward (pseud of Kenney, Edward H)
    47R
Herder, A.E. von 44L
Hermand, L. 20L
Herrmann, F. 69L, 85R
Herzer, Rudolf 32L, 44L, 97L
Hesse, J. 51L
Hesse-Wartegg, Ernst von 32L
Heyde, Doris 12L
Hickman, Money L. 136R, 159L
Highbaugh, Irma 76L
Hildebrand, Heinrich 148L
Hills, Tynette, Wilson 34L, 48R
Hinneberg, P. von 6L
Hinton, Harold C. 97L
Hiordthal, Th. 62R
Hirakawa, A. 113L
Hirayama, Amane 92R
Hirth, Friedrich 20R, 32L
Ho, Berching 93L, 100R
Ho, Chien 159R
Ho, Lien-kwei 105R
Ho, Ping-yü 62R, 63L, 65L
Ho, Wai-kam 151L
Ho, Wellington 97L
Hoang, Tzu-yue 32L, 51L
Hoare, J.C. 27R
Hobson, H.E. 150L
Hobson, R.L. 156L
Hodgson, B.H. 111L, 128R
Hodous, Lewis 20R, 32L, 47R, 65R, 66L, 69L,
    72R, 76L, 76R, 92R, 95L, 95R, 105R, 109R,
    128R, 165R
Hoech, G.T. 150L
Hoernle, A.F.R. 120L
Hoffman, Johann J. 92R
Hollis, Howard C. 20R, 151L
Holth, Sverre 9L, 129L, 169L
Holzman, Donald 59R
Holzmann, Ferdinand 51L
Hommel, R.P. 72R
Hong, Sheng-hwa 92L

Hoogers, Joseph 38L, 39R
Hooyman 76R, 100L
Hopkins, E. Washburn 13R, 32L, 47R
Hopkins, J. Castell 105R
Hopkins, Lionel C. 13R, 20R, 83L, 84L
Hornblower, G.D. 20R
Horning, Emma 66L
Horton, Walter M. 6R, 111L
Hosie, Lady 22R, 45L
Hotchkiss, Anna H. 157L
Houlné, Lucien 137L
Howe, P.W.H. 103L
Howey, M. Oldfield 20R
Hrdličková, V. 129L, 163L, 164L
Hsiang, Paul S. 27R, 32R, 37L
Hsiao, Kung-ch'üan 44L, 92R
Hsiao, Paul S.Y. 32R, 51L, 56L
Hsieh, E.T. 87L
Hsieh, Tehyi 32R
Hsieh, Yu-wei 37L, 38L
Hsiung, Pin-ming 51R
Hsu, Francis L.K. 6R, 38L, 40L, 69L, 85R, 87L,
    103L
Hsü, Pao-chien 37L
Hsü, Shin-yi 72R
Hsü Ti-shan 47R
Hsü, Vivian 140L, 164L
Hsu, William 167L
Hu, Chang-tu 6R
Hu, Hsien-chin 40L
Hu, Shih 24R, 27R, 44L, 51R, 129L, 137L,
    138R, 164L
Huang, Chia-cheng (François Houang) 111L,
    129L
Huang, K'uei-yen 44L
Huang, Lucy Jen 97L
Huang, Shou-fu 158L
Huang, Tzu-ch'ing 63L
Huang, Wen-shan 13R, 20R
Huard, Pierre 87L, 164L
Hubbard, Elbert 32R
Hubbard, Gilbert E. 79R
Huber, Éd. 120L, 142L, 164L
Hubert, Ch. 44L
Hubert, Henri 9L
Hubrig 42L
Huby, Joseph 10R
Hudson, B.W. 79R
Hudson, G.F. 22R, 45L
Hudson, W.H. 27R
Hudspeth, W.H. 72R
Huebotter, Franz 54R, 87L
Huebsch, Daniel A. 8R
Hugh, Albert Y. 92R
Hughes E.R. 6R, 24R, 136R
Hughes, K. 6R
Huizenga, Lee S. 72R, 87L
Hull, R.F.C. 63L
Hulsewé, A.F.P. 129L, 163L
Hume, Edward H. 87L
Hume, Robert E. 32R, 47R, 103L

Hummel, Arthur W. 120L, 122L
Hummel, Margaret G. 76R
Hummel, Siegbert 51R, 56L, 72R, 154R, 161R
Humphreys, Christmas 6R, 114L, 138R
Humphreys, H. 16R
Hundhauser, Vincenz 51R
Hurd, William 6R
Hurst, R.W. 148L
Hurvitz, Leon 51R, 120L, 124R, 129L, 133L,
    134L, 135L, 137R
Hutchinson, John A. 6R
Hutson, James 65R, 72R, 92R, 105R
Hwang, Teh-shih 98R

I, Ying-ki 129L
Ianson, Meredith 50L
Ibara, T. 114L
Idumi, Hokei 115L
Ikeda, Suetoshi 27R
Ildephonse, Dom Prior 79R
Imbault-Huart, Camille 44R, 58L, 76R, 79R, 89R,
    129L, 144R, 160R
Imbert, Henri 76R
Ingalls, Jeremy 6R
Inge, W.R. 122R
Inglis, James W. 111L, 161R, 169L
Ingram, J.H. 13R
Innes, Kathleen E. 13L
Inquirer (pseud for Happer, A.P.) 44R
Inveen, Emma 159L
Irving, Christopher 158L
Irving, E.A. 60R, 79R, 140L
Ito, C. 20R, 148R
Ivanovski, A.O. 120L
Iwai, Hirosato 120L, 144R
Iwamoto, Yutaka 115L
Izushi, Yoshihiko 16R
Izutsu, Toshihiko 56R

J. 40L, 81R
J.M. 44R
Jacquet, E. 59R
Jaltso, Shirob 167L
James, Edwin O. 6R, 16R, 27R, 103L
James, F. Huberty 27R, 69R, 92R
Jameson, R.D. 90L
Jan, Yün-hua 120L, 129L, 129R, 134L, 142L,
    144R
Jang, Ching-schun 51R
Javorsky, Dorothea 154L
Jaworski, J. 115L
Jayne, H.H.F. 151L, 160R
Jenyns, Soame 154R
Jeremias, Alfred 6R
Johnson, Obed S. 63L
Johnson, Samuel 7L
Johnston, Charles 95R
Johnston, E.H. 115L
Johnston, Reginald Fleming 7L, 32R, 69R, 72R,
    81R, 85R, 95R, 105R, 111L, 111R, 134L,
    144R, 158L, 164L, 165R, 169L
Jong, J.W. de 115R, 120L

Joos, G. 32R, 51R
Joyce, T.A. 151L, 151R
Julien, Stanislas 52R, 54R, 58R, 85R, 90L, 108R,
    109L, 133L, 134L, 142L, 142R, 144L, 163L,
    169L
Jundt, Pierre 5R
Jung, C.G. 55R, 63L, 65L
Jung, Hwa Yol 37L
Jung, Moses 35L, 105L
Jurji, Edward J. 7L, 24L, 32L, 32R, 47R, 105R
K. 44R
K.F. 72R
Kahlenbach, Gerhard 51R, 53R
Kaiten, Nukariya 137R
Kaizuka, Shigeki 32R
Kaler, Grace 20R
Kalff, L. 40L
Kaltenmark, Maxime 7L, 12L, 16R, 24R, 32R,
    47R, 51R, 55L, 58L, 59R, 63L, 81R, 87L,
    105R
Kaltenmark, Odile 7L
Kalvodová, Dana 90L
Kamstra, J.H. 129R
Kanaoka, Shuyu 146R
K'ang Yu-wei 95R
Kao, Chü-hsün 25L, 73L
Karlgren, Bernhard 14L, 19R, 20R, 86L, 120L
Karutz, Richard 144R, 161R
Kasugai, Shinya 129R
Katō, Jōken 27R
Katschen, Leopold 92R
Kaul, T.N. 157L
Keep, Ann E. 146L
Kellett, E.E. 32R
Kelley, Charles F. 151R, 154R
Kennedy, J. 129R
Kennelly, M. 4R, 66L
Kenney, Edward H. (see Herbert, Edward, pseud)
Kenny, P.D. 7L
Kermadec, H. de 66R
Kern, Maximilian 7L, 32R, 47R
Kershaw, F.S. 156L
Kervyn, Joseph 87R
Kiang, Alfred 140L, 167L
Kiang, Chao-yuan 14L, 85R
Kiang, Kang-hu 37L
Kielhorn, F. 120L
Kim, Chewon 13R, 16R, 103L
Kimm, Chung Se 120L
Kimura, Eiichi 25L, 32R, 51R, 58L
Kimura, Mitsutaka 120L
Kimura, Ryūkan 129R
King, Gordon 157L, 160R
King, Winston L. 47R, 103L, 111R, 169L
Kingman, S. 151R
Kingsmill, Thomas W. 16R, 51R
Kishi, Masakatsu 157R
Kitagawa, Joseph M. 7L, 96R, 118R, 167R
Klaproth, Julius H. 47R, 48R, 81R, 111R, 140R,
    142R

Klatt, Werner 97L
Klee, Th. 151R, 156R, 157L, 157R, 160R
Klügmann, Karl 32R, 79R
Knodt, E. 71L
Kobayashi, T. 44R
Koehn, Alfred 38R, 73L
Koeppen, George von 14L, 83L
Koerber, Hans Nordewin von 161R
Komor, Mathias 20R
König, Franz 5L
König, H. 84L
Konow, Sten 129R
Kopsch, H. 58L
Körner, Brunhild 20R, 66R, 69R
Körner, Theo 84L
Köster, Hermann 7L, 14L, 20R
Kraemer, H. 7L
Kramer, Gerald P. 98R
Kramer, Ilse 32R
Kramer, Samuel N. 15R
Kramers, R.P. 2R, 32R, 51R, 97L
Kranz, P. 7L, 40L
Krause, Friedrich E.A. 7L, 33L, 44R, 47R,
    111R
Kremsmayer, Heimo 84R
Krieg, Claus W. 16R
Krieger 159L
Kroker, Eduard Josef M. 56R
Krone, Rudolf 48L, 79R, 111R
Kronfuss, Wilhelm 88L
Krueger, H.E. 157L
Krueger, R. 109L
Ku, Hung-ming 37L, 95R
Kuan, Chiung 165R
Kubayashi, Yukio 45R
Kubo, Noritada 58L, 129R
Kühnert, J. 17L, 28L
Kulp, Daniel Harrison II 69R
Kung, Chan-yuen 100L
Kung, Hsien-lan 20R, 33L
Kung, Tien-min 124R, 169L
Kuntze, Hertha 153R
Kuo, Chü-ching 38R
Kuo, Huo-lieh 167R
Kuo, P.C. 14L
Kuong-hoa (Li, Joseph) 103R, 105R
Kupfer, Carl F. 79R, 159L, 165R
Kuroda, C. 120L
Kurz, H. 14L

L.M.N. 83L
Labadie-Lagrave, G. 92R
Lacouperie, Albert J.B. Terrien de 17L, 73L,
    120L, 129R, 142R
LaDany, Ladislao 97L
Lahiri, Miss Latika 110R, 111R
Laidlay, J.W. 142R
Lair, H.P. 33L
Laird, P.J. 87R
Lalou, Marcelle 2R, 109R, 121R, 154R
Laloy, Louis 59R
Lamairesse, E. 111R

Lamiot, Louis 142R
Lamotte, Étienne 115L, 120R, 129R, 158L,
    161R
Lancashire, Douglas 33L, 95R, 129R, 169L
Lancaster, Lewis R. 120R
Lanciotti, Lionello 14L, 84R, 137R
Lanczkowski, Günter 51R, 103R
Landon, Perceval 144R
Landor, A. Henry Savage (see Savage-Landor, A H.)
Landresse 140R, 142R
Langerhans, Heinz 167L
Lanjuinais, J.D. 71L
Lanöe, F. 76R, 81R
Lao, Kan 151R, 159R
Lapicque, P.A. 42L
Laprairie, Père 69R
Lartigue, J. 148L, 157R
Latham, A. 148L
Latourette, Kenneth Scott 7L
Laufer, Berthold 21L, 25L, 40L, 84R, 120R,
    134L, 142R, 154R, 161R
Laurence, Y. 136L
La Vallée Poussin, Louis de 2R, 109L, 112L,
    115L, 115R, 120R, 124R, 145L
Lavollée, C. 7L, 81L
Lay, W.T. 25L
Leboucq, P. 92R, 93L
Le Coq, Albert von (see Coq, Albert von le)
Lecourt, H. 73L
Lee, André 17L
Lee, Charles L. (pseud for Yen, P'u-sheng) 83L
Lee, Dana 35L
Lee, H.T. 33L, 167R
Lee, Peter H. 129R, 134L
Lee, Pi-cheng [Lü, Pi-ch'eng] 73L, 124R, 161R
Lee, Rensselaer W. III 97L
Lee, Shao-chang 33L, 120R, 163L
Lee, Sherman E. 151R
Lee, Siow Mong 164L
Lee, T'ao 73L, 79R, 87R
Lee, Teng Hwee 37L
Lee, Tim 130L
Lee, W.J. 33L, 97L
Lees, G.F. 21L
Legge, James 7L, 26L, 33L, 44R, 48L, 51R,
    55L, 103R, 141R, 142R
Lehmann, Edward 5R
Lemaître, Solange 28L
LeMoine, A. 33R
Lenormand, Ch. 39R, 140L
Leon, Mariette 142L
Leong, Y.K. 40L, 66R, 163L
Leprince-Ringuet, M.F. 79R
Lerner, Martin 156L
Leslie, Daniel 33L
Lessa, William A. 40L, 83L
Lessing, Ferdinand D. 21L, 33L, 109L, 145L,
    147L, 154R, 164L
Letourneau, Charles 7R
Leung, A.K. 69R, 76R
Leung, Tit-sang 88L

Leuridan, Thre. 151R
Levenson, Joseph R. 25L, 96R, 97L
Lévesque, Léonard 98R
Lévi, Sylvain 108L, 114L, 115R, 120R, 122L,
    126R, 129R, 130L, 143L, 161R, 162R
Levy, Howard S. 25L, 58L
Levy, Isidore 9L
Levy, Marion J. jr. 106L
Levy, Paul 143L
Li, Hsin-tsung 143L
Li, Huan-hsin 87R
Li, Joseph (see Kuong-hoa)
Li, Shih-yü 69L, 79L
Li, Wei-tsu 69R, 73L
Li, Yih-yuan 98R
Li, Yung-hsi 143L
Liang, Ch'i-ch'ao 95L, 124R, 130L
Liang, Si-ing 33L
Liang, Ssu-ch'eng 148L, 148R, 150L, 155R
Liao, T'ai-ch'u 93L
Liebenthal, Walter 28L, 52L, 103R, 111R, 115R,
    120R, 124R, 130L, 133L, 134L, 134R, 137R,
    151R, 164L
Liétord 87R, 143L
Life Magazine Editorial Staff 7R
Lillico, S. 33R
Lim, Boon Keng 33R
Lim, K.W. 147L
Limpricht, W. 158L
Lin, Li-kouang 115R, 120R, 134R
Lin, T.C. 48L
Lin, Wen-lang 99L
Lin, Yueh-hwa 76R, 81R
Lin, Yutang 52L
Lindsay, J.H. 151R
Ling, Jui-tang 17L
Ling, Peter C. 59R
Ling, Shun-sheng 14L, 17L, 40L, 44R, 73L,
    90L, 103R
Link, Arthur E. 58R, 121L, 130L, 134R
Linossier, Raymond 147L
Lion, Lucien 21L, 87R
Liou, Tse Houa 55L
Little, Alicia Bewicke 7R, 140L
Little, Archibald J. 7R, 158L
Little, D.B. 151R
Liu, Chi-wan 73L, 79R, 99L
Liu, Chiang 69R, 76R, 81R
Liu, Chün-wang 98L
Liu, Guan-ying 137R
Liu, Hua-yang 55L
Liu, James T.C. 44R
Liu, Ts'un-yan 25L, 37L, 63L, 90L,
    164R
Liu, Wu-chi 33R
Liu, Wu-long 109R
Llewellyn, Bernard 93L
Lo, Ch'ang-p'ei 164R
Lo, Dorothy 76R, 100L
Lo, Hsiang-lin 100L, 130L, 133L, 155R
Lo, Jung-pang 36R

Lo, L.C. 63L
Lobsiger-Dellenbach, W. 151R
Loehr, Max 21L, 155L
Loewe, Michael 25L
Loewenstein, Prince John 21L
Lohmann, T. 7R, 97L
Loi 140L
Lombard-Salmon, Claudine 100R
London, Ivan D. 97L
London, Mariam B. 97L
Long, Charles H. 118L
Lou, Dennis Wing-sou 14L, 73L, 103R
Lounsberry, G. Constant 138R
Lovegren, L.A. 148L, 150R
Lovelock, B. 21L
Löwenthal, Rudolf 95R
Lu, Gwei-djen 3L, 87R
Lu, Hung-nien 79R
Lu, K'uan-yu (Luk, Charles) 55L, 63L, 65R,
    115R, 137R
Lubke, A. 28L
Lucius 145L
Ludwig, Ernst 146L, 148L
Luk, Charles (pseud of Lu, K'uan-yü) 115R, 133L,
    134R, 137R
Lum, Chung Park 83L
Lum, Peter 76R
Lust, John 2R
Lüth, Paul E.H. 52L
Lutschewitz, W. 69R, 93L
Lyall, Alfred C. 44R
Lyman, Stanford M. 93L, 100R
Lyon, D. Willard 33R
Lyon, David N. 73L
Lyon, Quinter M. 7R

MacCulloch, John A. 16R
MacGowan, D.J. 83L, 130L, 145L
MacGowan, John 90L
MacInnis, Donald E. 97L
MacIntosh, Charles Henry 48L
MacIntyre, John 69R
MacKenzie, Donald A. 17L
MacKenzie, Norman 94R
MacLagan, Patrick J. 28L, 48L, 69R, 71L, 76R,
    103R, 145L
Maclure, M. 89R
Madrolle, Claudius 158L
Maejima, Shinji 130L
Mahdihassan, S. 63L, 63R
Maître, Ch. E. 121L
Maki, Itsu 121L
Makita, Tairyō 10L, 134R
Malebranche, Nicolas 33R
Malan, Saloman C. 103R, 169L
Mallman, Marie Thérèse de 147L, 161R
Malval, J. 43R
Manabe, Shunshō 85R, 147L
Mangrin, Ignace 93L
Mansfield, M.T. 66R, 90L
Mao, W.E. 7R
Marceron, Désiré J.B. 2R

March, Andrew L. 42L
March, Arthur C. 3L
March, Benjamin 150L, 151R, 155L, 159R
Marchal, H. 147L
Marin, J. 21L
Martin, Alfred W. 33R, 52L
Martin, Ernest 40L, 44R
Martin, Ilse 70L, 77L
Martin, James A. jr 6R
Martin, W.A.P. 7R, 28L, 37L, 40L, 63R, 90L,
    106L, 111R, 150L
Martinie, J.A. 87R, 111R
Maryon, Herbert 21L
Masaki, Haruhiko 130L, 145L
Masdoosi, Ahmad Abdullah al 33R, 48L
Maspero, Henri 5L, 7R, 13L, 14L, 17L, 21L, 25L,
    46R, 48L, 52L, 60L, 60R, 64L, 66R, 73L,
    87R, 103R, 121L, 128L, 130R, 140L, 159L,
    164R
Masson, J. 98R
Masson-Oursel, Paul 7R, 10R, 13L, 64L, 115R
Masters, Frederic J. 93L
Masuda, Jiryo 115R
Masunaga, Reiho 130R, 137R
Mateer, Calvin W. 79R
Matgioï (pseud. of Pouvoirville, A. de) 33R, 48L
    93L, 95R
Mather, Richard B. 121L, 130R, 153R, 160R,
    164R
Matignon, J.J. 7R, 40L, 40R, 140L, 145L
Matsubara, Saburo 156R
Matsumoto, Yeiichi 155L, 159R
Matsunaga, Alicia 124R
Matthias, Leo L. 97R
Maurer, Herrymon 52L
Mayers, William Frederick 40R, 73L, 81R,
    130R, 145L
McAleavy, Henry 134R
McCaffree, Joe E. 14L, 83L
McCarland, S. Vernon 7R
McCartee, D.B. 33R, 73R, 80L
M'Clatchie, M.T. 25L, 28L, 73R, 103R
McDaniel, C. Yates 165R
McFarlane, Sewell S. 21L
McGovern, William M. 111R, 124R
McGowan, D.J. 63L
McGreal, L.F. 4R, 66L
McNair, H.F. 46R, 66L, 111L
McOmber, Douglas 77L
Mead, G.R.S. 48L, 58R, 111R
Mears, Dewey G. 17R
Mears, W.P. 25L, 48L, 103R
Mecklenburg, F.A. 3R
Mecklenburg, K.A. 3R
Mecquenem, J. de 40R
Medhurst, C. Spurgeon 25L, 52L, 103R
Meech, Samuel E. 45L, 160R
Mégroz, R.L. 83L, 104L
Mei, Y.P. 40R
Meier, F.J. 121L
Meister, W. 21L
Meister, Peter Wilhelm 124R, 147L
Melchers, Bernd 148L, 151R

Mély, F. de 64L
Mensching, Gustav 8L
Menzel 8L
Menzies, Allan 8L
Merkel, R.F. 3L
Merton, Thomas 137R, 139L, 169L
Mertz, James E. 85R, 86R 87L
Messing, Otto 33R, 45L
Metzger, Emil 84R
Meunié, Jacques 130R
Meurs, H. van 150L
Meuwese, C. 143L
Meyer, Henriette 117R
Meynard, A. 45L, 115R
Miao, D.F. 17L, 21L, 73R
Michael, Franz H. 97R
Michihata, Ryoshu 130R
Michaud, Paul 25L, 58R
Migéon, Gaston 151R
Migot, André 111R, 158L, 167L
Miles, George 93L
Millard, R.A. 21L
Millican, Frank R. 93L, 95R, 134R, 165R
Milloué, Léon de 8L, 14L, 21R, 30R, 40R, 42L,
    50L, 81R, 83L, 104L, 111R, 146L, 147L
Milne, William C. 25R, 58R, 93L, 150L
Minamoto, H. 147L
Minayeff, I.P. 111R
Minnaert, P. 84R, 85R
Mironov, N.D. 84R, 121L, 161R
Mitchell-Innes, Norman G. 40R, 81R
Mitrophanow, Igor 75L
Mitsunori, Okuno 90L
Miyabe, Tadashi 97R, 105L, 106L
Miyahara, Mimpei 48L
Miyamoto, S. 116R, 123L
Miyazaki, Ichisada 83L
Mizande, François 159L
Mizuno, Kogen 109L
Mizuno, Seiichi 151R, 152L, 157L, 157R, 159R,
    160R
Modi, J.J. 130R
Moebius, P. 83L
Mok, P.R. 163L
Mollard, Sidney G. jr. 81R, 99L, 100R
Möller, N. 52L, 56R
Monestier, Alphonse 134R
Mong, Lee Siow 71L
Montell, G. 71L
Montucci, Antionio 58R
Montuclat 45L, 77L
Moor, de 17L
Moore, Charles A. 26R, 125L
Moore, Frederick 95R
Moore, George F. 8L
Moreau, J. 28L
Morgan, Evan 14L, 55L, 56R, 59R
Morgan, Harry T. 21R, 77L, 85R
Morgan, Kenneth W. 3L, 8L, 112L, 112R
Morgan, W.P. 93L, 100R
Mori, Sodō 77L, 121L

Morisse, Lucien 81R
Morley, Arthur 14R
Moroto, Sojun 40R
Morris, Aldyth V. 26R
Morrison, Mrs H.M. 80L
Morrison, John Robert 17L, 86L
Morrison, Robert 45L, 58R, 93L, 112L
Morse, William R. 87R
Mortier, Florent 14R, 48L, 60R, 64L, 73R, 83L, 86L, 87R, 124R
Mortier, Raoul 7R
Mou, Tseng-san 33R
Moule, A.C. 80L, 150L
Moule, G.E. 45L, 90L, 163L
Mueller, Herbert 60R
Mukherji, Probhat Kumar (Mukhopādhyāya, Prabhāta-Kumārā) 121L, 130R
Mukhopādhyāya, Sujit 130R
Müller, F. Max 5L, 8L, 33R, 48L, 52L, 55L, 112L, 113L, 116L, 121L
Müller, F.W.K. 121L, 164R
Mullie, J. 14R
Mullikin, Mary Augusta 80L, 157L, 160R
Munn, William 40R
Munsterberg, Hugo 14R, 21R, 152L, 156L
Murakami, S. 112L
Murakami, Yoshimi 56R, 104L, 137R, 169L
Muralt, Raoul von 137R
Muramatsu, Yuji 93R
Murata, J. 130R
Murdoch, W.G.B. 152L
Murphy, Gardner 48L, 106L
Murphy, John 8L
Murphy, Lois B. 48L, 106L
Murphy, Maynard 98R
Murray, A.S. 70L
Mury, Francis 93R
Mus, Paul 121L, 125L, 161R

Nagahiro, Toshio 155L, 157L, 157R, 160R
Nagao, Gadjin M. 121L
Nagel, August 73R, 77L
Naitō, Torajirō 116L
Nakagawa, Tadayori 157R
Nakamura, Hajime 37L, 121L
Nakamura, Keijiro 37L
Nakaseko, Rokuro 62L
Nakayama, Shigeru 83L
Nakayama, T. 87R
Nambara, Minoru 2L, 101R
Nance, F. N. 21R
Nanjio, Bunyiu (also written Nanjō Bunyū or Buniyu) 109L, 109R, 116L, 121L
Natsume, Ikken 60R, 83L
Natz, Marie 159L
Needham, Joseph 3L, 61L, 62R, 63L, 64L, 65L, 87R, 131L, 164R
Neef, Hans 52L
Nettle, Gillian 91R

Neumann, Carl (Charles) F. 116R, 143L
Newbold, Lt. 93R
Newell, William H. 81R
Ng, Yong-sang 70L, 73R, 77L, 90L
Nguyen-Van-Quan 87R
Nicolas-Vandier, Nicole 25R, 131L
Nicouleau, M. 66R
Niida, Noboru 106L
Nikhilanda, Swami 35L, 105L
Nilakantasastri, K.A. 143L
Nitschkowsky 40R
Nivison, David S. 37L, 97R
Nobel, Johannes 108R, 116L
Noguier, A. 52L
Noss, John B. 8L, 33R, 48L
Nott, Charles Stanley 21R

Oberle, A. 70L, 90L
O'Brien, Paul W. 116L
Ōchō, Enichi 112L
O'Connor, Patrick 97R
Odontius, L. 90L, 163L
Oehler, W. 37L, 66R, 165R
Oelmann, F. 150L
Ogiwara (see Wogihara)
O'Hara, Albert R. 80L, 99L
Ohara, Masatoshi 116L
Ohashi, Kaishun 131L
Ohlinger, Franklin 83R
Okakura, Kakuso or Kakuzo 116L, 133R
Olschki, L. 131L, 169L
O'Neill, Frederick W.S. 8L
O'Neill, John 17L
Ono, Gemmyō 133R, 134R
Opitz, Peter-Joachim 52L
Orcet, G. d' 145L
Orelli, Conrad von 8L
Osgood, Cornelius 70L
Oshawa, Georg 88L
Osk, Ewald 52L, 52R
Ottewill, H.A. 65R, 73R, 77L
Otto, Johann H. 88L
Otto, P. 77L
Ou, I-Tai 17L
Ou, Yun-joei 64L
Owen, G. 14R, 73R

Pachow, W. 52R, 58R, 104L, 116L, 121R, 169L
Pacifique-Marie, P. d'Aingreville 40R
Pai, Hui 121R
Pal, Pratapaditya 153R
Palatin, W. von 131L
Palatre, Père 81R, 86L, 93R
Palen, Lewis S. 70L
Paléologue, Maurice 40R
Pálos, István (Pálos, Stephan) 64L, 88L
Pang, Tzu-yau 48L
Pantoussoff, N. 148R
Paravey, Charles-Hippolyte de 52R, 55L, 56R

Parker, A.G. 66R
Parker, A.P. 83R
Parker, Edward Harper 8L, 14R, 33R, 37L, 40R,
    45L, 48L, 48R, 52R, 73R, 81R, 84R, 88L,
    112L, 121R, 131L, 169L
Parmentier, H. 148R
Parnell, J. 21R
Parrinder, Edward G. 8R, 33R, 52R, 112L
Parrish, Fred L. 8R, 14R
Parry, D. 59R
Parsons, James B. 25R
Partington, J.R. 64L
Patai, R. 8R, 104L
Paton, William 8R
Paulus, A. 39L, 101R
Pauthier, Georges 28L, 48R, 52R, 58R, 104L, 169L
Pauthier, M. 58R
Pavie, Théodore 8R, 60L, 90L, 163R
Peachey, Paul 136R
Peat, Wilbur D. 153R
Peeters, Hermes 8R, 34L, 48R, 66R, 112L
Peeters, Jan 25R
Peisson, J. 8R
Peisson, Z. 34L
Pelliot, Paul 6L, 20L, 21R, 23R, 28L, 43L, 52R,
    54L, 55L, 58R, 64L, 93R, 108R, 109L, 114R,
    121R, 123R, 125R, 126R, 131L, 141R,
    143L, 145R, 152L, 155L, 159R, 160L,
    161R
Penniman, T.K. 21R
Peri, Noël 140L, 159L, 161R
Pernitzsch, Max G. 8R
Perrot, Albert 34L, 45L, 95R
Perry, John 17R
Perry, John W. 17L, 45L
Perzynski, F. 71L
Petit, J.A. 8R
Petrucci, Raphaël 146L, 155L, 159R
Petterson, Richard 21R, 99L
Petty, Orville A. 94R
Petzold, Bruno 121R, 125L, 133R, 137R
Pfizmaier, August 55L, 60L, 64L, 73R, 82L
Pfleiderer, Otto 8R
Phelps, Dryden Linsley 158L
Philastre, P.L.F. 55L
Philosinensis (pseud of Gützlaff, Charles, q.v.)
Pichon, Jean-Charles 14R, 21R
Pickering, W.A. 93R
Pike, E. Royston 37R
Pillai, A. Balakrishna 131L
Pitcher, P.W. 40R
Piton, Charles 112L, 131L
Planchat, Edmond 34L
Plath, J.H. 14R
Playfair, G.M.H. 45L, 93R
Plopper, Clifford H. 90L
Plumer, James M. 22L, 152L, 159R, 160R
Pohlman, W.J. 37R, 162L
Poirot 7R
Pokora, Timoteus 64L, 131L
Politella, Joseph 34L, 48R

Polonyi, P. 156L
Pommeranz-Liedtke, Gerhard 22L, 66R, 155L
Pomonti, M. 19R
Pompignan, R.H. Assier de 111R
Poon, Eddie K.K. 2L
Poor, Robert 152L, 162L
Poore, Major R. 40R, 104L
Pope, John A. 156L
Porkett, Manfred 88L, 90R
Porter, Henry D. 70L, 93R
Poseck, Helena von 41L, 90R
Pott, William S.A. 37R
Potter, Charles Francis 34L, 52R
Potter, Jack M. 41L, 42L, 70L
Pouvoirville, Albert de (see also Matgioï, pseud)
    93R
Pratt, James Bissett 112L, 125L, 165R
Préau, André 48R, 64L
Preston, John 80L, 86L
Price, A.T. 116L
Price, Frank W. 8R, 167L
Price, P.F. 41L
Priest, Alan 22L, 73R, 152L
Prinsep, James 22L
Prip-Møller, Johannes 140L, 140R, 145L, 149L,
    150L
Pruden, Leo M. 121R
Průšek, Jaroslav 164R
Przyluski, Jean 22L, 83R, 104L, 121R, 122L,
    145L, 147L, 164R, 169R
Puech, H.C. 8R

R., S.C.B. (see also Reitz, S.C.B.) 14R, 22L
Rachewiltz, Igor de 25R, 131L, 134R
Radloff, W. 116L
Raguin, Yves E. 131L, 167L, 167R
Rahder, Johannes 109L, 116R
Raja, C.K. 143L
Rall, Jutta 88L
Ramanan, K. Venkata 116R
Randall, J. Herman 32L
Rankin, Mary L.B. 93R
Rao, M. Basava 152L
Rape, C.B. 93R, 169R
Ratchnevsky, Paul 12L
Ravary, P. 41L
Ravenholt, Albert 97R
Rawlinson, Frank J. 8R, 28L, 37R, 93R, 95R
Re, Arundel del 169R
Read, Bernard E. 64L, 88L, 157L
Reece, John H. 10R
Reed, John H. 99R
Rees, J. Lambert 8R, 164R
Regnault, Jules 42R, 86L
Reichelt, Karl Ludvig 9L, 112L, 145L, 165R,
    166L
Reid, Gilbert P. 34L, 48R, 56R, 96L
Reid, J.M. 112R
Reischauer, August Karl 9L, 28L
Reischauer, Edwin O. 131R
Reitz, S.C.B. 152L, 152R
Rémusat (see Abel-Rémusat, J.P.)
Renondeau, G. 165L

Reuss, Alfred 161L
Reuter, J.N. 116R
Réveillère, Contre-Admiral 28L
Réville, Albert 6L, 9L
Reynolds, M.E. 50L
Rhie, Marylin M. 152R, 157R
Rhys-David, T.W. 144L
Riboud, Mme Krishna 159R
Richard, Timothy 77L, 88R, 90R, 93R, 112R,
    116R, 122L, 163R, 164R
Richardson, Ernest Cushing 3L
Riddel, W.H. 17R, 22L
Ring, George C. 9L
Ringgren, Helmer 28R, 66R
Ringgren, Inga 66R
Roberts, L. 22L, 41L
Roberts, Laurance P. 153R
Robinson, Lydia G. 59L
Robinson, Richard H. 112R, 116R, 133R, 134R
Robiou, F. 3L, 14R
Rochline, Marianne 91R
Rock, Joseph F. 84R
Rockhill, William W. 158L
Rogers, Millard 22L
Roi, J. 64L
Roll, Christian 97R
Rondot, Natalis 159L
Rosenberg, Otto 109L, 166L
Rosenkranz, Gerhard 17R, 34L, 48R, 104L,
    112R
Rosny, Léon de 9L, 48R, 52R, 55R, 58R,
    109L, 112R
Ross, E. Denison 109R
Ross, Floyd H. 34R, 48R
Ross, John 14R, 28L, 34L
Rosthorn, A.V. 143R
Rostovtzeff, M.I. 73R
Rotermund, W. 37R, 52R, 125L
Rotours, Robert des 14R, 34L, 73R, 104L
Roussel, Alfred 166L
Roussel, Romain 80L, 143R
Rousselle, Erwin 14R, 17R, 28L, 34L, 42R, 45L,
    48R, 53L, 56R, 64R, 65R, 73R, 77L, 96L,
    133R, 134R, 137R, 138L, 145L, 155L, 162L
Rowland, Benjamin jr. 147L, 152R
Rowley, Harold H. 9L, 14R, 104L, 106L
Roy, A.T. 34L, 34R, 96L
Rudd, H.F. 37R
Rué, M. 93R
Rule, Paul A. 25R, 104L
Ruyer, R. 28R
Rychterová, Eva 22L, 41L
Rydh, Hannah 15L, 22L, 74L, 82L
Rygaloff, Alexis 34R

S.v.F. 80L
Sach, E. von 102R
Sachse, H. 38R
Sadler, J. 70L
Saglio, Charles 93R
Saha, Kshanika 131R

Saint-Denys, le Marquis d'Hervey 34R
Saint Ina, Marie de 28R, 34R
Saint-martin, Vivien de 144L
Saintyves, P. 145R
Saitschik, Robert 34R, 53L
Sakamaki, Shunzo 138L
Sakamoto, Yukio 125L
Salmony, Alfred 22L, 22R, 152R
Sampson, Theos 82L
Sargent, Galen E. 25R, 131R, 134R
Sarkar, B.K. 9L, 104L, 169R
Sarre, F. 156L
Sasaki, G. 133R
Sasaki, Genjun H. 133R
Sasaki, Nobuji 61L
Sasaki, Ruth Fuller 136R
Sasaki, Shigetsu (see Sokei-an)
Saso, Michael R. 48R, 58R, 64R, 77L, 99L
Sastri, S.S. Suryanarayana 122L
Sato, Mitso 140R
Saunders, E. Dale 147L
Saunders, Kenneth J. 131R, 140R, 166L
Saussaye, P.D. Chantepie de la 9L, 110R
Saussure, Léopold de 22R, 28R, 104L
Savage, Katherine 9L
Savage-Landor, A. Henry 80L, 158R
Sawamura, Sentarō 150L
Scaligero, Massimo 64R, 104R
Scarborough, William 80L, 90R
Schaeder, Hans H. 149L
Schaefer, Thomas E. 37R
Schaeffer, Phil 116R, 166L
Schafer, Edward H. 9R, 15L, 82L, 83R
Schalek, Alice 41L
Schang, Tscheng-tsu 84R
Scherman, Lucian 147R, 152R
Schindler, Bruno 15L, 28R
Schipper, Kristofer M. 55R, 59L, 61L, 64R, 80L,
    90R, 99L
Schlegel, Gustave 45L, 66R, 74L, 77L, 94L, 100R,
    109L, 122L, 131R, 141L, 143R, 162L
Schloss, Oskar 3L
Schmeltz, J.D.E. 82L
Schmidt, Charles 34R, 80L
Schmidt, H. 147R
Schmidt, K.O. 53L
Schmidt, P. 28R, 104R
Schmitt, Erich 6L, 9R, 34R, 60R
Schneider, Herbert W. 35L, 105L, 110R
Schneider, Laurence A. 34R
Schneider, Louis 131L, 164R
Schnitzer, Joseph 155L, 163R
Schnupftabaksdose 45L
Schoeps, Hans-Joachim 9R
Schott, Wilhelm 112R, 122L, 125L
Schram, Stuart R. 94L, 97R
Schröder, C.M. 66R
Schroeder, Dominik 70L, 77L
Schubert, J. 131R
Schubert, Renate 55R

Schüler, Wilhelm 45L, 60R, 82L, 90R
Schultze, O. 22R, 74L
Schulz, Bernard 53L
Schuster, C. 22R, 104R
Scidmore, Eliza R. 77L
Scott, Alexander C. 41L, 146L
Ščuckij, J. 125L
Seckel, Dietrich 138L, 146L, 147R, 152R, 155L
Sedgwick, Ellery 122L
Segalen, Victor 146L
Seidel, Anna K. 59L, 60L, 64R
Sekino, Tadashi 156R
Selby, T.G. 125L, 163R
Semenoff, Marc 34R
Sen, Satiranjan 88L, 122L
Serebrennikov, J.J. 41L
Servus 125L
Seu, A.C. 143R
Seu, Kshtiti Mohan 131R
Shastri, H.P. 55R, 104R
Shaw, R.D.M. 138L
Sheffield, D.Z. 37R, 104R
Shen, C.T. 125L
Shen, Ting-su 77L
Sherley-Price, Lionel D. 34R, 104R
Shibata, Masumi 138L
Shields, E.T. 158L
Shih, Chao-yin 30L
Shih, Ching-ch'eng 15L, 41L
Shih, Joseph 28R, 34R, 56R, 104R
Shih, Robert 131R, 135L
Shih, Sheng-Kang 109R
Shih, Vincent Y.C. 28R, 94L
Shinkai, Taketarō 157R
Shinmi, Hiroshi 97R, 105L, 106L
Shirokogoroff, S.M. 84R
Shoku, Soyen 116R
Shor, Franc 159R
Shor, Jean 159R
Short, Dorothy 30L, 54L
Shryock, John K. 16R, 34R, 44L, 45L, 68L, 70R,
    76L, 80R, 85L
Shu, Seyuan 37R
S[huck], J.L. 74L
Sickman, Laurence 146L, 149L, 152R, 155L
Silabhadra, Bhikkhu 143R
Silva-Vigrier, Anil de 160L, 161L
Simbriger, Heinrich 28R
Simmons, P. 22R, 156L
Simon, Eugène 40R, 104L, 104R
Simpson, William 145R
Sims, Bennett B. 34R
Sinensis 17R, 42R
Siren, Osvald 138L, 145R, 146L, 148R, 152R,
    155L
Sivin, Nathan A. 64R, 88L
Skinner, G. William 3L
Slater, N.B. 96L

Sjöholm, Gunnar 15L, 28R, 106L
Smalley, Frank A. 9R
Smart, Ninian 9R, 34R, 48R
Smith, Arthur H. 34R, 66R
Smith, Carl T. 34R, 53L, 104R
Smith, D. Howard 9R, 15L, 28R, 74L, 104R
Smith, G. Elliot 74L
Smith, Helmer 122L
Smith, Huston 28R, 34R, 48R, 104R
Smith, J.L. Gardner 32L
Smith, Mrs J. Gregory 9R
Smith, Stanley 9R
Smith, Wilfred C. 28R
Sneath, E. Hershey 29R, 36L
Söderblom, Nathan 9R, 15L, 104R
Sohier, A. 97R
Sokei-an (Sasaki, Shigetsu) 163R
Solomon, Bernard S. 56R, 104R
Soon, Tan Tek 22R
Soothill, William E. 9R, 22R, 45L, 45R, 109R
Soper, Alexander C. 22R, 146L, 147R, 148R,
    149L, 150L, 152R, 153L, 153R, 154L, 155L,
    155R, 156L, 156R, 160L
Soper, Edmund D. 9R
Soulié, Charles George de Morant 35L, 86L, 88L
Sowerby, Arthur de Carle 70R, 77R
Soymié, Michel 3L, 17R, 22R, 60R, 80R, 83R,
    135L, 147R, 161L
Sparham, Charles G. 104R
Sparling, G.W. 94L
Specht, Édouard 122L
Speed, John G. 94L, 100R
Speer, Robert E. 9R, 104R
Spencer, Sidney 35L, 49L
Spiegel, H. 41L
Spiegelberg, Frederic 9R, 138L
Splitter, Henry W. 77R
Spooner, Roy C. 64R
Sprague, Roger 148R, 153L
Spruyt, A. 74L, 157R
Stadelmann, Heinrich 64R
Staël-Holstein, A. von 121R, 122L, 131R, 143R,
    162L
Staiger, Brunhild 35L, 97R
Stange, H.O.H. 9R
Stanley, Arthur 159L
Stanley, Charles A. jr 35L, 41L, 80R
Stanton, William 94L
Starr, Frederick 35L
Stauffer, M.T. 95R
Stein, Mark Aurel 108R, 119R, 143R, 154L, 155R,
    160L, 161L
Stein, O. 65L
Stein, Rolf A. 10L, 22R, 25R, 59L, 65L, 149L
Steininger, Hans 29L, 45R, 55R, 65L, 90R, 131R
Steinkirk, Martin (see Tao-chun, pseud)
Stenz, Georg M. 70R
Stevenson, J. 131R
Stewart, James Livingstone 10L, 104R
Stewart-Lockhart, J.H. 67L

Stiassny, M. 83R, 147R
Stirling, W.G. 83R, 86L, 94L, 94R, 100R, 101L
Stolberg, Baron 38R
Storrs, Christopher 35L
Strausz 29L
Strickmann, M. 65L
Stringer, H. 42R
Ström, Ake 66R
Stronath, Alexander 10L
Stroup, Herbert 112R
Stuart, J. Leighton 77R
Stübe, Rudolf 10L, 15L, 35L, 53L
Stuhr, P.F. 45R, 169R
Su, Jyun-hsyong 37R
Su, Ying-hui 160L
Sudzuki, Osamu 153L
Sullivan, Michael 22R, 80R, 161L
Sumiya, Kazuhiko 97R, 105L, 106L
Sun, Chan-ko 77R
Sun, E-tu Zen 24L, 127L
Sung, H.C. 77R
Sung, Lung-fei 99L
Suppaner-Stanzel, Irene 37R, 56R, 105L
Sutton, S.C. 109L
Suzuki, Beatrice Lane 125L, 162L
Suzuki, Daisetz Teitaro 74L, 90R, 109R, 116R,
    122L, 125L, 131R, 133R, 138L, 138R,
    139L, 145R, 162L
Swallow, Robert W. 70R, 77R, 158R
Swann, Peter C. 45R, 146L, 153L, 156R
Sykes, William H. 109R, 122L, 165R

T.C.A. 21R
Taam, Cheuk-woon 3L, 35L
T'ai-hsü (T'ai-hü) 125L, 131R, 166L
Takakusu, Junjirō 108L, 116R, 122L, 122R,
    125L, 132L, 135L, 143R, 162L, 163R,
    169R
Takasaki, Jikido 122R
Takata, Ninkaku 125R
Takeuchi, Teruo 35L, 37R
Takezo, Y. 114R
Tamaki, Kōshirō 125R, 135L, 169R
Tamura, Zitsuzo 45R
T'an, Chung-yo 158L
Tan, J.M. 17R
T'an, Yün-shan 10L, 105L, 112R
Tang-che, Colonel 37R
T'ang, Chün-i 35L, 105L
T'ang, Leang-li 94L
Tang, Peter S.H. 70R
T'ang, Yung-t'ung (also Tang Yong-torng) 122R,
    123L, 130L
Tani, Nobukazu 153L
Tao-chün (pseud of Steinkirk, Martin) 161L
Tao, Frank 77R
Tao, L.K. 40L, 66R, 163L
Tao, Pung-fai 86L
Tapper, H. Allen, jr. 30R, 49L
Tarling, Nicholas 95R
Taussig, H.C. 97R
Tavernier, E. 41L
Taylor, G. 143R
Tchang, Mathias 41L

Templer, William 67R, 89L
Ten Broek, Janet Rinaker 59L
Teng, Chien-wu 161L
Terrill, Ross 97R, 105L, 106L
Tetlie, Joseph 9L
The, Sian Giap 100R
Thelin, Mark 99L
Thiel, Joseph (P.I.) pseud of Matthias Eder 41L,
    59L, 70R, 74L, 80R, 82L, 84R, 86L, 132L
Thiersant, Dabry de 38R
Thomas, F.W. 116R, 117L, 123L, 132L, 143R
Thomas, Henry 35L
Thomas, M.M. 97R
Thompson, Laurence G. 10L, 99L
Thompson, Sylvanus P. 21R
Thornberry, Mike 35L, 105L
Thrupp, Sylvia L. 23R
Thurn, E. 169R
Tiberi, Fortunato 41L
Tiele, C.P. 15L
Tien, Antoine Tcheu-kang 29L
Tien, Tsung 60L, 77R, 94L
Ting, Chung 96R
Ting, Su 83R
Ting, W.Y. 10L
Titsch, F. 3L
Tizac, H. d'Ardenne de 153L
Todo, Kyoshun 132L
Tokiwa, Daijo 153L, 156R
Tomii, M. 15R
Tomita, Kojirō 22R, 23L, 153L, 155R, 160L
Tomomatsu, E. 123L
Tomonobu, A. Imamichi 56R
Tompkinson, Leonard 37R, 106L
Tonn, W.Y. 55R, 77R
Too-yu 35L, 105L, 112R, 169R
Topley, Marjorie 3R, 25R, 35L, 67L, 80R, 86L,
    88L, 94L, 100R, 101L, 167R
Torney, D.V. von 29L
Torrance, Thomas 41L, 82L
Touan, Tchang-yuan 37R
Tourchier, Louis 10L
Tournois 148R
Trager, Frank N. 97R
Tran-Ham-Tan 45R, 74L, 80R, 82L
Trask, Willard R. 27L, 83R
Trautz, F.M. 145R
Tredwell, Winifred Reed 23L
Trève, Jacques 53L
Trevor, M.H. 138R
Trimborn, Hermann 24L
Trippner, P.J. 70R, 74L, 88R, 168L
Tröltsch, Charlotte Freifrau de 53L
Trood, S.M.E. 35R, 49L
Trubner, H. 153L
Ts'ai, Yuan-pei 96L
Ts'ao, T'ien-ch'in 63L, 65L
Tsao, Wen-yen 35R
Tscharner, Eduard Horst von 10L, 29L, 38L, 53L,
    57L
Tschen, Yin-ko 88R, 135L

Tschepe, A. 35R, 80R, 148R
Tseng, Lai-ting 109R
Tseung, F.I. 83R, 101L
Tsu, Yu-yue 96L, 140R, 166L
Tsujimura, Kōichi 138R
Tsukamoto, Zenryū 10L, 112R, 120R, 129L,
    132L, 134R, 135L, 157R, 166L
Tsumaki, Naoyoshi 49L
Tubyansky, M. 123L
Tucci, Giuseppe 29L, 117L, 123L, 132L, 147R,
    162L
Tung, Tso-pin 15L
Turnbull, Grace H. 35R, 53L
Turner, F.S. 42R
Turner, Gerald 156L
Turrettini, François 90R
Twinem, P. de W. 94L, 96L
Twitchett, Denis C. 128L, 132L, 140R

Ui, Hakuju 117L, 123L, 125R, 135L
Ular, Alexandre 53L
Underwood, Horace Grant 10L
Unkrig, W.A. 124L
Unno, Taisetsu 125R, 135L
Uno, T. 105L
Utsuki, Nishū 117L

Vail, Albert 10L
Vail, Emily M. 10L
Valbert, G. 35R, 38L
Vale, Joshua 67L
Valentino, Henri 144L
Vallée Poussin (see La Vallée Poussin, Louis de)
Vallerey, Gisèle 17R
Van Buskirk, William R. 35R, 53L
Van der Sprenkel, O.B. 10L
Vanderstappen, Harry 157R
Vandier-Nicolas, Nicole 49L, 67L, 117L
Vargas, Phillipe de 96L
Varma, S.C. 98L
Vassiliev, Boris 123L
Vaudescal 43L
Vaughan, J.D. 101L
Veith, Ilza 88R
Ventakasubbiah, A. 123L
Verdeille, Maurice 140R, 158R, 163R
Vial, Gabriel 159R
Vichert, Clarence G. 57L, 84R, 86L
Vincent, Irene Vongehr 159R, 160L
Vincent, J.B. 159R
Vinson, Julien 10L
Visser, Marinus Willem de 23L, 123L, 162L, 169R
Vlar, Alexandre 105L
Vleeschower, E. de 67L, 82L
Vogel, J. Ph. 153L
Vogelaar 76R, 100L
Vogt, E.Z. 40L
Volpert, Ant. 41L, 70R, 74L, 77R, 82L
Voskamp, C.J. 29L
Vuilleumier, B. 23L

W. Dr J. 27R, 41L

Waddell, N.A. 35R, 49L, 138R
Wai-dau 138R
Waidtlow, C. 15L, 25R, 45R
Waite, Arthur E. 160L
Wakeman, Frederick jr. 94R
Waldschmidt, Ernst 117L
Wales, H.G. Quaritch 80R
Waley, Arthur 25R, 59L, 65L, 84R, 86L, 117L,
    125R, 132L, 138R, 144L, 155R, 156L, 159R,
    160L, 163R
Walker, J.E. 41R
Walleser, Max 117L, 135L
Walshe, W. Gilbert 10L, 26L, 41R, 49L
Wang, C.H. 64R
Wang, Chao-hsiang 93L
Wang, Hsun 159L
Wang, L.C. 33L
Wang, Ngen-jong 45R
Wang, Tch'ang-tche 57L
Waong, P.L. 41R
Ward, Barbara E. 94R
Ward, C.H.S. 112R
Ward, John S.M. 94R, 101L
Ward, W.E. 147R
Ware, James R. 59L, 65L, 117L, 123L, 132L
Warneck, Johann 15L
Warner, Langdon 145R, 146L, 153L, 154R,
    159R, 160R
Wasson, R. Gordon 65L, 106L
Watanabe, Kaikyoku (or Kaikioku) 123L, 123R
Waterbury, Florance 23L
Watson, Burton 114L
Watson, William 23L
Watters, Thomas 45R, 53R, 90R, 112R, 123R,
    143R, 144L, 147R, 162L, 164R
Watts, Harold H. 35R, 49L, 138R
Weber, Max 35R, 49L
Weber-Schäfer, Peter 26L, 45R
Webster, James 90R
Weddingen 53R
Wegner, M. 147R, 153L, 162L
Wei, Francis C.M. 10L, 112R, 169R
Wei-huan 166L
Wei, Hwei-lin 15L
Wei, Louis Tsing-sing 41R
Wei, T.F. 77R
Wei, Tat 29L, 35R
Wei Wu Wei 168L
Weinstein, Stanley 123R, 135L
Welch, Holmes 49L, 59L, 96L, 96R, 98L, 99L,
    140R, 166L, 167L, 167R, 168L
Welch, William 153L
Weller, Friedrich 117L, 117R, 121R, 123R,
    132L, 138R, 144L
Wen, Ch'ung-i 70R, 74L, 77R, 90R
Wenley, Archibald G. 23L, 45R
Wentworth, Erastus 112R
Werner, E.T.C. 10R, 17R, 26L, 29L, 41R, 45R,
    74R, 82L, 96L
Wethered, H. Newton 144L
Wetterwald, Albert 91L

Weygandt, J.W.H. 15L
Whitaker, K.P.K. 91L, 163R
White, Hugh W. 29L
White, William Charles 23L, 23R, 155R
Wickersham, James 105L
Widgery, Alban G. 35R
Wieger, Léon 10R, 38L, 55R, 59L, 88R, 91L,
   110L, 112R, 117R, 133R
Wieman, Henry N. 6R, 111L
Wiese, J. 145R
Wiethoff, Bodo 46L, 74R
Wilhelm II (German emperor) 23R
Wilhelm, Hellmut 15L, 65L, 65R, 83R
Wilhelm, Richard 10R, 29L, 35R, 41L, 49L, 53R,
   55R, 57L, 59L, 65L, 124R, 125R, 135L, 166L,
   166R
Willetts, William 153R
Williams, C.A.S. 23R
Williams, David Rhys 36L, 53R, 106L
Williams, E.T. 36L, 38R, 46L, 49L, 74R, 78L,
   86L, 96L, 112R
Williams, Mrs E.T. 91L
Williams, F. Wells 91L
Williams, S. Wells 4R, 10R, 41R, 46R, 74R, 94R,
   150L
Willmott, W.E. 93L, 100R
Willoughby-Meade, Gerald 67L, 91L
Wilson, B.D. 41R, 101L
Wilson, David A. 33R
Wilson, H.H. 140R, 144L
Wilson, Major-General 93R
Wilson, Thomas 147R
Wilson, William J. 65L
Wimsatt, G.B. 70R, 74R
Winance, Eleuthère 29L
Winkworth, Susanna 4L
Winston, Clara 9R, 165L, 166R
Winston, Richard 9R, 165L, 166R
Winter, H.T.J. 49L, 105L, 112R
With, K. Suiko 156L
Witte, H. 166R
Witte, Johannes 132L, 166R, 169R
Wittfogel, Karl A. 132R
Wogihara, Unrai (also Wogiwara or Ogiwara)
   109R, 123R, 125R
Wohlgemuth, Else 123R
Wolcott, Carolyn 106L
Wolcott, Leonard 106L
Wolf, Arthur P. 41R, 82L
Wolf, Marion 156L
Wolfers, M. 78L
Wong, C.M. 70R
Wong, C.S. 78L, 101L, 148R, 168L
Wong, K. Chimin 23R, 74R, 88R
Wong, Ming 87L
Wong, Mou-lam 117R, 138R
Woo, Kang 57L
Wood, C.F. 163R
Woodbridge, Samuel I. 80R
Woodin, S.F. 26L
Woog-Garry, Valentine 10R

Worcester, G.R.F. 78L
Wright, A.R. 67L, 74R
Wright, Arthur F. 26L, 93R, 126L, 128L, 131R,
   132R, 135L, 135R, 164R
Wright, Harrison K. 26L, 160R
Wright, Hope M. 24R, 126L
Wu, Chi-yü 55L
Wu, Feng-p'ei 147R
Wu, George 98R
Wu, John C.H. 36L, 105L, 137R, 139L, 169L
Wu, Joseph S. 29L
Wu, K.T. 123R, 132R
Wu, Lien-teh 88R
Wu, Lu-ch'iang 62L, 65R
Wu, Mi-feng 159L
Wu, S. 36L
Wu, Tso-jen 161L
Wu, Yao-tsung 98L
Wurm, Paul 106L
Wyder, H. 10R
Wylie, Alexander 94R, 132R
Wyman, Mary 105L
Wynne, M.L. 101L

Ya, Han-chang (or Zhang) 98L
Yamaguchi, Susumu 117R
Yamaïzoumi (also Ymaïzoumi) 15R, 41R
Yamamoto, Akira 157R
Yamazake, Hiroshi 132R
Yamata 117R
Yampolsky, Philip 114L, 134R, 139L
Yang, C.K. 10R, 29L, 38L, 98L, 106L
Yang, Ching-schun 53R
Yang, I-fan 167R
Yang, Kun 41R
Yang, Lien-sheng 129L, 132R, 140R
Yang, Ming-che 36L, 49L, 49R, 113L, 132R,
   168L
Yang, Richard F.S. 60L
Yang Yu 148R
Yang, Yung-ch'ing 10R
Yao, Ruth 80R, 99L
Yao, Shan-yu 29L
Yashiro, Yukio 157R
Yates, M.T. 41R, 42R
Yeates, T. 10R
Yeh, George K.C. 36L
Yeh, Theodore T.Y. 10R, 36L, 105L
Yen, P'u-sheng (pseud for Lee, Charles L. q v.)
Yetts, W. Perceval 17R, 20L, 23R, 36L, 54R,
   60L, 91L, 145R, 153R, 155R
Yewdale, Merton S. 49R, 53R, 65R, 88R
Ying, Ignatius 132R
Yiu, Tung 59L
Ymaïzoumi (see also Yamaïzoumi) 15R, 41R,
   53R, 117R
Yoo, Yushin 3R
Yoshioka, Yoshitoyo 55R
Youn, Laurent Eulsu 36L
Young, W. 78L, 101L
Yu, David C. 7R
Yu, Feng 78L
Yu, Hsiang 98L

Yu, Pung Kwang 36L
Yu, Shih-yu 94R, 96L
Yü, Tzu-tan 158L
Yü, Ying-shih 29L
Yuan, H.B. 61L
Yuan, T.L. 3R
Yule, Henry 113L, 144L
Yung, Hsi 139L

Zaborowska, Gilberte 84R
Zach, E. von 16R, 102R, 117R, 123R, 132R
Zacher, J. 80R
Zen, Sophia H. Chen 24R
Zenker, Ernst Victor 38L, 57L, 59L
Zia, N.A. 10R, 105R
Zia, Rosina C. 36L, 49L, 105R
Zimmerman, Werner 88R
Zürcher, Erik 113L, 131R, 133L
Zwaan, J.P. Kleiweg de 88R